WILLIAM WILBERFORCE

ROBIN FURNEAUX

William
Wilberforce

HAMISH HAMILTON
LONDON

First published in Great Britain, 1974
by Hamish Hamilton Ltd
90 Great Russell Street London WC1
Copyright © 1974 by Robin Furneaux

SBN 241 02202 9

Printed in Great Britain by
Western Printing Services Ltd, Bristo

TO

C. E. WRANGHAM

Contents

List of Illustrations

between pages 414 *and* 415

Preface

WILLIAM WILBERFORCE spent much of his life writing. He wrote a book, letters that grew into books, articles, pamphlets and reviews. When faced with a difficult decision he would put the arguments on both sides down on paper. He kept a diary for most of his adult life and also various journals to which he would commit his religious thoughts. He did not intend these works to be published, and they are full of abbreviations. He wrote memoranda on different subjects, the most famous being his unfinished sketch of Pitt. He started an autobiography. But his correspondence alone would have buried most men. He often wrote and received as many as twenty letters a day and few of them were short. In addition to his own papers, two of his sons kept notes of his conversation in their commonplace books.

His life was therefore unusually well documented, and the greater part of his papers have survived, though they are now dispersed. When his sons came to write their biography of him, they plunged bravely into this sea of documents and emerged with a five-volume digest linked by a brief narrative. They drew extensively on Wilberforce's diary and journals, but later restored the balance by publishing two volumes of his correspondence. At the end of the nineteenth century an important new collection of documents was discovered, edited and published under the title of *The Private Papers of William Wilberforce*. These Private Papers included many letters to and from Pitt and Wilberforce's sketch of Pitt. They also contained family correspondence which the brothers might have considered too intimate for publication.

With eight published volumes to draw on, almost exclusively composed of Wilberforce's papers, the biographers who followed his sons have left the original documents undisturbed. Only Mr. Newsome, in his authoritative study of the lives of Wilberforce's sons, has delved beneath the surface.

This is a pity· although the sons did their work thoroughly, they were jealous of their family's privacy. Nineteenth-century readers did not expect a detailed account of family life; they would rather learn about

Wilberforce the statesman, the philanthropist, the enemy of slavery, the religious leader. Apart from this different attitude towards the scope of biography, the sons were also inhibited by a decision that the monument they would create to their father's memory should be untarnished by the intrusion of their own personalities. They carried out this task so successfully that even when they quoted a letter from Wilberforce to one of them, it would appear as 'to a son', though they would sometimes add 'aetat—' so that he could be identified with a little effort. Since Wilberforce himself regarded his family as being the most important of his many responsibilities, this treatment makes it hard to base a balanced biography on the published sources.

His sons changed some documents—a practice which was considered less reprehensible then than now. Salacious matter was never a feature of Wilberforce's correspondence, and it is a measure of the changing times that his sons occasionally felt obliged to act as censors when they thought his comments too earthy for inclusion. When discussing his religion their editing assumed a constructive aspect and they quite often substituted, for example, the word 'Christian' for 'Evangelical', an alteration which can only be calculated to mislead their readers.

In spite of their many omissions and occasional inaccuracies, any biographer of William Wilberforce must lean heavily on the printed sources, especially the biography. Some of the manuscripts have disappeared and the diary is illegible in places. On the whole the manuscripts reveal little that is new about Wilberforce's political life; but they are indispensable for any study of his other aspects.

Mr. C. E. Wrangham, Wilberforce's great-great-grandson, has been a model of kindness and hospitality to me throughout the preparation of this book. He has allowed me complete access to his collection of manuscripts, helped me decipher Wilberforce's lamentable handwriting, let me quote from his own privately published studies and read and criticised the final draft. Mrs. Wrangham and he have entertained me and had me to stay for many nights. Wilberforce's own table sometimes caused complaints; one of his more eccentric guests remarked that he preferred spiders to his host's food. I am delighted to report that this is one quality that has not been inherited by his descendants.

I would like to thank the Librarians and staff of the Bodleian Library, the William R. Perkins Library, Duke University, North Carolina, and the Wilberforce Museum, Hull—the other owners of Wilberforce's papers for their kindness and help, and for permission to quote from their documents. I am also indebted to the staff of the London Library and the British Museum.

Among the families of the Abolitionists I am particularly grateful to Lord Wilberforce, Mr. Granville Sharp and Mrs. Sandwith. I must also thank Sir William Pennington-Ramsden, the owner of Muncaster Castle, and Mrs. Patterson, the owner of Rayrigg, for allowing me to see their houses, Miss Mair Griffiths, Miss Anne Pope, and Miss Susan Avid for their research, and Secretarial Assistance for their typing.

I would also like to thank Canon Raby for showing me the church where the Clapham Sect worshipped, and Mr. E. E. Smith of the Clapham Antiquarian Society, Mr. and Mrs. Adrian Berry, Mr. Edward Cazalet, Mr. Christopher Chope, Mr. Adrian Fortescue, Mrs. Louie Holdsworth, Lord Longford, Mr. John Patterson, Professor SamKange and Professor Rambert Stokes.

WILLIAM WILBERFORCE

CHAPTER I

EARLY LIFE

THE house in Kingston-on-Hull where William Wilberforce was born is now a museum dedicated to his memory. The visitor leaves the busy town centre of Hull, follows a narrow lane between warehouses and finds himself suddenly opposite a Jacobean red-brick house with a statue of the philanthropist in front of it. The house had passed into the possession of the Wilberforce family in 1732, and as soon as they owned it they installed great Georgian windows which let in the light but spoilt its proportions, though it still retains much of its charm and warmth. Behind the house a long narrow garden leads down to the river Hull. It is a typical home of a prosperous eighteenth-century merchant, comfortable, spacious but unpretentious and conveniently close to his business; indeed after Wilberforce moved down to London it became the office of his family firm.

Inside Wilberforce House there are exhibits showing the development of Hull since the Middle Ages, there are Georgian rooms with furniture lent by the Victoria and Albert Museum, a Victorian bedroom with William Morris wallpaper, a magnificent rococo ceiling above the staircase, a children's museum and a banqueting hall, whose panelling seems to have been spared when the Wilberforce family decided to let the light in. The room in which Wilberforce was born carries the inscription: 'Statesman, Orator, Philanthropist, Saint; one of the greatest Parliamentarians in a great age, a friend of Pitt and Burke, of Fox and Canning—he did more than any other man, by his eloquence and courage, his industry and pertinacity, to bring about the abolition of slavery throughout the British Empire. No Englishman has ever done more to evoke the conscience of the British people and to elevate and ennoble British Public life.' After reading this it is something of a shock to turn to the glass cases around the side of the room and see the Court dresses inside which seem cut for a child rather than the man who had earned such an imposing tribute. Two portraits of Wilberforce look down enigmatically at the scene.

A room nearby gives us a glimpse of the enemy. All the gruesome paraphernalia of slavery are exhibited here. There are silver branding irons, which were considered more humane than those made of iron, but this is

the only touch of humanity in the room. There is a murderous collection
of whips, shackles, runaway slave collars and a plantation's inventory with
a poignant entry 'Quamina, a good watchman, but bad legs' valued at
sixpence. There are posters advertising slaves for sale and rewards for run-
aways, there is a model of a slave ship used by Wilberforce to demonstrate
the cruelty of the trade to the House of Commons. The rest of the Museum
has a pleasant, light atmosphere but visitors in this room are usually silent
except for occasional exclamations of disgust. They are in a receptive mood
when they move on to a room next door where they are startled to see a small
figure in dark clothes seated behind a desk and looking up as though surprised at being disturbed. The effigy, although not a good likeness of
Wilberforce, is extraordinarily lifelike. He sits in his own chair underneath
a painting of a negro in chains, which he used to illustrate lectures; his books
and table are in front of him as he sits playing with his lorgnette. The
picture of the slave in chains hangs alongside portraits of Wilberforce and
Clarkson, two men who devoted their lives to removing them.

When Wilberforce was born the approaches to his house must have been
very different. Hull was then, as it is today, a prosperous and important
port, but it was, of course, a much smaller place, centred on the corner of
its two rivers, the Hull and the Humber. Wilberforce's house was therefore
in the heart of eighteenth-century Hull. He was often to thank Providence
later in his life for preserving him from any connections with the Slave
Trade or the West Indies, and if he had been born into a merchant family
in a West Coast port his fortune would probably have been drawn in part
from these tainted sources. But the merchants of Hull drew their wealth
from the Baltic Trade, timber from Norway for Hull's shipyards, high-
grade iron from Sweden, and, later in the century, wood, hemp, flax and
iron from Russia and Prussia. They bought luxury goods from Holland
and tobacco and rice from America, and sold textiles and metal goods.
According to the port's historian no slave ship ever cleared from Hull.[1] In
the latter half of the century, Hull became one of the main whaling ports.
During the summer months the smell of whale oil would become offensive
and the merchants would retire to their villas outside the town.[2]

Hull did not throw up any merchant princes of spectacular wealth as did
Bristol and Liverpool, but the town was dominated by an oligarchy of
solid, prosperous mercantile families, of whom the Wilberforces were one.
They were a sporting group, fond of their hunting, racing, shooting and
fishing. Many of them bought land and some, like the Sykeses, great
houses. The Wilberforces contented themselves with buying odd pieces of
land. In Hull itself life was gay and pleasant for the merchants. They entertained lavishly and met on the racecourse, at the Assembly and in the
theatre. Wilberforce remembered that the society there was as lively as in
any place except for London, so much so that members of West Riding

county families would keep a town house in Hull in the same way that the merchants kept country houses outside it.

The Wilberforces were an old family, one of the few, according to the editor of Burke's Peerage, who can trace their ancestry back to Saxon times.[3] Family tradition has it that a Wilberfoss was the spearman who slew Harold Hardrada at Stamford Bridge. In any case the Wilberfosses held lands in the North Country at the time of the Norman Conquest, and the characteristic family names of William and Robert appear soon afterwards. They lived for many generations in the town of Wilberfoss, eight miles to the east of York, and they used this spelling of their name until it was changed to Wilberforce by William's grandfather. In the middle of the sixteenth century a younger son settled in the neighbouring town of Beverley. This branch of the family prospered while the parent stock in Wilberfoss declined. A William Wilberfoss was mayor of Beverley at the time of the Great Rebellion, and his great-grandson, the first William Wilberforce, was twice mayor of Hull. The family's prominence in the Baltic Trade seems to have dated from the mid-seventeenth century, so that when William was born in 1759 he was the heir to a hundred years of successful trading. His father, Robert Wilberforce, was the mayor's second son, the eldest, naturally, having been given the family name of William. Robert Wilberforce was a partner in his father's house in Hull and it was here that his son was born.

William's father, who died in 1768, remains an obscure figure and the family was dominated by the elder William. Wilberforce when an adult could still remember two of his grandfather's stories, both to do with a somewhat inglorious military career. Once the great Duke of Marlborough had invited him to watch a battle from the safety of a neighbouring hill, an offer which he had prudently declined. In 1745 when the Young Pretender had invaded England, the citizens of Hull had been threatened with a battle that could not be avoided so easily, and he had helped to strengthen the defence of the town. But the attack never came. The old man must have been a fine raconteur to have made such stories memorable.

We know too little of Wilberforce's childhood. The skeleton is there but there is no flesh and blood to complete our picture. We can read the few anecdotes about him, see where he was brought up, what schools he went to and what he thought of them, without getting any idea of the kind of boy he was. Although he sometimes referred to his childhood in various memoranda, his modesty was such that he adds little to our knowledge. His great friend James Stephen once challenged him: 'I should like you to write a life of yourself, and I would write another; and it would be curious to see the different renderings which would be given to the self-same facts.' Wilberforce at once began: 'I was so small of stature when a youth that Milner put me on a table to read to the boys.' Stephen interrupted him, his point proved: 'Why, Wilberforce, Milner himself has told me that it was that your elocution might be a model to the school.' The only letters that survive are those written to his aunt and uncle during the harrowing period of his first religious crisis. And only then can we see him as a human being rather than the little paragon that people remembered sixty years later.

He was an only son but he had three sisters of whom two died in their childhood. Wilberforce often used to reminisce about his early days, and it is extraordinary that his second son, Robert Isaac, should have been eighteen when he discovered that his father had had more than one sister. 'He spoke of his sisters,' Robert Isaac remembered. 'I said I thought he had only one. "Yes", said he, "I had three, the eldest died at about fourteen when I was about eight, she was at one of the great boarding schools in London." "What was her name?" "Elizabeth, the youngest Ann was I think one of the sweetest children that ever was born; she was quite born, I know my mother thought, to be a comfort to her, for she lived with her all the time my sister Mrs. Stephen (Sarah) was about for her education. She was only born just before my father's death, and she only lived about eight years." '

From his first days William was a weak child. He was small, feeble and shortsighted. In Classical times, he often reflected, he would infallibly have been exposed. But he soon showed the qualities that were to raise him above these handicaps, a vigorous mind, an affectionate, considerate nature and a voice which struck all who heard it with its range and beauty. A guest at his mother's house remembered a degree of thoughtfulness unusual in so young a child. 'I shall never forget how he would steal into my sickroom, taking off his shoes lest he should disturb me, and with an anxious face looking through my curtains to learn if I was better.'

At the age of seven he was sent to Hull Grammar School, where, through the good offices of his grandfather, Joseph Milner was soon to become headmaster. Wilberforce was lucky in his first teachers, for Milner, although only twenty-four, was a man of great ability who was to become famous through his monumental *History of the Church of Christ*. Wilberforce was also fortunate in that, during his time at Hull Grammar School, Milner had still to start his magnum opus. John Venn, who came there in 1773, complained that Milner neglected his pupils in favour of his *History*. Joseph Milner's younger brother Isaac also taught at Hull and he was destined to play a great part in Wilberforce's life. Isaac Milner had himself been educated at Hull Grammar School, but he had been removed at the age of ten to earn his living as a weaver, and he would sit morosely at his loom with a copy of Tacitus open in front of him. It must have come as an unspeakable relief when Joseph obtained his headmastership and enrolled Isaac as an usher. He was a vast, ungainly man with a genius for mathematics.

In 1768 Robert Wilberforce died and his son was transferred to the care of his elder brother William, who lived in London at St. James's Place and owned a villa in Wimbledon. The school in Putney which William now had to attend must have come as a shock to a pupil of the Milners. 'Mr. Chalmers, the master, himself a Scotsman, had an usher of the same nation, whose red beard—for he scarcely shaved once a month—I shall never forget. They taught writing, French, arithmetic and Latin . . . with Greek we did not much meddle. It was frequented chiefly by the sons of merchants, and they taught therefore everything and nothing. Here I continued some time as a parlour boarder: I was sent at first amongst the lodgers and I can remember even now the nauseous food with which we were supplied, and which I could not eat without sickness.'[5] He considered it 'a very indifferent school' and in a more critical memorandum 'a most wretched little place', and the Scottish usher 'a dirty disagreeable man'.[6]

William remained two years at this school, spending his holidays with his aunt and uncle. Religion was to give his life its driving force and it was here that he first came under its influence. His uncle had married a Miss Thornton, a half-sister of the great lay Evangelical, John Thornton. The line between Evangelicals and Methodists was still loosely drawn and William's aunt was an ardent admirer of Whitfield. William's affectionate nature was easily trained into a religious course; he accompanied his aunt and uncle to church and chapel, listened, enthralled, to the sermons, and became a devout and surprisingly mature Methodist.

The tone of his letters home to Yorkshire must have altered after his conversion, which was greeted in Hull with great alarm. Wilberforce later explained to his second son the horror caused by this news. 'It is impossible for you to have any idea of the hatred in which the Methodists were then held by the common people. I cannot better explain it to you than by saying that it is more like the account given in *Ivanhoe* of the persecutions against the Jews, than anything else I know.'[7] His mother descended on Wimbledon and, much to his distress, removed the young Methodist. The scene was charged with emotion, both sides feeling certain that they were in the right. His aunt implored her not to deprive her son of the opportunity of a religious life. Wilberforce's own High Church sons and biographers record the answer with relish. 'You should not fear,' replied his mother with a caustic allusion to her peculiar tenets; 'if it be a work of grace, you know it cannot fail.' William's grandfather's comment was more practical. 'Billy,' he said, 'shall travel with Milner as soon as he is of age; but if Billy turns Methodist he shall not have a sixpence of mine.'

But Billy had turned Methodist and his Methodism proved surprisingly tenacious against all the efforts of his family and friends to wean him away from it. He was only twelve and the diversions of life in Hull were fatally attractive. He later recalled: 'It was then as gay a place as could be found out of London. The theatre, balls, great suppers, and card parties, were the delight of the principal families in the town. The usual dinner hour was two o'clock, and at six they met at sumptuous suppers. This mode of life was at first distressing to me, but by degrees I acquired a relish for it, and became as thoughtless as the rest. As grandson to one of the principal inhabitants, I was everywhere invited and caressed: my voice and love of music made me still more acceptable. The religious impressions which I had gained at Wimbledon continued for a considerable time after my return to Hull, but my friends spared no pains to stifle them. I might almost say, that no pious parent ever laboured more to impress a beloved child with sentiments of piety than they did to give me a taste for the world and its diversions.'[8]

His mother had sent him to Pocklington, an exceedingly expensive school if it really cost the £300–£400 a year that Wilberforce remembered. It was not the kind of place where he might renew his acquaintanceship with 'serious' religion. Its headmaster, who bore the pleasant name of the Rev. K. Basket with grace and polish, seems to have been too much the sauve man of the world even to have insisted on his pupils working.

Wilberforce remembers having a room there to himself 'and one or two such distinctions'. There were twenty-eight boys in the school whom he remembered, collectively, as being 'a sad set'. As far as work was concerned, 'I did nothing at all there'. This statement does not seem to have been entirely true. By some miracle a few of his essays have survived from Pocklington.[9] They show that he was at least made to cultivate an impeccable copperplate hand (an accomplishment which, unfortunately, did not survive his schooldays), and that he was made to think.

The Methodist influence is most evident in the early essays. In August 1772 when he was asked to write about companions, the sentiments which glow through his twelve-year-old's prose—itself no bad advertisement for Pocklington—are the same as he might have expressed in his adult life.

'Nothing gives a greater tincture to the Mind or Morals of Man than either the good or bad Qualities possessed by those with whom they associate. A Person by being very intimate with another and being constantly in his Company naturally imbibes his Manners, and the same Sentiments occur to him; which tho' perhaps they may be in some Measure wrong yet having the Sanction of a friend it is very likely that they will be winked at and overlooked.

'In nothing is there a greater difference than in a good or a bad Companion whether one considers it in regard to his Morals or Understanding. A real good Companion is not one who can sit over so many Bottles, or play so many pools at Quadrille; but one whom Good Sense, Good-Nature, a good education and improved understanding have all conspired to render truly agreeable. He must in his behaviour be free and open without Plasticity, genteel and complaisant without flattery. He must not affect to appear ignorant of what he really knows or fond of displaying his Superior Knowledge. A person famous for any particular Art to be ranked in this class must not conceal his Thoughts upon it if asked yet must not with an over bearing haughtiness seem so fully persuaded that what he says is right or not to give Ear to any Sentiment which may in the least differ from his own opinion. A person possessed of these Qualifications may be called a truly good Companion, and it is amazing the effect which the company of such a person may produce. On the contrary a Companion unworthy of the name in a manner rusts and corrodes every one with whom he is intimate. Since there is so much to be got by the Society of a good Companion and as much to be lost by that of a bad one we ought to take the greatest care not to form any improper connections never to go into bad Company because by that our manners may be tainted. We never ought to admit any one into that class till we are perfectly acquainted both with his Morals and Abilities.'[10]

Poor William! a companion who could share his trials and fortify his beliefs was exactly what he needed and could not find. With everyone at Pocklington and Hull determined to erase his Methodism he had no one to turn to or trust. In such circumstances to ask him to write on companions was the equivalent of telling a starving man to describe his idea of a perfect meal.

This period must have been one of the two most wretched in Wilberforce's life, the other being the months after his second and final conversion. On that occasion we can follow the full course of his mental agony. While groping for the strength and faith to lead a life that he knew to be right, he committed all his heartsearching, his doubts, his pathetic lapses and crushing remorse to the pages of his diary. But he then had friends, advisers, confidants: he could consult those who were sympathetic to his religious beliefs; he had some experience of life on which to draw. During this first crisis he had none of these solaces. He kept no diary and he could share his inmost thoughts with no one, for everyone around him was an enemy of his religion. His faith was being sapped, not built up, until he allowed himself to live in a way which, at first, he knew to be wrong, but which he finally accepted as normal. It must have been a terrible ordeal for a child of twelve. 'It almost broke my heart,' he remembered fifty years later. A reader of his son's biography or his own recollections might be forgiven for thinking that, at any rate, it was not a long one and that 'the considerable time' his Methodism lingered was no more than a few months. But William continued a clandestine religious correspondence with his aunt and uncle for nearly three years after his removal from their house.

On November 15, 1771 he wrote to both of them:

Dearest Aunt,

I was very sorry to hear that you are not better and that you was obliged to go to Bath; as I am sure you would not like it. I hope however you can hear the gospel there and that is everything: though sometimes I have comfortable seasons in prayer: sometimes I can taste the sweetness of redeeming love; and when I do then I should not fear anything.[11]

To his uncle:

Comfort yourself you Dearest that they who are in Jesus must suffer Persecution and it is just as it should be; if we suffer with him we shall also reign with him; and let what will happen he is blessed who has the Lord for his hope, who can look unto him as unto a loving father being reconciled to him by the blood of Jesus. May the blessing of the living God keep you and preserve you in this world and may he bring you unto his Kingdom of bliss and joy. I am your dearest, dearest son.

W. Wilberforce.

P.S. I cannot write more because it is seen where the letter is to.[12]

The pain caused by his removal and 'persecution' and the defiant strength of his faith are there on the surface for anyone to see.

On November 29 he writes again to his uncle:

My dear uncle,

How good God is to me, what reason have I to be thankful; it is impossible to sum up all his mercies and his benefits are innumerable. I own I will give anything in the world to be with you again yet I trust that everything is ordered for the best and if we put our whole trust and confidence in him we shall never be confounded.[13]

In August 1772 to his aunt:

One of the greatest misfortunes I had whilst at Hull was, not being able to hear the blessed word of God, as my mama would not let me go to high church on a Sunday afternoon;* but the Lord was everyday granting me some petition, and I trust I can say that I increased in the knowledge of God and Christ Jesus whom he had sent, whom to know is life eternal.[14]

In September he takes 'the opportunity of writing by the maid who goes away tomorrow; thinking it a better way than sending it to my uncle, since grandpapa might perhaps see the letter'.[15]

In December: 'This morning I received my uncle's letter and was very sorry to find that I displeased both him and you by not writing; but I hope you will both excuse me, and I will never do so any more. I had as leave if not rather not go home at all for the Clares are at Hull during the holidays and I am much afraid that they will force me to go.'[16]

The pain has been replaced by a resignation, but the faith is as firm as

---

* Mrs. Wilberforce must have been in a dilemma. She was not an irreligious woman. Wilberforce later described her as 'a pious woman in her way. She was what I should call an Archbishop Tillotson Christian: she always attended Church Wednesdays and Fridays and had family prayers on Sunday.'[17] But to take her son even to High Church was to stoke his Methodism.

ever. This attitude continues until the end of the correspondence preserved in the Wrangham MSS., the last religious letter to his aunt being on May 19, 1774.[17]

When he was thirty-seven Wilberforce could look upon his removal from Methodism as a blessing in disguise.

'How eventful a life has mine been, and how visibly I can trace the hand of God leading me by ways which I knew not! I think I have never before remarked, that my mother's taking me from my uncle's when about twelve or thirteen and then completely a methodist, has probably been the means of my being connected with political men and becoming useful in life. If I had staid with my uncle I should probably have been a bigoted despised methodist; yet to come to what I am after so many years of folly as those which elapsed between my last year at school and 1785, is wonderful. On the depths of the counsels of God! what cause have I for gratitude and humiliation.'[18]

It is fair to say that he also felt cause for resentment whenever he recalled the efforts made to separate him from his early faith. One can be grateful to Providence and angered with its agent.

His later essays from Pocklington reflect the change. In March 1773 he was set to write about Popularity, an interesting question since it was one of the subjects which he later treated in his religious book *Practical View*. After his conversion he regarded it as a useful quality which should be cultivated but sacrificed when required for a more important cause. But in 1773 he wrote with an aristocratic paganism which must have brought a smile to the face of the Rev. K. Basket. 'Noble' has replaced 'moral' as his favourite adjective of approval. The first sentence sets the scene. 'There are some people who spend their whole time and use their utmost Endeavour and Application in gaining the short-lived and empty praises of a thoughtless and vulgar Rabble, always fluctuating from one extreme to another, ignorant of its real interest, and perhaps preferring the Man who secretly attempts to destroy it.'[19]

Even when he wrote on religious subjects he showed no signs of that intense personal involvement which was a characteristic both of the Methodism of his youth and of the Evangelism of his manhood. When asked to re-write the first nineteen verses of Psalm 136 in couplets he produced a poem[20] which, though technically excellent for a boy just fifteen, lacked any depth of feeling. An essay on Patience written shortly afterwards shows the change in his approach even more clearly.

'We must learn to bear whatever befalls us,' he wrote, 'so as on the one hand, not to be too much elevated or overjoyed by the Smiles of Prosperity, nor on the other too much depressed or cast down by the Frowns of Adversity. The stings of Fortune, how severe soever they may seem to us, it is most likely we deserve; for we ought to learn to bear with Patience, what we cannot possibly avoid. Life is a very uncertain thing at best, therefore we ought not to rely upon any good Fortune, since perhaps this moment we may enjoy the greatest Worldly Happiness; the next be plunged into the Deepest Abyss of unutterable Misery.'

While the sentiments expressed here are not inconsistent with Christianity they could no more have been written by a converted Wilberforce than Thomas Paine's *Age of Reason*. The passage was full of opportunities for introducing the subject of Divine intervention in human affairs, of how all our trials were the dispensations of God and how we must greet them with gratitude rather than that negative pagan virtue, patience. And yet he never mentions Providence. If we can date his lapse from Methodism it is in 1774, between his last letter to his aunt on May 19 and this essay, which is undated but probably some time in the autumn.

It had been a long struggle but by October 1776, when he went up to St. John's College, Cambridge, Wilberforce was as worldly as any of his friends from Pocklington.

He had grown up to be a very charming young man. He was small, little over five feet to judge by his clothes in the Hull Museum, and so slight that he inspired such whimsical descriptions as 'all Soul and no body'. None of his features were handsome but they had a liveliness which was attractive. His movements were very fast and he was seldom still. His conversation followed the same pattern. He would pick up an idea very quickly, play with it, and turn to another only to abandon it in its turn. All this was done with a speed and pleasure which entranced his listeners. He took an obvious and innocent joy in meeting people, in talking to them and exchanging ideas. This pleasure later seemed sinful to him because the ideas were frivolous and he could have been spending his time and gifts to better effect, but it continued to be a characteristic until the end of his life. Pocklington, while fatal to his Methodism, had put a polish on his manners. His mind was so quick that his contemporaries found it difficult to gauge his intellectual powers. He was facile and fast to grasp a point but too interested in other things to worry away at it for long. He could keep up a reasonable standard with little effort; it was to be many years before it could be seen what he might achieve when he immersed himself in a subject.

He found nothing at the University to turn him away from his course of innocent hedonism. John Venn, who went up a few years after Wilberforce, commented that 'the very air of Cambridge seems infected by the breath of anti-Christ', but this was an exaggeration. From a religious or moral point of view Cambridge was neutral rather than corrupt. Devout young men like Gisborne and Babington and industrious undergraduates like Milner and Clarkson pursued their studies without interference or mockery. But those who wished only to enjoy their lives at University were allowed to do so without being chivvied by their tutors. To his lifelong regret, remorse and resentment Wilberforce fell into this category and was allowed to idle away his years at Cambridge as a dilettante. All Methodist seriousness forgotten, he abandoned himself to a life of pleasure for which his wealth, gaiety and charm made him perfectly equipped.

'I was introduced,' he wrote, 'on the very first night of my arrival, to as licentious a set of men as can well be conceived. They drank hard, and their conversation was even worse than their lives.' After his first year he severed connections with this group and lived much with the Fellows of his College in a state which he later described as one of 'sober dissipation'. 'But those with whom I was intimate did not act towards me the part of Christians, or even of honest men. Their object seemed to be to make and keep me idle. If ever I appeared studious, they would say to me, "Why in the world should a man of your future trouble himself with fagging?" I was a good classic and acquitted myself well in the College examinations; but mathematics, which my mind greatly needed, I almost entirely neglected, and was told I was far too clever to require them. Whilst my companions were reading hard and attending lectures, card parties and idle amusements consumed my time. The tutors would often say within my hearing, that "*They* were mere saps, but that I did all by talent". This was poison to a mind constituted like mine.'[21]

William Pitt, who was the same age as Wilberforce, had already been in residence at Pembroke three years when the latter arrived. He and Wilberforce were to become intimate friends soon after leaving Cambridge, but, while there, they enjoyed no more than a passing acquaintance with each other. Pitt, although he chose at the end of his academic career to take the honorary M.A. to which his rank then entitled him, was a serious scholar and moved in more staid circles than Wilberforce.

Thomas Gisborne's rooms were next to Wilberforce's. He, too, was to become a great friend, once Wilberforce's conversion had given them something in common. But even at Cambridge they were on friendly enough terms. Gisborne spent his time studying and emerged the sixth wrangler of his year. Wilberforce spent his in play and sometimes their aims conflicted. 'By his talents, his wit, his kindness, his social powers, his universal acceptability, and his love of society, he speedily became the centre of attraction to all the clever and idle of his own college and of other colleges. His room swarmed with them from the time when he rose, generally very late, till he went to bed.' Wilberforce, he remembered, kept a great Yorkshire pie in his rooms for his many guests. He was, Gisborne writes, 'by far the most agreeable and popular man amongst the undergraduates of Cambridge . . . He spent much of his time visiting, and when he returned late in the evening to his rooms he would summon me to join him by the music of his poker and tongs—our chimney pieces being back to back—or by the melodious challenge of his voice. When I did go in he was so winning and amusing that I often sat up half the night with him, much to the detriment of my attendance at lectures the next day.'[22]

Gisborne would undoubtedly have been thought a 'mere sap' by the worldly fellows of St. John's. His testimony shows that Wilberforce's friendships at Cambridge were not entirely confined to the idle and self-indulgent.

Wilberforce's vacations, too, were spent in the pursuit of pleasure. The gaiety of Hull Society had been lifted to an even higher level by the arrival of a garrison, and when not amusing himself there, Wilberforce would travel, in search of diversion, with his mother and sister. The shame with which he later remembered these idle but innocent years is perhaps no more than a measure of how much he enjoyed them at the time.

Before his departure from Cambridge in the summer of 1780, Wilberforce had decided to enter politics. The family business had been run during his minority by his cousin, Abel Smith of the banking family. Wilberforce was happy with this arrangement as his own inclinations were towards public life. A dissolution was expected and his greatest worry was that it might take place too soon, while he was still a minor and ineligible to sit in Parliament. The prominence and popularity of his family in Hull made this town a natural choice as his constituency. After a successful canvass there he went to London to woo the three hundred Hull free men who lived by the Thames. He entertained them to lavish suppers in public houses in Wapping and afterwards found his legs as a public speaker in front of these simple, friendly audiences.

In the evenings he would repair to the gallery of the House of Commons and listen to the great debates on the American War, to North's cool defence against the eloquence and fire of Fox and Burke. Here he discovered William Pitt, who like Wilberforce hoped for a seat after the next election. Night after night as they found themselves sitting together, their casual acquaintanceship ripened into a deep friendship, which was to survive every difference and strain until Pitt's death in 1806. They would look down together on to the small, panelled room in which the House of Commons sat. It had a more intimate atmosphere than the great debating chamber which has taken its place. Oratory and repartee were both highly regarded arts and members expected to be impressed as well as convinced. The style of the speaker, the grace of his diction and phrases, the facility with which he could produce classical allusions to illuminate his theme were considered as important as the soundness of his arguments. They were the characteristics that distinguished an orator from a mere debater. The House was responsive, appreciative and stimulating when the speaker was good, but merciless to a bad one. It was an arena where an individual could show his brilliance: oratory there, as well as being an art, was a competitive sport. Pitt brought to the Gallery a smouldering resentment against the war that had destroyed so many of his father's achievements. His passionate feelings on this subject could always be fed by the terrible memory of his father's appeal against it in the Lords. Chatham, who had only a short time to live, had fainted at the end of his speech and Pitt had helped carry him from his place. Wilberforce, of course, had no such political inheritance. It is likely that, when making his first political decision to oppose the American War, he was influenced, as he never ceased to be, by Pitt's opinions. There is no evidence that Wilberforce thought much about politics during his Cambridge career, but it is probable, as Professor Coupland points out, that his youth and character would have enlisted him on the side of the Opposition.

Pitt was in some ways a forbidding figure, a strange mixture of precocity and immaturity. From his childhood he had been set apart by the brilliance of his mind. He had been brought up to seek and to claim the political power that he was so well equipped to exercise.

Wilberforce knew most of the leading figures of his day and they were an impressive group by any standards. Fox, Sheridan, Ricardo, Milner, Canning, Brougham, Erskine, Bentham, Southey, Wordsworth, Walter Scott, Humboldt, Madame de Staël and Macaulay—but of all the people he ever met he considered Pitt to have had the finest brain. His mind was versatile, quick and flexible. When fresh from Cambridge he defeated Gibbon in argument and caused the great historian to leave the room in fury.[23] He was an adept classical scholar; his grasp of mathematics was such that after he had solved a difficult problem Dr. Playfair, the eminent mathematician, said that for an amateur it was the most extraordinary achievement he had ever seen.[24] Sir Charles Middleton, a leading agriculturalist, was equally astonished by the speed of his mind. In Parliament he was able to adapt his speech to answer all his opponents' points without disturbing or distorting the flow of his own.

He was less adept at handling people. His shyness—'I am the shyest man alive,'[25] he once confessed to Wilberforce—and awkwardness often made him seem cold, stiff and arrogant. Unlike his great rival Fox he could inspire respect more easily than affection. He neither made nor lost friends quickly. But those who were his friends thought of him as a paragon of all human virtues, 'something between God and Man'.[26] Wilberforce also thought him the wittiest man he had ever met, 'far more so than Sheridan, Jeckyll, or any other of his contemporaries . . . There was this peculiarity in Mr. Pitt's wit: all the others seemed to say a witty thing just as it arose from the collision as it were of the steel with the flint . . . [but] Mr. Pitt was systematically witty . . . the others were often run away with by their wit. Mr. Pitt was always master of his. He could turn it to any end or object he desired.'[27]

Pitt's character was complementary to Wilberforce's and it is not strange that they became such close friends. Wilberforce had the vivacity, charm and gregariousness that Pitt lacked, but he tended, at the beginning of his career, to see politics as a game, a contest of eloquence and wits in which victory was its own reward. Pitt introduced Wilberforce to the serious side of politics; until his conversion all of Wilberforce's political ideas were taken from Pitt and even after it they seldom found themselves in disagreement. In return Wilberforce helped Pitt to relax and unbend, something that he could only do with his closest friends. On these occasions Pitt would become a different man. He would lay aside his rigid self-control and indulge in horseplay, gambling, singing and practical jokes. He would also talk with a warmth, sensitivity and humour which would have astonished many members of parliament. Those who knew him well realised that the public must have a very misleading impression of him. He hid his emotions so successfully that they might wonder if he had any.

The date of the election which had threatened to postpone Wilberforce's political debut might, in the event, almost have been chosen with his convenience in mind, for he was able to work the celebration of his coming of age into his campaign. On August 24, his birthday, an ox was roasted whole and many hogsheads of ale were consumed in one of his fields. To our eyes eighteenth-century elections seem a strange mixture of fastidiousness and corruption. The vote of a resident elector was rewarded by a gift of two guineas, a 'plumper'* by four. The travelling costs of electors who lived outside the constituency had to be met by the candidates. The expense of bringing a Hull free man from London would be about £10. It was also customary for the successful candidate to give each of his supporters a present of £2.[28] While as willing as his opponents to pay these dues, Wilberforce shrank from shaking the hand of the local butcher, Johnny Bell, 'a fine athletic fellow', on the grounds that 'I thought it going rather too low for votes'. But when Wilberforce made this complaint to a supporter he was told, 'Oh sir, he is a fine fellow if you come to bruising.' The day after the election Johnny Bell showed himself worthy of this tribute; approaching Wilberforce privately he disclosed, 'I have found out who threw that stone at you and I'll kill him tonight.' Wilberforce was horrified at the thought of such a bloody start to his public life and persuaded him that a good fright would be punishment enough. After this Johnny Bell became his friend and the hero of many of what Wilberforce's sons call 'anecdotes characteristic of society at that time'.[29]

The poll was on September 11. Wilberforce's connections, charm and purse were strong enough to defeat the powerful interests of Lord Rockingham and the Government. He received exactly the same number of

---

* In seats which had two members electors might vote for two different candidates. To give a candidate a plumper was to vote for him alone.

votes (1,126) as his two opponents combined. The election cost him between £8,000 and £9,000.

Pitt had stood for the University Seat at Cambridge, where, through poor preparation and formidable opposition, he finished bottom of the poll. But his connections were strong enough to see him into Parliament. At the request of the Duke of Rutland, Sir James Lowther, the great northern boroughmonger, presented him with Appleby and waived his usual demand for political obedience. Pitt was thus able to enter the House after the Christmas Recess. Twenty months later he was to become Chancellor of the Exchequer.

CHAPTER II

MEMBER FOR HULL

WILBERFORCE had approached London with some trepidation, for nothing in his life so far had prepared him for its society. When he arrived, he later remembered, he 'knew not a single person above the rank of commoner, scarcely of a merchant. Some time before when an uncle of mine had got in Parliament, I recollect thinking it a very great thing. I used to consider a country gentleman a very great thing.'[1] But he need not have worried; as a young, rich, personable and charming member of parliament Wilberforce found the doors of London Society open to him. When he came down from Cambridge he had expected its tone to be serious and intellectual and 'so little did I know of general society, that I came up to London stored with arguments to prove the authenticity of Rowley's poems'.

He found instead a Society full of wealth and talent but devoted to the pursuit of pleasure. It was dominated by the great political families, the Cavendishes, the Howards, the Russells, the Foxes, the Greys, the Crewes, the Portlands—these families and many others had palatial houses in or near London. Wilberforce found the atmosphere of slightly jaded hedonism very far from the earnest intellectual exchanges he had expected. Later in his life he remembered an evening in the Duke of Queensberry's house.

'I always observe,' he wrote, 'that the owners of your grand houses have some snug corner in which they are glad to shelter themselves from their own magnificence. I remember dining, when I was a young man, with the Duke of Queensberry, at his Richmond villa. The party was very small and select. Pitt, Lord and Lady Chatham, the Duchess of Gordon and George Selwyn "who lived for society and continued in it, till he looked really like the wax-work figure of a corpse" were among the guests. We dined early that some of our party might be ready to attend the opera. The dinner was sumptuous, the views from the villa quite enchanting and the Thames in all its glory—but the Duke looked on with indifference. "What is there," he said, "to make so much of in the Thames. I am quite tired of it. There it goes, flow, flow, flow, always the same." '[2]

He patronised the theatre, the opera and concerts and was lucky enough to arrive in London when Garrick and Mrs. Siddons were in their prime. But as a young member of parliament, he spent as much of his time in clubs as anywhere else.

The clubs then fulfilled three functions; they were political societies in which members could meet and make their plans, social clubs where they could see their friends and dine with them, and casinos where they could lose their estates. White's was the Tory stronghold and Brooks's, on the other side of St. James's Street, the headquarters of the Whigs. As was fitting for an independent member Wilberforce joined both. He also belonged to Boodle's and Miles and Evans.

To step into Boodle's for the first time and win twenty-five guineas from the Duke of Norfolk, to meet and play with old George Selwyn, the renowned rake, wit and morbid connoisseur of executions, must both have been exhilarating experiences for a young man from the provinces, even if he knew 'they considered me a fine, fat pigeon whom they might pluck'.[3]

Wilberforce has left us an account of the second occasion. 'The first time I was at Brooks's, scarcely knowing any one, I joined from mere shyness in play at the Faro table, where George Selwyn kept bank. A friend who knew my inexperience, and regarded me as a victim decked out for sacrifice, called to me, "What, Wilberforce, is that you?" Selwyn quite resented the interference, and turning to him, said in his most expressive tone, "Oh sir, don't interrupt Mr. Wilberforce, he could not be better employed." Nothing could be more luxurious than the style of these clubs. Fox, Sheridan, Fitzpatrick, and all your leading men, frequented them, and associated upon the easiest terms; you chatted, played at cards, or gambled as you pleased.'[4]

In his short existence as a clubman Wilberforce most often patronised Goosetree's. This was a small club in Pall Mall with some twenty-five members, mainly Wilberforce's contemporaries from Cambridge. Pitt, who dominated its proceedings, dined there every night during the winter of 1780–1. Other members became close friends of Wilberforce, Pepper Arden, Bankes, Eliot and Grenville. They gambled at Goosetree's, like most young men of their age and class, though the stakes never seem to have reached the terrifying level of Brooks's. But Pitt found that the play was beginning to fascinate him too much and, wiser than Fox, he abandoned it. Wilberforce, too, gave it up, but for different and typical reasons. He was persuaded to take the bank one evening at Goosetree's and rose from the table a winner of £600. He was shocked to find that some of the losers had difficulty in paying. He did not as yet have any feeling that gambling was wrong, but if to lose was unpleasant and to win was to cause suffering, there was no pleasure left in play.

Wilberforce's first speeches in Parliament were on behalf of his constituents. On May 17, 1781 he presented a petition from Hull against the

revenue laws; no record of his maiden speech survives. On December 5 he
spoke on the motion of Mr. Hussey to increase the strength of the Navy by
10,000 seamen. This does not seem to have been his finest hour. After a
hackneyed patriotic oration—the ministers' declaration that the British
Navy was inferior to the French 'went to harrow and tear up by the roots
all those ideas of glory of the country which he had been taught to adopt
in his infancy, and which made every Englishman's breast glow with the
noblest ardour whenever he heard of Great Britain being involved in a
contest with France and Spain'[5]—he descended to more local loyalties
with the suggestion that more ships should be ordered from a yard in
Kingston-upon-Hull. Lord Mulgrave, replying to Wilberforce, pointed
out that this yard had already built two ships for the Navy, the *Temple* and
the *Ardent*. The *Temple* after three years' service went down on a fine,
calm summer's day and was lost. Almost as soon as the *Ardent* had been
fitted out, she had had to be sent into dock, where she had cost nearly as
much to repair as she had to build. The Admiralty would do well to
approach new contracts with this yard with caution. Lord Mulgrave's
speech was later shown to be somewhat distorted.[6]

Wilberforce probably spoke in between these two performances. Parliamentary reporting in his day was anything but accurate and the less important speakers were lucky if they were mentioned at all. The reporters
cannot always be blamed for this. They had to turn up early to get seats in
the crowded gallery and then work, often without relief, for a debate that
might last over ten hours. It was sometimes impossible for them to identify
members, sometimes they had to leave the Commons altogether, either
because a debate in the Lords claimed their attention, or because a Member
had 'spied strangers'. Then the wretched reporter had to build up some
sort of version of an important speech by asking Members what had been
said. The next day, exhausted, he tried to make sense of this mixture of
notes, memory and hearsay. His editor then re-wrote the whole report to
make sure that his own political patrons had the better of the exchanges.*
Many of the best speeches were impromptu so that Members could not
always protect themselves by preserving a copy of what they had said. In
these circumstances even 'Memory' Woodfall, the prince of parliamentary
reporters, could give only a rough sketch of a speech.

Pitt's parliamentary career began more impressively than Wilberforce's
with a speech on financial reform which made Burke describe him as 'not
just a chip of the old block: he is the old block itself'. Fox congratulated
him; North claimed it was the finest maiden speech he had ever heard. In
May 1782 he spoke again and Wilberforce described the scene to a friend
in Hull. 'The papers have informed you how Mr. William Pitt, second son

---

* 'I took care that the Whig dogs should not have the best of it.' Dr. Johnson.

of Lord Chatham, has distinguished himself; he comes out as his father did a ready-made orator, and I doubt not but that I shall one day or other see him the first man in the country. His famous speech, however, delivered the other night, did not convince me, and I staid in with the old fat fellow [Lord North]: by the way he grows every day fatter, so where he will end I know not.'*⁷

We have seen that Wilberforce's first speeches were concerned with the interests of Hull and it was not until February 22, 1782 that he spoke on wider issues. He had entered Parliament as an opponent of the American War which was now tottering towards its inglorious close. Wilberforce supported General Conway's action for putting an end to the war and launched into a vigorous attack on Lord North's administration. While this ministry existed, he declared, there were no prospects of peace or happiness in the kingdom. The ministers' conduct had resembled the career of furious madmen rather than the prudent exertions of statesmen. From what the government said, it was clear that they intended to pursue the ruinous war in the former cruel, bloody and impracticable manner.

Lord North's Government could not survive the loss of the war and in March 1782 he was succeeded by Lord Rockingham, supported by Shelburne. Rockingham was First Lord of the Treasury, Fox and Shelburne Secretaries of State. The King showed a preference for Shelburne as the least obnoxious of his new ministers, but his influence was at its lowest and he could do nothing to prevent the Government being dominated by Rockingham, Fox and Burke.

Lord Rockingham's interests were paramount in Yorkshire and he seems to have formed a high opinion of the young member for Hull, the courtesies he showed to Wilberforce being so marked that the latter received several applications for the supply of his robes in anticipation of his transfer to the Upper House. But if Rockingham had any such intentions, which would surely have been premature, they were cut short by his death on July 1, 1782. Fox had already resigned from the Government, so Shelburne succeeded. Pitt became his Chancellor of the Exchequer at the age of twenty-three.

As a politician Wilberforce always loathed the idea of 'party', a word which in his day carried factious connotations. He regarded himself as an independent member, and the fact that he invariably supported Shelburne and Pitt did not detract from his independence, because he was tied to them only by friendship with Pitt and agreement on a number of issues. That Pitt both relied upon and valued his support can be shown by his request to Wilberforce to second the Address on the Preliminaries of Peace with America.

* Dr. Johnson commented more elegantly on Lord North's figure with the words, 'he fills a chair'.

Shelburne's plans for peace were most imaginative; before the war the American colonies had been one of the largest importers of British goods. He thought it essential to restore this position and the obvious means was free trade. America's territorial claims should be satisfied at once, and the peace treaty followed by a commercial treaty offering the United States the freest possible trade with British territories. Access to British colonies was essential because the Americans' surplus on their trade with the West Indies enabled them to pay for British manufactured goods. Another advantage of being generous to America was that France and Spain would then be put under pressure to agree to a reasonable peace.

Shelburne's proposals, while subtle and intelligent, were also ahead of his time and beyond the influence of his party in the Commons. The commercial treaty, which ran against the protectionist philosophy of the day, was in any case a separate measure. The territorial concessions, taken by themselves, seemed to the ordinary member of parliament to constitute an abject surrender. Shelburne's colleagues began to desert and rumours of a coalition between Fox and North circulated.

On February 17, 1783 Wilberforce seconded the Address on the Preliminaries of Peace. He took the opportunity of denouncing the impending coalition. He did not get to bed until nine in the morning. On February 21 he spoke again in defence of the Peace Treaty, but his effort was outshone by an astonishing performance by Pitt. Wilberforce wrote: 'Pitt's famous speech on second day's debate —first day's not so good. Spoke three hours, till four in the morning. Stomach disordered, and actually holding Solomon's porch door open with one hand, while vomiting during Fox's speech to whom he was to reply.'[8]

In spite of Pitt's brilliance Shelburne was twice defeated on the Peace Treaty and it became clear that his Government was doomed. The nature of the next ministry was not so obvious. There were three groups in Parliament, led by Shelburne, Fox and North; all were to some extent discredited. In the words of J. Steven Watson, 'no one political group could command general support to maintain a stable government, for Shelburne would bear the stigma of losing the peace, North of losing the war, and Fox of losing self-control'.[9] There were also personal antipathies. Fox would not serve with Shelburne, nor Pitt with North. But North believed that Fox and Shelburne might be reconciled, and, backed by the King, leave him and his followers isolated. To protect himself and them he must form a coalition with one of the other groups. Shelburne would allow him only a menial role, while Fox would accept him as an equal partner.

Fox also shrank from an alliance with Shelburne. He could foresee a recurrence of the situation reached under Rockingham, when the King would deal only with Shelburne among his ministers. His following could be disrupted by an alliance between his colleagues and the King. North, on the other hand, was an easy-going man who would allow Fox the first place.

Shelburne resigned on February 24. The new Coalition seemed so monstrously unnatural to the King that he refused to summon its nominal leader, the Duke of Portland, until April 2. For Fox to join with North, the victim of his magnificent denunciations for so many years, seemed to Wilberforce and many of his contemporaries the very epitome of party spirit. In fact the Coalition was less iniquitous than it had been painted. The cause of Fox's vituperation was North's American policy and this became a matter of past history when the Coalition, after destroying its author in February, ratified his peace treaty in March.

*

During these years Wilberforce derived enormous pleasure from his social life. His wit, polish and generosity won him many friends as did that abundant charm to which all his contemporaries bear witness, but which none of them has been able to capture in their descriptions. His voice, as fine in song as in rhetoric, was a social grace much in demand. 'Wilberforce, we must have you again, the Prince says he will come at any time to hear you sing' was the reaction from Devonshire House after his first appearance there. He was also an adept mimic, with Lord North as his favourite butt, until he was cured by old Lord Camden of this 'dangerous art'. 'When invited by friends to witness my powers of imitation, he at once refused, saying very slightly for me to hear it, "It is but a vulgar accomplishment." "Yes, but it is not imitating the mere manner; Wilberforce says the very thing Lord North would say." "Oh," was his reply, "everyone does that." '10

In the intimate society of Goosetree's he could behave more freely. We see him with Pitt, Euston and other members in a room off the House of Commons, singing and laughing *à gorge déployée*, so that George Selwyn, looking on, 'could wish for one day to be twenty'. At Pitt's house, we find him 'laughing so heartily' that Harriot Pitt in the next room could hardly finish her letter. Pitt unbent among this small group of intimates as he never would again. He could forget for a moment that he was Chancellor of the Exchequer, lay aside his coldness and stiffness and behave like any young man in his early twenties. It is not always easy to reconcile the horse-play which he should already have outgrown with his astonishing political precocity. But Wilberforce later remembered the Pitt of those days as 'the wittiest man I ever knew'.

Wilberforce had inherited the villa in Wimbledon on the death of his Methodist uncle. It had eight or nine bedrooms and a large garden. As the only member of his set with a country house conveniently close to London, his hospitality was much in demand and his friends would often dine or sup with him and spend the night there. He wrote to his sister:

My dear Sister,
   From my retirement at Wimbledon, I write to you in your retirement at Drinkston, and I wish you may find as much comfort in one as I do in the other. The existence I enjoy here is of a sort quite different from what it is in London. I feel a load off my mind; nor is it in the mighty powers of Mrs. Siddons, nor in the yet superior and more exalted gratifications of the House of Commons . . . to compensate me for the loss of good air, pleasant walks, and what Milton calls 'each rural sight, each rural sound'.[11]

Pitt liked to sleep in the country air enough to leave London at midnight to join Wilberforce at Wimbledon. 'Eliot, Arden and I', he wrote, 'will be with you before curfew, and expect an early meal of peas and strawberries.' Once at Wimbledon, Pitt could indulge his taste for horseplay. One morning his fellow guests rose to find that the Chancellor of the Exchequer had strewn Wilberforce's flower beds with the shreds of a silk hat one of them had worn down from the opera the night before. A lieutenant of Shelburne's was frustrated in his search for political news. 'I have had no opportunity of particular conversation with Mr. P since yr Ldship left London . . . He passes, as usual, most of his time with his young Friends in a Society very lively—some little excess happen'd lately at Wimbledon . . . In the Evening some of the Neighbours were alarmed with noises at their doors, but Nobody, I believe, has made any ill natured reflection upon a mere frolic—It has only been pleasantly remarked, that the Rioters were headed by Mr. P, later Chancellor of the Ex-, and Master Arden, late Solicitor Genl.'[12]

*

In the autumn of 1783 Wilberforce accompanied Pitt and Eliot on a visit to France. Their journey was preceded by some good-natured bantering, which shows that, even then, he had a reputation for vagueness. After telling Wilberforce to meet them at Bankes's Pitt adds, 'I hope you will bear all these things in mind, and recollect that you have to do with punctual men who could not risk their characters by being late for any appointment.' Pitt may later have regretted giving this warning, for Wilberforce arrived on time, was taken out shooting and, hopelessly short-sighted and inexperienced, nearly succeeded in depriving himself of his best friend and England of her next Prime Minister.

Wilberforce's foreign trips always fortified his gratitude to Providence for permitting him to be born an Englishman. He made many friends on these visits; he admired the beauty of the scenery; he enjoyed moving in a different society; but somehow he was always glad to be home again. His first journey abroad began dismally. The three friends had all confidently left it to one another to provide introductions. It was with the greatest difficulty that they obtained a letter to a M. Coustier in Rheims, where they planned to spend a few weeks improving their French and sampling the local vintages, before moving on to Paris. They assumed M. Coustier to be a pillar of the local nobility and it was, therefore, with some surprise that they found him behind a counter distributing figs and raisins. Wilberforce, who had heard that it was usual for continental gentlemen to practise some handicraft or hobby, took this playing the greengrocer to be a harmless eccentricity. But before long they discovered him to be a 'véritable épicier' and M. Coustier, although the soul of courtesy, could scarcely be expected to supply introductions to the local nobility. They spent a miserable ten days in their inn, during which their knowledge of the French language made little progress, since they spoke only to one another and to their Irish courier.

At length they screwed up their courage, returned to M. Coustier and persuaded him to 'put on a bag and sword and carry us to the Intendant of police, whom he supplied with groceries'. The Englishmen considered this manoeuvre to have worked admirably and they would have been startled to have known the impression that they had made on the policeman.

Rheims was still ruled by an episcopal government that had lasted since the days of Clovis. In the absence of the Archbishop, his authority was wielded by the secretary to the Council of State, the Abbé de Lageard, 'a fellow of infinite humour and extraordinary humanity'. Many years later de Lageard remembered their arrival.

'One morning when the Intendant of police brought me his daily report, he informed me, there are three Englishmen here of very suspicious character. They are in a wretched lodging, they have no attendants, yet their courier says, that they are "grands seigneurs", and that one of them is son of the great Chatham; but it is impossible, they must be "des intrigants".' The Intendant wished to make an official investigation, but de Lageard, who knew something of England, decided to visit them himself. 'As I was at once satisfied by their appearance I asked whether I could be of any use to them, and offered whatever the town of Rheims could afford for their amusement. Amongst other things Mr. Pitt complained, "Here we are in the middle of Champagne, and we cannot get any tolerable wine." "Dine with me tomorrow," I replied, "and you shall have the best wine the country can afford." They came to dine with me, and instead of moving directly after dinner, as we do in France, we sat talking for five or six hours.'[13]

De Lageard proved a perfect host. To prevent time from hanging heavily on their hands he would visit them for six hours at a stretch. He introduced them to his friends and arranged for them to hunt over the Archbishop's lands. Wilberforce's diary reflects the change. 'A sad party—drunken prior—sang—seventy three [years old].' At this house they were the victims of one of those preconceptions that plague Anglo-French relations. Their hosts did ample justice to their meal, but noticed that the Englishmen did not eat as much as they had. They attributed this to distaste for the delicate and subtle dishes that had been served and after an orgy of winks, hints and laughter, a gigantic joint of almost raw roast beef was placed upon the table. They were unable to tackle this monstrous dish at the end of an already adequate meal, but their reluctance was attributed to shyness. If they had been alone, the French agreed, they would have made heavy inroads into their national fare.

They were presented to the Archbishop on his return. After entertaining them to dinner he offered to have them to stay for a week. He seems to have impressed Wilberforce, who noted 'N.B. Archbishops in England are not like Archévêques in France; these last are jolly fellows of about forty years of age, who play at billiards, etc., like other people'.[14]

They sometimes had more serious conversations, usually with de Lageard. Pitt, who spoke the best French of the three, would enquire carefully about political institutions in France. The Abbé remembered his conclusion. 'Monsieur, vous n'avez point de liberté politique, mais pour la liberté civile, vous en avez plus que vous ne croyez.' De Lageard in return asked him which part of the British constitution might first be expected to decay. Pitt replied, 'the prerogative of the King and the authority of the House of Peers'. The Abbé once expressed his surprise 'that a country so moral as England can submit to be governed by a man so wanting in private character as Fox; it seems to show you to be less moral than you appear'. 'C'est que vous n'avez pas été sous la baguette du Magicien', was Pitt's answer, 'but the remark,' he acknowledged, 'is just.'[15]

When they arrived in Paris they found that the story of their embarrassments in Rheims had preceded them. Marie Antoinette often teased Pitt by asking if he had lately heard from his friend the grocer. Wilberforce was much taken by the Queen, whom he described as 'a monarch of most engaging manners and appearance'. But he found her husband less impressive, 'a clumsy, strange figure in immense boots' and 'so strange a being (of the hog kind) that it is worth going a hundred miles for a sight of him, especially a boar hunting'.[16]

They were in fact taken boar and stag hunting, and also to Court, to the theatre and opera, to suppers, to cards, backgammon and billiards. They were entertained to dinner by the Marquis de la Fayette and met Benjamin Franklin in his house. Necker gave Pitt to understand that he would be an acceptable suitor for the hand of his daughter, the future Mme de Staël. Pitt is said to have replied, 'I am already married to my country.' It might not have been a comfortable match, but, if there is anything in heredity, they should have had phenomenal children. There were many English visitors in Paris and at one party they behaved in the oafish, insular manner all too often adopted by our countrymen abroad. A dozen of them monopolised a table throughout the evening and admitted only one Frenchman to it, the Marquis de Noailles, who qualified by virtue of his perfect command of the English language. Wilberforce was later ashamed of this episode and particularly by the presence at their table of the British Ambassador, who was, he felt, old enough to know better. When they were allowed to approach him, the French 'crowded round Pitt in shoals; and he behaved with great spirit though he was sometimes a little bored when they talked to him about the parliamentary reform'.[17]

A special messenger to Pitt cut short their visit, and on October 24 they returned. Wilberforce found himself 'better pleased with his own country than before he left it'.

*

Pitt did well to hurry home. The years of political chaos that separated the periods of North's and Pitt's dominance were drawing to their close, and the country was on the brink of a crisis in which he would be able to play a decisive part. George III had always detested the Fox-North Coalition. He had accepted it only after all his protests, even the threat to return to Hanover, had failed to produce any alternative. He was determined to put an end to it as soon as he could and Fox's India Bill gave him his chance. This Bill contained many useful features, but it transferred all political power to a board of seven Commissioners in London, while the commercial affairs of the Company were to be run by nine Assistant Commissioners. These sixteen Commissioners were all to be supporters of the Government. The vast powers of patronage that Fox proposed to create for his own use outraged the King, the Company and the Opposition.

Wilberforce joined Pitt in attacking the Bill in the Commons. His speeches began to attract more attention and his eloquence was described as one of Pitt's mainstays. But in spite of the Bill's unpopularity the Coalition won the vote in the Commons with ease. The King was now ready to use any expedient to rid himself of the Coalition. But before acting he needed an alternative Government with a chance of survival. Shelburne, North and their associates were discredited, but Pitt's reputation was unsullied by the disastrous American War and, although only twenty-four, he had great ability and a great name. Robinson, the supreme political calculator of the times, produced analyses of the Commons, showing how they would vote before and after a General Election. This document persuaded both the King and Pitt that the risk was worthwhile. The King sent a note to the Lords, where the India Bill was about to be debated, declaring 'he would consider all who voted for it as his enemies'. He was not without enemies in the Upper Chamber, but the Coalition was defeated, first by 87 votes to 79, then, on December 17, by 95 to 76. On December 18 the Government was dismissed and Pitt became First Lord of the Treasury.

Wilberforce's diary shows something of the intrigues, confusion and tension that filled the last months of 1783.

'20th. House—spirited debate about putting off India Bill. Dined Goosetree's.

'27th. Great day in the House. Sat till past four in the morning.

'28th. No House. Dined Tom Pitt's—Mrs. Crewe—charming woman.

'29th. Went to see Mrs. Siddons—Mrs. Crewe at play.

'30th. Dined Lord Chatham's—meeting. Wrote for ladies to go to the gallery, but disappointed.

'Dec. 1st. House—late night. Home about five, immediately after debate. Fox spoke wonderfully.

'3rd. Dined Goosetree's. Supped Duchess of Portland's, Downing Street. Charles Fox came in—whispering over chair. Heavy evening.

'6th. Dined Hamilton's—opera. Supped Burlington House—Mrs. Crewe—Duchess of Portland. Mrs. Sheridan sang old English songs angelically—promised her our votes.

'8th. House sat till near four. Spoke ill—confused.

'22nd. Lord Temple resigned. No dissolution declared. Drove about for Pitt—"So your friend Mr. Pitt means to come in," said Mrs. Crewe: "well, he may do what he likes during the holidays, but it will only be a mince-pie administration, depend on it."

'23rd. Morning Pitt's. Dined Sir C. Middleton's. Pitt nobly firm. Evening Pitt's. Cabinet formed—"We had a great meeting that night of all Pitt's friends in Downing Street. As Pratt, Tom Steele, and I were going up to it in a hackney coach from the house of Commons, 'Pitt must take care,' I said, 'whom he makes Secretary of the Treasury, it is rather a roguish office.' 'Mind what you say,' answered Steele, 'for I am Secretary of the Treasury.' At Pitt's we had a long discussion; and I remember well the great penetration showed by Lord Mahon. 'What am I to do,' said Pitt, 'if they stop the supplies!' 'They will not stop them,' said Mahon, 'it is the very thing which they will not venture to do.'"

Lord Mahon's comment was right. To hamstring the Government by withholding financial grants would have been an unprecedented demonstration of 'party spirit' calculated to upset the independent members. But this was the only limit Fox felt bound to observe. When Parliament reassembled on January 12, 1784 he set out to show his strength. He twice defeated the new Government and carried five other resolutions without division. His personal domination of the House was as complete. He subjected Pitt to the full power of his matchless rhetoric and tempered his fury only with contempt. Pitt was shaken by the violence of this attack, but he held on under a series of defeats and did not ask for a dissolution. The tide soon began to turn in his favour. When in office Fox had enjoyed a majority of 106; on January 12 it had been 39 and 54; on January 12 it fell to 21 and a week later to 8. By March 1 it was 1. Pitt now easily obtained his supplies and asked for a dissolution.

There was never any doubt about the result of the next election. No government lost one throughout the eighteenth century. What was remarkable about 1784 was not the swing to Pitt, but the kind of seat in which it occurred. Wherever the opinion of the electorate could make itself felt the story was the same. Fox's supporters were ousted from counties and open boroughs and forced back on the Whig nomination boroughs for survival. Public opinion, the Royal Influence and the great financial institutions were united in their support for Pitt, and his victory was complete and overwhelming. Nowhere was this more clearly shown than in Yorkshire.

*

Yorkshire, with some 20,000 voters, was the most populous as well as the largest constituency in the country. It was also a sounding board for national public opinion, for its electorate was diverse. The influence of the great aristocrats, particularly that of Lord Rockingham, was unusually strong because of a local arrangement under which most tenants farmed their land on short leases. In the days of open ballots, the landlords' power to terminate leases at six months' notice made their tenants exceptionally amenable to their wishes. But Yorkshiremen have never been noted for their servility and the magnates' influence was limited by the great number of country gentry and freeholders in the County who had a reputation for independence. The agricultural interests, in their turn, were balanced by the weavers of the West Riding and the clothiers of Leeds. There were also many Methodists and Quakers qualified to vote.

Elie Halévy has advanced the theory that eighteenth-century politicians saw elections as an extension of their sporting life, a more exciting and often more expensive form of faro. Only this, he reasons, could have persuaded them to indulge in such ruinous contests, when they could have bought a closed borough for a fraction of the price. Representation of the County held great prestige, but hardly enough to compensate for the cost of fighting an election. The Duke of Norfolk, whose influence in Yorkshire elections was considerable, evidently took this view. 'What greater enjoyment can there be in life,' he asked, 'than to stand a contested election for Yorkshire and to win it by one?'[18]

But only the most extravagant and competitive candidate or patron could consider contesting the County of Yorkshire. It had cost Wilberforce about £8 for every vote he won in Hull in 1780. To be sure of the County a candidate needed about 12,000 votes and in a fiercely contested election, as we shall see, they could cost more than £8 each. But £100,000 in the late eighteenth century is equivalent of some £1,500,000 today. It is not surprising that in the century before the Reform Bill, only four Yorkshire elections went to the polls, those of 1734, 1741, 1807 and 1830. There were no shortages of challenges in other years, but these were settled after extensive canvasses, which were themselves more expensive than fighting most seats. In the days of open ballots such canvasses were far more accurate than any modern opinion poll and could, if carried far enough, give a guarantee of success or failure. The two political parties often agreed to share the seat, each putting up only one candidate. But if a party made a challenge and had a strong enough canvass, it would sometimes seize both county seats without a struggle.

In 1779 a new influence had appeared in the County's politics in the shape of the Yorkshire Association. This organisation, led by Christopher Wyvill, was dedicated to parliamentary and economic reform. In the 1780 election the Associators, mainly independent country gentlemen, allied themselves with Lord Rockingham. Together they installed Sir George Savile, one of Yorkshire's representatives since 1761, and Henry Duncombe in the place of Edwin Lascelles the other sitting member. The poet William Mason, one of the leading Associators, boasted that they had 'plucked every peacock's feather out of the tail of that strutting carrion crow Lascelles and frightened the Lord Paramount of the West Indies out of the contest!'[19] Savile greeted the appearance of the Association with the words 'hitherto I have been elected in Lord Rockingham's drawing room —now I am returned by my constituents'.[20]

After Rockingham's death in 1782, his political influence passed to his nephew, Lord Fitzwilliam. Fitzwilliam lacked Rockingham's political touch, but it is likely that nothing he could have done would have avoided a clash with the Association. In 1783 the Fitzwilliam candidate was humiliated in a by-election in York City. At the end of the same year the resignation by Sir George Savile of the County seat threatened a more serious crisis, but Fitzwilliam and the Associators agreed on a compromise candidate, Savile's nephew, F. F. Foljambe, and both sides claimed him for their own.

This precarious alliance could not be maintained at the General Election of 1784. Wyvill and his Associators recognised in Pitt their best chance for Reform, while Fitzwilliam was irrevocably committed to Fox. Wyvill forced the issue by calling for a County Meeting to carry an address to the King condemning the Coalition. This meeting was to be held in the Castle Yard at York on March 25.

Wilberforce went to York to speak in support of the motion, but he had other plans. 'I will tell you what I have hardly told anybody else,' he later confided to his friend J. S. Harford, 'that I had then formed in my own breast the project of standing for the County of York, though to anyone else it would have appeared a mad scheme. . . . It was very contrary to the aristocratic notions of the great families of the County to place the son of a Hull merchant in so high a situation.'[21] The outcome proves that Wilberforce's plan was no 'mad scheme', but it was certainly an ambitious one. In London his grace, polish, charm and wit could overcome any lingering prejudices against him as the son of a tradesman. London society would tolerate almost anyone who was amusing, civilised and rich. But he was at first sight far from an ideal representative for Yorkshire. This privilege was normally reserved for members of the great landed families, like Duncombe, Lascelles, Milton and Fawkes who later shared the seat with Wilberforce. These were the kind of men the squires could respect. The gulf that separated Wilberforce from the squires can be seen in his attitude after a visit to his estate: 'Went to look at my land; my land just like any one else's land.'

Apart from this social handicap, Wilberforce's prospects were hampered by the absence of any obvious opening. The County's two members, Foljambe and Duncombe, were both standing again. Foljambe had the backing of Lord Fitzwilliam's powerful interests and had proved an acceptable candidate to the Associators. In the event of a compromise between the two parties, Duncombe would be the representative of the Associators. Wilberforce's only chance was therefore in a contest in which the Associators would win both seats.

It was a foul day in the Castle Yard and the crowd was lashed by wind, rain and hail. The speakers were partly sheltered by a wooden canopy. Wilberforce spoke towards the end of this long meeting, so that when he rose even the hardy Yorkshire audience were cold, wet and bored. The weather was by now so bad that an eyewitness thought it seemed 'as if his slight frame would be unable to make head against its violence'. In these miserable conditions Wilberforce made one of the best and most important speeches of his life. It is no exaggeration to say that it won him the seat. He spoke for an hour and held his audience enthralled from beginning to end. Boswell, who was shivering in the rain, reported to Dundas, 'I saw what seemed a mere shrimp mount upon the table; but as I listened, he grew, and grew, until the shrimp became a whale.'[22] His speech was interrupted by a message from Pitt, telling him that Parliament was to be prorogued that day, enclosing a copy of the speech to be made from the throne and urging him to 'tear the enemy to pieces'. When this note was handed to him Wilberforce showed the adaptability that is the hallmark of the true orator. His flow was cut short by having to stop to read it, but he used the pause to raise the dramatic level of his speech. He studied it for half a minute and then, instead of resuming where he had left off, announced, with great effect, that the King had this very moment appealed to the decision of the nation.

The address was carried by acclamation and the two parties retired to confer in their respective taverns. Wilberforce found himself with an incongruous and tipsy group; there were Associators and non-Associators, Wnigs and Tories, aristocrats and clothiers, united only by their dislike for the Coalition. During dinner several quarrels broke out which Wilberforce prevented from spreading by 'reminding them of the great constitutional principles which we all maintained'. His companions decided that such a combination of eloquence and diplomacy should be rewarded with the representation of the County. At midnight there was a spontaneous cry of 'Wilberforce and liberty!'

The next morning their rivals proposed to share the County seats between their own nominee, Foljambe, and any other person. An acceptance would have been fatal to Wilberforce's chances, since Duncombe, not he, would have been his party's first choice. But the York Tavern group delayed giving an answer until they had sounded out their neighbours. Wilberforce's position was still thought too insecure for him to resign from his present seat. He therefore left York for Hull on the evening of March 26 and carried out a hurried canvass. On April 1 he won the seat, though by a less generous margin than in 1780.* The Hull electorate seemed to resent the likelihood that he would resign if elected for the County. Some of his constituents did not confine their protests to the ballot; 'snowballs, etc., thrown at me in chair,' Wilberforce records.

Wilberforce returned to York to find his cause well advanced. He had already shown his persuasiveness, eloquence and tact; he now revealed another weapon, replying to attacks at the nomination meeting with such withering sarcasm that his opponents were silenced and he and Duncombe easily elected on a show of hands. Their canvass was equally encouraging. They polled two-thirds of the electorate and found 11,173 friendly and only 2,510 doubtful or hostile. Such a response justified them in going all out for both seats. £18,670 was raised towards the cost of an election, and the candidates, in spite of their protests, were not allowed to contribute. But only a quarter of this sum was needed. Their opponents' canvass must have agreed with theirs, for on April 6 they withdrew. Wilberforce's diary for the next day reads: 'Up early—breakfasted tavern—rode frisky horse to castle—elected—chaired—dined York Tavern. Spencer Stanhope† spoke to me.'

Pitt wrote to congratulate him:

Downing Street, April 8, 1784.

My dear Wilberforce,

I can never enough congratulate you on such glorious success. I am going to dine at

---

* The voting was: Wilberforce 807, S. Thornton 751, D. Hartley 357.
† His successor at Hull.

Wilberforce House, with a statue of Wilberforce in the garden

William Wilberforce
aged eleven
after J. Russell

William Pitt by Thomas Gainsborough

Isaac Milner,
attributed to Archer Shee

Photo: Edward Leigh

William Wilberforce
by Rising

Clapham Common showing the church where the Saints worshipped

Wilberforce stands stooped in front of the fire in the
library which Pitt designed at Battersea Rise

Photo: John R. Freeman & Co

Wimbledon to-day, to mix my joy with Mrs. Dixon's, who has all the trophies of victory, such as handbills, ballads, &c. to adorn your kitchen, and your boy. I hope you will have a worthy successor in the person of Spencer Stanhope. I have seen Manners, who has no thought of standing, and will write to his friends in favour of Stanhope. I hope his accomplishments cannot fail to conciliate the previous confidence necessary for your sanction.

Ever yours,
W. Pitt.

P.S. Westminster goes on well, in spite of the Duchess of Devonshire and the *other women of the people*, but when the poll will close is uncertain.[23]

Lord Fitzwilliam saw his failure in social terms. 'We were certainly not deserted by the better part of it [the County] but beat by the ragamuffins.'

*

In London that summer Wilberforce regularly attended Parliament and voted with Pitt. He seemed certain of a brilliant political career: he was still only twenty-four, but he had already won, without great influence or connections, the most coveted seat in Parliament. He had proved his eloquence in debate and on the hustings. He was liked by both parties and he was the Prime Minister's most intimate friend. The only doubt about his future was whether his fragile health would interfere with his political career. At the end of the session he returned to York to spend his twenty-fifth birthday at what his sons call 'the top wave and highest flow of those frivolous amusements, which had swallowed up so large a portion of his youth'. He went to the races and the ball and his singing, as always, was much in demand. There was no sign that his life was about to undergo a complete and permanent change, but the first step towards making this change was taken during his holiday in York. Wilberforce was planning a continental tour, and asked a friend William Burgh, to be his companion. Burgh refused and shortly afterwards Wilberforce met his old schoolmaster Isaac Milner and asked him to come instead. Milner accepted.

CHAPTER III

THE CONVERT

ISAAC MILNER had known and taught Wilberforce before his Methodist phase. After two years as an usher at Hull Grammar School he obtained a sizarship to Queen's College, Cambridge. Here Milner soon showed how wasted his talents had been at the loom. He took his degree in 1774, came out Senior Wrangler of his year and was pronounced 'incomparabilis', a unique tribute. He was ordained the next year and became a fellow of his old college in 1776. Everything about Milner was larger than life. He was a huge man of great strength but extreme timidity, 'the most enormous man it was ever my fate to see in a drawing-room', according to Marianne Thornton.[1] His health was apparently robust enough; he certainly ate enough for three, but he frequently complained of headaches and trouble with his pulse. It is hard to say whether these ailments were genuine for Milner was an arch-hypochondriac, always haunted by imaginary illnesses and fleeing from such menaces to his well-being as the east wind and thunder.

Milner's mind was as massive as his body, ponderous yet versatile. The title of 'incomparabilis' is sufficient tribute to his mathematical genius. His talents developed early; as a boy of eight he is said to have designed and built a sundial; he was elected a member of the Royal Society when still a Bachelor of Arts. He studied Chemistry and became the Professor of Natural Philosophy as well as that of Mathematics. He was also a distinguished divine and an amateur of practical mechanics. He solved the 'contrivance of the invisible girl' which had puzzled all London when performed in Leicester Fields. As a conversationalist and wit he was regarded as Johnson's successor. His comical stories were enhanced by a broad Yorkshire accent that he kept all his life. His weaknesses, timidity and indolence, were as marked as his good qualities. Altogether he is rather a surprising companion for Wilberforce to have chosen; but the two men had not entirely lost touch with each other and Wilberforce used to obtain tickets for Milner in the Gallery of the House of Commons.

The party set off on October 20, 1784. Wilberforce and Milner travelled in one carriage; Wilberforce's mother, sister and two ailing female cousins in another. They crossed France to Lyons and sailed down the Rhône to Avignon, which he found 'sweetly situated, but a most dirty hole; particularly our inn, The St. Omers'. At this inn Mary Bird, one of his cousins, slept 'in a small chamber with a thin partition from a dining room and heard a party [Lady Rivers and her family] talking over Wilberforce. . . . They spoke of his abilities in the highest terms, but thought he was going to die at Nice, for one said "he was all soul and no body".'[2] They then took the 'execrable road' to Marseilles and followed the coast to Nice, 'the whole of Provence abounding in aromatics of all kinds,' Wilberforce noted: 'roads hitherto very bad—dusky olives—striking view from the Estrelles —formerly infested by banditti—trees cut down near road to prevent their sudden attack—the country more delightful than can be imagined—everything to constitute beauties of prospect, but rivers and verdure—the olives too almost the only wood except where you have pines.'[3]

Even in those days Nice was popular among English travellers, and Wilberforce found many of his friends from London there. 'Duke of Gloucester,' his diary reads, 'Lady Rivers, and G. Pitt, Sir. I. Wroughton, Bosanquet, Duchess of Ancaster and Lady Charlotte, etc. here.' This was as well for 'the natives were in general a wretched set'. Wilberforce was at home in this Society and Milner fitted in easily enough, his unpolished manners causing less stir than they would have in London. 'Pretty boy, pretty boy,' he exclaimed in his broadest Yorkshire accent, while ruffling the hair of the young Prince William of Gloucester, to whom he had just been presented. His cloth did not prevent him from attending Sunday parties and dinners and his wit made him a welcome guest. But Mrs. Wilberforce firmly refused all Sunday invitations for herself and the other ladies. The winter passed pleasantly and idly; they rode and walked, went to parties and gave dinners. They even tried, without results, the 'animal magnetisers' that were the fashionable toys of Nice Society. 'The Climate was so delightful,' Wilberforce remembered, 'that many times during the month of January we carried our cold meat into some of the beautiful recesses of the mountains and rocks by which the place is surrounded on the land side and dined in the open air as we should here in the summer.'[4]

But Nice was to mean more in Wilberforce's life than another round of entertainment and pleasure. In the carriage on the way there the conversation sometimes turned to religious subjects, which Wilberforce would treat with flippancy. Milner would resist these attacks and reply, 'I am no match for you, Wilberforce, in this running fire, but if you really want to discuss these subjects seriously, I will gladly enter on them with you.' Just before they left Nice, on February 5, 1785, Wilberforce picked up a book belonging to one of his travelling companions, Doddridge's *Rise and Progress of Religion*, and asked Milner if it was worth reading. 'It is one of the best books ever written. Let us take it with us and read it on our journey.'

In those days continental travel was uncomfortable and sometimes dangerous. The roads were bad, the inns filthy and the food, even in France, unspeakably vile. 'Milner and I,' Wilberforce wrote, 'attended by Dixon our courier, made the best of our way, setting out in the morning before it was light and travelling till after dark—the wretched inns in which we had to take up our quarters not being likely to afford any meat, we used to buy it where it was to be had during the day, carry it along with us, and when we came to our inn at night make it into soup with the addition of pearl barley, onions, etc. not a morsel of bread could we eat as it was all sour (indeed Milner and I never tasted bread but twice on the continent in both our expeditions) no wine except now and then a little Frontiniac, no brandy, no butter, or cheese; in short none of those things which in England we should deem indispensable for our comfort even our health.'[5]

The ordinary discomforts of the journey were increased by heavy snow-falls in the Alps. They travelled through eighteen days of snow, and once, as they were plodding after their coach up an icy hill, only Milner's herculean strength prevented it from sliding over a precipice. Saved from the loss of their belongings and their vehicle, the vast clergyman and the diminutive politician got into the coach at the top of the hill, wrapped themselves in their travelling rugs and resumed their studies of Doddridge. Wilberforce was sufficiently impressed to resolve to read the Scriptures himself at some future date.

At first the diary of his life in London during the summer session of 1785 shows little change. He worked with Pitt on the details of a Reform Bill which would have disenfranchised thirty-six rotten boroughs with compensation and given the extra seats to London and the Counties. 'At Pitt's all day—it goes on well—sat up late chatting with Pitt—his good hopes of the country and noble, patriotic heart—to town—Pitt's—House—Parliamentary Reform—terribly disappointed and beat—extremely fatigued—spoke extremely ill but commended. April 19th. Called at Pitt's—met poor Wyvill.' He dined with Pitt two or three times a week and his time passed pleasantly 'sitting up all night singing—shirked Duchess of Gordon, at Almack's—danced till five in the morning'.

But an unfamiliar note, the first germination of Doddridge's seed, soon intrudes. 'Dined Hamilton's—christening—very indecent—all laughing round.' On April 14 he writes, with exasperating reticence, 'Opera—shocking dance of Festin de Pierre, and unmoved audience.' 'S and I talked—strange that the most generous men and religious, do not see that their duties increase with their fortune, and that they will be punished for spending it in eating, etc.' There are also signs that he was fretting against conventional politics. When he was at Spa on his second tour with Milner,

Pitt wrote him a long letter telling him of the marriage of Harriot Pitt to Eliot, in which he refers to Wilberforce's 'constant call for *Something out of the Common Way*'.[6] These thoughts were still mere speculations which were without influence on his conduct, but at the end of the summer session he set out once more with Milner to the Continent. He was to be a different man when he next returned to England.

Wilberforce and Milner had arranged to meet the ladies in Genoa, having left them in Nice. 'When my mother is once set down in a place 'tis the most difficult thing in nature to remove her.'[7] They read the Greek Testament on the coach and Wilberforce later remembered 'by degrees I inbibed his sentiments, though I must confess with shame that they long remained merely as opinions assented to by my understanding but not influencing my heart'. His correspondence showed a new seriousness; in a letter to his friend, Lord Muncaster, he wrote, 'I fancy I see storms arising, which already "no bigger than a man's hand", will by and by overspread and blacken the whole face of heaven. It is not the confusion of parties, and their quarrelling and battling in the House of Commons, which makes me despair of the republic (if I knew a word half way between "apprehend for" and "despair", that would best express my meaning), but it is the universal corruption and profligacy of the times, which taking its rise amongst the rich and luxurious has now extended its baneful influence and spread its destructive poison through the whole body of the people. When the mass of blood is corrupt, there is no remedy but amputation.'[8]

The ladies joined them at Genoa after an adventurous passage across the Gulf in a felucca. Together they travelled to Geneva, being carried in chairs over the Mont Cenis, and to 'the paradise of Interlaken', Zurich and Spa. At Geneva they once more met the Gloucesters who sent Milner some of their own wine when he complained of the effects of the local vintage on his health. Wilberforce was by now utterly absorbed in his talks with Milner, so much so that his fellow-travellers complained of the infrequency of his visits to their carriage. He seems to have recognised little change in himself, but the difference is obvious to any reader of his diary. 'Began three or four days ago to get up very early. In the solitude and self-conversation of the morning had thoughts, which I trust will come to something—.' 'As soon as I reflected seriously upon these subjects the deep guilt and black ingratitude of my past life forced itself upon me in the strongest colours, and I condemned myself for having wasted my precious time, and opportunities, and talents.'[9] Spa, where they stayed for six weeks, was full of English and they could not fail to notice the change in him. 'Mrs. Crewe cannot believe that I think it wrong to go to the play.— Surprised at hearing that halting on the Sunday was my wish, and not my mother's.'[10]

On November 10 Wilberforce returned to Wimbledon, his mind in a turmoil. Parliament was not sitting; he was alone for much of the time and his thoughts fermented in solitude. His old life lay in ruins around him. Everything for which he had striven, every achievement, ambition and delight became worthless and even harmful when seen through his newly opened eyes. The more he brooded the more he became convinced of his own sinfulness in having neglected the mercies of God for so long.

This certainty of guilt cast him into a state of the deepest depression. He knew now what he ought to do but he was haunted by fears of relapse. He had no confidence in his strength and application. He knew himself and realised that the intense pleasure he could derive from worldly intercourse would always be a temptation. For many years after his conversion he would remind himself of this failing by writing in his diary after each purely social entry some such comment as: 'How ill suited is all this to me! How unnatural for one who professes himself a stranger and a pilgrim!' He was haunted by the memory of his first relapse from Methodism. He began a private journal to make himself 'humble and watchful'. A few extracts from this extraordinarily intense document show the state of his mind.

'It was not so much the fear of punishment by which I was affected, as a sense of my great sinfulness in having so long neglected the unspeakable mercies of my God and Saviour; and such was the effect which this thought produced, that for months I was in a state of the deepest depression, from strong convictions of my guilt. Indeed nothing which I have ever read in the accounts of others, exceeded what I then felt.'[11]

*

'Nov. 24th. Heard the Bible read two hours—Pascal one hour and a quarter—meditation one hour and a quarter—business the same. If ever I take myself from the immediate consideration of serious things, I entirely lose sight of them; this must be a lesson to me to keep them constantly in view. Pitt called, and commended Butler's Analogy—resolved to write to him, and discover to him what I am occupied about: this will save me much embarrassment, and I hope give me more command both of my time and conduct.'

'25th. St. Antholyn's—Mr. Forster's—felt much devotion, and wondered at a man who fell asleep during the Psalms: during the sermon I fell asleep myself.—Walked, and stage coach, to save the expense of a chaise.

'26th. —refused to go to Camden Place, and to Pitt's; but all religious thoughts go off in London—I hope by explaining my situation and feelings, to relieve myself from my embarrassment.

'Sunday, 27th. I must awake to my dangerous state, and never be at rest till I have made my peace with God. My heart is so hard, my blindness so great, that I cannot get a due hatred of sin, though I see I am all corrupt, and blinded to the perception of spiritual things.'

'28th. I hope as long as I live to be the better for the meditation of this evening; it was on the sinfulness of my own heart, and its blindness and weakness. True, Lord, I am wretched, and miserable, and blind, and naked. What infinite love, that Christ should die to save such a sinner, and how necessary is it He should save us altogether, that we may appear before God with nothing of our own!

'Tuesday, 29th. Pride is my greatest stumbling block; and there is danger in it in two ways—lest it should make me desist from a christian life, through fear of the world, my friends, &c; or if I persevere, lest it should make me vain of so doing.

'Nov. 30th. Was very fervent in prayer this morning, and thought these warm impressions would never go off. Yet in vain endeavoured in the evening to rouse myself. God grant it may not all prove vain; oh if it does, how will my punishment be deservedly increased! The only way I find of moving myself, is by thinking of my great transgressions, weakness, blindness, and of God's having promised to supply these defects. But though I firmly believe them, yet I read of future judgment, and think of God's wrath against sinners, with no great emotions. What can so strongly show the stony heart? O God, give me a heart of flesh! Nothing so convinces me of the dreadful state of my own mind, as the possibility, which, if I did not know it from experience, I should believe impossible, of my being ashamed of Christ. Ashamed of the Creator of all things! One who has received infinite pardon and mercy, ashamed of the Dispenser of it, and that in a country where his name is professed! Oh, what should I have done in persecuting times? (Forgot to set down that when my servants came in the first time to family prayer, I felt ashamed.)

'I thought seriously this evening of going to converse with Mr. Newton —waked in the night—obliged to compel myself to think of God.'[12]

On December 2 he wrote to Newton asking if he could call and have 'some serious conversation with you'. He finished: 'P.S. Remember that I must be secret, and that the gallery of the House is now so universally attended, that the face of a member of Parliament is pretty well known.'[13]

Wilberforce badly needed a spiritual rock to cling to in his turmoil. Milner was of no use to him, for when converting Wilberforce he seems also to have converted himself and come to a sudden realisation of his responsibilities and duties as a clergyman. Milner, too, was undergoing a spiritual crisis. In the autumn of 1785 Wilberforce needed a simpler, stronger guide and one who had already overcome his own doubts. In Newton he found such a man.

The Evangelicals came from diverse backgrounds: Hannah More was a poet and playwright, Zachary Macaulay a slave driver, James Stephen a lawyer, Thomas Babington a landed magnate, Henry Thornton a banker, Wilberforce a politician, Isaac Milner a don and Lord Teignmouth the

Governor-General of India, but none had led so colourful a life as John Newton.

Newton was the son of an officer in the merchant navy. He went to sea under his father's command at the age of eleven; he was pressed into a King's ship and rated as midshipman, deserted and was flogged and degraded to the rank of common seaman. At his own request he was exchanged into a slaver and taken to the coast of Sierra Leone. Newton's mother was a religious woman who did her best for her son but his enthusiasm was fitful. He confessed, 'I took up and laid aside a religious profession three or four times before I was sixteen years old.' So weak a growth could not survive the atmosphere of a slaver and he admits that at this time 'I was exceedingly vile'.

Newton left his ship to become overseer of a Slave Depot on the Plantain Islands off Sierra Leone but here he found himself in bondage. The trader to whom he acted as an unpaid serf had a black mistress who delighted in tormenting Newton. He was starved, feverish and deprived of shelter and water. For a time he was forced to work as a slave on a lime plantation. He survived only because of the scraps brought to him by the other slaves. His one relaxation was to study a copy of Euclid and trace out diagrams on the sand. He remained on the Plantain Islands from 1746 to 1748 until rescued by his father.[14]

Newton's experiences as a slave did not turn him against the trade but they did bring him back to God. He sailed as first mate on a slaver, married his childhood sweetheart, and in 1750 was given the command of a slaver. This ship must have been the most extraordinary ever to follow the Triangular Trade. All the ordinary horrors of the Middle Passage were present, for Newton was an insensitive, if not a cruel man. The crew, also, needed severe discipline and the rope's end was much used. But separated only by a few boards from his wailing, stinking, miserable cargo, Newton would spend hours in prayer or conducting services for his seamen. In this unlikely retreat he found 'sweeter and more frequent hours of divine communion' than he had ever known before. During one of his voyages he composed the hymn 'How sweet the name of Jesus sounds'. When faced with the contrast between the gentle beauty of this hymn and the abominable background against which it was written, one can only regard its author as being among the most insensitive men who ever lived. But one is then left with the paradox of how such a man could have written such lines. Newton left the trade for reasons of health rather than conscience. He looked back on it with nostalgia as affording, more than any other profession, 'greater opportunities to an awakened mind, for promoting the life of God in the soul'. He referred to himself, to the end of his days, as 'the old African blasphemer'.

Newton was ordained in 1764; his beliefs were as Calvinistic as was compatible with membership of the Church of England. His first charge was the curacy of Olney in Buckinghamshire, where he became the friend of Cowper. He left Olney sixteen years later because of his inability to restrain the 'gross licentiousness' of his parishioners. One cannot help feeling that the old slaver may have found the constraints available to a curate rather cramping. John Thornton placed him at St. Mary's Woolnoth, Lombard Street, where he remained until his death in 1807.

Newton is an interesting character. At first sight it is easy to dismiss him as an iron man who had exchanged the hard life of a slave captain for the hard faith of Calvinism. His self-discipline, lack of perception, the way in which he subordinated everything to his mission—all these give his life an almost inhuman quality. His industry was great, his will strong and his faith absolute. But there was a softer side to Newton's character. He loved his wife with an adoration that he feared might be idolatrous. His letters to her are models of beauty and tenderness. His affection for Cowper was almost as deep, though in this case his well-meaning attempts to help the poet plunged him deeper into his private hell. Newton could never understand that the faith that suited his own character so well could destroy a weaker man. He was confident enough to compose a collection of hymns (the Olney hymns) with Cowper as joint author, and surprisingly the hymns written by the old slaver bear comparison with those of the poet. 'Glorious Things of Thee are Spoken' written by Newton is the most jubilant hymn in the collection. He had a genuine sense of humility which gives his letters and epistles an attractive child-like quality, and this may also have been present in his sermons for although 'his utterance was far from clear, and his attitudes ungraceful', they were invariably well attended.

Newton's attitude towards slavery is as puzzling as any of the contradictions in his character. We have seen him look back with complacency at his days as a Christian slaver; he finally changed his attitude and testified against the traffic before the House of Lords. But he leaves us with the feeling that, even then, he had not appreciated its full monstrosity. Like the other Evangelicals he was seldom reluctant to air his sins in public, but the sins that plagued his conscience were nothing compared with the guilt he should have felt for his contribution to the miseries of the Slave Trade. It is probable that he was swept along by the Evangelical crusade against the trade without his deepest feelings being involved.

Not even Newton's certainty could give Wilberforce a speedy release from his agony, but the mere act of confiding in another seems to have allowed him some relief, and like Cowper before him, he was able to draw strength from the other man's steadfast faith. His remorse was unabated and even Newton sometimes failed to console him. 'I go off sadly—I am

colder and more insensible than I was—I ramble—O God, protect me
from myself—I never yet think of religion but by constraint—I am in a
most doubtful state. To Newton's, but when he prayed I was cold and
dead; and the moment we were out of his house, seriousness decayed.'
But rays of hope sometimes shone through. 'Colder than ever—very
unhappy—called at Newton's, and bitterly moved: he comforted
me.' 'Went to hear Forster [preach] who was very good: enabled me
to join in the prayers with my whole heart, and never so happy in my
life. . . . '[15]

Wilberforce's mental agonies continued for many years and his repentance over any pathetic backslidings was always intense. But the meeting
with Newton provided a sympathetic ear and sensible advice. Wilberforce
would certainly have left public life if Newton had urged him to, but
Newton told him instead to stay where he was and to try to do good there.
Newton was an old friend of Wilberforce's first spiritual mentor, the
Wimbledon aunt. He brought her and her brother John Thornton back
into Wilberforce's life. Thornton at first took a cautious view towards
Wilberforce's conversion: 'As in Nature so in Grace,' he wrote, 'what
comes very quick forward rarely abides long.'[16] He followed this gloomy
and inaccurate forecast with dismal advice. 'You can't be too wary in
forming connections,' he told poor Wilberforce, 'the fewer new Friends
perhaps the better.'[17] But reflection on Newton's chequered career must
have helped Wilberforce put his own past into perspective. If Newton
could rise to grace from such a cesspool his own salvation might surely be
achieved. With the comfort and sympathy provided by these people,
Wilberforce could begin the long passage from despair to serenity.

The strength of Wilberforce's emotions and the horror with which he
recoiled from his unregenerate days will strike most readers as excessive.
He was really a very innocent young man. The sins that so repelled him
were no more than idleness and taking too much enjoyment from the
frivolous pleasures of life. The contrast between the extravagance of his
remorse and the pathos of his faults is so extreme that one is tempted to
look for something more serious, but it would be wrong to do so. Those
who knew him before his conversion remembered Wilberforce as a gay,
charming, frivolous young man, without malice or viciousness of any sort.
If there had been dark secrets in his past, the opponents of Abolition
would surely have unearthed them and used them against him. And in any
case Wilberforce would have revealed them himself, pouring them out
with his lesser sins on to the pages of his religious Journal. A convert to a
dynamic and demanding faith often feels a need for confession, an urge to
contrast the splendours of his new religion with the hopelessness of his
old way of life. In these circumstances the last thing he will do is to conceal
his failings; he is more likely to exaggerate them, to wallow in them. If all

that Wilberforce could produce was a list of minor errors, we may be sure
that there was nothing else for him to confess.

*

The religion chosen by Wilberforce and practised by Newton, Milner
and the Thorntons was certainly demanding. In December he wrote to
his sister: 'There is no opinion so fatal as that which is commonly received
in *these Liberal* days, that a person is in a safe state with respect to a future
world, if he acts tolerably up to his knowledge and convictions, though he
may not have taken much pains about acquiring this knowledge or fixing
these convictions.'[18] This sentence is almost a synopsis of the book that
Wilberforce wrote in 1797, *Practical View*, which in its turn is the clearest
expression of Evangelical belief.

The Evangelical Succession was the Church of England's answer to the
Methodist Revival of Whitfield and Wesley. They had much in common
with the Methodists and were often confused with them. Their enemies
would call them Methodists to discredit them; Sydney Smith wrote, 'We
shall use the general term of Methodism to designate these three classes of
fanatic (the two groups of Methodists and the evangelicals), not troubling
ourselves to point out the finer shades and nicer discriminations of lunacy,
but treating them all as in one general conspiracy against common sense,
and rational orthodox Christianity.'[19] Newton responded to such attacks
with the claim that, 'one of the world's great engines in opposing the
truth, has been to brand the possessors of it with a name'.[20] But the distinction between Evangelical and Methodist was often hard to draw.*
Their message was simple; they were not concerned with doctrinal trivia,
but with leading a Christian life. They were solemn, earnest men whose
own expression for 'religious' was 'serious'. They were not original
thinkers; they threw up no great philosophers or writers; few of them
had the social connections or graces of the High Church party. But
they were effective and responsible for great changes, and this was because
their message was simple and timely. Their main theme was that it was not
enough for a man to be a 'nominal Christian', to conform to Christianity,
to avoid breaking any of the Commandments, to go to Church on Sunday
and then to forget about God for the rest of the week. Christianity should
instead be carried into every corner of life and allowed to fill it.

At the end of the eighteenth century such a doctrine was revolutionary,
for the Church had lapsed into a state of near paganism. Nepotism

* Even Wilberforce was sometimes muddled by this. Although he later thanked
Providence for rescuing him from the fate of being 'a bigoted, despised Methodist', on
June 12, 1786 he noted in his diary: 'Expect to hear myself now universally given out to
be a Methodist: may God grant it may be said with truth.'

abounded and plural livings gave some clergymen vast incomes and many parishes absentee vicars. When the great lawyer Blackstone had heard the best preachers in London he declared 'that not one of the sermons contained more Christianity than the writings of Cicero'.[21] Henry Venn commented on the sermons of the Prebendary of York, 'excepting a phrase or two, they might be preached in a synagogue or mosque without offence'.[22] Boswell once told Wilberforce that Johnson had confessed to him that he had never met a religious clergyman. Wilberforce answered sharply that serious clergymen were no doubt put off by the company Johnson kept, but there was substance in the complaint. After listening to an Evangelical sermon Lord Melbourne complained: 'Things are coming to a pretty pass when religion is allowed to invade private life.'[23] The higher offices of the Church were often awarded as part of political patronage. Thus Pitt appointed his old tutor Pretyman to the Bishopric of Lincoln. The bishops in their turn would fill their dioceses with their friends and families. When Bishop Sparke was appointed to the Diocese of Ely a wit suggested that a traveller could find his way home across the fens at night by the light of all the little Sparkes shining in their livings.[24]

In these circumstances many clergymen entirely neglected their duties, and even the best had a very lax idea of them. Archdeacon Paley represented everything admirable in the eighteenth-century Church. He was a man of humanity with a formidable intellect; even Wilberforce, who opposed his High Church principles, had to admire his *Moral Philosophy* and *Evidences of Christianity*. Paley was also a wit. When Pitt, just made Prime Minister at the age of twenty-four, came down to Cambridge, the Archdeacon suggested as a fitting text for the sermon: 'There is a lad here who hath five barley loaves and two small fishes; but what are they among so many?'[25] One would expect such a man, one of the most respected clergymen of his time, to submerge himself in his work and it comes as a surprise to read Paley's instructions to his clergymen suggesting rewarding ways of spending their free time. The degree of Paley's involvement with the poor can be seen in his pronouncements on them. The Evangelicals would sometimes claim to envy the poor on the grounds that they were exposed to fewer temptations and thus had an easier road to Heaven. Paley extended his envy from the spiritual to the gastronomic plane and claimed that when the poor ate a succulent dish, they must derive far more pleasure from it than those palates which were jaded and stomachs glutted by a succession of rich meals.

If Paley was representative of everything that was best in the eighteenth-century Church, it is not hard to imagine the worst. Jane Hill referred to them collectively as 'fat bulls of Bashan'.[26] Some parishes were seldom if ever visited by their vicars. The inhabitants were allowed to remain without religion, without education and in times of hardship, without assistance. This was the state in which Wilberforce and Hannah More found the people of the Cheddar Gorge.

The Evangelicals had a very different approach. If Paley made plans for the idle hours of his subordinates, they lamented that there were only twenty-four hours in a day. By Church of England standards they were mainly low church and Calvinistic, but it was in their attitude rather than their doctrine that they differed from the traditional clergy. 'Enthusiasm' was to be deplored in eighteenth-century clergymen; it conjured up pictures of tub-thumping dissenters of dubious social origins, but the Evangelists embraced it with fervour. They saw themselves as being placed in their parishes to cultivate their flock like a crop for a heavenly harvest. They threw themselves into this work; preached, visited, persuaded, educated, organised, bullied and cajoled their parishioners into the ways of righteousness.

The Evangelical Movement was unique in that its leaders were laymen. The man to whom Evangelicals looked for a lead was not to be any clergyman but William Wilberforce, and he and his Clapham friends were the organisers and leaders of the great Evangelical campaigns. The Pope, claimed Sydney Smith, had no such 'power over the minds of the Irish as Mr. Wilberforce has over the mind of a young Methodist converted the previous quarter'.[27] While men of the world used their influence to secure livings for their friends, the Evangelicals used theirs to install suitably 'serious' clergymen. They were always a minority in the Church and had few representatives in its higher ranks, but their energy gave them a disproportionate influence.

The success of the Evangelical Movement was due to its vigour and its positive and constructive approach. Its followers could feel that they were tackling the most important problems of their time. Its failure to produce any profound thinkers or writers eventually led to the movement's becoming sterile.

Gladstone describes it as 'beneficial as an impulse and a moral example [but] when considered as a system, incomplete and abnormal. It did not represent the whole of Anglicanism, or indeed any other whole. . . . It has not had, and in truth hardly could have what can with any strictness be called a Theology. For penetrating and exacting minds, it raises questions to which it can furnish no reply.'[28] Sir James Stephen is more caustic; after paying tribute to the early Evangelicals, he describes their successors as having 'dwarfish, sterile, rotatory minds'[29] which revolved 'through a narrow orbit, from which all variety and illustration is superstitiously excluded—the head giddy with the recurrence of certain threadbare dogmata'.[30]

The Evangelicals had a passion for education and produced a truly remarkable crop of children. W. E. Gladstone, Lord Macaulay, Cardinals

Manning and Newman, Robert Isaac and Samuel Wilberforce, Sir James and Sir George Stephen, the Brontë sisters and the Grant brothers all shared an Evangelical upbringing, but none of them remained Evangelicals. Each had his own reason for the change, but all felt a revulsion from the Evangelism* which succeeded that of their parents. Without any adequate philosophy to sustain them, its adherents were left mouthing stale catchwords and platitudes. The movement soured and became joyless, self-righteous and Calvinistic. It came to be dominated by men like Henry Carus Wilson so mercilessly exposed by Charlotte Brontë as Mr. Brockle-hurst in *Jane Eyre*. Thus intelligent and idealistic young men like the sons of Wilberforce and Stephen would find the doctrines of Evangelism childish and its exponents distressingly vulgar. They would have agreed with Charles II's description of Calvinism, 'Say what you will it is no religion for a gentleman.' It is part of Wilberforce's achievement that for a short time he made it one.

At the time of his conversion Evangelism was a growing movement, and he was able to do much to foster and shape its growth. It was not, Gladstone wrote, agreeing unexpectedly with Charles II, a movement 'well calculated to fit its agents for exercising social influence at large'.[31] The few Evangelicals who had social standing lacked social flair and were too intense and dull to have any influence. Wilberforce realised that until its leaders set an example there was no hope of the country leading a religious life.

Evangelism, being more an attitude towards religion than a faith with a particular doctrine, drew its supporters from different groups in the Church of England and Methodists. These people naturally differed on many points, but Evangelicals did have some distinguishing characteristics, two of which may seem peculiar today. They believed implicitly in the inter-vention of Providence in human affairs and they would go to extraordinary lengths to keep Sundays uncontaminated by work or pleasure.

The belief of intelligent, practical men like Wilberforce and the Thorntons in Providence is hard to explain but impossible to deny. They were ridiculed for it by more cynical contemporaries and they clearly carried this belief much further than any other group, but they were not alone in it. The Duke of Wellington, not a man notorious for his religious enthusiasm, wrote of his escape from the Cato Street conspiracy, 'We were saved certainly by Divine Providence.'[32] Wilberforce once wrote in his diary: 'But it is quite providential (how I abhor that word, fortunate, as if things happened by chance!).'[33] He compared the workings of Providence to the opening of the night-blowing cereus. 'It reminds me,' he said as the flower burst open in front of him, 'of the dispensations of Divine Provi-

---

* I have used 'Evangelism' throughout in preference to the cumbersome 'Evangeli-calism', which may, strictly speaking, be more correct.

dence first breaking on the glorified eye, when they shall fully unfold to the view, and appear as beautiful as they are complete.'[34] He would take particular pleasure in tracing its workings. His own life was too quiet to allow scope for spectacular providential intervention or interpositions, as the Evangelists called such events, but he seized on the flimsiest examples as evidence. Once the lynch-pin on his coach fell out and he was unharmed; once a bench by the Avon on which he was sitting collapsed and he just missed falling into the river. He could not swim. On both occasions he ascribed his survival to Providence.

Providence, he believed, intervened in individuals' lives to save the good and punish the wicked, and it acted no differently in the affairs of nations. Napoleon was both an instrument and a victim of Providence. In 1808 when there was a move to recall all missionaries from India he wrote to William Hey: 'Buonaparte, by all accounts, is preparing on a grand scale for an expedition to the East; and should this country use the powers of its government for the avowed purpose of shutting the scriptures out of our Indian empire, how could we hope that God would not employ his French army in breaking down the barriers we had vainly and wickedly been rearing, and thus open a passage by which Christian light might shine upon that darkened land.'[35]

In the same year he wrote of Napoleon: 'This man is manifestly an instrument in the hands of Providence; when God has done with him, He will probably show how easily He can get rid of him. Meanwhile may we be of the number of those who trust in Him, and all will be well.'[36] When Napoleon returned from Elba Wilberforce wrote to his eldest son: 'Able, and active, and wicked as Buonaparte is, he is no less under the Divine control than the weakest of human beings. He is executing, unconsciously, the Divine will, and it is probably because the sufferings which he brought upon the nations of Europe did not produce the intended effect of humiliation and reformation, that he is allowed once more to stalk abroad and increase the sum of human misery.'[37]

Sometimes the workings of Providence were puzzling. Wilberforce had claimed that the successful vote in the Commons on the Indian Missions in 1793 was the clearest example of its intervention he had ever seen. The Court of Directors at once rallied their forces and threw out the motion. Wilberforce did not speculate as to whether Providence might have changed its mind. Again when Henry Thornton was dying, Wilberforce wrote, 'The sudden removal of such a man would be a most mysterious providence.'[38]

He allowed Providence the best of both worlds. When the good were being rewarded and the wicked punished its presence was manifest; when the reverse took place he either ignored it, or described it as 'a mysterious Providence'. When considering this subject he seems to have abandoned his powers of reason. He could have asked why God should have exalted the atheists in France to punish the nominally Christian in England. There was no justice there and in any case, if He was all-powerful, why did He need an instrument like Napoleon? It would have been just as easy to find evidence of counter-Providence. If in Wilberforce's eyes Thomas Paine had been a saint and not a devil, there could have been no clearer evidence of Providential interposition than his miraculous escape from a Paris cell during the Terror. As it was he simply ignored such events. A more general objection could be raised to the theory that Providence constantly intervened in the affairs of men. If it had been at this work for so long, and was all-powerful, all-wise and all-good, then why was the world still in such a deplorable state? He allowed one area, duelling, where Providence did not intervene, and there may have been an element of special pleading in this exception. Most duels were obviously objectionable to a Christian, but there could be circumstances in which a man felt forced to fight by considerations of honour without having the least intention of harming his opponent. Wilberforce argued that even so it was wrong to lay a useful life and perhaps the welfare of a family on the altar of Chance.[39] But if Providence were substituted for Chance, to fight a duel could become almost an assertion of faith.

His belief in Providence did not lead him to rely on it entirely. He might advocate policies which on purely rational grounds were ridiculous in order to avoid tempting Providence, but his faith in it never stopped him from working hard to promote what he thought was right.

The Evangelists believed that every day should be filled with thoughts of God, and it is not surprising that on Sunday, the day set aside for Him, they should think of little else. Wilberforce found it an immense relief to be able to turn away from the cares of the world for one day in the week and it needed a crisis of the first order to make him break his day of rest. Sunday was a safety valve for a man who worked as hard as he did. He was to speculate after the suicide of Castlereagh whether it could have been prevented if he had allowed himself a rest on Sundays.

Wilberforce describes his own attitude to Sunday in his book, *Practical View*, which we shall examine later. What was more controversial was his desire to impose an Evangelical Sunday on the rest of the country. He went to great trouble to stop any kind of official entertainment on Sundays, a course of action which led to a clash with the Speaker, Addington, who was in the habit of giving innocuous Sunday parties. The Proclamation Society was always on the watch for breaches of the Sabbath. In 1792 he and Eliot considered a Bill for obstructing Sunday travel.[40] He lobbied Pitt for support for a measure to ban Sunday newspapers, and he persuaded Perceval not to recall Parliament on a Monday, so that members need not travel on Sundays. His campaign against Sunday entertainments led to there being few amusements which the poor could enjoy on their only day of rest. But if we count this against him, we should also remember that the fact that they had one day a week free from their work was partly because of his insistence on the observance of the Sabbath.

The Evangelicals took a severe line on other pleasures. Some, like the theatre, they considered sources of corruption, others like prize-fighting and bull-baiting cruel and degrading. Even the most innocent were tolerated rather than approved for they represented at the best, time which could have been devoted to religious pursuits. The more distractions that existed, the less likely people were to become 'serious'. This is why they tried to bring God into all their correspondence, books and speeches and looked for His presence in those of others, whatever the topic. Reminders of His presence would help the cause of serious religion in the same way that distractions and worldly amusements would harm it.

Although they were rigorous in their attitude towards the way in which men filled their lives, the Evangelicals were tolerant of other creeds. In the words of the great French historian of nineteenth-century England: 'The Evangelicals were not theologians, but men of motion and action. . . . This feature of Evangelism made it easy for adherents to work with Protestants of every denomination. For while Evangelicals maintained the theological principle which was the common foundation of all the doctrinal systems of Protestantism, they systematically refused to interest themselves in the theological differences which held Protestants apart.'[41] Political jealousies and the antagonism between laxity and enthusiasm might lead them into quarrels with the High Church party, but Wilberforce had close friends who were High Churchmen, Methodists, Unitarians and Quakers. When there were arguments about which body should send missionaries to India, he lamented, 'Alas! alas! let us have some substance before we differ about the form.' He once told his sons that he thought the difference between churchmen and dissenters unimportant. 'He no where found in scripture that it would be asked at the last day "were you Churchman or dissenter?" but "what were your works?" '[42]

With Parliament in recess and himself withdrawn from society, Wilberforce's conversion remained unknown to his friends until the beginning of December 1785. He had resolved, on November 24, to write to Pitt 'and discover to him what I am occupied about', but he did not send the letter until a week later. When the two friends met, less often than before, Wilberforce's sometimes lugubrious thoughts evidently remained unsuspected. 'At the levee, and then dined at Pitt's—sort of cabinet dinner—was often thinking that pompous Thurlow and elegant Carmarthen would soon appear in the same row with the poor fellow who waited behind their chairs.'[43]

At the moment of his spiritual crisis, just before his appeal to Newton,

Wilberforce wrote to his closest friends explaining his new beliefs. Some of them treated his attitude as a temporary depression; others thought that since his life had always been harmless he must now become an ascetic; one threw his letter in the fire. He explained himself fully to Pitt, 'I told him that though I should ever feel a strong affection for him, and had every reason to believe that I should be in general able to support him, yet I could no more be so much a party man as I had been before.' On December the 2nd he received Pitt's reply. It is a beautiful letter which reveals the strength of Pitt's friendship with Wilberforce, and the humanity hidden behind his icy façade.

Downing St.,
December 2, 1785.

My dear Wilberforce,

Bob Smith mentioned to me on Wednesday the letters he had received from you, which prepared me for that I received from you yesterday. I am indeed too deeply interested in whatever concerns you not to be very sensibly affected by what has the appearance of a new era in your life, and so important in its consequences for yourself and your friends. As to any public conduct which your opinions may ever lead you to, I will not disguise to you that few things could go nearer my heart than to find myself differing from you essentially on any great principle.

I trust and believe that it is a circumstance which can hardly occur. But if it ever should, and even if I should experience as much pain in such an event, as I have found hitherto encouragement and pleasure in the reverse, believe me it is impossible that it should shake the sentiments of affection and friendship which I bear towards you, and which I must be forgetful and insensible indeed if I ever could part with. They are sentiments engraved in my heart, and will never be effaced or weakened. If I knew how to state all I feel, and could hope that you are open to consider it, I should say a great deal more on the subject of the resolution you seem to have formed. You will not suspect me of thinking lightly of any moral or religious motives which guide you. As little will you believe that I think your understanding or judgment easily misled. But forgive me if I cannot help expressing my fear that you are nevertheless deluding yourself into principles which have but too much tendency to counteract your own object, and to render your virtues and your talents useless both to yourself and mankind. I am not, however, without hopes that my anxiety paints this too strongly. For you confess that the character of religion is not a gloomy one, and that it is not that of an enthusiast. But why then this preparation of solitude, which can hardly avoid tincturing the mind either with melancholy or superstition? If a Christian may act in the several relations of life, must he seclude himself from all to become so? Surely the principles as well as the practice of Christianity are simple, and lead not to meditation only but to action.

I will not, however, enlarge upon these subjects now. What I would ask of you, as a mark both of your friendship and of the candour which belongs to your mind, is to open yourself fully and without reserve to one, who, believe me, does not know how to separate your happiness from his own. You do not explain either the degree or the duration of the retirement which you have prescribed to yourself: you do not tell me how the future course of your life is to be directed, when you think the same privacy no longer necessary: nor, in short, what idea you have formed of the duties which you are from this time to practise. I am sure you will not wonder if I am inquisitive on such a subject. The only way in which you can satisfy me is by conversation. There ought to be no awkwardness or embarrassment to either of us, tho' there may be some anxiety:

and if you will open to me fairly the whole state of your mind on these subjects, tho' I shall venture to state to you fairly the points where I fear we may differ, and to desire you to re-examine your own ideas where I think you are mistaken, I will not importune you with fruitless discussion on any opinion which you have deliberately formed. You will, I am sure, do justice to the motives and feelings which induce me to urge this so strongly to you. I think you will not refuse it: if you do not, name any hour at which I can call upon you to-morrow. I am going into Kent, and can take Wimbledon in my way. Reflect, I beg of you, that no principles are the worse for being discussed, and believe me that at all events the full knowledge of the nature and extent of your opinions and intentions will be to me a lasting satisfaction.

Believe me, affectionately and unalterably yours,

W. Pitt.[44]

After this Wilberforce could hardly avoid a meeting. The two friends talked in private for two hours. 'He tried to reason me out of my convictions but soon found himself unable to combat their correctness, if Christianity was true. The fact is, he was so absorbed in politics, that he had never given himself time for due reflection on religion.'[45]

Pitt's and Wilberforce's friendship was to continue until the former's death in 1806. After his religion and family it was the deepest attachment of Wilberforce's life. But, although their friendship remained close, it could never quite regain the intimacy of the days before Wilberforce's conversion. Their conversation showed that religion would always represent some sort of barrier. It was not that their politics would be likely to differ. On his return to Parliament Wilberforce somewhat naively records, 'I was surprised to find how generally we agreed.' There were to be times when his conscience drove him into the Opposition lobby, but they were few. Wilberforce's political philosophy was largely derived from Pitt and it continued much the same long after Pitt's death. In addition to this common approach and the personal loyalty he felt towards Pitt, Wilberforce had inherited the country gentleman's belief that it was his duty, except in special cases, to support the Government of the day. Until 1801 this meant to support Pitt. The Opposition found Wilberforce's profession of independence of 'party' an exasperating affectation, and they could point to a long series of votes for Pitt to support their claim. Wilberforce's answer— that he was truly independent, but that, in his judgment, Pitt had been right on all these questions—can have done little to mollify them.

But each of the two friends now had a side to his life that was closed to the other. Pitt could not share Wilberforce's religious beliefs, nor Wilberforce Pitt's political machinations. There would be something incongruous, as Professor Coupland has pointed out, in urging the new Wilberforce to 'tear the enemy to pieces'. It was natural for them both to find new religious and political friends. They could not meet so often. Pitt was busy all day and liked to relax by sitting up late at night and talking with his old friends. But to keep such hours threw Wilberforce's self-imposed regimen out of joint, and to spend this leisure on idle conversation caused his conscience further agonies. Pitt still went out to Wimbledon for his country air, but he now went to Dundas's villa not Wilberforce's.

There were strains on their friendship. Pitt, as Prime Minister, had to manipulate the delicate machinery of influence so as to provide a continuous and constructive government. Wilberforce never fully understood this side of politics. To him 'influence' like 'party' was bad, although he was prepared, on occasions, to use it himself. When he looked back at Pitt's first years in office, he declared: 'No one who had not been an eye witness could conceive the ascendancy which Mr. Pitt then possessed over the House of Commons. If he had then generously adopted the resolution to govern his Country by *principle* rather than by *influence*, it was a resolution which he could have carried into success.'[46] This statement, Wilberforce's considered opinion, shows a startling ignorance of the nature of eighteenth-century politics. Pitt may have had a great personal ascendancy, but he did not have a large personal following. When Pitt embarked on 'non-party' legislation he was often defeated. Wilberforce understood well enough why Pitt could not use his official influence to help abolition of the slave trade. One cannot help feeling that he realised also that any Prime Minister needed to govern by influence and that his statement is at least part wishful thinking.

Wilberforce was constantly soliciting Pitt's help for his various causes, few of which were concerned with the mainstream of politics. Pitt's patience and understanding were extraordinary. He would oblige Wilberforce whenever possible and would listen to his demands, however outrageous, without ever asking for any quid pro quo. Wilberforce's conscience was an inconvenient and sometimes destructive factor in politics. He might present a motion in the Commons against duelling when Pitt himself had just fought a duel. He might oppose a war in which the country was struggling for its existence. He might demand that the militia should cease drilling on Sundays when Napoleon's army was massed in Boulogne. He might deprive the Government of its most valuable Minister at the most critical moment of the war. But Pitt never protested. Wilberforce admired him more than any other man in the world, a lack of religious principles being the only flaw he could perceive in Pitt's character. He was as great and as good as a man without religion could be.

The summer session of 1786 soon provided an example of how the two friends could still agree on an issue where political and moral considerations were inextricably entangled. Warren Hastings is now acknowledged to have been one of the greatest governors of British India. He held his empire through all the dangers of the American War and at the same time was able to lay the foundations by which it would be ruled by law. He did so when hamstrung by a Council which consistently overruled his measures for reasons of personal spite. Hastings maintained control by a rule that was always firm and sometimes high-handed and unjust. He was left in the awkward position where he had been given definite orders but not the means of raising the money to carry them out. He made good some of the difference by fining any princes who disobeyed him extravagant sums.

Philip Francis, Hastings's chief enemy on the Council, returned to England before him and poisoned the mind of the Opposition against him. Edmund Burke had a sincere and deep loathing for the corrupt type of Anglo-Indian known as 'nabobs', a group of men who systematically looted and cheated their way into vast fortunes. Francis managed to convince Burke that Hastings was the chief of all the nabobs, when he was on the contrary the first man to bring decorum to public life in India. Other members of the Opposition turned against Hastings on less pure motives. The opposition of India House had been seen as one of the main factors that contributed to their humiliation in the general election of 1784. When Hastings returned to England in 1785, confident of a peerage and ambitious of power in his own country, he found his enemies moving for an examination of his conduct in the House of Commons.

The debate on the preliminary motions showed Wilberforce in his new rôle, that of a man shorn of party attachments and anxious only to see that justice was done. After Burke had presented his charges on April 26 Wilberforce said of him: ' . . . Of that gentleman's head and heart, of his humanity and his abilities, his rectitude and his perseverance, no man entertained a higher opinion than he did [but] for the sake of national justice and for the sake of the character of the House he should so far restrain his feelings as to appear to conduct himself on so serious an occasion with the temper and moderation it so well deserved.'[47]

Hastings himself then appeared at the bar of the House; he either failed to appreciate his position or was unable to rise to the occasion. Instead of answering the accusations against him he read aloud for two days an account of his thirteen years' rule in India. The House emptied in boredom, while his arrogance and insensitivity left a damaging impression.

On June 2 the Opposition presented its case on the first of the charges against him, that of his conduct of the Rohilla War, the one action for which Macaulay found it impossible to forgive Hastings. Wilberforce agreed that Hastings had been at fault, but he would not care to see the Rohilla War made the basis of an impeachment. It had taken place over twelve years ago, since when Hastings had devoted his life and sacrificed his health to the public service. To impeach him now would be 'like eating the mutton of a sheep which we had previously shorn of its fleece'. Pitt agreed with Wilberforce and the House, taking its cue from him, defeated the motion by 119 votes to 67.

On June 13 the House debated a very large fine which Hastings had levied on Cheyt Singh, the Zemindar of Benares. When the Opposition was mounting its case, Pitt beckoned to Wilberforce and took him behind the Speaker's chair. 'Does not this look very ill to you?' he asked. 'Very bad indeed,'[48] Wilberforce replied. With this reassurance Pitt rose and made Hastings's impeachment a certainty. First, to the delight of Hastings's partisans, he demolished Burke's argument and showed it to be based on mistaken ideas of Indian customs. Hastings had been justified in fining Cheyt Singh, but he then went on to say that in our dealings with oriental powers we must conduct ourselves by higher than oriental standards. In deciding the amount of the fine Hastings had not been 'guided by any principle of reason or justice', and the sum had been 'beyond all proportion exorbitant, unjust and tyrannical'. If there was to be an impeachment this must be one of its articles.

Every kind of motive has been advanced for Pitt's abandoning Hastings. He is said to have wished to score off the King, who supported Hastings, to ruin a potential rival, to discipline India House, to placate Dundas, to divert the Opposition's energy from more important matters. Wilberforce never had any doubts about his motives. At the end of his life he remembered. 'Oh how little justice was done to Pitt on Warren Hastings business! People were asking, what could make Pitt support him on this point and on that, as if he was acting from political motives; whereas he was always weighing in every particular whether Hastings had exceeded the discretionary power lodged in him. . . . He paid as much impartial attention as if he were a juryman.'[49]

The Opposition's motion was duly carried and on its next motion Pitt again spoke against Hastings. Neither he nor Wilberforce took any part in the process of impeachment, though Pitt succeeded in having Francis, Hastings's most venomous enemy, removed from the list of Managers of the trial.

The impeachment started as Sheridan's greatest dramatic production for which seats in the gallery changed hands for fifty guineas. The fashionable world was there in full force: the Queen and foreign ambassadors, the Duchess of Devonshire and Mrs. Fitzherbert, while the arts were represented by Reynolds, Gibbon and Mrs. Siddons. When Sheridan launched into a superb denunciation of Hastings which lasted for five hours ladies fainted and grown men collapsed into one another's arms. But the trial soon became a bore; the prosecution became less scrupulous and less credible. Hastings was finally acquitted on all charges, but the fortune he had brought back from India, a fraction of what he would have made had he been the monster reviled by Burke and Sheridan, was exhausted in his own defence.

*

Wilberforce's internal struggle continued throughout the summer session of 1786. His diary remains full of self-reproach, but agony no longer leaps out from its pages. June 22: 'I do not think I have a sufficiently strong conviction of sin; yet I see plainly that I am an ungrateful, stupid, guilty creature.' July 2: 'I have not been examining myself with that seriousness with which we ought to look into ourselves from time to time. That wandering spirit and indolent way of doing business are little if at all defeated, my rules, resolved on with thought and prayer, are forgotten.'

At the end of this session Wilberforce slept almost every night in Wimbledon. Horseplay and roistering no longer disturbed his neighbours, though his delight in its 'rural sights and sounds' remained as strong as ever. But he decided that the villa was a luxury which would ill suit his new way of life. It was inconvenient for his servants, a cause of wasted time and it consumed money that could be put to better uses.

When Parliament went into recess he travelled up to Yorkshire, where an anxious family awaited him, for rumours of his 'enthusiasm' had already reached them. They may have expected a bible-thumping Methodist; if so they must have been delighted to find him with all his old virtues but with a new degree of humility, consideration and self-restraint. A friend commented to his mother, 'If this is madness, I hope he will bite us all.'

CHAPTER IV

NEW CAUSES

THE years 1785–7 saw a complete and irrevocable change in Wilberforce's life. At the beginning of 1785 he had been an ambitious and able politician, whose time was divided between the advancement of his own career and the pursuit of pleasure. In both of these fields he was supremely able and it seemed that a successful and delightful life lay in front of him. In 1785 he became converted; 1786 was a year of spiritual struggle in which he reconciled himself to his new beliefs; in 1787 he was to begin the career of 'usefulness' that was to occupy the rest of his life. For Wilberforce to remain in politics he had to use his position for something more than self-advancement. He had to make it a platform for his religious views and find causes that would wed his new beliefs with his old profession.

The first of these causes was the reform of the 'manners' or morals of the country. This enterprise was to be the most controversial and abused of all Wilberforce's many charities. The train of thought that led him to this measure is shown in a letter to Wyvill.

'The barbarous custom of hanging has been tried too long, and with the success which might have been expected from it. The most effectual way to prevent greater crimes is by punishing the smaller, and by endeavouring to repress that general spirit of licentiousness, which is the parent of every species of vice. I know that by regulating the external conduct we do not at first change the hearts of men, but even they are ultimately to be wrought upon by these means, and we should at least so far remove the obtrusiveness of the temptation, that it may not provoke the appetite, which might otherwise be dormant and inactive.'[1]

This passage sums up Wilberforce's attitude to the problem of vice: savage punishment was barbarous and futile and it was far better to remove the opportunities of sin. The absence of temptation did not mean that a man would lead a virtuous life, but it would make it easier for him to do so. The Proclamation Society's object was to see that laws against Sabbath-breaking, duelling, lotteries, drunkenness, unlicensed entertainment, blasphemy, obscenity and other unwholesome forms of behaviour in public were enforced.

The idea of such a society—a self-appointed guardian of the nation's morals, patronised by royalty and prying into the pathetic amusements of the poor, intolerant, destructive, rich and answerable only to itself—seems obnoxious to us. It was equally repellent to many of Wilberforce's contemporaries. In its two incarnations, as the Proclamation Society from 1787 to 1802 and afterwards as the Society for the Suppression of Vice, it was bitterly attacked in Parliament and the Press. Joseph Hume called it the Society for Vice, Sydney Smith in a brilliant satire, 'the Society for the Suppression of Vice among those with less than five hundred pounds a year'.

But to see the Proclamation Society in perspective we must look at it in its social setting. The late eighteenth century is in many ways one of the most attractive periods in our history. We can look back on it with nostalgia as an age in which taste was at its highest and in which every field was dominated by a man of genius. Although drawing its leaders from a minute proportion of the population, it could boast Pitt, Fox and Burke as its statesmen, Bentham as its philosopher, Gibbon as its historian, Reynolds and Gainsborough as its artists, Johnson as its wit, Boswell as its biographer, Walter Scott as its novelist, Goldsmith and Sheridan as its playwrights, Garrick and Mrs. Siddons as its actors, Malthus, Adam Smith and Ricardo as its economists, Wesley as its preacher, Wordsworth and Cowper as its poets, and the Adam brothers and Nash as its architects.

It was also an age of curiosity and experiments, in which the rigours of classical architecture and classical metre were both relaxed by new influences. Whatever their tastes the rich had the opportunity to indulge them. The ordinary country gentleman might live on his estate, follow hounds, shoot his coverts, and intervene in county politics at the time of elections. The more adventurous could enter Parliament or dabble in the arts or sciences. Knowledge was still at a stage where one man could become the master of many subjects, so that a naval officer and politician like Sir Charles Middleton could become one of the country's leading agriculturists, another naval officer, Lord Cochrane, a revolutionary leader and an inventor, while Gully, the prize fighter, rose to be Member of the House of Commons. The Whig aristocracy, closely connected, supremely self-confident, rich both in wealth and talents, are among the most attractive groups in our history, and if we were asked in what past age and class we would like to be reincarnated, we might well choose theirs. Although surrounded by every imaginable luxury and privilege, they retained an idealism, an attachment to liberty and a loathing of oppression most nobly exemplified in Charles James Fox.

There was a less attractive side to the period. Even the highest ranks of society were riddled with corruption. Ministers made fortunes out of their official positions and their sons lost them at the gaming tables of Brooks's,

White's, Boodle's or Almack's. George III had set a high standard of respectability which was followed neither by the nation nor by his own sons.
Prostitution became so common that at one time it was estimated that one
out of every four unmarried women in London was a prostitute,[2] and its
brazenness was equally alarming. Part of the Evangelical objection to the
theatre was because prostitutes would solicit their clients outside and even
from the boxes. 'No sooner is a playhouse opened in any part of the
Kingdom,' wrote Johnson's literary executor, 'than it at once becomes
surrounded by a halo of brothels.' Every age has its favourite vice and the
deflowering of virgins was the passion of the rakes of Wilberforce's day.
Special brothels were kept 'for the reception and seduction of female
infants under fourteen'. In the London female penitentiary the average
age of prostitutes was only sixteen.

Drunkenness was common. 'A statesman of the Georgian era,' wrote
G. O. Trevelyan, 'was sailing on a sea of claret from one comfortable official haven to another, at a period of life when a political apprentice in the
reign of Victoria is not yet out of his indentures. No one can study the
public or personal history of the eighteenth century without being impressed by the truly immense space which drinking occupied in the mental
horizon of the young and the consequences of drinking in that of the old.'[3]
Pitt, Dundas and Sheridan all appeared drunk in the House, while outside
it people would indulge in wild drinking bouts. They became known as
two, three or four bottle men according to their capacity. The morals and
language of London society were distressingly loose.

While the rich lived in this state of selfish, pagan hedonism the poor
were degraded, sottish and held down by a barbaric penal code. If Gilray's
cartoons give us a picture of the profligacy of the rich, the miseries of the
poor are immortalised in those of Hogarth. It is important to remember that
if anything the scenes in 'Gin Lane' fall short of the original. Their masters
may have been sailing on a sea of claret, they were drowning in an ocean of
gin. In the middle of the century the authorities became seriously worried
in case the poor drank themselves into extinction. Increases in the price of
gin had improved matters by Wilberforce's time but drunkenness was still
the first of the nation's problems. The entertainments open to the poor
were not far removed from those offered in the Roman amphitheatre, the
execution of criminals, prize fights and various forms of tormenting
animals being the most popular.

Prostitution, drunkenness, immorality, gambling and brutality, all
carried to horifying excess—this was the seamy side of eighteenth-century
life and one did not have to be a puritan to disapprove of it.

In the winter of 1786 and the next spring Wilberforce was busy organis-
ing the new Society. He, for one, never had any doubts about its importance. He later declared, 'God Almighty has set before me two great

objects, the suppression of the Slave Trade and the reformation of manners.' His method of securing the latter was to obtain a Royal Proclamation against vice and immorality and then to found a Society to implement the Proclamation. On May 29, his plans complete, he wrote to William Hey.

'It would give you no little pleasure could you hear how warmly the Archbishop of Canterbury expresses himself: the interest he takes in the good work does him great credit, and he assures me that one still greater* to whom he has opened the subject in form, and suggested the measures above mentioned, is deeply impressed with the necessity of opposing the torrent of profaneness which every day makes more rapid advance. What think you of my having myself received a formal invitation to cards for Sunday evening from a person high in the King's service?'[4]

The Proclamation was issued on June 1, 1787. Its launching had deliberately been made as quiet as possible. Horace Walpole remarked that the Proclamation was 'no more minded in town than St. Swithin's Day'. But by September the Society was well established with the Duke of Montagu as its chairman and many bishops among its supporters. Lord North lent his approval and Pitt was prepared to help. Fox, understandably, was not approached.

Wilberforce's feeble eyesight had been affected by all this exertion and even before it he had been told by his doctor that 'I have suffered from living too low'. The doctor had advised 'a strict adherence to meat and wine, as the most trusty and effectual restoratives . . . another part of his directions is, that I should try *with caution* the Bath water'.

In the autumn of 1787 Wilberforce left London for Bath. There he met Hannah More, who was to be one of his closest friends and most valuable allies. They took to each other at once. 'That young man's character,' she wrote, 'is one of the most extraordinary I ever knew for talents, virtue and piety. It is difficult not to grow wiser and better every time one converses with him.' Hannah More and Wilberforce had much in common. They had both been influenced by Newton, both were friends of Sir Charles and Lady Middleton. She, like Wilberforce, had lived a fashionable life before her conversion, although she had moved in literary rather than political circles.

Hannah More was one of five daughters of a Bristol schoolmaster; her father educated her himself, but refused to teach her Latin and Mathematics in case she became a female pedant. She became engaged to a rich, elderly merchant who, for some reason, kept putting off their wedding. In the end he offered her an annuity to be free of the match. This was as close as any of the five More sisters got to marriage. At the age of thirty Hannah went to London and joined the Blue Stocking circle. Although debarred by her sex from The Club she became a friend of many of its

* Presumably George III.

members, Johnson, Garrick, Reynolds and Burke. She wrote tragedies and poetry in which Johnson and Garrick found merit, though the former might have applied his own dictum about women's preaching to women's poetry, 'Sir, a woman's preaching is like a dog walking on his hinder legs. It is not done well; but you are surprised to find it done at all.' He seems to have settled into a gruff, affectionate and slightly patronising relationship with Hannah. When he heard that she lived harmoniously with her four sisters he roared, 'What! five women live happily together! God forever bless you, you live lives to shame duchesses!'

Johnson was a deeply religious man and the Blue Stockings were much concerned with propriety. Hannah More's conversion was a more gradual affair than Wilberforce's and it did not lead to such an alteration in her way of life. She remained a close friend of Garrick and his wife and continued to go to the theatre until his death. And she had always said she would be happy to abandon it once the incomparable Garrick had gone. She remained a friend of that disreputable rake Horace Walpole until his death in 1797. Walpole, to many Evangelicals, must have epitomised all that they loathed about the eighteenth century. He teased her about her religion; she, in return, scolded him.

Wilberforce was to turn Hannah More's energies into new channels. He stayed with the sisters in Somerset in 1786 and met Charles Wesley there. When the great Christian rose and gave him his blessing, 'I was scarcely ever more affected. Such was the effect of his manner and appearance, that it altogether overset me, and I burst into tears, unable to restrain myself.'[5] On another visit, the party went on a trip to the Cheddar Gorge, but Wilberforce was more distressed by the wretched state of its inhabitants than impressed by its beauty. He found the lack of any education or religious instruction particularly striking. He told Hannah More, 'If you will be at the trouble, I will be at the expense.' After some reflection she replied, 'I joyfully accept the honourable office of your Almoner, on condition that you will find fault with, and direct me with as little scruple as I shall have in disposing of your money.'[6]

She needed no more encouragement, but embarked on a tour of the Mendips to find the best places for her schools. Hannah More loathed subversion as much as the most reactionary Somerset landlord, and, since the main object of her schools was to make the poor more virtuous, they should have been welcomed by the rich on grounds of self-interest. But she found a hidebound prejudice against any form of education for the poor. All her persuasiveness was needed to fight this opposition and she never fully overcame it. Thus the story of the Mendip schools is interrupted by violent quarrels with their neighbours, and Hannah More, whose whole work was calculated to reconcile the poor with their station in life, was absurdly accused of inciting them to revolution. The Church, with more justification, called her a Methodist. In September 1789 she wrote a delightful letter to Wilberforce telling him of her progress.

24.9.89. The George Hotel, Cheddar.

You would laugh to see the bustle I am in. I was told we should meet with great opposition if I did not try to propitiate the chief Despot of the village,—who is very rich and very brutal; so I ventured to the Den of this Monster, in a Country as savage as himself, near Bridgewater. He begged I would not think of bringing any religion into the Country, it was the worst thing in the world for the poor, for it made them lazy and useless; in vain I represented to him that they would be more industrious as they were better principled, and that for my own part I had no selfish views in what I was doing; he gave me to understand that he knew the world too well to believe either the one or the other. . . . I found friends must be secured at all events, for if these rich savages set their forces against us and inflamed the people I thought nothing but hostilities would ensue. So I have made eleven more of these agreeable visits, but I was by this time improved in the arts of canvassing and had better success. Miss Wilberforce would have been shocked had she seen the petty Tyrants whose insolence I stroaked and tamed, the ugly children I praised, the Pointers and Spaniels I caressed, the cider I commended, the wine I drank, and the brandy I might have drank; and after these irresistible flatteries I enquired of each if he could recommend me to a house; said that I had a little plan which I hoped would secure their orchards from being robbed, their rabbits from being shot, and their game from being stolen and *might* lower the Poor Rates. If *effect* be the best proof of Eloquence then mine was a good Speech. . . . they (the *wealthy* poor wretches) are as ignorant as the beasts that perish, drunk every day before dinner and plunged in such vices as make me begin to think London a virtuous place. . . .

With the assistance of the wealthy wretches Hannah More found a house and garden suitable for her school. 'The House I have taken at once,' she continued, 'for six Guineas and a half per year. I have ventured to take it for *seven years*, there's courage for you!' She also found a mistress for the school. 'I hope Miss Wilberforce will not be frightened but I am afraid she must be a Methodist.'

The condition of the Church in the Mendips was altogether deplorable. 'I asked the Farmers if they had no Resident Curate. They told me they had a right to insist on one, which right they confessed they had never ventured to exercise for fear their *tythes should be raised*. I blushed for my Species. . . . ' Sometimes the presence of a clergyman did nothing to improve matters. In the living of Axbridge the incumbent 'Mr. Gould is drunk about six times a week, has kept a Mistress in his House, and very frequently is prevented from preaching by two black eyes got by fighting'.[7]

CHAPTER V

THE SLAVE TRADE

In the course of 1787 Wilberforce's attention became focused on a cause that was to occupy him for the next twenty years, and with which his name is indissolubly linked. It was both the greatest challenge and the most monstrous outrage of his time. Well established, profitable, a symbol of the country's naval and commercial greatness, the slave trade was regarded by the few who troubled to think about such things as an unavoidable evil. But it had not always been so. The British attitude to the trade started as one of distaste which changed to approval as soon as the profits to be made in it became apparent. In the later part of the eighteenth century a feeling of revulsion arose which the Abolitionists were able to cultivate and exploit.

To its first circumnavigators, Africa was no more than a gigantic obstruction on their way to the spice markets of the East. In the fifteenth century only the Portuguese bothered to set up trading posts on its West Coast. At first these stations conducted a brisk trade in gold, ivory and pepper, but the coastal tribes' hoarded supplies were soon exhausted. In 1444 the first human cargo was shipped back to Lisbon and sold at the auction block. A regular slave trade developed and each year carried about 500 negroes from Africa to Portugal. Conditions on the Coast were far from those of the idyllic pastoral societies later described by the Abolitionists, and for these first slaves their mild bondage in Portugal was probably an improvement on anything they had known before But this was only true until the discovery of America opened up vast areast for ropical agriculture on a scale that could at last satisfy all the demands of the Old World. From Carolina to La Plata there was the same opportunity and the same problem—labour. Europeans, who were in any case too expensive, would sicken and die in the fields. The native Indians were unsuited, both physically and psychologically, to slavery. This unsatisfied craving for labour began the long and tragic relationship between Africa and America.

The first consignment of negroes was sent from Lisbon to America in 1503. By 1515 the Portuguese were making direct shipments from Africa. At first the English stood aloof; Sir John Hawkins, it is true, made two exceedingly profitable slaving voyages, but this was exceptional. Queen

Elizabeth was horrified and told him that if any of the Africans had been
carried off without their free consent, 'it would be detestable, and call down
the vengeance of Heaven on the undertakers'. An agent of the African
Chartered Company maintained that Englishmen did not buy or sell 'any
that had our own shapes'. This scrupulous attitude did not survive the
acquisition of colonies in the Caribbean. After 1713, when she gained the
Asiento, or sole right to supply the Spanish Colonies with slaves, England
became the leader of the Trade. At first Bristol and London were the main
slaving ports, but in the second half of the eighteenth century they were
eclipsed by the rise of Liverpool. We will follow the Abolitionists as they
strip away the veils hiding the Trade's secrets, but their descriptions of its
horrors were inevitably exaggerated. They needed to shock the nation and
in their propaganda they emphasised the worst episodes in the experience
of the thousands of seamen they had interviewed. The ordinary, routine
slaving voyage was bad enough.

The slavers sailed on a Triangular course, taking trade goods to Africa,
exchanging them for slaves there, shipping the slaves for sale in the West
Indies and carrying a cargo of tropical produce home. The first captains
would cruise along the coast for weeks or months to complete their cargo.
But this wasteful system was replaced by one of agents and factories where
the slaves could be gathered together to await the ship's arrival.

These unhappy people had been acquired by a variety of means. Some
would be domestic slaves, about to exchange an easy life for the impersonal
drudgery of the plantations; some, prisoners of tribal wars and raids,
which increasingly were waged not over any quarrel but in order to
obtain captives for the Trade; others, criminals condemned to be sold into
slavery—almost any crime was now punished with this sentence; others
had been kidnapped or tricked into the barracoons where the slaves were
kept chained.

When the time arrived for them to be taken on board, the slaves became
hysterical with terror, for round the coffles and barracoons rumours had
sped that monstrous men from the sea would come to eat them. They were
subjected to medical examinations and the old, the sickly and the deformed
discarded and often killed as useless. The slaves who had passed the examination were branded with their new owner's mark; they hated leaving
Africa and had to be flogged into canoes to take them out to the slave ship,
where the first arrivals were sometimes playfully christened Adam and Eve.
Here they were crammed into the hold and kept chained each in a space
smaller than a coffin. Clarkson's diagram of the *Brookes* gives a better idea
of conditions in the Middle Passage than any number of words.* It is
necessary only to add that the *Brookes* as drawn by Clarkson carried 450

* See illustration 6, between pp. 94 and 95.

slaves, which was four less than the limit under the 1788 regulation. On an earlier voyage she had carried 609.

The slaves were kept chained in these crowded holds. It was in their owners' interest that their health should be as good as possible. When weather permitted they were taken up on deck and made to jump around under the threat of the lash. But when the weather was bad the buckets in the hold overflowed or upset and the slaves lay in their own filth for weeks on end in an atmosphere which gutted the seamen's candles and could be smelt across a mile of ocean. In these foul conditions they were ravaged by epidemics; but some captains would risk losing many of their slaves in exchange for the high profits that could be expected from 'tight packing'. In these ships the slaves were crammed in 'spoon-fashion' always lying on their right sides because this was thought to be better for their hearts. Slaves suffered more from seasickness than Europeans and sometimes died of this complaint. Others were driven mad by the conditions and by terror of the unknown future. Mad or dead they were thrown overboard to feed the sharks that followed the slave ships all the way across the Atlantic. Those who survived would have to endure a journey that averaged about one hundred days. At the beginning of the voyage the crew would take their pick of the slave women. The slaver who wrote, 'Once off the coast the ship became half bedlam and half brothel,'* has left us the pithiest summary of conditions in the Middle Passage.

If the crew's lust was allowed a free rein this was certainly the only indulgence permitted them. They were treated far worse than sailors in any other trade or service. It is an exaggeration to claim that their condition was worse than that of the slaves, but it was certainly of less concern to their owners. Mortality among the seamen was higher than among the slaves; they were subject to the same diseases to which they had less resistance and had to complete all three legs of the Triangular Trade. The dangers of the Trade were expressed in a seaman's rhyme:

> Beware and take care of the Bight of Benin
> Few come out, though many go in.

Floggings were severe and frequent. As they neared the West Indies the harshness of discipline on board was deliberately intensified. Only a small crew was needed on the last leg home and those who could be driven to desertion need not be paid.

When the ship arrived in the West Indies the slaves, their terror of being eaten re-awakened, spent a few days on board being prepared for sale. Their bodies were fattened and oiled, their sores and ailments hidden.

* Captain Drake of the *Gloria*—quoted in the most recent book on the Trade, Oliver Rainsford's *The Slave Trade*.

Finally they were paraded through the streets and auctioned, naked, on the block. Lower quality slaves were sold in a 'scramble'. Buyers would tender for a number at a price and then, at a signal, race to the yard where the slaves waited in terror, and seize the soundest-looking ones they could find. The sickest and weakest slaves of all were wanted by no one. They were unloaded, dumped on the quay and left there to die.

Once he had been bought, a slave began the process of 'seasoning', which might last for a year. This involved not only learning his new duties but unlearning his entire past. He had to adapt physically to the arduous labour of the cane fields and mentally to the role of a slave—without rights, without liberty, almost without identity. The psychological more than the physical shock of adjustment made the period of seasoning the most lethal of all the stages of enslavement.

Under kind masters and humane captains—and there were a few, even in the Slave Trade—conditions could be better than those described, though the state of the captives had, by the very nature of the Trade, to be miserable. Under the callous and sadistic they could be worse, much worse. It has often been asked why this repellent traffic should not have aroused more opposition before the Abolitionists formed their Committee, and why it should have been allowed to continue so long afterwards. We shall face the second question later. The first can be answered by pointing to the incredulous horror of the House of Commons when the full iniquity of the Trade was revealed to it. At the same time the House, although shocked, was not persuaded to vote for Abolition. It would mitigate the evils of the Trade by passing Dolben's Bill, but it would not abolish what it regarded as a profitable and necessary branch of commerce. If the House took this attitude after hearing all the facts we can understand why the public, while still ignorant of them, should be indifferent. In an age in which suffering abounded the Slave Trade was accepted as a painful necessity, as one of the many unpleasant facts of life.

The Trade was never without enemies. In England this opposition preceded the Trade itself and was never entirely extinguished. Richard Baxter, the Nonconformist divine, and Alexander Pope spoke against it. John Locke in his first treatise on civil government described slavery as 'so vile and miserable an estate of many, and so directly opposite to the generous temper and courage of our nation, that it is hardly to be conceived that an Englishman, much less a gentleman, should plead for it'. Mrs. Behn wrote *Oroonoko, or The History of The Royal Slave*, the first novel in the English language by a woman and the first to have a slave as its hero. John Wesley quarrelled about it with Whitfield who bought slaves on behalf of a charity and in his *Thoughts on Slavery* called it 'the execrable sum of human villainy'. Dr. Johnson, a passionate enemy, shocked his hosts at an Oxford college by toasting the next negro revolt in the West

Indies. He greeted the Declaration of Independence, from which Jefferson's clauses denouncing the Trade had been removed, with the question, 'How is it that we hear the loudest yelps for liberty among the drivers of negroes?' Robertson's influential *History of America* attacked slavery and Adam Smith's *Wealth of Nations* exposed it as inefficient. 'A person who can acquire no property, can have no other interest but to eat as much, and to labour as little as possible.'[1] Edmund Burke and Horace Walpole detested it. Cowper, Southey and Wordsworth lent their voices to the cause. Dr. Paley and Bishop Porteus denounced slavery from their pulpits.

But in this, as in so many noble movements, the Quakers were the first to act. In 1727 a Quaker Meeting censured any involvement with the Slave Trade. In 1761 they resolved that any Friends involved in the Slave Trade should be expelled. In 1763 they extended this order to embrace anyone who assisted the Trade indirectly. In 1783 they presented a petition to the Commons. The American Quakers also pioneered the movement in their country urging in 1754 and demanding in 1776 that Friends should emancipate their slaves.

Slavery was too entrenched and lucrative an institution to be hurt by the criticisms of poets, clergymen and philosophers or threatened by a sect with little political influence. It is ironic that when it suffered its first restriction, this defeat was inflicted upon it by a man who held the humble position of a clerk in ordinary in the Minuting Branch of the Ordnance Office. In the story of Abolition the name of Granville Sharp must rank with those of Wilberforce and Clarkson.

Like Wilberforce, Granville Sharp came from a Yorkshire family. His grandfather had been Archbishop of York, his father Archdeacon of Northumberland. Granville was the latter's ninth son. He was an extraordinary man, humble, brilliant, dogged, humane, energetic, upright and eccentric, and in him all these qualities were present in extreme forms. His humility was such that he never once took the chair of the Abolitionists' Committee during the many years in which he attended its meetings as president. Although humble he would never allow himself to be deflected or deterred once he knew that he was right. He fully earned Sir James Stephen's tribute: 'As long as Granville Sharp survived, it was too soon to proclaim that the age of chivalry was gone.'[2] His intellectual energy was phenomenal. As an apprentice to a linen draper he found himself working next to an aggressive Unitarian who engaged him in theological arguments and declared that Sharp's errors sprang from his ignorance of the Greek language. He had chosen the wrong man. Sharp at once taught himself Greek with such success that, after refuting his fellow-apprentice, he went on to discover and correct unsuspected errors in the translation of the New Testament. He later had similar arguments with a young Jew who told him that his misunderstanding of the Prophesies was due to his unfamiliarity with the Hebrew original. This deficiency, and the Jewish apprentice, were soon corrected. Sharp went on to publish a pamphlet on the 'Rules relative to the Hebrew Conversive Vau', in which he claimed to have demolished the accepted doctrine of the Rabbi Elias. The College of Heraldry, too, was grist to his mill. A friend of his, a retired tradesman, claimed to be the rightful heir to the title of Lord Willoughby de Parham. Sharp busied himself in the appropriate sources, and incredible though it may seem, soon had his friend installed in the House of Lords. He even had the temerity to enter into argument with Dr. Johnson over the morality of pressing seamen.[3]

Sharp's personal integrity was as strong as his kindness and sympathy for the suffering. He resigned his post in the Ordnance Department rather than be in any way involved in the American War. His superiors appreciated him enough to give him several years' paid leave in the hope that his conscience would allow him to return. But some of his views were surprising: he had a deep faith in the Anglo-Saxon institution of Frankpledge as a constitutional panacea. And it must have been one of the period's most enjoyable encounters when he lectured a flabbergasted but polite Fox on the identity of Bonaparte with the Little Horn in the book of Daniel. 'That man passes as a statesman,' Sharp later complained, 'and yet it is evident to me that he never before so much as heard of the Little Horn.'

Sharp's concern about slavery started by accident. In 1765 Jonathan Strong, a slave kept in London, was beaten, almost blinded, and abandoned as useless by his master; stumbling helplessly down the street he met Granville Sharp who took him to the surgery of his brother William. The two brothers restored him to health and found him a decent job. When two years later Strong was recognised by his old master, 'the patient, once more become sleek and strong, was an object on which Barbadian eyes could not look without cupidity'.[4] He was seized by two of the Lord Mayor's officers. Granville Sharp was summoned, and went to the Mansion House, where the Lord Mayor ruled that since Strong had stolen nothing he might go free. But as soon as Strong was dismissed a ship's captain seized him by the arm and claimed him as the property of a Mr. Kerr. Sharp immediately charged the captain with assault. A few days later he was himself issued with a writ for robbing the original master of his slave. This man, a Barbadian lawyer, called on him and challenged him to a duel. Sharp replied that 'as he had studied the law so many years, he should want no satisfaction that the law could give him'. Strong's owner did not pursue the matter, but as a result of the case Sharp was led to study the law on the matter. At first he found the results of his researches horrifying.

In the reign of William and Mary, Chief Justice Holt had ruled that a negro in England was free because 'one may be a villeyn in England, but not a slave'. But this judgement was effectively overruled in 1729 by an opinion published by York and Talbot, respectively Attorney and Solicitor General. They considered that slaves were not free by virtue either of being in England or of being baptised. Although slaves obtained favourable verdicts in 1732 and 1739 these were isolated and exceptional cases. Rewards were openly offered for the recovery of fugitive slaves and others were advertised for sale. *The Gazette* of April 1769 is typical when it groups together for sale 'at the Bull and Gate Inn, Holborn, a chestnut gelding, a tin whistle, and a well made, good tempered Black Boy'.

Sharp consulted many lawyers, including the great Dr. Blackstone, without finding one who would allow that a defence existed against the opinions of 1729. Almost anyone else would have been dismayed by the unanimous opposition of all legal authorities, backed by nearly forty years of precedent. A brave man might perhaps have tried to hide slaves, like organisers of the Underground Railroad in the Southern States many years later, while lobbying futilely for a change in the law. But Granville Sharp was happily described as having 'the most inflexible of human wills united to the gentlest of human hearts'.[5] He treated Blackstone as another Unitarian apprentice. He had never opened a law book, 'except the Bible', in his life, but he now embarked on an exhaustive study of the law as it affected the liberty of British subjects. After two years' work he published a pamphlet, 'A Representation of the Injustice and Dangerous Tendency of Tolerating Slavery in England'.

Other cases followed that of Strong without the fundamental legal issue being raised. The most dramatic of these concerned Thomas Lewis, a slave who was seized in Chelsea, near the house of Mrs. Banks, the mother of Captain Cook's companion. Lewis screamed for help as he was dragged to a boat on the Thames. Mrs. Banks's servants ran out too late, but, on being told what had happened, she summoned Granville Sharp and offered to pay for the case. Sharp obtained a writ of Habeas Corpus which was served, at sea, on the captain of the ship taking Lewis to the West Indies. Lewis's master persisted in his claim and the case was heard before Lord Chief Justice Mansfield on February 20, 1771. Sharp's counsel brandished his Tract and claimed that 'no man can be legally claimed as a slave in this country'. Lord Mansfield put to the jury the question whether Lewis's master had established a title to his property. If so he would have to consider whether such property could exist in England. The jury decided that the master had not established his claims. Several jurors, wildly excited, chanted, 'No property! No property!' Sharp was less pleased, being certain that he could have won the main point that slaves could not exist in England. But Lord Mansfield was happy to leave this unsettled. 'I hope it will never be finally discussed,' he added, 'for I would have all the masters think them free, and all negroes think they were not, because then they would both behave better.'

On February 7, 1772 the case of the negro Somerset was brought before Lord Mansfield and three other justices and the main issue could no longer be evaded, Somerset's owner having a clear title to him under Virginian law. Lord Mansfield, who still flinched from facing the question, made every effort to avoid the issue. He twice adjourned the case; he repeatedly recommended Somerset's owner to abandon it, or failing that to end it by setting him free; he urged settlement out of court and finally recommended that legislation be introduced to secure property in slaves. But Parliament was unobliging and Somerset's owner adamant while no consideration could now have deflected Sharp. When Mansfield's judgement came it was unequivocal: he declared the power claimed by Somerset's master 'never was in use here, or acknowledged by the law' and 'tracing the subject to natural principles, the claim of slavery never can be supported'.

Mansfield was reluctant to act for two reasons. There were some 14,000 slaves in England, who would become free as a result of his decision. They would be destitute and many would take to crime; their owners would blame the law for encouraging them to bring slaves over and then declaring them no longer to be their property. They might even have grounds for litigation. Mansfield was a great lawyer, with a deep veneration for English law. He cannot have been happy to see its foremost authorities including himself humiliated by an outsider. Neither of these feelings was allowed to upset his judgement, but before we give this unwilling hero of the Abolitionist movement too much credit we should remember the same mechanically legal verdict he was to give, probably with equal reluctance, in the case of the slave ship *Zong*.*

The years after the Somerset decision saw many attacks on slavery. Charles Wesley, Thomas Jefferson, Adam Smith and Dr. Johnson made their contributions to the cause. Cowper was inspired by the verdict to write:

> I would not have a slave to till my ground,
> To carry me, to fan me when I sleep,
> And tremble when I wake, for all the wealth
> That sinews bought and sold have ever earn'd.
> No; dear as freedom is,—and in my heart's
> Just estimation priz'd above all price,—
> I had much rather be myself the slave,
> And wear the bonds than fasten them on him.
> . . . .
> Slaves cannot breathe in England; if their lungs
> Receive our air, that moment they are free.

* See page 68.

Sharp also began lobbying bishops and archbishops. He made new allies, notably Anthony Benezet, the eminent American abolitionist. He was still aiming as much at the institution of Slavery as at the Trade. But in 1776 a motion against the latter was moved in the Commons by Wilberforce's predecessor for Hull. It failed to attract any significant support. Feelings on the subject were running high and all that was needed to make those opposed to slavery co-ordinate their efforts was a violent shock, one well-publicised atrocity. It was in the nature of the Slave Trade that such an atrocity was inevitable. It came in 1783 with the case of the slave ship *Zong*.

On March 19, 1783 a negro called on Granville Sharp with a horrifying story. One hundred and thirty-two slaves, he swore, had been thrown alive into the sea from an English slaver. The *Zong* had lost her way; sixty slaves and seven crew had died of an epidemic and the water supply was running uncomfortably, if not dangerously, low. As the rest of the slaves were in poor health, it was clear that many would die before the voyage was over and the survivors fetch low prices in Jamaica. The loss would then fall on the owner; but if they were jettisoned on any pretext concerning the safety of the ship, the underwriters would pay. The slaves were thrown alive into the sea in three batches. When the time came for the last thirty-six, they knew what was in store for them. Twenty-six were shackled and thrown overboard; the last ten broke away from the slavers and leaped into the sea themselves. One caught a rope trailing from the ship, pulled himself back on board and somehow survived to bring the story back to Sharp.

Sharp was outraged; this seemed to him a clear case of murder and fraud; even the story of the water shortage did not stand up—not that he would have regarded the most acute shortage as a justification for murder. No attempt had been made to ration the crew and, on the second day of the massacre, there had been a heavy downpour, after which thirty-six slaves were thrown overboard. The master of the *Zong* was rewarded for his initiative and thus benefited financially from his crimes. The underwriters brought a suit against the owners, which Sharp wished to follow with a criminal prosecution. But even the commercial action failed; the Solicitor General deplored his 'pretended appeals' to humanity and asserted the right of masters to drown their slaves 'without a surmise of impropriety'. Lord Mansfield ruled that it was 'as if horses had been thrown overboard'.

The only pleasant thought that one can derive from this appalling case is that it may have hastened the union of the Abolitionists. It is certain that they would have got together at some time, but it is likely that the *Zong* spurred them on. In 1783 the Quakers formed a Committee of six members—William Dillwyn, George Harrison, Samuel Hoare, Thomas

Knowles, John Lloyd and Joseph Woods, to co-ordinate efforts 'for the relief and liberation of the negro slaves in the West Indies and for the discouragement of the Slave Trade on the coast of Africa'. The activities of this Committee soon led to co-operation with Granville Sharp, who had been working on similar lines. The Movement now had an organisation to which sympathisers might gravitate, but its leaders, though able and energetic, lacked political influence and first-hand knowledge of the West Indies. Both these deficiencies were soon to be repaired.

James Ramsay had served as surgeon in the man-of-war commanded by Sir Charles Middleton. When they met a slave ship in which an epidemic was raging Ramsay was the only man prepared to board her and attend the sick. The miserable condition of the slaves made a deep impression on him and when, soon afterwards, an injury forced him to seek work on shore, he made up his mind to do everything he could for them. Ramsay, after being ordained, became rector of two parishes on St. Kitts, where he remained for nineteen years, during which his efforts to improve the slaves' lot made him loathed by their masters. He returned in 1781 to take up the living of Teston in Kent which was in the gift of his old commander Sir Charles Middleton. Ramsay told the Middletons about the horrors of slavery and convinced them that something had to be done about it. As a first step he wrote an *Essay on the Treatment and Conversion of African Slaves in the British Sugar Colonies*.

Ramsay's *Essay* was the first statement of the Abolitionist case to be based entirely on first-hand evidence. It was exceedingly difficult for the Abolitionists to get information from the West Indies, since almost everyone who worked there had some connection with slavery. Ramsay had seen the slave ships abandoning their pathetic 'refuse slaves' to die on the quays of St. Kitts. He had seen scrambles and auctions and calculated how many slaves had died in the Middle Passage and during their seasoning, but he attacked the Slave Trade more as a part of slavery than as a distinct evil. Ramsay's experience of the Trade, although greater than other Abolitionists', was slight compared to his knowledge of slavery. He argued that the brutal treatment of slaves would only stop when it was in their masters' interest that they should be well and happy. At present slaves who died could be replaced through the Trade, but if it were removed self-interest would force the planters to treat them better.

In the same year as Ramsay's *Essay* was published Sir Charles Middleton entered Parliament. He wanted to find an advocate for the slaves, a rôle for which he thought himself inadequate. Middleton was a supremely efficient administrator. He ran his wife's and his sister-in-law's farms, poured money into them, and ultimately made great profits. He was an innovator in the cultivation of hops; he was also responsible, under Pitt, for the modernisation of the Navy. Pitt did not like Middleton, but considered him 'the best man of business he ever knew'.[6] He did not, how-ever, have the stature as a speaker necessary for the advocate of Abolition. But he and Lady Middleton were to play an important part in the campaign by recruiting, bringing together, and encouraging the first Abolitionists.

In 1785 the cause gained an even more important recruit. Thomas Clarkson, like Wilberforce, was an undergraduate at St. John's College, Cambridge. In 1784 he had won the first prize for Latin essays by B.A.s of 'middle standing' and he was determined to repeat his success in 1785. Dr. Peckard, the examiner, as an opponent of the Slave Trade, chose the subject, 'Is it right to make men slaves against their will?' He presumably hoped to stimulate thought and therefore opposition to the Slave Trade; the result must have been beyond his wildest dreams.

Clarkson started work late, but his powers of concentration were phenomenal. He devoured every book on Africa and grilled everyone he could find who had been there. He slept with a candle in his room so that he could jot down any thoughts that occurred to him in the night. He won his prize, but at some stage this ceased to be all-important; an academic exercise had turned into a crusade. As he rode back to London Clarkson could not dismiss the horrors of the Slave Trade from his mind.

'I stopped my horse occasionally, and dismounted and walked. I frequently tried to persuade myself in these intervals that the contents of my essay could not be true. The more, however, I reflected upon them or rather upon the authorities on which they were founded, the more I gave them credit. Coming in sight of Wade's Mill in Hertfordshire, I sat down disconsolate on the turf by the roadside and held my horse. Here a thought came into my mind—that, if the contents of the essay were true, it was time some person should see these calamities to their end.'[7]

Clarkson decided to translate his prize essay and have it printed as a pamphlet. He was introduced by his publisher to Sharp, Ramsay, Dillwyn and other Abolitionists.

Ramsay invited him to Teston for a month in the summer of 1786. He introduced him to the Middletons and, heartened by finding these new allies, Clarkson declared at their dining table, 'I was ready to devote myself to the cause.'[8]

In May 1787 the different workers in the cause united to form a Committee for the Abolition of the Slave Trade. Granville Sharp was its Chairman, Clarkson a member and nine out of twelve of its number were Quakers. From this moment the Abolitionists' efforts were co-ordinated by a group of dedicated and brilliant men. In Clarkson they had a human dynamo, a detective of incredible energy, patience and perseverance, a man of genius who had found his vocation. All they lacked was an advocate to put their cause forward in Parliament.

In 1780 Edmund Burke had considered a measure to mitigate and finally abolish the Slave Trade. He had recoiled because of the strength of the West Indians in Parliament. In the face of their opposition he thought his motion might destroy the Whig Party without helping the slaves. The qualifications for a parliamentary leader of the Abolitionists were daunting. He could not be too much of a party man, or, like Burke, his resolve would be softened by party considerations. He had, similarly, to be independent enough to secure support from a wide range of political groups. But if the advocate needed to be independent he had also to be an independent man of ability, connections and reputation. He had to be important enough to have the ear and secure the sympathy of the great; he had to be an orator able to arouse pity, anger and disgust, capable of speaking often on the same subject without boring the House. He had to have the mind to master a complicated subject and to expose his opponents' lies. He needed, above all, to be prepared to devote himself, his time, his money, and, if necessary, his health, to the cause. Wilberforce fulfilled all these requirements.

The best causes are often plagued by bickering and Abolition was no exception. In the dispute between Wilberforce's sons and Clarkson one of the issues was the question of when Wilberforce decided to adopt the cause. His sons traced his interest to a letter which they claimed he wrote to a York newspaper at the age of fourteen, and they even gave this epoch-making event a place in their chronology of the abolition movement. Wilberforce himself remembers being sufficiently concerned about the problem in 1780 to ask a friend to investigate conditions in Antigua. But in those days, he confesses, 'I did nothing—nothing I mean to any good purpose; my own distinction was my darling object.' In the autumn of 1786 he stayed with Sir Charles and Lady Middleton and was urged by them to undertake the parliamentary leadership of the cause. Ramsay almost certainly took part in these discussions; Wilberforce had met him at Teston in 1783. Wilberforce, like Clarkson a few months earlier, was encouraged by their enthusiasm and promised to undertake the leadership of the Parliamentary campaign if nobody better could be found. In the spring of 1787 he was lobbied by Clarkson.

'On my first interview with him he stated frankly that the subject had often employed his thoughts and that it was near his heart. He seemed earnest about it and also very desirous of taking the trouble of inquiring further into it.'[9] Newton may also have influenced Wilberforce, but it is unlikely that he needed much persuasion. Convinced that he had squandered his talents and position on self-aggrandisement, he was desperate to find a more serious field for their use, 'the something out of the common way' he had discussed with Pitt in 1785. The Proclamation Society, founded as it was to enforce existing laws, was largely an extra-Parliamentary body. To justify his continuance as a member of Parliament he had to find some good cause that he could promote there. Pitt understood his difficulties, shared his concern about the Slave Trade, and wished to give him an incentive to remain in Parliament. 'Do not lose time,' he urged Wilberforce, 'or the ground may be occupied by another.'

'When I had acquired so much information,' Wilberforce remembered, 'I began to talk the matter over with Pitt and Grenville. Pitt recommended me to undertake its conduct, as a subject suited to my character and talents. At length, I well remember, after a conversation in the open air at the root of an old tree at Holwood, just above the steep descent into the vale of Keston, I resolved to give notice on a fit occasion in the House of Commons of my intention to bring the subject forward.'[10]

Soon after he had reached this decision a dinner was arranged by Clarkson, in the house of Bennet Langton, a friend of Dr. Johnson's and a member of the Committee, at which Sir Joshua Reynolds, Boswell, Windham and Middleton were present. All the guests, including Boswell and Windham, who later deserted the cause, urged Wilberforce to undertake it. But after his conversation with Pitt at Holwood on May 12 their pleas were superfluous. He replied that he would be happy to take up the cause in Parliament 'provided no more proper person could be found'. He had no objection to Clarkson's telling this to his 'friends in the City'.

The first thing that the Abolitionists had to decide was what, precisely, they wished to abolish. They were faced with two distinct evils, the Slave Trade and the institution of slavery. With the exception of Granville Sharp, who did not recognise the impossible, they agreed that their chances of success would be greater if they concentrated on one of these evils. They also agreed that 'it did not matter where they began, or which of them they took as far as the end to be produced was the thing desired'. If slavery were abolished, the Trade would clearly die at the same time. The Foreign Slave Trade would then stand out as a moral anachronism and economic folly. If the Trade were abolished, planters would be forced to treat their slaves well in order to preserve their numbers. Greater leniency must grow into greater privileges and rights and, at length, into freedom. The last argument seems weak even assuming that the planters, when faced with Abolition, would react logically; they had seldom done so in the past, nor were they to do so in the event. No such doubts seem to have struck the Abolitionists in 1787, and even if they had, they would still have been justified in concentrating their attack on the Trade. An attack on slavery would have been an open assault on 'property', a word which in the eighteenth century had deep emotional overtones. The Abolitionists would have been charged with letting loose an irresponsible race; they would have had slave revolts flung in their teeth and been challenged to prove that the slaves were ready for freedom, a statement with which few of them then agreed. There would have been grave constitutional questions of the powers of Parliament over the internal affairs of semi-independent colonies. Secession would have been threatened; more 'yelps for liberty' would have been heard from the drivers of negroes. On the other hand Parliament had an indisputable right to regulate or abolish any branch of commerce, and to prohibit the Trade would interfere with no one's property or security.

Another decision taken by the Abolitionists in the summer of 1787 was to gather as much evidence as possible about the Trade before it became known that there was to be a Parliamentary inquiry. Clarkson undertook this task. He called on Wilberforce before leaving and found him in bed, probably with a foretaste of the serious illness he was to suffer the next year. 'After conversing as much as he well could in his weak state, he held out his hand to me, and wished me success. When I left him, I felt much dejected. It appeared to me as if it would be in this case, as it is often in that of other earthly things, that we scarcely possess what we repute a treasure, when it is taken from us.'[11]

The Government was co-operative. In September 1787 George Rose wrote to Wilberforce: 'It is quite unprecedented to allow anyone to rummage the Custom House Papers for information who have no Employment in the Revenue; I will however without delay obtain for Mr. Clarkson all the information he wants though I am a West Indian Planter, would I were not!'[12]

In London Clarkson was able to get a general picture of the Trade, understand its economics and assess its importance. In Bristol when he began to discover its effects on its victims he found them more horrible than anything he had expected. On two occasions the stories told to him were so frightful that he thought that the slavers had discovered his purpose and were trying to foist false information on him, which later would betray his case. In both cases he confirmed the story as true. He found a small ship which carried seventy slaves. He measured its hold and found it to be thirty foot long and varying between ten foot four and five foot wide. He checked the builder's measurements to see if he had made a mistake. In this ship a grown slave would have had to sit all the way across the Middle Passage and contract his limbs so that they occupied only three square feet of the deck.

Clarkson was shunned in the street 'as if I had been a mad dog', but his list of witnesses slowly grew. A retired surgeon, Alexander Falconbridge, was particularly valuable. Falconbridge had been on four slaving voyages to Africa, but was now an opponent of the Trade. He told Clarkson everything he knew, helped prepare the evidence for the Inquiry and later acted as his bodyguard in Liverpool. Clarkson had expected to hear horrifying stories about the treatment of slaves, what surprised him was that the seamen seemed to suffer almost as much. Flogged, sometimes to death, mutilated, cheated and starved, their existence was miserable and their mortality rate far higher than in any other trade. This was an important discovery. It was predictable that one of the defences of the Slave Trade would be that it gave employment and training to seamen—a 'nursery for seamen' was the phrase later used. Armed with Clarkson's evidence documented with the muster rolls of slave ships, the Abolitionists could prove that the Trade was, instead, their grave.

Clarkson discovered that the retired captains who avoided him often had investments in slaving ships. But when the seamen heard that he was also interested in their grievances, they came flooding in to see him. The strain of hearing their stories, of sitting up all night in their taverns, finally became too much for him. 'I was agonised to think that this Trade could last another day. I was in a state of agitation from morning to night. I determined I would soon leave Bristol. I saw nothing but misery in the place.'[13]

Clarkson continued his journey through Gloucester, Worcester and Chester; in each of these places he converted the editor of the local newspaper to the Abolitionist cause, and founded an Abolitionist society. In Liverpool he bought various instruments, shackles, thumbscrews and devices for opening the mouths of reluctant slaves, all of which were used in the Trade. He studied the duties levied in the port and found, to his surprise, that they were less in 1772 when a hundred slavers used it than in 1779 when a mere eleven did so. It seemed that the prosperity of Liverpool was not dependent on the Slave Trade.

Clarkson stayed in a tavern where he had a private sitting-room, but he generally dined in public. As soon as his mission became known, people began coming in and studying him as he ate, 'as if I had been some curious creature imported from foreign parts'. These unwelcome visitors started to justify the Trade in an aggressive manner, saying 'they had heard of a person turned mad, who had conceived the thought of destroying Liverpool and all its glory'. Since Clarkson was the last man to allow such statements to stand unanswered, the tavern became a debating chamber in which he was invariably victorious. Falconbridge, who had accompanied him from Bristol, was able to answer the obvious question, 'have you been on the coast yourself?', by saying that he had and that all Clarkson's statements were true. His robust appearance and the fact that he always carried a pistol deterred the slavers from more direct arguments.

The gathering of evidence proceeded along the same lines as in Bristol, stories being easier to find than witnesses. Patience, perseverance and sometimes cunning were necessary. One of these cases led to a dangerous moment for Clarkson. He had discovered that a slave captain had flogged his steward for two and a quarter hours, as a result of which the man had died. He found that a member of the crew would tell the story, but not in his presence. Clarkson therefore hid in his room while the seaman told his story. But the secret leaked out. Shortly afterwards Clarkson when walking back from the head of the pier found his way blocked by eight or nine men. Instead of dividing and letting him through as he expected, they closed in on him. Suddenly he recognised the murderer of the steward and two other slavers with whom he had quarrelled at the inn. Clarkson dashed forward at them and at the cost of a few blows, pushed his way through to safety. He heard later that these men had been abusing him and that one of them had said that 'I deserved to be thrown over the pier head'.

Soon after this attack Clarkson left Liverpool, his task completed. He had gathered the evidence needed by the Abolitionists for the presentation of their case in Parliament. During his investigations he had acquired the names and histories of 20,000 seamen, so that the Abolitionists now knew more of the Trade than the slavers themselves. It was an outstanding piece of detective work, performed in circumstances that were always distressing and sometimes dangerous.

*

On February 11, 1788 the King directed that a Committee of Privy Council should investigate the African Slave Trade. Wilberforce summoned Clarkson to London to help prepare the Abolitionists' case. Although well armed with evidence they were short of witnesses. It took courage to stand up and testify against the Trade and then return to life in a slaving port. A man called Norris who had been helpful to Clarkson in Liverpool seemed a promising witness; but when Clarkson tried to find him he discovered, to his horror, that Norris was already on the way to London as a member of the delegation to defend the Trade. The pain of this betrayal was to be increased when Norris's evidence proved to be particularly damaging.*

When Counsel began their examination of the Trade witnesses a very different picture emerged from that uncovered by Clarkson. The witnesses denied outright that kidnappings took place in Africa, or that wars were waged, let alone fomented, for the purpose of obtaining slaves. They claimed that the only natives who became slaves were those captured in 'just' wars and those who had been sentenced to slavery for their crimes. The Trade was a blessing to these people; in earlier wars all captives had been slain, now, thanks to its kindly intervention, many were saved. Those who were transported to the West Indies were doubly fortunate in being alive at all and in being removed to a better life. Their happiness on the journey

* It seems likely that Norris was deceiving Clarkson throughout. In his evidence to the House Norris claimed that Clarkson only wanted a gradual abolition and that he had applied for a post as captain of a slaver for his friend Falconbridge; Norris must have known both these statements to be untrue. He was evidently a man of some standing in Liverpool, enough so to be mentioned in the correspondence of Stephen Fuller, the agent for Jamaica.

could be seen by the singing and dancing with which they expressed their delight.

Even at the beginning of the Inquiry this idyllic presentation of the Middle Passage was less than convincing. But the Trade witnesses also painted a grim picture of the despotism of some African princes, which visibly affected the Committee. Norris was especially eloquent on this subject and gave a horrifying description of the rule of the King of Dahomey. But much of this evidence was contradicted by that of two Swedish botanists produced by Clarkson. These men had kept journals during their African travels and they clearly had no interest in favouring either side. On the habits of the King of Dahomey and his colleague of Ashanti, the slavers had, for once, a reasonable argument. The barbarities practised by these tyrants were so frightful that their subjects would have done well to take their chances on the Middle Passage. Rather than playing down their atrocities, the honest answer to the slavers' case would have been to point out the great extent to which they had been increased by the Trade. Both these kings waged wars, destroyed tribes and ravaged provinces to find slaves. Their countries were transformed by the Trade from inland tribal states into slave empires.

It was clear that the Privy Council's investigation could only be a preliminary to a discussion of the matter by the House. At this critical time Wilberforce was laid low by an illness that made his doctors despair of his life. His digestion had always caused him trouble and from time to time he suffered agonising attacks of piles and constipation.* Early in 1788 these disorders became much worse. Throughout February and March he endured a series of attacks, recoveries and relapses. His appetite disappeared: he became feverish, could not sleep and felt 'constant thirst and heat'. His doctors, after a consultation, diagnosed 'an absolute decay of all the digestive tracts', and one of them, Dr. Warren, confided to a friend, 'That little fellow with his calico guts, cannot possibly survive a twelvemonth.'[14] Orthodox cures being unavailing he was sent to Bath at the beginning of April to take the waters. Before he left, Pitt, 'with a warmth of principle and friendship that have made me love him better than I ever did before', promised to take his place in promoting Abolition.

On May 8, 1788 Pitt therefore proposed that the matter should be debated in the next session, a motion that was carried without division. It would have been factious for the slave party to have opposed any discussion of the question, but an opportunity for a trial of strength did arise in this

---

* The first reference I can find to these disorders is in Wilberforce's Private Journal (Wrangham MSS.) on July 1, 1785, in which he writes. 'Last winter I had the piles again for a few days but only very slightly as to pain, though confined for ten or twelve days, and reclined—I rather believe that if they had not been neglected at first they would have come to nothing.'

session. Sir William Dolben, an old and much respected member, had been horrified by conditions on slave ships refitting in the Thames. He introduced a Bill to limit, for a trial period of a year, the number of slaves who could be carried in relation to the tonnage of a vessel. The drawing of the *Brookes* between pp. 94 and 95 would just have qualified under Dolben's proposals. The supporters of the Trade responded to this challenge by claiming that the Middle Passage 'was one of the happiest periods of a slave's life'. They maintained that the present system was designed to promote the slaves' comfort and health and that any restrictions would be unnecessary and ruinous.

The picture of the Middle Passage as a holiday cruise did not stand up to examination, and the witness who described the holds of slave ships as being 'redolent with frankincense'[15] can only have harmed his own cause when the truth became known. The spokesmen for the trade contradicted themselves and each other. On June 17 the House divided 56 to 5 in favour of Dolben's motion. But the reaction of the House of Lords was ominous. Dolben's Bill was the thin end of the Abolitionist wedge; it posed no threat whatsoever to the planters and demanded a minimal regulation of the Trade.

It was to last for an experimental period of a year, after which it would have to be renewed by Parliament. Its conditions were entirely reasonable, it tried only to alleviate a little of the suffering caused. The slavers themselves later admitted that, far from leading to the ruin they had predicted, it had in fact increased their profits. It was supported by Pitt and Fox and had passed through the Commons with only token opposition in a debate during which the defenders of the Trade had been discovered in numerous lies. The issues were clear and the ground could hardly have been more favourable. If the Abolitionists failed to carry this modest measure, they could not hope to succeed with anything more ambitious.

Pitt's Lord Chancellor, Thurlow, was openly hostile to the Bill and other Ministers in the Lords lukewarm. Admiral Rodney, the hero of the American War, spoke against it. Throughout the struggle, the greatest naval commanders opposed abolition. Most of them had spent many years in the West Indies and retained a strong impression of the planters' hospitality and the contentment of their slaves. Pitt rallied his forces, declaring that if the Bill were defeated, 'the opponents of it and myself cannot continue as members of the same government'. Thurlow, unsilenced by this threat, derided the measure as the result of a 'five days fit of philanthropy', and Dolben's Bill returned to the Commons much amended. A new Bill, containing most of these amendments, passed through the Lords a few days before the end of the session. Pitt was said to have prevented the King from proroguing Parliament until it was safe.

Pitt wrote to Wilberforce on June 28, 'The business respecting the Slave

Trade meets just now with some rub in the House of Lords. Even in the temporary regulations respecting the conveyance, which I wonder how any human being can resist, and which I therefore believe we shall carry, tho' it creates some trouble . . . there seems not a shadow of doubt as to the House of Commons next year. . . . '[16]

*

Pitt's encouraging letter found Wilberforce much recovered. The waters at Bath always agreed with him, but the credit for this cure must be given to another remedy. Much to his reluctance, Wilberforce was persuaded by his doctor to take opium, and the improvement in his health was almost immediate. Opium saved his life, but from 1788 to his death in 1833, it was to remain a necessity for him. Doctors in Wilberforce's time were still unaware of the dangers of this drug; there was no restriction on its sale and it was used in a soothing syrup for babies and a well-known children's tonic, Godfrey's Cordial. Wilberforce could never abandon the habit, for in his case the agonies of withdrawal symptoms would be joined by a recurrence of the intestinal disorders, which the drug alone could cure. But if Wilberforce had to depend on opium, he had the strength of character and will never to become its slave. 'If I take but a single glass of wine,' he would say, 'I can feel its effects, but I never know when I have taken my dose of opium by my feelings.' Although sometimes obliged by illness to increase his normal dose of one or two grains to five or six, he always was able to reduce his consumption again after he had recovered. Alethea Hayter in *Opium and the Romantic Imagination* conducted a fascinating study of the use of opium by nineteenth-century poets and its effect on their art. She describes Wilberforce's relationship with the drug:

'There is one class of addict, not a large one, who when they have discovered the dosage which preserves them from the wretchedness of withdrawal symptoms will restrict themselves to that amount and will continue for many years, perhaps for all the rest of their lives, taking only so much opium and no more. Opium now gives them nothing positive, nothing they could not have had if they had never taken it at all; it simply saves them from the pains of giving it up. They are like diabetics dependent on their regular injections of insulin to keep them in normal health. Addicts of this type can lead conventional, responsible lives, and their addiction may not be detected even by their family and friends. Examples of this type of addiction were William Wilberforce and the poet George Crabbe. Such men and women are rareties, because only strong and well-balanced characters can maintain such a regime, never yielding to the temptation to increase their dose, and strong and well balanced characters do not generally take to opium in the first place. . . . These confirmed but moderate addicts are called "users" in the jargon of the addict world.'[17]

This description should be qualified, in Wilberforce's case, only by the reminder that the drug was a medical necessity. Whatever his strength of mind and his resolve to rid himself of it, he could never succeed, since the result would be illness and the cure a return to its use. The fact that he was always able to reduce his dosage from dangerous levels argues that, had it not been for his intestinal condition, he could have abandoned it altogether. The greatest amount of opium ever taken by Wilberforce seems to have been about six grains per day. Isaac Milner, in 1799, wrote to him that he was finding it necessary to take 'almost twenty grains of opium daily'.[18]

CHAPTER VI

ABOLITION: INQUIRY

WILBERFORCE'S recovery was so quick that he was able to leave Bath after a month. He spent his convalescence first at Cambridge, then in Westmorland. He wrote to a friend asking him to prepare quarters: 'Beware, however, of a damp bed, and rather let me have one that has been slept in, sheets and all, for a month together.' After Cambridge Wilberforce travelled up to Rayrigg, the house he had rented on Lake Windermere.

He took delight in the beauty of the Lake District. He shared the passion of his age for spectacular scenery—lakes, mountains, precipices and waterfalls—and Windermere was as close as England could come to 'the paradise of Interlaken'. He remembered later: 'I never enjoyed the country more than during this visit, when in the early morning I used to row out alone, and find an oratory under one of the woody islands in the middle of the lake.'

He had first taken Rayrigg in the winter of 1780 and moved there for the summer recess of 1781. He kept up the lease, which only cost him £10 a year, until 1788. Rayrigg is a pleasant unpretentious little manor house occupying a superb position on the eastern shore of Lake Windermere. To the east it is cut off from the outside world by a belt of high trees, while the house looks out across the lake towards the west and the mountains. A small peninsula gives different views to the north and south. Its present owners have made a delightful garden. Its position is secluded and beautiful, its atmosphere one of peace; it should have been a perfect place for Wilberforce to restore his health and settle into his new way of life. But even in Rayrigg the outside world could not be forgotten. Three miles south at Storrs Hall there lived Colonel John Bolton, a wealthy slave trader. Wilberforce never mentions Bolton, but he must have known that he was there.[1]

More immediate distractions soon pursued him. He had brought his mother and Milner with him, and for a time they enjoyed a pleasant, secluded existence. But one day they were horrified to see the Duchess of Gordon and her daughter outside while they were still eating their dinner. Wilberforce was firm: 'Their tapping at our low window announced that they had discovered our retreat, and would take no denial. I went to them and told the Duchess, "I cannot see you here, I have with me my old mother, who being too infirm to make new acquaintances, is no more in your way than you are in her's." '[2]

A man seeking to subdue the worldly side of his character could hardly have been discovered by a more unwelcome visitor. The Duchess of Gordon was the leading Tory hostess of the day. She was a persuasive, importunate, obstinate woman who would not be put off by Wilberforce's excuses. Her flirtatious attitude towards religion would have jarred on an Evangelical more than honest paganism. She liked the idea of religion and would implore Wilberforce to come and rest and meditate in the peaceful atmosphere of Gordon Castle. He never did and warned his friends not to. One of them, his wife's cousin Lord Calthorpe, later disregarded this advice and paid the price. Calthorpe was carried away into thinking he might make a convert of the Duchess and was persuaded, against his better judgement, to spend a Sunday with her. He was, therefore, mortified when he saw the delight with which she greeted the news of another guest's arrival. In the few hours he had with her alone he sternly read her *Leighton's Commentaries*, only to look up and find her fast asleep. She teased him about his faults and threatened to report them to her friend Wilberforce. Although fascinated by her, Calthorpe had had to conclude: 'She seemed to be on the same kind of terms with Religion as she is with her Duke, that is on terms of great nominal familiarity without ever meeting each other.'[3]

The Duchess easily cajoled Wilberforce and Milner into taking supper that night and a long walk the next day. She soon left, but she was replaced by other unwelcome visitors and, as Wilberforce's body recovered, his conscience returned to the attack. By the end of July he was recording in his Journal:

'The life I am now leading is unfavourable in all respects, both to mind and body, as little suited to me as an invalid . . . as it is becoming my character and profession as a Christian. Indolence and intemperance are its capital features. It is true, the incessant intrusion of fresh visitors, and the constant temptations to which I am liable, from always being in company, render it extremely difficult to adhere to any plan of study, or any resolutions of abstemiousness, which last too it is the harder for me to observe, because my health requires throughout an indulgent regime. Nothing can excuse or palliate such conduct. . . .

'I am this week entering on a scene of great temptation—a perpetual round of dissipation and my house overflowing with guests. . . . '

He resolved:

'(1) To be for the ensuing week moderate at table.

(2) Hours as early as can contrive.'[4]

These expedients were not enough; we soon read, 'Milner and I had much talk about this being a most improper place for me, and resolved upon not continuing the house.' He complained in a letter to Newton: 'The tour to the lakes has become so fashionable, that the banks of the Thames are scarcely more public than those of Windermere. You little knew what you were doing when you wished yourself with me in Westmorland. At this moment my cottage overflows with guests.'[5] He never went back to Rayrigg.

Wilberforce took such matters seriously. Nearly a year earlier he had scribbled down a memorandum on 'The temptations of the table'.

'After dining with Pitt, tête à tête I find after a time I have been giving way to the temptations of the table against the sharpest convictions of the criminality of the compliances, for little as they might seem what sins are they seeing they disqualify me from every useful purpose in life.

'I see Bob Smith who is influenced by inferior considerations, I see Pitt too and others of my friends practising self denial and restraint in these respects, and when they exceed tis at times of jollity, whereas I do it merely from the Brutal Sensuality of animal Gratification. I trust I shall better keep than I have done the resolutions of temperance that I make at this moment.

No Dessert ⎱ One thing in first,
No Tastings ⎰ one in second course.

Simplicity. In Quantity moderate—as little thought about my eating and drinking as possible either before or after—Never more than 6 glasses of wine, my common allowance 2 or 3 . . . to be in bed always if possible by 11 and be up by 6 o'clock. The effect on my Health should be attended to; a full diet good for me, but a simple one, no sweet, no rich things, no mixtures.'[6]

He called gluttony 'The lowest and most debasing of all Gratifications'.[7]

All these confessions of intemperance sound like the complaints of a hungover penitent, but for Wilberforce the word had a much wider meaning. Over-eating or eating unsuitable food (vegetables were particularly dangerous) made him ill, and at times he could only manage a vile gruel. He seems to have used the word 'intemperance' as a synonym for 'self-indulgence'; in this category he could put not only over-eating and drinking but also the excessive enjoyment of worldly life. In fact all three usually went together. As far as drink was concerned, Wilberforce was a small man, little more than five feet in height and with a slight frame, and the size of his body is one of the factors that determine a man's ability to absorb alcohol. Wilberforce's confession that 'if I take but a single glass of wine I can feel its effect' confirms that he must have had a weak head, and when he exceeded his self-imposed limit of six glasses he must have been quite convivial. But wine, together with opium and Bath water, was prescribed by his physicians. When he dined out he had to drink in the company of friends who each needed a bottle of port to stir their jaded palates. In these circumstances it is not surprising that he should find intemperance so hard to master. But his failings seem to have been noticed by no one else; there is no reference to his being drunk in his contemporaries' memoirs.

*

In October he returned to Bath, but soon left again to attend a jubilee in York on November 5. He laid down carefully the conditions under which he was prepared to come. His friend Wyvill had urged the importance of the occasion on him. 'Your absence from the meeting would be peculiarly prejudicial, because many would consider it a proof of excessive scrupulosity ... but if you embrace this opportunity of meeting your constituents, and show them you are exactly the same person whose cause they lately espoused with so much zeal ... it is surely possible to mix in such assemblies with innocence and decency.'[8]

Wilberforce was put on his mettle by the inference that he had changed so little since 1784. 'I cannot say that I am by any means the same person,' he replied. '... I can assert with truth that I have a higher sense of the duties of my station, and a firmer resolution to discharge them with fidelity and zeal; but it is also true that I am under many restraints as to my conduct to which I was not then subject. Not that I would shut myself up from mankind and immure myself in a cloister. My walk, I am sensible is a public one; my business is in the world; and I must mix in assemblies of men, or quit the post which Providence seems to have assigned me.'[9] He goes on to ask, if the impression of 'excessive scrupulosity' was to be removed, would it not be necessary for him to behave in as abandoned a fashion as before? And this he could not do. He nevertheless decided to attend the jubilee, which seems to have passed without friction.

*

Wilberforce never entirely succeeded in disciplining his butterfly mind. The freshness and delight with which he flitted from subject to subject, although a handicap to a man of affairs, was a part of the charm that so impressed all who met him. He was aware of this trait and regarded it as a weakness. In the winter of 1788–9 he set out to introduce a more systematic note. His diary now includes a chart showing how every hour of the day was spent. He defined his headings:

'Squandered—waste or misappropriation—all unnecessary meals or bed time. House of Commons, business, etc., into all this is brought all time spent in going to and from public offices—letters of business—consulting, etc. Relaxation suâ causâ—here mealtimes when alone or quite

at liberty, etc.: the more this head can be reduced the better. Dressing, etc.
—all that is frittered away—all which I forget how to account for. Requi-
site company—going from place to place—waiting for people. Minor
application—study—reading for entertainment, or with no great attention
—familiar common letters, etc. Major application—study—reading for
use—composing—getting by heart. Serious—private and family devotions,
etc.'[10]

He also kept a note of the hours at which he rose and went to bed. The
figures are accompanied by comments usually of a penitent nature. The
whole was drawn up in tabular form. This analysis only lasted a few
months, but he would start keeping the chart again whenever he felt his
self-control slipping.

*

In the last months of 1788 a sudden unexpected crisis threatened to over-
turn Pitt's Government and throw the whole future of the Abolition
movement into confusion. On October 22 Pitt received a note from the
King's physician that George III was in a state 'nearly bordering on
delirium'.[11] After an apparent recovery the King lapsed into undoubted
madness. Some provision had to be made for the exercise of the royal
powers, but there was no constitutional precedent to follow. The Prince
of Wales was an irresponsible spendthrift and a committed supporter of
Fox, so that the prospect of his exercising the royal prerogative was
daunting. Pitt naturally hoped for the King's recovery, but his physicians
disagreed on the prospect; not surprisingly, since porphyria, the disease
from which he suffered, was unknown at the time. In their ignorance, they
made such exotic diagnoses as 'the flying gout'.[12] By the time that Parliament reassembled in December, the King's health seemed to have improved a little, but it was still necessary to make provisions for a Regency.

Pitt was anxious that the Regent's powers should be kept as small as
possible; he was, however, not prepared or able to force any plan on the
House. The Opposition came to his rescue. The Prince had at first gained
sympathy by his grief at his father's illness; he lost it as quickly as he
regained his spirits and returned to quarrelling with his mother and leading
a wild life with his cronies from Brooks's Club. In view of his conduct the
King's attempt to throttle him at one of their meetings might have been
taken by a cynic as evidence of restored sanity. His advisers were equally
foolish. Fox's first reaction when the matter was raised was to deny that
the House had any right to examine it. This sudden espousal of the royal
prerogative by a man who had spent much of his life fighting it repelled
members by its hypocrisy. Aided by these mistakes, Pitt carried through
both Houses severe restrictions on the Regent's power. Having done so he
could only await his own dismissal. But at the last moment the King began

to recover. On February 27, 1789, the medical bulletins ceased and the crisis was over. Wilberforce had served on a committee examining the Royal Physicians, a fruitless task when none of them had the means to diagnose the King's malady. He supported Pitt loyally and willingly in the debates.

*

At this time the Committee considered sending agents to Africa and the West Indies to obtain information. The reason why they decided against this proposal casts an interesting light on their characters. Such agents, they reasoned, would have to tell falsehoods to find out anything useful, and this they could never countenance. At no stage in their struggle do the Abolitionists seem to have considered the doctrine that the means justify the ends. Wilberforce would later show the same attitude when opposing the use of informers by the Proclamation Society, and when refusing to play politics over Abolition.

The first months of 1789 were occupied with preparing the case against the Slave Trade. Wilberforce was helped by a new ally, who had a deep knowledge of the subject and who was soon to become, with Pitt, his closest friend. James Stephen practised at the West Indian bar, but during eleven years' residence there he never owned a slave. His first acquaintance with the institution had been more than enough for him. On his way to St. Christopher he arrived in a Barbadian court and watched, with mounting horror, a travesty of a trial that ended with two slaves being sentenced to be burnt alive.[13] Stephen, more than any other man, gave passion to the Abolitionist movement. He was impetuous, emotional and combative; if Wilberforce's greatest temptation was towards the frittering away of his time, Stephen's was towards duelling; although a religious man he would have derived a deep satisfaction from putting a bullet into the skins of owners, drivers or shippers of slaves.

The depth of his hatred of the Slave Trade can be seen in one quotation. 'I would rather be on friendly terms with a man who had strangled my infant son than support an administration guilty of slackness in suppressing the Slave Trade.' Stephen meant this, like everything else he said, quite literally. He was a formidable man with as great a capacity for work and as vigorous a mind as any of the other Evangelicals. He was an expert in commercial matters and responsible, under Perceval, for drafting the Orders in Council as an answer to Napoleon's economic blockade of the country. But of the other Evangelicals only Wilberforce and Hannah More shared his gift of being able to express their thoughts forcibly and eloquently. He had a striking hawklike appearance with his eyes deeply sunk beneath a tremendous brow. When he was angry it was impossible to subdue him. Until 1794 when he settled in England, Stephen's help had to be anonymous; he was not a rich man and a large family was dependent on his success at the West Indian Bar.

The Privy Council's inquiry was finished early in 1789 and presented to Parliament in April. Members did not have long to read it before the debate on May 12. It was a formidable document, and although full of the witnesses' contradictions and rumours, it offered the careful reader a detailed account of the African Slave Trade. The Privy Council made no judgements; its report was divided into six sections: (1) A detailed description of the different kingdoms along the Slave Coast and the way in which slaves were obtained in each. (2) The carrying of slaves to the West Indies. This section included an analysis of the mortality rates among both slaves and seamen. (3) The treatment of slaves in the West Indies. (4) The extent of the Trade and the population of the West Indies. (5) The advantages said to be enjoyed by the French sugar colonies. (6) The Slave Trade as conducted by other countries.

The first three sections were the most important. The slavers' witnesses did their utmost to establish that Africa was a hell from which slaves should be grateful for being rescued, while the Abolitionists' testified to the kidnapping of natives and the enslavement of prisoners of war and minor criminals. They showed the brutality of the African end of the Trade. Newton and others testified that the slaves driven mercilessly to the coast thought that they were to be eaten by the white men. Those that were not sold as slaves were murdered or reserved for human sacrifice. They also went to great pains to produce specimens of African products and manufactures to prove that other forms of commerce could replace the Slave Trade. An expert witness from Manchester praised the quality of African cotton.

The descriptions of the Middle Passage given by defenders of the Trade could not be reconciled with statistics for the death rates of slaves and seamen. Not all their witnesses need have been lying, for some slave ships and captains were clearly worse than others. But the general impression must have been that conditions on board slave ships were vile, and the conclusion was confirmed by the figures.

As the day of the debate approached the West Indians stepped up their agitation. If carried, they claimed, this Bill would ruin not only the Trade, but the Colonies, not only the Colonies but the very commercial prosperity of the nation. Wilberforce, naturally, came in for his share of abuse. His old Cambridge friend Gisborne wrote an amused letter. 'I shall expect to read in the newspapers of your being carbanadoed by West Indian planters, barbecued by African merchants, and eaten by Guinea captains; but do not be daunted, for—I will write your epitaph.'

*

On May 12, 1789, Wilberforce rose in the Commons. He had been unwell, and had not had time to polish his phrases or prepare his speech properly. He felt bound to cover the whole subject and he was not sure that his stamina would be strong enough. He spoke for three and a half hours, with no worse effect than 'my breast sore'. He later complained of 'a most inaccurate report' of his speech, and we must judge it, not by what remains on paper, but by the effect it had on an audience which included the greatest orators of that golden age.

He went through the leading features of the Slave Trade. In Africa many innocents were condemned, wars were fomented and countries ravaged—all to obtain slaves. He went on to describe the Middle Passage. 'This, I confess, in my opinion, is the most wretched part of the whole subject. So much misery condensed in so little room is more than the human imagination has ever before conceived.' He quoted with contempt the renegade Norris's account of shipboard life, showing in detail where it differed from the truth. Sometimes Norris was twisting the truth, as in his description of the slaves dancing, when he omitted to add that they did so under threat of the lash. But there was one kind of evidence that was beyond argument or perversion and that was the death rate of slaves on the Middle Passage. Of the slaves shipped $12\frac{1}{2}$ per cent* had died on board, $4\frac{1}{2}$ per cent on shore before their sale and another third in the seasoning.

He declared the wickedness of the Slave Trade to be so enormous, so dreadful and so irremediable, as to admit of no solution short of its abolition. However necessary the Trade might be, however powerful the arguments for its continuance, justice demanded that it should be stopped at once. But in this case he hoped to prove that justice could be reconciled with expediency.

His analysis of mortality among slaves in the West Indies led him to believe that their numbers could be kept up without the introduction of new stock. For the decline in the slave population was now running at a rate of less than 1 per cent each year. The abolition of the Trade and the removal of the discrepancy between the sexes that would follow should allow the slaves' numbers to remain at their present level. But, without fresh stocks, the planters would be given every incentive to treat their slaves better and the 'natural increase' in their numbers would then be restored. He described the various factors working against an increase in the slave population† which could have been expected to have led to a far

---

* Figures for fatalities on the Middle Passage vary greatly. Wilberforce's, which are probably too high, were taken from the average of all ships on which evidence had been heard before the Privy Council.

† This argument was always contested by Wilberforce's opponents and up to a point they were right, for the slave population continued to fall after Abolition in 1807. But this was because the planters failed to respond in the rational way expected by Wilberforce. None of the abuses of which he complained was removed. After Emancipation their numbers at once started to rise again.

sharper decline than was in fact taking place. In these circumstances the Trade was unnecessary as well as evil. Its abolition would leave few scars even on the city of Liverpool, for only 13,000 of its 170,000 tons of shipping sailed on the Triangular Trade.

Clarkson's investigations enabled him to refute the argument that to abandon the Slave Trade would lead to the ruin of the British Navy. Wilberforce showed conclusively that it was the cause of the death of far more seamen than any other trade, and he quoted naval captains to show that those who survived were often useless and corrupt. 'Instead of being a benefit to our sailors as some have ignorantly argued, I do assert it is their grave.'

The next objection that Wilberforce anticipated was more substantial. If we were to relinquish the Slave Trade, would not our rivals, the French, then take it up? At this point in Wilberforce's speech 'a cry of assent was heard from several parts of the House'. We would lose a valuable branch of our commerce but the evil would continue unabated. Wilberforce described this as a very weak argument, and in moral terms he was right, but it was much the strongest practical argument levied against the Abolitionists. The same objection, he replied, could be made against stopping any form of wickedness. But when he descended to a practical answer, he was less convincing. Even if the French took over our rôle, they would still have to buy trade goods from us. But he believed that, if we abolished it, France, under Necker, would not be far behind: '. . . let this enlightened country take precedence in this noble cause, and we shall soon find that France is not backward to follow, nay perhaps to accompany our steps'.

An honourable trade in natural products could replace the Slave Trade, and this would increase once the impediment to progress in Africa represented by the Trade had been removed. Britain had enslaved the minds and blackened the characters of Africans until some had claimed 'the very apes are of a higher class, and the orang-outang has given them the go by'. But only three centuries ago the people of Britain were in the same state of barbarism. The citizens of Bristol sold their own children to the Irish as slaves. But after some calamity which they attributed to a judgement from on high, the latter abolished the traffic. All that he asked the House was to show that they were now as enlightened as the Irish had been three centuries before.

He finished with a rousing patriotic oration. It had been a polished and masterful performance; as the introducer of the motion Wilberforce had had to touch on every aspect of the Slave Trade and even extend his range to include slavery. He had to mention and answer all the objections that would be raised in the course of the debate. He did all this and succeeded at the same time in shocking and moving the House, without ever allowing his subject to lead him into hysteria or personal bitterness.

After he had finished, Wilberforce laid on the table of the House twelve propositions that he had deduced from the Privy Council Report.

One: That the number of slaves annually carried from the coast of Africa in British vessels was about 38,000, of which 22,500 were carried to British islands.

Two: That these slaves consisted of four groups: prisoners of war, persons sold for debts or for crimes, domestic slaves sold for the profit of their masters, persons made slaves by various acts of oppression.

Three: That the trade so carried on had a tendency to cause frequent wars among the natives, to produce unjust convictions and oppressive punishments and to obstruct the natural course of civilisation.

Four: That Africa in its present state furnished several valuable articles of Commerce peculiar to itself and that it could easily produce others. Trade with Africa if these commodities could be substituted for the Slave Trade.

Five: That the Slave Trade was peculiarly destructive to the seamen employed in it.

Six: That the method of transporting slaves from Africa to the West Indies exposed them to many sufferings for which no regulations could provide an adequate remedy.

Seven: That many also died in Barbados and in the West Indies as a result of their treatment during the voyage.

Eight: That many others died during the first three years after their importation.

Nine: That the natural increase of population among the slaves in the islands had been prevented mainly by the inequality of sexes imported from Africa, by the dissoluteness of manners among the slaves and lack of encouragement of marriages, by disease attributable to severe labour, bad treatment or insufficient food.

Ten: That the whole number of slaves in Jamaica in 1768 was 167,000, in 1774 193,000, 1787 256,000. Comparing these figures with the numbers imported and retained in the island during all these years the excess of deaths above births was about seven-eighths of one per cent. In the first six years of this period it was higher, the last thirteen it was about three-fifths of one per cent and during these thirteen years about 15,000 slaves had died as the result of repeated hurricanes.

Eleven: In Barbados the story was the same.

Twelve: Records from the smaller islands are not full enough to make any similar comparisons. But there was no reason why the natural increase of slaves in the West Indies could not be restored and the Slave Trade rendered unnecessary.[14]

Lords Penrhyn and Gascoyne, the two members for Liverpool, spoke after Wilberforce. Both prophesied that ruin and misery would follow

Abolition. Penrhyn said that Wilberforce's misrepresentations were such that no reliance could be placed on any part of his speech. Gascoyne suggested that the Trade should be made a greater source of revenue than at present.[15]

Edmund Burke praised Wilberforce's speech: 'The House, the nation and all Europe, were under very great and serious obligations to the hon. gentleman, for having brought the subject forward in a manner the most masterly, impressive and eloquent. Principles so admirable, laid down with so much order and force, were equal to any thing he had ever heard of in modern oratory; and perhaps were not excelled by any thing to be met with in Demosthernes'.[16] Pitt claimed that Britain had the resources to prevent an illegal trade with her colonies. When Wilberforce's propositions were debated one by one, the House would be forced to agree with him.[17] Fox considered 'a trade in human kind so scandalous that it was to the last degree infamous to let it be openly carried on by the authority of the government of any country'. He commented angrily on the suggestion that the trade needed regulation rather than abolition, that he knew of no such thing as the regulation of robbery and murder.[18]

The debate was resumed on May 21, when the West Indians succeeded in postponing a vote until counsel had been heard and evidence tendered before the bar of the House. This decision, although bitterly disappointing to the Abolitionists, was not unreasonable. The House could hardly be expected to take such an important step without hearing evidence for itself. There is no doubt that fears of the French taking over the trade played a part in their indecision. Two future Prime Ministers, Grey and Jenkinson (later Lord Liverpool), were prevented from voting for the Bill by this consideration.

The hearing of evidence against the Bill continued throughout the summer, and at the end of the session it was still unfinished. The Abolitionists were overpowered by the thought that Parliament could delay, even for an hour, let alone a year, the abolition of a trade which caused such misery.

*

France was the Abolitionists' Achilles heel, but many French statesmen, including Necker the Prime Minister, were known to be sympathetic. If France would promise to abolish the Trade at the same time as England, the main objection to Abolition would be overcome. The day after the hearing of evidence was postponed, Wilberforce recorded in his diary: 'June 24 . . . Evening. Almost determined to go abroad about slave business.' He explained more fully in a letter to a friend. 'Does it not seem a most preposterous determination to which I am come, of spending some time in and about Paris? Yet such is my plan, and I propose to cross the

water in a very few days. You will readily conceive that though the present
state of politics in that quarter is justly interesting to the highest degree,
I am not attracted solely or indeed chiefly, by this consideration. This is
professed to the million, but the slave business is mainly in my view, and
I do not feel myself at liberty to decline any path wherein I see a probability, however faint, of forwarding this great object. I need scarcely suggest
to you, however, that you must be secret as the grave. My errand will be
suspected of course, and the least hint from you will be caught at and
circulated with avidity.'[19]

This naïve plan horrified Wilberforce's friends who found no difficulty
in predicting the attitude of the French to the presence of an important
English politician during such a crisis. Apart from its effect on Anglo-
French relations, and thus on the very measure he wished to promote, his
visit might also expose him to some danger. 'If you had shown your face in
Paris,' Gisborne wrote to him, 'the populace might very probably have
chaired you on their shoulders to the frowns of the monarch and the
bullets of his Swiss guards.'[20] It was thought that a less conspicuous figure
should be sent to Paris, and Clarkson was chosen.

Clarkson was intoxicated by the atmosphere of Paris during the summer
of 1789 and he was soon bombarding Wilberforce with optimistic letters.
'I should not be surprised if the French were to do themselves the honour
of voting away this diabolical traffic in a night.'[21] His liberal spirit soared
at the sight of the rusty shackles of despotism being dismantled and replaced by the will of the people. It seemed to him impossible that the new
leaders of France could fail to recognise the evils of the Slave Trade. He
was received with enthusiasm by the leading liberals, notably by La
Fayette, the hero of the American Revolution. He associated with a newly-
formed society, les Amis des Noirs, and with them received threats that if
he did not stop his activities he would be stabbed to death. Mirabeau was
so impressed by Clarkson's cross-section of the *Brookes* that he had a
model made in wood which he kept in his dining-room. Clarkson was
encouraged by his interest and wrote to Mirabeau a letter of sixteen to
twenty pages in his minute handwriting every day for a month until his
exhausted correspondent begged him to stop. The King was shown specimens of African goods and seemed suitably impressed, but his health was
thought too delicate for him to be exposed to the drawing of the *Brookes*.[22]

Not all the politicians Clarkson met were so sympathetic. He was told
that the Revolution was more important to France than Abolition and that
interfering with the Slave Trade could injure the Revolution by alienating
the citizens of the great ports. And the French were as reluctant as the
English to make a moral gesture which could help only their rivals. Clarkson was often pressed for a commitment that, if France abolished, England
would follow suit. It was, of course, quite impossible for him to make such

a promise. Pitt himself could not have guaranteed how the House of Commons would vote, let alone the House of Lords. But it slowly dawned on Clarkson's optimistic mind that without such a guarantee there was no prospect of France abolishing the Trade. Before he left Paris, a bitterly disappointed man, Clarkson had a last interview with the Deputies of Colour, who represented the mulatto community of St. Domingue. He urged moderation on them, but they replied that the oppression of the white colonists and the National Assembly could no longer be borne. Three months after Clarkson's departure there was an abortive rising in St. Domingue which ended in its leader, one of these Deputies, being broken on the wheel. After this barbaric reprisal, reconciliation between the two parties became impossible.

Clarkson's task in France was more difficult than he realised; if he and Wilberforce could have persuaded the French to agree to some form of reciprocal abolition, they would both have deserved a fêting by the Jamaican planters and the freedom of the City of Kingston. Wilberforce had shown Parliament that the British West Indies no longer needed the Slave Trade; for the British colonists it was a luxury paid for by their neglect of their slaves, but for the French it was still essential. The French possessions in the Caribbean were bigger, more fertile, more efficient and less exploited than the British. In 1788 sugar production in St. Domingue* was double that of Jamaica, in 1789 a third more than the combined production of all the British colonies, and St. Domingue still had virgin land suitable for cultivation. Until the Napoleonic Wars France also owned Guadeloupe, Martinique and Grenada. The only unfulfilled need of these French colonies was a sufficiency of slave labour. In the ten years between 1782 and 1792 the slave population of St. Domingue nearly doubled. In France, unlike England, there were compelling commercial reasons for retaining the Trade. On the other hand for Britain to continue to carry slaves to the French colonies was to cut the throats of the planters who voted, lobbied and agitated against such a traffic being stopped.

While Clarkson was in Paris the cause acquired its first martyr. The defenders of the Trade had singled out James Ramsay and attacked him with poisonous virulence and an utter indifference to the truth. He may have been treated so viciously because the West Indians regarded him as a traitor after his long residence in St. Kitts. Ramsay was ill at the time of the debate in May and it seemed to his friends that the lies and slanders heaped upon him hastened his end. Molyneux, the leader of the attack in Parliament, agreed. 'Mr. Molyneux,' Stephen reported from St. Christo-

---

* St. Domingue is now Haiti. The Spanish colony of St. Domingo, which occupied the rest of the island, has become the Dominican Republic. Wilberforce and his friends would call both colonies 'St. Domingo', but I have preserved the distinction except in quotations.

pher, 'announced the decease of the public enemy to his natural son in this island, in these terms "Ramsay is dead—I have killed him".'

In the winter of 1789 and the first months of 1790, most of Wilberforce's time was spent improving his knowledge of the Slave Trade. For, when the hearing of evidence was resumed, the hostile witnesses would be examined, not by counsel, but by him and his friend and fellow abolitionist, William Smith.

The witnesses were concerned to establish that only criminals and prisoners of war were sold as slaves, that they were treated well on the Middle Passage and in the West Indies, that there were no other commercial opportunities on the Slave Coast and that the Trade was not particularly dangerous to seamen. They were more defensive than in their evidence to the Privy Council. The Trade witnesses suffered from two great disadvantages. They were meeting specific and horrible accusations with general statements that in their experience everything was well. Unless they could contradict some of the Abolitionist accusations, any impartial tribunal would have to regard such statements as worthless. They were also, inevitably, prejudiced, almost all of them being connected either with the Trade or with the sugar colonies. The only exceptions to this rule were the naval witnesses, of whom the most distinguished were Lord Rodney and Sir Peter Parker. The former obstinately referred to the Trade as 'a considerable nursery for seamen'.[23] He had never heard of cruel treatment to any slave on an English island and he attributed the French naval strength in the American War to her growing share of the Slave Trade. There is little doubt that Rodney was a sincere if superficial observer, but apart from his view of the Trade as a nursery for seamen, an argument that was soon to be abandoned by its defenders, his evidence was concerned with Slavery, which was a peripheral issue in the debate on the Trade. Parker held stronger views, 'The Abolition of the African Trade would, in his opinion, cause a general despondency among the negroes and gradually decrease the population, and consequently the produce of our islands, and must in time destroy near half our commerce, and take from Great Britain all pretensions to the rank she now holds of being the first maritime power in the world.'[24] The Abolitionists could meet these generalisations, advanced by those whose interest in the matter was clear, with first-hand evidence of atrocities and a mass of statistics given by witnesses without ulterior motives.

Clarkson and Dickson—his 'white negroes', Pitt called them—were constantly with Wilberforce, analysing, checking and exposing their opponents' evidence and preparing their own. Sometimes Clarkson would be sent out on a long journey to clear up a difficult point or find a vital witness. The trouble he would take on these occasions was extraordinary. Clarkson once boarded 320 ships and interviewed about 3,000 seamen in order to find a single witness, whose name no one knew. He found his man, and, in the course of his investigations, three other witnesses.

During these months Wilberforce's already chaotic life became quite unmanageable. 'I cannot invite you here,' he wrote to a friend, 'for, during the sitting of Parliament, my house is a mere hotel.'[25] But there was never a hotel with such a clientèle as Wilberforce's house in Palace Yard. The Prime Minister and his friends dined there so often that the rumour spread that Wilberforce received a pension for entertaining them. Once a week the Slave Committee dined, and 'the white negroes' did much of their work there. His ante-room was full from the early morning until he left for business. The first arrivals would be asked in to take breakfast with him, and they could be an extraordinary assortment. There were Yorkshire constituents, petitioners for charity, Africans, missionaries, politicians, preachers; perhaps a Haitian professor might find himself sitting between a young Yorkshireman, for whose education Wilberforce was paying, and an eminent statesman who had been forgotten in the confusion. One young man presented himself at the door and Wilberforce's Lincolnshire footman, when asked what he was like, replied, 'Oh sir, he's a rough one.' The walls of the ante-room were originally lined with books of a size that Wilberforce could put in his pocket and study on his walks. But what would go into his pocket also fitted others' and after losing many of his books, he had to replace the remainder with massive folios. Hannah More described it as a 'Noah's ark, full of beasts clean and unclean'.[26]

*

The examination of the Trade witnesses lasted until April 1790. It was never possible for Wilberforce to relax his vigilance. The planters first tried to prevent the Abolitionists' witnesses being heard at all; then, thwarted in this attempt, they took advantage of a thin House to amend Dolben's Bill, increasing the number of slaves that could be carried. This amendment was rejected the next day by the exertion of Pitt's influence. The hearing of the Abolition witnesses continued throughout the summer session.

All this was frustrating work. The Abolitionists felt acutely that every day the Trade was allowed to continue, more human lives were being squandered. But the hearings in front of the Commons might be the only opportunity for establishing an indelible record in favour of their case. At the end of the summer session of 1790, only half their evidence had been presented and they decided to hold over the rest. There were encouraging signs that the country was at last becoming aroused. The Slave Party had lost the war of pamphlets; the circulation of the *Brookes* print had had great effect.

The Abolitionists were swift to exploit the popularity of Cowper's *The Negro's Complaint*. They circulated special copies of the poem throughout

Thomas Clarkson by C. F. von Breda   Granville Sharp by George Dance

FOUR ENEMIES OF SLAVERY

Zachary Macaulay   James Stephen

Fig. 1

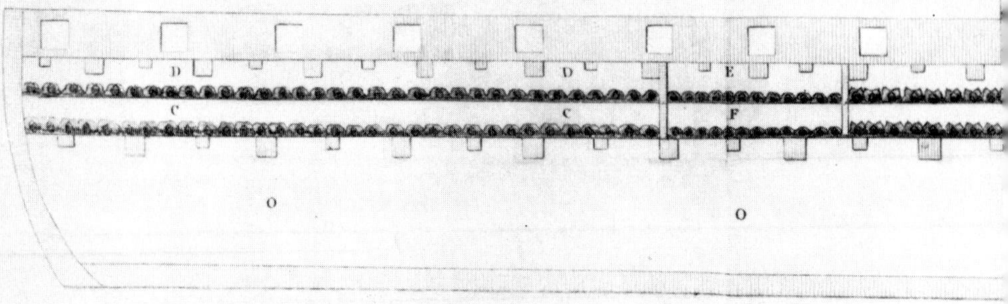

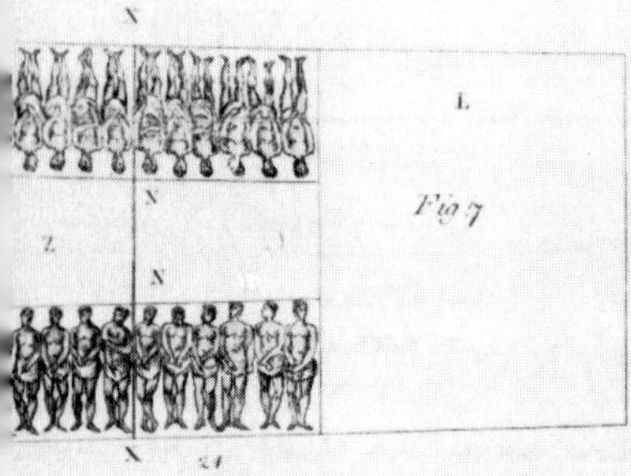

Fig. 7

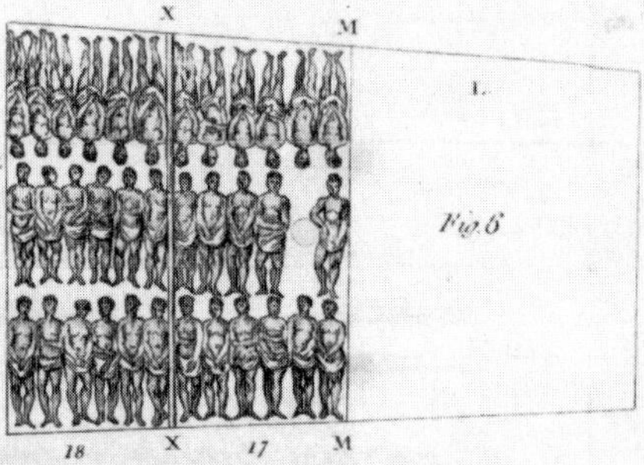

Fig. 6

Fig. 2

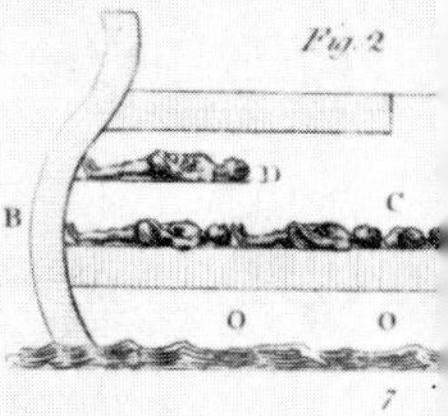

Fig. 5

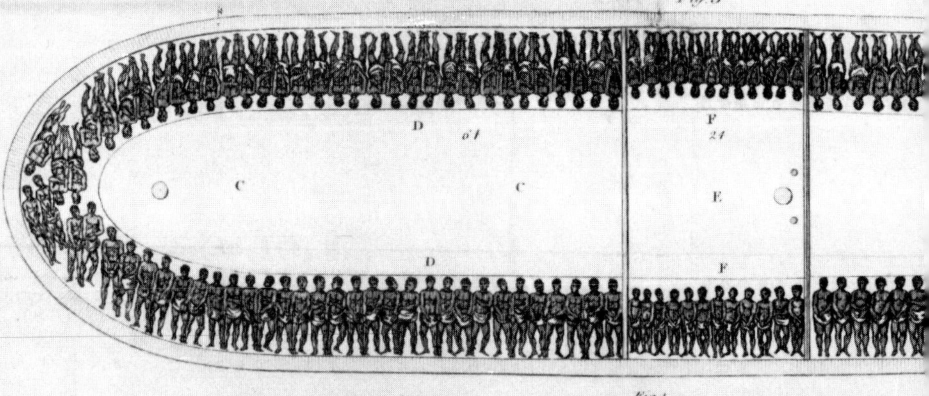

Fig. 4

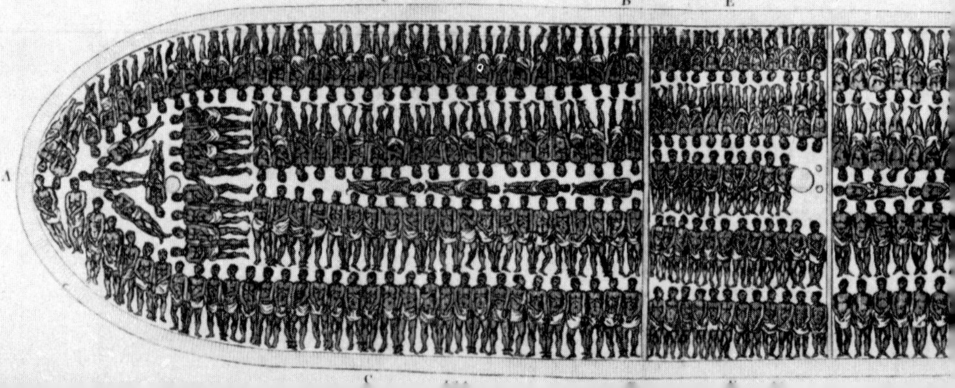

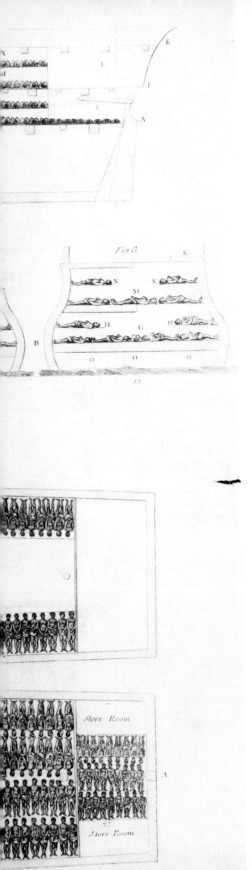

Clarkson's drawing of the *Brookes*.
Loaded like this she would just
have qualified under Dolben's
regulations

Photo: John R. Freeman & Co

Philanthropic Consolations. Gilray's satire on Wilberforce
and the Bishop of Rochester after losing the Slave Trade Debate in 1794

Scene on the Slave coast by A. F. Biard

the country, with the inscription 'A Subject for Conversation at the Tea-table'. To some readers this will seem all too apt a description of *The Negro's Complaint*. Cowper was a passionate Abolitionist and a poet who could often carry his own burning emotions and agonies into his verse. But in *The Negro's Complaint* he reduces the most horrifying question of his time to the levels suitable for 'conversation at the tea-table'. The passion that inspired *The Castaway* and *The Morning Dream* is missing and he is not helped by an insipid rhythm. The fourth and the last are possibly the best of its seven stanzas.

> Is there, as ye sometimes tell us,
>   Is there One who reigns on high?
> Has He bid you buy and sell us
>   Speaking from His throne, the sky?
> Ask Him, if your knotted scourges,
>   Matches, blood-extorting screws,
> Are the means that duty urges
>   Agents of His will to use?
>
> Deem our nation brutes no longer,
>   Till some reason ye shall find
> Worthier of regard and stronger
>   Than the colour of our kind.
> Slaves of gold, whose sordid dealings
>   Tarnish all your boasted powers,
> Prove that you have human feelings,
>   Ere you proudly question ours!

Josiah Wedgwood had produced a cameo of a negro in chains imploring for compassion with the same inscription as the Committee's seal, 'Am I not a Man and a Brother?' Wedgwood distributed these cameos liberally and, set in bracelets and ornamental pins, they were sported by ladies of fashion. Clarkson comments, rather pompously, 'And thus fashion, which usually confines itself to worthless things, was seen for once in the honourable office of promoting the cause of justice, humanity and freedom.'[27] The growth of local Abolitionist societies gave a more reliable guide to the movement's progress.

Wilberforce had to go to Yorkshire for an election at which he was returned unopposed. He felt that he had neglected his constituents; he had no house on his scattered Yorkshire property and he did not visit the county so often as in the days before his conversion. He records his gratitude in a written memorandum. 'I must mention the uncommon kindness and liberality which I experienced from my constituents. In former times the county members displayed their equipages annually at the races and constituted a part of the grand jury at the Summer assizes, the latter, indeed, I should have been glad to attend but for the unseemly festivities which annually take place at that period. I was not, however, wanted . . .

I could not consistently with my principles frequent the theatre and the ball-room, and I knew I should give offence by staying away, were I actually in York; but no discontent was ever expressed at my not presenting myself to the county on those occasions.'[28]

In fact Wilberforce's conversion probably strengthened his hold on the county. He may have lost the support of some sporting squires, but his religious seriousness must have attracted much of the Methodist vote. Abolition, too, would have appealed to a county which had contributed so much to the movement. Wilberforce with all his causes, was an exciting member and he was also a conscientious one. However busy he was with other matters, he never forgot his constituents' interests, and his closeness to Pitt allowed him to do them many favours. He did not feel able to fulfil all the social obligations of a county member, but within the rules he had made for himself, he was active in his search for support. The pains he took over details can be seen in a letter to William Hey written on November 3, 1790:

'I inclose a scheme . . . on which Mr. Grey and I have determined for the County Election Book . . . I do not wish the names of any persons to be inserted, whose supposed real property is less than £100 per annum, or personal than £2,000 sterling, except in any case wherein the influence is greater in proportion than the property, and may be deemed equal to the influence ordinarily accompanying the above amount; also, let the blank column for supposed influence be filled with the initials "Li" for little, —"Mi" for middling,—"Gr" for great,—and "V.Gr" for very great. The column for observations should contain remarks concerning the party's connections, etc. . . . e.g. whether he likes the leg or the wing of a fowl best, that when one dines with him one may win his heart by helping him, and not be taken in by his "just which you please, sir".'[29]

After the election Wilberforce went for a tour of Wales with Thomas Babington. They had been contemporaries at St. John's College where Babington had been a great friend of Gisborne's. But, unlike Gisborne, he had been put off by Wilberforce's frivolity. Since his conversion, however, they had become close friends. Most of Wilberforce's first group of friends, the young disciples of Pitt who met at Goosetree's, belonged to the aristocracy. Many were peers or the sons of peers. They owned land and had political connections and traditions in their families. His second group of friends came from the same social background as he did, the middle and upper middle classes. Many of them were rich but their wealth was based on business rather than land and they all worked, as bankers, merchants, lawyers or clergymen. There were two aristocratic exceptions, Lord Muncaster and Thomas Babington. The latter could trace his ancestry back to the Babington who plotted against Queen Elizabeth. His house in Leicestershire, Rothley Temple, with Gisborne's Yoxall Lodge, became Wilberforce's main country residence until his marriage. Wilberforce thought he had never met a man who 'exhibited the Christian character so fully and so uniformly'.

Babington was a serious man with a deep and literal respect for the truth. Once Henry Thornton visited him unexpectedly and asked, rather nervously, if it would be convenient for him and his family to stay. Babington thought for a moment and then pronounced that it would indeed be very inconvenient, since his house was already full, but that the pleasure of Thornton's company would more than compensate him for the trouble. Knowing that he meant every word he said, Thornton was able to enter with a clear conscience. Babington had much of Thornton's seriousness, but, unlike his friend, he had a playful side, especially with children and he showed great ingenuity in devising games for them. Although he lived in Leicestershire, he did not permit his children to hunt, because of the low moral standards of those who then followed hounds. But he realised that their adventurous instincts needed some outlet and designed a series of tasks for them which were very similar to Outward Bound courses. Wilberforce consulted Babington about the education of his children. Babington married the aunt of Lord Macaulay and the great historian was born in Rothley Temple and named Thomas Babington after his uncle.

After their holiday in Wales, Wilberforce and Babington closeted themselves in Gisborne's house and studied the Slave Trade. Wilberforce had to extend his mastery of an indictment that never ceased to grow. By the time the Abolitionists had finished presenting their case he had assimilated 'a giant folio volume from the Privy Council and near 1,400 pages of evidence delivered before the House of Commons'. These documents were, of course, full of discrepancies and contradictions all of which he had to be able to recognise and explain. The two friends rarely went out and in the peace of Yoxall Lodge they made rapid progress. It was less easy when Wilberforce returned to London in the middle of November. His diary resumes its complaints of wasted hours while the examinations before the House both added to the amount of detail to be mastered and made less time available for this purpose. In the spring of 1791 he abandoned everything else and settled down in John Thornton's house in Clapham to devote his time to the Slave Trade. Even Sunday was neglected. 'Sunday as a working day—did not go to Church—Slave Trade.' 'Gave up Sunday to Slave business.' This, for Wilberforce, was the ultimate sacrifice.

Prospects were not encouraging; the Abolitionists had, it was true, won the argument and exposed the defenders of the Trade in a number of lies. Their case in Parliament would be presented and supported by the greatest speakers of the day, Pitt, Fox, Burke, Sheridan and Wilberforce, while not a single orator of renown would oppose them. There was a rising groundswell of feeling in the country. But two events outside England had done the cause such damage that even Wilberforce could not go into this debate with his normal optimism.

Wilberforce himself had observed, when opposing the Repeal of the Test Act in 1789: 'I am convinced that if public feeling had not been altered by seeing how soon every other kind of plunder followed the destruction of tithes in France, our clergy would by this time have lost their property.' He was now to see the same reaction working against his own cause. It is almost impossible to exaggerate the impact of the French Revolution on the ruling classes of England. Pitt's administration had started as one sympathetic to reform—electoral, financial, administrative and, in the case of the Slave Trade, moral. Its policy was changed by the French Revolution to one of almost mindless repression and reaction. The ordinary country member supported it at every stage. Samuel Romilly commented: 'If any person be desirous of having an adequate idea of the mischievous effects which have been produced in this country by the French Revolution and all its attendant horrors, he should attempt some reform on humane and liberal principles. . . . He will then find not only what a stupid spirit of conservation, but what a savage spirit, it has infused into the minds of his countrymen.'[30]

'Democracy' became as pejorative a word as 'atheism' or 'Republicanism'. Wilberforce himself was far from immune from this feeling, and although he could recognise and deplore it when it worked against Abolition, he found it less easy to diagnose the same symptoms in himself. He shared the horror of the rest of his class at the excesses of the Revolution; he watched, with equal fear, the formation of radical societies in London; like them he regarded the very fabric of society as being threatened. But for him the Revolution posed a more ghastly threat through its militant atheism, which menaced not only the security of the country, but the immortal souls of its inhabitants. To prevent the atheists from seizing power, severe measures were justified, indeed demanded. Tolerance, kindness, even justice were expendable in the face of such an enemy. This terror of the French Revolution explains, if it does not excuse, Wilberforce's support of repressive legislation at home.

It is hard for us now to see a connection between the Abolition of the Slave Trade and the encouragement of a Revolution in England. Even in 1791 few members can have seen the matter in that light. There was simply an instinctive and mass withdrawal from any measure that could conceivably be called progressive. The King, as so often, exemplified the feelings of his subjects. He had once sympathised with the Abolitionists. 'How go on your black clients, Mr. Wilberforce?' he had whispered at the levée, but after the Revolution he was a determined enemy. These feelings had not fully matured by the time of the Debate in 1791; attitudes in

England naturally reflected events in France and it was not until the outbreak of the Revolutionary Wars in 1793 that reaction reached its peak.

The second setback for the Abolitionists took place in the West Indies.
The rebellion of Clarkson's friends in St. Domingue was followed by slave
revolts in Martinique and Dominica. These insurrections, which inevitably
were blamed on the Abolitionists, gave the planters an emotional argument. They could now give descriptions of slave uprisings that rivalled in
horror the Abolitionists' accounts of the Middle Passage. Fortunately for
the Abolitionists, the rebellions, like the Revolution, did not reach their
climax until after the Debate. Once the great and successful slave revolt
in St. Domingue had taken place, the planters were able to point to its
example as a warning against tinkering with the Slave Trade. In this, as in
their support of the foreign Slave Trade, they showed a stupidity which,
had it been displayed by their charges, they could have used to demonstrate
that 'the orang-outang had given them the go by'. It was common knowledge in the colonies that slaves imported from Africa were far more
dangerous than those born in the New World. Before the American War,
the States of Virginia and South Carolina had vainly petitioned for the
suspension of the Trade, not because of any hostility to it, but for fear of
negro revolts led by Africans.[31] The connection was so clear and had been
marked so long, that one would have thought that the successful slave
rebellion in St. Domingue in August 1791 would only be attributed to the
unprecedented imports of slaves over the last ten years. The best way to
avoid such insurrections was first to abandon the Slave Trade and secondly
to treat the existing slaves better. The planters were instead to use St.
Domingue's example as an excuse to retain the Trade and to continue to
abuse their labour, and, in spite of all evidence to the contrary, they were
to impose their views on the House.

On February 24 Wilberforce received a moving letter from the death-
bed of John Wesley. It is possibly the last ever written by the great man.

My dear sir,
    Unless the Divine power has raised you up to be as Athanasius contra mundum, I
see not how you can go through your glorious enterprise, in opposing that execrable
villainy, which is the scandal of religion, of England, and of human nature. Unless God
has raised you up for this very thing, you will be worn out by the opposition of men and
devils, but if God be for you who can be against you? Are all of them together stronger
than God? Oh be not weary of well-doing. Go on in the name of God, and in the power
of his might, till even American slavery, the vilest that ever saw the sun, shall vanish
away before it. That He that has guided you from your youth up may continue to
strengthen in this and all things, is the prayer of,
                            Dear Sir,
                        Your affectionate servant,
                            John Wesley.[32]

CHAPTER VII

ABOLITION: DECISION

ON April 18, 1791 Wilberforce moved the Abolition of the Slave Trade. He did not have to range so widely as when he had introduced the motion the year before. As a result of the hearings, the House was now well informed on the matter. His speech[1] was designed to show how the evidence supported the claims he had made in 1790. Its emphasis, too, was different. Fewer pleas of the Trade's humanity would be heard in this debate, more assertions of its expediency. Wilberforce had to shift his ground to answer these arguments without allowing the House to forget the moral issues. He cited new evidence on the seizure of slaves in Africa and on the anarchy and perversion of justice brought about there by the Trade. Rather than repeat his description of the Middle Passage he singled out a slave captain who had given evidence for the defence. This witness, Captain Knox, had assured the House that 'the slaves slept during the night in very tolerable comfort'. But, when pressed, Knox had admitted to carrying 290 slaves in a vessel of 120 tons, and in these conditions there was not room for all of them to lie on their backs. Their comfort on other voyages under his command must have been less than tolerable, for he had carried 450 slaves in a ship of 108 tons and 600 in one of 150.

Wilberforce asked the House on whom these cruelties fell and answered, 'on a people with feelings and intellect like ourselves.'

He then dealt in great detail with the claim that Abolition would ruin the West Indies. The planters, by using this argument, had brought the institution of slavery into the debate. He showed how the slaves were, in practice, unprotected by law and how those guilty of their mutilation or murder were punished, if at all, by derisory fines. He went through all the factors that should have led to a heavy decline in the population and showed that this decline was in fact very small. He quoted the opinion of the Assembly of Jamaica that, once the numbers of the sexes had become equal, the slave population would grow.

After dismissing, with a salvo of gruesome statistics, the 'nursery for seamen' argument, Wilberforce explained why legislation could not be left in the hands of the West Indian Assemblies. No law passed by these bodies could be effective so long as the evidence of negroes was not accepted against that of whites. Such laws as existed were consistently evaded; where there was a limit to the number of lashes that might be given a slave for a single offence, this was circumvented by the repeated infliction of the maximum penalty.

It had been said that the negroes were happier as slaves than they would be as free men. But if one of them in extraordinary circumstances saved enough money he always purchased his release from 'this situation of superior happiness by the sacrifice of his last shilling'.

At present, he admitted, the negroes were unfit for freedom; but they must be restored to the level from which they had been so unjustly degraded. Abolition would achieve this by ensuring better treatment and milder discipline. The planters, too, would benefit from it, for all insurrections were led by imported slaves.

He declared himself comparatively indifferent to the present decision of the House. Whatever its verdict he was certain that the people of the country would demand the Abolition of the Trade, once its full iniquity had been laid before them. It was a nest of serpents, which would never have existed so long, but for the darkness in which they lay hid. The light of day would now be let in on them and they would vanish from sight. As for himself, he would never abandon the work, and he would be carried forward by the knowledge of the justice of his cause.[2]

Wilberforce's speech was a powerful indictment of the Trade and many of his arguments were unanswerable; this did not, of course, prevent them from being answered. The opposing speakers seemed either to misunderstand the evidence they had heard, or wilfully to ignore it. They repeated, ad nauseam, their old exploded dogmas. The Trade was an absolute necessity to our commercial interests, a nursery to our seamen; its discussion caused discontent and revolts among the slaves. But there was some progress. Wilberforce had established, in the debate in 1790 and in the Parliamentary Enquiry, that the Trade caused great suffering and that its abolition was therefore desirable. The debate in 1791 was more concerned with whether it was practicable. A spokesman for the trade put the issue in its bluntest form by acknowledging that it was not an amiable traffic, but neither was that of a butcher, yet a mutton chop was a good thing.

James Martin, who had interests in the West Indies, and William Smith spoke strongly against the Trade; Pitt was calm and persuasive, pointing out how much its abolition would help the West Indies. But Fox spoke with passion and caustic wit. If members, knowing what the Trade was from the evidence, did not abolish it, they would consign their souls to eternal infamy. After Wilberforce's and Pitt's arguments, the only reason for keeping up the Trade would be to give planters the liberty of misusing their slaves so as to check their population.

Fox examined the means of obtaining slaves and amused himself at the expense of those who had justified enslaving criminals including adulterers: 'Was adultery, then, a crime which we needed to go to Africa to punish? Was this the way we took to establish the purity of our national character? . . . It was a most extraordinary pilgrimage for a most extraordinary purpose!' One can imagine uneasy glances being exchanged during this passage. Fox dealt mercilessly with the plea that the slaves had been taken from a worse to a better state. He reminded the House of selections from the evidence given by William Smith, including a horrifying account of a slave captain flogging a ten-month-old baby to death because it would not eat. He added equally terrible stories of his own. The House was visibly affected and Fox was quick to take advantage of the change in atmosphere. Would they now sanction enormities, the bare recital of which made them shudder? Humanity did not consist in a squeamish ear, nor in shrinking and starting at such tales as these, but in the disposition of the heart to remedy the evils they unfolded.

He switched from this emotional appeal to ridicule. Mr. Alderman Watson had declared the trade to be essential because of its connections with our fisheries. What was this but an acknowledgement of the way in which these miserable beings were treated? The Trade was to be kept up, with all its enormities, so that there should be people to consume the refuse fish from Newfoundland which were too bad for anyone else to eat.[3]

After attacking members who had claimed a difference in intellectual powers between Africans and Englishmen, and those who had cited Christianity in defence of the Trade, Fox finished by declaring that the whole world should rejoice that such a Bill had been presented, not merely as a matter of humanity, but as an act of justice; could it be called humanity, to forbear from committing murder?[4]

Fox's speech had been magnificent; he had displayed the full range and power of his oratory—majestic force and language, devastating wit and deep emotional appeal. Stanley, a member for Lancashire, rose to his feet at the end of Fox's speech, and announced that, though he had intended to vote against Abolition, the impression made on his feelings was such that he was now convinced that total Abolition was the only course to take.

Too few members had Stanley's sensibility; at half past three in the morning the House divided. Wilberforce's motion was lost by 88 votes to 163. One of his opponents had earlier described this debate as a war between the giants and the pygmies of the House. The giants had had the best of the debate, but as he had forecast the pygmies were left with the last word. A disgusted Horace Walpole gave a shorter explanation: 'Commerce clinked its purse.'

*

Pitt had described Dolben's Bill as one 'which I wonder how any human being can resist'. The same could be said with even more force of the motion for Abolition in 1791, for if the scope of the second measure was more ambitious, the information available to members had increased greatly since 1788. Two inquiries had taken place with witnesses from both sides examined first by the Privy Council then by the House. There had been lengthy debates both in 1790 and 1791. Before 1788 most members were ignorant of conditions on the Middle Passage, and if they heard anything disquieting they could regard it as an unfortunate necessity. The Slave Trade, they would have thought, was no crueller than much that was tolerated in their own country. It did a service to the Africans by removing them from barbarism to civilisation, often saving their lives in the process. It was a necessity to the West Indies, a pillar of our naval greatness, and if we abandoned it our role would be taken up by others. By 1791 all but the last of these arguments had been demolished. Any impartial person reading the evidence and the debates must conclude that the Trade was unjust, that it caused boundless misery, that it was ruinous to Africa, of little benefit to the West Indies, and of none to the Navy. The leaders of both parties denounced the Trade with great eloquence while its defenders were reduced to advancing arguments which had already been lost. But the vote against Wilberforce was decisive.

The French Revolution and the slave revolts undoubtedly played their part in this defeat. It has been argued that if the Abolitionists could have obtained a decision before these unfavourable events had influenced opinion, they would have carried the motion. This seems unlikely. The Slave Trade, however odious, was a profitable and long-established branch of commerce, supported in Parliament by the full weight of the West Indian lobby. A complete and irresistible case had to be made out before it could be abolished, and the inquiries lasted until the Commons debate of 1791. The argument that the French would take up our share of the Trade remained good throughout this time. Even if the French Revolution and slave revolts had been delayed until after the debate it is unlikely that the motion would have passed the Commons and almost certain that it would have failed in the Lords. An institution which has been in existence as long as the Slave Trade acquires a certain inertia and is unlikely to be voted into extinction so early in the campaign.

To see the matter in perspective we should examine what the other side was doing when the Abolitionists were mounting their offensive. The Slave Traders themselves were of little political consequence, being able to command only the votes of the members for Liverpool and Bristol. The defence of the Trade was organised by a much more influential body, the West Indies lobby.

Each West Indian island appointed an agent in London to look after its interest, by far the most important being the agent for Jamaica, Stephen Fuller, who organised the campaign against Wilberforce. Fuller was an intelligent man with a strong bent for scientific and medical subjects; he was also far from callous. He approved of the new regulations for the treatment of slaves in Jamaica, not only as being effective ammunition for Parliament but also as reforms which were necessary and right. He recommended that murder of a slave should be made a felony without benefit of clergy, that a Council for the protection of slaves should be founded in every parish of Jamaica, that old ugly penal laws should be repealed and every means of improving the slaves' condition pursued.[5]

One would expect such a man to look on some aspects of the Trade with misgivings, and to suggest that it, too, could put its house in order. But when faced with Dolben's Bill he organised a petition against it on the extraordinary grounds that 'whatever nation should be restrained from the Slave Trade, will of course be restrained from the cultivation of sugar'. Fuller regularly attended both inquiries and his reaction to the evidence was not horror but boredom. As he made no attempt to understand his enemy the Abolitionists remained in his eyes 'enthusiasts and fanaticks' and their arguments 'that horrid mass of calumny'. When he first heard of the motion for Abolition this polished and cultivated man was reduced to a state of near-hysteria. He pleaded in a scribbled postscript for evidence to use in the inquiries, begged for arms for the West Indies and tried to get the motion withdrawn by some unlikely exercise of the royal prerogative.

Fuller's papers correct some misconceptions. The Abolitionists thought that their opponents were trying to draw out the issue and prevent an early vote, but at this stage the West Indians were as anxious as anyone to bring the matter to a head. Once the inquiries had begun both sides were victims of the slow parliamentary processes. One is struck when reading Fuller with the thought that he never paused to assess the damage which Abolition would do to the West Indies. He opposed Dolben's Bill and abolition of the foreign trade which, respectively, would have done no harm and some good to his employers, for fear of alienating the slave traders 'who will certainly leave us if we leave them'.

Fuller had no statistics available to prove that the Trade was essential to the West Indies and had to send to Jamaica for them. Thus at the very moment when he was protesting that Abolition or even regulation would finish the cultivation of sugar, he had no idea whether either would make any difference. But in his eyes Abolition itself was not the real menace; what terrified him was the effect that the discussion of Abolition might have on the slaves in Jamaica. He wrote to Lord Sydney, one of his strongest parliamentary supporters, on January 29, 1788:

'Your Lordship may depend upon it, that during the time this business is agitated in Parliament, the slaves will be minutely acquainted with all the proceedings. . . . I submit to your Lordship, whether it is not probable that they will wait with patience for a tardy event, or whether they will not strike while the iron is hot, and by a sudden blow finish the business themselves in the most expeditious and effectual manner, without giving their zealous friends here any further trouble.

'Fearing this may be the event of this perilous undertaking, pregnant with mischief out of the reach of human foresight, it becomes my indispensable duty to call upon your Lordship for your interference with His Majesty, graciously and in good time, to lay such commands upon his governors as may prevent it. And if by an early interference or any means whatsoever, it were possible to prevent this dangerous matter from being agitated at all in Parliament, it might tend to quiet the minds of a great number of His Majesty's subjects.'[6]

The whites in Jamaica were outnumbered sixteen to one by their slaves. In these circumstances they lived in constant terror of slave revolts. Fuller was probably right when he forecast that the slaves would not distinguish between Abolition and Emancipation, but would realise that something was being done on their behalf which their masters were thwarting. This is the reason why he was so anxious to bring the matter to a speedy end, and Wilberforce's declaration after his defeat that he would continue to raise Abolition every year must have come as an unpleasant shock to the West Indians. Fuller wrote to his masters, 'He is blessed with a very sufficient quantity of that enthusiastical spirit, which is so far from yielding that it grows more vigorous from blows.'[7] A few days later he was complaining, 'It is very unpleasant to be kept in perpetual hot water.'

The Abolitionists had a rational answer to the problem of slave revolts. These uprisings were usually led by Africans and provoked by maltreatment. The way to stop them was to cease importing Africans and to improve the slaves' conditions. Fuller repeatedly urged the latter course on the Committee of Correspondence in Jamaica and suggested many measures which were put forward by the Abolitionists in their amelioration campaign over twenty years later. Slaves should be encouraged to marry; families should not be separated by sale; provision should be made for the hearing of slave complaints; long and satisfactory service should entitle a slave, first to wages and then to the right to purchase his freedom with his savings; married slaves who had four or more children should be given their freedom as a reward.

These reforms, he said, expressed 'the universal wish' of the members who had voted down Wilberforce's motion.[8] While recognising the need for reforms and obsessed by the terror of slave revolts, Fuller and his fellow West Indians never seem to have made the connection between them and imported slaves, although in the past other colonial planters had

petitioned for suspension of the Trade on these grounds. The Abolitionists, of course, could never afford to recognise that their campaign might
cause slave revolts, although on occcasions it must have done so. After the
debate in 1791 3,000 slaves gathered in Jamaica to celebrate Wilberforce's
birthday. They came with ample supplies of food and drink but were persuaded to disperse peaceably before their celebrations had become too
convivial. This was the sort of episode which, if events had taken a different course, could have led to a sudden and violent uprising; when their
grievances were festering any large assembly of slaves was dangerous.

The West Indian lobby, then, was committed to opposing Abolition for
a number of reasons; fear of disturbing the slaves and of alienating the
slavers, the belief that they needed more slaves to cultivate their plantations
and, perhaps, the suspicion that Abolition was no more than the thin end
of a wedge aimed at the extinction of slavery. The lobby was one of the
most powerful parliamentary groups with some sixty votes at its command.
This solid base, the unpromising political background, the fear that only
the French would benefit, and the view that if the Trade had been going
on undisturbed for so long there could be no great urgency in abolishing
it, between them explain the defeat of Wilberforce's motion. Judging from
their speeches, more members were frightened of the effect of Abolition
on the West Indies than on the traders, who would have suffered more but
who had less representation in Parliament.

*

After losing the battle in the Commons, the Abolitionists set out to rally
the country to their cause. They had already established a network of local
associations which could agitate, organise petitions and distribute literature. In the summer of 1791 the Committee produced a single-volume
abridgement of the evidence which had a great effect and stimulated
activity by the local societies. This type of political lobbying was new to
England and deeply disturbing to some members of Parliament who could
foresee its being extended to every kind of issue. But so long as Parliament
remained unreformed its effectiveness was limited, although on issues
where there was indifference rather than active hostility it could be decisive. Two examples of the successful use of mass petitions can be seen in
the lobbying for the admission of missionaries to India in 1813, and in the
pressure on the British Government to arrange an international ban on the
Slave Trade after the end of the Napoleonic Wars.

In 1791 this weapon was still strange and it lay uneasily in Wilberforce's
hands. After the publication of the Committee's abridgement a movement
to boycott West Indian sugar spread through the local societies. Some of
his friends embraced it with gusto. 'We use East Indian sugar entirely,'
wrote Babington, 'and so do full two-thirds of the friends of Abolition in

Leicester.'⁹ Poor William Smith somehow missed this loophole and gave up sugar entirely. 'Though I am not yet at all reconciled to the deprivation of the most favourite gratification of my palate.'¹⁰

Clarkson, on his travels, found that a great number of people had given up sugar, often as many as 500 in a single town. Wilberforce's instinctive reaction was to support this movement, but he later decided that it might do more harm than good at this early stage. The boycott was a new tactic—the word did not even exist in those days. It could be interpreted as an attempt to bypass Parliament and thus give offence to uncommitted members. Its use could only be worthwhile when the orthodox Parliamentary campaign had proved hopeless.

In both the Abolitionist and emancipation campaigns there was to be a difference between those who wished to use the normal processes of legislation and those who were determined to put every sort of pressure on Parliament. The danger of the first strategy was that the desire to remain on friendly terms with the Government of the day, whose good offices were indispensable to any legislation, should become an end in itself; if no steps beyond discreet personal lobbying were taken, there was no reason, other than gratitude, for the government to support the Abolitionists.

But during a period when the fear of riots, revolution and democracy was obsessive, a violent popular campaign could bring the cause into disrepute and make its passage through Parliament impossible. When Wilberforce was faced with this kind of choice, his background, character and religion combined to urge caution on him. His adult life had been spent as a Member of Parliament; he understood the delicate workings of influence. He was less familiar with the effects of popular agitation and he initially exaggerated its dangers and underestimated its effects. He almost always chose the familiar path, and there is no doubt that he was often over-cautious and too anxious to avoid giving offence to governments which needed and had his support on other issues. These considerations do not apply to the beginning of Pitt's administration. Until his last years in office Pitt was a strong supporter of Abolition, but unable to unite his own Government on the issue. Even then he was prepared to go to great pains because of his belief in the cause and his personal friendship with Wilberforce. Nor did Wilberforce then have a substantial political following of his own.

The Abolitionists were plagued by ill-fortune. The French Revolution had prevented their case from receiving a fair hearing in April and now, when popular feeling was rising in their favour, another event added to the prejudices against them. The crushing of the mulatto revolt had left the island of St. Domingue simmering with discontent. To the mulattos who were still underprivileged and the slaves who remained in bondage it seemed that the revolution in France would bring them nothing. The

general state of confusion and resentment was fed by a series of contradictory decrees from the National Assembly in Paris. On August 22 the
slaves rose, massacred their masters and seized much of the country. The
situation was complicated by the hatred that already existed between
the whites and mulattos. A three-cornered war ensued between whites,
mulattos and blacks, which all sides waged with ferocious barbarity. This
war was to last, with many fluctuations and interventions by the British
and Spaniards, until the Peace of Amiens in 1803 forced the French to
evacuate the islands and left the Haitians the victors of the one entirely
successful rebellion in the history of slavery.

The revolution in St. Domingue could have been interpreted in a light
favourable to the Abolitionists. It might have been seen as evidence that
the slaves were capable of organisation and of carrying out their designs
with courage and efficiency. It could equally have acted as a warning
against importing too many slaves. But, overshadowed by the greater
revolution in France, it merely hardened the prejudices of Englishmen
against reform. Stories of blood-crazed slaves burning, looting and committing bestial atrocities convinced many waverers that a firm hand was
necessary to stop the infection from spreading to Jamaica.

The full horror of events in St. Domingue did not reach England until
early in 1792. Then Wilberforce wrote to Babington,[11] 'People here are
all panic-struck with the transactions in St. Domingo, and the apprehension or pretended apprehension of the like in Jamaica and other of our
islands. I am pressed on all hands, except by W. Smith and the committee
who hear little of the matter, to defer my motion till next year.' A more
serious defection threatened to take place on the same score. 'Pitt threw
out against Slave motion on St. Domingo account.' He records in his
diary: 'I must repose myself in God. The insincerity of my heart has been
shamefully evinced to me today, when I could hardly bring myself to do
my duty and please God at the expense (as I suspect it will turn out) of my
cordiality with Pitt, or rather his with me.' But he steeled himself and
wrote to Babington, 'Do not be afraid lest I should give ground. . . . This
is a matter wherein all personal, much more all ministerial, attachments
must be as dust in the balance.'[12] In the event it was Pitt who came round
to Wilberforce.

If opposition to the Abolitionists had been swollen by the revolutions in
France and St. Domingue, the numbers of their supporters had also increased. By the time of the next motion against the Trade an unprecedented
number of petitions had been laid before Parliament, 310 from England,
187 from Scotland and 20 from Wales demanding the end of the Trade.
Only four were presented in its favour and one for its regulation. In spite
of Wilberforce's disapproval mass abstentions from sugar continued, and
some of these supporters were uncomfortable bedfellows. It was natural

for radicals to be in favour of Abolition and it sometimes seemed that the reverse was equally true. Clarkson's enthusiasm for the French Revolution could be particularly embarrassing because of the prominent place he occupied in the Abolitionist movement. His dangerous habit of praising the Revolution in the wrong company caused Milner to comment in a letter to Wilberforce, 'I wish him better health and better notions in politics; no government can stand on such principles as he appeals to, and maintains. I am very sorry for it, because I see plainly advantage is taken of such cases as his, in order to represent the friends of Abolition as levellers. This is not the only instance where the converse of a proposition does not hold: levellers certainly are friends of Abolition.'[13]

On April 2, 1792 Wilberforce again moved the Abolition of the Slave Trade.[14] His survey of conditions in the West Indies and Africa contained little new, apart from answers to objections that had arisen since the previous debate. He related various atrocities that had taken place in the last year. The House was shocked by some of these horrifying stories and there were shouts of 'Name! Name!' Wilberforce, with apparent reluctance, gave the names of the guilty captains. He quoted figures to show that Dolben's regulations, although relieving the Middle Passage of some of its miseries, could not ensure a low mortality rate. The House could not reach the cause of this mortality by any regulations. 'Until they could cure a broken heart—until they could legislate for the affections, and bind both by their statutes the passions and feelings of the mind, their labour would be vain.'

He pointed out that Denmark had now abolished the Trade and she, far less than Britain, could afford a reduction in her commerce. The petitions on the table, unprecedented in their numbers, proved that the people of Britain wished to follow Denmark's lead.

It was a hard speech to make. Almost all the arguments had been won in the last two debates and there was some repetition this year with an inevitable loss of freshness. It was not, however, necessary for him to end it with a passage of such complacency. 'In his exertions for the cause,' he said, 'he had found happiness though not hitherto success; it had enlivened his waking and soothed his evening hours; he carried the topic with him to his repose and often had the bliss of remembering that he had demanded justice for millions who could not ask it for themselves.'[15] Such egocentric smugness was a pitfall for the Evangelicals, but in all fairness to Wilberforce it should be pointed out that humility almost always preserved him from the consciousness that his virtue was its own reward. This statement is indeed in so stark a contrast to the agony he records in his diary at the continuation of the Trade, that it seems possible it represented what he thought he should feel rather than what he was in fact feeling. All the evidence suggests that failure to carry Abolition did anything but contribute to the bliss of his repose.

The defenders of the Trade spoke with a new confidence and aggression. They blamed the massacres at St. Domingue on Abolitionist agitation. So much mischief, they declared, should have satisfied anyone, but now the Abolitionists were demanding the total destruction of Britain's West Indian colonies. They were a group of sectaries, sophists, enthusiasts and fanatics. As for their petitions, itinerant clergymen, mendicant physicians and other undersirable people had extorted signatures from the sick and indigent. Schoolboys were bribed to sign them with the promise of a holiday.

The Abolitionists held their own in the debate until Dundas rose and made a decisive intervention. Up to this moment the dispute had been, firstly was the Slave Trade an evil, and, if so, could it be brought to an end without doing great harm to the colonies? The Abolitionists had won the first point; no one in 1792 claimed that the Trade was anything but unpleasant; the dancing, singing slaves and the holds 'redolent with frankincense' had joined the nursery for seamen among the planters' abandoned positions. The Abolitionists had also won the second argument, though not so decisively. Their opponents still maintained that the labour force in the West Indies was inadequate without fresh supplies of slaves, but the statistics were against them. The defenders of the Trade could still fall back on the argument that to abandon the Trade would be to benefit France, not Africa, and they could capitalise on feelings aroused by the revolutions in France and St. Domingue. But the appeal of the first argument was entirely cynical and that of the second seemed likely to be temporary. Feeling in the country was evident from the number of petitions against the Trade, and it was remarkable that, in 1792, Liverpool itself failed to present one in its favour. This depth of opinion must sooner or later be reflected in the House. Although their danger was slight so long as the revolutions kept members clear of progressive causes, the defenders of the Trade were in an intellectually indefensible position, with no lines of retreat and with the country against them. Dundas rescued them from this uncomfortable perch.

He declared that he had always been a warm friend of Abolition, though he differed from Wilberforce as to the means of achieving it. So far the only opinions heard had been from those who wanted immediate Abolition and from those who considered the Trade vital to the prosperity of the West Indies. He agreed with Wilberforce that the Trade was not necessary and that newly imported slaves were likely to lead revolts; but he thought Abolition should be gradual and accompanied by measures to revive the numbers and begin the education of the negroes in the West Indies. He would like to see the last movement lead to an end of hereditary slavery. If there were enough members sympathetic to this 'moderate' view, they might put the question to the House.[16] Addington, the Speaker, and Jenkinson, both future Prime Ministers, supported Dundas. The atter pushed the foreign slave trade argument to its limits. He pointed out that the death rate on British ships, although distressing, was much lower than on foreign slavers; it was therefore in the negroes' interests that Britain should continue the Trade.

Fox ridiculed Dundas's proposals with his usual fire and brilliance, but if the honours in the 1790 debate were Wilberforce's and in 1791 his own, in 1792 they must be awarded to Pitt. The Prime Minister had 'thrown out against' having the debate that year, but once committed he made one of the finest speeches ever heard in Parliament.[17] He dissected the arguments of Dundas and Jenkinson without ever losing the thread of his own. He went over the whole ground again, showing the advantages of immediate over gradual Abolition. He tackled the problem of presenting the Trade to other nations and gave the best answer yet heard to it. 'This miserable argument, if persevered in, would be an eternal bar to the annihilation of the evil. How was it ever to be eradicated, if every nation was thus prudentially to wait until the concurrence of all the world should be obtained?' The argument would also work in reverse. If we failed to abolish, other nations would say, 'Great Britain has not only not abolished, but has refused to abolish, the Slave Trade. She has investigated it well. Her senate has deliberated on it. It is plain, then, she finds no guilt in it.'[18] We would become guilty, not only of our own crimes, but of those of all Europe.

He compared the position of Africa with that of Britain when it provided the Romans with a slave market. The Romans could have used arguments heard in the House tonight about the 'natural incapacity' of Britons. They could have said, 'There is a people destined never to be free.' Now we had raised ourselves from barbarity, and one thing only remained to complete the contrast, for we still wilfully perpetrated barbarity in Africa.

Pitt chose Africa as the theme for his peroration, Africa as it might be once the blight of the Slave Trade had been removed. He pictured its natives, transformed by peace and prosperity, absorbing all the benefits of science and philosophy. It was an imaginative tour de force, marked by extraordinary eloquence. He finished his speech with a quotation from Virgil to illustrate the dispelling of darkness and its replacement by light and all its attendant blessings. They had sat all night, and as Pitt reached this point in his speech, a shaft of sunlight came through the window and lit up his face. The effect, on a House already mesmerised by his eloquence, must have been devastating. After it was all over Windham, Fox and Grey walked home together. They agreed that Pitt's speech was 'one of the most extraordinary displays of eloquence they had ever heard. For the last twenty minutes he really seemed to be inspired.'[19]

After Pitt's speech the House divided on the question of whether the

Chairman should leave the chair. This, the equivalent of rejecting any form of Abolition, was voted down by 234 to 87. A second vote was held on Dundas's amendment that the word 'gradual' should be inserted into Wilberforce's motion and carried by 193 to 125. Dundas then put the amended motion, which was carried by 230 to 85.

On April 23 Dundas revealed the details of his plan. He intended to abolish the foreign Slave Trade at once and to continue the Trade to British Colonies until 1800. Other nations would be invited to join in the Abolition. He also proposed that slaves in the West Indies should hence-forth be attached to the land rather than their masters, and that they should receive religious instruction. Lord Mornington, Wellington's elder brother, who was shortly to become Lord Wellesley, moved a series of amendments bringing the date of Abolition forward; after defeats for January 1, 1793 and 1795, he succeeded in carrying an amendment abolish-ing the Trade as from January 1, 1796. But now, for the first time since Dolben's motion, the matter came up before the House of Lords. In spite of the exhaustive inquiries already made by the Privy Council and the Commons, the Lords decided that they should hear their own evidence. The leisurely manner in which they did so gave notice of their intention to let the Bill die a slow death. So long as their inquiry continued it could be used as an excuse to reject any other legislation controlling the Trade, on the grounds that the whole matter was under scrutiny. The Lords' inquiry was therefore a more effective and, superficially, a more reasonable reply to the Commons' proposals for gradual Abolition than they could have achieved by rejecting the Bill.

After the debate in April 1792 the Abolition issue was never to be the same. The House had decided, by an overwhelming majority, that some form of Abolition was necessary, and this, at first sight, seemed to be a triumph for Wilberforce and his friends. But their victory was delusive. So long as the only alternatives were Abolition and the indefinite retention of the Trade, the 'moderate men' to whom Dundas appealed might be convinced that the former was preferable. The new choice posed by Dundas gave such members a chance of satisfying their consciences with-out disturbing the existing state of affairs. He created a third group. On April 3 the planters mustered 87 votes, the Abolitionists 125; but 106 more members voted for Dundas's motion than for permanent retention.

The appeal of his proposals was insidious and calculated to seduce not only moderate men, but also lukewarm Abolitionists. Any uneasiness about promoting reforms in such turbulent days could now be reconciled with a complaisant conscience. There was always to be some reason for putting off the measure, and if it slipped through the Commons the House of Lords could be trusted to send it back. Dundas also took the sting out of the Abolitionists' attack. By agreeing that the Trade was odious and unnecessary he deprived them of their strongest arguments. Their opponents were given an intellectual smokescreen. They no longer needed to defend a discredited Trade, but merely to discover reasons why its immediate Abolition was inadvisable. The 'warmth' of the friendship Dundas possessed for the cause can best be judged from his record.

In 1794, when Wilberforce introduced a Bill for the abolition of the foreign slave trade and asked Dundas for his support, the latter replied:

'I know with absolute certainty that the Bill will be regarded by the colonies as an encroachment upon their legislative rights, and they will not submit to it unless compelled. Upon this ground I have used all the influence I possess to prevent any question on the subject being agitated, at least during the war. My opinion does not prevail, and therefore the only thing to which I can reconcile myself is being perfectly quiet on the subject; and even to that I should feel it very difficult to reconcile myself, if I did not believe that your Bill will not pass the House of Lords.'[20]

In 1797 when he should, for consistency's sake, have supported Abolition for January 1, 1800, he was instead the leader of an attack on a Bill of Wilberforce's which would have allowed it to continue beyond that date. But Dundas, though he saved the West Indians, was not acting in collusion with them. If any group was more disgusted than the Abolitionists by his intervention it was the West Indian lobby. Stephen Fuller wrote a gloomy letter to the Committee of Correspondence in Jamaica breaking the 'unwelcome news'. 'I am persuaded,' he wrote, 'that if it had not been for Mr. Dundas's amendment by adding the fatal word *gradual*, we should have had a majority in the House.'[21]

*

Shortly after this debate Wilberforce's life was threatened by two West Indian captains, one of whom had developed a hatred for him after being humiliated in cross-examination. This man challenged him to a duel. Wilberforce was later to develop very strong views against duelling, but these were still germinating in his mind. He discussed the matter with friends, but he never seems to have seriously considered responding to the challenge.

The second threat was less easily avoided. During his speech Wilberforce had been persuaded to name the officers responsible for the worst atrocities that had been discovered since the last debate. One of the most horrifying of these cases concerned a Captain Kimber, who had flogged a pregnant girl of fifteen to death for no reason other than wilful sadism. After the debate Kimber was tried for murder and acquitted, a verdict which seems a scandalous miscarriage of justice even from the account of the trial prepared by his friends. Boswell was in the gallery, gloating over the outcome. Not content with the clearing of his character, Kimber wrote to Wilberforce demanding compensation for the inconveniences he had suffered. 'A public apology, £5,000 in money, and such a place under government as would make me comfortable,'[22] were his modest demands. When these were rejected he took to calling at Wilberforce's house and waylaying him in the street, where he would abuse and threaten him. When Wilberforce went to Yorkshire in the summer of 1792, one of his friends thought it prudent to accompany him as an armed bodyguard. Wilberforce himself took a more philosophical view in a letter to Muncaster in July, 'I can't say I apprehend much, as I really believe, that if he were to commit any act of violence it would be beneficial rather than injurious to *the cause.*' Lord Sheffield, the Member for Bristol, finally persuaded Kimber to leave Wilberforce alone.

In the summer of 1792 the French Convention bestowed on Wilberforce what his sons describe as 'the doubtful honour of French citizenship'. Any association with the Revolution could be damaging to Abolition and the identity of the other honorary citizens made the compliment more embarrassing.

Jeremy Bentham, who was honoured at the same time, could afford to be amused. He wrote to Wilberforce on September 1: 'Looking over the list, among the 17 of which it is composed I observe 6 British: and among these 6, none but *yourself* and your humble servant that are not *reputed Republicans*, unless it be your journeyman labourer in the Vineyards of the Slave Trade, Mr. Clarkson, of whose sentiments in constitutional matters I am not apprised. What say you then, to an expedition to Paris upon occasion—properly dubbed and armed—not à la J—n to *devour* the country, but à la Wilberforce to *give peace* to it . . . ?'[23]

But Wilberforce had to take a more serious view of the matter. Bentham and Clarkson could not be objected to, Benjamin Franklin could be borne at a pinch, but the name of Thomas Paine, another of the honorary citizens, was anathema to Wilberforce and to the British Parliament, and any association with him was dangerous. On September 11 William Mason wrote to him from Yorkshire, 'I was provoked lately to see your name registered among the list of citizens by the French savages. . . . ' Wilberforce was aware of the dangers of his new citizenship and found a congenial way of disarming critics by joining a committee for the relief of émigré clergymen.

CHAPTER VIII

THE CLAPHAM SECT

DURING the years 1789–92 most of Wilberforce's time was consumed by the demands of Abolition. In the summer recesses he would go down to Bath and take the waters; from there it was an easy journey to the More sisters' house at Cowslip Green. His summer visits to Rayrigg were replaced by tours of his friends' houses. Apart from the Mores he would stay with Muncaster in his Cumberland castle, Gisborne at Yoxall Lodge in Staffordshire and Babington at Rothley Temple in Leicestershire. When Parliament was sitting he was able to escape from the turmoil of Westminster to rest and work in John Thornton's house in Clapham.

During his spiritual crisis Wilberforce had been advised by Newton to see as much as he could of the Thorntons, and this was excellent advice. There was a solid quality about the Thorntons' religion and all their good works, which must have been reassuring to a nervous convert. In spite of his undoubted piety and generosity, Henry Thornton remains a somewhat aloof figure. He inherited a banking business from his father, but he was also a Member of Parliament, representing Southwark for eight sessions. He never offered his electors any inducement to vote for him, and regarded their opinion of him with contempt. 'I would rather have a shake of the hand from good old John Newton, than the cheers of all that foolish mob, who praise one, they don't know why.' He was rewarded by their consistent loyalty. Thornton, although no orator, was remorselessly logical in his reasoning. He spoke often on financial subjects and had a gift for explaining them in simple, easily understood terms. These qualities, and his unquestioned honesty, made Henry Thornton a respected figure. Judged even by Evangelical standards he was an extraordinarily generous man, giving away five-sixths of his income when a single man and a third when he had a large family to support. He voted sometimes for Pitt, sometimes for Fox, and although influenced by Wilberforce and his supporter on most issues, Thornton continued to think for himself and make his own calm, balanced decisions.

Thornton and Wilberforce were both exceptionally generous. The way in which they gave makes an interesting contrast, for the two men, though steered into the same paths by their faith, had very different characters. Wilberforce's generosity was warm-hearted and impetuous; he could not restrain himself when he saw someone in distress, even though he knew that his money would be squandered. Thornton's charity was more effective if less attractive; in the words of Zachary Macaulay, he would set himself to 'weigh the best mode of imparting relief so as to raise no false hopes, and to produce no future unhappiness, and to join, if possible, the interests of eternity to those of time'.[1] Wilberforce, Macaulay thought, was a warmer, more imaginative and affectionate man with superior talents; Thornton had the better judgement and greater self-discipline. Macaulay admired these two men as much as any in the world, and of the two his own morose seriousness led him to prefer Thornton.[2]

The Thorntons, like the Wilberforces with whom they were connected by marriage, were a family of prosperous Hull merchants, but they had moved south earlier. Robert Thornton, Henry's grandfather, had been a Director of the Bank of England as well as a merchant in the Baltic trade, and had bought an estate to the south of Clapham Common with boundaries two miles long.

The very un-Evangelical magnificence of this estate was probably a result of his wife's tastes. 'Mrs. Thornton,' Wilberforce remembered, 'though a woman of good understanding had somewhat of a turn for the splendid in all particulars.'[3]

After his father's death Henry Thornton bought Battersea Rise, an upright Queen Anne house on the west side of the Common, while his two elder brothers, Samuel and Robert, lived on the family estate. The grounds at Battersea Rise were less extensive than on the main Thornton property, but as a garden they were large enough to encourage Henry Thornton not only to increase the size of his own house, but also to build two more, Glenelg and Broomfield, for his friends Charles Grant and Edward Eliot. He asked Wilberforce to share Battersea Rise with him.

Thornton added two wings to Battersea Rise, which trebled its size and gave it no less than thirty-four bedrooms;[4] but the house's central feature was its oval library, designed by William Pitt. When Thornton was discussing the problems of making a library with him, Pitt showed a keen interest and said that he had always wanted to design one.[5]

The library at Battersea Rise could be seen by his admirers as an extension of its designer's mind, lofty, symmetrical and exquisitely proportioned. Three sides were filled with bookcases and the fourth looked out through high glass doors on to lawns, the trunks of giant tulip trees and elms and distant views of farmland. There was a ceiling and a mantelpiece in the style of Adam and there were busts of both Fox and Pitt, as if to emphasise its owner's independence. Sir James Stephen, a strong Whig, considered that 'few of the designs of the great Minister were equally successful'. Battersea Rise, Glenelg and Broomfield have long been destroyed, their gardens torn up and their trees cut down, to make way for the houses of a more crowded and less elegant age, but the scene in Pitt's library is preserved in the sketches of Henry Thornton's children, and from what we can see there it seems that Sir James Stephen's tribute was not undeserved.

Battersea Rise was to be the centre of the Clapham Sect and its library their meeting place until Henry Thornton's death in 1815. Wilberforce lived there with him for four years and after Henry Thornton's marriage and Eliot's death he moved to Broomfield and stayed until 1808. There was already a small nucleus of Abolitionists in Clapham, Henry Thornton's brothers who were both Members of Parliament, William Smith and Granville Sharp, who lived there in his brother's house. In 1793 they acquired an ideal clergyman in John Venn, a leading Evangelical preacher, and Clapham's attractions as a religious haven were much increased. Venn came from a long line of clergymen who, on the paternal side of his family, stretched back without interruption to the Reformation.[6] His father, Henry Venn, had been a pioneer of Evangelism and John Venn, like Wilberforce, had been educated by Joseph Milner. Henry Venn, too, had been Rector of Clapham,* where his wife had been urged 'to repress the disgusting earnestness of her husband'.[7] John Venn was more fortunate in his parishioners; his sermons never ceased to delight and inspire Wilberforce. Venn's first sermon at Clapham lasted for twenty-five minutes, a time which his father considered 'five or seven minutes too short'.[8] Wilberforce was less critical. 'Venn preached an excellent introductory sermon—I received the sacrament and had much serious reflection. Oh may it be for good! I renewed all my solemn resolves, and purpose to lay afresh my foundations.'

There seems no doubt that Henry Thornton deliberately planned a colony of Saints at Clapham. He wrote to Grant in 1793: 'On the whole I am in hopes some good may come out of our Clapham system, Mr. Wilberforce is a candle that should not be hid under a bushel. The influence of his conversation is great and striking.'[9] The living of Clapham was in the Thornton family's gift; by persuading Wilberforce, Grant and Eliot to move there and by seeing that a suitable Evangelical clergyman was

---

* He was also the only Evangelist of his time to be a first-class cricketer. I cannot resist an irrelevant quotation from *The Intellectual Aristocracy* by N. G. Annan, p. 287:
'Henry Venn, Rector of Yelling, after playing victoriously for Surrey against All England a few days before his ordination, gave his bat to the first comer, saying, 'I will never have it said of me, "well struck, Parson". But the old Adam rose up in his descendants and his great-great grandson, Dr. J. A. Venn, bowled out Victor Trumper twice using a bowling machine invented by himself and his father the logician.'

installed, he had taken the first step towards creating the Clapham Sect.*
Other Evangelicals were drawn to the place by a combination of good company, an admirable vicar, and pleasant countryside within a convenient
distance of London.

Clapham was an isolated village, infested with footpads and highwaymen, until its Common was drained in 1751. By 1760 it had 1,000 inhabitants, by 1791 2,700 and by 1811 over 5,000. The roads into London were
improved and regular coach services installed. The Common was planted
with trees, some of which were said to have been cotton trees brought back
by Captain Cook from the Pacific.[10]

The Grants and Eliot were both in residence by 1794 and they were
soon to be joined by James Stephen on his return from St. Christopher. In
the first years of the nineteenth century Lord Teignmouth and Macaulay
moved there and the Sect can be said to have been complete. There were
also regular visitors who attended the Clapham cabinets and must be
allowed honorary membership of the Sect. Hannah More, Babington,
Gisborne and Milner were the most important and frequent visitors.

The Claphamites lived in great intimacy. They would wander into one
another's houses and gardens and always find themselves welcome. There
seemed to be a general assumption that a friend could come in at any time.
They would also call on one another unexpectedly in the country and
expect and receive the same welcome. They liked to spend their holidays
with other members of the Sect, often in a series of prolonged visits to one
another's houses. The Grants, Thornton, Eliot and Wilberforce were so
close to one another that although each of their houses on Henry Thornton's property had its own garden allotted to it there was no attempt to
make any demarcation and they all treated the garden as a form of common
property. It was perhaps natural that, living so closely together, the Clapham Sect should marry into one another's families and they did so to an
almost incestuous degree. Wilberforce was first cousin to the Thornton
and Smith brothers; Stephen married Wilberforce's sister, Gisborne
Babington's, Babington Macaulay's, Charles Eliot Venn's. Macaulay, the
supply of sisters having been exhausted, married one of Hannah More's
pupils. The relationships of the next generation were even more complicated.†

Living in such proximity to one's friends was both pleasant and useful.
Wilberforce always found 'the very prospect [of returning to Clapham]
mends, fixing and solemnizing my mind'. The enthusiasm for one another's

---

* The Claphamites themselves never used this expression, which is in any case a
misnomer since 'sect' implies dissent, while except for William Smith they were all
members of the Church. It seems to have first been applied to them, posthumously, by
Sir James Stephen in the *Edinburgh Review* in 1844 (see Howse 187–9).

† See Annan, *The Intellectual Aristocracy*, F. K. Brown 72–3 and Newsome 24–5.

good causes with which the group became infected led to the birth of a mass of societies for the relief of every class of unfortunate from Russian sufferers to Irish serving women. Wilberforce has been compared to a Prime Minister of a cabinet of philanthropists,[11] in which each of his ministers held a particular portfolio, Stephen and Macaulay the Slave Trade, Lord Teignmouth the Bible Society, Thornton the Exchequer, Grant India, Macaulay and Hannah More public relations. Milner, Venn and Simeon were his spiritual consultants, and he looked perhaps more to Babington than anyone else for general advice. Even if one excludes the contribution made by those who did not live in Clapham, it is safe to say that never in the history of the Church did the inhabitants of a single parish have such an effect on the world. For the Clapham Sect's good works were not limited to England and Africa. They intervened on behalf of the convicts of Australia, the victims of the Napoleonic wars, the Greeks struggling for freedom, the Haitians, the North American Indians, the Hottentots and the slaves. They distributed bibles and sent out missionaries to every corner of the world. They have been criticised for concentrating so much of their energies on religious campaigns, though it would be unrealistic to expect such religious men to do anything else. But the drive behind their campaigns was so great that their temporal achievements were enough to put any other group to shame. If they had never succeeded in anything else, their share in either of the great victories of Abolition and Emancipation would have guaranteed their place in history.

The Clapham Sect had many virtues, of which a combination of humanity and application of the highest order stands out. It also had its faults and the most serious of these—one to which Evangelicals, even in isolation, were prone—was spiritual pride. It was all too easy to look down from the rarefied heights of Clapham Common on to the rest of mankind. It was not a trap into which Wilberforce fell as often as some of his friends, but it shows itself occasionally in his writings. He lived so much in the society of the religious and considered religion of such over-riding importance that, whatever the evidence to the contrary, he could not bring himself to expect good of men of the world. A perfect example of this fault was provided when one of the Claphamites suggested that Gibbon should be employed to write propaganda for Abolition; 'a fee,' he added contemptuously, 'would be a sufficient motive'.

*

The Clapham Sect had scarcely assembled before they launched their first crusade and it was one which was exclusively their own. Charles Grant had lived a dissolute life as a young man in India before being converted as a result of a family tragedy. He then conceived the idea of establishing Christian missions in India under government patronage. He found an ally in John Shore, another rising official in the East India Company, and sympathetic ears in Clapham. When Wilberforce was told of the situation in India, he found it doubly distressing. Not only were its millions denied the opportunity of embracing the true religion and left to the worship of a rabble of unwholesome deities, but the Company's servants themselves were said to be 'unbaptised' on their voyage to the East and to lead a pagan life after their arrival.

It was normal for them to keep a string of native mistresses. As late as 1810 a book for the instruction of young servants of the Company included a chapter on this subject. The manual quoted approvingly the reply of an elderly gentleman who kept a harem of sixteen Indian girls, and, asked how he looked after such a number, answered, 'Oh, I give them a little rice and let them run around.'[12] Such sentiments were not calculated to appeal to Clapham.

In 1793, when the East India Company Charter was due for renewal, Wilberforce took the opportunity of presenting two resolutions drafted by Grant, that the Company should appoint chaplains in India and on board their merchantmen. Once these innocuous clauses were passed he introduced another, that the Directors should send out suitable people to act as schoolmasters and missionaries. This too was passed and Wilberforce wrote triumphantly in his Journal: 'The hand of Providence was never more visible than in this East Indian affair . . . how properly is Grant affected.'[13] But this 'Providential interposition', a name which the Evangelicals would give to any favourable development, and Grant's reaction to it, were both premature by twenty years. The Court of Proprietors of the East India Company became aroused by this foray of enthusiasm into their property, and, at the third reading of the Bill, they showed their power by rejecting, with ease, all Wilberforce's motions. His protestations and eloquence were swept aside; he wrote, bitterly, to Gisborne, 'The East India Directors and Proprietors have triumphed, all my clauses were last night struck out on the third reading of the Bill and . . . twenty millions of people . . . are left . . . to the providential protection of—Brama.'[14]

This setback showed how sanguine Grant had been in hoping for a mission patronised by the Company, for the resolutions that were rejected did not go nearly so far. But it was not in the nature of the Clapham Sect to accept a defeat when they knew themselves to be in the right. They would be better prepared when the Charter next came up for renewal in 1813. Meanwhile their attention had been drawn to the need for missionary activity. They had recently founded a colony for freed slaves in Sierra Leone and this and the convict settlements of Australia were the first areas in which they established missions. India, for the time being, remained closed to them. Under the Charter Act of 1793 entry without a licence into British India became a high misdemeanour. Even after Grant became a

Director of the Company in 1794 he was unable to arrange passage for missionaries. But Shore built churches and set a standard for Europeans in India by the austerity and integrity of his own life. Although very far from being a great Governor-General he was unquestionably an honest one. Grant used his position to send out suitable chaplains and, as time went on, these men began a process of clandestine proselytising, so that, when the matter was next debated by Parliament, there were already missionaries working in India.

CHAPTER IX

SIERRA LEONE

On February 1, 1793, war broke out with France; it was a conflict which for some time had seemed inevitable. Wilberforce opposed the war. He did not regard his own country as being the aggressor, but thought she could have gone to greater pains to avoid it. On the day that war was declared he was on his feet in the House of Commons, about to make some such statement, when an urgent message from Pitt silenced him. It was one of the few occasions on which he allowed himself to be deflected.

One result of the war was to kill the Abolitionist movement. We have seen the French Revolution turning opinion in England against reform. This reaction was intensified by civil unrest in England in the autumn of 1792. The execution of Louis XVI on January 21 and the outbreak of war on February 1 completed it. All the nation-wide agitation of the Abolitionists appeared to have been wasted; no more petitions flooded in to embarrass Parliament. A friend wrote to him from Hull, 'I do not imagine that we could meet with twenty persons in Hull at present, who would sign a petition, that are not republicans.' Instead of appealing confidently to the nation, the Abolitionists now had to struggle to keep the Cause alive.

The war frustrated all progressive causes, but its effect on the Abolition campaign was threefold. Not only did they suffer from the general change in atmosphere, but the war also added two new and special arguments against them. Pitt, like his father before him, hoped to remain a paymaster in Europe while using the war to seize French colonies, the most valuable of which were the sugar islands. If this policy were successful, the arguments used by the Abolitionists to show that the Slave Trade was unnecessary would no longer apply, for England would have acquired new and fertile possessions with virgin land, which needed massive imports of slaves to be developed. Fortunately for the Abolitionists the matter was never fully put to the test. St. Domingue was the greatest prize, but yellow fever and the heroism of the slaves repelled all British attempts at its conquest.

The removal of St. Domingue from the ranks of the sugar-producing colonies altered the balance of trade and restored prosperity to her less efficient competitors, while British naval supremacy prevented the produce of her enemies' colonies from reaching Europe. The result was a sharp rise in the sugar price, a revival in the British West Indies and the cultivation of new and marginal lands. This caused a demand for more slaves; as foreign colonies were conquered the demand intensified and led in 1798-1802 to the greatest shipments the British ever made across the Middle Passage.[1]

The gradual Abolition agreed on by the Commons in 1792 had then seemed a cruel protraction of the Trade. A year later it was the best the Abolitionists could hope for. To expedite proceedings in the Lords, Wilberforce moved, on February 26, the further consideration of Abolition, but he was defeated by eight votes.* The Lords' inquiry proceeded at a dismal pace, only seven witnesses being examined that session. The Duke of Clarence opposed further consideration of the matter until after the Easter Recess; he was abusive and called Wilberforce, by name, a fanatic and a hypocrite. In the hopes of achieving something in this unhappy year, Wilberforce introduced a Bill to abolish the Trade with foreign colonies, which was defeated on its third reading. The attendance of members shows how interest in the matter had waned; the first motion was defeated by 61 to 53, the second by 31 to 29.

In 1794 Wilberforce carried his Foreign Trade Bill through the Commons, but even staunch Abolitionists refused to support it in the Lords so long as the inquiry there continued. But the Lords heard only two more witnesses before abandoning their investigations. The Abolitionists were left in a desperate position; if the Lords would not abolish the foreign part of the Trade, nor the Commons renew their motion, there was no chance of progress. Clarkson's nervous system broke under the strain of an accumulation of overwork and disappointment. In seven years he had travelled more than 35,000 miles and maintained a correspondence, in his own hand, with 400 people. Now the nightmare of the barbarity, against which he had fought so hard, continuing for ever was too much for him, and he had to retire from the struggle.

There was, however, one Abolitionist enterprise which continued throughout these depressing years. It was a sickly plant in need of constant attention and plagued by every kind of misfortune, but it survived, finally flourished and remains a permanent achievement, the free negro country of Sierra Leone.

At the time of the Somerset case there were some 14,000 Blacks in England. One of the reasons behind Lord Mansfield's prevarication had been the fear of what would happen when all of them were declared free. After the case it was clear that many needed help and, with his usual generosity, Granville Sharp supported all those who came to him. But this

---

* Some planters had misgivings and wished to allow this Bill to pass, but they were defeated at a planters' meeting by a large majority. Stephen Fuller Papers, June 5, 1793.

was not enough. In 1783 the Blacks themselves proposed a solution. Let them be sent back to Africa and settled in a free colony there.

This proposal had a double appeal to the Abolitionists. The project in itself was worthy of support and its success would advance the greater cause of Abolition by showing the Blacks capable of responsible behaviour and Africa a source of goods other than slaves. For Granville Sharp it had an added attraction. Perhaps mercifully, few Utopians have a chance of drawing up a constitution. Sharp made sure that that of the colony fairly bristled with frankpledges and laws derived from those of ancient Israel. Unfortunately the practical details of founding a colony were less thoroughly investigated.

The first colonists sailed from England on April 8, 1787. There were 400 Blacks and 60 Europeans, mainly women, and they were to settle on a quarter of a million acres which had been bought from a neighbouring chief. But their landing coincided with the beginning of the rainy season and they had scarcely set foot on shore before being tormented by hunger, fever and dysentery. In the first year half of the settlers died or deserted, but the survivors built a small town and slowly improved their position. Sharp's comments were severe. 'The greatest blame of all,' he wrote, 'is to be charged on the intemperance of the people themselves; for the most of them became so besotted during the voyage that they were totally unfit for business when they landed, and could hardly be prevailed on to assist in erecting their huts.'[2] To add insult to injury many of those who deserted the colony went to work for its enemies in slave ships or factories. Sharp was especially pained to hear that Henry Demane, whom he had rescued from a ship on the Thames, had himself become a dealer in slaves.

The disintegration of the first colony was as much his fault as theirs. If Sharp had spent less time laying down his frankpledges and more investigating the climate of Sierra Leone, he would have discovered that the beginning of the rainy season was scarcely an ideal moment to arrive. The colonists did not have enough money to buy from neighbouring tribes the livestock they needed to survive, and without arms they were at the mercy of any petty chief. This weakness was exposed in the winter of 1789, when a chieftain sent them notice of his intention to burn down their town in reprisal for some outrage committed by an English warship. The colonists, unable to resist, had to leave their homes and allow him to carry out his threat.

In 1790 the St. George's Bay Company was formed to salvage the colony. Sharp was its president, Henry Thornton chairman and Wilberforce and Bankes among its first directors. From this time onwards, although the settlers would have to face a daunting series of hazards, a shortage of finance would not be among them. Wilberforce's first action on the Company's behalf seems to have taken place in January 1790, when he negotiated for Sharp the purchase of a ship from the Treasury.[3] In February he was invited to join the Board and soon afterwards we find him canvassing subscribers with some caution, emphasising 'the uncertainty of its turning out a profitable concern'. The new Company chose Clarkson's martial friend Falconbridge to reorganise the colony. He collected the fugitives from the burnt settlement, gave them arms and settled them in a new town which he named Granville Town.

In 1792 the colony received massive reinforcements, 100 whites being sent out from England in February. But the largest consignment of settlers came from a surprising source. After the American War of Independence many Blacks who had fought on the British side were left without homes for they could not return to America without being enslaved. These black loyalists were an embarrassment to the British Government, which settled 4,000 of them in Nova Scotia, where they were promised but not given land. On hearing of the Sierra Leone colony they sent a spokesman to London and obtained permission to join it. John Clarkson, the brother of Thomas and an ex-naval officer, was sent to choose the new settlers. He took 1,131 Nova Scotians across the Atlantic and brought them to Granville Town which he renamed Freetown. The newcomers gathered to sing hymns of gratitude under a vast silk cotton tree, which still stands and is pointed out with pride to any visitor to the city of Freetown.

The arrival of the Nova Scotians gave the colony a more solid appearance which was appreciated in London. The company had aimed at raising £100,000, but its subscriptions finally amounted to £235,280. Although the St. George's Bay Company was ostensibly a commercial investment, its subscribers must have realised 'the uncertainty of it turning out a profitable concern'. As a charity its appeal to subscribers was a combination of the imaginative nature of the project, and the possibility that, if things went well, they would see some of their money back.

After his replacement by Clarkson, Falconbridge brought back with him the son of the local paramount King, a young man called Naimbana. His father must have been a curious and intelligent chieftain, for he sent another son to be educated in France and a third to be taught the Moslem faith by the Mandingo tribe. Naimbana took the names Henry Granville at his christening as a tribute to Sharp. He seems, however, to have become generally known as the Black Prince. He was a shy, studious, diffident man and very sensitive to any slights on his country. He became a devout Christian during his visit to England and he endeared himself to all the Clapham Sect. With such a man as paramount King, the colony would have had no problems with its neighbours and a section of the coast could have been rid of the Slave Trade. It seemed that this moment had come in 1793 when the old King died and Naimbana returned to Africa to claim his inheritance; but he fell ill and died during the voyage.

Clarkson returned to England at the end of 1792. He had been popular with the colonists, but, through taking their side in every dispute, less so with the board in London. He was replaced by William Dawes, an officer in the Marines, and Zachary Macaulay, the father of the historian, who was soon to become an intimate friend of Wilberforce.

*

Francis Jeffrey, the editor of the *Edinburgh Review*, once told Thomas Babington Macaulay, 'The more I think, the less I can conceive where you picked up that style.'[4] He certainly had not inherited it from his father. His great-nephew, Sir George Otto Trevelyan, wrote of Zachary Macaulay, 'Nature had denied him any sense of the ridiculous.' He was the archetypal Evangelical, without any extraneous features, and if Evangelism, even in the hands of so effervescent a man as Wilberforce, could be a sad faith, in those of Zachary Macaulay it was positively morose. His seriousness overlapped into every field; surely no one else could have written thus to his fiancée to compliment her on her dress: 'I really cannot resist the propension I feel to pay you a compliment on your very just taste in that article, I have always admired it, and been pleased with it, not because I lay particular weight on external appearance, but because I insensibly attach to it the idea of a well-ordered mind. I must say that you were the only person that I met who could so follow the reigning mode as to avoid singularity, and yet preserve the grace that it was so much calculated to outrage.'[5]

Dreary, humourless, cold and pedestrian, Macaulay nevertheless had qualities that made him loved by his friends and admired by the world. Even in the Clapham Sect his industry was outstanding; he got up at four o'clock each morning to begin his day's work and he was a superbly efficient worker who could gut a document of its essentials more quickly than any of his colleagues. A phenomenal memory and an acuteness in detecting fallacies were both qualities that he passed on to his more famous son. He was among the stoutest of Wilberforce's 'intellectual walking sticks'; Wilberforce indeed treated him as a sort of walking encyclopaedia and would say, 'Let us look it up in Macaulay.' He was indefatigable and immune to despair; he was indifferent to his own comfort, safety and health when faced with demands imposed by the cause. He risked his health for many years serving, first as Deputy Governor, then as Governor of Sierra Leone. He was the only leading Abolitionist to have crossed the Middle Passage in a slave ship. He took on the thankless task of editing the *Christian Observer*. Late in his life he found that he lacked the time to run his business and work on the Emancipation campaign. He handed the business over to his nephews and allowed it to become ruined and his family destitute.

Macaulay had been an irreligious youth when, at the age of sixteen, he went to seek his fortune in the West Indies. He stayed in Jamaica eight years and was promoted from overseer to manager of the plantation on which he worked. He is said to have done everything possible to improve the slaves' lot, but it seems from his own account that he soon became reconciled to the system. At first shocked by the condition of the slaves, 'I resolved to get rid of my squeamishness as soon as I could . . . and in this I had a success beyond my expectation'.[6] In 1792 Sierra Leone gave him a chance to return. Macaulay was still unregenerate. An expert card and backgammon player, he gave some gamblers an expensive lesson on the voyage home. But in England he found his father dead and his sister married to Babington. He went to Rothley Temple and was converted there.

Under Dawes and Macaulay Sierra Leone was run on stricter lines than in the past. But their discipline, while severe after Clarkson's indulgent regime, was mildness itself compared to the English Penal Code. The settlement's progress during the next two years was impressive; it became self-sufficient in rice and vegetables; the level of literacy was high and good relations were established with neighbouring tribes. This advance was not achieved without some friction, for the colonists constantly demanded more rights and the governors more work. A mutiny was suppressed without blood being shed and its six ringleaders punished by expulsion from the colony. But in September 1794 Sierra Leone was struck by a blow that wiped out most of the progress it had made.

A fleet of seven or eight ships sailed into the bay, flying the English colours. The settlers were unsuspicious until it suddenly began to bombard the town. The ships were French piloted by an American slave trader and they pillaged Freetown, stealing or destroying everything of value. They cut down any plants in the Governor's garden that looked either beautiful or useful, they burnt the houses and slaughtered the livestock. The Swedish botanist had his specimens destroyed and his collection ruined. Nothing escaped them. The French officers listened sympathetically to Macaulay's complaints and then explained that they could not control their men. The French only stayed in Freetown for a fortnight, but they cost the colony £50,000. The only benefit of their visit was to show the settlers how vulnerable they were and thus to dampen their rebelliousness.

In 1795 Macaulay's health broke down and he had to return to England. Almost anyone else would have taken the first ship home, but Macaulay saw his sickness as providing an opportunity to study conditions on the Middle Passage at first hand. Macaulay kept notes in Greek script so as to fool the ignorant slavers. He seems to have chosen an unusually well-run slave ship. 'The Captain,' he wrote, 'told us that a slave ship was a very different thing from what it had been reported. He accordingly said a few words to the women, to which they replied with three cheers and a laugh. He went forward on the main deck and spoke the same words to the men, who made the same reply. "Now," he said, "are you not convinced that Mr. Wilberforce has conceived very improperly of slave ships?" [7] He was shown where to sling his hammock and asked if he would mind a few slaves sleeping underneath it. He was warned that 'the smell would be unpleasant for a few days; but when we got into the Trade Winds it would no longer be perceived'. The Captain never swore in Macaulay's presence and stopped his officers from doing so. Discipline was milder than usual, but Macaulay sternly concluded that the slaves' cup 'is full of pure, un-mingled sorrow, the bitterness of which is unalloyed by almost a single ray of hope'. [8]

In England Macaulay was introduced to the More sisters and went to visit them at Cowslip Green. He fell in love with one of their teachers, Selina Mills. But Selina, who lived with the sisters, had made a pact with Patty More who had suffered from an unhappy affair that neither of them would ever marry. Macaulay asked Hannah More for advice and she must have been influenced by concern for Patty when she told him, with most un-Evangelical lack of candour, that Miss Mills was entirely indifferent to him.* Macaulay would have left but for a chance meeting with Selina Mills who was weeping at his indifference. He returned to confront the sisters and a distressing scene took place. Patty More, who had also dis-covered the truth, when asked about Selina showed 'such a repulsing cold-ness which quite surprised me, and made me soon quit the subject. One thing indeed I regret having said, because it was silly. It was an involun-tary expression of surprise that those women who possessed the greatest share of intrinsic worth did not seem to possess that degree of estimation in the eyes of men which they merited. I could have bit my tongue in vexation, but the words were irrevocable.' [9] The Babingtons joined in on Macaulay's side, and the whole affair was probably as near as the Clapham Sect ever got to a nasty squabble.

In the spring of 1796 Macaulay returned to Sierra Leone as Governor, leaving Selina engaged to him but working still for the Mores. He remained there for three years and left an apparently thriving community behind him. There were 1,200 inhabitants, half of whom were supported by their

---

* As Miss Mills's superior and guardian she had other reasons for discouraging the marriage. There had been a scandal at the school run by Selina Mills, involving the abduction of one of her pupils. She was thought to have been negligent and Hannah More may have considered her bound to stay on until the matter was tidied up. She also knew that the Mills parents would not regard Macaulay as a suitable match. But neither of these reasons seems as likely to have provoked her into a lie as a protective sisterly love.

farms. Freetown had become a compact little settlement with 300 houses neatly laid out beside public buildings. There were mechanics, shop-keepers, seamen and fishermen; three wharves had been built to help the colony's growing trade.

But underneath its prosperity the colony was riddled with discontents and once Macaulay's firm hand was removed, its troubles returned. The settlers, particularly the Nova Scotians, had always found the authority of the Governor excessive. In 1800 the Directors of the Company replied by applying for a Charter, which gave legal recognition to their powers. Discontent in the colony reached a climax in the autumn of that year, when the Governor was besieged by rebels. He was rescued only by the providential arrival of 550 new settlers, the warlike and disciplined Maroons* from Jamaica. The rebels were easily routed and the Maroons given land as a reward for their loyalty. Three of the revolt's ringleaders were hanged and thirty-two exiled. After this eruption of violence peace was restored; the Maroons proved a stabilising influence in a society previously dominated by the volatile Nova Scotians and the colony was untroubled by revolt or invasion until its transfer to the Crown in 1807.

The Sierra Leone colony was of the utmost importance to the Abolitionists. It was not only an experiment which, in its immediate results, justified the time and money lavished on it: it was also a weapon of propaganda and a means of accumulating information about the Trade. In the loneliness of the Coast, slavers and Abolitionists met on surprisingly friendly terms and little could happen there that was not reported, sooner or later, to Sierra Leone. When there were debates on the Slave Trade or Slavery, the Abolitionists could point to Sierra Leone as a proof of how slaves could hold positions of responsibility and how Africa could furnish more wholesome products than human flesh. Their opponents, of course, seized on every incident in the colony's troubled history as an example of the futility of such experiments. After Abolition Sierra Leone found a new role as a home for slaves freed from captured ships and as the base for naval squadrons hunting the slavers.

---

* The Maroons were descendants of slaves freed by the Spanish during the Cromwellian invasion of Jamaica. They held out in the mountains of Jamaica and proved impossible to conquer. The British authorities recognised their freedom on condition that they returned runaway slaves. This group of Maroons had surrendered after a revolt in 1795 and been deported, in spite of the Government's promises, to Nova Scotia. Maroons still enjoy some autonomy in the Cockpit Country of Jamaica under the rule of their own Colonel.

CHAPTER X

WAR AND THE BREACH WITH PITT

THE war with France caused the first serious difference between Pitt and Wilberforce. The latter explained his attitude, much later, in a letter to William Hey. 'Our government had been, for some months before the breaking out of the war, negotiating with the principal European powers for the purpose of obtaining a joint representation to France, assuring her that if she would formally engage to keep within her limits, and not molest her neighbours, she should be suffered to settle her own internal government and constitution without interference.

'I never was so earnest with Mr. Pitt on any other occasion, as I was in my entreaties before the war broke out. That he would declare openly in the House of Commons, that he had been, and then was negotiating this treaty. I urged on him that the declaration might possibly produce an immediate effect in France, where it was manifest there prevailed an opinion that we were meditating some interference with their internal affairs. . . . At all events, I hoped that in the first lucid interval, France would see how little reason there was for continuing the war with Great Britain.

. . . 'How far this expectation would have been realised you may estimate by Mr. Fox's language, when Mr. Pitt, at my instance, did make the declaration last winter [1799]. "If," he said, "the right hon. gentleman had made the declaration or delivered it to France as well as to Russia, Austria, and Prussia, I should have nothing more to say or to desire." '[1]

Pitt's urgent message had stopped Wilberforce from speaking out at the beginning of the war, but for some time there was little difference in their views. Although Wilberforce may have thought that Pitt had failed to take every step to prevent the war, he still saw him as a man who wanted peace. In September and October the two friends met often and discussed the war at length. While Wilberforce's diary gives us no details of these conversations, it also shows no signs of discord. Wilberforce continued to support Pitt in the first months of 1794, though 'witnessing with deep solicitude and not without some gloomy anticipation, the progress of the war'.[2] But by the summer he had found a change in Pitt's attitude:

'July 10th,' his diary reads, 'To the House of Commons . . . Pitt much too strong for war.' By the end of the year his resolve was beginning to harden. 'November 19th. Off at ten to Pitt's—heard that Parliament would be prorogued until December 30th, giving me time to make up my mind—strongly at present disposed to peace.' He still hesitated to make his views public. He prayed for divine guidance and sought the advice of his friends. He wrote to Bankes, asking him to come and discuss the matter.

'. . . From what I can collect on this subject Pitt's ideas are as warlike as ever. I allow much of the argument that any peace we could make with a French republic would be insecure, and require an immense peace establishment, etc.: but then I see no grounds to hope for a better issue from prosecuting the war. There appears to me, humanly speaking, no probability of a limited monarchy being established in France by means of it. I am inclined to believe it might be our best plan to declare our willingness to make peace on equitable terms . . . Remember, all the French know of the intentions of Great Britain is from our declarations and from Pitt's, speeches, and these have been uniformly point-blank against any accommodation with the existing system of government in France, or in other words, against a republic. Therefore unless we make some new declaration, they can have no idea but that we mean to fight against the republic *usque ad internecionem*. . . . I am quite sick I own of such a scene of havoc and misery, and unless I am quite clear I shall not dare vote for its continuance.'[3]

He also consulted Grant, Henry Thornton and Muncaster; with their agreement he decided to move an amendment to the King's speech. It was not a comfortable decision. Wilberforce knew that by moving this amendment he would be encouraging an opposition, both in and outside Parliament, which wished to go very much further than he. On the other hand his motion would make the majority of conservative citizens regard him and his cause as tarred with the Jacobin brush. Above all he dreaded the pain he would suffer as a result of opposing Pitt. We have seen how he had to steel himself to persevere with his Slave Trade motion when Pitt threw out against it 'on St. Domingo account'. Pitt had given way then, but he could scarcely be expected to stop the Revolutionary War as a gesture of friendship. Wilberforce was also less sure of his ground than before. At the last moment he was attacked by nagging doubts about his own motives. 'It is a proof to me of my secret ambition that though I foresee how much I shall suffer in my feelings throughout from differing from Pitt, and how indifferent a figure I shall most likely make; yet that motives of ambition still insinuate themselves.'[4]

December 30 was the day of the debate. Wilberforce's diary reads: 'A disturbed night—full of ambition. How small things confound human pride! why not small things God's agents as much as locusts?—worse this morning. Prepared amendment at Bankes's. Moved it in a very incoherent speech; good arguments, but all in heaps for want of preparation; had no plan whatever when I rose.' He needed to tread a narrow line. On the one hand he had to be moderate in statements to avoid encouraging popular unrest, on the other he was 'forced to adopt an amendment stronger than he himself liked'[5] by the bellicose attitude of the Government. The amendment was easily defeated, but Wilberforce's sons claim that there were 'but two events in the public life of Mr. Pitt which were able to disturb his sleep—the mutiny at the Nore, and the first open opposition of Mr. Wilberforce'. Wilberforce was equally affected.

'Wednesday, Feb. 4th. Dined at Lord Camden's—Pepper and Lady Arden, Steele, etc. I felt queer, and all day out of spirits —wrong, but hurt by the idea of Pitt's alienation'. And poignantly, '12th. Party of *the old firm* at the Speaker's; I not there.' The New Year saw a series of divisions on the question in each of which Wilberforce, much to his distress, sided with the Opposition. On every other issue he loathed their politics. His state of mind cannot have been improved by a friendly remark of Fox's: 'You will soon see that you must join us altogether.'[6] His old allies were critical. 'Mr. Wilberforce,' Burke told Pitt, 'is a very respectable gentleman, but he is not the people of England.'[7] Windham called him a 'wicked little fanatical imp',[8] and told Lady Spencer, 'Your friend Mr. Wilberforce will be very happy any morning to hand your Ladyship to the guillotine.'[9] The King cut him at the levée.

The loss of old friends was not balanced by any new alliances. If the Government was offended by his motions for peace, the Opposition saw his support of the supplies (he maintained that, if war must be waged, it should be carried on with vigour) and his defence of the suspension of Habeas Corpus as acts of apostasy. He had never been so unpopular. One of the most distressing aspects of his situation was the disagreement of almost all his close religious friends. Milner, now Dean of Carlisle, wrote to reproach him on January 4, 1795.

'... On Friday night I read over the debates, and I can truly say I never was so much concerned about politics in my life; I was quite low, and so I continue. There was not any one of the speeches that I liked. In the first place, I never conceived that you had intended to take so decided a part in this business as to lead the Opposition against Pitt. There is not the slightest doubt but you will be presented as having gone over to the Opposition, nor will it be easy to do away with the impression; for, 1st, you opposed government in the great question of peace or war. 2nd, you made the motion. 3rd, the opposition approved of it and hailed the accession of their new forces.... I wish I may be mistaken, yet as I understand your Amendment and the consequent division, it will certainly tend to weaken the government and divide the sentiments of the country, to strengthen a factious opposition, and to encourage the French convention.'[10]

Dr. Burgh, a close friend and supporter of Wilberforce's since he became Member for Yorkshire, thought he might have underestimated his own importance. 'The eyes of the world are upon you, and look to your sentiments as a rule for their own. I have seen your authority weigh in minds that before considered every merit of the question to be on the other side. Is not this a reason for pausing and trembling over every step you advance? . . . Faction begins to claim you; you are quoted, and are growing into the subject of a panegyric. It is of infinite importance that you should not appear to the country as a leader of opposition.'[11] William Hey wrote in a similar strain, and although Duncombe, his fellow-member for Yorkshire, had seconded his amendment, the reaction of the county was overwhelmingly hostile.

The reasons Pitt had given for opposing Wilberforce's peace amendment were, firstly, that a reasonable peace was impossible after the French victories in Europe; secondly, that a secure peace could not be achieved with the present French Government; thirdly, that to make peace now would be to betray Britain's allies and thus frustrate any future coalition. But his fourth and main reason for fighting on was that Britain could afford to do so while France could not. Her success so far had been financed by the confiscation of property and issues of paper money, but such expedients could not be repeated. Pitt believed he could calculate the month, almost the day, on which France would collapse into bankruptcy. Wilberforce had no answer to this argument. He was too concerned with the moral issues, too conscious that war was an evil, to become involved with intricate arguments about its expediency. But a mutual friend of Pitt's and Wilberforce's exploded all the Prime Minister's calculations with one devastating question. The Abbé de Lageard had found his way to London after being hunted through thirty departments by the Committee of Public Safety. When he heard Pitt's argument advanced at Wilberforce's dinner table, he asked, 'I should like to know who was Chancellor of the Exchequer to Attila.'[12]

The vulnerability of the French West Indian islands to British sea power was another temptation to Pitt. The policy of financing his continental allies while seizing France's colonies, pressed upon Pitt by Dundas, represented a continuation of his father's strategy of winning Europe in America. After the Seven Years War Britain had seriously considered keeping the island of Guadeloupe rather than Canada. St. Domingue, which seemed to lie at Britain's mercy, was a more tempting prize than all the great territories Chatham had captured from France. British troops were landed in the island, where they found, in yellow fever, an invincible enemy. Wilberforce was utterly opposed to these adventures as part of, and a justification for, a war which he thought unnecessary, and as a policy which, if successful, would make Abolition more difficult to achieve. For, if the British ever took St. Domingue, it would at once outweigh all their other West Indian possessions in importance. The demand for slaves to cultivate its virgin lands would give a new impetus to the Trade and the Abolitionist argument that it benefited rich foreign colonies would vanish when Britain herself possessed the richest colony of them all.

Wilberforce differed with Pitt on another matter during this summer. The Duke of Wellington was later to describe the sons of George III as 'the damnedest millstones about the neck of any Government that can be imagined'. Of all these millstones the heaviest was the Prince of Wales. By the time that he had come of age in 1783 the Prince had already accumulated debts of £29,000. In 1787 Parliament had to contribute another £160,000 towards his debts. By 1795 he was married* and deep in debt again.

There were two proposals in front of the House, to raise the Prince's income either to £100,000 a year or to £125,000. Both sums excluded his income of some £12,000 from the Duchy of Cornwall. It was also suggested that his debts should again be paid. Pitt, while moving for a sum of £100,000, seems to have wished to agree to Fox's figure of £125,000, for Wilberforce noted in his diary on May 11, 'Pitt is furious about our meaning to resist the Prince's additional £25,000.'

Wilberforce spoke strongly in favour of the lower figure.[13] He reminded the House of the vast debts the country had incurred through the war. Should the poor, already distressed, be taxed and impoverished to supply the luxury and prodigality of the Court? His recommendation of 'a certain chaste and dignified simplicity' may be judged, considering the tastes and character of the Prince, as being a counsel of perfection. But Wilberforce's plea struck a chord with other members who were revolted by the Prince's lack of self-control and his long record of broken promises. The lower figure was adopted.

In the summer recess Wilberforce toured his constituency and found that some of his old supporters had been turned against him by his advocacy of peace. 'In one family of my most zealous partisans,' he wrote, 'when I visited Yorkshire even as late as the middle of the summer, the ladies would scarcely speak to me.'[14] It was a temporary coldness and a rare one, but where it existed it was bitter so that it comes as a shock after reading Wilberforce's diary of his tour, most of which could have applied to any year, to find an entry such as: 'August 18th. Called on T—s. They violently incensed by my political conduct. G. would not come down—poor woman, how foolish! The coldness of the others seemed to give way

---

* His marriage to Mrs. Fitzherbert in 1789 was not legal under the Royal Marriage Act.

by my being unaffected, and apparently undiscerning.' His charm and persuasiveness could usually heal such rifts and when he returned to London he found the cause for them disappearing.

Wilberforce had not looked forward to the next parliamentary session with any relish. In October he had written to the Speaker, 'Oh, this vile meeting of parliament! when we shall have to discuss again about governments capable of maintaining the relations of peace and amity. Poor fellow —Pitt I mean—I can feel for him from my heart, particularly on a Sunday.'[15]

He was pleasantly surprised to find a letter from Pitt hinting at a change in attitude. 'It is hardly possible to form any precise opinion of what is to be done till we see the immediate issue of the crisis just now depending, but I cannot help thinking that it will shortly lead to a state of things in which I hope our opinions cannot materially differ. I need not say how much personal comfort it will give me if my expectation in this respect is realized.'[16]

The breach was soon healed. 'Monday October 26th. Kept myself open for Pitt. 27th. Saw Pitt at breakfast this morning, and had a most satisfactory conversation with him. Gave dinner to Duncombe, Samuel and Henry Thornton, and Muncaster—all pleased with my report. 29th. Meant to go to Battersea Rise, but Pitt wished to see me on West Indian subject (Address)—another confidential and satisfactory conversation with him. . . . Walked down to Westminster Hall and then to the House. Pitt spoke capitally, and as distinct as possible on the main point. Duncombe, and Muncaster, and Sir Richard Hill appeared to me to be won by his frank avowal.'[17]

Pitt's change in attitude was due to a number of reasons. The allies whom he had been so reluctant to betray had not hesitated to betray him. Prussia had made her own peace and Holland was now an enemy, while Austria, his only remaining ally, was as anxious for peace as he. France showed no signs of collapsing into bankruptcy. The argument which Pitt had advanced, and Wilberforce acknowledged, that no peace with the French régime could be secure, was beginning to look thin. The moderate government of the Directoire was now in control of France, the Jacobins dead or in exile. A disastrous harvest in England, followed inevitably by riots and discontent, provided another reason for seeking peace.

*

In 1794 the country suffered from the first of a series of bad harvests, followed by one of the hardest winters ever known. The harvest of 1795 was again disastrous and these strains were imposed on a society already under the pressure of social change and the burden of a war. Scarcity gave a new impetus to the discontents caused by enclosures and inadequate poor relief systems in the country and by Jacobin agitation in the towns.

The radical clubs in London had first become prominent in 1793 when 200,000 copies of Paine's *Rights of Man* were sold. The London Corresponding Society was the largest and most influential of these bodies. Its agitation in 1794 had provoked the Government into suspending the Habeas Corpus Act and retaliating with a series of ill-calculated and unsuccessful prosecutions of its leaders. This enemy within, demanding peace and a People's Convention, distributing seditious literature and inspiring the Parliamentary Opposition to new extremes of irresponsibility, would have been intolerable to any wartime government.

Matters reached a climax in October 1795, when the London Corresponding Society held a meeting, attended by 150,000, at which they virtually called for a civil war. Two days later the King was jeered and stoned on his way to Parliament and a window of his coach was broken by a pellet from an air gun. 'My Lords,' he announced as he entered the House, 'I have been shot at.' On his way back to the Palace the guards had difficulty in keeping the mob away from his coach. But the reaction was not slow in coming.

London was still an unpoliced city, vulnerable to riots, which could only be controlled by calling out the army. Many Londoners could remember the great Gordon Riots of 1780, when Parliament and the Bank of England had been threatened and the city had narrowly escaped being burnt to the ground. This memory explains much of the terror aroused by threats of rioting. But Gordon was a maniac and his followers inspired only by religious hatred. If they could bring London close to ruin, what could be expected of the Corresponding Society, with the example of Paris behind it and two terrible harvests to spread discontent? The night after his rough reception by the mob the King went to the opera where he was received with wild enthusiasm, the National Anthem being played six times. It was the first demonstration of affection for any Hanoverian monarch and it was inspired by fear. Burke, plunged into despair by his terror of revolution, daily expected a guillotine to be erected on Tower Hill. Pitt told Wilberforce, 'My head would be off in six months were I to resign', and Wilberforce noted, 'I see he expects a civil broil.'[18]

The horror aroused by the mobbing of the King gave the Government a chance to introduce legislation. Bills were drawn up against Treasonable Practices and Seditious Meetings. Political meetings of more than fifty people must now be reported to the magistrates in advance and any seditious speeches at them became grounds for immediate arrest. The Commons debated these measures for the first time on November 10. Wilberforce supported Pitt with a speech that was all the more effective because of the obvious distaste with which he approached the Bills. He looked on them, he said, as a temporary sacrifice, which would pass on our liberties to our children unimpaired.[19]

He turned to the radical clubs and societies and to the claim that they somehow embodied a part of the liberties of the nation. These clubs, he argued, could do no good and might do great harm. And if their death would mean the extinction of national liberties then where were these liberties before the clubs were born? It was one of the glories of the British Constitution that it possessed, in the House of Commons, a popular assembly where grievances might be discussed and champions found for the injured and oppressed. The system of petitioning, unaffected by the Bills, was designed to allow the people of the country to present their grievances to Parliament and thus to prevent their discontents from being bottled up. He could solemnly declare that in voting for this measure he would invigorate the Constitution.

The Bills were passed against a background of popular unrest, and Wilberforce's journal reflects the uncertainties of the time. 'How vain now appears all successful ambition! Poor Pitt! I too am much an object of popular odium. Riot is expected from the Westminster meeting. The people I hear are much exasperated against me. . . . How fleeting is popular favour! I greatly fear some civil war or embroilment; with my weak health and bodily infirmities, my heart shrinks from its difficulties and dangers.'[20]

In Yorkshire, agitation against the Bills was led by Wilberforce's old friend Wyvill. The sheriff, when asked to convene a public meeting, refused to do so on the grounds that it 'would only tend to raise riot and discontent'. The opponents of the Bills then summoned a meeting in the Castle Yard at York, the scene of Wilberforce's first triumph in Yorkshire politics. They called this meeting at short notice so as to surprise the friends of the Government. Wilberforce received the news on a Sunday morning on his way to church. He sat through a 'sad sermon' then hurried over to Pitt's. Pitt urged him to attend the meeting and lent him his own carriage for the journey. One of their friends commented 'if they find out whose carriage you have got, you will run the risk of being murdered'. The meeting was to be held that Tuesday, and for one of the few times in his life, Wilberforce had to sacrifice his Sunday to political necessity. Pitt's coach, with four horses and two outriders, sped up the North Road, reaching Ferrybridge on the first night and Doncaster on the second.

On Monday, November 30 an immense number of freeholders flocked into York. An observer from Leeds,[21] the Reverend Miles Atkinson, wrote, 'There went through Hatton Turnpike above three thousand horsemen.' The Government party suggested that the meeting should take the form of a debate in the Castle Yard or any other convenient place. Their opponents proposed that an equal number of each side should be admitted to a debate in the Guildhall. They rejected each other's suggestions. The next morning the two meetings clashed and the Government party, to their surprise and delight, found themselves in a three to one majority. They invaded their opponents' meeting, moved and carried an adjournment to the Castle Yard amidst scenes of angry disorder. The opposition refused to move and the Government party, though triumphant, were leaderless and uncertain as to what to do next. At this moment a great roar was heard outside the Guildhall as Wilberforce's muddy carriage turned the corner. Thirty-two years later he took the same road with his sons and told them, 'What a row did I make when I turned this corner in 1795; it seemed as if the whole place must come down together.' The city resounded with shouts at his arrival and 'hats filled the air'. Wilberforce made his way to the hustings and tried to persuade Wyvill to move with him to the Castle Yard. The latter, certain of being out-voted and out-argued, prudently refused.

Even without the opposition the meeting in the Castle Yard was described by the York paper as 'perhaps the largest assemblage of gentlemen and freeholders which ever met in Yorkshire'. 'Here,' Atkinson wrote, 'we had three good speeches from Colonel Creyke, Mr. Spencer Stanhope and Mr. Wilberforce. The last I think, and so I believe think all that heard him, was never exceeded. A most incomparable speech indeed. All went on quietly, till that mad fellow Colonel Thornton stood up in his regimentals and would speak in favour of the Jacobins.' Thornton declared that many soldiers were eager to join the revolutionaries as soon as they rose. To show himself among their number he proceeded to remove his regimentals and threw them to the mob who chaired him, undignified but triumphant, back to the opposition meeting at the Guildhall. During this exhibition a petition was carried against seditious meetings and in favour of King and Constitution.

Wilberforce's speech remained in the memory of one of his audience for many years. In 1810 Colonel Cockell wrote to him about the meeting in Castle Yard: 'I never felt the power of eloquence until that day. You made my blood tingle with delight. The contrast of your address, and the mellow tone of your voice, of which not one single word was lost to the hearers, with the bellowing, screaming attempts at speaking in some others was most wonderful. You breathed energy and vigour into the desponding souls of timid loyalists, and sent us home with joy and delight.'[22]

He was himself less satisfied. 'I should have said much more," he wrote to William Hey on December 7, 'if we had got into debate, for I really had not natural elasticity enough to expand, without opponents, to such a size as I should have swelled to if I had been as large as I was prepared to be.' But his friends and opponents both attributed the success of the Government party in Yorkshire to his speech. In this they surely exaggerated, for the Government party was in a three to one majority before his arrival. What he did achieve was to rescue this majority from a confused situation in which it did not know how to use its own strength, and to turn what might have been a nominal victory into a triumph. More than 7,000 signatures appeared on Wilberforce's loyal petition, less than 300 on his opponents'. Other counties followed Yorkshire's lead, 'proving,' Wilberforce maintained, 'the justice of what Fox would often say, "Yorkshire and Middlesex between them make all England".'

The Bills were effective; membership of the radical clubs fell sharply, and this in itself gave some substance to the Opposition's arguments. Dedicated revolutionaries would have not been deterred so easily.* But of all the severities imposed by Pitt's Government in the name of national security, the Seditious Meetings and Treasonable Practices Acts are the easiest to defend. No nation occupied with a war that threatens its survival can tolerate an enemy within. The restrictions left the Press free, the Parliamentary Opposition untouched and the right of petition unimpaired. The Government had good grounds for thinking them necessary. The trouble with the Acts was that they could be used for purposes which their authors had never envisaged, to check, not revolutionary activity, but the airing of reasonable complaints. In the turmoil and bitterness of the French Wars the distinction was not always easy to draw.

*

1796 was the year in which the Slave Trade should have ceased, had the Commons' motion for gradual Abolition been endorsed by the Lords, but circumstances could scarcely have been less favourable for its renewal. In the winter of 1795 the French had sent agitators to the British West Indies to spread rebellion. These agents had some success which, with the unabated terror of Jacobinism, made prospects for Abolition bleak. On the other hand Wilberforce, by his vigorous support of Pitt's Bills, had cleared himself of any suspicion of Jacobin sympathies and his policy on the war no longer differed from that of the Government. Dr. Burgh made these points in a letter on December 12, 1795.

'They who make sale of their brethren will hardly stick at Falsehood; and accordingly diligence has been used to associate Jacobinism, equality, and the abolition of a trade that preserved the gradations of society. At this time you stand in a situation peculiarly favourable to the refutation of all this unchristian stuff. Last year you had not half the advantages you now possess. To what nonsense were my ears then a frequent witness. Your desire to terminate the war was a result, forsooth, of dissenting principles, principles hostile to all good government, and your zeal to abolish the Slave Trade was of course included in the same silly charge.'[23]

In September 1795 the Abolitionists gained a powerful recruit with the

* By 1798 the London Corresponding Society was sufficiently disillusioned with the revolutionary cause to debate a motion that it should raise a loyal Corps to resist invasion by the French (Watson, p. 361).

return of James Stephen from the West Indies. He brought with him three
turtles and wrote to Wilberforce: 'The best is designed for you; for I know
nobody more worthy of the good things of the West Indies, nor one who,
as matters stand, has a worse chance of often receiving them.'* Stephen
did not join the inner circle of Wilberforce's friends until his wife died in
1796 leaving him desolate and pathetic. His hatred of slavery, and a love
for her that had lasted since he was fourteen, were the two great emotions
which dominated his life. Wilberforce comforted him in his misery and
slowly coaxed him out into the world. During this time they became close
friends and in 1800 Stephen joined Wilberforce's family by marrying his
widowed sister Sarah. Underneath the occasional sharpness of Stephen's
tongue their relationship was one of deep tenderness. 'You are and ever
have been kind to me, beyond a brother's kindness,'[25] Wilberforce wrote
to him much later. Kindness remained at the root of their friendship.
Stephen worried over Wilberforce's health almost as much as Barbara, his
own wife, while Wilberforce, if he saw Stephen looking unhappy, would
drag himself away from a mountain of correspondence to write, and ask
why.

Stephen was a perfect foil for Wilberforce. His obsessive loathing of the
Slave Trade led him to regard all other issues as subordinate to its abolition and he would reprove Wilberforce, almost savagely, when he allowed
himself to be diverted. Wilberforce had been a politician and a partisan of
Pitt's before he became an Abolitionist. He relied on parliamentary arguments and lobbying to gain his ends because these were the weapons he
understood. Stephen disliked Pitt and distrusted his attitude toward
Abolition. He was prepared to use any means of putting pressure on the
Government.

On December 15, 1795, Wilberforce gave notice that he would again
move the Abolition of the Trade in the next session. He reminded the
House that it had once decided that the Trade should end on January 1,
1796. Meanwhile the Christmas recess provided a welcome rest after the
exhaustion caused by the passing of the Bills. 'The last fortnight or three
weeks,' he complains in his diary,[26] 'have been severe trials to a man
weakly like me; and I have lost ground in health which I must recover.'

He made his motion on February 18 in a speech which he thought 'cold
and indifferent', but the debate aroused him to reply 'warmly and well'.
Jenkinson's speech with its proposal that the matter should be postponed
until the end of the year was particularly provocative. 'There is something

* Wilberforce sent the turtles to the Bishop of Durham who gave a banquet for
fifty-five people at which they were consumed. All his guests, he wrote to Wilberforce,
were supporters of Abolition, 'yet I cannot flatter you with the same unanimity were
you to extend your benevolent zeal to the emancipation of the turtles'. Wilberforce considered this joke to be in the worst of taste and wrote on the letter, 'Very facetious'.[24]

not a little provoking,' he answered, 'in the dry, calm way in which gentlemen are apt to speak of the sufferings of others. The question suspended! Is the desolation of wretched Africa suspended? Are all the complicated miseries of this atrocious trade—is the work of death suspended? No sir, I will not delay this motion, and I will call upon the House not to insult the forbearance of Heaven by delaying this tardy act of justice.'[27]

He was roused to a fury by West Indian claims that their slaves were well fed, clothed and lodged and by the inference that this was all they could require. 'What! Are these the only claims of a rational being? Are the feelings of the heart nothing? Where are social intercourse and family endearment? Where the consciousness of independence, the prospect often realised, of affluence and honour? Where are willing services and grateful returns? Where, above all, the light of religious truth, and the hope full of immortality? So far from thanking the honourable gentleman for the feeding, clothing, and lodging of which he boasts, I protest against the way in which he has mentioned them, as degrading men to the level of the brutes, and insulting all the qualities of our common nature.'[28]

Wilberforce was surprised and delighted when a motion to adjourn the debate was defeated by 26 votes. On March 3 an opponent moved the second reading of his Bill in the hope of catching the Abolitionists unprepared. Wilberforce hurried round to the House from his supper at Palace Yard and spoke to fill in time until enough of his supporters arrived to carry the motion, but on the third reading he was less successful. *The Two Hunchbacks*, a new comic opera with music by Portogallo, was being performed in London. This production seemed to have a particular appeal to Abolitionists, and enough of them attended it instead of the House, to allow the Bill to be lost by 74 votes to 70. Another ten or twelve Abolitionists were in the country. The distaste with which Wilberforce regarded all theatrical performances must have increased the pain of this desertion. 'I am permanently hurt,' he declared, 'about the Slave Trade.'

*

He had been taking two grains of opium daily throughout the winter, double his normal dose. In April he contracted a severe fever accompanied by excruciating intestinal troubles. He kept a private journal[29] at this time, mainly of his medical symptoms. 'After excellent night on Tuesday 12th —large loose stool—blood and mucus—I never suffered so much in that way. I felt as if my bowels would force their way through the anus. Not wine—opium—chalk. About one quarter of a pint of starch with thirty drops of laudanum have been very useful.' During this agonising illness he took up to four grains of opium daily and three grains for some time afterwards. On May 6, 'I feared a relapse and took in the twenty-four hours five grains of opium—today four grains—I have caught cold.'[30]

It says much for Wilberforce's courage that throughout this illness he kept working as best he could. 'I have lately felt and now feel a sort of terror on re-entering the world,' he wrote in his journal on April 17, but he had never really left it. He was most concerned over a Bill to relieve Quakers of the obligation of paying tithes and to allow them to make affirmations in criminal courts. This Bill was passed on May 10.

He could not take the same pleasure from the state of Abolition. After the main motion had been lost in March an attempt was made to relieve the Trade of some of its worst features. This Slave Carrying Bill was supported by members who had consistently opposed any form of Abolition. There was no real opposition, but there was, equally, no interest. The Bill was presented three times and every time the House was 'counted out'. It seems extraordinary that 70 members should have voted for Abolition in March when, even if the opera-goers had forsaken *The Two Hunchbacks*, the motion would have been lost in the Lords, while only 36 attended the Slave Carrying debate in May, which could and should have prevented great suffering.

CHAPTER XI

RELIGIOUS LIFE

WILBERFORCE would often take a religious friend on holiday with him; in 1793 it had been Venn's turn. Wilberforce reported to Hannah More:

My dear Madam,
    After having been detained day after day for above a fortnight in or near London, I at length emerged with Mr. Venn on Tuesday last, and arrived here yesterday afternoon. The heat is such as to render the Bath waters a potation as little suited to health as pleasure, and unless the weather changes, we must withdraw from this roasting without stewing within whilst we have strength to get away, and seek a more genial climate amongst the mountains of Wales. Meanwhile we cannot quit these parts without being gratified, and I hope profited, by a survey of your operations; and therefore we propose, if it be convenient, to be with you to-morrow evening. Both Mr. Venn and I prefer being witnesses of your Sunday lecture before your week-day conventicling. You must not engage a pulpit for him, as all his sermons are in his trunk and he does not extemporize before strangers; but if his trunk arrives in time, he will put one or two sermons in his pocket, and perhaps you could get a pulpit on short notice for the Rector of Clapham, M.A. though not for one of Miss Patty's lank-haired favourites. I am sure you will thank me for making you acquainted with so good and so agreeable a man.[1]

After they joined the More sisters, Wilberforce wrote in his diary: 'Off betimes for "the round" with Venn and two Miss Mores. He preached at Axbridge and Cheddar—wonderful scenes—God is with them. Walked in evening amongst Cheddar rocks with Venn and home late.' Back in Bath he continued: 'I have had Venn with me near a fortnight; he is heavenly-minded, and bent on his Master's work, affectionate to all around him, and above all to Christ's people, as such how low are my attainments! Oh let me labour with redoubled diligence to enter in at the strait gate. An indolent, soothing religion will never support the soul in the hour of death. Then nothing will buoy us up but the testimony of our conscience that we have fought the good fight. . . . '[2]

There was certainly nothing indolent or soothing about Wilberforce's religion. It set him standards that he could never attain and left him self-critical at every stage of his progress. He despised the doctrine which held regular attendance at church and decent behaviour outside it to be enough to satisfy the demands of religion. This easy-going approach posed a more insidious danger than the theory, popular in the eighteenth century, that 'honour' could provide a substitute for religion. No one who believed in God could hold the latter view, but he might be seduced by the former into becoming a 'nominal Christian'. Wilberforce had long toyed with the idea of writing a book on Christianity to refute these dangerous heresies. On December 6, 1789 he had drawn up a list of the arguments in favour of and against such a book. The reasons for publication were obvious, but he thought them outweighed by the damage a religious book could do to the power for good he possessed through his position.

'A. The dread of an over-righteous man would deter people from co-operating with me for national reform.

'B. My influence with P. and other great men, even G. himself, would be lessened: few if any livings obtained: few great men would attend to my recommendations in all the ways wherein I now have influence: few private men, etc. I should be looked on as morose and uncharitable. Bishops would fear me.

'C. To publish in defence of religion not my particular province.

'D. Were I to express all I think I should be deemed an enthusiast, and were I to withhold I might mislead.

'E. My connexion with P. and my parliamentary situation put me into the capacity of doing much good in the private walks: I may carry bills of reform, I may get a bishop.'[3]

None of these objections could apply for long, for Wilberforce's was not the kind of religion that could be hidden or played down to accommodate the worldly. His behaviour in Yorkshire, his slow withdrawal from society, his cautious proselytising, his support of religious and humanitarian measures, in all these ways his life spelt out the change in his views long before the publication of his book. His influence with Pitt had been un-affected; it is possible that in 1789 some members might have been turned against Abolition by its sponsor's religious views, but by 1793 these views were known to all the Commons and Abolition itself had become a lost cause. Perhaps because of the unfortunate result of his first bout of enthusi-asm Wilberforce always anticipated a more hostile attitude to his religious opinions than was probable. But by 1793 any such hostility was spent and the publication of a religious book could only help his causes by creating a solid body of support in the country.

Wilberforce may not have gone as far as this in his own mind when, on August 3, 1793, he recorded in his diary, 'I laid the first timbers of my tract.' But a change in his attitude to society at this time shows that he was now less frightened of his religion offending others and that it was mature enough for him to risk exposing himself to worldly scenes. He had at first avoided society because he enjoyed its pleasures too much and was frigh-tened of being corrupted by them. He now made deliberate forays into it in search of converts; later in August he wrote to Hannah More about his experiences.[4]

' . . . Though with Lord Y. I had some little serious [i.e. religious] conversation (God grant that the seed may remain and spring up hereafter), I had no opportunity of any such intercourse with the others; and I fear I seemed to them a gay, thoughtless being. My judgement prescribed cheerfulness, but perhaps my temper reduced me into volatility. How difficult it is to be merry and wise! yet I would hope that even by this gaiety, though somewhat excessive, a favourable entrance may have been provided for religious conversation, if any future opportunities of explanation occur, as I think they will. You see how honestly I open myself to you. But this is the result neither of vanity nor emptiness, but because I really wish you would perform that best office of friendship, advising me upon the subject in question, and telling me whether I ought or ought not to endeavour to adopt a more staid or serious demeanour . . . '

He had his eye on bigger game than Lord Y. 'Doubtful whether or not I ought to go to Windsor tomorrow to take the chance of getting into conversation with some of the royal family. . . . Yet I distrust myself: I fear my eye is not simple, nor supremely set on God's glory in this scheme. Perhaps I should do better to attend to my proper business, and this is Satan's artifice to draw me off. Yet on the other hand, if any good is done it is great. I will pray to God to direct me—Thought over the Windsor scheme and resolved against it.'[5]

At the beginning of 1794 Wilberforce started a new method of keeping a check on himself. From January 1794 to May 1800 he wrote at the top of each page of his diary headings of the various faults to which he considered himself to be prone—volatility, wandering in prayer, christianity forgetting, Holy Spirit forgetting, regulation of company and Conversation, friends' spiritual good, truth erring, humility, self-denial, etc., etc.[6] It was a formidable list. He would write under each heading his performance in this particular. He was very critical; his entries vary from 'indifferent, little in mind, middling, baddish, very bad, sadly neglected, forgot sadly' to an occasional 'better, rather better' or 'better I hope'.[7]

In the summer of 1794 he continued his social tactics. 'Spent the evening at Mrs. A's . . . declined playing cards (I had played there before), but not austerely.' 'Dined at Hampstead to meet Jay,* his son, etc.—quite Americans, sensible. . . . I fear there is little spirit of religion in America; something of French, tinctured with more than English simplicity of manners; very pleasing, well-informed men. . . . '

In the summer recess he resumed work on his book. On July 17 his diary reads, 'After dinner I set off for Betchworth, and reaching it at

* The American Ambassador.

night, began next morning thinking in earnest about my tract. Here for
the first time I have got a little quiet, and have resumed my work diligently; yet I doubt whether I can do anything worth publishing. Henry
Thornton, Venn and Farish came to me on different days for discussion
about it. I cannot receive their ideas, and get no benefit from them. I
began to think that help must come either from thinking over a subject
together, or criticizing one's productions when done.'

He moved on to Teston, but although conditions were ideal, his book
progressed slowly. 'I stare at my subject instead of closing with it,' he complained. He read Tom Paine's *Age of Reason* and penned the outraged
comment in his diary, 'God preserve us from such poison.' But even this
did not seem to inspire him to a counterblast. He described his intention,
in a letter to Hey, of writing 'a sort of protest against the religion of the
higher, and, indeed, of the middling orders'.

The rift with Pitt and his tour of Yorkshire kept him from work on his
book in the recess of 1795. His religious self-reproaches continue, though
in a more philosophical tone. He is no longer dashing down his despair on
to paper, but conducting a self-analysis. Society was still a problem. 'July
15th [1795]. The result of examination shows me that though my deliberate plans are formed in the fear of God, and with reference to His will,
yet that when I go into company (on which I resolve as pleasing to God) I
am apt to forget Him; my seriousness flies away; the temptations of the
moment to vanity and volatility get the better of me. If I have any misgivings at the time they are a sullen, low grumbling of conscience, which
is disregarded. Although, therefore, I am not defective in external duties
to God, or grossly towards my fellow-creatures, but rather the contrary,
yet I seem to want a larger measure, 1st, of that true faith that realizes
unseen things, and produces seriousness; and, 2nd, of that vigour of the
religious affections, which by making communion with God and Christ
through the Spirit more fervent and habitual, might render me apt and
alert to spiritual things. My finding no more distinct pleasure in religious
offices (vide David's Psalms every where) argue a want of The Holy
Spirit.'[8]

The last sentence is contradicted by an entry in his journal for the same
period. 'My eyes are very indifferent—tears always make them so, and this
obliges me to check myself in my religious offices.' As far as society is concerned, Wilberforce now felt that no truly religious man could derive real
pleasure from it, and that his enjoyment of social functions was a sign of
his own shallowness. After a Royal Academy dinner on May 2 he entered
in his diary: 'Sat near Lord Spencer, Windham, etc.—too worldly-minded
—catches and glees—they importunate for Rule Britannia—I doubt if I
had much business at such a place. What a painted shadow! It is not right
for me entirely to abstract myself from the world; yet what a gay dream

was this! Oh God, do thou for Christ's sake fill my soul with the love of Thee, and all other things will grow insipid.'[9] Insipid: this was the last word that could be used to describe Wilberforce's attitude to society; so long as it was used as a yardstick he would never be satisfied with the state of his soul.

*

On May 20, 1796 he set out again to Yorkshire for the elections, in which he wished to secure his own return for the County and that of two members favourable to Pitt in his old constituency, Hull. Samuel Thornton, a brother of Henry and a member of the Clapham Sect, seemed sure of election and the other Pittite candidate, Stanhope, likely. But the early optimism of Wilberforce's diary gives way to 'great discontent now against Sam Thornton'. The Opposition candidate, Sir Charles Turner, headed the poll and Thornton just beat Stanhope into second place.

Duncombe found himself in an uncomfortable position in the County election. He had spoken against the Bills which had been presented by his party and endorsed by his constituents. He was old and unwilling to enter a contest for his seat; after an unpromising canvass he withdrew. Three candidates came in to replace him, Charles Duncombe, his nephew, Henry Lascelles, the son of the 'carrion crow' plucked by the Associators in 1780, and Walter Fawkes. All three agreed to give their second votes to Wilberforce. Charles Duncombe soon dropped out of the contest leaving Lascelles, a Pittite, and Fawkes, a Whig, to dispute the second seat. Fawkes seemed to have the better of the preliminaries and Wilberforce came under pressure from his supporters to unite with Lascelles and thus ensure his return. This put him in an awkward situation. Lascelles was a firm Pittite and the roots of his strength in the County were much the same as Wilberforce's. On the other hand his immense fortune came from plantations in the West Indies. By joining with him Wilberforce would be donating another vote to the West Indian lobby, and at the same time, dealing his own reputation a severe blow. In the 1807 election an Opposition squib was to take up the rumour of an alliance between Wilberforce and Lascelles.

> What! Shall the friend of human kind,
>   The Advocate of Freedom,
> *Join* with the M A N, *whose fetters bind,*
>   *Whose guilty lashes bleed 'em!*[10]

Wilberforce foresaw this danger. 'Evening most distressing,' he wrote in his diary on May 30, 'all the West Riding men wishing me to join Lascelles. . . . Much distressed to resist the importunity of my friends to join. Lloyd declared that a motion about to be made that they should leave me. I more cool, thank God, than usual. What a mercy I did not yield! My character would have had a lasting blot.' Fawkes's canvass was promising but not decisive and he did not feel it strong enough to enter the contest against a much richer man.[11] Wilberforce, although his seat was safe, was spared the expense of a contested election by one of Fawkes's committee who mislaid a letter promising the support of the Dukes of Norfolk and Devonshire and Lord Fitzwilliam. With such impeccable backing Fawkes would surely have contested the seat.

CHAPTER XII

'PRACTICAL VIEW'

THE summer and autumn of 1796 were busy months for Wilberforce and work on his book was restricted to a few spare moments. Now that peace with France seemed possible he was anxious to have included in the treaty a convention against the Slave Trade. He spent much of his time trying to persuade Pitt and Dundas to adopt this clause. He was active in raising contributions for distressed émigrés and he lobbied patrons and corporations to build more churches. He had been shocked by the state of some London hospitals and was now concerned with their reform. He threw himself, with enthusiasm, into the affairs of Jeremy Bentham.

The great philosopher had designed a 'panopticon' or model prison which had involved him in heavy losses. But Dundas, when Home Secretary, had been pleased with the plan and had obtained Pitt's permission to continue the experiment. Bentham then entered into contracts for building the panopticon, only to find Lord Spencer complaining loudly and successfully of its proximity to his estate. Wilberforce did his best to find him another site. 'Never was any one worse used than Bentham,' he complained, 'I have seen the tears run down the cheeks of that strongminded man through vexation at the pressing importunity of creditors and the insolence of official underlings, when day after day he was begging at the Treasury for what was indeed a mere matter of right. How indignant did I often feel, when I saw him thus treated by men infinitely his inferiors! I could have extinguished them. He was quite soured by it, and I have no doubt that many of his harsh opinions afterwards were the fruit of this ill-treatment.'[1]

Bentham was an amusing, if expansive, correspondent. When in difficulties with the Government over his panopticon he finished a letter to Wilberforce with the words:

The next time you happen on Mr. Attorney General in the House or elsewhere, be pleased to take a spike, the longer and sharper the better, and apply it to the seat of honour by way of memento that the Penitentiary Contract Bill has, for I know not what length of time, been sticking in his hands, and you will much oblige,

your humble servant to command,
Jeremy Bentham.

N.B. A corking pin was yesterday applied by Mr. Abbot.[2]

Bentham in turn took up Abolition, 'if to be an anti-slavist is to be a Saint, Saintship for me'.

On October 6 Parliament met again and Wilberforce became embroiled in a new controversy. Malmesbury had gone to Paris to negotiate peace, a journey which, according to a disgusted Burke, he had made 'the whole way on his knees'. While suing for peace the Government tried also to prepare for invasion by introducing legislation to strengthen the militia. The Opposition's attacks on these bills struck Wilberforce as so factious that he allowed himself one of his rare sharp retorts. 'I will not charge them with desiring an invasion,' he said in Parliament on November 2, 'but I cannot help thinking that they will rejoice to see just so much mischief befall their country as would bring themselves into office'.[3] Although he supported the Government on this issue he took exception to one detail. 'Dundas,' his diary reads, 'is now clear that it would shock the general morals of Scotland, to exercise their volunteers on a Sunday; but I can scarce persuade Pitt, that in England it would even in serious people, excite any disgust.' He was to return to this question at singularly inconvenient moments. It is a measure of Pitt's friendship and detachment that he was able, when the Grand Army was massed for invasion at Boulogne, to listen with patience to Wilberforce's pleas that the militia should not be permitted to drill on Sundays.

At the end of the session Wilberforce noted: 'The recess for six weeks is commencing. I once meant to try to finish my tract, but I now rather think that, the time being too little for so very serious a work, I shall devote it to preparation for the House of Commons—improvement in speaking, which sadly neglected, and in knowledge.' He had never forgiven himself for his idleness at Cambridge, which had prevented him from acquiring the thorough grounding in the Classics that was then so important a part of the orator's armoury. While education still rested on the two pillars of Classics and Mathematics great speakers like Pitt or Fox could always produce an apposite quotation from the Classics to point their argument. Wilberforce, though a fair classical scholar, never reached this stage, but he would set himself reading courses to improve his knowledge. The Classics, history, philosophy, poetry, economics, politics and theology all had their place in these courses. For relaxation he would allow himself a ration of novels, memoirs and lighter works. All this was a labour of love for Wilberforce, who devoured books with immense enthusiasm, finding the same inspiration and delight in Herschel's *Astronomy*, Owen on *Spiritual Mindedness* and Walter Scott's *Lady of the Lake*.

But in the first days of 1797 this pleasant programme was upset by illness. On January 2, 'I had a severe seizure of complaint in bowels, I used the usual remedies. I thank God, they succeeded. . . . I took in the twenty-four hours six grains of opium.'⁴ By the 8th he was well enough to endure the journey down to Bath where his improvement was rapid. 'I have now been drinking the Bath waters three days,' he wrote in his private journal, 'and God be praised, they seem to agree with me much— restoring my appetite which was quite extinguished, whether from opium or illness. I have been reducing my opium and am now at about four grains daily. My eyes uniformly better than formerly.'⁵

He did some work on his book at Bath in spite of bad health and the claims of society. 'Calls, of which I make about sixty, and receive as many —water drinking—dinings out with people, who expect me to stay— many letters to write;—all this leaves me, through hurrying much and I hope not idling, very little time.'⁶ But when he returned to London, on February 14, it was ready for the printer.

Religious works were little in demand and his publisher received him cautiously: 'You mean to put your name to the work? Then I think we may venture upon 500 copies.'⁷ Wilberforce's book was published on April 12 under the formidable title of *A Practical View of the Prevailing Religious System of Professed Christians in The Higher and Middle Classes in this country contrasted with Real Christianity*. After a few days *Practical View* had sold out and within six months it had been through five editions and 7,500 copies. Its success continued; by 1826 fifteen editions had been printed in England and twenty-five in America; it had been translated into French, Italian, Spanish, Dutch and German. Such a reception from the public was pleasant enough, but Wilberforce must have found the response of his friends even more gratifying.

One of the disadvantages of friendship with an author is that one has, from time to time, to find something pleasant to say about his books. Wilberforce's friends, with their scrupulous Evangelical regard for the truth, suffered from no such inhibitions, especially when the book was on a religious subject. Praise from them was a genuine tribute and they were unanimous in their praise of *Practical View*. Muncaster wrote: 'As a friend I thank you for it; as a man I doubly thank you; but as a member of the Christian world, I render you all gratitude and acknowledgement. I thought I knew you well, but I know you better now, my dearest excellent Wilber.'⁸*

Newton wrote to Grant: 'What a phenomenom has Mr. Wilberforce sent abroad! *Such* a book, by *such* a man, and at *such* a time! A book which must and will be read by persons in the higher circles, who are quite in-accessible to us little folk, who will neither hear what we can say, nor read what we may write.'⁹ The old African blasphemer knew how to write to authors. 'I have *devoured* it,' he told Wilberforce, 'I think you know by this time, that I do not much deal in Ceremonials and compliments—but

* Only Muncaster and Dr. Burgh seem to have used this nickname.

I should stifle the feeling of my heart were I wholly to suppress mentioning the satisfaction, the pleasure, the joy, your publication has given me.'[10]

Bishops, archbishops, aristocrats and Royalty added their praises, the Duchess of Gloucester called it 'your inimitable Book',[11] but Wilberforce may have been more pleased by a verbal tribute. Edmund Burke was dying; the message was passed through his doctor that he 'spent much of the last two days of his life reading Wilberforce's book, and said that he derived much comfort from it, and that if he lived he should thank Wilberforce for having sent such a book into the world. So says Mrs. Crewe, who was with Burke at the time'.[12]

The most welcome praise of all came from strangers. A competent preacher may take the praise of the converted for granted, but to bring religion home to the worldly is a higher achievement. An anonymous correspondent 'had purchased a small freehold in Yorkshire, that by his vote he might offer him a small tribute of respect'.[13] A libertine, once an admirer of Hume, Voltaire and Gibbon, wrote to say that he had been reformed by reading *Practical View*.[14]

It is often hard to understand the appeal of the best-sellers of long ago, but that of *Practical View* is obvious. The book is rambling, diffuse and untidily finished, as one would expect from a work written in the spare moments of a busy life. The passage on the theatre is interrupted by an irritating excursion into the generosity of nominal Christians. But it was written by a national figure at a time of national emergency. Disaster had followed disaster in the continental war and the French had rejected peace on any terms that could be acceptable. The suspension of payments by the Bank of England, just before the book's publication, and the Mutiny at the Nore just afterwards, could alarm the most sanguine. In such circumstances people turn to religion. 'It was a wonder for the lower orders,' wrote the *Annual Register* for 1798, 'throughout all parts of England, to see the avenues to the churches filled with carriages. This novel appearance prompted the simple country people to enquire what was the matter?'[15]

It should also be remembered that by his leadership of good causes, particularly Abolition, Wilberforce had built up a large following of the faithful. *Practical View* also had many merits. It was written with burning sincerity and, while Wilberforce showed a firm intellectual grasp of his subject, it was never too theoretical or high flown. His approach to Christianity was essentially practical. His message was that it was not enough to profess Christianity, to lead a decent life and to attend church on Sundays, but that Christianity must rather be allowed to pervade every aspect, every corner of the Christian's life. He develops his theme by stating the various arguments against his case and by pointing out their fallacies. The book is the fullest statement of Wilberforce's beliefs and philosophy. It also contains his views on how Christianity should affect the rich, the poor and the statesman, and his own vision of Utopia. It is, therefore, worth examining in some detail.

Wilberforce argues that it is not easy to be a Christian. In a passage which is clearly a self-portrait, he claims that any diligent Christian would admit 'that hourly he sees fresh reasons to deplore his want of simplicity in intention, his infirmity of purpose, his low views, his selfish unworthy desires, his backwardness to set about his duty, his langour and coldness in performing it'.[16]

The nominal Christians' religion is so nominal, that 'if Christianity were disproved their behaviour would alter little as a result'. Unless religion plays a vital part in a man's daily life it becomes no more than a series of prohibitions and restraints and there is no sense of sin. To regard religion in this way means that it will soon come to be considered as being about external actions rather than habits of mind: 'It is indeed true and a truth never to be forgotten, that all pretentions to internal principles of holiness are vain when they are contradicted by the conduct; but it is no less true, that the only effectual way of improving the latter, is by a vigilant attention to the former.'[17] The nominal Christian's interest is concentrated on temporal, the true Christian's on eternal, things. The latter's attitude 'hardens him against the buffets of fortune, and prevents our being very deeply penetrated by the cares and interests, the goods and evils, of this transitory state'.

He contrasts all the failings of nominal Christians with the lives of their more serious brethren. 'Their bodily and mental faculties, their natural and acquired endowments, their substance, their authority, their time, their influence; all these, they consider as belonging to them and not for their own gratification, but as so many instruments to be consecrated to the honour and employed in the service of God. This must be the master principle to which all others must be subordinate. Whatever may have been hitherto their ruling passion; whatever hitherto their leading pursuit; whether sensual, or intellectual, of science, of taste, of fancy, or of feeling, it must now possess but a secondary place, or rather (to speak more correctly) it must exist only at the pleasure, and be put altogether under the control and direction, of its true and legitimate superior.'[18] To feel towards any person or thing or cause that supreme love which God reserves for himself was idolatry, the sin admitted by John Newton in his feelings for his wife.

Nowhere is the difference between the two kinds of Christian more evident than in their treatment of the Sabbath. He asks the rhetorical question of how nominal Christians were employed on this day. 'Are they busied in studying the word of God, in meditating on his perfections, in tracing his providential dispensations, in admiring his works, in revolving in his mercies? . . . Do their secret retirements witness the earnestness oɩ their prayers and the warmth of their thanksgivings, their diligence and impartiality in the necessary work of self-examination, their mindfulness of the benevolent duty of intercession? Is the kind purpose of the Sabbath answered by them, in its being made to their servants and dependents a season of rest and comfort? Does the instruction of their families, or of the more poor and ignorant of their neighbours, possess its due share of their time? If blessed with talents or with affluence, are they sedulously employing a part of this interval of leisure in relieving the indigent, and visiting the sick? . . .

'Surely an entire day should not seem long amidst these various employments. It might well be deemed a privilege thus to spend it, in the more immediate presence of our heavenly Father, in the exercises of humble admiration and grateful homage.' After spending Sunday in such a way, 'the mind thus quieted, purified, enlarged, ennobled, partaking almost of a measure of the heavenly happiness, and becomes for a while the seat of love, and joy and confidence, and harmony'.[19]

But for nominal Christians, even for those 'of the graver and more decent sort', the Sabbath is 'a heavy day'. 'How glad are they to qualify the rigour of their religious labours. How hardly do they plead against being compelled to devote the *whole* of the day to religion, claiming to themselves no small merit for giving up to it a part, and purchasing thereby, as they hope, a right to spend the remainder more agreeably!'[20] He sums up their attitude towards Christianity. 'If the truth must be told, their notion is rather a confused idea of future gratification in heaven, in return for having put a force upon their inclinations, and endure so much religion while on earth.'[21]

After demolishing the wretched nominal Christians Wilberforce turns to one of his own constant temptations, 'the desire for human estimation and applause'. This longing, he points out, is nurtured in schools and universities as honourable ambition. But public opinion varies from age to age and is calculated to produce the appearance rather than the reality of excellence. The Christian is clearly taught by the Bible not to seek the praises of the world. Nothing shows the prevalence of this emotion in the world of nominal Christians more clearly than the example of the House of Commons, where resentment, arrogance and vengefulness are widespread. These are qualities that 'too often change the Character of a Christian deliberative assembly into that of a stage for prize fighters'.

Duelling is an example of 'that excessive valuation of character, which teaches, that worldly credit is to be preserved at *any rate*, and disgrace at *any rate* to be avoided'. The chief offence of duelling is 'that it is a deliberate preference of the favour of man, before the favour and approbation of God'. It is the only vice in which men resolve to indulge themselves whenever the opportunity arises. To covet honour is as dangerous as the more obvious fault of coveting wealth.

The true Christian must often forfeit the esteem even of good men by following his conscience. When he does acquire such esteem, he should treat it 'like the precious metals, as having rather an exchangeable than an intrinsic value, as desirable not simply in their possession, but in their use'. He should treat fame as a windfall, to be relinquished, if necessary, with cheerfulness. 'He will studiously and diligently use any degree of worldly credit he may enjoy, in removing or lessening prejudices, in conciliating goodwill and thereby making way for the less obstructive progress of truth.'

He next deals with the claim that it was enough for a man to lead a good life without the benefit of religion and finds it no more satisfactory than that of someone who was scrupulous with his religious observances to atone for an evil life. But he really begs the question by denying that, in the absence of religious feelings, good qualities could ever thrive to their fullest extent and become 'moral virtues' rather than 'amicable instincts'. The best that could be expected of such men was 'a cold sense of duty'. Those who were prepared to deny the express commands of God could go on to refine away all moral obligations. Wilberforce's low opinion of the virtues of the ungodly is surprising for one who benefited so much from their support in the Abolition campaign. Could the passionate speeches of Fox, Sheridan, and Pitt, the unwavering support of Brougham, be performed in 'a cold sense of duty'?

His views on the theatre are also less than complete. He condemns it on the grounds that it is frequented by the ungodly and that the performances there are directly hostile to Christianity. He does not seem to consider that the theatre could be used for anything except the productions of the devil. He launches into a violent diatribe: 'Should we seek our pleasure in that place which the debauchee, inflamed with wine, or bent on the gratification of other licentious appetites, finds most congenial to his state and temper of mind? In that place from the neighbourhood of which . . . decorum and modesty, and regularity retire, while riot and lewdness are invited to stop, and invariably select it for their chosen residence; where sentiments are often heard with delight, and motions and gestures often applauded, which would not be tolerated in private company.'[22] He remarks that, since the Revolution, the number of theatres in Paris has multiplied greatly.

It would have been more interesting, and revealing, if Wilberforce had stated his views on the theatre under ideal conditions, for one did not have to be a religious enthusiast to deplore its present state. But what would have been his attitude to the performance, on weekdays, of unexceptionable or even moral plays, by say Hannah More? One of his friends,

Thomas Bernard, once planned to found a 'moral theatre', but Wilber-force has not left us his views on the project. Some Evangelicals would not have hesitated in condemning these with the same rigour as they would the bawdiest Restoration comedy. A play, they would have argued, diverts attentions and absorbs feelings which should have been devoted to God. In this sense a good play was more dangerous than a bad play, a moral story more insidiously damaging than an immoral. Wilberforce would have been unlikely to take such a kill-joy attitude. Many of the same objections could be made to novels which he read with avidity, and he did not mind his children performing in school plays. He did object to the theatre's influence on actors' morals. Even a religious play could have evil effects through attracting decent young Christians to the stage and all its corruptions.

'It is an undeniable fact,' Wilberforce writes, 'for the truth of which we may safely appeal to every age and nation, that the situation of the per-formers, particularly those of the female sex, is remarkably unfavourable to the maintenance and growth of the religious and moral principle, and of course highly dangerous to their eternal interests. Might it not then be fairly asked, how far, in all who confess the truth of this position, it is consistent with the sensibility of Christian benevolence, merely for the entertainment of an idle hour, to encourage the continuance of their fellow creatures in such a way of life?'[23]

The greatest evil in political communities is selfishness. 'In the great and the wealthy, it displays itself in luxury, in pomp and parade, and in all the frivolity of a sickly and depraved imagination which seeks in vain its own gratification and is dead to the generous and energetic pursuits of an enlarged heart. In the lower orders, when not motionless under the weight of a super incumbent despotism it manifests itself in pride, and its natural offspring, insubordination in all its modes.'[24] Christianity set itself in opposition to selfishness in all its aspects. The welfare of political com-munities was, therefore, dependent on its prevalence.

He saw his Utopia in a truly Christian state. 'A man, whatever might be his employment or pursuit, would be furnished with a new motive to prosecute it with alacrity, a motive far more constant and vigorous than any human prospects can supply; at the same time . . . he would not be liable to the same disappointments as men who are active and laborious from the desire of worldly gain or of human estimation. Thus he would possess the true secret of a life at the same time useful and happy. Follow-ing peace also with all men, and looking upon them as members of the same family, entitled not only to the debts of justice, but to the less definite and more liberal claims of fraternal kindness, he would naturally be respected and beloved by others, and be in himself free from the annoy-ance from those bad passions, by which they who are actuated by worldly principles are so commonly corroded. If any country were indeed filled with men, thus diligently discharging the duties of his own station without breaking in upon the rights of others . . . all would be active and harmonious in the goodly frame of human society. There would be no jarrings, no discord. The whole machine of civil life would work without obstruction or disorder, and the course of its movements would be like the harmony of the spheres.'[25]

Such a state would be perfectly compatible with true patriotism. Wilberforce maintains 'true Christian benevolence is always occupied in producing happiness to the utmost of its power, and according to limit to the extent of its sphere, be it larger or more limited; it contracts itself to the measure of the smallest; it can expand itself to the amplitude of the larger. It resembles majestic rivers, which are poured from an unfailing and abundant source. Silent and peaceful in their outset, they begin with dispensing beauty and comfort to every cottage by which they pass. In their further progress they fertilize provinces and enrich kingdoms. At length they pour themselves into the ocean, where, changing their names but not their nature, they visit distant nations and other hemispheres, and spread throughout the world the expansive tide of their beneficence.'[26]

Until this state of affairs was achieved it was right for the rich to behave with magnanimity and the poor with gratitude. In a famous passage on the latter he explains that Christianity 'renders the inequalities of the social scale less galling to the lower orders, whom also she instructs in their turn to be diligent, humble, patient: reminding them that their more lowly path has been allotted to them by the hand of God; that it is their part faithfully to discharge its duties, and contentedly to bear its inconveniences; that the present state of things is very short; that the objects about which worldly men conflict so eagerly are not worth the contest; that the peace of mind, which Religion offers indiscriminately to all ranks, affords more true satisfaction than all the expensive pleasures which are beyond the poor man's reach; that in this view the poor have the advantage; that, if their superiors enjoy more abundant comforts, they are also exposed to many temptations from which the inferior classes are happily exempted; that, "having food and raiment, they should be therewith content," since their situation in life, with all its evils, is better than they have deserved at the hand of God; and finally, that all human distinctions will soon be done away, and the true followers of Christ will all, as children of the same Father, be alike admitted to the possession of the same heavenly inheritance. Such are the blessed effects of Christianity on the temporal well-being of political communities.'[27] Wilberforce, writing to Pitt about this book, described the chapter which contains this passage as the 'basis of all politics'.

Such behaviour on the part of the poor would, of course, have left them completely at the mercy of the rich. Society would have been ossified in the mould of the turn of the century.

To promote a revival in religion, which was in every way essential to the nation, men of power and position should set an example. They should foster virtue and discourage vice. 'Above all let them endeavour to instruct and improve the rising generation, that, if it be possible, an antidote may be provided for the malignity of the venom which is storing up in a neighbouring country.' For Wilberforce saw France as a place where 'it is to be feared, a brood of moral vipers, as it were, is now hatching, which, when they shall have attained to their mischievous maturity, will go forth to poison the world'.

*

In the same year as the publication of *Practical View*, Wilberforce became involved in a scandal concerning a very different book, in the course of which he gave a rare exhibition of callousness. Thomas Paine had published the first part of his *Age of Reason* in 1794. It was a deliberately violent and coarse attack on Christianity and Atheism, for which he had equal contempt, and a justification of his own Deism. Wilberforce read it and exclaimed in horror, 'God defend us from such poison,'[28] but the book had little impact. Paine was dismayed by the lack of interest aroused by the first half of his work and made the second even more outspoken. If a book had been written with the sole object of infuriating the Proclamation Society, it would have been hard to improve on *The Age of Reason*.

A small bookseller called Thomas Williams had published *The Age of Reason* and he was duly prosecuted by the Proclamation Society. Thomas Erskine, whom Brougham described as 'the greatest advocate, perhaps, the world ever saw',[29] was briefed by the Society. Erskine was a deeply humane man who almost always appeared for the defence, and had indeed defended both Thomas Paine after the publication of *The Rights of Man*, and Williams's counsel, Stewart Kyd, who had been a defendant in the treason trials of 1794. Erskine's appearance for the prosecution was due to his strong Christian faith. Although Kyd put up an able defence, Williams's conviction was inevitable.

The trial took place in June 1797 but for some reason Williams was not sentenced or confined until 1798. In the interval Erskine had a strange experience:

'I happened to pass one day,' he says, 'through the Old Turnstile, from Holborn, on my way to Lincoln's Inn Fields, when, in the narrowest part of it, I felt something pulling me by the coat, when, on turning round, I saw a woman at my feet bathed in tears, and emaciated with disease and sorrow, who continued almost to drag me into a miserable hovel in the passage, where I found she was attending upon two or three unhappy

Pitt addresses the House of Commons. Wilberforce sits in front of the right-hand pillar. Painting by K. A. Hickel

Barbara Wilberforce by Russell

William Wilberforce by Russell

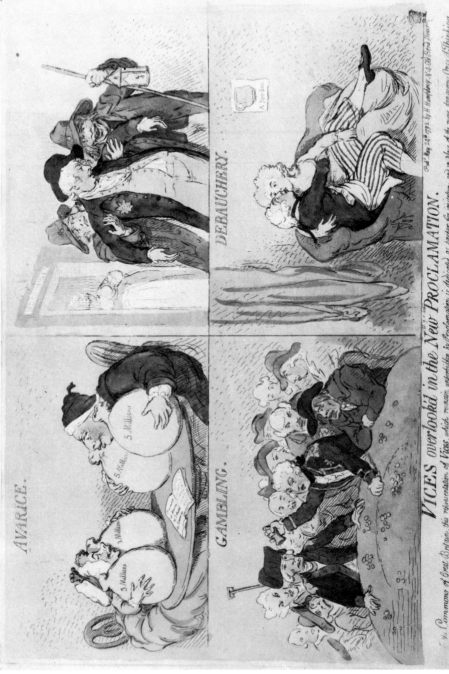

AVARICE.

DEBAUCHERY.

GAMBLING.

VICES *overlook'd in the New* PROCLAMATION.

To the Commons of Great Britain, this representation of Vices which remain, unforbidden by Proclamation, is dedicated, as proper for imitation, and in place of the more dangerous Vices of Thinking, Speaking & Writing, now forbidden, by Authority.

Pub.ᵈ May 24ᵗʰ 1792 by H Humphrey N.º 18 Old Bond Street

Gilray's caricature of the *Vices overlook'd in the New Proclamation* shows the Royal Family indulging in their habitual vices. The King and Queen personify avarice, the Prince of Wales drunkenness; the Duke of York gambles, while the Duke of Clarence whores children in the confluent small-pox, and in the same apartment, not above ten or twelve feet square, the wretched man whom I had convicted was sewing up little religious tracts, which had been his principal employment in his trade; and I was fully convinced that his poverty and not his will had led to the publication of this infamous book, as, without any kind of stipulation for mercy on my part, he voluntarily and eagerly engaged to find out all the copies in circulation, and to bring them to me to be destroyed.'[30]

Erskine was deeply affected by this sight and convinced that need rather than desire had brought Williams to publish *The Age of Reason*. He wrote to the Society urging it to relent, a move which he saw as being right in itself and as vindicating Christianity. 'Mercy,' he wrote, 'being the grand characteristic of the Christian religion which had been defamed and insulted, it might be here exercised not only safely, but more usefully to the object of the prosecution than by the most severe judgement which must be attended by the ruin of this helpless family.'[31]

The Society met to discuss the matter. Up to this point it is difficult to criticise its actions, for the *Age of Reason* was grossly provocative and anyone who sold it must have known the risks he was running. If they had now followed Erskine's advice and shown compassion they would have demonstrated the value of the Christian ideals which they had defended. But the Society met and refused to show any mercy. Erskine at once returned his brief and fee and never again acted for it. Williams finally came up for sentence on April 28, 1798. He was given one year's hard labour and then required to give security of £1,000 for his good behaviour during the rest of his life. This sum was so clearly beyond Williams's means that, unless the Government released him or he could find a friend to put up the money, he was in fact doomed to lifelong imprisonment.*

The Williams case shows Wilberforce at his very worst; only attacks on Christianity could make him suspend his normal kindness, and of all such attacks none during his lifetime was delivered by so pitiable an assailant as Williams. In such circumstances Wilberforce could not see the dividing line between protection of the public and persecution of an individual. The scene of a gathering of bishops, baronets and well-fed philanthropists deciding on the ruin of a destitute and sickly family is disturbing enough, but when they do so in the course of defending Christianity, it becomes nauseating.

Apart from Erskine's noble attitude there are only two redeeming features in the Williams case. Williams may not have been such an innocent as he seemed, and though abandoned to his fate by the Proclamation Society, he still had friends. Francis Place, 'the radical tailor', had

---

* He was released after two years.

persuaded Williams to publish *The Age of Reason* and had shared the expense and risk of publication. Williams not only refused to give Place his share of the profits on the first edition of 2,000, but printed a second and larger edition on his own account. But when Williams was in prison Place and Erskine raised enough money to support his family.[32] Place, who detested Erskine, denies that the Williams family was as distressed as he had claimed.[33]

CHAPTER XIII

MARRIAGE

THE publication of *Practical View* found its author back in Bath taking the waters. Wilberforce was now thirty-seven and his name had never been associated with that of any woman. The London Society in which he had first moved, that of Pitt and Goosetree's Club, was entirely masculine, so much so that the Opposition hacks had not hesitated to accuse Pitt of impotence or even homosexuality. When he moved in a wider social circle, his wit, charm and good nature clearly made him attractive to women, but there is no hint of any affair. Sir James Stephen describes him before his conversion as being able to pass for the brother of every man and the lover of every woman with whom he talked, but this impression would seem to have been deceptive. He was now past the normal age for marriage, in bad health and so occupied that he had abandoned the idea. He had expressed these thoughts in a letter in the winter of 1796.

'I doubt if I shall ever change my situation. The state of public affairs concurs with other causes in making me believe I must finish my journey alone. I much differ from you in thinking that a man such as I am has no reason to apprehend some violent death or other. I do assure you that in my own case I think it highly probable. Then consider how extremely I am occupied. What should I have done had I been a family man for the last three weeks, worried from morning to night? But I must not think of such matters now, it makes me feel my solitary state too sensibly.'[1] The last sentence turns the whole letter upside down, for he is clearly unhappy with his 'solitary state' and his pretexts for remaining in it are flimsy. Wilberforce sometimes seems to have taken a lugubrious satisfaction from the probability of his dying a violent death. He was really in no great danger; the threat to his life was always from his constitution rather than from his enemies. But his wish, perhaps a subconscious one, to trace the working of Providence in preserving him from a violent end led him to exaggerate the dangers.

On April 13 he wrote, 'Babington has strongly recommended Miss Spooner for wife for me. We talked about it.' It is the first mention of her or of marriage in his diaries.* On April 15 he dined with her in a party and underlined the words '*Pleased with Miss Spooner*'. From this moment his courtship developed with whirlwind speed.

At church on Easter Sunday, April 16, he was 'very much affected by my own meditations about Miss Spooner and mind sadly rambling at the dinner. . . . I in danger of falling in love with creature of my own imagination. But Religion'. He also kept a private journal[2] at this time; he seems to have written in this journal almost as a spectator of his own courtship and to have used it to offer himself the advice he might have been given by a prudent friend. But at Easter his diary and journal were still in step. He wrote in the latter, 'April 16th: I humbly bless God, that I have enjoyed part of the morning a very large degree of internal comfort and that my heart has been tender, but I fear it has been too much animal *heat* and emotion, partly from ideal forms of conjugal happiness to which Miss Spooner has led me. What a blessed Sunday have I been permitted to spend, how happy at dinner and in love.'

'Monday Evening. Miss Spooner much irritated and I discomposed about her. She [? told] Babington that it was public news.

'Wednesday. Miss Spooner called on Thos. Babington to go with her to Pump Room and I accompanied them. . . . Miss Spooner came in evening. Latish. Began to be much pleased with her.

'Thursday. Miss Spooner to Pump Room morning. Then home Miss Spooner. More pleased with her.

'Friday. Morning. Miss Spooner did not come. For first time slept well tonight. Every other kept awake thinking of Miss Spooner.

'Saturday. Morning. Miss Spooner to Pump Room. . . . Supped with Spooners—captivated with Miss Spooner. My heart gone, but that would forbear openly for a while, as advised by Henry and H. More, tho' they imperfect judges.'

After waiting thirty-seven years for marriage, Wilberforce was in no mood for further delays. He learnt of Barbara Spooner's existence on April 13, first met her on the 15th, fell in love by the 22nd and proposed, not without misgivings, on the 23rd. This day's entry is frantic with anxiety.

'Sunday 23rd April. After sad night haunted with Miss Spooner rose to prayer. Miss Spooner to Pump Room, Randolph's. Much affected and at length I fear too hastily wrote, I fear rather too hastily declaring to Miss Spooner state of my mind and she dined with us. Afternoon. Babington rather advised me to put off for 2 or 3 days. I vexed, having got over the Struggle. But at length gave way. When going to Miss Babington found

---

* The following quotations are taken from his diary in the Wrangham MSS. His sons considered the entries too private for publication.

that my letter had actually gone. That night I had a formal favourable answer—kept awake all night.'

He wrote in his private journal for the same day:

'This last week seems a month. Alas—I fear I have been too eager about earthly things. It seems as if I have been in a fever. I have constantly however prayed to God for his direction and read his word—yesterday had resolved to wait before I determined about Miss Spooner, but she quite captivated me last night by her behaviour to her parents, the Lillingstones and myself and the Babingtons. Such frankness and native dignity, such cheerful waggish innocence from a good conscience, such mutual confidence and affection towards her parents . . . her modesty and propriety. . . . I could not sleep for thinking of her, and being much agitated this morning at and after Church, wrote a long rambling letter to her which she has just returned with favourable answer. Jacta est alea. I believe indeed she is admirably suited to me, and there are many circumstances which seem to advise the step. I trust God will bless me; I go to pray to Him. I feel sadly too absorbed in the love of her, but I trust this will go off by use. I believe her to be a real Christian affectionate, sensible, rational in habits, moderate in desires and pursuits, capable of bearing prosperity without intoxication, and adversity without repining.'

His friends were alarmed by the speed of his engagement. Babington, who had persuaded him to delay his proposal for a few days, no doubt felt a special responsibility for having recommended Barbara in the first place. Milner and Hannah More both advised him to pause, but there was now no stopping him.

'Tuesday,' his diary continues. 'Called Miss Spooner's middle of day and explained and dined. Delightful interview at night for an hour, one of Barbara's hands in mine; the other in her mother's. . . .'

He sent for Milner to come and see Barbara who was unwell, but before he arrived Wilberforce received from Pitt an urgent summons to London. Poor Milner arrived from Cambridge to find Wilberforce's carriage at the door and Barbara perfectly well, but he accepted the situation with his usual good humour.

Wilberforce was deeply upset by being called away from Barbara, but when he reached London he was dismayed by the state of the country. Napoleon's victories in Italy had forced Austria to make a separate and humiliating peace, leaving England without an ally on the continent. Only bad weather and incompetence had prevented the French from landing troops in Ireland the previous December. The Dutch, now allies of France, were known to be preparing another invasion. The Irish themselves were becoming increasingly rebellious, while the English army there was described by its commander as being 'in a state of licentiousness which must render it formidable to everyone but the enemy'.[3] Only the navy stood between England and the invincible armies of France and in April the Channel Fleet at Spithead had mutinied and refused to put to sea. The Spithead mutineers were concerned with specific and well-founded grievances. They were disciplined, firm and prepared to put to sea at any time to meet an enemy attack. Their demands were met within a week. But the mutiny at Spithead was followed by another at the Nore, where the sailors were more political and less organised. There was talk of blockading the Thames.

Wilberforce reached London before the second naval mutiny, but he was so depressed by the state of affairs that he wrote to Barbara telling her that he would not hold her to the engagement against her will. This offer received the treatment it deserved. 'May 5th. Delightful letter of my dearest Barb's today kindly reproving me for mine.'[4]

Excitement brought back his fever and he suffered also from heavy colds for the next week. On May 7 he looked back on this momentous period in his life in his familiar mood of self-criticism.

'Sunday May 7th. Alas! What cause for deep humiliation do I find in myself on looking back over the last fortnight at Bath, sadly too sensual about Barbara. Too *sure* of happiness with B. I still fear I may have been too precipitate, not so much in offering to Barbara, as in resolving to marry at all. I remember well on this day fortnight, I durst not fairly to weigh the arguments, on both sides and then determine honestly. It is now too late to retract if wrong. Oh Lord God do thou forgive me for I have yielded too hastily to the Forces of affection or the impulse of appetite. . . . She, I really trust, is a dear child of God, and I derive very great comfort from the reflection.'[5]

After the outbreak of the mutiny at the Nore there was some discontent among the soldiers in London which led to Wilberforce being the victim of a ludicrous misunderstanding. A rumour circulated that he had written to the soldiers to express his sympathy and intention of raising their grievances in the House. On May 13 'Pitt sent to me about soldiers'. Wilberforce replied that to have supported the soldiers at that moment would have amounted to 'little short of positive insanity'. An inquiry then uncovered the truth. A Church of England clergyman called Williams had fallen into want through his own excesses. Wilberforce had given him money and continued to do so even after Williams molested and insulted him and once spat in his face. But at last even Wilberforce had to admit him to be irreclaimable. He wrote a letter to 'wicked Williams', as he was called henceforth, telling him to expect no more money. Williams had visited the barracks with this letter, read an imaginary message of support and shown the signature to the soldiers as proof of its authenticity.

After this comical mystery had been solved Wilberforce called on Pitt to persuade him to make a liberal offer to France. Pitt, who had been making increasingly liberal offers for the last six months, agreed to try again and Wilberforce left at once for Bath and Barbara.

*

He had been sustained during his illness and the political crisis by his correspondence with Barbara. On May 14 he was able to turn with relief from 'wicked Williams' to 'her sweetest letters—for Piety, just views of Religion, dear sweet old Bab'. A few days later he was distracted and kept from his sleep by re-reading her letters. On May 28 he reproached himself for 'consuming my time in writing to B and reading her letters',[6] when he should have been devoting it to politics. Can his failure to recover from his illness be a punishment from God? '*B is above all women who ever lived, I believe, qualified to suit me, and I hope, I in some degree to suit her.*'

On May 29 he reached Bath to find 'my dearest Barbara in my arms—wished still to put over marriage to Wednesday. . . .' 'Tuesday 30th May. Writings signed to Church about 11 o/c and married—Miss Anne Chapman and Miss Lillingstone for Bridesmaids and my dearest Barbara, composed but inwardly agitated—suddenly moved to tears at service much affected. I but queer in my feelings all day. Dined Mr. Spooner's. In evening to Beacon Hill. My dearest B desired me to join in prayers with her. Retired to bed early.'

At this point in the diary a pious hand has been busy with its eradicator, leaving us, as Wilberforce's sole reflection on his wedding night, 'Oh that I might be worthy of her.'

His friends were worried that Wilberforce's critical faculties might have been suspended during the elation of his courtship, but they need not have concerned themselves about Barbara. Although far from being suited to all tastes, she was serious enough to satisfy the most demanding Evangelical. They gave their cautious approval. Hannah More wrote, 'She is a pretty, pleasing pious young woman, and I hope will make him happy'; Zachary Macaulay, 'Her exterior indicates great sweetness of temper, considerable humility, and a mind rather highly embellished than strongly cultivated'; Henry Thornton, 'She is a very pleasing young woman about twenty-five, rather handsome than otherwise, with character, and unquestionably of a pious disposition. Her fortune is small (£5,000) and the family is not by any means grand, her father being merely a thriving merchant and a country banker with a large family. They live six miles from Birmingham—the name is Spooner. The match is not what the world would account to be a good match—that is to say he has not insisted on some things which the world most esteems, because he has thought it indispensable that the lady should have certain other qualities.'[7] Henry Duncombe wrote from Yorkshire on rather different lines: 'You will perhaps judge my way of thinking old-fashioned and queer but I am greatly pleased that you have not chosen your partner from among the titled fair ones of the land. Do not however tell Lady C so.'[8]

She was an attractive woman, to judge by the portrait by Russell, dark with almost gipsy good looks and very large and beautiful eyes. Wilberforce had gone outside the inner circle of Evangelism in choosing her and some of his friends thought he had married beneath him. But the Spooners were a respectable and thoroughly serious Evangelical family from Birmingham. Barbara's brother, William Spooner, became Archdeacon of Coventry and his daughter, Catharine Spooner, married Archibald Campbell Tait, later Archbishop of Canterbury. Lord Calthorpe, a cousin of the Spooners, was an Abolitionist.

It is difficult to be fair to Barbara. Her marriage to Wilberforce gave him thirty-five years of undiluted happiness. If he lost his critical faculties when he married her, then, so far as she was concerned, he never regained them. Marianne Thornton, who loathed and envied Barbara almost as much as she loved Wilberforce, saw his marriage to her as giving him an opportunity to display his own angelic character. But Wilberforce simply accepted and loved Barbara as she was and the faults that grated on others he found endearing.

Marianne presents the case against poor Barbara with deadly skill. She writes of her own mother, 'I once heard him [Wilberforce] say that the union between her and my father gave him such a delightful idea of domestic life that it made him determine to marry also, but he was not equally fortunate in his choice. He fell in love very suddenly with a Miss Barbara Spooner, the only religious member of a worldly family, and she confided to Mr. W all her persecutions and difficulties. She was extremely handsome and in some ways very clever, but very deficient in common sense, a woman with narrow views and selfish aims, that is if selfishness can be so called when it took the form of idolatry of her husband, and thinking everything in the world ought to give way to what she thought expedient for him. Instead of helping him forward in the great works which it appeared Providence had given him to do, she always considered she was hardly used when he left her side, and instead of making his home attractive to the crowds of superior people that he invited, her love of economy made her anything but a hospitable hostess. Yet the oddity and queerness of the scenes that went on there often made up, especially to young people, for all other deficiencies.'[9]

Apart from her claim that the Spooners were not a religious family there is truth in all of Marianne's accusations. Barbara was an intensely domestic woman who existed only for her family. Wilberforce looked on his health, his money and his reputation as assets which should be nurtured when possible, but which should always be expendable. But to

Barbara the existence and the well-being, physical and moral, of the family was the great cause in which she submerged herself and to which all others must be subordinated. Thus she was never able to enter into Wilberforce's political life or to understand its importance. It took him away from the family and was a constant menace to his health.

She was also too careful with money to share Wilberforce's easy hospitality. The food at their houses was both inadequate and disgusting. Wilberforce remembered how one of their guests, 'poor W', 'declared most seriously that he liked spiders better than my dinner. "Spiders are very good food", and looking round the corners of the room, "you have no spiders here."—a singular man—appears a strong predestinarian.'[10] But his guests did not have to be eccentric to object to Wilberforce's food. Marianne describes Isaac Milner's reaction to it:

'One of Mr. W's constant inmates was Dr. Milner, the Dean of Carlisle, the most enormous man it was ever my fate to see in a drawing-room. He was a rough loud and rather coarse man, but he used to say all he thought and ask for all he wanted, in a way no one else ever ventured to do, in the many Wilberforce homes he visited. The real bond of union between him and Mr. W was that he was a deeply religious man, and how clever he was the records of Cambridge honours shew. "Now W listen, for no power on earth will make me repeat what I am going to say" used to be his rough exclamation when Mr. W was flitting after a child, a cat or flower or a new book, when they had met to discuss some important point. At the W breakfast, when he chiefly received company, there was the most extraordinary mixture of guests, and an equally strange want of the common usages of life. To use a Yorkshire expression of his—Everyone was expected to fend for themselves. He was so short-sighted he could see nothing beyond his own plate, which Mrs. W. took care to supply with all he wanted till the Dean's stentorian voice was heard roaring "There was nothing on earth to eat", and desiring the servants to bring some bread and butter, he would add "and bring plenty without limit", while Mr. W. would join in with "thank you, thank you kindly Milner, for seeing to these things, Mrs. W is not strong enough to meddle much in domestic matters". I remember my mother saying to someone who wished he had married a different woman "That no one would have known how much of the angel there was in him if they had not seen his behaviour to one whose different tastes must have tried his patience so much". But never for a moment did it fail, he was always throwing his shield over her, bringing forward her best points and trying to persuade other people that if they knew her well they would value her more. It was one of the bright parts of my mother's character that she was always so kind to Mrs. W. In a fearful infectious fever my mother nursed her like a sister and always shewed her affection for her old friend by doing all she could for his wife, and taking the whole party into our house whenever they could come, which was often.'

The most irritating of Barbara's faults was her obsessive worrying. She worried about everything and was unable to keep these worries to herself, but health and hell-fire were her greatest concerns. Haunted by nightmares of disaster striking the family, she suffered agonies brooding about the perils that lay in wait for their bodies and their souls. Up to a point she was justified, for children, of course, were less likely to survive in those days and Wilberforce was always too preoccupied with matters he thought more important to pay proper attention to his own health. Barbara supplied the deficiency, fussed over him, made him rest and forced him to eat, sometimes giving him violent indigestion as a result.

She showed an equal concern about her own health and even worried herself into illness; but she was at her most fearful with her children. Almost any action on their part brought on her nightmares. If they travelled abroad they would drown in the equinoctial storms, or catch cholera, or be poisoned by foreign food. When they went to university she was terrified of their being seduced by prostitutes; when winter came she thought they might forget to put on warm underwear and catch chills; when they stayed at home the state of their bowels and their morals caused her equal and acute anxiety. She expressed this anxiety in letters which were often hysterical in tone and always excessive in length and she continued long after her children had grown up. It was an Evangelical convention that no letter was complete without a passage of religious exhortation. Both Wilberforce's and Barbara's letters to their children follow this rule, but their tones were very different. Wilberforce's were hopeful and encouraging, Barbara's shrill and despairing; she constantly reminded her children that to fall from grace would both endanger their souls and disappoint their father. Neither of their letters are concise, but hers ramble on interminably. It is extraordinary that their children remained so religious and, if Barbara's letters had been unrelieved by anything better, they would surely not have done so.

Her unfortunate trait of always expecting the worst must have caused Barbara great pain. But one can sometimes detect a certain morbid relish. After her eldest daughter's death she started keeping a commonplace book[11] in which she would enter memorable stories and reminiscences. Half of the book is taken up by an extremely interesting account of the More sisters, but the other half is unrelieved deathbed gossip, in which wholesome examples of the deaths of sinners abound. Death by fire seemed to hold a peculiar fascination for Barbara; she gives two lengthy descriptions of such deaths, those of Lady Salisbury and Lady Mary Fitzgerald. After describing how Lady Salisbury's charred bones were discovered with the skeleton of a little dog which had been in her room, Barbara quotes lugubriously:

Just as the Tree cut down that fell
To North or Southward there it lies,
So Man departs to Heaven or Hell—
Fix'd in the state in which he dies.[12]

Lady Mary's burning is also capped by a quotation, in this case the tasteless epitaph bestowed on her by John Thornton. 'Dear Lady Mary Fitzgerald is gone to Heaven in a Chariot of fire.' Barbara adds, 'The saying I remember greatly pleased my husband.'

Barbara, in her morbid vein, should be quoted sparingly. But her book ends with a story that is so splendidly representative of this side of her character that it can be retold in full.

'The last recollection,' she wrote, 'recalled to my mind a sad history told to your father in my hearing by Spencer Stanhope Esq. M.P.—the Father of the present gentleman of that name who lives I believe at the family place in Yorkshire and who married the youngest daughter (I think it was) of Mr. Coke of Norfolk—Father also to the Clergyman of the name of Stanhope whom I met at Mr. James'. There was a large young family when the Father and Mother used to visit us—Many daughters but I do not know what became of any of them who survived their Father—I have sometimes thought the history I am going to narrate might make a useful Tract—Mr. Stanhope mentioned that a very respectable and nice looking young woman had lived with them as Housemaid for sometime and at last was addressed by a Man in a better line of life and good circumstances— employed in some place of trust (I think) in the Management of the concerns of some prosperous Navigation Company. It was thought a great match for her, but the most important of all considerations was overlooked both by her and her friends, for he was an immoral man and one who had made a practice of proposing marriage to young women of good credit and character only with the purpose of drawing them into Sin and Shame and leaving them to misery and disgrace, distress, and a reproaching conscience and so often had he succeeded in this dreadful wickedness that hardly anyone would believe his intentions towards Mr. Stanhope's Housemaid were not of the same atrocious kind. Her friends, whose sense either of religion or morality could not be high, did not advise her against the marriage but only bid her beware of the snare they feared he was laying to entrap her. This time, however, his wish to marry was sincere—the day was fixed—the morning arrived—she was dressed in her bridal attire and waiting in the kitchen at Eight O'clock, the hour he had appointed tho' she feared to let her fellow servants know the exact time and had mentioned Nine—but Nine, Ten, Eleven came and no Bridegroom appeared. At last the Postman came and drawing the Housekeeper aside asked her if they had heard the dreadful news that this unhappy Man had destroyed himself during the Night. The Housekeeper attempted to break it to the unhappy Woman and began saying that the Bridegroom had—she was informed, met with an accident. Oh cried his poor victim, then I am sure he is drowned, for I have been dreaming all night of dead bodies being dragged out of the water. It was *almost even so* for stung as is supposed by Conscience, recalling the many young persons he had deceived and ruined, he had first swallowed a quantity of Gin and then having entangled his hands and feet in some such manner as to render himself incapable of extrication by his own efforts he had thrown himself into some shallow water where he was rather suffocated by the effect of the Gin rising into his throat and meeting the water, than by actual drowning—on his Table was found a Note addressed to a pious Man, who had been his friend and had vainly endeavoured to reclaim him containing only these words, Dear — pray for my poor Soul—.'[13]

Poor Barbara! She does not leave a happy impression on paper. One cannot help feeling, when reading her, that she would have done better to have married an extreme Evangelical clergyman. But to judge her by her letters and memoirs alone is unfair. We must also take into account her relationship with the rest of her family, and here we see her in a more attractive light. Although unable, through lack both of inclination and of ability, to enter into many of her husband's interests, she fulfilled in every way his idea of a perfect wife. He was blissfully happy with her, loved her to distraction and worried himself into a hysterical state when she was ill. If she jarred on him at any time in the course of their long marriage he never complained about it in the pages of his most intimate journals. Her sons, particularly Robert Isaac, would sometimes become irritated when, as responsible adults, they received advice from her which would have been better suited to five-year-old children. But they, too, loved and cherished her and readily forgave her faults. 'Never was there a tenderer or more loving mother,' wrote Samuel, 'rarely one more sensible or more really able.'[14] Many of the qualities in Barbara which inspired such love cannot be recaptured. But one outstanding characteristic was the utterly unselfish nature of her own love for her family. However tiresome they may be there is something deeply attractive about those who live for others.

It was fortunate that Barbara was so well matched to Wilberforce. Not every bride would have been suited by a honeymoon that consisted of a tour of the More sisters' schools. Wilberforce always looked on the sisters and their schools with undiluted approval. His friendship with Hannah dated back to the days of his conversion and he was partly responsible for the Cheddar schools being founded. When Barbara visited them she was sympathetic to their aims, but rather mixed in her approach to the More sisters. She respected their piety and wished to like such old and dear friends of her husband; on the other hand she was shaken by their unconventional behaviour and, perhaps, a little jealous. She was also a gossip and, unlike Wilberforce who shared this fault, prepared to put it on paper.

When Barbara first met the More sisters she noticed that 'Miss Patty was the only one of the sisters who had had any pretensions to beauty'.[15] She noted down a story which does not appear anywhere in the long correspondence between Wilberforce and Hannah More, but which may give some clue as to why Patty More behaved so hysterically when Zachary Macaulay and Selina Mills became engaged. 'I knew she had endured a very painful trial,' Barbara wrote, 'having relinquished an attachment very strong, and which was mutual, in order to gratify her Sisters, who for some cause which I could never learn could not endure her becoming the wife of the individual for whom she felt this decided predilection.'[16]

The sisters welcomed the Wilberforces 'with a frankness and cordiality and almost overwhelming expressions of delight but seldom met with in the more polished circles and which owed their charm to being believed to be truly sincere. The ladies were not polished characters excepting Mrs. H. More, who had been accustomed to the highest society.'[17]

Hannah More described to Barbara her decision to leave this society and devote herself to good works in the West Country as 'relinquishing the Greeks for the Barbarians'. Barbara thought that she loved Patty the most of her sisters, all of whom worshipped her.

'That her sisters should consider her as they evidently did as the first of human beings is not to be wondered at,' Barbara complained, 'tho' it would have been more according to the general usages of Society to have repressed a little of their extreme admiration before visitors and strangers and I often thought when your Father and other mutual friends of theirs were present that the excess of her sisters' expressions of overflowing praise and delight in her and her works caused her considerable uncomfortableness.'[18] Barbara may have been critical of the sisters' manners, but she accepted their work with enthusiasm. She has left a record of their tour of the More sisters' schools.[19] They were idyllically happy until, less than a week after his marriage, Wilberforce's conscience stirred itself from its brief slumber. 'I most wretched and haunted on account of wasting of time for the last week,' he writes on June 3. 'May God forgive me. Home at night and sweet ride with B and Mrs. More.' On June 6 they returned to Bath on their way back to London. 'Dearest B all kindness and comfortably composed. Her mother much agitated in parting with her.'

CHAPTER XIV

RECONCILIATION WITH PITT

WHEN Wilberforce and Barbara returned to London they made their headquarters in Palace Yard. In the summer session of 1797 Wilberforce introduced a Bill and carried it through the Commons to allow Roman Catholics to serve in the militia. He disliked their religion intensely but saw them as loyal men who should not be prevented from serving their country. Whether such service should be rewarded by a removal of the civil disabilities imposed upon them was a problem which perplexed him for many years. He was opposed to persecuting Catholics for their religion. 'Persecution for religious opinions is not only the wickedest, but one of the foolishest things in the world.'[1] But he was to oppose, in 1807, the Maynooth grant, by which a Protestant State would have subsidised a seminary for Catholic priests. The issue as to whether they should sit in Parliament was less clear-cut, and one which split his closest friends. Henry Thornton supported Catholic Emancipation when Wilberforce still held back; Dr. Burgh wrote him a series of impassioned letters urging that while freedom from persecution was a right which belonged to every human being, the vote and eligibility for Parliament were privileges that must be earned.

Pitt's support and its obvious good sense saw Wilberforce's Bill through the Commons, but in the Lords it met with violent opposition from the Bishops and lukewarm support from the Government. Its defeat made Pitt furious with Grenville, and Wilberforce with the Bishops.

In the summer recess he took Barbara to his mother's house in Hull and then on to Rothley Temple. His brother-in-law, Dr. Clarke, had died; he found his sister 'pretty well and more composed than I could have expected'. Dr. Clarke's death had left his vicarage vacant and Wilberforce successfully urged the Corporation of Hull to appoint his old master, Joseph Milner. It must have been pleasant for Wilberforce to have done his old friend a good turn and at the same time to supply such an impeccable vicar. But Milner caught a severe cold on the way to York for his institution, which must have developed into pneumonia for he died soon afterwards.

Wilberforce complained, as always, of a shortage of time, 'late morning hours and early dining, many calls, a vast many letters, and attention to my mother, prevent my getting anything done. Reading the Bible with my wife'.[2] But his happiness was transparent. 'It is hardly in human nature, I fear,' wrote Isaac Milner 'to continue as happy as you are at present.'[3] Wilberforce agreed in a letter to Macaulay: 'My cup was before teeming with mercies, and it has at length pleased God to add the only ingredient almost which was wanting to its fullness. In this instance, as in many others, His goodness has exceeded my utmost expectations.'[4]

At Rothley Temple he heard the news of Eliot's death. 'Deeply hurt by Eliot's death,' he wrote, 'kept awake at night by it.' He had valued Eliot's advice more highly than that of any member of the Clapham Sect with the possible exception of Henry Thornton. Eliot had married Pitt's sister Harriot and this provided a useful link between the world of politics and religion. Apart from the personal loss that Wilberforce felt, his death had disrupted the Claphamites' plans for India. Eliot's position and relationship to Pitt had made him an acceptable candidate for the post of Governor-General, an office in which he could have been trusted to do everything possible to encourage the establishment of missions.

Eliot's death left Broomfield empty, and Wilberforce moved there soon afterwards. Palace Yard had been an ideal pied à terre for a bachelor, but the noisy and chaotic life there was unsuited to Barbara's fragile health. A political headquarters could not also be a home. Broomfield provided a haven where they hoped that she could rest and he could work without distractions.

*

Ever since his rapprochement with Wilberforce, Pitt had been prepared to make peace on any reasonable terms, and as the position on the Continent deteriorated, his terms became more and more reasonable. He was willing to acknowledge the French conquests in Italy, the Ionian islands, Belgium and Holland. He would return every possession that he had captured from the French, retaining only the Dutch colonies of Ceylon and the Cape and Spanish Trinidad. At first it seemed that France might agree to these terms. Then Malmesbury, the British envoy, was secretly approached and urged to wait for the triumph of the peace party in France. This event failed to materialize; indeed, on September 3, the coup of Fructidor brought the war party to power, and their opponents to a miserable end, in one of France's few remaining colonies, Cayenne. The new French delegate demanded the immediate surrender of all British conquests as a condition of talks, and indicated that any peace would also involve the surrender of the Channel Islands, Canada, India, Gibraltar and Newfoundland.

After this even Wilberforce recognised that war was inevitable. He wrote to Babington on November 6. 'I once was ready to give up all we have conquered, either from France or her allies; *now*, after the hostile mind she has discovered towards us, and our recent experience of the effrontery of her rulers, I would not make peace without reserving either Ceylon or the Cape; no both. I rather think of declaring this publicly. As for Trinidad, it is not worth having.'

He still thought, against all the evidence, that if the negotiations had been handled properly, peace might have been achieved. He expressed this view in a letter to Muncaster:

'I wish we had taken a different course, and instead of sending over a man of diplomatic note who considered his character as a negotiator at stake, that we had employed some plain man of known firmness and simplicity both of manners and conduct. I wish also that we had at once named the lowest terms on which we would treat, declaring that we had gone as far for the sake of peace as we could do consistently with the honour and safety of the country, and making public too our offers. Even yet I think there would have been a chance, though speaking impartially, I fear not a great one that we should have got peace on the spot; and that even if the Revolution of the 4th of September had taken place the new directory would not have dared to recommence the war. But I am clear that these fellows now in power have been resolved ever since they came into authority not to make peace with us at all. Well, there is then nothing left for us but to go on, waiting for a moment of returning sanity in our enemies. But I confess my apprehensions are great. Our expenses are the first cause of alarm, and though I trust reforms will be made, and even our establishment curtailed, yet all that can be saved that way will be inconsiderable in a practical view.'[5]

The war had indeed reached a critical point so far as Britain's finances were concerned. Pitt was faced with a deficit which he could not continue to meet by borrowing without imposing a crippling burden on future generations. He decided to triple the existing indirect taxation assessed on windows, servants and other luxuries; he introduced, for the first time, a graduated rate into these taxes. He reformed the land tax; at the same time he brought forward an entirely new imposition, the income tax.

Pitt broke the news to the Commons on November 24. Wilberforce wrote in his diary, 'Pitt let off on tripling the assessed taxes. Vexed that I could not get an opportunity of answering Tierney. Pitt foolish though, and wrong, to crush him.' The country's reactions to the taxes mirrored Wilberforce's own. Outrage and horror were replaced by a grim sense of purpose. Only a series of disasters seems to arouse patriotic fervour in the English and the winter of 1797 certainly came at such a moment. Austria, Britain's last ally on the continent, had signed a humiliating peace, but peace for England, on equally humiliating terms, had been refused. The navy had mutinied twice and might do so again. The greatest army ever seen was massed for invasion under a military genius. The Bank had stopped payment; England had abandoned the Mediterranean; taxes were being increased by an unprecedented amount; Ireland was seething with discontent. Only Duncan's victory over the Dutch fleet at Camperdown on October 11 stood against all these disasters.

Adversity made the war popular for the first time. When Pitt announced that his overtures had been rejected by the French the House rose and sang 'Britons strike home'. Canning, the most brilliant of Pitt's young followers, started a magazine, the *Anti Jacobin*, into which he poured his great powers of ridicule and invective. During the debates on the subsequent taxes the Speaker suggested that, in addition to them, a voluntary contribution should be raised. This fund proved amazingly popular.* The Duke of Bedford, a Whig who had hitherto opposed the war, contributed £100,000, the King £20,000 a year, Wilberforce one eighth of his income, Pitt, deep in debt, £2,000. Each seaman of H.M.S. *Argonaut* subscribed ten shillings—'to drive into the sea all French scoundrels and other blackguards.'[6] Wilberforce spent much of his time persuading his friends in the City to subscribe. He seems to have been slow in detecting the changed mood of the country. He was hesitant, gloomy and lacking in confidence over the war. He wrote to William Hey, 'Nothing can make me support it, but the consciousness that we have no alternative. I dread the venomous ranklings which it will produce.'[7]

His support was undoubtedly appreciated by Pitt; on this kind of issue Wilberforce could swing many votes, but his advice may have been less welcome. 'Saw very little of Pitt this last week,' his diary reads on November 26, 'vexed him by plain dealing.' Taxation was one of Pitt's, but not Wilberforce's, strongest points. On the night that the Bill passed through committee this led to an exchange which caused Wilberforce pain then remorse. 'December 30th. House very late on Assessed Taxes. I sparred with Pitt and he negatived several exempting clauses. I much cut and angry.' The next day his attitude was different. 'Alas! alas! with what shame ought I to look at myself! What conflicting passions yesterday in the House of Commons—mortification—anger—resentment, for such conduct in Pitt, though I ought to expect it from him and can well bear with his faults towards God—all these feelings working with anger at myself, from the consciousness that I was not what a Christian should be. . . . Yet even still I find my heart disposed to harbour angry thoughts. I have found the golden rule useful in quieting my mind putting myself in Pitt's place, etc.'[8]

Neither Wilberforce nor his friends had caught the full wind of change,

* In all some £2½ million was subscribed.

although in some ways he was borne along by it. His diary in December shows a state of extreme anxiety. '7th Dinner at home—Morton Pitt, Colquhoun, and others—storm louder and louder, Colquhoun speaks of it as a most unfortunate plan. 13th. Anxious in the night about politics . . . much discussion with Henry Thornton, who sadly worried about assessed taxes. . . . 14th. Fox speaking well on assessed taxes: much shaken. I think Pitt must give them up.' His view of the Opposition hardened. He had once supported their peace policy, now it seemed to him treason. 'December 6th. Fox's language at the Whig Club throws light, if any were wanting, upon their secession. . . . It is my firm opinion that a conviction of their weakness alone prevents their taking up the sword against government.' Throughout his life Wilberforce was to feel warmth and affection for anyone who had supported Abolition. Sheridan, Brougham and Bentham were all men of humanity and genius, but to many religious enthusiasts of Wilberforce's day they would have seemed to be a drunken playwright, an unprincipled Scottish adventurer and an atheist. But after their services to Abolition Wilberforce could regard them all with indulgent affection. He was probably the only man in England who read the works of Lord Byron in the hopes of finding 'good feeling'. It is a measure of the times that he could forget the gratitude and the wary admiration he normally felt for Fox.

Parliament's reception of the taxes reflected the change of feeling on the war. The taxes were resented and criticised but accepted by both Houses. To pass such laws would have been unthinkable at any earlier stage.

*

Before his marriage Wilberforce had maintained that he could never have devoted so much time to his causes if he had family responsibilities. The winter of 1797–8 proved that, on the contrary, his family life could be adapted to meet his public duties. The time that he could spare from supporting and lobbying for the Taxation Bills and pressing Pitt to allow exemptions was filled by a number of new and old causes. The Proclamation Society was involved in the prosecution of the unfortunate Williams. There were meetings with Simeon, the Cambridge Evangelist, Grant and Venn to promote missions. Joseph Milner's death had again left the Hull vicarage vacant, and there was Isaac Milner to be comforted. James Stephen had now openly joined the Abolitionists; he was a powerful ally but a demanding correspondent. There were the 'Carib lands' in Trinidad to be defended from the slave system, the Abolitionist case to be prepared for the debate in the spring. The Sierra Leone colony seemed to stagger from crisis to crisis.

One cause which could be sure of his support was an attempt to legislate for the better observance of the Sabbath. But the bishops lobbied by Wilberforce were unenthusiastic and he adopted instead a voluntary declaration, which he urged people of influence to make. Even this was too much for George III who 'turned the conversation' when the Bishop of London explained the plan to him. An institution which particularly offended Wilberforce's Sabbatarian feelings was the Sunday entertainment given by the Speaker of the House of Commons. The approach to the Speaker seems to have been handled ineptly; news of the declaration reached him before he was sounded out by the Bishop of Durham and he took umbrage. 'Evening to Speaker on Sunday declaration plan: he very unreasonably angry—I deeply moved and much hurt. Staid late with him, and afterwards could not get to sleep.'[9] His second attempt was equally unsuccessful. 'Interview with Speaker, who extremely offended with declaration, and being asked to change day [of his entertainments]. "Personal insult", etc. I told him that it was not so meant. The attempt has failed, but I hope God will accept it.'

Wilberforce's charitable contributions made calls on his time as well as his purse. Even before his conversion he had been a generous and warm-hearted man, who, in 1783, gave away between five and six hundred pounds. Religion increased his sense of obligation and until his marriage he regularly gave away at least one quarter of his income, often more. Much of this charity was dispensed through intermediaries; a clergyman would be given a regular annual sum for distributing among the poor of his parish, a reliable friend £100 to disburse as he thought best. He contributed generously to charitable institutions, not only in London and Yorkshire, but all over the country. He gave very substantial sums towards the expenses of the Abolition campaign and paid for the education of young men for Holy Orders. He used to tear fifty-pound notes in half and send them, by different posts, to Hannah More for her schools.

Like any philanthropist he was a target for rogues; he recognised and accepted this, and he would often lend money which he knew would never come back. To Wilberforce the likelihood of its being squandered was preferable to the possibility of a needy and deserving applicant coming to him in vain. His diary shows shrewdness, insight and humanity in these dealings.

'Given W.C. £63 to enable him to refund what he has taken of the Board's money. I do it only because it would be ruin to him to withhold it. I have solemnly assured him that it should be the last time of my assisting him. . . . As I have told him plainly, I fear he cannot be saved from ruin. . . . He dislikes me and feels no gratitude to me I know for what I have done.' How many philanthropists are so perceptive?

'Captain Pearce £5. 5s. He is but a moderate hand I fear, but in urgent want.'

'Lent Robert Wells £13, which never expect again—he has a wife and six children to maintain, and ekes out a scanty income by a trade in old clothes.'

'Sent Dr. Chapman six guineas for a book which not read, and impertinently sent me, but Irving says he is a worthy man, and he must be distressed to act in this manner.

'Lent W.C. £55 on a solemn promise that he will never again issue a Bill, and not borrow of any one without previously informing me. He is not economical, but has a claim on me from having lived in my service, and imprudence must be pardoned. He is sure that from his salary he can gradually repay me, but I cannot believe it.'[10]

He also recognised that money was not the answer to every problem. 'Giving is not always the best charity,' he wrote to his son Samuel in 1824, 'far from it; employing people is often a far preferable mode of serving them.'[11]

Not all the recipients of his charity were undeserving. Two future judges received £300. Debtors were released from prison to lead useful lives through his intervention. His secretary remembered one of the most gratifying of these cures. 'Mr. Ashley,' Wilberforce once said to him, 'I have an application from an officer in the Navy who is imprisoned for debt. I do not like to send Burgess* to him, and I have not time to go myself; would you inquire into the circumstances?' 'That very day I went, and found an officer in gaol for £80. He had a family dependent on him with no prospect of paying his debt; and as a last hope, at the governor's suggestion, had made this application. The officer had referred him [Wilberforce] to Sir Sidney Smith, to whom he wrote immediately. I was in the room when Sir Sidney called on the following morning, "I know the poor man well," he said, "we were opposed to each other in the Baltic, he in the Russian, I in the Swedish service; he is a brave fellow, and I would do any thing I could for him; but you know, Wilberforce, we officers are pinched sometimes, and my charity purse is not very full." "Leave that to me, Sir Sidney," was his answer. Mr. Wilberforce paid his debt, fitted him out, and got him a command. He met an enemy's ship, captured her, was promoted; and within a year I saw him coming to call in Palace Yard in the uniform of a post captain.'[12]

On the whole Wilberforce's gifts to naval officers were rewarding. 'E. forced his way in to see me—the poor midshipman who about eight months ago wrote to me from Morpeth gaol, at the suit of a tailor for uniform, whom I got released, and sent him a few pounds. He called to thank me, and said he should never forget my kindness, not ashamed of it, and would subscribe five pounds per annum to Small Debt Society.'

* His almoner.

Charles Wesley's widow was given a pension for life. There is a revealing sentence in a letter he wrote to Hannah More asking about her
character. 'Unless she is something very bad indeed, the widow of Charles
Wesley ought, if health, not luxury required it, to feed on ortolans.'[13]

Lord Clarendon remembered a case which showed Wilberforce's
kindness and sympathy in a most attractive light. 'I was with him once
when he was preparing to make an important motion in the House of
Commons. While he was most deeply engaged, a poor man called, I
think his name was Simkins, who was in danger of being imprisoned for a
small debt. Wilberforce did not like to become his security without inquiry; it was contrary to a rule which he had made but nothing could
induce him to send the man away. "His goods," said he, "will be seized,
and the poor fellow will be totally ruined." I believe at last he paid the
debt himself; but I remember well the interruption which it gave to his
business, which he would not resume till the case was provided for.'[14] It
might irritate Wilberforce's serious friends to see him diverted from his
work to deal with the needs of an unknown beggar, and to do so spontane-
ously required a warmth of human feeling and sympathy quite beyond the
ordinary calculations of generosity.

*

In the atmosphere of defeat and disaster that hung over the country
Abolition seemed an irrelevance: Clarkson, broken in health, had retired
from the conflict; the Committee seldom met; only Wilberforce continued,
year after year, with his motions.

In 1797 the cause was threatened by the loss of its most indispensable
supporter. Pitt had stood by Abolition through all the tribulations of the
last eight years, flinching only once 'on St. Domingo account'. In February C. R. Ellis, a member of a distinguished West Indian family, brought
forward a motion which, he hoped, could be accepted by Abolitionists
and West Indians alike. Ellis maintained that the West Indian assemblies
would not accept legislation from the mother parliament on a subject so
vital to their interests. They should be given a chance to make their own
contribution towards Abolition. The Governors should be instructed to
encourage the West Indian legislatures to improve the conditions of the
slaves until their natural increase had made the Trade superfluous.

Ellis's motion was a transparent attempt to prolong the Trade by
passing the responsibility to Assemblies which would be certain to do
nothing. Wilberforce called it 'the abominable motion'. He was therefore
horrified to find, on April 1, that Pitt wished him to accept some modifi-
cation of it. 'Called at Speaker's where Mornington. Discussed about
Ellis's motion. Ellis's motion till very late—much hurt. Pitt wanted me to
close with it modified, but when I would not, stood stiffly by me.'[15]

Pitt had torn to pieces Dundas's proposals for gradual Abolition in 1792, and compared to Ellis, Dundas was an enthusiast for the Cause. Some kind of case could be made for his arguments, none for Ellis's. Pitt cannot have failed to realise that the result of Ellis's motion must be the indefinite continuation of the trade. It was not even a compromise, more a face-saving device, and this must have been what Pitt wanted. He realised that there was little chance of any Abolition motion passing through the Commons and none of its being accepted by the Lords. The issue divided his Government at a time when its unity was essential. There was nothing to gain and something to be lost by continuing. Acceptance of Ellis's motion would have passed responsibility on to the West Indian legislatures. If they failed Parliament could return to the matter when the situation in Europe was less menacing. His vision of a free Africa which had dazzled the Commons in 1792 had faded away. He no longer believed in Abolition as a practicable policy. From now on he had to be pushed, cajoled and bullied into helping the cause.

Having lost Ellis's motion, Wilberforce on May 15 introduced his own; he did so more to keep the issue alive than in the hopes of any success. The planters were unusually aggressive. Their opportunity came when Wilberforce rather foolishly declared that 'such were the odious effects of this baleful system that he could attribute the present state of the colonies, and the terrible mortality that had taken place there, to nothing but divine vengeance for the guilt of continuing it'.[16] Bryan Edwards, a planter and the historian of the West Indies, had just taken a seat in Parliament. He ridiculed Wilberforce's statement to some effect and reminded him of the lines:

> Let not this weak, unknowing hand
> Presume thy bolts to throw,
> And deal damnation round the land
> On each I judge a foe.

He recommended Wilberforce 'if he was desirous of exercising his humanity, to look in his own country' where 'he would even meet a race of blacks as worthy of his benevolent attention as those in the West Indies, namely, the chimney-sweepers'. Abolition, he claimed, 'would emancipate the negroes. It would do more; it would cause them to rise in insurrection'.[17] The motion was lost by the surprisingly narrow margin of 82 to 74.

At the beginning of 1798 James Stephen openly declared his adherence to the cause of Abolition. His loathing of the trade had been bottled up for many years; now it came flowing out in a series of impassioned letters to Wilberforce. Stephen, even more than Wilberforce, saw in his country's misfortunes a divine retribution for her role in the Slave Trade. 'It remains only,' he wrote in September 1797, 'that Great Britain, certainly their [the negroes'] most implacable enemy, should feel the last disabling inflictions of the scourge she has well deserved. My views of the event are awful and alarming, but only, I confess, under this aspect. It is not in our party divisions, in our falling credit, our broken Bank (for such in spite of delusion it is), nor in the force of our enemy; but it is in the marriage of our national interests to the detestable commerce of Liverpool and the oppression of the West Indies, that I foresee our political destruction. . . . But you will think me half mad and wholly presumptuous. I cannot help it. I must divulge these thoughts to somebody, and who is likely to make more allowance for them than you? you who are the Moses of these Israelites, though at the same time a courtier of Pharaoh.'[18]

Stephen's knowledge of the West Indies alerted him to a danger that might otherwise have escaped Wilberforce. New lands in Trinidad and St. Vincent had been opened up for planting. Pitt had almost agreed to an arrangement under which, although African slaves would not be imported to these lands, slaves from the other islands might. This would allow the Slave Trade to enter the new lands at one remove, for the stock in the older islands would, of course, be replenished by the Trade.* Wilberforce used all his influence with Pitt to have this order reversed, but Stephen was not satisfied and delivered to Wilberforce a rebuke in his most splendid style:

'I still clearly think that you have been improperly silent, and that when you see the government loading the bloody altars of commerce, the idol of this Carthage, with an increase of human victims, and building new altars for the same execrable purpose, while the sword of Almighty vengeance seems uplifted over us for that very offence, you are bound by the situation wherein you have placed yourself to cry aloud against it. You are even the rather bound to do so, because those high priests of Moloch, Lord Liverpool and Mr. Dundas, are your political and Mr. Pitt also your private friend.'[19] Wilberforce always accepted criticism from Stephen with disarming humility. 'Go on my dear sir and welcome,' he replied, 'Believe me, I wish you not to abate any thing of the force or frankness of your animadversions. . . . Openness is the only foundation and preservative of friendship and though by it I have lost some friends, or I should rather say have discovered that I never possessed them, yet it has cemented and

---

* Trinidad and, to a lesser extent, other West Indian conquests were to cause the Abolitionists acute anxiety. Trinidad had a greater acreage suitable for the cultivation of sugar than Jamaica and only just over 10,000 slaves. To bring the island to the same state of concentrated sugar production as Jamaica would require the importation of a million slaves. Until the proclamation against this branch of the Trade in 1805 this nightmare was held at bay only by an arrangement which could be revoked at any time. But between 1797 when it was acquired and 1807 when the British Slave Trade was abolished, the slave population of Trinidad grew by a mere 11,000, evidence that smuggling must have been on a small scale.[20]

attached me still more closely to the two best I have in the world. Let me therefore claim from you at all times your undisguised opinions. I promise on my part as impartial a deliberation as I am able to exercise, and I hope if I am convinced I shall be able to act up to my convictions. I will even concede that I ought studiously to guard against a bias to which I am liable, if not from personal connexion, yet from an apprehension of mischief from weakening government, and strengthening the hands of opposition.'[21]

He brought forward his motion on Abolition again on April 3, 1798. In this debate Bryan Edwards and the other defenders of the Trade were joined for the first time by Windham, who had until then spoken in favour of Abolition. Windham had adopted Burke's attitude of implacable hostility to the French and this had gradually poisoned his views on other subjects. A replacement for his eloquence was found in the voice of Canning, who now spoke for the first time for the Abolitionists. After a close debate, in which the cruelty of the Trade was not questioned, Wilberforce's motion was lost by 87 votes to 83.

*

Party politics have seldom been as bitter as at this time. The Government felt that the Whigs had overstepped the line between opposition and treason, while they considered the war was futile and unnecessary and the repressive measures at home tyrannical. This unfortunate state of affairs came to a head early in 1798 when the Duke of Norfolk, the premier peer of the realm, was deprived of his Lord Lieutenancy for giving a toast to 'the sovereign majesty of the people'. Fox was not the man to let his friends suffer on his behalf and after an inflammatory speech at the Whig Club he repeated Norfolk's toast. Pitt was so angry that he wished to prosecute him, but feared that an acquittal might make Fox more popular than ever. His sense of justice would not allow him to take the coward's way out and prosecute the printer instead of Fox. He wrote to Wilberforce for advice:

'With a Westminster jury, and an inflammatory speech from him versus the Attorney General, he would have a chance both of an acquittal and a triumph.'

After discussing the possibility of expelling Fox from the House Pitt continued: 'We might send him to the Tower for the remainder of the Session, which tho' doing little in fact, would assert the authority of the House. The chief objections to this last measure are that weak and moderate men might call it severe and vindictive, and that at the end of three weeks he might be led home in procession, and have the glory of breaking windows.'[22]

He asked for Wilberforce's advice by return. Unfortunately we do not know what it was, but if Wilberforce urged caution on him it would have been for reasons of expediency rather than principle. He had been as alarmed as Pitt by what he saw as the Whigs' disloyalty. He had written at the end of the previous year: 'A conviction of their weakness alone prevents them taking up the sword against the government.' In any case Pitt made no attempt to have Fox expelled or imprisoned but contented himself with removing him from the Privy Council.

Soon after this an episode occurred which was to put a strain on Wilberforce's and Pitt's friendship and provide a rare example of the former subduing his conscience. We have seen Pitt crushing Tierney, a radical member, in Parliamentary exchange. On May 25 Pitt accused Tierney of deliberately sabotaging the country's defence, a remark that was ruled out of order by the Speaker. When Pitt refused to apologise Tierney issued a challenge, which he at once accepted. Pitt's thin, almost cadaverous figure was a joy to cartoonists, but Tierney was a fat little man. The wits in Parliament therefore suggested that, to make the contest more even, Pitt's figure should be chalked on to Tierney and no shots outside it should count. Pitt himself took the matter more seriously; he made his will, asked Addington to attend the duel as a friend (thus preventing him from intervening as Speaker) and took care to keep the matter from Wilberforce until it was all over. On May 27 Pitt and his second Dudley Ryder left Downing Street and drove through Chelsea and Putney to Kingston Vale. Here they stopped their carriage and walked past the inauspicious sight of the highwayman Jerry Abershaw dangling on a gibbet. They met Tierney and his second General Walpole in a secluded dell. The two men fired at each other twice from twelve paces; on the second exchange Pitt discharged his weapon into the air. Neither man was hit and honour was satisfied.

Wilberforce was not. His disapproval would in any case have been severe, but the final blow was that the duel should have taken place on a Sunday. His own entry for the day has a certain irony: '27th Whitsunday. Pleasant day—spent as Sundays should be.' The next day the storm broke. '28th Ashley came in at my dressing time, and brought word of Pitt and Tierney's duel yesterday. I more shocked than almost ever. Pitt had provoked me much same Friday by lowering me in estimation by putting off slave carrying Bill. I resolved to do something if possible. 30th to town. Found people much alive about duel, and disposed to take it up. I gave notice [of introducing a motion on the subject in the House]. Letter from Pitt, evening.'[23] Pitt must have been alarmed about Wilberforce's reactions but he can scarcely have expected him to propose a motion in the House condemning duelling. He knew Wilberforce well and realised that he might not be aware of the effect that his motion would have. He sent him a letter that is as typical of Pitt as the motion was of Wilberforce. It is stiff, proud, logical and yet affectionate.

Downing Street, Wednesday,
May 30th, 1798, 11 P.M.
My dear Wilberforce,

I am not the person to argue with you on a subject in which I am a good deal concerned. I hope too that I am incapable of doubting your kindness to me (however mistaken I may think it) if you let any sentiment of that sort actuate you on the present occasion. I must suppose that some such feeling has inadvertently operated upon you, because whatever may be your *general* sentiments on subjects of this nature, they can have acquired no new tone or additional argument from any thing that has passed in this transaction. You must be supposed to bring this forward in reference to the individual case.

In doing so, you will be accessory in loading one of the parties with unfair and unmerited obloquy. With respect to the other party, myself, I feel it a real duty to say to you frankly that your motion is one for my removal. If any step on the subject is proposed in parliament and agreed to, I shall feel from that moment that I can be of more use out of office than in it; for in it, according to the feelings I entertain, I could be of none. I state to you, as I think I ought, distinctly and explicitly what I feel. I hope I need not repeat what I always feel personally to yourself.

Yours ever,
William Pitt.[24]

'Strange length to which he carries the point of honour' was Wilberforce's comment. But Pitt's appeals always moved him and he soon found that his motion would meet with no support. He wrote back.

Broomfield, Sat. June 2, 1798
My dear Pitt,

I scarcely need assure you that I have given the most serious and impartial consideration to the question, whether to persist in bringing forward my intended motion or to relinquish it. My own opinion as to the propriety of it in itself, remains unaltered. But being also convinced that it would be productive on the whole of more practical harm than practical good, and that it would probably rather impair than advance the credit of that great principle which I wish chiefly to keep in view, (I mean the duty of obeying the Supreme Being, and cultivating His favour) I have resolved to give it up; and when thus resolved, I cannot hesitate a moment in sending you word of my determination. At the same time I shall be much obliged to you if you will not mention my resolution generally, though you may think it necessary; but for many reasons I do not wish it to be publicly known till it is heard from myself. The Speaker is the only person of our town friends, to whom I shall open myself at present.

I am sure, my dear P. that I need not tell you that the idea of my being compelled by duty to do any thing painful or embarrassing to you has hurt me not a little; but I know you too well not to be sure that even you yourself would not wish me to be influenced by this consideration against the dictates of my conscience. I will only hint the pain you have been the occasion of my suffering on the subject itself, which I had intended to bring into discussion. I will only say, that whatever mischiefs may hereafter flow from it, will not be imputable to me. It is my sincere prayer, my dear Pitt, that you may here be the honoured instrument of Providence for your country's good, and for the well-being of the civilized world; and much more that you may at length partake of a more solid and durable happiness and honour than this world can bestow. I am, and I trust ever shall be,

Your affectionate and faithful friend,
W. Wilberforce.[25]

Pitt replied with warmth.

Downing Street, Saturday, 6 P.M.
My dear Wilberforce,

   I cannot say to you how much I am relieved by your determination, which I am
sincerely convinced is right on your own principles, as much as on those of persons who
think differently. Much less can I tell you how sincerely I feel your cordial friendship
and kindness on all occasions, as well where we differ as where we agree.

Ever affectionately yours,
W. Pitt.[26]

At one stage in the affair Pitt had told Wilberforce that the King
approved of his conduct. If Pitt really believed this he was deluding himself, for George III was too sensible a man to wish his Prime Minister to
become involved in such dangerous escapades. 'Public characters,' he
pronounced, 'have no right to weigh alone what they owe to themselves,
they must consider what they owe to their country.'[27]

The last word on Pitt's duel was in a more flippant vein. Lord Mornington had just captured the fortress of Seringapatam from 'the Tiger of
Mysore', Tippoo Sahib. After hearing the news he wrote to Pitt, 'I send
you by Henry a pair of pistols found in the palace of Seringapatam. They
are mounted in gold and were given by the late King of France to the
"Citizen Sultan". They will, I hope, answer better for your next Jacobin
duel than those you used under Abershaw's gibbet.'[28]

Wilberforce's disapproval of duelling was more complex than it appears
at first sight, and he never really analysed his feelings in *Practical View*. A
much later essay on the subject, dated 'Summer 1820', exists among the
Wrangham manuscripts. In this paper he argues that duelling 'is perhaps
the only crime which by far the greater number of the higher classes
of Society live in the habitual determination to commit whenever the
occasion for committing it shall occur, or at least be enforced on them'.
The very ideal of 'living with an habitual determination to break any one
of the commands of God exhibits the face and involves the criminality of a
direct and habitual denial of His authority'. There have been fallacious
arguments advanced against duelling; it is urged that all revenge is
criminal, that we are bound to love and not to injure our fellow creatures.
Wilberforce replies that duellists are brought to the field not by the desire
for revenge, but by fear of being thought cowards. Many of them have no
wish nor intention of injuring their opponents. 'I verily believe that there
is many a one who would rather lose his own life than take away that of his
antagonist.'

The motives which make men fight duels—desire for esteem and fear of
contempt—are inadequate reasons for any Christian. It is monstrous that
two men's lives should be staked against each other, one of which may be
of the utmost value to his family or country, the other of none. But however necessary it may be for a man to live and bring up his children, the

law of honour does not allow him to refuse a challenge on such grounds. 'And what must that system be which imposes on a man so fearful an alternative as that of exempting himself from such opprobrium, at the risk of clouding the prospects of the whole of their future lives of a number of his fellow creatures, whom Providence has committed to his charge and of whom he was to have been a protector and a blessing?'

Duelling was inherited, he claims, from the system of Chivalry. In its original form it was acceptable to Christians, for the duel in those days 'recognised the great principle of the overruling providence of God. It was expressly founded in the persuasion that the Almighty was the arbiter of the combat and would assign the victory as justice would require'. But no one now believed in Divine intervention in such matters, and without such beliefs, for a man who duels, 'the standard of duty is to be ascertained not by the will of God but by the opinion of man'. And the law of honour is 'the principle by which we make the preservation of the favour of man the supreme object of our solicitude'. It would have been interesting if Wilberforce had pursued the idea of Providential supervision of duels, for he had already disposed of the obvious objections to duelling. Such interpositions would have been as plausible as many in which he believed, but, while he often traced the workings of Providence on the battlefield, he was content to leave the field of honour to Chance.

*

June 1798 saw Wilberforce settled at Broomfield. Barbara was expecting her first child; the uproar about Pitt's duel was over, little parliamentary business remained and he was as near idleness as he ever allowed himself to be. 'Books, letters, a little dictating, and many friends' passed his time. In these pleasant surroundings, he received the news of his mother's death. She had lived in Hull and he had only seen her on his summer visits there. Their relationship had come full circle since she had rescued him from the clutches of his Methodist aunt. After his second conversion Wilberforce had made sure that she followed him; he would write her admonishing letters when he felt that she was slipping. One of these[29] reproves her for her 'fretfulness' and refers with elephantine lack of tact to her failing faculties. Wilberforce regarded senility, like grey hairs, as part of God's dispensation, and he was to be equally frank in observing the same symptoms in himself.

He went up to Hull for the funeral. He wrote to Barbara on July 7: 'My dear mother did not suffer in death, and I trust she is happy. The change gradually produced in her over the last eight years was highly gratifying to all who loved her and looked forward. It was a solemn and affecting scene to me, yesterday evening, to be in my mother's room, and see the bed where I was born, and where my father and my mother died, and where she then lay in her coffin. I was alone, and I need not say to you, or seek to conceal from you, I put up my prayers that the scene might work its due effect. It is late, and I must retire.'[30]

Life at Broomfield continued at its easy pace that summer. 'July 11th. Burgh came to dinner—Henry Thornton, after it rational conversation. 12th. Malta taken, and no other news of Buonaparte. La Fayette talking of assisting the oppressed people of Ireland. Thornton and Grant to evening council, about Sierra Leone. 16th. After breakfast at Auckland's, and then on to Pitt at Holwood. Tête à tête with Pitt and much political talk. He is better—improved in habits also—beautifying his place with great taste—marks of ingeniousness and integrity. Resenting and spurning the bigoted fury of Irish Protestants.'

The improvements in Pitt's habits must be a reference to his drinking. A rumour had been circulated by the Opposition that he had become mad, but Wilberforce was at pains to deny this; he wrote to Muncaster:

'You ask me concerning the report about Pitt. Altogether without foundation is my answer. But our oppositionists either know human nature well, or they pursue instinctively the means adopted to produce their malevolent end. Report and calumniate confidently and diligently: no matter if the report be proved false and the calumny be at once formally, distinctly, and authoritatively rebutted its authors go on reporting the same tale, more confidently and more diligently. It will gradually sink into the minds of men, and there leave a depositum which will permanently tincture them; and if, from our friends foolishly neglecting these rumours when first propagated, they are suffered to diffuse themselves without contradiction, as if too foolish to be believed (but the folly is ours nothing is too foolish to be believed), then the business may be done in less time, and the story will soon gain credit. . . . I spent a day with him lately, tête-à-tête, and he appeared better than he has been all the winter, and his *habits* much more wholesome.'[31]

CHAPTER XV

REPRESSION AND ABOLITION, 1799–1800

WILBERFORCE'S first child, a son, was born on July 21, 1798, soon after his father's return from Hull. He was, of course, christened William. In September Wilberforce took Barbara to Warwickshire to join her family. After a visit to Yoxall Lodge, they went on to Bath, where they heard the news of Nelson's victory over the French fleet at Aboukir Bay. Wilberforce was deeply gratified by the words with which he had announced his triumph. Nelson, blinded in his good eye by a wound in the forehead, thought that he was dying when he started his dispatch with the words 'Almighty God has blessed His Majesty's arms. . . .' Wilberforce wrote to Hannah More, 'Are not you almost as delighted with Nelson's letter as with the victory itself?'

The defeat of the French fleet, and the failure of the Irish rebellion in the summer, had removed the two most urgent threats to the country's security. Nelson's victory was followed by the capture of much of the French fleet that had sailed, too late, to support the Irish. Pitt's ambassadors were busy arranging a second coalition against France.

'So much success,' Wilberforce wrote to Grant, 'makes me almost tremble.' He was called back to London early in November on a less momentous issue. Sunday drilling had just been introduced into the Channel Islands to the annoyance of the Wesleyan Methodists who served in the militia. Their refusal to take part in this desecration of the Sabbath was rewarded by fines or imprisonment. They appealed to Wilberforce, who obtained Dundas's assurance that he would intervene. On his return to London Wilberforce found that Dundas had done nothing and that the authorities in Jersey were proposing to make refusal to drill on Sunday punishable by banishment. He exerted his influence and was able to write on December 8: 'The Jersey Methodists cause decided in their favour— Banishment Bill assent refused.'

*

Madame de Staël once called Wilberforce the most loved man in England, but in some quarters he was one of the most detested. Members of the

188

High Church saw his Evangelical zeal in narrow doctrinal terms and utterly misunderstood the effect of what he was doing. High Tories might object on similar grounds to his freeing the slaves or teaching the poor to read. More serious criticisms can be levelled against his support of repression at home, first by Pitt during the French wars, and then by Liverpool, Sidmouth and Castlereagh in the hard years after the peace. In both these periods he had to make decisions on two different kinds of issues; the Government would ask for the suspension of certain liberties on the grounds that the security of the Constitution as a whole demanded it. Wilberforce, together with his fellow members of Parliament, would have to decide whether such sacrifices were necessary. When they were imposed, as they invariably were, individuals would suffer some injustice. They might be imprisoned without trial under the Habeas Corpus Suspension Acts or other repressive legislation carried during these years. They might be cut down by the cavalry at Peterloo or denounced by a government spy. In any case their grievances were likely to be raised in Parliament.

A threat to the fabric of the Constitution and therefore the religion of the country was the only thing that could make Wilberforce suspend his normal humanity. It is difficult to blame him for supporting the emergency powers claimed by the Government. The House of Commons was fed with stories of conspiracies and secret distributions of arms. The numbers and inflammatory language of the Jacobin clubs had been equally alarming. Even the Parliamentary Opposition often seemed to be verging on treason, while across the Channel he could see the hideous atheist strength of France ready to exploit any discontent. Wilberforce was convinced of the Government's good faith; he believed their evidence of subversion and conspiracy and trusted them to apply their measures with justice. But when the issue was one of a particular injustice done to an individual the claims of justice and the Constitution did not clash, and there was no reason why the case should not be examined on its merits. We have already seen Wilberforce actually instigate one such prosecution in the action that the Proclamation Society brought against Thomas Williams for selling *The Age of Reason*. At the end of 1798 he became involved in another case which is still raised against him, that of the prison at Cold Bath Fields.

On December 21, 1798 the House was debating the second reading of a bill to continue the Habeas Corpus Suspension Act. Courtenay, a radical member who had supported Abolition in the past, rose to oppose the Bill. He claimed that seventy or eighty people had been arrested under this Act in 1797 and that none of them had yet been brought to trial. Their conviction, he urged, could have justified the continuation of the suspension, but their being held so long without trial argued that the Government was abusing its powers. There was another reason why the suspension should cease. He had heard disquieting rumours about the conditions in which these prisoners were held and had decided to discover the truth for himself. The prison where they were kept was said to be known as the Bastille. To test this Courtenay found a coach and asked the driver to take him to the Bastille. 'Very well, sir' was the answer.

'You know it then?'

'Oh yes, I know it—everybody knows the Bastille in Cold Bath Fields.'[1]

He found the prisoners' conditions miserable, though one would not have thought Cold Bath Fields as he describes it much worse than other eighteenth-century prisons. 'I found them,' he said 'without fire and without candle—denied every comfort, every innocent amusement excluded from all intercourse with each other, and every night locked up from the rest of the world.'[2]

The prisoners included a man sentenced for selling a pamphlet called 'Duties of Citizenship', a boy confined for disobedience to his master, a prostitute shut up in a cold damp cell when suffering from the illness of her calling, and a querulous warrior, Colonel Despard, who in spite of receiving the preferential treatment due to his rank, kept the issue alive by his incessant complaints and petitions.

Courtenay's speech did not contain any deeply shocking indictment of conditions in Cold Bath Fields, but it ended with a passage calculated to arouse Wilberforce. He had already been provocative. 'I understand,' he had said earlier in his speech, 'that some reverend gentlemen are among the magistrates who manage it. Perhaps they kindly subject these prisoners to so much pain in this world, that the less punishment may be inflicted on them in the next. (Hear, hear!)' He finished by saying: 'I cannot conclude without lamenting that an honourable gentleman, celebrated for his humanity, has not visited this prison. I am convinced that the honourable gentleman's principles of "Vital Christianity" would have induced him to exert himself to ameliorate the condition of these unhappy people. I am certain, however, that the honourable gentleman will no longer suffer it to be said by the unfortunate "I was in prison and you visited me not." '[3]

Wilberforce had not only inspected the prison himself, but had been in constant communication with one of the visiting magistrates. He replied in a flippant tone which must have been most irritating. 'The honourable gentleman tells us the prisoners are starved. But what says a visiting magistrate who lately sent me the result of his own observation? With the permission of the House, I will read his very words. "I saw their dinner: better I would not wish on my own table. It was roast beef and plum pudding." Aye, sir, and my friend is a doctor of divinity!'[4] He compared Courtenay to Fielding's simpleton clergyman, Parson Adams. At the end of his speech Pitt leaned over and asked how long it was since he had read *Joseph Andrews*.

On December 26 Courtenay raised the matter again and complained of the 'Christian rancour and religious facetiousness' with which Wilberforce had treated him. Wilberforce produced the devastating retort that 'a religious man might sometimes be facetious' while 'the irreligious did not of necessity escape being dull'.[5] Wilberforce at once regretted his self-indulgence. 'In what a fermentation of spirits was I on the night of answering Courtenay!' He laments in his journal: 'How jealous of character and greedy of applause! Alas! alas!'[6]

He could not have known it but he would have done better to have deplored speaking from a deficient brief, though the truth was still well hidden. Sir Francis Burdett had taken over the attack from Courtenay, and on March 6, 1799 he succeeded in having a select committee appointed to investigate Cold Bath Fields. This committee, which made its report on April 19, gave its complete approval to the management of the prison, with qualifications only on its record-keeping and failure to hang up the prison regulations in a prominent place. The cells were dry and airy, the food 'sufficient, good and wholesome', the health of the prisoners 'remarkably good', and all statements to any other effect 'absurd and wicked reports'.[7]

The Opposition did not give up; on February 19, 1800, when the Suspension of Habeas Corpus was again debated by the Commons, we find Sheridan denouncing 'the infamous conduct of Aris', the Keeper of Cold Bath Fields.[8] After the House's report such persistence seems pigheaded, but their case was soon to be corroborated in full by the report of a grand jury. Aris and his sons had systematically illtreated any prisoners who lacked the funds to buy immunity. Short rations to the verge of starvation, solitary confinement in miserable conditions, beatings and forced labour all played a part in their persecution of prisoners.

There are a few villains and sadists who can pose convincingly as honest men; it seems certain that Aris was one of them. He not only duped Wilberforce so successfully that the latter described him in Parliament as 'a pattern of humanity, and indeed too good for his station',[9] but he also deceived his own prison chaplain, from whom Wilberforce drew his information, the visiting magistrates, and the Committee of the House. It is hard to blame Wilberforce for a gullibility so widely shared. No one suggested that he knew of the barbaric conditions in Cold Bath Fields when he spoke against an inquiry in December 1798—no one, that is, until the Hammonds wrote their account of the affair in 1918.[10] Courtenay's case in 1798 was miserable, consisting of rumours, cabmen's gossip and the crotchety complaints of Colonel Despard. As if to compensate for his flimsy evidence he presented it in a grossly provocative manner, but even if everything he said was believed, it did not amount to a very dreadful indictment by the penal standards of the day. Cold Bath Fields was one of those rare scandals where the truth was much more frightful than any rumour. Wilberforce had been to the prison at least as often as Courtenay and he drew his information from its chaplain so that he had every reason for considering his own sources more reliable.

Aris was dismissed and died many years later in poverty, but contrary to the general impression he does not seem to have been prosecuted.* Indeed the only legal case that I can find concerning him was one in which Aris successfully sued someone who had accused him of starving two prisoners to death. No defence was offered and the jury awarded him £700.[11] The other point to be made is that, ghastly though the conditions in Cold Bath Fields were, they were little worse than those in other English prisons of the time, nor did they improve much after Aris was dismissed. G. L. Chesterton, who was appointed governor of Cold Bath Fields in 1829, and who finally reformed its administration, found conditions there utterly deplorable. There had been a severe outbreak of typhoid in 1818 due to blocked-up drains. The rich prisoners were often drunk, the poor always brutally treated and underfed. The turnkeys were petty and corrupt tyrants. After he had taken his position Chesterton was often pestered by Aris and his sons who 'would come and importune me for assistance, and the former never failed to aver that he was unjustly sacrificed to popular clamour. I do not know that the Middlesex Governor was, at this epoch, a worse specimen of his craft than others of his brother functionaries throughout the country, for all our penal establishments were then such sinks of iniquity that Aris may possibly have been not a whit more guilty than his compeers.'[12]

'Be it remembered,' Chesterton writes later in his book, 'the disclosures which then set the seal of infamy upon the prison at Cold Bath Fields, would equally have been elicited by an inquiry into the details of almost every other prison in the Kingdom. Such establishments reeked of corruption.'[13]

If Wilberforce was misled over Cold Bath Fields his general attitude to penal reform was immensely in advance of his times. He supported the efforts and experiments of Elizabeth Fry, Howard, Bentham and Romilly. He opposed savage penalties or transportation for any but the most serious offences. He favoured corrective training in the place of transportation and above all he regarded the great object of imprisonment to be the reform rather than the punishment of the offender. When speaking on Romilly's motion respecting Penitentiary Houses on June 5, 1810 he

* This impression is probably drawn from Sir Samuel Romilly's speech on February 17, 1818 in which he claimed that Aris was 'afterwards convicted of the grossest delinquency'. The conviction seems to have been moral rather than judicial.

declared of corrective training: 'The great and cardinal excellence of this system is to restore to society the unhappy wretch whose vices have brought him to premature ignominy and disgrace.' Discipline, religious instruction and moral example must play their part in this reform, while he must be kept away from the more contaminating influences in the prison. Wilberforce did not follow other nineteenth-century prison reformers who, to avoid corruption, prevented prisoners from having any communication with one another, either by permanent solitary confinement or by 'the silent system'. The prisoner must be taught to read and write, instructed in a trade and have a portion of his earnings laid up for his release, so that he would not lack the means of making an honest living.[14]

If one cannot blame Wilberforce for his defence of Cold Bath Fields one might expect the discovery of the truth to have changed his attitude towards the Suspension of Habeas Corpus. It is true that he was silent during the next series of debates on the subject, but in the post-war crisis he again defended its suspension. It was a difficult act to defend, because, in both periods of emergency, the Government had already armed itself with such powers that it could disperse the most innocuous assemblies and convict anyone who posed the smallest threat to the stability of the State. The Government, particularly in the later period, gathered its information from a network of spies and agents provocateurs. In such circumstances the only point of suspending Habeas Corpus was to allow the Government to detain people against whom they had no evidence whatsoever. When they first sought this power, they solemnly promised not to abuse it and pleaded the imminence of a French invasion as their excuse. Romilly in 1818 reminded Wilberforce that he and the House had been deceived once about such abuses and that they had in front of them evidence of new cruelties at least as strong as those presented by Courtenay in 1798.[15] Habeas Corpus was the only safeguard against new Arises, but Wilberforce still voted against it.

*

Cold Bath Fields, though aggravated by the suspension of Habeas Corpus, was an example of the persecution of individuals. The second repressive cause forwarded by Wilberforce during these years led, instead, to the persecution of a class.

In April 1799 the master millwrights presented a petition against a Trade Union which had been formed by their journeymen. A committee asked for leave to bring in a Bill to prevent this unlawful combination, but Wilberforce rose and suggested that it would be better to have a general Combination Law. Combinations of workmen were 'a general disease in our society; and for which he thought the remedy should be general; so as not only to cure the complaint for the present, but to preclude its return'.[16]

On June 18 a Bill was introduced into the Commons; it passed rapidly through its various stages and received the Royal Assent in July. The Combination Act attracted so little attention at the time that its passage into law is not even recorded in Hansard. Only Hobhouse in the Commons and Holland in the Lords spoke against it. But it was the most severe measure of its kind ever enacted. Its prohibitions were so minute that it seemed to some that for one workman to talk to another about his job would be unsafe in future. He could be sent to jail for three months by a single magistrate, possibly his own employer, if he infringed any of its clauses. Those found in possession of illegal union funds were forced to answer questions on oath, a new and sinister legal development by which a man might face the choice of incriminating himself or being found guilty for failing to do so.

In 1800 many petitions against the Bill were received, and some of its worst features removed by a Parliamentary Committee which, ironically, included those two stout Liverpudlian defenders of the slave trade, Gascoyne and Tarleton. But the laws remained strong enough to put the workman at the mercy of his master until 1824 when they were surreptitiously repealed by Francis Place. Although Wilberforce took no part in the debates he was responsible for suggesting a general Combination Law in the first place. His attitude towards the working classes is a perfect illustration of how, although ahead of his age in many ways, he was firmly rooted in it in others. By all means, he would have said, let the workmen's conditions be improved: let them be educated, cared for in sickness, fed in times of famine, let their hours of work be made bearable. But such concessions must be granted, not demanded. Magnanimity from the rich and resignation from the poor were the two qualities required in *Practical View* and, to its author, Trades Unions seemed a step on the road to revolution.

*

The Abolition of the Slave Trade was again debated in the spring of 1799. Canning and Pitt made powerful speeches in its favour; Wilberforce demonstrated the futility of leaving Abolition to the Colonial Assemblies; he then produced an interesting and new argument to show the harmful effect that the Trade was having on Africa. He pointed out that in any continent it was natural to expect the coastal areas to be more advanced than the interior, for they have the advantage of contact with other civilisations. In Africa, and only in Africa, was the reverse true. In spite of long contacts with the most cultivated of European nations, the Africans of the coast were backward and uncivilised compared with those of the interior.

Contrary to all experience the civilisation of the interior was three centuries more advanced. 'Yet even there, may be perceived some fatal influence from this deadly traffic. The storm upon the surface stirs slightly even the still depths of the ocean.' He warned again against provoking the anger of Heaven. Perhaps remembering Bryan Edwards having scored off him on this point, he made it clear that he did not expect the country to be engulfed by some great catastrophe. 'But there is an established order in God's government, or sure connexion between vice and misery, which through the operation of natural causes, works out His will and vindicates His moral government.'

The motion was defeated by 84 to 54, but Wilberforce still felt he was gaining ground. The other measures were revived; bills to regulate the Middle Passage (Slave-carrying Bill) and to confine the Trade to certain parts of the African coast (Slave Limitation Bill). The latter had among its objects the protection of the colony of Sierra Leone. The Slave-carrying Bill was proposed by William Smith and carried through the Commons, but on the second reading of the Limitation Bill 'Pitt coolly put off the debate, when I had manifested design of answering P's speech, and so left misrepresentations without a word'. But this Bill too passed through the Commons.

The Lords, as always, were more difficult. They insisted yet again on hearing witnesses. Wilberforce produced Macaulay, Dawes and other experts, and had Stephen examine them. Poor Macaulay had just returned from Sierra Leone. He was ill and his only wish was to see Selina Mills at once. Instead he was told to give evidence at the bar of the House of Lords. It was the only time in a life devoted to fighting slavery that he needed persuasion to do his duty. His temper was visibly ruffled. Pitt exerted himself and Grenville defended the Slave Limitation Bill with all his ability, but other members of the Government could not be persuaded to support it and the Duke of Clarence was speaking for the Royal Family as well as the Royal Navy when he repeatedly attacked it. On July 5 the Slave Trade Limitation Bill was defeated on its second reading in the Lords by 27 to 32 with 36 proxies on each side. The Abolitionists had lost fourteen votes through mistakes over proxies and would otherwise have carried the Bill. Wilberforce was bitterly disappointed. 'Thurlow profane balderdash. Westmorland coarse. Bishop of Rochester, ill-judged application of Scripture. Grenville spoke well. Never so disappointed and grieved by any defeat.'[17]

Pitt was encouraging and hoped to carry the bill next year. The King, he claimed, had not used his influence against the Bill, although as Wilberforce knew he disapproved of it. Stephen returned much of his professional fee.

*

Macaulay, once his services were no longer required by the House of Lords, left for the West Country and married Selina Mills on August 26. After some anxious discussion together they decided to ask Patty More to the wedding. Her answer, Macaulay thought, 'was certainly a very strange one and contained a mysterious intimation that they would never meet again in this world'.[18] But this was Patty's final fling and after the wedding friendly relations were restored.

Macaulay had brought back forty African children, mostly the children of chiefs, to be educated in England. He had them all inoculated at the small-pox hospital at St. Pancras and then took them to Clapham, where they lodged at Henry Thornton's house. The first time that they were taken for a walk across the Common many of them disappeared. The astonished inhabitants of Clapham had sent menservants out to try to bring an African child in for inspection. The Africans were pathetically trusting and fancied everyone to be their friends. Their story had a sad ending. After six years the English climate had taken its toll and only six of the forty remained alive.

While the Limitation Bill was being considered by the Lords, Wilberforce was sponsoring a very different measure in the Commons. This was a motion introduced by Lord Belgrave to ban Sunday newspapers. Later in his life Wilberforce once took and read all nineteen newspapers to judge their contents for himself, 'and assuredly such a collection of ribaldry and profaneness never before disgraced my library'. In 1799 he evidently felt no need for this sort of examination; the Sunday newspaper like the Speaker's Sunday receptions might be harmless in itself, but it distracted its readers from their observance of the Sabbath.

Pitt had been lobbied and it says much for Wilberforce's influence with him that he was at first prepared to support the Bill. But Dundas soon recalled him to his senses by pointing out that three-quarters of the Sunday newspapers supported his Government. Without his support the Bill was lost on its second reading.

These defeats may have been made less painful for Wilberforce by the birth of his first daughter on July 21, 1799, exactly a year after the birth of his son. Just as his own family always called their eldest son William, so his wife came from a long line—eight in succession—of eldest daughters called Barbara. Their baby accordingly became the ninth. Both Barbaras were doing well; *Practical View*'s sales continued and the war seemed to be coming to an end. 'Pitt sanguine,' he wrote, 'Buonaparte quite defeated'.[19] After reflecting with gratitude on the good state of his family and country, he declared: 'How gracious is God through Christ, to fill my cup with blessings, yet not to lessen or commute in what is still more important!'[20]

But in August and September he suffered from a series of fevers which left him too weak to work. He succumbed to Milner's bullying, which took the form of 'a most serious and forcible lecture on the necessity of taking care of myself and of living a more quiet life', and left with his family for temporary retirement in Bath. Henry Thornton gloomily forecast that he would find no rest there. 'For he is a man,' he wrote to Hannah More, 'who, were he in Norway or Siberia, would find himself infested by company, since he would even produce a population, for the sake of his society, in the regions of the earth where it is the least. His heart also is so large that he will never be able to refrain from inviting people to his house. The quiet and solitude he looks to will, I conceive, be impossible and the Bath house will be troubled with exactly the same heap of fellows as the Battersea Rise one.'[21] But Wilberforce seems to have led a quiet life in Bath, reading, writing many letters and following, from a distance, the defeats of the Second Coalition. He returned to London on January 23, 1800.

He found that the international situation had changed disastrously. The English expedition to the Helder had been an expensive fiasco. The allies had been defeated in Switzerland and Germany. Napoleon returned to France and was appointed First Consul. One of his first actions was to write to King George proposing peace. Wilberforce was concerned by the way in which this letter was treated. The British Government saw Napoleon as an upstart without the power to hold France to a secure peace. Accordingly they left his letter unanswered and sent a memorandum to Talleyrand the French Foreign Minister, saying that the King saw no reason to depart from the normal means of conducting business with foreign states and that France's best hope of peace was to restore the Bourbon dynasty. Windham put their view bluntly in a letter to Pitt: 'A Government such as the present, dropt from the clouds or rather starting underneath the ground, is in no state to offer anything. It cannot answer for its own existence for the next four and twenty hours.'[22]

Wilberforce disapproved of any rejection of peace proposals. 'I am grieved to the heart,' he wrote when he had heard the news,[23] 'fearful that I must differ but leave off consideration until indispensable, and I can hear what Pitt says.' He elaborated his views in a letter to Muncaster. 'I must say I was shocked at Lord Grenville's letter; for though our government might feel adverse to any measure which might appear to give the stamp of our authority to Buonaparte's new dignity, yet I must say that, unless they have some better reason than I fear they possess for believing that he is likely to be hurled from his throne, it seems a desperate game to play to offend, and insult, and thereby irritate this vain man beyond the hope of forgiveness.'[24]

On January 24 he met Pitt and discussed the correspondence. 'He shook me,' Wilberforce confessed. The next day he 'slowly came over to approve of the rejection of Buonaparte's offer, though not of Lord Grenville's

letter'. After much heart-searching he decided to support the Government
and he spoke, in their favour, on February 17. He was unhappy with this
speech, which failed to reflect his torn mind and was 'too earnest and
strong'. But he and the Government were probably right, although Pitt's
hopes for victory in 1800 proved to be misplaced. Napoleon had declared
to Junot on New Year's Eve, 'What I need is time, and time is just the one
thing that I cannot afford. Once conclude peace, and then a fresh war with
England!'[25] But Wilberforce was right about Grenville's letter. By infer-
ring that only through a Bourbon restoration could peace be achieved it
left the French people with no alternative to a war which they loathed.

*

Early in 1800 an entirely different crisis threatened. There had been what
Wilberforce described as 'gathering clouds', before his illness in 1799. The
increasing number of 'itinerant home missionaries' had caused alarm, and
it was proposed to tighten the Toleration Act so that licences to preach
would be more difficult to obtain. 'I saw this storm brewing in the spring,'
Wilberforce wrote to Babington, 'and warned Pitt against any infringement of perfect toleration.' In March 1800 the issue was raised again in a
far more menacing way.

Wilberforce was not the only man who influenced Pitt on religious
matters. His old Cambridge tutor Pretyman had been elevated to the
diocese of Lincoln, and Pretyman represented the extreme High Church
Party. A Bill had been drafted, to which Pitt, influenced by Pretyman, had
pledged his support, providing for magistrates the power to withhold
licences. There was also some regulation of the nature of their preaching.
Wilberforce used all his powers of persuasion on Pitt and Pretyman. 'To
see this design drawn out in a bill! Never so much moved by any public
measure.'[26] He realised that his best chance of stopping the Bill was to
persuade Pitt. 'I place more dependence on Mr. Pitt's moderation and
fairness of mind (though less in this instance than in any other) than either
on the House of Lords or Commons. In short, so utterly ignorant in all
religious matters is the gay world, and the busy and the high and the
political, that any measure government should propose would be easily
carried.'

Wilberforce urged on Pitt that, within a few weeks of the Bill becoming
law, many of the best dissenting ministers would be in prison, where they
would become martyrs. Finding Pitt adamant in the Bishop's presence,
Wilberforce ate supper with him alone. 'And I confess I never till then
knew how deep a prejudice his mind had conceived against the class of
clergy to whom he knew me to be attached. It was in vain that I mentioned
to him Mr. Robinson of Leicester, Mr. Richardson of York, Mr. Milner
of Hull, Mr. Atkinson of Leeds, and others of similar principles; his

language was such as to imply that he thought ill of their moral character, and it clearly appeared that the prejudice arose out of the confidence he reposed in the Bishop of Lincoln.'[27]

This passage, from a memorandum written by Wilberforce long after the event, is of great significance, for all the men he mentions were Evangelicals, not dissenters.* The reference to 'the class of clergy to whom he knew me to be attached' reinforces the evidence that the Bill would have affected the Evangelicals. Wilberforce argued and pleaded with Pitt in vain. The most he could secure was an assurance that the motion would not be introduced without his having another opportunity of talking over the matter. Other issues occupied Pitt's attention and the Bill was never revived. Wilberforce was more than happy to let it rest.

The whole episode is mysterious and intriguing. We do not know exactly what 'regulations' were contained in the Bill, nor why Pitt's attitude should have been so hard. He was normally amenable to Wilberforce's pleas and prepared to accept or at least to accommodate his judgement on moral matters. He was always ready to go to great lengths to avoid a split and would only stand out against Wilberforce when compelled to by affairs of State, or, as in the case of his duel, by personal pride. For the Prime Minister who had once agreed to shut down Sunday newspapers for the sake of friendship then to support a persecution of his friend's religion, the very core of his being, is an extraordinary departure. And Pitt, always open to reason, had refused to allow an impartial inquiry into the characters of the Evangelicals cited by Wilberforce. But his failure to proceed was probably due to Wilberforce's intervention.

In April, Wilberforce was hurt and disappointed by the defeat of a Bill which made strong appeal to his humanity. We are so used to regarding ourselves as a nation obsessed with the welfare of animals, so accustomed to the sallies of foreigners on this subject, that it is hard to remember that this has not always been so. In Wilberforce's time animals enjoyed no legal protection except as a form of property. There was nothing to stop their owners misusing them as they wished, and very few people felt that cruelty to animals was wrong in any way. As a result animals suffered from terrible abuses. Badgers were nailed down by their tails to be baited to death by dogs; horses, too old to justify having money spent on them, were worked to death. Post horses and hunters were galloped until they dropped dead, sheep intended for slaughter had their faces slashed and their tendons cut, and the details of their slaughter were nauseating. At country fairs cruelty to animals was perpetrated in grotesque forms. A man would eat five live fox cubs as an exhibition; a similar feat was sponsored by the

---

* It also shows the danger of relying on Wilberforce's memory. 'Milner of Hull' would not have suffered unduly from any persecution at Pretyman's hands; he had been dead for nearly two years.

Duke of Bedford and Lord Barrymore, when the latter bet, successfully, £500 that he could produce a man who would eat a live cat. An impression of wanton sadism can be gained from Hogarth's *Four Stages of Cruelty*. Blake, Wordsworth, Coleridge and Cowper all protested against this cruelty. John Wesley condemned brutal sports and wondered: 'What if it would please the All-Wise and All-Gracious Creator to raise [animals] higher in the scale of beings? What if it should please Him when he makes us equal to angels to make them as we are now?' The Methodists became known and mocked for their kindness to animals, a compassion which was shared by the Evangelists.

Bull-baiting was one of the most revolting forms of cruelty to animals, but its suppression could also appeal to those who were indifferent to the bull's suffering. Apart from its inherent offensiveness, it shared many of the objections that could be made against the theatre. Riotous assemblies gathered to see the baiting; labourers and servants left their employment to watch. Bull-baiting was premeditated and purposeless torture, and an easier target than the callous or hot-blooded cruelties that were so common. If the bulls failed to show spirit they were tormented by fire or acid. The dogs were no better treated. Quite apart from the wounds they suffered from being tossed by the bull, they were sometimes tortured by their owners. Sheridan in 1801 told the House the story of a bull-baiter who showed the courage of his bitch by cutting off her feet one by one as she clung to the bull. When she still kept her grip he cut her throat and sold her puppies to the audience for five guineas each.[28]

On April 18, 1800 Sir William Pulteney introduced a Bill to ban bull-baiting. Windham went to great pains in defence of the sport and, in spite of Sheridan's eloquence and sarcasm, the Bill was lost. Wilberforce did not introduce the motion 'because I am a common hack in such services', but he considered that Pulteney had mishandled the debate. He 'argued it like a parish officer, and never once mentioned the cruelty. No summonses for attendance were sent about as is usual. In consequence not one Thornton, nor many others, were present, any more than myself. I had received from some country magistrates an account of barbarities practised in this generous pastime of Windham's, which would be surpassed only by the tortures of an Indian warrior. A Surrey magistrate told a friend of mine yesterday, that some people met for a boxing match, and the magistrates proceeding to separate them, they threw their hats into the air, and declaring Mr. Windham had defended boxing in parliament, called out "Windham and Liberty". A strange and novel association, by the way!'[29]

Wilberforce consistently supported every effort to improve the treatment of animals. Outside Parliament the Society for the Suppression of Vice (the successor to the Proclamation Society) campaigned against cruelty to animals. In January 1809 its efforts brought a withering rebuke from the pen of Sydney Smith in the *Edinburgh Review*. Smith's theme was the contrast between the Society's tolerance of the vices of the rich and its persecution of those of the poor. 'The trespass, however, which calls forth all the energies of a suppressor, is the sound of a fiddle. That the common people are really enjoying themselves, is now beyond all doubt and away rush secretary, president and committee to clap the cotillon into the compter, and to bring back the life of the poor to its regular standards of decorous gloom. The gambling houses of St. James's remain untouched. The peer ruins himself and his family with impunity; while the Irish labourer is privately whipped for not making a better use of the excellent moral and religious education which he has received in the days of his youth!'

The Society, he claims, cannot be ignorant of the fashionable gaming houses. 'Is there one,' he asks, 'they have suppressed, or attempted to suppress? Can anything be more despicable than such distinctions as these? Those who make them seem to have for other persons' vices all the rigor of the ancient puritans—without a particle of their honesty or their courage. . . . At present they should denominate themselves a society for suppressing the vices of persons whose income does not exceed five hundred pounds per year; and then, to put all classes upon an equal footing, there should be another society of barbers, butchers and bakers, to return to the higher classes that moral care, by which they are so highly benefited.'

He criticises the Society's use of informers ('a ratcatcher loves to catch rats'), and its kill-joy attitude. Its bulging purse and august patronage prejudiced the outcome of its prosecutions. 'Lord Dartmouth, Lord Radstock, and the Bishop of Durham, versus a Whitechapel butcher or a publican!—is that a fair contest before a jury?' When he deals with cruelty to animals he points out the same double standards.

'Of cruelty to animals, let the reader take the following specimens;—running an iron hook in the intestines of an animal; presenting this first animal to another as his food; and then pulling the second creature up and suspending him by the barb in his stomach.

'Riding a horse till he drops, in order to see an innocent animal torn to pieces by dogs.

'Keeping a poor animal upright for many weeks, to communicate a peculiar hardness to his flesh.

'Making deep incisions in the flesh of another animal while living, in order to make the muscles more firm.

'Immersing another animal, while living, in hot water.

'Now we do fairly admit, that such abominable cruelties as these are worthy of the interference of the law: and that the Society should have punished them, cannot be a matter of surprise to any feeling mind—But stop gentle reader! these cruelties are the cruelties of the Suppressing Committee, not of the poor. You must not think of punishing these.—the first of these cruelties passes under the pretty name of *angling*:—and therefore there can be no harm in it—more particularly as the President himself has one of the best preserved trout streams in England.—the next is *hunting*:—and as many of the vice Presidents of the Committee hunt, it is not possible that there can be any cruelty in hunting. The next is a process for making brawn—a dish never tasted by the poor, and therefore not to be disturbed by indictment. The fourth is the mode of crimping cod; and the fifth, of boiling lobsters; all high life cruelties, with which the justice of the peace has no business to meddle.

'Any cruelty may be practised to gorge the stomachs of the rich,—none to enliven the holidays of the poor. We venerate those feelings which really protect creatures susceptible of pain, and incapable of complaint. But heaven-born pity, nowadays, calls for the income tax and the court guide; and ascertains the rank and fortune of the tormentor before she weeps for the pain of the sufferer.'[30]

It is a fair criticism. Wilberforce was realistic enough to know the hopelessness of trying to litigate against the vices of the rich. And the reaction against any such attempt could cripple his whole campaign of reform. The rich must be argued, shamed and cajoled out of their wickedness, the poor could at times be coerced; still, it was not an attractive contrast.

Others have carried the charge against Wilberforce much too far, and he has been accused of indifference towards cruel sports, and of aiming at their suppression solely because they represented a diversion from the path of true religion. His diary gives the lie to such accusations. A story told by Lord Teignmouth shows his compassion in cumbersome but endearing language.

'In one of his last visits to Bath, the little dwarfish figure, twisted now into a strange conformation, was wending its way up one of the steep streets by which loaded carts bring coals to the inhabitants of Bath from the port on the Avon. Two rough carters* were urging their feeble horses up one of the steepest of these streets, when one of the horses slipped and fell. The man to whom the cart belonged, a burly specimen of a savage race, infuriated by the stoppage, rained blows and kicks, mingled with hoarse curses on the prostrate animal. Wilberforce who was near, and who forgot everything in his sympathy rushed forward when the giant had

---

* The advocates of kindness to animals had a number of clashes with brutal carters. Lord Erskine, the Lord Chancellor, once reprimanded a carter for misusing his horse and received the answer, 'Can't I do what I like with my own?' 'Yes, and so can I, this stick is my own,' Erskine replied and gave the man a good beating with it.[31]

raised his hand for a further blow, and interfered, pouring upon him at the same time a torrent of eloquent rebuke. The fellow arrested in the very height of passion, and furious at the language used, stood with his face like a thundercloud, as if meditating to turn his stroke on the puny elf who appeared before him. At this moment his companion, who had recognised Wilberforce stepped up to him and whispered his name. The word acted like a charm. In an instant the lowering face cleared, and from rage and sullen hatred the look passed at once into wondering reverence as if, in the midst of his brutal passions and debasement, there was suddenly presented to him an object that awakened the better feelings of his nature, and drew forth his slumbering sympathies.'[32]

In 1824 Wilberforce together with Thomas Fowell Buxton, his successor in the struggle against slavery, became a founder member of the Society for the Prevention of Cruelty to Animals (now the R.S.P.C.A.).

*

In May one of his greatest friends joined his family. Wilberforce's sister had been left a widow by the death of Dr. Clarke, whom Wilberforce had been grooming for the Deanery of York. James Stephen, too, was a widower. Wilberforce's comment on their marriage is less enthusiastic than one might expect. 'I trust,' he wrote to his cousin, Mary Bird, 'that it will please God to bless the union. Stephen is an improved and improving character, one of those whom religion has transformed, and in whom it has triumphed by conquering some strong natural infirmities. He has talent, great sensibility, and generosity. My chief objection was, that it seemed like my sister's beginning life again, and going to sea once more in a crazy vessel.'[33]

His own family life continued to entrance him. He wrote to Muncaster in July: 'How I pant for Windermere and Derwentwater! What delight should I feel in carrying my dear wife to that land of wonders and beauties!' Instead they went to Bognor at the end of the summer session 'that my wife and children may breathe sea air, after repeated illnesses'. Henry Thornton and his daughter joined them. 'Here we are,' Wilberforce wrote to Hannah More, 'reading and discussing and through the mercy and overflowing goodness of God, enjoying ourselves not a little.' They read mainly history, a study which confirmed Wilberforce's content. 'What blessings,' he wrote to Stephen,[34] 'do we enjoy in this happy country! I am reading ancient history and the picture it exhibits of the vices and miseries of man fill me with mixed emotions of indignation, horror, and gratitude and when I look on the water and consider that the sea only is interposed between me and France. . . .!' Milner evidently received a rapturous letter, for he replied; 'Perhaps these wonderful smiles are for some future trial: continue to watch.'

By the time Milner's letter arrived his warning was already too late. Wilberforce wrote to Grant on September 27:

'It has pleased God to visit me with one of the severest of human trials in the dangerous illness of my dearest wife. The final issue is not likely to be very speedy, but from the violence of the symptoms, and especially of the delirium (this is very affecting), at the outset of the disorders, I am frankly and properly told that there is every reason for apprehension, though not for despair. Blessed, a thousand times blessed be God that I humbly trust I may believe death would be her unspeakable gain.'[35]

He also wrote to Hannah More on the same day. This letter starts much the same as the one to Grant, then continues:

How soothing to reflect that her sufferings are not only allotted but even measured out by a Being of infinite wisdom and goodness, who loves her, I trust! aye, better than a dear child is loved by an earthly parent. I am sure you will all feel for me and pray for me, and for my poor dear sufferer.

Mr. & Mrs. Henry Thornton are all kindness and consideration for us. I am not sufficiently used to sickness, and it is extremely affecting to me to hear her wildness and delirious distress, and sometimes fancies, mixed with her usual kind looks and gentle acquiescence. May we all be ready, and at length all meet in glory, meanwhile, watch and pray, be sober, be vigilant; strive to enter in and assuredly we shall not be shut out. I had used to say such words as these, not I hope wholly without meaning; but how much more forcibly are they impressed on the mind by the near view of death to which I am brought! God bless you all. The grace of our Lord Jesus Christ and the love of God, and the fellowship of the Holy Ghost, be with *us* all.
Yours always,
W. Wilberforce.[36]

There are hysterical overtones here which are absent from Wilberforce's correspondence except in the first months after his conversion. Henry Thornton describes his condition: 'Poor fellow! he cleaves now to his old friends, and he finds a relief in employing a little time in writing to them, which is what we encourage and especially as the sick-room is not the place either for him or for her. He seems more softened and melted than terrified or agonised and shows the truly Christian character under this very severe and trying dispensation.'[37]

By October 1 the worst of the fever had passed. Once Barbara was out of danger, he wrote to William Hey: 'God has in His chastisement remembered mercy, and my beloved wife is spared to me, and is gradually recovering her health and strength. May I improve from the discipline through which I have gone; but it is truly melancholy and humiliating to observe, how the strong feelings of the mind in the moments of suffering decay and grow cold after it is over. This hardness of heart towards God, in spite of the uniform and unvarying dictates of the judgement, is a sad proof of corruption.'[38]

Mrs. Thornton wrote during Barbara's illness: 'Mrs. Wilberforce is perfectly rational but deaf and indisposed to talk. She has had two good nights with opium and her appetite is very well, but we starve her for her strongest food is veal-tea, anything beyond that raises her pulse in a few minutes. . . . It has been a very awful and distressing scene, and while we only had the Apothecary I did not know whether the medicine she took might kill or might cure her.'[39]

*

The Slave Trade still flourished in 1800. Almost every way of removing or relieving it had been rejected by Parliament: outright and gradual Abolition, Abolition of the Foreign Trade, limitation of the area that could be raided, improvements on the Middle Passage, all had been turned down. Nothing had been achieved except the improvements made in Dolben's Bill and the empty gesture of referring the matter to Colonial Assemblies. But Wilberforce had felt, through his last series of defeats, that he was making progress. The terror of Jacobinism, which since 1793 had prevented Abolition from being seriously considered, was now receding and would continue to recede as the enemy became identified not as a cause but a man.

The economic arguments against Abolition were also looking thin. The war and above all the revolt in St. Domingue had revived a British plantation industry which had seemed on the point of succumbing to richer and more efficient competitors. By 1794 the price of sugar had advanced from 32/- per hundredweight to 58/-. By 1798 it was 87/-. In these conditions the plantations and with them the Trade thrived. Marginal lands were planted and all of Wilberforce's influence was needed to prevent the Trade being extended to captured colonies. But in the middle of 1799 the market broke. Cuba was beginning her rise to the position she occupied for many years as the greatest sugar producer in the West Indies. American ships imported the sugar of enemy colonies and re-exported it under her own flag in ships chartered from the French and Spanish for the duration of the war. In Europe new experiments with beet sugar were beginning to bear fruit. This increase in supply came at a time when the British planters had greatly expanded their production. In the middle of 1799 the price of sugar plummeted from the 87/- reached in 1798 and in 1800–1801 it varied between 50/- and 28/-. Wilberforce's aphorism was again proved true. 'Of West Indian, even more truly than of any other riches it may be affirmed that they are apt to make themselves wings and fly away.'

In these circumstances the planters from the old islands should have wanted to stop the Trade to prevent their rivals from adding to a position of ruinous oversupply. The planters in both old and new British colonies should have united to demand the end of the Foreign Slave Trade. For a moment they seemed to act under the influence of reason. Wilberforce recounted the episode in a letter to Gisborne:

'I have suffered great chagrin on the subject of the Slave Trade. Pitt listened too easily to the assurance of several of the principal of the West Indian proprietors, who declared themselves willing to support a suspension [of the Trade] for five years; till at length, when we hoped all was going on prosperously, a public meeting of the West Indian body, at which a strong anti-abolition spirit was manifested, shook the resolution of our timid converts, and all, except Sir William Young, turned around. I wished Pitt to come forward with the measure notwithstanding and tried to prevail on Dundas to support us in it. But the latter, though extremely angry at the Jamaica people, who, in a report recently come over, talk big and dispute our right to abolish, etc. will not, I fear, consent to support us now. Lord Grenville is very earnest for laying a tax on all negroes imported into the island, to be applied in the encouragement of population, but I am clear that the regulation would be futile. Negroes have risen in price from £76 to £120 per head, and yet they have been bought in greater numbers than ever, so that on the whole any tax would be of no avail. Pitt declares that he will by an order of council, stop the importation of negroes into the new settlements, into which three-fourths, speaking loosely, of the whole importation have been brought.'[40]

In spite of the failure to reach agreement on a suspension of the Trade, Wilberforce must have been immensely encouraged by the offer, which represented a complete change in the planters' policy. Why they should make and then withdraw it is less clear. Their consistent opposition to the abolition of the foreign branch of the Trade makes it absurd to treat them as creatures of logic. One suggestion is that Wilberforce was tricked by them into agreeing to a suspension, so as to deprive him of the opportunity of debating the matter in 1800. While the planters' actions certainly had this effect, it seems a devious means of preventing a debate which could have achieved nothing. Many accusations were thrown at the planters during the Abolition campaign, but that of excessive subtlety was not among them. The obvious explanation is probably the right one, that they did recognise the link between the Trade, overproduction in the Indies, disastrous prices and bankrupt plantations, and that they asked for a suspension of the Trade to stop it. Their withdrawal may have been due to an emotional reaction or to opposition from representatives of the newer islands and plantations, who still needed fresh labour. This class of planter was in a dilemma; he had sunk a large sum of capital into his plantation during the euphoric years of the sugar boom, he was almost certainly indebted to the loan sharks for more than he could now raise by the sale of his plantation. On the other hand credit was easy and to stay solvent he must harvest his next crop of sugar. But at present prices to continue a marginal plantation was merely to postpone ruin. The planters lived in hopes, for which, by refusing to suspend the Slave Trade, they had themselves removed all grounds.

After this reverse it was too late to arrange for Wilberforce's annual motion to be debated and in 1800 it went by default for the first time since 1791. Wilberforce instead explored the possibility of an international Abolition. Peace, he thought, could not be far off and the peace treaty would present a chance for including a general renunciation of the Trade among its terms. He wrote to Hare Naylor, an Englishman who knew Napoleon, to find out his reaction. 'Would I were the starling to hollow "Abolition" in the Grand Consul's ear.' The letter includes an interesting assessment of Napoleon's genius:

'It is the particular in Buonaparte's character which has always most impressed me with a sense of his possessing extraordinary powers, that he wins over people of acknowledged eminence in various lines, attaches them to his cause and renders them subservient to his purpose. This power of gravitation, if I may so call it, is absolutely necessary where any one is to be the centre of a system. Without it all would be confusion. But it is the infallible proof of a great man.'[41]

CHAPTER XVI

PEACE

THE Napoleonic wars were accompanied by a series of disastrous harvests, and that of 1800 was one of the worst. On his return from Bognor Wilberforce threw himself into working for the relief of the poor. In 1796 he had sent out to his friends a detailed questionnaire under twenty-three headings,[1] the answers to which provided him with a knowledge of the conditions and needs of the poor in different parts of the country. He sat on the House of Commons Committee examining the matter, but he was not content with their efforts.

'Our first report is made,' he wrote to Muncaster on December 6. 'Alas! it does not go far enough. I wish that we should gain the hearts of our people by declaring our determination to abridge our luxuries and comforts and superfluities not merely our bread. This way of establishing a distinction between the poor and rich in times like these is neither prudent nor feeling. They compare our situation to that of a ship at short allowance; but then officers are at short allowance too, not the men only.'

Wilberforce was particularly concerned about the distress of the manufacturers in the West Riding. He sent money to many friends in Yorkshire, asking them to disburse it to the needy as they thought best. He lobbied the Government incessantly to obtain relief for the poor from public funds. Milner described his effort to Hey: 'Our dear and benevolent friend absolutely exhausts his strength on this subject. He is the most feeling soul I ever knew; and also the most patient and indefatigable in endeavouring to lessen the miseries of the people: and how he does get misrepresented and abused! But you may kick him as long and as much as you please; if he could but fill the bellies of the poor, he would willingly submit to it all.'[2]

His diary for the first part of 1801 gives some idea of his efforts. 'March 10. Addington wavering about plan and not for giving public money.' 'March 19. The committee about the poor makes no progress. People half-hearted in general.' 'March 31. I find more persons approving my idea about the poor. I am nearly resolved to move for a million for their relief.' 'April 1. Poor relief put off most shabbily till after Easter. Sad work—whilst we hear of increasing distress and even tumult and insur-

208

rection. Much hurt by coldness and dilatoriness of government.' The most that he was able to achieve was to obtain permission for parishes to borrow on their rates for poor relief. His own contribution was exceptionally generous even by the standards of Evangelical charity. During 1801 he gave away a sum more than £3,000 in excess of his income.

*

At the beginning of 1801 Pitt had been in office for nearly seventeen years. It was easy to forget on how slender a base his power rested. Although supreme in his administration, he had never built up a great personal following. This was due partly to the coldness of his character and partly to the distaste with which he viewed the sordid side of politics. His rule had been unchallenged only because he had done what the country and the King wanted. He had never adopted as a government measure any issue on which they would oppose him. In his early days in office, Pitt had been the only alternative to Fox and the Whigs; but this, his strongest security, no longer applied. The Portland Whigs, Grenville and Windham, although holding office under Pitt, in fact led a party of their own whose distinguishing characteristic was its extreme hostility to France. New men had come up in Pitt's own party. Although George III preferred Pitt to any other Prime Minister, he was not the only candidate.

After the Irish rebellion of 1798 had been quelled, Pitt and his Governor-General, Cornwallis, reviewed the situation there. So long as Ireland festered with grievances she would remain a danger. The brutality with which the uprising had been suppressed ensured that her discontent would increase. Pitt himself felt unhappy about the methods used in Ireland, as is shown in one of the Conversational Memoranda kept by Wilberforce's sons.[3]

'When a statement had been made to the House of the cruel practices, approaching certainly to torture, by which the discovery of concealed arms had been enforced, John Claudius Beresford rose to reply and said with a force of honesty, the impression of which I never can forget, "I fear and feel deep shame in making the avowal. I fear it is too true—I defend it not—but I trust I may be permitted to refer, as some palliation of these atrocities, to the state of my unhappy country, where rebellion and its attendant horrors had roused on both sides to the highest pitch all the strongest passions of our nature." I was with Pitt in the House of Lords when Lord Clare replied to a similar charge—"Well, suppose it were so, but surely, etc." I shall never forget Pitt's look. He turned round to me with that high indignant stare which sometimes marked his countenance, and stalked out of the House.'

Pitt resolved to cure Ireland's troubles by generosity. The Irish parliament was dominated by the nominees of a few great landowners and

Catholics were not allowed to sit in it. Pitt and Cornwallis agreed that until the Catholics enjoyed the full rights of citizenship there would be no peace in the country, but to attempt to give emancipation in Ireland would be dangerous. The Protestants, more militant than ever since the rebellion, would be left in a minority and control over the country would have been lost. A Union with England would solve this problem, for in a British Parliament the Catholics would always remain in a minority. While the mischief they could do would be limited, they would constitute an important interest, and would have more voice in their own affairs. Union would also benefit Ireland's commercial interests, who could then export their products free of duty to any part of the Empire. Wilberforce was not an admirer of the Roman Catholic religion and he did not become an advocate of Emancipation until much later. He feared that the Catholic members would speak for the hierarchy, not for themselves. But he soon came to recognise that, in the case of Ireland, Emancipation was a precondition of any reasonable settlement. 'I do not like it,' he had written in his diary on January 7, 1799. By February 10, 'my judgement at length made up for the Union'.

It was an issue that divided Wilberforce's friends. Humanity and political sense argued for one side, fear of Catholicism for the other. From Yorkshire Dr. Burgh thundered against the Union. Bankes, Milner and William Hey all opposed it while Henry Thornton sided with Wilberforce.

Pitt saw Emancipation as a necessary part of the Union. When Cornwallis's son was asked who would succeed his father if Emancipation were rejected, he replied 'Bonaparte'. The Irish Parliament was persuaded and bribed to end its own existence and they did so under an implied promise of Emancipation. Pitt believed that he could persuade his own country to accept Emancipation as a part of the Union, which was popular, but he failed to carry his own cabinet with him. Loughborough, his Lord Chancellor, was particularly disloyal and would report to the King on the arguments used against Emancipation in cabinet. Pitt's own brother, Lord Chatham, sided against him, but George III's attitude was decisive. He thought Emancipation 'the most Jacobinical thing I ever heard of'. He felt deeply and sincerely that to agree to Pitt's plans would be to break his Coronation Oath. Although Pitt had been in power for so long, his position on this issue was weak for his cabinet was divided and the King's views, more than his, represented those of the country. The King, moreover, had a successor; he had already approached Addington, the Speaker, and found him willing to form a government. On March 15, 1801 Pitt left the office he had held for seventeen years. He was accompanied by Dundas, Grenville, Windham, Spencer, Cornwallis and Castlereagh.

Wilberforce felt that Addington might have been guilty of duplicity, and, typically, he told him so. 'I set off for Addington,' he remembered, 'and told him honestly what was said of him—well I acted the part of an honest man. I told him that it was universally said that Pitt had employed him to prevent misunderstanding with the King and that he had used his situation to gain the King's confidence for himself and had been too ready to receive his favour. I told him that I did not believe it was so. He was very angry at first; but we parted good friends. I was with him till late in the morning, of a Saturday night. Your mother [Barbara] was much alarmed at my long stay, a gentleman having been found dead in Westminster a few days before, murdered either by himself or some one else.'[4]

*

The failure of the Second Coalition and the League of Armed Neutrality had left France in undisputed control of the continent, while Britain's domination of the seas was as complete. Neither country seemed able to achieve anything in the other's element, and it was natural that both should look for peace. But the terms of any peace had now to reflect France's continental victories to an extent beyond what would be sanctioned by the more bellicose members of Pitt's Government. Addington had no such legacies, and there seems to have been a general understanding both that his Government would be more favourable to peace than Pitt's and that it was too weak to survive for long as a war ministry. Their common desire for peace led to Wilberforce's name being mentioned as a candidate for office under Addington. He admits to being excited by the prospect—'I was for a little intoxicated and had risings of ambition.' But he was too much a man of principle to have made a comfortable colleague, especially when a gulf separated his position on Abolition from that of Addington.

Wilberforce would have liked to have linked the two issues of Peace and Abolition by having a general renunciation of the Slave Trade incorporated in the Peace Treaty, but Addington did not wish to add to the number of issues that had to be negotiated, and he was, in any case, cool about Abolition. Wilberforce could never have fitted into any government that was not committed to his most important cause, but he was human enough to feel disappointed at his exclusion and honest enough to feel shame at his disappointment. He wrote in his private journal later that year, 'I believe that retired, domestic life is by far the most happy for me, blessed as I am with affluence, etc. Yet when I see those who were my equals or inferiors rising above me into stations of wealth, rank, etc., I find myself tempted to desire their stations, which yet I *know* would not increase my happiness.'[5]

At every stage of the negotiations Wilberforce worried that the Government was not earnest enough for peace. He did not expect any peace to be lasting or secure; he simply saw nothing to be gained by continuing the war. He was staying with Gisborne when the news of peace reached him, and, to the children's delight, they let off fireworks in celebration. He moved on to Bath, where he found 'the people *intoxicated* with joy here and everywhere'. The politicians he met were less enthusiastic, Lord Rosslyn assuring him that not one member of Pitt's cabinet would have approved the terms. Wilberforce reflected that, if this had happened, he would once more have found himself in opposition.

On his return to London he found that the old cabinet had indeed been split over the peace terms. Grenville, Windham and Spencer attacked them, but Pitt spoke strongly in their defence. 'His character now appears in its true light,' Wilberforce wrote triumphantly. He considered Pitt's support of Addington 'one of the noblest instances of true magnanimity that was ever exhibited to the admiration and imitation of mankind'.[6]

*

Wilberforce has been described as a 'Minister of Public Charity': the lull afforded by the Peace of Amiens gives us an opportunity to examine this side of his life, which was now occupying a great deal of his time. His activities during 1802 show the range of his good works.

Much of his time was occupied with familiar causes. On May 24 he spoke in defence of the Bull-baiting Bill, which was again defeated. We find him conferring with Joseph Lancaster, the educational pioneer, promoting the distribution of Bibles in Paris, determining to write another book to enlighten new members, particularly the Irish, on the evils of the Slave Trade. Abolition, the Carib lands issue, Sierra Leone and the Proclamation Society all claimed their share of his time. Together with Thomas Bernard and the Bishop of Durham he had founded the Society for bettering the conditions and increasing the comforts of the poor. This Society, which is mainly associated with Bernard, founded numerous hospitals, including some specialising in particular diseases. It aimed at establishing a system of special hospitals for those suffering from infectious complaints. Sir Robert Peel, a hard-headed philanthropist, had called on the Society's office and been so impressed by its work that he gave it £1,000. Wilberforce, with equal enthusiasm, supported Sir Robert's Bills to improve the lot of children working in factories.

But new societies had bloomed in the forcing houses of Clapham. At the beginning of the year the establishment of the *Christian Observer* had given the Evangelical movement a voice. Wilberforce was concerned lest it should prove too monotonous a drone to last. When urging Hannah More to contribute 'some religious and moral novels, stories, tales call 'em what you will',[7] he hoped to lighten its tone. 'The truth is, it is heavy, and it will be heavy from the very nature of the case. If it be not enlivened it will sink.'[8] If the content was heavy, and under the editorship of Zachary

Macaulay, likely to remain so, the price was light. The *Christian Observer* cost its readers 1/– an issue, its cheapest rival 2/6.

Macaulay was always landed with thankless jobs; in 1806 he complained to Hannah More, 'I wish I could find someone to relieve me of the editorship of the *Christian Observer*. On one side it is attacked as Calvinistic, while even our ally Scott stigmatises it as Arminian. The Dissenters make a violent clamour against it as being High Church, while the High Church abuse it as being favourable to the Methodists. The sale, however, is prospering.'[9] But his tribulations as an editor had hardly begun. In February 1809 the *Christian Observer* reviewed Hannah More's anonymous novel, *Coelebs in Search of a Wife*, which had already provided a Roman holiday for the young literary lions of the *Edinburgh Review*. Hannah More had expected no better at their hands, but she was outraged by the review in the *Christian Observer*. The reviewer did not know that she had written the book, and while praising much of it, he thought the work 'apt to be vulgar' and discovered 'some want of taste and strict moral delicacy' in it. He also took a strong and understandable dislike to the character of its hero. 'Three years' excruciating illness' she wrote to a wretched Macaulay, 'which has battered my body has probably injured my mind, and I can take this Review as an admonition to write no more.' He had no sooner absorbed this letter than he received another from her, apologising for the first.

Later still, in 1816 the correspondence column of the *Christian Observer* was to be thrown into confusion by the first published work of Thomas Babington Macaulay who was then sixteen. In a letter signed 'Candidus' he defended the practice of reading novels, and although prudently citing the spurned works of Hannah More, he also spared a good word for those of Fielding and Smollett. An avalanche of furious replies from 'Northern Vicar' and others cascaded in on Zachary Macaulay and the correspondence continued for a year.

These were dramatic moments in the life of a dull, though eminently 'useful'* magazine. The *Christian Observer*'s main function was to keep the Evangelicals' case in front of the public. Thornton was a frequent and Wilberforce an occasional contributor.

In the West Country the More sisters' schools had become an institution and a model for others to copy. 'The old bishop in petticoats', as Cobbett called her, had been busy since Wilberforce's visit to the Cheddar Gorge in 1789. Her attitude to the poor must seem as offensive to the modern reader as the patronising tone of her tracts, but both were probably not resented by the wretched peasants of the Mendips. Behind all her teaching lay the assumption that the existing social order was sanctioned

---

* The Evangelicals used this word to describe something likely to advance their cause.

by God and that to tamper with it was an offence against Him. Thus Hannah More scarcely drew a distinction between reform and revolution, between the grievances of the ill-used and the agitation of the seditious. She loved Thomas Babington Macaulay like a son and left him her valuable library in her will. He made his mother promise not to send her a copy of the speech he made in support of Reform in 1831; 'If you do,' he warned her, 'she'll cut me off with a prayer book.'[10] But the news leaked out; Hannah More revoked the bequest and 'not even a prayer book escaped the ban'.[11]

If one accepts, as she did, the divine sanction of the social order, one can only praise what Hannah More achieved within this framework. Her instruction was always practical, her pupils were taught to read, so that they could study the Bible, but not to write, as this might have given them ideas above their station. She taught the poor how to make ends meet. She deplored their eating extravagant food, through greed or ignorance, at the expense of fuel and clothing. She gave them detailed instructions on how to manage on a shilling a day. She was a connoisseur of cheap cuts of meat, grey beans, sheep's heads and skimmed milk.

In times of want Hannah More's philosophy was inadequate. No one knew better than she what famine meant to the poor, but she never uttered a word of criticism of the system that caused such misery. There is no parallel in her writings to Wilberforce's statement that the officers, as well as the crew, should be on short rations. On the other hand she and her sisters did everything within their power to alleviate the suffering of the poor. In the terrible winter of 1817, 300 calamine miners were thrown out of work when the brass foundries closed down. The sisters first provided them and their starving families with food and clothing, then, in an extraordinary industrial departure from their usual methods, they put the men back to work, bought up their ore and stockpiled it against better times.[12]

'You do not know that I have turned *Merchant*,' she wrote to Wilberforce. 'These are not very prosperous days to begin trade. But after having devised every means to assist out poor miners at Shipham, etc., etc., Mr. Addington, another neighbouring gentleman and myself have entered into partnership, and purchase every week a certain quantity of the dead stock of ore which has lain on their hands. Thus for a short time we are giving them employment. . . . If times mend we will hope to sell our stock, but we must stand the chance of other traders.'[13]

Hannah More's relationship with the poor was paternalistic and the good she could do them limited by her belief that the social order was divinely ordained, but her goodwill and kindness towards them, like her courage, were boundless. The same could not be said for her relationship with the Established Church. We have seen her disgust at finding a clergyman drunk, keeping a mistress and 'prevented from preaching by two black eyes got by fighting'. When she first established her schools she could not find enough teachers who belonged to the Church of England. Following Wilberforce's advice on 'comets'—'Whitfield has them at his command and John Wesley is not unprovided'—she engaged a number of Methodists. Although a member of the Church she was closer in beliefs and enthusiasm to the Methodists than to the dissolute clergy of the Mendips. She said as much in 1794 in a letter to Wilberforce:

'Mr. Boak returns many thanks for his book. I think he is going on well for he is dismissed from one of his curacies for being a Methodist by a Rector who keeps a mistress, gets tipsy before dinner, and last week treated 40 of the poorest wretches he could find to a strolling play because Boak had preached against plays the Sunday before. This Rector is our chief Magistrate! Don't we stand in need of a little visit from the French?'[14]

What she eventually received was a little visit from the High Church. In 1800 Bere, the curate of Blagdon, published an attack against Hannah More and her Methodist schoolmaster in his village, as a result of which the latter had to be removed. Bere then indulged himself in an orgy of unseemly and unchristian gloating which so disgusted his bishop that he, too, was removed. Bere now became a martyr. He was an adept controversialist, soon proved that he had not been guilty of any offence and was reinstated. The school, which had returned in his absence, was again dissolved. A bitter war of pamphlets ensued in which Hannah More was accused of spreading Jacobin principles, praying for the success of the French and trying to overthrow the Church; her real faults had been arrogance and lack of tact, to which she now added disingenuousness. While declaring with one breath that she intended to remain silent and that she would not deign to answer Bere's scurrilous pamphlets, with the next she unleashed a stream of vitriolic abuse. Wilberforce's part in the affair was confined to a little lobbying in London and maintaining a lengthy correspondence with Hannah More.[15]

In 1802 the controversy began to die down. The new Bishop of Bath and Wells was a man of tact who seems to have persuaded both sides that they had won a moral victory.

Hannah More was cursed with an unspeakable biographer, Roberts, of whose book Marianne Thornton has this to say:

'She [Hannah More] calls Sir Thomas Acland in one of her notes to me "The recreant Knight of Devonshire" which Roberts thinking uncivil I suppose, has altered into "the excellent and estimable Sir T. Acland"—two words that playful woman never used in her life. Somewhere else she began to me, "When I think of you I am gladerer and gladerer and gladerer", which he, thinking bad English, has done into "I am very glad".

Now if such an oaf as that will write a book at least he should be honest.'[16]

To Roberts even Hannah More's social views seemed excessively adventurous. He accordingly edited her letters and remarks to suit his own ironclad pedestrianism. An excellent life of Hannah More by Dr. Jones has at last restored the balance and we can see her again as a kind and great-hearted woman whose failings were those of her age. Although she exhibited, far more than Wilberforce, the unattractive side of the Evangelical movement, his admiration for her was apparently without reservations. When complaining of the lack of religion in Walter Scott's novels, he said of her most famous tract, 'I would rather go to render up my account at the last day, carrying with me "The Shepherd of Salisbury Plain", than bearing the load of all those volumes, full as they are of genius.'[17] It was because of the More sisters' work that he was later able to claim, 'there is no class of person whose condition has been more improved in my experience than that of unmarried women. Formerly there seemed to be nothing useful in which they could naturally be busy, but now they may always find an object in attending the poor'.[18]

Clapham did not lag behind Somerset in education. Venn established enough schools in his parish so that every child could be taught to read. Henry Thornton and Wilberforce supported schools in Southwark and Turngate out of their own pockets. Macaulay made the level of literacy in Sierra Leone far higher than in England. He and Wilberforce helped the educational pioneers, Bell and Lancaster; Grant founded Haileybury, a college for training Indian Civil Servants. The same pattern was imitated by Evangelicals in other parts of the country. It is ironical, considering their extreme conservatism and the religious emphasis of their teaching, that these schools should have been criticised as 'seditious'. But in the long run the most conservative schools were revolutionary in their effect, for only education could give the workers the means to improve their lot.

The Church Missionary Society, another key Evangelical charity, had its origins in the efforts made by Grant and Wilberforce to let missionaries into India. Wilberforce, though asked to be President of the Society, consented to serve only as its Vice-President. The Church's attitude towards it was cautious, but, when asked for his blessing, the Archbishop of Canterbury issued a somewhat tepid endorsement. The Society was not founded until April 12, 1799 and it was thus preceded by some missionary activity in Sierra Leone and among the convict settlements of Australia. But India was its main target and here it had two problems: to obtain permission for missionaries to enter the country, and to find suitable missionaries to send out. The first problem was not solved until the revision of the East India Company's charter in 1813, but as we have seen, much missionary work was done before then by the earnest chaplains sent out by Grant and Shore. The idea of life as a missionary failed to appeal even to the serious young men who studied under Simeon and Farish at Cambridge. With these two restrictions the Society had a slow start, sending out in its first fifteen years twenty-four missionaries of whom seventeen were German.

The British and Foreign Bible Society, which was founded in 1804, complemented the other Societies. It supported the Sunday Schools and helped the early missionaries by sending out translations of the Bible. After his return from India Lord Teignmouth found in this Society the main interest of his life. He retained the presidency until his death and declared that he would willingly be forgotten as the Governor-General of India if he might be remembered as President of the Bible Society. The Bible Society had narrow aims, to which it was hard for any Christian to object. It thus escaped the stormy beginnings of other Evangelical charities. By the time Wilberforce retired from Parliament in 1825 it had distributed 4,250,000 Bibles, translated into 140 languages and dialects including 55 in which it had never appeared before.[19]

These were the main pillars of Evangelical benevolence: the Abolition movement, with its offspring in Sierra Leone, the educational experiments in the Mendips and elsewhere, the Society for the Bettering of the Poor, the Proclamation Society, the Church Missionary Society and the British and Foreign Bible Society. But the movement was swollen by a host of smaller societies, religious and humanitarian, which ranged from the eminently useful Climbing Boys Society, formed to protect chimney sweeps, to the absurd, 'a maritime female penitent refuge for the poor degraded females'. These societies continued their mushroom growth throughout Wilberforce's lifetime. At one stage he was a contributor to sixty-nine, the Patron of one, the Vice-President of twenty-nine, the Treasurer of one, the Governor of five and on the Committee of five; and these figures take no account of auxiliary and branch associations or of anonymous contributions.[20]*

*

On February 3, 1803 when Parliament reassembled Wilberforce found to his horror that the French were chartering British ships to ferry their troops over to St. Domingue. Addington did not seem interested. 'He half-defended the merchants for helping Buonaparte with ships for transport, which most monstrous.'[21] Pitt had not come up to London and even Fox 'did not seem to feel the full enormity of our helping Buonaparte as he ought'.[22] Pitt wrote him a sympathetic answer: 'To aid the French in their present measures is as contrary to all general ideas of policy, as it is revolting to our feelings; and I think there must be some legal mode of

* Wilberforce often gave anonymously. He once made three separate anonymous donations to the same charity so as to avoid attracting attention.

preventing British merchants from being concerned in such a transaction.'[23] If there was such a 'legal mode' even James Stephen was
unable to find it. Nearly a month later Wilberforce was writing to Babington, 'I have ascertained that the French Government have actually engaged some English ships to carry over troops and stores to St. Domingo,
whether to serve as stiflers or drowners I know not.' Only the renewal of
war prevented this expedition.

The Peace of Amiens had never looked secure. Napoleon's efforts to
re-establish a colonial empire were matched by his reluctance to let go any
of his European conquests. The peace had scarcely been signed before he
had accepted the presidency of the Cisalpine Republic; he next annexed
Piedmont and thus brought northern Italy firmly under his control. He
invaded Switzerland, meddled in Germany and intrigued with the Bey
of Tunis. His vassal, the King of Spain, seized the property of the Knights
of St. John and assumed the mastership of the order. In these circumstances England could hardly return Malta to the Knights as she was
bound to do by the terms of the peace.

Wilberforce had heard news from Paris of Buonaparte's raging against
Lord Whitworth, the British envoy. 'He spoke loud enough to be heard by
two hundred people, and his countenance was perfectly distorted with
passion.'[24] France had used the peace to build up her navy, England to
run down hers. The army too had been greatly reduced in numbers, but
the country was eager for war. Even Wilberforce felt 'a sort of intoxicating
flush' on hearing that Lord Whitworth was returning from Paris.

Wilberforce admired Addington whom he regarded as 'a man of sense,
of a generous mind, of pure and upright intentions, and of more religion
than almost any other politician'. But he was sadly disappointed by his
performance in office. Sir Charles Middleton produced an emergency
plan to destroy any French invasion flotilla.* The Government was shown
this plan and approved of it, but did nothing to implement it. Wilberforce vainly demonstrated to them various abuses in the naval department.
He was dismayed by the chaotic measures taken to rearm the country.
Addington had underestimated enthusiasm for the war and when he
called for volunteers, he was submerged by the response.

Wilberforce received complaints from a number of bellicose but spurned
constituents. The greatest meeting ever assembled in the East Riding had
congregated at Beverley to offer their services as volunteers, only to have
their offer rejected. Thomas Grimston, an old friend of Wilberforce's, had
recruited, commanded and paid for a troop of yeomanry cavalry through-

---

* This plan was to requisition a hundred large merchantmen, equip them with
carronades and use them to run down the flotilla. Middleton's expertise in naval
affairs was unquestioned and the plan was probably the cheapest and quickest way of
meeting the threat of invasion.

out the war. His services, too, were declined, without any reason being given. Ralph Creyke wrote from Marton complaining that the new levies were being provided with no firearms and an inadequate number of pikes:—'I have heard much talk of the advantages of a pike, but the firelock is the only weapon to put into the hands of a gentleman soldier.'[25] Other volunteers had been denied even the courtesy of an answer. There were no firearms for the new levies and few plans for providing any. Even after war was declared on May 17, 1803 this state of idle confusion continued. The defences of the Thames remained flimsy and, while half a million veterans camped the other side of the Channel, nothing was done to implement Middleton's plan or to raise a defence force at home.

Wilberforce's attitude towards war was consistent. If it must be waged, he believed that it should be waged energetically, but he was always anxious to clutch at any straw that might lead to peace: 'I pant for peace,' he wrote to a naval officer at this time. He was thus opposed to the retention of Malta, both as a provocation to the French and as a breach of a promise. 'Malta,' he said in the Commons on May 23, 'is indeed a valuable possession, but the most valuable of all the possessions of this country is its good faith.' Wilberforce felt deeply on this subject and published his speech. On June 4 he spoke again, against a censure on Addington moved by Pitt's friends.

Although Pitt could achieve little in Parliament he was active in his role of Lord Warden of the Cinque Ports. Wilberforce worried about him. 'Pitt is about to take command of 3,000 volunteers as Lord Warden; I am uneasy at it. He does not engage on equal or common terms, and his spirit will lead him to be foremost in the battle. Yet as it is his proper post, one can say nothing against it.'[26] He was concerned not only that Pitt might be killed, but that he would die before experiencing true religion. He expressed his anxiety in a letter to Gisborne. 'I feel a good deal for him on account of the danger to which he is exposed, while, I hear, so little prepared for the event which may ensue. For Pitt to close his life in resisting the enemies of his country, would indeed be in history a brilliant catastrophe; but how differently must we think and feel, who see through a Scriptural medium!'

The strain of the summer session was too much for Wilberforce's health. He retired to Bath and improved greatly, but he found his 'frame was not susceptible of that thorough repair which it used to receive at Bath in earlier days'.[27] Babington, seriously concerned about his health, implored him to retire from politics, but Wilberforce refused; he compared himself to a mouse, or pony, which though not able to pull a cart, might yet perform some service that would justify its not being put out to grass for the rest of its life. He wrote in a similar vein to William Hey: 'I often think how little I should have done in a state of society in which muscular force was the main point of superiority.' His health prevented him from serving his country in any military capacity; he must therefore do what good he could as a civilian.[28]

After the renewal of war the rift between Pitt and Addington widened rapidly. This distressed Wilberforce who recognised the latter's limitations, but admired him in spite of them. No one, including Wilberforce, expected him to make a forceful War Minister, but the speed with which he ran down the navy shocked many members; Wilberforce, among others, was influenced by Middleton's expert opinion that he had been 'strangely negligent'.

Pitt attacked this negligence in his first open act of opposition. On March 15, 1804, he tabled a motion on the state of the navy; during the debate Tierney launched a 'low attack' on Pitt, which Wilberforce answered 'as I was told extremely well'. The motion was lost, but the fact that it had been made spurred the Admiralty out of its lethargy.

The next month Pitt decided to go into more systematic opposition, although without allying himself to Fox. Wilberforce attributed the change in his attitude to the influence of 'men of party spirit'. 'I fear he has been urged forward by people of less wisdom than himself. I am out of spirits,' he wrote in his journal, 'and doubtful about the path of duty in these political battles.'[29] He never seems to have considered that Pitt could just as well have been acting from patriotic motives. If he thought, as he must, that he could conduct the war better than Addington, it was surely his duty to work to replace him. But if Addington had acted with more purpose he would have had Wilberforce's support against his greatest friend. 'I cannot help regretting,' Wilberforce reflected, 'that Addington's temperance and conciliation should not be connected with more vigour.'[30]

Torn by loyalty to his friend and duty to the Ministry, Wilberforce tried to effect a compromise by promoting a coalition between Pitt and Addington, but his efforts came to nothing. Addington was not prepared to fight to remain in power and Pitt had already scented victory. At the end of April he was in communication with the King and by May 10 he formed a new Government.

But Pitt was never to recapture the power he had wielded during his first period in office. He wished to include Fox in his Government, but was not prepared to force him on the King. With Fox excluded, Grenville and his followers declined to serve. Pitt had no great personal following and for the next two years he was to be dependent on Addington and the King for his majority in the Commons. He could no longer rely on automatic support from a patriotic House. His old relationship with the King was also impossible to renew. We have seen that, in his first administration, a no man's land existed between their areas of power. They had been bound together by mutual need, but from 1804 Pitt was no longer the only acceptable Prime Minister. His basis for bringing pressure to bear on the King had gone, and even if it remained he would have had to act cautiously for the King's state of health was such that, if upset, he would again go mad.

CHAPTER XVII

PITT AND THE SLAVE TRADE

PITT's return was welcome to the Abolitionists; the first fire of his support for their movement had burnt out long ago, but he could still be counted as its friend, while Addington had hardened from a gradual Abolitionist to an opponent.

The issue had not been debated since 1799. In 1800, as we have seen, Wilberforce was deflected by hopes of achieving an agreed suspension of the Trade. He had allowed 1801 to pass without renewing his motion because he did not wish to prejudice the chance of a general, international Abolition. He had learnt in November from Otto, the French Foreign Minister, 'that if our government would propose to negotiate for the Abolition, theirs would probably consent to it'.[1] This statement, encouraging though it seemed to Wilberforce, must have been insincere. By the terms of the peace France had regained all her West Indian possessions; she had also acquired Louisiana from Spain. She was at that very moment equipping an expedition of 25,000 men to reconquer St. Domingue. With the richest island in the Indies and a great new continental territory in her grasp, she cannot have contemplated an end to the Trade. Wilberforce ignored these factors when he unburdened himself in a long letter to Addington:

'Can any thing be more reasonable than to expect, now that our islands have been saturating themselves with slaves for near six years longer than you consented to fix, and two years beyond Dundas's period . . . than to expect, I say, that you should now adopt that measure which he (whose sentiments, you will admit, were at least not more favourable to Abolition than yours) publicly recommended in 1792. . . . I scarce need suggest that all the European powers by whom the Slave Trade has ever been carried on, will be engaged in the negotiation at Amiens; and that the ascendancy possessed by Great Britain and France over their respective allies, affords means and facilities for effecting the desired object, which may never again occur. . . . I have good reason to believe that America would gladly unite in the engagement. . . . The proposal will with far more propriety be made by us to France, than by France to us, for many reasons; but especially for this, that we alone of all the European nations know any thing of the real nature of the mischievous effects of the Slave Trade. France most likely conceives, as I myself thought before I had gone into the business, that the conditions of the slaves in the colonies is the grand concern (as it was of their society, called Amis des Noirs), and not the detention of Africa in barbarism and misery.

'I will only add a few words for myself. It is not (to a friend I may make the avowal) without emotion that I relinquish the idea of being myself the active and chief agent in terminating this greatest of all human evils; but *you* will readily believe me when I say, that any unpleasant sensations on this head vanish at once before the prospect of effecting the desired object far more radically and completely than by any springs I could set in motion. I hope I can truly assure you also, that it helps to reconcile me to *my* loss on this occasion, that it would be *your* gain; and I should look on with joy, if the Disposer of all human events, who has already rendered you the instrument of good to mankind in the termination of one of the most bloody wars that has raged in modern times, should further honour you, by making you His agent in dispensing to the world this greatest and most extended of all earthly benefits.'[2]

Addington was not ready for such glory. He had already endorsed the French expedition to St. Domingue and he now showed signs of indecision about the uncultivated lands in Trinidad which, unfortunately for the Abolitionists, remained in Britain's hands after the peace. It was further evidence of the planters' foolishness that they should wish to bring vast new areas under cultivation at the very moment when the French were reclaiming the richest plantations in the world. Pitt agreed with Wilberforce, who used him as an intermediary; Canning introduced a motion against importing slaves to cultivate new lands. Wilberforce wrote to Muncaster: 'Oh what an eternal blot would it be on the character of parliament, if after having resolved by an immense majority that the Slave Trade should be gradually abolished, we should enter on the cultivation of a new settlement, the complete peopling of which with negro slaves, reckoning the number always lost in opening uncleared lands, would take near a million of human beings!'[3]

Canning's Bill was postponed until late in the summer session of 1802 and it was debated in a flat, unfriendly atmosphere. Addington had shocked Wilberforce, who never ceased to expect better things of him, by declaring his sympathies with the French efforts to crush St. Domingue. Wilberforce's own view of those who planned this expedition was that 'there is scarce any thing to be found equal to them in the annals of human villainy'.[4] Canning's motion was lost in a House shaken by reports of slave rebellions. Wilberforce had intended to follow it with one for Abolition, but having failed to put an end to a part, the House could not be expected to abolish the whole of the Trade. The rebellion of the Nova Scotians in Sierra Leone had added to feeling against the Abolitionists and it was, in any case, too late in the session to achieve anything.

The summer of 1803 had seen the country so preoccupied with the renewal of the war that to have introduced a motion on Abolition would have been damaging to the cause. But in 1804 prospects were more encouraging than at any time since the first debates on the subject.

A military empire having succeeded Jacobinism as the enemy in France, the issue could be considered on its merits for the first time since the outbreak of the French Revolution. The House of Commons that was to debate it would be very different from that of 1799, for since the Act of Union it had been joined by Irish members without West Indian connections and with a strong predilection for liberty. The planters in 1800 had shown signs of grasping the fact that to flood the New World with slaves might not be beneficial to their property there. In 1804 they were still wavering over a decision to suspend the Trade. 'Some of the principal West Indian proprietors,' Wilberforce wrote to Hannah More in February, 'begin themselves to relish the idea of suspending the Slave Trade for three or five years. They have not the assurance to pretend to be influenced by any principles of justice (this is literally true), but merely by a sense of interest.'[5]

This letter is really more revealing about Wilberforce than about the West Indians. To have felt obliged to pretend to be influenced by principles of justice, they would first have to be convinced that the Trade was wrong. Wilberforce's letter shows him to have been astonished at their failure to realise this, but it would have been truly astonishing if they had.

He was approached by West Indians about a suspension, first in the winter of 1803, then in the spring of 1804. They assured him they could carry this motion unanimously; he planned to make it palatable to the House by having Addington introduce it and appear 'the sober practical man in opposition to the wild enthusiasts who are for total Abolition'. But Addington, though doubtless sober and practical, was without any interest in Abolition and declined this flattering role. It was the second time that he had rejected Wilberforce's overtures, but Wilberforce persisted in believing him sympathetic to the cause. His failure to accept was due to 'a natural aversion to come forward just at this moment'. Wilberforce had built up an imaginary picture of Addington in his mind which was not supported by anything he had ever said or done. Because he liked Addington and saw signs of religion in him Wilberforce thought he must have Abolitionist leanings, and he clung to this belief long after it had been shown to be false. When Addington finally declared his views on Abolition Wilberforce's self-deception added to his sense of betrayal. On this occasion the West Indians had again failed to gauge the feelings of their colleagues. A meeting of planters on May 17 voted by a large majority against any suspension of the Trade.

On May 20, 1804 Wilberforce moved the Abolition of the Trade. He was unhappy with the stiffness and lack of fluency with which he spoke, though the Speaker told him 'he hoped I had satisfied myself, as I had done every body else'.[6] His opponents made no showing in the debate, but nothing can have prepared him for the result. Wilberforce's motion was carried by 124 votes to 49; every Irish member voted for him and they celebrated with a great Irish dinner at which he was toasted. This triumph was marred for Wilberforce only by two jarring notes. 'I fear the House of Lords,' he wrote to Newton in answer to the old man's congratulations. The other matter was more personal. Wilberforce had thought that by offering Addington the role of the practical but humane statesman who would move the suspension of the Trade, he was doing him a great service at the cost of allowing himself 'to be stigmatized as [a] speculative visionary'. He could not believe that a man with Addington's good sense, such 'noble and upright' qualities and even the glimmerings of religion, could be on the wrong side over Abolition. He was therefore deeply wounded when Addington rose and in a 'speechling' of forty seconds said that Wilberforce's plan was impracticable.

He was consoled by messages of encouragement from all quarters. None can have pleased him more than John Newton's letter. The old slaver doubted if he, 'within two months of entering his eightieth year, should live to see the accomplishment of the work, but the prospect will give me daily satisfaction so long as my declining faculties are preserved'.

On June 7 and 27 Wilberforce's Bill passed through its Second and Third Readings. In the last debate Addington was 'most vexatious' and provoked him into sarcasm. 'I am glad,' Wilberforce reflected afterwards, 'that some rather severe remarks I made on him and his warm zeal for Abolition, in which he declared none of us surpassed him, did not get into the newspapers.'[7]

After such success in the Commons it was heartbreaking to hear Pitt, Grenville and Bishop Porteous agreed against trying to force the Bill through the Lords until next year. 'I own,' he wrote, 'it quite lowers my spirits to see all my hopes for his year at once blasted, *yet I can't help myself*. To be sure, one session in such a case as this is not much; yet as we know not what may happen in the interval, I tremble lest some insurrection, or other event with two handles, should turn men against us.'[8] 'It is truly humiliating,' he wrote to Muncaster,[9] 'to see in the House of Lords, four of the Royal Family come down to vote against the poor helpless, friendless slaves.'

Wilberforce still hoped to use Parliament's favourable mood to force through some legislation against the Trade. The obvious target was the branch that supplied slaves to Surinam and other conquered colonies. But Pitt much preferred to stop this traffic by Royal Proclamation. 'Very strong on this,' Wilberforce noted 'and against any vote of Parliament.'[10] Wilberforce had to be content with this promise, for he had no chance of winning the vote against Pitt's opposition. Proclamation was in any case a preferable weapon. The West Indians might regard legislation against this branch of the Trade as permanently removing the threat of the virgin lands being cultivated and this was one of the few prospects that could soften their opposition to Abolition.

Proclamation may have been the best policy for the Abolitionists, but Pitt seemed to shrink from applying it. On July 3, 1804 he had promised to act and this promise was repeated time and again without anything being done to implement it. On September 14 Wilberforce wrote to him the sort of personal appeal that seldom failed. 'Let me beg you, my dear Pitt,' he implored, 'to have the Proclamation issued. It will not cost you an hour to settle this. I beg you will remember how much I myself am personally concerned in it, if any other excuse be necessary for my boring you so about it than the merits of the subject itself.' But his pleas, like his reminders, were ignored and it was over a year before the Proclamation was issued, and then only under threat of legislation.

*

After the postponement of Wilberforce's motion on Abolition, the most colourful of its supporters came into prominence for the first time. Henry Brougham, a Scotsman of versatility and genius, had burst upon London in 1802 when he was one of a group to set up the *Edinburgh Review*. Brougham was a perfect example of a brilliant man who failed to achieve the highest political offices. He could master subjects so easily and with such speed that he seldom troubled to add any depth to his knowledge. He was bursting with ideas, some brilliant, some almost insane, and his arrogance was too great for him to distinguish between them. He did not argue, he lectured, and his great demagogue's voice would drown any opposition. Brougham's conceit was such that Samuel Rogers commented after he had left him, 'Solon, Lycurgus, Demosthenes, Archimedes, Sir Isaac Newton, Lord Chesterfield and a good many others went away in one postchaise!'[11] He was a careerist who at one time or another let down almost all his colleagues, until he became so distrusted that for the last thirty years of his long life he was excluded from all political power, but there were some causes in which he believed with passion and which he never betrayed. Abolition and Emancipation were among them. He was capable of great kindness as he showed when the Macaulay and Wilberforce families fell on hard times. Wilberforce remembered him for his exemplary conduct towards his own family. 'Of his extraordinary powers,' he wrote, 'no one ever entertained a doubt. There are also very pleasing traits of private character: I have been assured of his incessant and kind attentions to his old mother. On his brother's failing, I believe, in business, he paid his debts to a large amount and took on himself, I am assured, before being in office, the charge of his eight or nine children.'

This statement and the long friendship between the two men show Wilberforce to have been much more tolerant than other members of the Clapham Sect. Stephen had called Brougham 'the dupe of his [own] vanity',[12] while Henry Thornton, a severely critical man, made him the subject of a typical denunciation. 'It is my clear and deliberate opinion,' he wrote, 'that Brougham tho' clever and in some respects useful to our cause and also to the Government is so rash, so unreasonable in his expectations and above all has such accommodating principles that he is neither a very pleasant, a very safe, nor a very creditable instrument.'[13]

Apart from the *Edinburgh Review* Brougham was one of the founders of London University and the Penny Cyclopedia; he has also left us the Brougham carriage.

Brougham planned to tour the continent in the autumn and winter of 1804. He had become interested in Abolition in 1803 and was elected to the Committee, together with Stephen and Macaulay, in 1804. He was now willing 'to shape his course' to suit the needs of the Abolitionist movement. There was in fact little he could do except hector his hosts on the iniquities of the Slave Trade, as the European Trade had ended for the duration of the war; though he did extract a rather wistful offer from the Dutch to abolish the Trade if England would give them back their colonies. Brougham travelled as an American and seemed to enjoy taking chances. Wilberforce was worried to hear of him quartered in the same lodgings as several French generals.

An unprecedented effort was made to prepare the Abolitionist argument for the Lords in 1805. Their case must be convincing on every front and leave no opening for their opponents that could not be overwhelmed by a deluge of facts, quotations and figures. Stephen's study of slavery in the West Indies brought all the arguments up to date, and Wilberforce was anxious in case the African side of the matter should be neglected. Everyone was put to work. Stephen had already prepared a collection of admissions made by opponents of Abolition. Young Robert Grant was set the task of going through classical writers for quotations, Muncaster of providing quotations from African travellers. He set out a list of propositions for which he needed supporting quotations. A less thorough man would have regarded most of them as having been established in earlier debates. The table itemised the harm done by the Slave Trade.

PROPOSITIONS TO BE PROVED BY EXTRACTS FROM AFRICAN TRAVELLERS.

A. The African negroes not inferior to the natives of other countries, under similar circumstances, in intellectual or moral qualities. There is nothing either in their under-standings, or hearts, or tempers, which makes it impossible to civilize them—

2. or establish a commercial connexion with them. Contra, they are naturally in-genious, commercial, &c.

B. The Slave Trade is the source of great misery to Africa—

1. by producing or prolonging wars.

2. by causing the chiefs to commit acts of depredation on their own subjects or their neighbours—village breaking.

3. by causing innumerable acts of individual depredation, as kidnapping, &c.

C. The Slave Trade produces unjust convictions for crimes, excessively severe punishments, prosecutions for witchcraft, &c.

2. The Slave Trade has gradually rendered the penal code of Africa, from being mild, very severe. (This you proved admirably.)

D. The Slave Trade renders person and property insecure in Africa, and thereby is a standing obstruction to civilization.

E. It is not true that the Slave Trade prevents on the whole much misery; captives being killed, &c.

F. It is not true that the slaves if not bought by the Europeans would be murdered, instead of being set to work.

G. It is not true that slaves are ill off in their own country, or worse off than in the West Indies.

H. The Slave Trade corrupts the morals of the Africans, so that they are rendered the worse, not the better, for their connexion with us.

Muncaster's daughters were asked to copy out their father's quotations. 'I beg you will tell your daughters,' Wilberforce finished his letter, 'with my respects, that they will reflect as long as they live with pleasure, on any time or pains they may expend in behalf of the poor Africans.'[14]

*

On his return to London at the beginning of 1805, Wilberforce found Pitt and Addington reconciled.

Wilberforce was delighted both with this development and with Pitt's eagerness to acquaint him with it. 'It showed me that he understood my real feelings.' He called on Pitt and walked with him in the Park. ' "I am sure," he said, "that you are glad to hear that Addington and I are at one again." And then he added, with a sweetness of manner which I shall never forget, "I think they are a little hard upon us in finding fault with our making it up again, when we have been friends from our childhood, and our fathers were so before us, while they say nothing to Grenville for uniting with Fox, though they have been fighting all their lives." '[15]

It did not occur to Wilberforce that Pitt's sweetness might have been intended to sugar a pill. Pitt had this new alliance in mind and wished to put aside all questions that could divide it. Since Abolition was one of these he asked Wilberforce if it might be postponed, a request which was sternly refused. Wilberforce had waited sixteen years for this moment; no personal considerations could allow him to delay it any further. The First Reading passed smoothly enough but on the Second Reading he suffered the most surprising and painful defeat of the entire campaign. For the first time in sixteen years Pitt did not declare his personal desire for Abolition. He rose, denied 'any intention of entering into the debate' and confined himself to answering a charge that the Government had issued an official contract for the purchase of slaves.[16]

'Beat, alas, 70 to 77,' Wilberforce wrote in his diary. 'Sad work! Though I thought we might be hard run from the face of the House, I could not expect the defeat, and all expressed astonishment. The Irish members absent, or even turned against us. . . . Some Scotch, I believe, who last year neutral, voted against us. Great canvassing of our enemies and several of our friends absent* "from forgetfulness, or accident, or engagement preferred from lukewarmness".'[17] He was tormented by this failure. 'I never felt so much on any parliamentary occasion. I could not sleep after waking the first night. The poor blacks rushed into my mind, and the guilts of our wicked land.'[18] He wrote to Muncaster, 'From the fatal moment of our defeat on Thursday evening, I have had a damp struck into my heart. I could not sleep either on Thursday or Friday night, without dreaming of scenes of depredation and cruelty on the injured shore of Africa, and by a fatal connexion diffusing the baleful effects through the interior of that vast continent. . . . I am almost ashamed of being so well and comfortable, when I think of the misery of my poor clients. . . .'[19]

His resolve was unshaken. He was approached after the debate by Hatsel, the Clerk of the House, and told: 'Mr. Wilberforce, you ought not to expect to carry a measure of this kind. . . . You and I have seen enough of life to know that people are not induced to act upon what affects their interest by any abstract arguments.' 'I *do* expect to carry it,' Wilberforce replied, 'and what is more, I feel assured I shall carry it speedily.'[20]

A defeat on the main issue and resentment at Pitt's speech may have hardened the Abolitionists' attitude towards the Guiana branch of the Trade. Wilberforce met Pitt on March 9 and declared that if nothing was done he must bring it before the House and seek the assistance of the Opposition. Three days later Pitt told him the Government had unanimously agreed to stop the Trade and asked him to draft regulations. But the delay had destroyed Wilberforce's trust. On March 28 there was a meeting of leading Abolitionists at Lansdowne House. Fox and Grey were

---

* Nine Abolitionists who had not missed a debate for sixteen years were absent because they thought the motion safe (Clarkson Abolition II 499).

there and the Opposition was in a majority. They were in no mood for delays. When Wilberforce told them that he hoped Pitt would soon issue the Order in Council, 'I saw certain significant winks and shrugs, as if I was taken in by Pitt, and was too credulous and soft, etc.; but I of course saw them as if I had seen them not.'[21] 'Bankes and I charged with message to Pitt, whether he would effect Guiana Abolition, or we should.'[22] They were able to return with an answer that the Government would stop the Trade by Order in Council.

This promise was made at the end of March, on behalf of a cabinet that had been consulted, to an important group of members including the leaders of the Opposition, but it was not implemented until September 13. Pitt's coldness towards Abolition can be attributed to a reluctance to offend the Addingtonians, but his delay in issuing the Order in Council must be due to other reasons, since Addington had been consulted about the Order and had agreed to it. There was therefore no one of importance who would be offended by its being made and however much Pitt had cooled towards Abolition, he must have retained a preference for it, so long as it had no ill-effects politically.

The most likely explanation is that Pitt was unwell and no longer as capable as he had been. He had to organise and finance another coalition in Europe, while the basis of his Government in England became impossibly thin when the loss of Melville in April was followed by the resignation of Addington in July. The King still refused to hear of the inclusion of Fox and Grenville. These responsibilities were too much for his waning powers and it is not surprising that, submerged by them, he should have lost sight of the Guiana branch of the Slave Trade. When the Order was issued it was not because of Pitt's insistence but because of the efficiency of one of his anti-Abolitionist ministers, Lord Castlereagh.

*

Wilberforce's life at Broomfield and in London continued at its hectic pace. Apart from the Slave Trade he had enough political and philanthropic business to fill a working day. One sentence in his diary sums up his way of life: 'I feel tired today as a man whose general work overdoes him.' His good causes sometimes led him into unlikely company. 'July 30th. Morning breakfast—friends about sending the gospel to the Indians. Mr. Norton's Mohawk's dance—Venn, Dealtry, Cookson, John Thornton—much discussion. We are all extremely struck with Mr. Norton, the Mohawk chief (Teyoninhokarawen); his blended modesty and self-possession; his good sense and apparent simple propriety of demeanour. May it be a providential incident thrown in my way to send the gospel to those ill-used people. He again danced his war dance more moderately.'[23] There is something very appealing in the thought of those solemn and worthy Evangelicals requesting a Mohawk Chief to moderate his war dance.

He had moved to Broomfield to escape from the chaos of Palace Yard, but Henry Thornton had been right when he said that Wilberforce would have found no peace in Siberia, let alone Clapham. His hospitality and his reluctance to offend visitors soon transformed Broomfield to the same state as Palace Yard. He would have moved to the country had he not valued the religious society of Clapham so much. He took his responsibilities as a father very seriously and dreaded the evil influences to which his children might be exposed elsewhere.

The references to them in his diary and correspondence have become more frequent. Although they were still young,* he noticed them to be 'very sagacious and attentive observers and shrewd in detecting inconsistencies. Often when they seem to be playing about the room heedless of all that is going forward, it appears afterwards, that they heard and remembered the conversation which was going forward'.[24] He took his family on holiday to Lyme Regis and although the demands of his children filled much of his time—'I am irresistibly summoned to a game of marbles,' he wrote to Hannah More—he was still able to work more effectively than at Broomfield. He wrote an article for the *Edinburgh Review* about the Slave Trade and articles and reviews for the *Christian Observer*. He read, criticised and amended Stephen's book on Slavery and Hannah More's *Education of a Princess*.

---

* William had been born in 1798, Barbara in 1799, Elizabeth in 1801 and Robert Isaac in 1802. They were to be joined by Samuel in 1805 and Henry in 1807.

CHAPTER XVIII

PITT AND MELVILLE

WILBERFORCE was not a decisive man. His speeches were often hedged with minute qualifications while his ability to see the merits of both sides of an argument, and his loathing of partisan, 'party' politics both made decisions more difficult to take. Later in his life it became a joke that 'you might safely predicate his vote, for it was certain to be opposed to his speech'.[1] But on some matters he was adamant, and corruption in high office was one of these.

In February 1805 a Committee of Navy Inquiry presented a report which included disturbing accusations against Dundas, now Lord Melville. Wilberforce was in Pitt's office when this report arrived. 'I shall never forget,' he wrote, 'the way in which he seized it and how eagerly he looked into the leaves without waiting even to cut them open.'[2]

Pitt's eagerness was understandable, for Melville was the most indispensable member of his Government. Under his leadership the navy had been rebuilt from the disgraceful state in which it had been left by Addington and St. Vincent. He was also Pitt's closest political friend and adviser, his manager in the House and the man who kept Scotland loyal to his Government.

Wilberforce's attitude towards Melville had always been uncertain; friendship with Pitt was the only thing the two men had in common, but, in spite of Melville's disastrous introduction of gradual Abolition, they seem to have got on well enough. Dundas signed one letter to Wilberforce in 1793, 'Adieu my dear little Fellow.' Wilberforce sometimes applied to him for political favours: he admired and envied his capacity for hard work, but deplored his influence on Pitt's 'unsullied mind'. Perhaps because his admiration for Pitt was so complete, Wilberforce blamed his failings on Melville. Although a worldly man Melville was never a vicious one and apart from bearing the heavy responsibility of introducing Pitt to drink, we may doubt if his influence was as harmful as Wilberforce supposed.

'His connexion with Dundas was Mr. Pitt's great misfortune,' he wrote. 'Dundas was a loose man, and had been rather a disciple of the Edinburgh

School in his youth, though it was not much known. Yet he was a fine fellow in some things. People have thought him a mean, intriguing creature, but he was in many respects a fine, warm-hearted fellow. I was with him and Pitt when they looked through the Red Book, to see who was the properest person to send as Governor-General to India; and it should be mentioned to Dundas's honour, that having the disposal of the most important office in the King's gift, he did not make it a means of gaining favour with any great family, or of obliging any of his countrymen, but appointed the fittest person he could find [Sir John Shore].'[3]

The case against Melville was not that he had been guilty of improperly applying Admiralty funds for his own benefit but that he had allowed his subordinates to do so. An Alexander Trotter, paymaster of the Navy when Melville was its treasurer, had used Naval funds to enrich himself. Thomas Raikes, the Governor of the Bank of England, had protested to Pitt about these abuses in 1798 and Pitt had passed the complaint on to Melville, who convinced him that everything was in order.

Wilberforce later wrote several memoranda to prove that, by this time, Pitt and Melville were 'scarcely upon speaking terms'. He claimed to have seen for over a year that Melville's power over Pitt's mind had decreased. But the stories he quoted[4] to illustrate his point are less than convincing and Wilberforce's adoration of Pitt coloured his opinion of his friendship with Melville to such an extent that he is not a reliable witness on this matter. Pitt, he maintains, could not forgive Dundas for involving his honour in the scandal by his lies after Raikes's accusation. 'In truth Pitt was chiefly led into supporting Melville by that false principle of honour, which was his great fault—he fancied himself bound in honour to defend one who had so long acted with him.'[5] He does not seem to have realised that Pitt might be angry with Melville and have lost much of his affection for him—and we can accept Wilberforce's evidence that this was the case —without ceasing to need him as his most valuable minister and his most able political supporter. But this is the kind of issue on which Wilberforce's judgement is wholly unreliable. It seemed so simple to him. Melville had broken the rules and allowed corruption in his department; he must therefore be punished—if the great Pitt supported him then he must have been led astray by 'that false principle of honour'. Members who voted against Dundas were demonstrating integrity, those who voted for him, 'party spirit'. But few other members saw the matter in such sharp tones of black and white, and Wilberforce's explanation of their behaviour is of little use for he did not begin to understand how they thought.

On April 8 Samuel Whitbread moved resolutions censuring Melville; Wilberforce listened intently to the debate, in the hope of hearing some argument that might divert him from his unpleasant duty, but there was none. As he rose to speak he caught Pitt's eye and saw his friend watching him with anguish, for the vote would be close and Wilberforce's speech could be decisive. 'It required no little effort to resist the fascination of that penetrating eye—from which Lord Erskine was always thought to shrink.'[6] He steeled himself and put the issue in its simplest form. 'Here is my Lord Melville publicly declaring on his oath that he has tolerated his dependent in a gross breach of an Act of Parliament for the purposes of private emolument. I really cannot find language sufficiently strong to express my utter detestation of such conduct.'[7] But for Wilberforce's speech, Whitbread's resolutions would have been rejected by about forty votes; after it the voting was tied with 216 members in favour of the motion and 216 against it. The Speaker gave his casting vote against Melville. The blow was too much for Pitt. He had been unable to hide his emotions when he saw Wilberforce siding with the Opposition and after the vote his self-control broke. He had endured more disasters, military and civil, than any Prime Minister in British history and he had met each one with unflinching courage. But now tears poured down his face; his friends gathered round him to shield him from the taunts of the Opposition and led him out of the House.

Wilberforce's diary reflects little of this drama. 'Stormy night,' he wrote, 'I spoke late, and from the state of men's minds, with a great deal of effect . . . adjourned at half-past five. Could not get cool in body or mind. Bed, and slept till twelve.'

He explained Pitt's collapse in the same almost anthropomorphic terms as he had interpreted his friendship with Melville. 'I never saw him so *quailed* as on Wednesday night,' he wrote to Muncaster. '. . . and this in my opinion did him honour, by proving, that though so invincibly firm when all was well within, he could not put a good face on it when his own conscience told him he was defending a bad cause.'[8]

The debate of April 8 was followed by others in which the Commons discussed the form of trial to which they should subject Melville. Wilberforce's interventions were mainly to insist that there must be a trial of some sort. He was always free with his superlatives, but even in the heat of the moment few members could have agreed with his statement that 'perhaps there never was a time when Parliament was called on to intervene in a matter of such importance'.[9]

He was relentless in the interests of justice, but he was also anxious that the issue should not be pre-judged and he was never personally vindictive towards Melville. When pressed to join the deputation which carried the Resolution up to St. James's he made the dignified reply: 'Christianity enforces no such sacrifice. She requires us indeed to do justice, but to love mercy. I learn not in her school to triumph even over a conquered enemy; and must I join the triumph over a fallen friend?'

He also took the opportunity to discuss the disadvantages of a system of 'strong government'. If Fox, Windham, Grenville and their followers had been in Pitt's cabinet, as he had wished, the motion would never have stood a chance of success. 'In short, what is called a strong government, and is eulogised as such in high terms, is often, in my opinion, the most corrupt of all others; as it is able to carry through any measure, however objectionable and support any man, however justly obnoxious.'[10]

It was finally decided to impeach Melville. There was no evidence that he was guilty of anything more serious than negligence and, as this was not among the charges against him, the impeachment duly failed. Wilberforce's intervention made him enemies. Melville's partisans blamed him for their hero's downfall. 'Bankes tells me I am much abused by Melville's friends, especially the ladies.'[11] Pitt never mentioned the affair to Wilberforce, but he would have had to be more than human not to feel deeply wounded by his speech, however much he understood and expected it. Whether it shortened Pitt's life is impossible to say, though the collapse of his health must have been hastened by the political strains caused by losing Melville. One of Wilberforce's constituents thought so. Sir John Legard wrote to Wilberforce on December 10, 1806, explaining why he could not vote for him in the next election, in a letter that shows the degree of adulation which Pitt could inspire in his followers:

'You must know (I think) that I was very much attached to Mr. Pitt, as a public Man; but You cannot know, for it is difficult to conceive the enthusiasm I felt for him, and still feel for his memory. I am almost disposed to repeat, what I once heard Lord Muncaster say, "that he considered him as something supernatural, something between God and man." Without going quite that length, I consider him the greatest Statesman this, or any other Country ever produced; and moreover, as good, and as honest as a public man could be. With these sentiments it is natural that I should be hurt by everything which gave him pain.

'When the unhappy delinquency of Lord Melville became the subject of investigation, I was particularly interested about it, as it was obvious that such a subject, involving the character of one of Mr. Pitt's most intimate Friends, and, as it were, his coadjutor in every political measure of importance, would agitate him extremely, and I felt some satisfaction in being able to satisfy my reason, that the Lord Melville was certainly culpable; yet in no way so as to involve his Friend, and, as he was punished, most severely, by the loss of his Honours, his Reputation, and his fortune I hoped the Country would be satisfied, and the matter left at rest.

'This, however, did not satisfy the Pure Patriotism of the Opposition. They had got the Man down, and they were determined to kick him on the ground. The motion for Impeachment was brought forward; the success of it seemed doubtful; or rather, I believe, appearances indicated that it would be thrown out, when, You Sir arose, and supported by a well earned reputation for integrity and independence, You made a luminous speech, which was said, at the time, to influence forty votes, and the question was carried by the Speaker's deciding voice. I believe the concurrence of these circumstances, the delinquency of Lord Melville and the desertion of some of his oldest Friends, inflicted a wound upon the Mind of Mr. Pitt, which it never recovered; and, as the mind never fails to influence the body, I cannot divest myself from the idea that they contributed to his premature death. I was told, by a Member of the House of Commons, who was present at the debate, that Mr. Pitt could not conceal his agitation, when he saw the turn Your Speech was taking. He found it difficult to be resolved, if Brutus so unkindly knocked or no. But, when the noble Caesar saw him stab: Ingratitude more strong than Opposition venom, quite anguished him: "Then burst his mighty heart!" The stab, that was then given to Mr. Pitt's feeling, have ever since rankled in my bosom.

'And then, a train of thoughts (perhaps the pure instigation of the Devil), rushed into my mind, and I have kept possession of it. I saw Mr. Pitt declining in popularity, because *all* his measures had not been successful. I saw him deserted by some of his oldest, and most attached Friends, merely as I thought from ambitious causes, because our Good Old King, was in a very declining state of health, and, upon the melancholy event of his death, there would be, of course, a change in Administration. I then said to myself, "Mr. Wilberforce is courting popularity, for if it were not so, as a Christian he would spare a fallen man; as a Friend to Mr. Pitt, he would spare Mr. Pitt's Friend, and decline voting at all, if he cannot give a vote in his favour." I have now performed this painful duty, which I should have declined for ever, had I not received Your second letter. I venerate the character of Mr. Pitt, and I resent any injury done to him as if it were done to my father, my Brother, and my Friend, at once. I am convinced You know how to pardon me, if I am in error, if I am not I have no pardon to ask.'[12]

It was the kind of letter, reluctantly undertaken, conciliatory in tone and yet damning in verdict, which must have been painful to write and agonising to receive. Wilberforce was more used to writing such letters than receiving them, and it clearly shook him. Where he would normally have docketed the letter with some brief comment, he now covered it with remarks, many of which, unfortunately, are illegible. But we can still read, 'Sir J. Legard—very frank—blaming my conduct about Lord Melville. It did not injure Pitt's health.'[13] Wilberforce was prepared to concede that Pitt might have died of a broken heart, but if so it was caused by Austerlitz, not by him. According to Macaulay he even used to call the expression of exhausted misery that Pitt wore in his last days 'the Austerlitz look'.[14] It is astonishing how ruthless the kindest of men can become when driven by a sense of moral purpose.

Apart from one truculent speech to the Commons Melville himself behaved magnificently. He recommended Sir Charles Middleton, the best possible choice, as his successor.* The most attractive side of his character is shown in a meeting with Wilberforce five years afterwards. 'We did not meet for a long time,' Wilberforce remembered, 'and all his connexions most violently abused me. About a year before he died, we met in the stone passage which leads from the Horse Guards to the Treasury. We came suddenly upon each other, just in the open part, where the light struck upon our faces. We saw one another, and at first I thought he was passing on, but he stopped and called out "Ah Wilberforce, how do you do?" and gave me a hearty shake by the hand. I would have given a thousand pounds for that shake. I never saw him afterwards.'[15]

*

In November Wilberforce heard the welcome news of Trafalgar which removed the threat of invasion that had hung over the country since war was resumed. He was so overcome by the news that tears ran down his face until he had to stop reading. But the next month brought the disastrous defeat of the allies' armies at Austerlitz and this blow was too much for Pitt. A minor attack of gout developed complications and he died on January 23.

Wilberforce returned to London on January 21 where he heard from Rose that 'all was hopeless'. On the 23rd Bishop Pretyman told him that Pitt had died at 4.30 that morning. 'Deeply rather than pathetically affected by it. Pitt killed by the enemy as much as Nelson. Babington went to dine at Lord Teignmouth's, but I had no mind to go out.'

Very religious people can sometimes seem inhuman to the rest of us in their apparent indifference to the death of those they love. Wilberforce believed in a Heaven in which he would meet his old friends again. To lose them in this life was therefore no more than a brief parting and cause for nothing beyond a few nostalgic pangs. If this belief is deeply held there is no reason to fear death so long as the person who is to die is ready to meet his Maker. Only when Barbara was dangerously ill did his fear get the better of his faith and allow him to express himself like an ordinary man in terror of losing what he loved most.

Wilberforce's friends wrote him letters of condolence over Pitt's death as if he had lost a close relation and Wilberforce was moved by it as much as by deaths in his family. But he was as upset that Pitt had died unregenerate as that he had died at all. It had always been his dearest wish to convert Pitt. His intellectual powers had been greater than those of any other man Wilberforce had known. In addition his quality of 'moral

* Creevey described the appointment as that of a 'superannuated Methodist in order to catch the votes of Wilberforce & Co.' 1905 edition p. 36.

purity' made him not only as great but as good as any man without religion could be. Wilberforce dreamed of what Pitt could achieve if his gifts could be harnessed to the cause of true religion. He told Muncaster: 'I own I have a thousand times (aye, times without number) wished and hoped that a quiet interval would be afforded him, perhaps in the evening of life, in which he and I might confer freely on the most important of all subjects. But the scene is closed—forever.'[16]

*

Pitt's sincerity in supporting Abolition has been the subject of much argument. There is no doubt that at the beginning he was an enthusiast. He encouraged Wilberforce to take up the cause and gave official assistance, on an unprecedented scale, to Clarkson's investigations. He was prepared to take up the leadership of the campaign when Wilberforce was dangerously ill. When Dolben's Bill was being mauled by the Lords, Pitt used all his influence to force it through before the end of the session.

His support continued to be vigorous until 1792, when he 'held out on St. Domingo account' though he followed this hesitation with the finest speech he ever made on the Trade. Clarkson, who admired Pitt, wrote a tantalising passage in his *Abolition*: 'A difficulty still more insuperable presented itself in an occurrence which took place in the year 1791, but which is much too delicate to be mentioned. The explanation of it, however, has convinced the reader that all the evidence of Mr. Pitt from that day were rendered useless, I mean as to bringing the question, as a Minister of State, to a favourable issue.'[17]

At first sight it seems that Clarkson must be referring to the offer in 1791 by the French planters in St. Domingue to give the island to Britain. The acceptance of such an offer—and Pitt did accept it in 1793—would have added to the strength of the West Indian lobby and increased the importance of West Indian interests in the country. It would equally have killed the economic argument against the Trade. By supplying slaves to foreign colonies, it could be urged, England was helping her rivals, who had larger, more fertile, but less populated islands, to ruin her own West Indian possessions. Abolition, by contrast, would remove the British supplies of slaves to these islands, and if foreign powers could be persuaded to join England in Abolition, the slave population of the West Indies would be frozen in a pattern favourable to her interests. If St. Domingue were acquired these arguments fall to the ground. Events were soon to prove that the last thing the island needed was more slaves, but with it in her possession, Britain would have had no reasons of self-interest to stop the Trade.

But the text of Clarkson's sentence argues against this interpretation. The offer of St. Domingue may have been highly delicate in 1791 when it was made, it could scarcely have been so in 1807 when Clarkson wrote his book. If Pitt had betrayed the cause because of greed for St. Domingue's tainted riches, Clarkson would hardly have been so charitable in his judgement on him. He considered that if he could have exerted himself 'as a Minister' he would have carried the measure. But Clarkson admits that Pitt, ham-strung by a divided cabinet, could never do so, and he admired his efforts as an individual for the cause. This distinction is implicit in Clarkson's sentence. Something happened in 1791 to prevent Pitt from ever moving the matter 'as a Minister of State'. It is a reasonable guess that the only sort of incident Clarkson would consider too delicate to mention twenty-five years afterwards would be some kind of intervention by the King. But he would have needed to be as positive a supporter of Abolition as his Prime Minister to force it on a reluctant cabinet. And in 1791 he was still far from being an enemy. This explanation, though no more than a guess, would be consistent with the verdict given by the Agent of Jamaica. 'His Majesty,' wrote Stephen Fuller, 'is a true friend to the Colonies. I am of the opinion we owe more to him than is generally known to the defeat of the absurd attempt of abolishing the Slave Trade.'[18]

Once the war with France had started, prospects of Abolition faded away. There were two reasons for this: firstly, the widespread reaction to Jacobinism and slave revolts, and secondly the fact that Britain's war effort was, to start with, confined to an attempt to seize the French West Indian islands. Sir J. W. Fortescue, the historian of the British Army, wrote: 'The secret of Britain's impetus for the first six years of war may be said to lie in the two fatal words, St. Domingue.'

Critics of Pitt's behaviour maintain that when he 'threw out against slave motion on St. Domingo account', Wilberforce meant that he was aiming at acquiring St. Domingue and that this goal and Abolition were inconsistent. It seems very unlikely that Wilberforce did mean this. He would have found such an exhibition of 'interest' on the part of a friend, whose purity he admired, unspeakably shocking. He wrote several memoranda on Pitt and Abolition, and he would surely have mentioned such a betrayal had it taken place. Again Pitt's protest came nearly a year before the war with France and the first attempt to take over the island. The obvious explanation is more likely to be right: Pitt knew that the House would be shocked by the outrages reported from St. Domingue and that, in this mood, they would again reject Abolition. If Britain had succeeded in taking and holding St. Domingue Pitt's devotion to Abolition would have been put to the test. But during the early years of the French wars the island and the cause were equally unobtainable.

Wilberforce had no criticism of Pitt's conduct towards Abolition during his first period in office. He gave his all in 1791 and 1792 and afterwards the cause was hopeless. Wilberforce's task in these bleak years was to keep

the issue alive but Pitt had too many responsibilities to concern himself
with lost causes. His support from 1794 to 1801 may have been perfunc-
tory but it was also consistent and that was all that could be required of
him. He spoke in every debate and, after one defeat, offered to introduce
the matter himself the next year. His only lapse was when he urged Wilberforce to accept some method of referring the question to the Colonial
Assemblies as suggested by Ellis. This move, useless in itself, would have
kept the cause dormant at a time when nothing positive could be achieved
and established a lack of goodwill on the part of the planters. The same
process, with Amelioration taking the place of Abolition, was to play an
important part in the Emancipation campaign. But Wilberforce, however
hopeless the prospects, insisted on keeping the cause alive and, on this
occasion, he seems to have had little difficulty in persuading Pitt to
support him.

When Pitt returned to office in 1804 everything had changed. Abolition
was acceptable to a majority of the Commons; the Lords' attitude,
although untried, was less promising, but the menace of Jacobinism
having been removed, the matter could again be considered on its merits.
But Pitt had lost the support of Grenville and his followers, who were loyal
Abolitionists, and been forced to rely on the Addingtonians who were not.
He was not the man he had been in 1801. His personal ascendancy had
gone for ever, together with his exclusive call on the votes of patriotic,
uncommitted members. He found the effort of conducting the war and
maintaining a majority in the Commons too much. He could no longer
take Abolition, too, under his wing. This decline in Pitt must account for
the delay in issuing the Order in Council, while his lukewarm performance
in the 1805 debate can be attributed partly to the same reason, partly to a
general loss of interest. He certainly never reached the stage of being
opposed to Abolition.

Brougham put the case against Pitt best:

'How could he, who never suffered any of his coadjutors, much less his
underlings in office, to thwart his will even in trivial matters—he who
would have cleared any of the departments of half their occupants, had
they presumed to have an opinion of their own upon a single item of any
budget or an article in the year's estimates—how could he . . . after
shaking the walls of the Senate with the thunders of his majestic eloquence, exerted with a zeal which set at defiance all suspicions of his
entire sincerity, quietly suffer, that the object, just before declared the
dearest to his heart, should be ravished from him when within his sight,
nay, within his reach, by the votes of the secretaries and under-secretaries,
the puisne Lords and the other fry of mere placemen,—the pawns of his
board? It is a question often anxiously put by the friends of the Abolition,
never satisfactorily answered by those of the Minister; and if any addi-

tional comment were wanting on the darkest passage of his life, it is
supplied by the ease with which he cut off the Slave traffic of the conquered colonies, an importation of thirty thousand yearly, which he had
so long suffered to exist, though an order in Council could any day have
extinguished it. This he never thought of till 1805, and then, of course, the
instant he chose, he destroyed it for ever with a stroke of his pen. Again,
when the Whigs were in power, they found the total abolition of the traffic
so easy, that the measure, in pursuing which Mr. Pitt had for so many
long years allowed himself to be baffled, was carried by them with only
sixteen dissentient voices in a house of 250 [sic] members. There can then,
unhappily, be but one answer to the question regarding Mr. Pitt's conduct on this great measure. He was, no doubt, quite sincere, but he was
not so zealous as to risk anything, to sacrifice anything, or even to give
himself any extraordinary trouble for the accomplishment of his purpose.
The Court was decidedly against abolition; George III always regarded
the question with abhorrence, as savouring of innovation—and innovation
in a part of his empire connected with his earliest and most rooted prejudices,—the Colonies. The courtiers took, as is their wont, the colour of
their sentiments from him. The Peers were of the same opinion. Mr. Pitt
had not the enthusiasm for right and justice, to risk in their behalf losing
the friendship of the mammon of unrighteousness; and he left to his
rivals, when they became his successors, the glory of that triumph in the
sacred cause of humanity, which should have illustrated his name, who in
its defence had raised all the strains of his eloquence to their very highest
pitch.'[19]

Brougham's arguments were refined and perfected by Sir James
Stephen and W. E. H. Lecky, and throughout the nineteenth and early
twentieth century the Whig view of Pitt's conduct prevailed—that,
although in favour of Abolition, he was too tepid, timid and enamoured
of office to force it through Parliament. The Whig historians forgot that
the greatest of all the Whigs had disagreed with them. A distinguished
group of Whigs once dined with William Smith* in the spring of 1796.
Fox, Tierney, Courtenay, Mackintosh, Francis Baring, Philip Francis and
Samuel Rogers were among the guests. The conversation was literary for
a time, then it suddenly turned to Wilberforce. Philip Francis said that
'Wilberforce, if it was left for him to decide whether Pitt should go out of
office for ten months and the Slave Trade be abolished for ever, or Pitt
remain in—with the Slave Trade, would decide for Pitt—"Yes," said Fox,
"I'm afraid he would be for Barabbas".'[20] Rogers thought this a joke,
since he knew Fox respected Pitt's sincerity on the Slave Trade, and so
long as Pitt was sincere, the conflict could not arise.[21] The modern school

* Not Sydney Smith, as stated by Professor Coupland. (See Rogers, *Recollections*
7–10, *Table Talk* 83.)

of historians has shown that Pitt did not have the power to make Abolition a Government measure, and that after 1792, with the Royal Family, his own ministers in the Lords, a great part of the country and even personal friends like Pepper Arden and George Rose turned against it, he had no chance of success.

It is conceivable that if Pitt had staked his own career on Abolition in 1791 or 1792, had bullied Dundas and soothed Thurlow, he might have been successful. But it would have been a desperate gamble, more desperate than Brougham as a Whig could recognise, for Pitt would have been hazarding what he himself must have regarded as the sound government, the very constitutional stability of the country, on a single issue. And he could not know that it would be the last chance to achieve Abolition for another twelve years. Pitt was a man with a deep faith in the powers of reason. Once convinced of the need for Abolition he was confident that sooner or later a majority of both Houses would come to share his views. It was not a prospect to encourage him to risk everything for a quick victory.

It is less easy to find excuses for Pitt during his second period in office. A majority in the Commons was certainly available for Abolition at any time between 1804 and 1806, and the prospects in the Lords were more favourable than before. There is no doubt that Pitt was handicapped both by ill health and by a dependence on anti-Abolitionist votes. But it is equally clear that his own enthusiasm for the cause had vanished. His performance in 1805 both in his speech on Wilberforce's motion and in his prevarication over the Order in Council is evidence enough. The factious conduct of Grenville and the obstinacy of the King must share some of the blame.

The most serious accusation against Pitt is concerned with his failure to prevent an extension of the trade into conquered colonies until forced to do so by the Lansdowne House ultimatum. It is, however, worth noting that Pitt both steadfastly refused to allow Crown lands in these places to be sold and stocked with new slaves and managed to keep the Trade out of Trinidad. His failure to act before the Lansdowne House meeting may have been due to divisions within the cabinet, and his slowness afterwards to difficulty in drafting a satisfactory Order, together with the inefficiency of Lord Camden, Castlereagh's predecessor. But he would never have tolerated such delays if he had retained his old Abolitionist zeal.

Even Wilberforce's enthusiasm for the cause had its limits. He was happy to sacrifice his health, his leisure and, if necessary, his life in its service, but he was not prepared to make the least accommodation of principle. There were times when Pitt was in difficulties and when Wilberforce's help would have been invaluable, but the latter, at the cost of great pain, would turn away from his friend and follow his conscience instead. Wilberforce might have used the Saints' votes in Parliament either to bribe or coerce the Government towards Abolition, but he refused to do so when Stephen suggested it. The vote against Lord Melville provided a perfect opportunity for bargaining; Pitt would surely have been willing to advance a cause to which he was sympathetic in return for the saving of the most important member of his Government. The threat of systematic opposition might equally have frightened Addington into a more favourable attitude. But Wilberforce refused to subordinate the means to the end. Pitt, too, had his principles and his priorities, the most important of which was to keep a strong Government in being. To do so he had to make accommodations to the views of his colleagues. It would have been easier for him to support Abolition with vigour if he could have expected something in return.*

Pitt's death marks a turning point in Wilberforce's political life. He never felt the same admiration and love for any other political leader. He would support the King's Government as a matter of duty, but he became more and more the independent he had always imagined himself to be. His political philosophy continued to be that of Pitt, shorn of its 'party' features and with a religious colouring.

*

Pitt's death gave Wilberforce one last legacy, for the man who had run the nation's finances with such efficiency was quite incapable of managing his own. This cannot have come as a surprise to Wilberforce, who had been called in to deal with similar crises in the past. Pitt had always been cheated mercilessly by his servants and tradesmen. Wilberforce's cousin Robert Smith (later Lord Carrington) was called in to examine his affairs in 1786. He found that three or four hundredweight of meat was being sent in every Saturday. In a second letter he complained to Wilberforce, 'I can scarcely conceive a private house in the Kingdom where such a quantity of provisions, as are charged, could be consumed. . . . Can it be possible that 3,800 pounds of meat could be dressed in twenty-eight days?'[22] Hardly in the house of a bachelor who seldom entertained.

Pitt's appointment as Warden of the Cinque Ports did something to relieve his financial embarrassment and gave him an income of £10,000. But in 1801 Pitt's friends, including Wilberforce, had raised £12,000 to pay his debts. By the time of his death they had again mounted to £40,000. 'This must have been roguery,' Wilberforce comments, 'for he really has not for many years lived at a rate of more than £5 or 6,000 per annum.'[23]

* Pitt's role in the Abolition campaign, particularly for his first period in office, is best analysed in 'William Pitt and the Abolition Question: A Review of an Historical Controversy' by Patrick Lipscombe. Leeds Philosophical and Literary Society. Vol. XII 87–128.

The idea was advanced that the nation should pay Pitt's debts, but Wilberforce preferred them to be met by private subscription. The precedent, he thought, would be a dangerous one which might lead to 'sad party practices'. 'But again,' he argued, 'to whom are the debts due? If to tradesmen, they ought to be paid, but might not debts to other sort of people, rich connexions, etc. be suspected; and the very idea of the people's paying these is monstrous. I must say, however, that considering the number of affluent men connected with Pitt, some of whom have got great and lucrative places from him, I cannot doubt but that, with perfect privacy and delicacy, a subscription might be made adequate to the purpose.'[24]

But Wilberforce, as so often, had taken too generous a view of human nature. Spencer Perceval, who more than any other politician was to succeed Pitt in his esteem, at once contributed £1,000, although he was not a rich man and had nine children to support. Perceval warned Wilberforce to be quick. 'That warmth of sentiment, which opens and softens the heart, certainly has a tendency to remove all strictures, even those of the purse; but the frame has a tendency to return to its habitual contraction.'[25] Wilberforce took this excellent advice to heart and tried for three days to raise the sum by private subscription. But on the third day, when he had made little progress, a motion was carried in the House that Pitt's debts should be paid by the nation. Wilberforce was only able to prevent the £12,000 contributed by his rich friends in 1801 from being included in this settlement by the threat of opposition.

On January 27 it was proposed that Pitt should be given a public funeral. In an astonishing display of the 'party spirit' that Wilberforce detested, both Windham and Fox opposed the motion, which was nevertheless carried by an immense majority. Wilberforce was one of those who bore the banner in front of the coffin. The nearby statue of Lord Chatham seemed to him to be gazing with consternation into the grave of his favourite son.

CHAPTER XIX

ABOLITION: TRIUMPH

LORD HENRY PETTY, the Chancellor of the Exchequer in the new Government, and an ardent Abolitionist, had been the organiser of the Lansdowne House meeting which forced Pitt to issue the Order in Council. After Pitt's death he stood for his old seat at Cambridge. Wilberforce gave him his support without thinking very much about it because of his services to Abolition. His Cambridge friends were horrified. Milner wrote him a series of long letters; 'I am vexed from the heart,' he claimed, at Wilberforce's support of a man who consorted with the worst sort of democrats and unbelievers. The good dean was so angry that he digressed and ended by criticising Wilberforce with equal vehemence for '*bearing too much with what was decidedly unjustifiable in Pitt's administration*'.[1] He finished in an acid vein, 'Did I tell you, they say Lord H. Petty must have gained you by praying extempore?'[2] Simeon wrote on the same lines and the affair produced what Wilberforce called 'a sad degree of rufflement'. Lord Henry won his election in a most satisfactory manner, Lord Palmerston, his opponent, suffering, Wilberforce believed unjustly, from being considered hostile to Abolition, and many graduates withholding their votes from him for this reason alone.

The new administration included many friends of Abolition. Fox, Grenville, Grey and Petty were among its leading advocates and Fitzwilliam, Spencer and Erskine were well-disposed towards it. Only Addington, now Lord Sidmouth, and Windham could be counted on as certain enemies. Best of all, the balance in the House of Lords was more favourable than at any time during the campaign. Fox's influence with the Prince of Wales ensured his neutrality; Grenville was available to shepherd the measure through the House, where Sidmouth was the only member of the Government certain to oppose it. Stephen wished to use the Saints' position in Parliament to ensure a friendly reception for Abolition. Wilberforce's rejection of this plan is worth reprinting, as showing the way he treated a problem which must sooner or later confront any parliamentary reformer:

'Stephen had a plan suggested by his warm zeal, that we should send a

245

deputation to the new ministry, to make a sort of contract that we would befriend them as we did Pitt, i.e. give them the turn of the scale, etc. if they would promise us to support the Abolition as a government measure. The idea is inadmissible, both on grounds of rectitude and policy (the two parties would infallibly have different ideas of the practical extent of the obligation, and mutual misunderstanding would ensue), yet I think we ought to contrive that the effect intended by it may be produced; and though I dare scarcely be sanguine when I recollect with whom we have to do, yet I cannot but entertain some hopes that the wish to mollify, and even conciliate, a number of strange impracticable and otherwise un-comeatable fellows by gratifying them in this particular may have its weight; at least it will tend to counteract the fear of offending the West Indians.'[3]

He demonstrated the independence of his position on March 3 when he criticised allowing a politician, Lord Ellenborough, to be appointed Lord Chief Justice. He admired and liked Ellenborough, whom he had first met on his continental tour in 1785. But he feared that by making a party man Lord Chief Justice, the Constitution might suffer the worst blow it had sustained since the revolution through the decisions of the courts being or seeming to be influenced by 'party attachments'. Ellenborough took his criticism seriously and was anxious to convince Wilberforce that he had behaved with propriety. He wrote an eight-page letter justifying his taking office in which he repeatedly promised not to allow his judgements to be influenced by political considerations. 'If after this explanation . . . you shall still retain your unfavourable opinion of the step I have taken I shall learn it from you with inexpressible pain.'[4] A year later, after he had left office, Ellenborough wrote more lightheartedly, 'Well Wilberforce, I hope I have not done much mischief after all.'

It was only when the Ministry of all the Talents came into power that the weakness of Pitt's support for Abolition became evident. Wilberforce found Fox 'quite rampant and playful, as he was twenty-two years ago, when not under any awe of his opponents'. Fox and Petty assumed that they would be successful in the Commons but not in the Lords, though Fox had obtained a promise of neutrality from the Prince of Wales. Feeling in the country was behind the Ministry. Clarkson had returned to his labours and in a journey, which he himself pronounced to be out-standingly successful, he found the younger generation passionately opposed to the Trade.

On March 31 a Bill was introduced to forbid the Trade with any cap-tured colony or foreign power, the first clause of which gave legislative effect to Pitt's Order in Council. The Attorney General Pigott sponsored the Bill in the Commons, Grenville in the Lords. Apart from correcting some inept drafting Wilberforce was able, for the first time, to sit back and be swept along with the tide. 'How wonderful are the ways of Providence!' he wrote in his diary. 'The Foreign Slave Bill is going quietly on. How God can turn the hearts of men!'[5] By May 18 the Bill had passed both Houses. Grenville did not wish to put the main question until the next year, for the Bishops had left town and the House of Lords was still uncertain without them. He wrote to Wilberforce that he would press on with total and immediate Abolition if he thought there was a fifty-fifty chance of success. He thought that this was not yet the case, and that Parliament would resent any attempt to rush the main question through before the summer recess.[6] Instead a general resolution for Abolition was introduced in both Houses. 'How wonderful are the ways of God,' Wilberforce wrote in his journal, 'and how are we taught to trust not in man but in Him! Though intimate with Pitt for all my life since earliest manhood and he most warm for Abolition and really honest; yet now my whole human dependence is placed on Fox, to whom this life opposed, and on Grenville, to whom always rather hostile till of late years, when I heard he was more religious.'[4]

The resolution, moved by Fox, declared the Trade to be 'contrary to the principles of justice, humanity and sound policy'. It resolved that the House would abolish it with all expediency. At the same time Wilberforce moved an address calling on the King to use his influence to obtain the co-operation of other countries. The debate was marred by a truculent and absurd speech by General Gascoygne in which he attempted to justify the Trade on scriptural grounds, and declared that it was so useful that, if it did not exist, it would have been right to start a new one. A final Bill, suggested by the alertness of Wilberforce and Stephen, prevented a last orgy of slaving by forbidding any new ship from entering the Trade. All these measures were carried with ease. 'If it please God to spare the health of Fox,' Wilberforce wrote, 'and to keep him and Grenville together, I hope we shall next year see the termination of all our labours.'[8]

The next month Fox became gravely ill. 'William Smith with us after the House,' Wilberforce wrote in his journal on June 29, 'and talking of poor Fox constrainedly; when at last, overcome by his feelings, he burst out with a real divulging of his danger—dropsy. Poor fellow, how melancholy his case! He has not one religious friend, or one who knows any thing about it. How wonderful God's providence. How poor a master the world! No sooner grasps his long-sought object than it shows itself a bubble, and he is forced to give it up.' Fox must have seemed a contradiction to Wilberforce. It was part of the latter's creed, laid down in *Practical View* and confirmed elsewhere, that little good could be achieved by men of the world. Wilberforce wrote at this time to William Hey, 'I have myself long ceased to expect much from any men who are destitute of true religion,' and this description fitted Fox all too well. But the sincerity of his support for Abolition was as obvious as his religious failings.

Fox bore the torture and humiliation of his last illness with great dignity. He never complained of his pain, but he did express a longing 'to go down to the House once more to say something on the Slave Trade'. 'I quite love Fox for his generous and warm fidelity to the Slave Trade cause,' Wilberforce confided to his journal. But the two men were so different that they could not do each other justice.

Wilberforce warmed to Fox's humanity and kindness and recognised his genius, but he was repelled by the profligacy of his life and appalled by his unpatriotic policies. But Fox's personality was overpowering; to meet him was to pass under the magician's wand, as Pitt had told the Abbé de Lageard. George III, who for most of his life hated Fox, ended by regretting his death more than that of Pitt, his most faithful servant. Wilberforce may have felt ashamed at feeling more affection for him than he should have for such a worldly man. On his part Fox had respected Wilberforce's humanity until the war with France began. Then he saw it replaced by what seemed to him to be a servile support for Pitt's policies accompanied by frequent expressions of independence. In 1806 Abolition brought them together again but they were never able to appreciate each other fully. Wilberforce's qualifications about the good that might be achieved by worldly men were no more unfair than Fox's forecast that he would 'be for Barabbas'.

At the end of the summer session Wilberforce 'slipped into the snug and retired harbour of Lyme, for the purpose of careening and refitting'. He used the peace he found there to write a pamphlet against the Trade, which he planned to publish just before the next debate on it in the House of Lords. 'A pamphlet thrown in in just such circumstances, may be like a shot which hits between wind and water,' he wrote to Bankes; 'it might prove of decisive efficiency. It will be well to supply people who wish to come over, with reasons for voting with us. For all men are not of the liberal or rather lavish, turn of Lord de Blaquiere who, when a friend who had asked him to vote with him on a certain private member's bill, was going on to state the reasons he had to urge his Lordship to give, "Oh," replied the peer, "let alone your reasons, surely it is the part of a friend to give my vote without reasons or against them." My idea is to state the chief arguments that may be urged to prove the injustice and cruelty of the Slave Trade; its pernicious effects on the happiness of Africa, and its obstruction of her civilization. Then to be very short on the middle passage, and more particular on the West Indian branch of the subject.'[9]

Wilberforce's tract came out on time, but it had sprouted from a pamphlet into a full-length book. *A letter on the Abolition of the Slave Trade; addressed to the freeholders and other inhabitants of Yorkshire* consolidated and summarised all the arguments that the Abolitionists had been using since they began their crusade. It contained little that was new, but it was an opportunity to present the case against the Trade in more detail than was possible in any speech. All the arguments ever urged by his opponents were refuted with the utmost care. He even went back to the Flood, in which he implicitly believed, to disprove the theory that Africa had never produced any civilisation. He surveyed the attitudes of the Greeks and Romans towards slavery and contrasted the very different impressions of the African character formed by travellers in that continent and planters in the West Indies. He showed Abolition to be desirable on grounds of morality, compassion, justice and 'that fluctuating, and often vicious instructress', expediency. It was a powerful document and an example of the pains to which Wilberforce was prepared to go to make his case complete.

The impetus behind the Abolitionist movement was now so great that not even the death of Fox in the summer of 1806 could affect it. On his death-bed Fox had said, 'Two things I wish earnestly to see accomplished —Peace with Europe and the abolition of the Slave Trade. . . . But of the two I wish the latter.' It was also a measure of the Abolitionists' strength that they should choose to introduce their Bill in the House of Lords. Wilberforce had had the cup dashed from his lips too often not to be concerned about the result. After Fox had gone they had to rely increasingly on Grenville, particularly in the Lords, and although Grenville had been loyal to the cause since the day that he, Pitt and Wilberforce sat beneath the Holwood oak, Wilberforce had never liked him. The reasons are rather mysterious since Wilberforce disliked very few people and might have been expected to appreciate Grenville's contributions to the cause. In any case at the end of his life Wilberforce remembered, 'Pitt once sent me word—"You don't like Grenville. I know and Grenville knows too".'[10] But a few years before the Talents took office, when he heard that Grenville had been reading Gisborne's sermons, his dislike melted away. This was as well for he now had to work closely with Grenville and trust him absolutely. On January 31 he wrote: 'Grenville told me yesterday he could not count more than fifty-six, yet had taken pains, written letters, etc. The Princes canvassing against us, alas.'[11] But on the morning of the debate Grenville showed him a list of over seventy peers who would vote for Abolition.

Most of the movement's old enemies turned out to deliver their last protests and the Duke of Clarence again denounced it on behalf of the Royal Family, though Wilberforce thought that he did so with less eloquence than usual. Lords St. Vincent and Eldon paraded their old arguments in favour of the Trade. Sidmouth 'fretted and hurt me', Wilberforce complained, for he still could not recognise him as an enemy of

Abolition. Hawkesbury, once a gradual Abolitionist, now spoke against the motion. But the finest speech of the evening was made by Grenville, 'Grenville's famous speech', Wilberforce called it in his diary. In a letter to Muncaster he added that it 'was one of the most statesman-like I ever heard, and it was universally acknowledged to deserve this character'.[12] Grenville's arguments were familiar and contained nothing that was not incorporated in Wilberforce's letter to the freeholders of Yorkshire, but they were presented with admirable clarity and force. He ended, not with the usual patriotic peroration, but with a highly personal passage in which he praised Wilberforce's steadfastness in the Cause:

'If your Lordships should agree to the abolition of this inhuman trade in blood, as I trust you will feel it due to your own character and to the character of the country to do, it will meet in the other house of parliament with the strenuous support of a person to whom the country is deeply indebted for having originally proposed the measure, and for having followed up that proposition by every exertion from which a chance could be derived of success. I cannot conceive any consciousness more gratifying than must be enjoyed by that person, on finding a measure to which he has devoted the labour of his life, carried into effect—a measure so truly benevolent, so admirably conducive to the virtuous prosperity of this country, and the welfare of mankind—a measure which will diffuse happiness amongst millions, now in existence, and for which his memory will be blessed by millions yet unborn.'[13]

This tribute infuriated Lord Westmorland, an implacable enemy of Abolition, whose contributions to earlier debates on the subject had been characterised in Wilberforce's diary as 'coarse'. He now unleashed a violent diatribe against Wilberforce. 'Though I should see the Presbyterian and the prelate, the Methodist and the field-preacher, the Jacobin and the murderer unite in support of it, in this House I will raise my voice against it.'[14] 'Westmorland out-blackguarding the blackguard', Wilberforce commented in his diary. But he later wrote to Muncaster, 'Westmorland bespattered me; but really it was a double pleasure to be praised by Lord Grenville and abused by Lord Westmorland.' The Duke of Gloucester and Lords Moira and Holland spoke with distinction in favour of Abolition. The Bill was carried at four o'clock in the morning of February 4 by 72 votes and 28 proxies to 28 votes and 8 proxies. It passed through Committee and its third reading without incident.

The debate in the Commons was fixed for February 23; Wilberforce's diary for the intervening period reflects his hopes and anxieties: 'I receive congratulations from all, as if all done. Yet I cannot be sure. May it please God to give us success. Lord Grenville's speech concluded with a most handsome compliment to me, and several peers now speak with quite new civility. How striking to observe Pitt and Fox both dead before Abolition effected, and now Lord Grenville, without any particular deference from Court, carried it so triumphantly! But let us not be too sure.'[15]

'Looking at the list of the House of Commons. A terrific list of Doubtfuls. Lord Grenville not confident on looking at Abolition list; yet I think we shall carry it too. Several West Indians with us. How popular Abolition is, just now! God can turn the hearts of men.'[16] By February 20 the outlook had become clearer and more encouraging. 'Lord Howick [Grey] in earnest and very pleasing. Our prospects brighten.' He spent the morning of the 23rd with Howick, who was to introduce the motion, dined with friends and entered the House in a mood of wary optimism.

The atmosphere there was so tense that Howick, an experienced speaker, became nervous and ill at ease and his introductory speech, though persuasive, was not a polished performance. He maintained that the injustice and cruelty of the Slave Trade, the miserable conditions on the Middle Passage, and its flouting of all Christian principles, had been established in earlier debates. The remaining arguments against Abolition were those of expediency. A minute statistical examination of the Slave Trade convinced him that its abolition would do little harm to Liverpool and much good to the West Indies. It had been claimed that the Slave Trade should be allowed to continue because it was sanctioned by great men of the past. He demolished this argument by showing that it could equally be used to condemn the Reformation and justify the use of torture. In any case 'the names of Pitt and Fox are not inferior to any other . . . let us rear this monument, more dear and splendid to their memory than any other that can be erected. This measure these great men left as a legacy to this house and to their country. . . . Upon this great question which was no less than to give peace and happiness to Africa, all other differences for a moment subsided.'[17]

General Gascoygne in his reply lamented that he had to deal with prejudice as well as argument, but his speech, too much of which was concerned with the House's scandalous refusal to hear yet more evidence, cannot be said to have contended successfully with either. Conditions did not favour him. It was difficult for supporters of the Trade to gain a hearing and impossible for them to impress the House. Many of its regular defenders including Windham remained silent, while others, like Rose and Castlereagh, did not even vote. But speeches for Abolition were greeted with enthusiasm and every telling expression in them applauded. After each speaker sat down another six or eight would spring to their feet eager to hammer their own nail into the coffin of the Trade.

Many were young men, returned to Parliament in 1806, who had given pledges to their constituents to vote for Abolition. Most of them followed Grenville's example and devoted their perorations to the praise of Wilberforce, and Fox's warmth for the Cause was remembered by his friends.

There was a general assumption of success which Wilberforce, after so many disappointments, must have found alarming. Praise and premature congratulations were showered upon his head from every part of the House; some tributes were elegant and moving, others couched in what now seems absurdly flowery language; Sir John Doyle lapsed into the latter school at the end of a strong speech for Abolition—'Let me congratulate the hon. member,' he finished, 'upon the effects produced by his unwearied industry, his indefatigable zeal, and his impressive eloquence, in thus bringing to a happy conclusion, a measure, which does so much honour to his heart and head, and which washes out this foul stain from the pure ermine of our national character.'[18]

The cumulative effect of all this praise, together with the certainty that the Trade was now doomed, was too much for Wilberforce. He sat almost in a trance, while a part of his mind, as a reflex action, assessed the different speeches. 'Lord Howick . . . embarrassed and not at ease, but argued ably. Astonishing eagerness of House.—Lord Milton very well. Fawkes finish, but too much studied and cut and dried. Solicitor General excellent.'[19]

Sir John Doyle produced an amusing argument against the plea that if Britain abandoned the Slave Trade her place would be taken by others and all the equipment so expensively ordered would be wasted. The first half of this old stumbling block was no longer convincing, for America was in the course of abolishing her Trade, Denmark had already done so, France and Spain were firmly blockaded and Portugal had not the resources to take over Britain's share. But Sir John took a more moral line.

'Suppose', he said, 'a highwayman should urge as an excuse, that it is true he did rob the man, but it was because he knew that if he did not, Will Bagshot's gang would, and that moreover it turned out a profitable job; and suppose that when pressed to relinquish so disgraceful an occupation, he should answer, "but I have gone to great expense in purchasing horses, which would be fit for nothing else but the highway. I have built stables, but they will suit none but highwaymen's horses, and I have purchased pistols and blunderbusses at a great expense, which would be useless in any other calling.' I mention this, merely to show how far the argument might be carried, and not as a comparison; for though no man has been more unhandsomely treated by highwaymen than myself, yet I would not degrade their profession by comparing it with the Slave Trade.'[20]

Each of these sallies and every tribute to Wilberforce was greeted with loud applause, but the most moving moment of the Debate came when Sir Samuel Romilly made his famous comparison between Wilberforce and Napoleon.

'When he looked to the man at the head of the French Monarchy, surrounded as he was with all the pomp of power, and all the pride of victory, distributing Kingdoms to his family, and principalities to his followers, seeming, when he sat upon his throne to have reached the summit of human ambition, and the pinnacle of earthly happiness, and when he followed that man into his closet or to his bed, and considered the pangs with which his solitude must be tortured, and his repose banished, by the recollection of the blood he had spilt, and the oppressions he had committed; and when he compared with these pangs of remorse, the feelings which must accompany his hon. friend from that house to his home, after the vote of that night should have confirmed the object of his humane and unceasing labours; when he should retire into the bosom of his happy and delighted family, when he should lay himself down on his bed, reflecting on the innumerable voices that would be raised in every quarter of the world to bless him; how much more pure and perfect felicity must he enjoy in the consciousness of having preserved so many millions of his fellow-creatures, than the man with whom he had compared him, on the throne to which he had waded through slaughter and oppression.'[21]

It had seemed impossible for any of the speakers in this one-sided debate to equal the eloquence which had been lavished on Abolition by the great orators of the age, by Fox, Pitt, Sheridan, Burke, Grenville, Wilberforce, Brougham and Canning. When Romilly did so, and at the same time made a tribute of incomparable elegance and beauty to Wilberforce, the whole House rose to its feet and burst out into deafening applause. It was a reward that had never within living memory been given to a member of either House and it overcame Wilberforce completely. He sat there with tears streaming down his face, barely conscious of what was happening. William Hey later asked him if the House had given him three cheers after Romilly's speech. 'I can only say,' he replied, 'that I was myself so completely overpowered by my feelings when he touched so beautifully on my domestic reception that I was insensible to all that was passing around me.'[22]

He had time to compose himself during the next speech, a foolish and exceedingly long defence of the Trade by a Mr. Hibbert, enlivened only by the revelation that during a war between two African states 'the slaves were compelled to carry over these mountains each a weight of 100 lbs. on their heads, for a space of ten miles, and sometimes twice a day, so that they became bald with the grievous pressure'.[23] The point of this and other historical digressions seems to have been to prove that slavery existed in Africa before the Trade.

Wilberforce answered in a short speech 'distinguished', according to the *Annual Register*, 'for splendour of eloquence and force of argument'. He refuted Hibbert's arguments and praised the younger members who had spoken out in favour of Abolition.

The House then divided and the majority in favour of Abolition was majestic. 283 members voted for it, only 16 against; some of its oldest supporters deserted the Trade. 'How astonishing is our success,' he wrote in his diary, 'and the eagerness and zeal of the House now, when members have been so fastidious as scarce to hear a speech about it! . . . Everybody taking me by the hand; and several voting with us for the first time.'[24]

The Bill had still to pass through the Committee Stage, but after such a majority there was no doubt of its success. Its supporters returned with Wilberforce to Palace Yard. The Thorntons were there, the Grants, Macaulay, Sharp, Robert Bird and William Smith, all delirious with joy. 'Well, Henry,' Wilberforce asked playfully, 'what shall we abolish next?' 'The lottery, I think,' replied Thornton with his usual seriousness. 'Let us make out the names of these sixteen miscreants; I have four of them,' said William Smith. Wilberforce, caught in a characteristic pose kneeling at the crowded table and writing a note, looked up and said, 'Never mind the miserable sixteen, let us think of our glorious 283.' Reginald Heber,* a High Churchman, was there. It was his first meeting with Wilberforce, to which he had brought a strong suspicion of his Evangelism. Afterwards he said to his friend John Thornton, 'How an hour's conversation can dissolve the prejudices of years!'[25]

The Bill came up for its third reading on March 16. Wilberforce had agreed to drop the expression about 'Justice and Humanity' in its preamble. The moral censure contained in these words seemed to annoy some opponents more than the fact of abolition, and its abandonment cost nothing. But the Bill was strengthened in a more important respect. The Abolitionists had thought that all they could possibly achieve would be a prohibition of the Trade, but the size of their majority now persuaded them that they could enact specific penalties against its continuation. Lord Grenville and Lord Howick wished to introduce a second Bill which would contain these penalties; the other Abolitionists gave way, but Wilberforce, horrified by the prospect of beginning legislation all over again, insisted that the penalties should be tacked on to the existing Bill. They were therefore inserted when the Bill passed into Committee; continuation in the Trade after January 1, 1808 was made to incur fines and the confiscation of the ships involved.

On March 16 Lord Henry Petty moved the third reading of the Bill, but everything after the great debate of February 23 was an ante-climax. Windham voiced his opposition to the Bill in a speech which Wilberforce thought 'sophistical' and to which he gave a spirited answer. Castlereagh broke his silence to predict heavy slave smuggling and discontent in the

* Afterwards Bishop of Calcutta and the author of the hymn 'From Greenland's icy mountains'.

West Indies, while Sheridan and Thornton were among those who spoke for the Bill, which was then passed on to the Lords without a division.

The assent of the Lords could be taken for granted, but it seemed for a moment that the success of Abolition might even now be imperilled. The Government had introduced legislation to allow Catholics to hold commissions in the Army. The present law, that they could only do so in Ireland, prevented Irish officers from serving elsewhere. The King had reluctantly agreed to the Bill's going forward, but he was now nearly blind and had not understood all its implications. When they had been explained to him he demanded that it should be withdrawn. The Government agreed but in turn asked for the right to show the benefits that would have arisen from their Bill. The King took this to mean that they would renew it and demanded a written promise never to raise the question again; no Government could agree to such terms.

It was a terrible possibility that Abolition might be lost in between the Talents leaving office and the new Government assuming it. But Wilberforce was soon reassured by Perceval who was to lead the Commons in the next administration. Perceval himself was committed to Abolition; he now revealed that Castlereagh, Eldon and Hawkesbury, all opponents, recognised that the recent votes in both Houses had decided the matter and they would be prepared to take it under their wing.

This offer was comforting but not necessary. An error in the Bill was hurriedly corrected, it was returned to the Lords on March 23, and after a final gesture of 'coarse opposition' from Westmorland, passed by them on the same day. It received the Royal Assent two days later on March 25. The Government had handed in its seals of office the day before.

Wilberforce's feeling was one of overwhelming relief and gratitude. 'God will bless this country,' he declared, and he wrote to the Rev. Francis Wrangham: 'I really cannot account for the fervour which happily has taken the place of that fastidious well-bred lukewarmness which used to display itself on this subject, except by supposing it to be produced by that almighty power which can influence at will the judgements and affections of men.'[26]

Sir James Mackintosh heard the news in Bombay, where he was serving as a judge. 'We are apt, perpetually to express our wonder,' he wrote, 'that so much exertion should be necessary to suppress such flagrant injustice. The more just reflection will be, that a short period of the short life of one man is, well and wisely directed, sufficient to remedy the miseries of millions for ages.'

*

The Abolition of the Slave Trade was one of the great moments of human history. As far as England was concerned it brought to an end perhaps the most monstrous evil in which she has ever been involved and paved the way for the removal of another great evil, the institution of slavery. For Abolition and Emancipation were to be linked, although in a very different way from that expected by the Abolitionists in 1807. It would be pleasant to leave Mackintosh's magnificent tribute as the last word on the subject but we must face the question; why did Abolition succeed in 1807 when it had failed so often before?

The traditional answer to this question is that the achievement of Abolition was postponed by the troubles in France and St. Domingue. In the first Debates the case received a sympathetic hearing and the support of the leaders of both parties. In 1792 the principle of Abolition was established, even though the date set was disappointing. It is hard to believe that, in conditions of peace, the Abolitionists would have had to wait another fifteen years for their triumph. Pitt's presence in office must also have played its part. Whatever his own enthusiasm, and in the early years it was great, he was hampered by having in his cabinet a succession of strong supporters of the Trade, notably Thurlow, Westmorland and Addington. He did not have the Whigs' influence with the Royal Dukes and peers, nor could he assume that the majority of his followers would vote for Abolition as a matter of course. The composition of the House of Commons also played its part. After the Union with Ireland the House received an influx of new members predisposed in favour of any cause associated with liberty. When the Talents came into power all these factors were pulling together in favour of the cause. There was also the craving of Fox and Grenville to leave one great achievement on the statute book.

A different interpretation of Abolition was advanced in 1944 by Mr. Eric Williams, the Prime Minister of Trinidad. In many ways his book, *Capitalism and Slavery*, came as an overdue corrective. Study of the economic background in the West Indies, Great Britain and the rival sugar producers had been neglected in favour of the political and moral sides of the campaign. This was a balance ill-suited to our times. We view with scepticism those who seem to be moved by moral forces, while readily believing that anyone will do anything for money, and all too often we are right. Mr. Williams traces the decline in importance of the West Indies from the days when Guadeloupe was considered as valuable a possession as Canada. The development of larger and more fertile sugar plantations elsewhere had made the British West Indian islands economic anachronisms while the new industries of the Industrial Revolution required a less restrictive system of Trade. We also need occasional reminding of a tiresome national trait—that of gloating over our own good works. Mr. Williams fulfils this last function by showing that the British Parliament which abolished the Slave Trade in 1807 and Slavery in 1834 went on in 1846 to encourage these two evils in other parts of the world by removing the duty on slave-grown sugar.

If he had stopped there Mr. Williams would have made a valuable contribution to the study of the question, but he follows his own arguments too far. The beginnings of the Abolitionist movement become a plot by which Pitt intended to ruin the French West Indian islands. This theory does not stand up to the most cursory examination. It is a poor plotter who allows his schemes to be ruined by those who stand to gain most from them; St. Domingue was already well stocked with slaves, and any deficiency left by the end of the British Slave Trade could soon have been made good by the French. This was, indeed, one of the most persistent and effective points made in Parliament by the enemies of Abolition. Once the French had refused to abolish, Pitt should, according to Mr. Williams's theory, have dropped general Abolition but firmly abolished the foreign part of the Trade.

Where personalities are involved Mr. Williams shows prejudices as extreme as those which he castigates so freely in others. His hatred of the Abolitionists overflows to engulf anyone who has ever praised them. Professor Coupland is found an ignorant, sentimental hero-worshipper of Wilberforce; there is condemnation of 'men who have sacrificed scholarship to sentimentality and, like the scholastics of old, placed faith before reason and evidence',[27] but if 'cynicism' is substituted for 'sentimentality' and 'prejudice' for 'faith' this sentence describes its author as accurately as it does his targets. Thus Wilberforce has 'an effeminate face'; as a leader he was 'inept, addicted to moderation, compromise and delay'. He is also described as 'smug', surely the last epithet that could be applied to him with justice. Thornton and Macaulay are discovered to have held small amounts of East India Company Stock, and although they would habitually give more than the value of these holdings to Abolition, the innuendo is allowed to lie.*

These faults should not blind us to the constructive side of *Capitalism and Slavery*. There is no doubt that the miserable state of the plantations, the rise of new industries and their demand for Free Trade played important parts, both in the Abolition and Emancipation campaigns, while the expansion of other forms of commerce led to the Slave Trade representing in 1807 only 1/24th of Liverpool's tonnage.[28] But to treat either campaign in exclusively economic terms is not only as unhistorical as to ignore economic factors altogether, but also inclined to founder on the planters' obstinacy. Their opposition to all attempts to abolish the Foreign Slave Trade showed that they were unable to appreciate their true interests. If all planters would have benefited from an end to the Foreign Trade, those

* Wilberforce, too, held this stock, but this seems to have escaped Mr. Williams. See Account Books, Duke MSS.

in the older colonies would have gained from a general Abolition, and they on the whole controlled the votes of the West India lobby. But apart from their quarrels when Wilberforce tried to negotiate a temporary ban on the Trade, both classes of planter consistently opposed both kinds of Abolition. It is therefore dangerous to ascribe their resignation to it in 1807 to a realisation that it would do them little harm.

The debates on the Slave Trade in 1806 and 1807 are notable for the absence of economic arguments. The West Indies were in a distressed state at the time, but neither Abolitionists nor planters openly connected this with the Slave Trade. Members clearly should have been influenced by economic considerations, but there is no evidence, other than the existence since 1804 of a group of planters prepared to suspend the Trade, to suggest that they were. If the economic interpretation is to be given much weight there should have been a correlation between the price of sugar and the Abolitionist minority in the Commons: there is no such correlation, indeed 1796, the year in which the Abolitionists came nearest to success and were thwarted on the Third Reading only by the *Two Hunchbacks*, lay in the middle of the post-St. Domingue sugar boom,* when the planters' influence should have been at its strongest. Those who feel inclined to disregard economic considerations should, however, note that 1796 was a year in which the political background was equally forbidding.

Abolition offered no material advantages to those who passed it. It menaced entrenched interests, which, although diminished in importance, were still well represented in an unreformed Parliament. It could also be taken, in the atmosphere of the times, as encouraging revolution and Jacobinism. For it to succeed all the Abolitionist stars had to be in conjunction. Most crucially the fear of revolution must be removed, and by 1807 the Jacobins were a nightmare of the past. Secondly the enemy must be at its weakest, and in 1807 the plantation industry was on its knees. Thirdly Parliament must be prepared to accept the measure, and in 1807 the Whigs were in office and the Irish at Westminster together with a great number of new members freshly elected with pledges to vote for Abolition.

These factors constituted the necessary background for success. They would have been useless without the presence of the Abolitionist Movement which had been waiting for such a moment for nearly twenty years. During this time every conceivable argument for and against the Trade had been aired and every possible step to mobilise public opinion taken. Without the Abolitionist Campaign the Trade would have survived and the fact that they had to wait for success until conditions were entirely

* For an authoritative appraisal of these arguments see Robert T. Anstey's 'Capitalism and Slavery, a critique', *Economic History Review*, 2nd series, XXI. no. 2. August 1968.

favourable should not detract from their achievement. There is no reason
to adjust Lecky's verdict: 'The unweary, unostentatious, and inglorious
crusade of England against slavery may probably be regarded as among
the three or four perfectly virtuous pages comprised in the history of
nations.'[29]

CHAPTER XX

THE YORKSHIRE ELECTION

THE triumph of the Abolitionists made Wilberforce a national hero. He was a unique figure in politics, attached to no party, for he had given the Talents the same support as he had Pitt, yet a power to be reckoned with. His moral stature was immense and he was respected as a man who would be swayed by principle rather than interest. This view of his character was by no means universal. We have seen Fox claim that if forced to choose between the slaves and Pitt 'he would be for Barabbas'. Conservatives and High Churchmen still thought of him as a dangerous meddler who threatened to upset the existing state of things, while some radicals looked on him as a sanctimonious reactionary. Nevertheless Wilberforce's reputation and prestige in the country as a whole were never higher than in 1807.

Wilberforce's scruples handicapped him as a Parliamentary candidate. He would not use his influence in ways which would have seemed perfectly reasonable to a more worldly man. His fastidiousness was most evident in religious matters: he often lobbied ministers to appoint particular clergymen but these were always men who would further the cause of 'true religion' rather than those who would cement Wilberforce's political alliances. We find him refusing a living to a connection of as influential and loyal a supporter as Sir Christopher Sykes (though why Sir Christopher should have asked Wilberforce for this favour is rather puzzling, as he must have had plenty of livings in his own gift), and another applicant provoked Wilberforce into a rare display of severity.

Sir,
   My having been much occupied I must apologise for my not returning an immediate answer to your letter, I am sorry to be now under the Necessity of informing you that I am so circumstanced at present as not to have it in my Power to comply with your Request without Impropriety. I feel it however my Duty not to conclude without frankly avowing to you the Circumstance of yourself and your Friend having some Interest in Yorkshire would in no degree influence me in your Favour on the present Occasion, and I confess that I wonder you should suggest this consideration in such a connection. Upon reflection you cannot I think but disapprove of it as a Sentiment equally dishonourable to me to whom it is suggested, and to yourself from whom it

comes. Having said this with a Freedom I think it right to use, I will add that I am conscious there are many Persons who conceived themselves at liberty to employ for the advancement of their Political Interest, any Influence they may possess in the disposal of ecclesiastical preferments, and you may without much thought have then given in to a Practice, which from what you tell me of your Connections you cannot I think but condemn on more mature deliberations.[1]

A letter to Pitt in January 1805[2] declares, as a matter of principle, that he never asks favours for constituents. But his religious views attracted votes from many Methodists and Quakers, who would not otherwise have been drawn into politics. And though he might be unsatisfactory as a disburser of patronage, he looked after his constituents' interests very carefully. In 1806 he was largely responsible for defeating a Bill that sought to impose a duty on unwrought iron—a measure which would have harmed Yorkshire manufacturers.

In the same year he sat as Chairman of the Woollen Trades Committee, and in spite of the great demands on his time made by Abolition, he only missed one of its sessions. His connection with this Committee could have been disastrous, for it had to adjudicate between the woollen manufacturers and the clothiers, both of which groups constituted powerful interests in Yorkshire. The clothiers operated a cottage industry from their homes and sold their goods in the cloth halls. They wished to restrict the use of mechanised methods of mass production by their competitors. The Committee could not cripple an important industry to suit the clothiers' interests and their report was, accordingly, in favour of the manufacturers. But Wilberforce, when approached by the clothiers, was considerate, sympathetic and polite. Henry Lascelles, his colleague for Yorkshire, who also sat on the Committee, insulted them when they called on him and made them his implacable enemies. This blunder was soon to cost him his seat.

Fawkes had been laying his plans for the next Yorkshire election; he had not forgotten the defeat of 1796 when he had withdrawn because of the lost letter. This time he secured Lord Fitzwilliam's support well in advance and canvassed energetically. The grievances of the clothiers may have prompted him to come forward in 1806 when he had held back in 1802.

At the end of October Wilberforce heard of the contest and hurried up to Yorkshire where he found that Lascelles had alienated all the clothiers but that most of them were prepared to split their votes between himself and Fawkes. If he united with Lascelles they would give plumpers to Fawkes. After a few days' canvassing he wrote to Barbara:

'It seems pretty clear already that I shall be first on the poll, if it comes to one, and I am sorry to say it, Mr. Fawkes second. Some of Mr. Lascelles's friends have been in a degree the bringers-on of this business, from over-estimating their strength, and thinking that they could turn me out without great difficulty; whereas almost all the respectable people who are not connected with great men when it comes to the point of choosing between Lascelles and me, give him up without hesitation.'[3]

When Lascelles, belatedly, came to the same conclusion, he offered to join forces with Wilberforce; but Lord Fitzwilliam, under pressure from Grenville, had instructed his supporters to cast their second votes for Wilberforce, whose independent instincts would in any case have prejudiced him against an alliance with Lascelles; now Fitzwilliam's gesture made it impossible. There was nothing left for Lascelles to do but withdraw. But before he did so the election had provided Wilberforce with some excitement and more exertion than was welcome.

'Thursday [October 30th] up early and off before breakfast for Bradford. Fifty or sixty gentlemen on horseback met me a little way from town, and conducted me to the inn. After cold collation and breakfast, to Cloth Hall and speechified: afterwards wrote letters; and they escorted me a mile or more on horseback on the road to Leeds. On Friday, off with William Hey to Wakefield—met a mile off, and drawn by people into town to inn, where addressed the people in the marketplace—vast crowd, and dragged in carriage again to Naylor's, and thence to Dawson's. Letters, and off for Dewsbury, where dragged, and addressed again. Carriage broke and stopped. Called Mr. Pooley's. Heckmondwyke, dragged, and speechified again—dreadful roads. Reached Pye-nest, two miles beyond Halifax (Edward's), by a quarter past seven, evening—found party of fifteen or sixteen just sitting down to dinner, having waited for me. I grazed hard against loaded waggon when dark, going opposite directions. One inch nearer, had infallibly been broken, and probably overset. Providential; but astonishing not an accident of any kind to speak of since leaving Lyme; and I have borne little inclemencies of weather and fatigue, much beyond what I thought possible.

'Saturday, after breakfast large party of gentlemen came on horseback from Halifax to Pye-nest to convey me to town, though a very rainy morning. The horses drew me up the hill, and the people to Cloth Hall, about a mile. Much hurt on first entering to read account of Samuel Thornton's defeat. Some hissed, and kept crying, Fawkes for ever; I walked round the Hall—immense concourse, and afterwards addressed the people from the steps. They would chair me to the inn. One man threw something which hit me on the forehead, happily not hard, and I kept watching afterwards. Amazing squeeze, and a very awkward operation. Taken to the Talbot. Bad, especially going through the gorges of the gates and narrow streets. Wrote letters till dinner, and Mr. W. Lawson came in about three, and told me report that Lascelles had resigned.

'Monday. After breakfast Huddersfield to inn, where R. H. Beaumont and many others. Went round Hall and back to inn where speechified the people.'

After it was all over Wilberforce wrote to Matthew Montagu, one of his closest supporters

My dear M,

Lascelles has declined the contest—Indeed it was clear he must have fallen and it is certainly better for a man be he ever so wealthy not to squander, indeed worse than squander, £50,000 in a hopeless contest. My old friends have exerted themselves in the most honourable manner and had there been a poll I must have been very far the foremost—The Noblemen in general and most of the foxhunters against me.[4]

*

The next election was not to be so easy. Lascelles's father, Lord Harewood, was willing 'to spend in it his whole Barbadian property'. Fawkes shrank from such a contest and he was replaced by Lord Milton, Fitzwilliam's heir. Since Fitzwilliam was as determined to win as Harewood, Wilberforce found himself trapped in the clash between these two great electoral anachronisms. It must seem extraordinary to us now that people should have been prepared to spend on such a scale. Lascelles's and Milton's fathers between them laid out a total of £200,000 on the election —the equivalent, very roughly, of one and a half million pounds each in modern currency. Although membership for Yorkshire carried great prestige, there was certainly no advantage to be derived from it which could justify such expenditure.

Wilberforce would once have revelled in such a challenge. But now there was not a single shameful 'rising' to be felt and he 'sickened at a contest'. But he could not withdraw without insulting his constituents and shaming himself. He had represented the County for nearly twenty-three years and to allow himself to be hustled out of his seat without a fight would have been an act of cowardice. It would also have implied that his constituents could be weaned from their loyalty and admiration for him by his opponents' money. He did not, in any case, expect to lose.

Although a rich man by normal standards, Wilberforce could not afford to compete on level terms with his two rivals. He also lacked the efficient party organisations which they controlled. When he entered Yorkshire at the end of April he found that 'Mr. Lascelles and Lord Milton had already engaged canvassing agents, houses of entertainment and every species of conveyance in every considerable town'.[5] His own supporters did not meet until May 4 when they established a painfully amateurish organisation.

The nomination was held at York on May 13 and Wilberforce's prospects improved, nearly every hand being held up in his favour. He now felt confident enough to call on the subscriptions that had been offered. 'It is impossible,' said one supporter, 'that we can desert Mr. Wilberforce and therefore put down my name for £500.' About £18,000 was raised at once, and on the motion of Spencer Stanhope and Charles Duncombe (now Lord Feversham) he was debarred from making any contribution to his own expenses. The fund finally grew to £64,544, over half of which was returned to subscribers.

Wilberforce's position should have been impregnable. He had a large following of his own built up over twenty-two years as the representative of the County. His prestige as champion of Abolition was at its zenith and Yorkshire had played a leading part in the struggle. One distinguished voter who did not always see eye to eye with Wilberforce supported him because of Abolition. 'Your letter followed me here, where I had come after voting for Lord Milton, one of the most ungainly looking young men I ever saw,' Sydney Smith wrote to Creevey. 'I gave my other vote for Wilberforce, on account of his good conduct in Africa, a place returning no members to parliament, but still, from the extraordinary resemblance its inhabitants bear to human creatures, of some consequence.'[6] Wilberforce lacked his opponents' organisation but he was immeasurably their superior at the hustings; he had cut his teeth as a speaker on Yorkshiremen in Wapping when he stood for Hull in 1780. His first triumph as an orator was in the Castle Yard in 1784 and he had followed it with another when he routed the opposition to Pitt's Seditious Meetings Bill. Wilberforce was well attuned to Yorkshire audiences. He knew exactly how to sway them and he thrived on their interruptions and questions.

Wilberforce should also have benefited from the bitter party and personal rivalry between his opponents. Lascelles was still loathed by the clothiers and tarred with the West Indian brush—a stain which he pathetically tried to remove by publishing bills and verses entitled 'Lascelles and Liberty'. Milton was only twenty-one, a sprig of the Fitzwilliam line that had so notably failed to preserve Rockingham's grasp on the County. He seems to have been such an admirable young man that Lascelles's pamphleteers had to attack him for his youth rather than any shortcomings in his character. But the accusation that he was expecting to inherit the representation of the County revived the hostility towards his family that had led to the triumph of the Associators twenty-two years before, and he also lost votes through being suspected of excessive sympathy towards Roman Catholics. The animosity between Lascelles and Milton was fed by local rivalry between their families and by the bitter atmosphere in national politics after the dismissal of the Talents. Both were strong party men, Lascelles a firm Pittite, Milton a Whig. Wilberforce as an Independent should have profited from this state of affairs, for supporters of both sides could be expected to give their second votes to him. Together with the votes of his own followers this would have seen him an easy leader of the poll.

At first it seemed that he was indeed safe. Both his opponents produced electoral poems, one entitled *Wilberforce and Milton for ever*, the other *Wilberforce and Lascelles for ever*,[7] while he called his *Wilberforce for ever*. While his opponents were libelling each other he was content to rally his supporters.

WILBERFORCE FOR EVER!
NO SLAVERY

Fame let thy trumpet thro Yorkshire resound
And gather the Friends of fair Freedom around;
Unawed by the Great and unbribed by the Court
The pride of our Country shall have our support.

Chorus—Wilberforce is the Man, our Rights to maintain,
The longer we prove him,
The better we love him;
We'll support him for Yorkshire again and again.

Shall he, who has serv'd us the best of our days,
Unstain'd by a Bribe without Pension or Place;
Whose conduct to come we may judge by the past,
Be rejected, dishonour'd, deserted at last?

Chorus—Ah! no, we'll maintain Wilberforce to a Man;
Him we can confide in,
We've proved and we've tried him,
We'll support him for Yorkshire again and again.

Let the foes of our Friend and his noble Designs,
Repeat their worst charge that he *cants and he whines;*
O we've heard of his Cants in Humanity's Cause
While the Senate was hush'd, and the land wept applause.

Chorus—Then shew us the Man, that talk like him can,
Our Interest we find in
Such canting and whining,
He shall cant for the County again and again.[8]

But he lost his advantage through a damaging rumour that swept across the County. Wilberforce, it was claimed, had secretly united with Lascelles, thus breaking a promise he had made to Milton to remain neutral. It would, of course, have been lunacy for him to have done so, for he could already rely on Lascelles's second votes and by uniting with him he would forfeit Milton's. His moral stature would have been diminished by an alliance with a leading slave owner. All that he stood to gain was the use of Lascelles's organisation which he did not need so long as he received second votes from both sides. After the election he described the story as 'that abominable report of a compromise between Mr. H. Lascelles and myself, which would have been highly dishonourable to us both, though far more so to me than to him'.[9]

But the rumours were believed, and not merely by the mob, but also by

Milton himself. 'There never was a doubt in the minds of the gentlemen of Lord Milton's Committee that Mr. Wilberforce both during his canvass and throughout the whole election, had joined his interest with that of Mr. Lascelles.'[10] So writes Grimston, a partisan of Lord Milton's. He cites joint canvasses and dinners and the acceptance, by Wilberforce's committee, of Lascelles's proposal that they should share the expense of split votes, while they refused to do the same for Milton. There is no doubt that the Miltonians sincerely believed that Wilberforce had betrayed them. Any other explanation of their behaviour is improbable for it was likely to force Wilberforce into an alliance with Lascelles, if he had not already formed one, and this would have been disastrous for Milton.* Part of the blame for this must lie with Wilberforce himself. His organisation was amateurish and uncohesive, most of his agents Pittites and therefore well-disposed towards Lascelles. This could not have been avoided, but they should have been firmly told to make no pacts. There is little doubt that, at a local level, there were alliances between Wilberforce's and Lascelles's agents and there is no doubt at all that Wilberforce knew nothing of this. As it was he made enemies of the Fitzwilliam interest from his supposed alliance with Lascelles. Milton had the best organisation of the three candidates and he had hired the best pamphleteers who now enjoyed a Roman holiday at Wilberforce's expense.

Some of their efforts were merely scurrilous. A wretched Mr. Ware was described as 'A Clergyman distinguished for his *Piety* and Morality in every brothel in York'. Wilberforce was similarly abused in 'The Unnatural Union!'[11]

> How much it will shock
> The whole Methodist flock
>   To learn that the *Saint* they take pride in
> To gain a few votes
> His time now devotes
>   To the VICE of the wicked West Riding!

* Wilberforce had given a promise of neutrality in return for the support of Lord Fitzwilliam and the Duke of Norfolk. He regarded this promise as unconditional and binding even when their support turned into bitter hostility. It could be argued that Milton, with Machiavellian subtlety, knew that Wilberforce would feel bound by his promise and decided to isolate him by withdrawing his support. If so he was running a grave risk. Wilberforce could have reasoned that since Milton had broken the agreement he was no longer debarred from forming an alliance with Lascelles, and such an alliance would have been more damaging to Milton than anything he stood to gain through betraying Wilberforce. Even without Milton's second votes Wilberforce was favourite to head the poll. He was certain to do so if he united with Lascelles. Milton stood a good chance of beating Lascelles so long as Wilberforce remained neutral, but his prospects would be greatly harmed by an alliance between his two opponents. Milton would thus be gambling a slight chance of putting Wilberforce out against a strong likelihood of

But the alliance with Lascelles was the main target.

The Monstrous Coalition!!12

We've heard of Coalitions strange
  Between a *Whig & Tory*;
But, Nature sure herself must change,
  E'er you believe *This Story!!*

What! Shall the friend of human kind,
  The advocate of Freedom,
Join with the MAN, *whose fetters bind,*
  Whose guilty lashes bleed 'em!!

Shall HE who *purged us from this ill*
  Join with a Negro Dealer;
Who of *his ever honour'd* BILL
  Would fain *be the* REPEALER!!

What! Shall the Patriot condescend
  (Lord MELVILLE'S firm Detector)
To join with TROTTER'S *bosom friend,*
  And MELVILLE'S warm PROTECTOR!!

Such junction can have no excuse;
  And future times will wonder
How e'er the *Foe to all abuse*
  Should *join* the FRIEND OF PLUNDER!

'The Gentle Denial' was even more offensive.

The Gentle Denial13
A New Ode

'Tickle me', says pious BILLY,
  'Tickle me', good LASCELLES, do.
'If you but tickle pious BILLY,
  'He, in return, will tickle you.'

To it then, They fall a tickling,
  Tickling pink & tickling blue.
'Colleague Lascelles!' . . . 'Colleague Billy!'
  Runs the whole COMMITTEE thro'

LAS   *'Plainest of all pious creatures*
       'Quakers are not plain as you'
WIL   'Gentlest of WEST INDIAN NATURES!
       'I must give the Devil his due'.
LAS   'But DEAREST SAINT! *our plans concealing,*
       'Tho joined, we must appear as Two:'
WIL   'Sweet *Sugar Cane!* at double dealing,
       You need not furnish me my cue.'

       'Tickle me' etc.

being beaten into third place by Lascelles. It is far more probable that he believed Wilberforce had betrayed him. He had, after all, grounds for this belief, and Grimston's evidence gives strong support for this interpretation.

This propaganda had its effect. The clothiers, who had been friendly to Wilberforce the year before, now saw him as the ally of their arch-enemy, Lascelles. Their standard was an old leather apron, which, if one of them appeared on the wrong side, they would shake in his face with the cry, 'What Thee vote against t'apron!' Very few of them did. The clothiers gave 1,081 votes to Milton, 331 to Wilberforce and 273 to Lascelles. It was a bad start in a poll of just over 30,000.

The poll at York remained open for fifteen days during which the campaigns of the rival candidates rose to a crescendo. On the second day the superior organisation of his rivals showed and Wilberforce was bottom of the poll. Lascelles and Milton between them had engaged all the carriages in the County and Wilberforce's supporters were left without transport. A barrister from London whom Wilberforce had engaged as adviser was plunged into gloom. 'I can see, gentlemen, clearly enough how this will turn out,' he pontificated, 'Mr. Wilberforce has obviously no chance and the sooner he resigns the better.'[14] But on the third day his friends were aroused by his danger. 'No carriages are to be procured,' wrote a supporter from Hull, 'but boats are proceeding up the river heavily laden with voters, farmers lend their wagons, even donkeys have the honour of carrying voters for Wilberforce, and hundreds are proceeding on foot.'[15]

A great number of freeholders under the leadership of Sir Robert Hildyard entered York on the third day of the poll. They would have divided their votes between Wilberforce and Lascelles, but seeing Wilberforce's danger, they all gave him plumpers. Another great body of voters from Wensleydale was met by a member of his committee.

'For what parties, gentlemen, do you come?'

'Wilberforce to a man,' they replied.

The devotion of some of his supporters was touching. A clergyman of very small means had travelled, often on foot, from one of the farthest corners of the County to vote for Wilberforce. He refused all reimbursement until the committee pressed him to accept a certain sum, he then took it only on condition that it was added at once to Wilberforce's election fund. A countryman who had come from Rotherham to give Wilberforce a plumper denied having spent any money at all on his journey. 'Sure enow I cam all'd-way ahint Lord Milton's carriage!'[16]

On the third day of the poll Wilberforce overtook Lascelles, on the fourth Milton, and on the fifth day he increased his lead. Milton's party retaliated, as Wilberforce remembered, still with a sense of grievance, some time afterwards:

'Owing to the assurances I had received of the friendly wishes of Lord Fitzwilliam, the Duke of Norfolk, and others, and the promised support of all the clothiers, and of nine-tenths or more of Lord Milton's supporters, I had given a pledge to remain neutral. This was quite wrong.—I should have made a conditional engagement, and then the Miltonians would not have dared to act as they did. All possible tricks were played to deprive me of votes. First I was safe. When the effect of this, which made me lose the votes both of Lascellites and Miltonians, was expended; then my committee would not pay the travelling expenses of any of Milton's split votes. This was defeated; though positive falsehoods told, and printed in handbills, to colour and sustain it. And at last the cry of my having joined Lascelles was raised. This conduct of Lord Milton's friends was shameful; since, by seeing the poll books, they must have known that I was not connected with him. Then, "No coalition, and Milton a plumper" was mounted; and he would bring up none else. Then the mob-directing system—twenty bruisers sent for, Firby the young ruffian, Gully, and others. With all this was combined great regularity and method in arrangement, numerous agents, and constant returns, and canvassing, and even economical expenditure, so far as compatible with immense establishment.'[17]

Gully* and his mob worked to such effect that it was almost impossible for Wilberforce to obtain a hearing after the first few days of the poll. Henry Thornton, Stephen and the Grants had hurried up to Yorkshire when they heard he was in danger. Thornton remembered one of his rowdier meetings. 'While Wilberforce was speaking the other day,' he wrote, 'the mob of Milton interrupted him: he was attempting to explain a point which had been misrepresented; he endeavoured to be heard again and again, but the cry against him always revived. "Print, print," cried a friend of Wilberforce in the crowd, "print what you have to say in a handbill, and let them read it, since they will not hear you." "They read indeed," cried Wilberforce; "what, do you suppose that men who make such a noise as those fellows can read?" holding up both his hands; "no men that make such noises as those can read, I'll promise you. They must hear me now, or they'll know nothing about the matter." Immediately there was a fine Yorkshire grin over some thousand friendly faces.'[18]

He was seldom so lucky, each time he rose there was a chorus of 'No Coalition! No Coalition!' a cry which had some irony, since it was on this slogan that he had himself wrested the County from the Fitzwilliam interests twenty-three years before.

Although greatly incensed with the conduct of his opponents, he went through the bustle of electioneering with extraordinary calm. Russel, his agent, remembers that 'it was necessary that I should have some private communication with him every day. I usually put myself in his way

* John Gully, rescued from a debtor's prison by his skill with his fists, became champion of England and later the owner of a country estate, coal mines and the Derby winner and father of twenty-four children. He was himself a Member of Parliament, 1832-7.

therefore when he came in from the hustings to dress for dinner. On each day as he entered I perceived that he was repeating to himself what seemed the same words: at length I was able to catch them, and they proved to be that stanza of Cowper's.

> The calm retreat, the silent shade
> With prayer and praise agree,
> And seem by Thy sweet bounty made,
> For those who follow Thee.'[19]

In a letter to Barbara, written in the middle of the polls, his mind seems even further from the contest. 'I have twice been at The Minster,' he writes, 'where the sublimity of the whole scene once nearly overcame me. It is the largest and finest gothic building probably in the world. . . . How beautiful Broomfield must be at this moment! Even the lilacs and hawthorn are in bloom. I imagine myself roaming through the shrubbery with you and the little ones.' He did mention the election, but only to say that the concourse of freeholders reminded him of the great Jewish Passover in the Temple in the reign of Josiah.[20]

Meanwhile Lascelles's poets, less talented than Milton's but every bit as industrious, had introduced a scatological element into the contest with a rhyme that came to be known as 'The Dirty Epigram'. By now Wilberforce was well in front and Lascelles held a comfortable lead over Milton. But the rumour of the 'Unnatural Alliance' began to take effect. According to Grimston, 'everyone was now so firmly convinced of the coalition between Mr. Wilberforce and Lascelles that even the Quakers gave plumpers to Lord Milton, so disgusted were all honest people by his deceitful behaviour.'[21] Even if this is as untrue as many of Grimston's statements the rumour certainly cost Wilberforce votes.

Milton's position at the bottom of the poll encouraged his supporters to give him plumpers in the same way as Wilberforce's had in the first days of the election. Helped by these factors and his superior organisation and propaganda Milton slowly gained ground. Lascelles was miserably served by his agents, the principal of whom gave his second vote to Milton.[22]

Wilberforce did not see the final result. On the twelfth day of the poll, when his own victory was certain, he was laid low by a gastric attack. His enemies at once circulated a rumour that he was dead, but it was too late to affect his election. He did not however escape without a last salvo from Milton's hacks:

> How came it that Willy, so fitted to grace
> A triumphant procession, refused to appear?
> Why The Doctor had gravely considered his case
> And prescribed him a *stool*, sir, instead of a chair.

The final voting figures were:

Wilberforce	11,806
Milton	11,177
Lascelles	10,989

'Had I not been defrauded of promised votes,' Wilberforce wrote to Hannah More, 'I should have had 20,000. However, it is unspeakable cause for thankfulness to come out of the battle ruined neither in health, character, or fortune. . . .'[23] It had been a desperately close fight; it is often represented as one in which the underdog triumphed, perhaps because of the advice given by Wilberforce's silly lawyer at the beginning of the contest. Wilberforce in fact started as an overwhelming favourite who expected to poll two out of every three votes. His very independence of party was an advantage which would attract second votes from both sides. In the event Wilberforce lost all Milton's second votes, had no electoral organisation comparable to his opponents', was shouted down whenever he tried to speak, and yet still managed to win. And he did so while spending little over a quarter of what each of his opponents had lavished on the election. He could not bear to waste other people's money on any of the fripperies of electioneering, and his caution was such that it endangered his success. Lascelles and Milton each spent £100,000 on the contest, Wilberforce £28,600. But the circumstances rather than the fact of his victory proved that, in a Yorkshire election, money was no substitute for merit.

CHAPTER XXI

THE SAINT

DURING the Yorkshire election Wilberforce's path crossed with that of another Yorkshireman who was to become pre-eminent in a very different world. Squire Osbaldeston lived for his sports, his horses, his hounds, his guns and his bets. But his mother was a strong partisan of Lord Milton's, and as eighteenth-century elections seldom seem to have been held during the hunting or shooting seasons, the Squire became a reluctant visitor to the hustings. Wilberforce must by then have been the most famous Yorkshireman alive, but the Squire's knowledge of him was hazy. He 'believed' he was a Tory and 'was not sure' if he was a Dissenter. 'He was a thin little man,' the Squire wrote with more confidence, 'and looked exactly like a Primitive Methodist parson; his voice corresponded with his appearance.'[1] He has left us two pleasant stories which illustrate the social background to the election.

Lord Fitzwilliam, being a great friend of Lord Carlisle, applied to the latter to use his influence on his son's behalf during the election. 'My dear Fitzwilliam,' Carlisle is said to have answered, 'whatever votes I can command you shall have; but I could not stoop to ask a favour of any plebeian.'[2] Lady Carlisle shared her husband's lofty social attitude. She was once ill and had to be examined by the doctor. She insisted on her maid being present throughout the interview and acting as interpreter. When the doctor finally said that bleeding was necessary, she turned to the maid and said: 'Tell the doctor he may bleed the Countess of Carlisle.'[3]

Unfortunately the Squire was tempted away from the election by a race meeting. His horse slipped in a street and he was injured in the fall, thus missing the rest of the contest. He remained convinced to his dying day that Lord Milton had beaten Wilberforce.

There was really little excuse for Osbaldeston not having heard of Wilberforce in 1807 and there would have been none at all afterwards, for from this time Wilberforce may be said to have assumed the somewhat daunting role which he filled for the rest of his life, that of the conscience of the nation. His reputation had grown first with the success of *Practical View*, and then through his leadership of the Abolitionist Movement. **The** triumph of this campaign had left its partisans in a state of euphoria. 'What shall we abolish next?' Wilberforce had asked Henry Thornton and he was not left short of answers. Thornton himself proposed the lottery, Sydney Smith wrote to plead for the oppressed in Ireland, and Wilberforce's correspondence contained a mass of other suggestions. Abolition had left him in a unique position, with a highly organised and enthusiastic body of supporters who could be mobilised in any new crusade. The *Christian Observer* acted as a means of communication between the Evangelical High Command and its adherents in the country.

As time went on Wilberforce became more and more a moral father figure to his country. He was a legend in his own time; when Sir Home Popham was cruising off the coast of Haiti one of his ships boarded a boat that had come out under a flag of truce. Almost the first question asked by the Haitians was, 'How is Mr. Wilberforce? He is our friend, and benefactor, and we are all interested about him.'[4] Their interest was widely shared; a visit to him featured in the itinerary of almost every distinguished foreigner who came to Britain. He was presented to the allied monarchs; he became a close friend of Marshal Blücher through his efforts for the 'suffering Prussians', and the Marshal sent him a personal dispatch after Waterloo. Madame de Staël lured him out to dinner, to his immediate delight and subsequent remorse. More humble tourists were taken to look at him, and in 1817 one of them described this experience: 'Another little man, as thin as a shadow, and drawing one side of his body after him, as if paralytic, hurried across the floor with a tottering brisk step, an awkward bow, and said, in substance, that schools in Ireland were most desirable, and should be organised by all means. These few words were extremely well spoken, with peculiar energy of feeling, and in a manner graceful and impressive. This was Mr. Wilberforce. Nothing can surpass the meanness of his appearance, and he seems half blind.'[5]

Wilberforce's friend, John Harford, was kinder in his description of him at their first meeting in 1812. He wore powder then and up to the time of his death, although it had long gone out of fashion. 'An eye-glass, of which he made constant use, and a diamond brooch, were appendages of his person. . . . His dress and appearance were those of a thorough gentleman of the old school.'[6] If so the old school was an eccentric one. Wilberforce had his coats cut so that he could carry Dalrymple's State Papers in their pockets. He was a perambulating library. Just as some smokers cannot turn out their pockets without discovering a dozen boxes of matches, so Wilberforce would always carry an astonishing number of books with him. He liked to walk, and he liked to read on his walks, aloud if he was with a friend. 'We were often amused by the capacity of his pockets,' Harford wrote, 'which carried a greater number of books than would seem, if enumerated, possible, and his local memory was such that, on drawing out any author, he seemed instantaneously to light on the passage which he wanted.'[7]

He stooped like most very short-sighted people and when he was an old man his head was bowed down until it sank almost on to his chest, so that he seemed even smaller than he was. But the strongest impression most people carried away was one of liveliness, speed and vitality, both of body and mind. He never seemed to be still for a moment. 'Who can fail to recall the rapid movements of his somewhat diminutive form,' wrote Joseph John Gurney, a Quaker friend of Wilberforce, 'the illuminations of his expressive countenance, and the nimble finger with which he used to seize on every little object that happened to adorn or diversify his path? Much less can we forget his vivacious wit—so playful, yet so harmless— the glow of his affections—the urbanity of his manner—and the wondrous celerity with which he was ever wont to turn from one bright thought to another.'[8] Southey put it better. 'He frisks about,' he wrote after Wilberforce had visited him in 1818, 'as if every vein in his body were filled with quicksilver.'[9] But Bishop Jebb's description of him was better still: 'He moved 'with the look of an angel and the agility of a monkey.'[10]

Wilberforce was an avid reader and one whose books served him in a number of ways. Religious works, particularly those of Doddridge and Baxter, reinforced his faith. The classics, Adam Smith, Hume and Malthus and a great number of books on Africa equipped him for debates in the Commons. History, philosophy, astronomy and poetry could be studied both for pleasure and for self-improvement. Lighter forms of literature fell into the realm of 'mere chit-chat', but enjoyable and tempting chit-chat for all that.

An extract from his diary in 1807 gives the flavour of his reading. 'Paley's Natural Theology, Adam Smith, popular pamphlets, Bisanquet's Value of Commerce—clever, but rash, and in parts unfair, but not designedly; a man should always have a friend to run over his writings— Cobbett too, and Edinburgh Review, and Eclectic; Mrs. Hutchinson's Memoirs of Colonel H.—beautiful; Spence against Foreign Commerce— sad stuff, a vile mingle mangle of blundering conclusions from Adam Smith, Economists, etc.; Lowe on State of West Indies—oil without vinegar; Concessions of America the Bane of Great Britain; excellent critique on Malthus in Christian Observer, which Bowdler's I am sure; Lay of Last Minstrel, Looking over East India documents for civilizing and converting natives, Buchanan's Ecclesiastical Establishment, and Wrangham's Civilization of Hindoos.'[11]

His reading, Sir James Stephen considers, 'was an ill-assorted and heterogeneous mess, made up of history, morals, philosophy, poetry, statistics, ephemeral politics and Theology, all in turn either lightly scanned, or diligently studied. . . . He would controvert, interrogate, or applaud in the form of marginal notes, when he was alone, or, if an auditor was at hand, in spoken comments, at one moment so arch and humorous, at the next so reverend and affectionate . . . [that the people in the book] became so many characters in a sort of tragi-comedy.'[12]

The Evangelicals believed that anything unconnected with true religion was a distraction and this explains their opposition to theatres and other forms of entertainment, even when such entertainments were harmless. Wilberforce carried something of the same attitude into his reading. Cowper was his favourite poet, not only because of the beauty of his verse, but also because it had much religion in it. 'His piety gives unfading charms to his compositions,' he wrote in 1809 to John Jay, the retired American Ambassador.[13] Hannah More's remark on Cowper could equally well have been made by him. 'I have found what I have been looking for all my life, a poet whom I can read on Sunday.'[14] The drearier type of Evangelical would judge a book purely on the basis of its 'usefulness' to the cause of true religion. Wilberforce and Hannah More loved literature far too much to be able to do so. Instead they applied double standards of criticism, literary and moral, to anything they read. Hence the pre-eminence of Cowper, the one poet who could pass both tests with flying colours.

In Wilberforce's eyes a great work of literature which lacked any religious exhortation was a waste of talents, and to that extent a failure. Apart from the theatre, which was a special case because of its threat to the actors' morals, he was broadminded about literary form. He would never have echoed Hannah More's denunciation of all novels, before she began writing them herself, as 'the most pernicious source of moral corruption'.[15] She wrote the ill-fated *Coelebs* for the subscribers to circulating libraries 'to raise the tone of that mart of mischief and counteract its corruption'. Wilberforce knew that novels could be as improving as any other form of literature, though he also realised that they seldom were.

His habit of examining a work which had nothing to do with religion on religious criteria led him to some extraordinary conclusions; at times he reminds us of the legendary review in a sporting magazine which described *Lady Chatterley's Lover* as 'an interesting account of the life of a gamekeeper'. His judgement on Swift is the most famous, though by no means the only example. 'What a thoroughly irreligious mind,' he exclaimed, 'no trace of Sunday to be found in his journals or letters to his most intimate friends.'

Sir Walter Scott was then at the height of his fame and Wilberforce, whose literary views were rather conventional, shared the general admiration of his works. In 1810 he wrote to Muncaster, 'Have you read The Lady of the Lake? Like a good economist I waited till it should come out in octavo, but had I tasted it before, though it had been folio instead of quarto, I could not without extreme difficulty have restricted the impulse to gratify my appetite for it without stint. Really I did not think that I continued in such a degree subject to the fascination of poetry. I have been absolutely bewitched. I could not keep the imaginary personages out of my mind when I most wished to remove them. How wonderful is this dominion over the heart which genius exercises! There are some parts of the poem that are quite inimitable—all that precedes and follows, "And, Saxon, I am Roderick Dhu!" I regret there not being so much of moral as in Marmion.'[16]

For Wilberforce the exasperating feature of Scott's works was that he always seemed to be on the verge of writing a truly moral book. He once despondently recorded his pain 'that a man of such evidently superior talents should not seem to have directed one thought towards doing good but mainly towards gaining money'.[17] But he examined each of Sir Walter's novels with a new hope. 'Scott's new poem, Halidon Hill, very beautiful,' he wrote in 1822, 'I have been running over the Fortunes of Nigel, the best, I mean the more moral in its tendency of any of Walter Scott's stories which I have heard, illustrating the ways of Providence, the character of men of the world, and their unfeeling selfishness.'[18] Again in 1825: 'Too much time taken, and interest too, in Walter Scott's Heart of Mid-Lothian. Yet I only hear it in afternoon and evening. Much the best of his novels that I have heard, Jeanie Deans a truly Christian character, and beautiful, as far as it goes. . . .'[19]

In spite of these redeeming features he had to conclude that Sir Walter was wasting, though not abusing, his genius. This led him to his famous judgement on Scott's works, that they reminded him of a giant using his strength to crack nuts and that he would rather bring Hannah More's Shepherd of Salisbury Plain up to the Last Judgement with him than all the products of Sir Walter's genius. In a letter to Hannah More he added, 'Aye or of all the plays of Shakespeare.'[20]

This judgement was inevitable, given Wilberforce's priorities. He loved literature, but like every other form of art, it was so inferior to religion that a humble work which served the cause of religion was better than the most brilliant one which did not. He made the point explicitly in 1813: 'I do not know a finer instance of the moral sublime, than that a poor cobbler working in his stall should conceive the idea of converting the Hindoos to Christianity; yet such was Dr. Carey. Why Milton's planning his Paradise Lost in his old age and blindness was nothing to it.'[21]

A few writers like Paine and Sterne were so corrupting or seditious that they drew upon themselves a violent attack from Wilberforce, but he always looked for good in a writer so long as there was any chance of finding it. One might have thought that Gibbon's gibes at the expense of the early Christians would have put him beyond the pale, but Wilberforce's objections seem to be directed almost as much against his style as his paganism. He wrote to Bankes in 1802, 'I have been running over Gibbon's Decline, etc. He is an extraordinary man. Coxcomb all over; but of great learning as well as very great show of it. He also has the merit of never declining a difficulty. But his style is abominably affected and perfectly accords with Lord Sheffield's (of Great Britain and Ireland) account of his mode of composition—and then his paganism is vastly more confirmed than that of Tully, or any other of the old school.'[22]

Byron, apart from his support of the anti-slavery campaigns, can have had little appeal to Wilberforce. It would be hard to imagine a more perfect example of the 'profligacy' of the age which he so often deplores. But in 1828 when his neighbour, Lady Raffles, brought him a copy of Moore's life of Byron, she remembers: 'I brought it with me from Murray's, to read parts of it to him at night, while he was pacing up and down the room with all the quickness and gaiety of a child. What struck me particularly, was his anxiety to find out anything in Lord Byron's favour. "There now," he would stop and exclaim. "Surely there is good feeling there?" ' He was able to read such provocative authors as Lord Chesterfield and Smollett without erupting, though Mackenzie's *Man of Feeling* and *Man of the World* caused a few rumbles. Goldsmith's *Vicar of Wakefield* trod on more delicate ground. 'What utter ignorance does it show of true Christianity?' he complained in his diary. 'Morality is its vital principle; yet the story though strangely unnatural, is beautifully told and inimitably interesting.'[23]

He admired Thucydides and confessed, 'I cannot help feeling for the Athenians although they were no more than a nest of wasps.'[24] But his tolerance of historical characters had its limits; when a friend told him that he had bought a history of the court and manners of Charles II Wilberforce replied that he would have done better to have burnt it.[25] He regarded this monarch with particular loathing. He told his son Samuel: 'There was no man he had such a thorough contempt and hatred for, that with the smoothest and kindest manner he had the most cruel heart. When he was told of the cruelties Lord Dundee had exercised among the Scottish Puritans, instead of feeling any indignation that his people were thus butchered, he calmly replied, "You tell me these things, but I do not perceive that he has done anything to *my* disadvantage." He forgot his friends invariably. The only thing that can be said for him is that he was not bitter in carrying out his hatreds, but that arose not from generous feelings but merely from the easiness of his natural temper which led him to forget everything and yet he was so smooth in manner. I do think he was one of the basest of men.'[26]

Among the poets, his favourites, apart from Cowper, seem to have been Shakespeare, Milton and Sir Walter Scott, and his *bête noire* Dryden. He knew Wordsworth, Southey, Scott, Mason and Rogers (who was always referred to in his diary as 'poet Rogers'). He found Wordsworth 'very manly, sensible and full of knowledge, but independent almost to rudeness'.[27] Southey was 'very pleasing, light as a bird in body and till the loss of his son, I hear his flow of spirits astonishing. He is a man of extraordinary method and punctuality; hence booksellers love to have to do with him. His library is excellent; fitted with curious Spanish and Portuguese manuscript volumes. He allots one time (before breakfast) to poetry, another to history and so on. His History of Brazil is that to which he looks for fame. He is kind, hospitable, generous, virtuous, and I hope, religious, but too hasty in his judgements, and too rash in politics. Hence he would be a dangerous counsellor though an able defender.'[28]

He was at his most critical where religious books were concerned. Doddridge, who had changed his life, would always remain 'super-excellent', Baxter and the 'eminently useful' Owen on *Spiritual Mindedness* might follow close behind, but other writers on religious subjects were examined with rigour. 'Oh how unlike is this to the Scripture!' he exclaimed after reading the Calvinist Romaine. 'He writes as if he had sat at the Council Board with the Almighty!'[29] The great High Church writer, Dr. Paley, came under more detailed criticism. Wilberforce recognised Paley's merits. 'He is assuredly a charming writer,' he wrote to Ralph Creyke who had praised him fulsomely, 'unequalled in perspicuity, and that, I doubt not, from superior clearness and precision in his conceptions. His language is as forcible as the great doctor's . . . without its turgid sesquipedality, if I may describe the Johnsonian style with a Johnsonian epithet. Above all, his illustrations are inimitably happy; nor can I deny that we owe him the highest obligations for his masterly explication of the various evidences of Christianity . . . yet must I say it, he appears to be a dangerous writer, likely to lead his readers in errors.'[30] He does not 'produce in us that true and just sense of the intensity of the malignity of sin, and of the real magnitude of our danger'. He also 'seems to have too low a standard of moral right and wrong and a standard which does not assign the true scriptural place or the moral scale to those sins which respect the Supreme Being'.[31]

Later in 1803 he returned to the same theme in a letter to Muncaster. 'The view of the divine character, which is there [in Paley's works] exhibited is very erroneous and very mischievous. His wisdom, power and goodness, are indeed enforced by many new proofs, but another attribute of the Supreme Being. . . . I mean His justice or His holiness, is entirely overlooked or neglected. The practical consequences of this error are most pernicious; it tends to flatter men into a false estimate of their own character, of the claims of God on them, and therefore the necessity and value of The Redeemer and Mediator between God and Man,'[32]

*

A list of Wilberforce's reading matter would be impressive in its size and scope, all the more so when we remember the fullness of his days and the weakness of his eyesight. As Sir James Stephen put it: 'After having lost the sight of one of his eyes, and while sorely annoyed by the ailments of the other, he ran over with eagerness and appreciated with curious felicity, a greater body of literature than is usually compassed by those who devote themselves exclusively to letters.'

But his reading had rather startling gaps, particularly in contemporary poetry. Reading Wilberforce's papers one finds no mention of Keats, Shelley or Coleridge and the only reference to Byron is the quotation already given, when Lady Raffles read Moore's life to him. Among writers of prose, Jane Austen seems to have been read only in the last year of his life, and although he was devoted to young Tom Macaulay and admired his oratory, he never made any serious comment on his essays in the *Edinburgh Review*.

His taste in literature was catholic but conventional; the same could be said about his appreciation of beauty. He was as moved by the sight and the smell of a flower as by the most stirring speech of Roderick Dhu. He had a deep love of nature in all her aspects, but his tastes were those of his age and he liked best spectacular scenery with mountains, tumbling waterfalls, valleys and boulders. Compared to 'the paradise of Interlaken' he found the English countryside slightly insipid, 'peaceful' and 'rural' rather than beautiful. But in the hills around Windermere and Muncaster, in the mountains of Wales and in Devon by 'the beautiful opening into Linton Vale, and the romantic valley of Rocks', he was entirely content.

Like the rest of the Clapham Sect his tastes were literary and intellectual rather than artistic; he has left us with no views on painting and, considering the range of his surviving papers, it is safe to say that he had little interest in it. His musical tastes were rather different for he had a fine voice and loved to sing. He appreciated good music and once confessed himself to be 'quite overpowered by the Hallelujah Chorus in The Messiah, a flood of tears ensued, and the impression on my mind remained through the day'.[33]

He once told his son Samuel why he did not attend more concerts. 'He thought it might be said "As you see he indulges himself in music because he is very fond of it, if he *himself* loved the theatre he would not condemn that." Besides he thought it right to show the world that a Christian was not obliged to go to the utmost limit of his letter as it were, for his pleasures; that he had many causes of joy and delight in religion itself that he need not go to seek for them as near as possible to the amusement of the world. He then spoke of the effect of music upon him. He could not go and spend a whole morning doing nothing but sitting to hear the performance of music: that if he was about to do anything which required all the efforts of his mind as to make an important public speech that then nothing could be so delightful as beautiful music. That it calmed all his feelings and produced a sort of tranquil happiness in his Mind.'[34]

He appreciated many different schools of architecture, though his preference seems to have been for the medieval. When he rented the great eighteenth-century castle of Hurstmonceux he wrote to Muncaster comparing it unfavourably with the latter's castle. 'This is a very good private gentleman's habitation, yet when one sets it against a complete castle, one side of which was 200 feet long, and which was in the complete costume of the age in which it was reared, it dwindles into as much insignificance, as one of the armed knights of the Middle Ages, fully accoutred, who should suddenly be transformed into the curtailed dimensions of one of the box lobby loungers of the Opera, or even one of the cropped and docked troopers of some of our modern regiments.'[35] Blaise Castle near Bristol, the home of James Harford, was the only building he would compare to Muncaster. It was 'your Paradise', 'your magnificent place', its beauties were 'romantic and sublime'.[36]

He found York Minster 'the largest and finest Gothic building probably in the world'; at Blenheim, 'the first spectacle gorgeously magnificent, like the Duke of Marlborough at the head of his 100,000 men'. The perpendicular church in Cirencester was 'beautiful', the pavilion at Brighton 'beautiful and tasty . . . though it looks very much as if St. Paul's had come down to the sea and left behind a litter of cupolas'. He wrote to Muncaster of the Middletons' house: 'It has none of the grand features of your northern beauties, but for the claims of softness and elegance I never beheld a superior to Barham Court.'

*

In Parliament Wilberforce's prestige was sustained by his own talents, by his position as member for Yorkshire and by his leadership of the Saints, a small compact group of friends who generally voted together. This party included Stephen, the Thorntons, Babington, the Grants, William Smith and, in its first days, Muncaster and Eliot. They were represented in the Lords by Bishop Porteous, with the Duke of Gloucester and Lord Barham as close allies. The strength of the Saints in the Commons was probably no more than twenty-five, but on questions of conscience other members would look to them, and particularly to Wilberforce, for a lead.

Somewhere in between the Saints and the ordinary Members lay a group of reformers who could not be called members of Wilberforce's party since their motives were humanitarian rather than religious, but who often found themselves allied with the Saints on particular issues. Sir James Mackintosh, Whitbread, Sheridan, Sir Samuel Romilly and Sir

Robert Peel all fell into this group. The Saints and humanitarians often supported each other's causes. Wilberforce spoke for Romilly's motions to remove the death penalty for minor crimes, for Peel's efforts on behalf of factory children, on the relief of chimney boys, for Burdett's bill to limit flogging in the army, against the Game Laws and in favour of Penal Reform. The humanitarians were firm Abolitionists, Emancipators and supporters of other causes sponsored by Wilberforce. But the two groups came into conflict, particularly in the years 1816–20, over the repression of discontent at home. They looked on this problem from two different standpoints. The humanitarians saw the anguished protests of the suffering being ground down with brutal force, the Saints saw the very fabric of Society threatened by agitation, and, obsessed by their memories of the French Revolution, lent their moral authority to the oppressors. As early as 1792 Courtenay, on hearing that Wilberforce had been made a citizen of France, told his French friends, 'If you make Mr. Wilberforce a citizen, they will take you for an assemblage of negroes, for it is well known he never favoured the liberty of any white man in all his life.'[37]

It was this aspect of the Saints' activities which earned them enemies. Radicals were outraged to find their efforts to achieve improvements in the condition of the poor frustrated by men who used their moral stature to prevent moral necessities. The sanctimonious tone sometimes used by the Saints was peculiarly ill-suited to justifying tyranny. It was natural to accuse them of hypocrisy. How was it possible for the leaders of the crusade against the Slave Trade to support Pitt's Combination Act, which did more than any other single measure to make the British workman miserable and helpless, to vote for the Corn Laws, which made the poor pay more for their bread, to justify the Peterloo massacre, to make excuses for the use of the industrial agent provocateur and spy, Oliver, and to turn inquisitor whenever some defenceless wretch sold one of Tom Paine's books?

The contrast has probably been over-emphasised. Wilberforce's record in home affairs was nothing like as reactionary as has been claimed, but the contradiction exists and one aspect of it is rather puzzling. Wilberforce often expressed his gratitude for being born in the England of his time. Phrases like 'Oh what blessings we enjoy in this country' recur in his correspondence. He spelt out these beliefs in his speech on Indian missions in 1813. 'Much of the large mass of comforts which we in this country enjoy, beyond those, I believe, of any other nation in ancient or in modern times, is owing to our invaluable constitution.'[38] It is partly a matter of perspective; looking at the social conditions of his time we are struck by the contrast between ostentatious wealth and degrading poverty, and in times of industrial or agricultural distress by the miseries of the poor and the indifference of the rich.

But in Wilberforce's eyes these injustices and calamities were part of the natural order of things, which always had existed and always would. He could look back at the history of his own country or compare its state with that of others and conclude, quite reasonably, that the England of his day was uniquely showered with blessings. Even so he sometimes seemed to be carrying his thankfulness to extremes. This is particularly true in his views on rural life, which he often seems to have seen as a pastoral idyll. He wrote to Lord Galloway in 1800: 'I assure you from my heart that no man respects more than myself the character of a nobleman or gentleman who lives on his own property in the country, improving his land, executing the duties of the magistracy, exercising hospitality, and diffusing comfort, and order, and decorum, and moral improvement, and, last though not least, religion.'[39] He docketed a letter from Ralph Creyke: 'A true picture of an English country gentleman, the very cement of our society.' Under the country gentlemen he saw great numbers of contented 'honest rustics' and 'sturdy yeomen'.

This picture, of course, bore little resemblance to reality, though judging by their correspondence Wilberforce's tribute to Creyke may have been well earned. All over the country honest rustics starved every time there was a bad harvest, while the 'very cement of our society' were busy enclosing the land of the sturdy yeomen and driving them into the new slums of the Industrial Revolution. Pitt was shocked when he saw for himself the conditions of the poor in the country and Wilberforce, too, reacted strongly on his first visit to the Cheddar Gorge. But, with his hosts of correspondents in every part of the country, he must soon have realised what was happening. In January 1796, he circulated a questionnaire[40] inquiring under twenty-three headings into the condition of the poor. When there was a famine he would require detailed information on what was needed and show vigour and compassion in relieving distress, but he never recognised, let alone tackled, the underlying reasons which made the life of the rural poor so miserable.

His attitude to poverty in the cities was the same. He dispensed charity with great generosity, encouraged education and fought against a number of abuses. But he suggested no changes in the system beyond that the poor should cultivate patience and the rich generosity. When he saw a movement threatening the existing order of things he condemned it without hesitation, and in doing so he set himself against many worthy causes, and lent his voice to inexcusable acts of repression.

This contradiction would have been less striking if Wilberforce's support for repression had been given with reluctance. It would have been understandable if he had weighed the dangers to Society against the suffering of individuals and decided that the measures were unpleasant but necessary. Sometimes he did so; his speeches on Oliver and the Corn

Laws are hesitant and indecisive, but he could approach other measures
of repression in the spirit of a crusade. His handling of his constituents
was never more able than when he rallied their support for the Seditious
Meetings Bill. After Pitt's Combination Act he coined the memorable
phrase: 'He stood between the living and the dead and the plague was
stayed.' His most devastating retorts were administered to Courtenay in
the debate on Cold Bath Fields and Burdett in the debate on the Seditious
Meetings Bill. On other occasions he seemed to be able to shut out his
instinctive sympathy for the suffering. In the 1817 debate on the suspension of Habeas Corpus Burdett reminded Wilberforce of the saying of
Christ, 'I was sick and in prison and he visited me not', and asked him
what a Christian should think of those who not only failed to visit the
prisoner, but would not even allow others to do so. Wilberforce replied
that Christianity had taught him to value the blessings the country
enjoyed and to pass them down to posterity.[41]

The contrast between Wilberforce's passionate support for freedom for
the slaves and his opposition to his countrymen's efforts to achieve
freedom has jarred on many of those who have written about him. It has
been called 'the Wilberforce enigma'. He has, not unnaturally, been
accused of hypocrisy and double standards, most notably in Hazlitt's
essay on him, which declared: 'His patriotism, his philanthropy are not so
ill bred, as to quarrel with his loyalty to or banish him from the first
circles. He preaches vital Christianity to untutored savages; and tolerates
its worst abuses in civilised states.'[42] In this Hazlitt was unfair. Wilberforce valued good relations with the great for their usefulness, but he
believed that they, like other forms of capital, should be expended when
duty required. His speeches in the debates on the Prince of Wales's
income, the Royal Divorce and, most of all, in the Duke of York scandal
in 1809, showed that, when necessary, he was not afraid of offending the
greatest.

Others carried these accusations further, and he received more than his
share of sheer abuse. Francis Place called him 'an ugly epitome of the
devil', Boswell wrote some wretched doggerel verse at his expense.

> Go, W— with narrow skull,
> Go home and preach away at Hull.
> No longer in the Senate cackle
> In strains that suit the tabernacle;
> I hate your little wittling sneer,
> Your pert and self-sufficient leer.
> Mischief to trade sits on your lip,
> Insects will gnaw the noblest ship.
> Go, W—, begone, for shame,
> Thou dwarf with big resounding name.[43]

He was suspected of hypocrisy even in his leadership of the Abolitionist movement. 'Something of this fluctuating, time-serving principle was even visible in the great question of abolition of the Slave Trade,' wrote Hazlitt, while John Rickman produced this splendid diatribe: 'Do you suppose that the verminous Wilberforce really expected to carry through his Slave Trade Bill,' he wrote to Southey in 1804, 'or that he introduced it so late in the session that he might augment his odour of sanctity and philanthropy etc. among his devotees, and yet the slaves might still be carried to the West Indies? You will observe that, had he introduced it directly after Xmas, it might e'er now have been law. Oh! Smithfield and fiery faggots for that Holy Man! I would willingly exalt him into a martyr.'[44]

But these voices, however eloquent, were in a minority, and, in spite of their denunciations of him, Wilberforce was perhaps the most respected member of the House. His reputation was supported by outstanding ability as an orator. Sir Samuel Romilly called him 'the most efficient speaker in the House of Commons'.[45] Pitt maintained that 'of all the men I ever knew, Wilberforce has the greatest natural eloquence'.[46] Buxton, who never knew him at his best, thought, 'Wilberforce has more natural eloquence than any of them, but he takes no pains and allows himself to wander from his subject: he holds a very high rank in the estimate of the House'.[47] Sir James Stephen, too, can only have heard Wilberforce speak in his declining years, and thought that he was not at his best in the House of Commons: 'The habit of digression, the parenthetical structure of his periods, and the minute qualification suggested by his reverence for truth impeded the flow of his discourse, and frequently obscured its object. . . . With these disadvantages he was still a great parliamentary speaker.' But Sir James considered him to be a greater one on the hustings and at his very best at the meetings of his charitable and religious societies. He warns his readers that 'the students of history of those times, who shall read some of the discourses which won for him so high a reputation, will scarcely avoid the belief that it was very ill-merited. But if he had *heard them fall from the lips of the speaker*—if he had *seen* him rising with a spirit of self-reliance which Mercutio might have envied, and had listened to those tones so full, liquid, and penetrating, and had watched the eye sparkling as each playful fancy crossed his field of vision, or glowing when he spoke of the oppressions done upon earth—the fragile form elevating and expanding itself into heroic dignity—and the transition of his gestures, so rapid and so complete, each successive attitude adapting itself so easily to each new variation of his style—he would no more have wondered at the efficacy even of ordinary topics and of commonplace remarks from such a speaker, than at the magic of the tamest speech from the lips of Garrick or Talma.'[48]

Brougham remembered one of the few occasions when Wilberforce, goaded beyond endurance, poured out a strain of sarcasm which none who heard it can ever forget. 'A common friend of the parties having remarked to Sir Samuel Romilly, beside whom he sat, that this greatly outmatched Pitt himself, the great master of sarcasm, the reply of that great man and just observer was worthy to be remarked,—"Yes," he said, "it is the most striking thing I almost ever heard; but I look upon it as a more singular proof of Wilberforce's virtue than of his genius, for who but he ever was possessed of such a formidable weapon, and never used it?" '

Buxton remembered his restraint: 'Often during a debate would he whisper to me hints and witticisms which would have filled the House with merriment, and overwhelmed his opponent. But when he rose to speak, though he went close to the very thoughts he had poured into my ear, he restrained himself from uttering them, nor would he ever give vent to any one allusion which might give another pain.'[49]

James Stephen chided him for another shortcoming. 'Your great defect has always been want of preparation . . .' he wrote, 'that you stand so high as you do, is because you could stand much higher if you would, i.e. if you could and would take time to analyze your matter.'[50]

Here we must make the distinction between self-improvement as an orator and the preparation of individual speeches. Wilberforce was often too short of time to prepare a speech properly, but the impression that he had great powers which he neglected was a mistaken one. Few speakers can have taken more trouble than Wilberforce in cultivating their ability. He advised young orators from his own experience not to attempt to make 'fine' speeches, but to attend as many committees as possible and thus gain experience and learn useful facts, to aim at a logical sequence of ideas and cultivate elegant writing, to memorise a few striking thoughts on the subject, on which to fall back if in difficulties. Wilberforce himself would persuade a friend to read him passages from a distinguished author, which he would then repeat back as closely as possible. He studied the classics to arm himself with telling quotations.[51] He analysed the art of speaking and, in his later years, would delight his audience by comparing the great orators of the past.

Canning was the most polished speaker he had ever known, but he was inferior to Fox or Pitt 'for he never drew you to him in spite of yourself'. 'Whitbread was a rough speaker; he spoke as if he had a pot of porter at his lips and all his words came through it. I remember him drawing tears from me on the lottery question.' 'Our general impression of Sheridan was, that he came to the House with his flashes prepared and ready to let off. He avoided encountering Pitt in unforeseen debate, but when forced to it usually came off well.' 'Burke was a great man. I never could understand how he grew at one time so entirely neglected. In part, undoubtedly it was that, like Mackintosh afterwards, he was above his audience. He had come late into Parliament and had had time to lay in vast stores of knowledge. The field from which he drew his illustrations was magnificent. Like the fabled object of the fairies' favours, whenever he opened his mouth pearls and diamonds dropped from him.'[52] 'Fox was truly wonderful. He would begin at full tear, and roll on for hours together without tiring either himself or us.' Fox and Pitt both enjoyed phenomenal memories. 'Often in the earlier part of my Parliamentary life I have heard him [Fox] at a very late hour speak, without having taken any notes, for two or three hours, noticing every material argument that had been urged by every speaker of the opposite party: this he commonly did in the order in which those arguments had been delivered, whereas it was Mr. Pitt's habit to form the plan of a speech in his mind while the debate was going forward, and to distribute his comments on the various statements and remarks of his opponents according to the arrangement which he had made.'[53]

Wilberforce could not emulate such feats of memory. But he could, when fired, produce a stream of eloquence the equal of anything of Pitt's or Fox's. He was also a fine debater, capable, when he allowed himself the indulgence, of withering sarcasm. He also had one asset which they lacked, the voice that had beguiled its hearers from his first schoolmaster to the Prince of Wales.

'His voice itself was beautiful; deep, clear, articulate, and flexible,' remembered one observer.[54] 'Melodious' was a word often applied to it, and at the very end of Wilberforce's life Gladstone found that it still had 'silvery tones'. It was also so well pitched that it could carry through a gale to the back of a great crowd, as it did in the Castle Yard in 1784. When he grew older and his voice deteriorated its melody would jar on unsympathetic ears. Brougham recognised its magic but admitted it would sometimes degenerate into a whine. Hazlitt, as always, was more abusive. 'It winds and undulates,' he complains, 'and glides up and down on texts of Scripture, and scraps from Paley, and trite sophistry, and pathetic appeals to his hearers in a faltering inprogressive, sidelong way, like those birds of weak wing, that are borne from their straightforward course "by every little breath that under heaven is blown".'[55]

He spoke on an amazingly wide range of subjects. In 1806, for example, when one would have expected him to be preoccupied with the final stages of Abolition, he found time to speak on the following matters: Funeral honours to Mr. Pitt, Monument to the memory of Marquis Cornwallis, Lord Ellenborough's seat in the Cabinet, Woollen Manufacturers, Commission of Naval Revision, Affairs of India, Lord Hamilton's motion for papers relating to India, Property Duty Bill, Stipendiary Curates Bill, Pig Iron Duty Bill, Repeal of the Additional Forces Bill,

Messrs. Chalmers & Cowie's Petition, Grant to the Family of Lord
Nelson, Vote of Thanks to Earl St. Vincent, Unaudited Accounts, Abandonment of Tax on Private Brewers, Mutiny Bill, Slave Trade, Affairs of
India—Oudh charge, Vaccine Inoculation, Vote of Thanks to the Volunteers, and Lord Nelson's Annuity Bill.

*

Wilberforce was fortunate in his colleagues, but he shared to some extent
that attribute of great men which he had called 'the power of gravitation'.
When in need he could lean on a number of as stout 'intellectual walking
sticks' as any leader could have wished. Macaulay, Stephen, Clarkson,
Dickson and Babington were a redoubtable team of researchers by any
standards and their efforts could always be augmented by those of a great
number of auxiliaries. Even Muncaster's daughters could be set to work
for Abolition. He received information from a vast network of correspondents in every part of the country.

Without all this help Wilberforce would have been lost, for he needed
his intellectual walking sticks, his white negroes, more than most leaders.
When he had a complicated problem to tackle his brain was clear and
incisive, though not sufficiently so to satisfy him. 'When I look into my
mind,' he once complained, 'I find it a perfect chaos, wherein the little
knowledge which I do possess is but confusedly and darkly visible.'[56] But
his days were invariably fully occupied, and all too often he ended them
bewailing unfinished business or unanswered correspondence. 'No man
has a right to be idle,'[57] he had written in *Practical View*, and he followed
his own precept. But if he never had an idle moment he cannot be said to
have arranged his busy ones very efficiently. His working hours were
interrupted by a stream of uninvited and unwelcome callers, whom he was
too kind to turn away. Every time he changed his home he pathetically
looked forward to a time of peace, but he achieved it only in 1808 when he
moved from Broomfield to Kensington Gore and bought a small and
secret house next door, which he called 'The Nuisance'. 'And even there,'
he admitted, 'I would be no more safe if it were known I had such a
lurking-hole, than a fox would be near Mr. Meynell's kennels.' His
scrupulous honesty did not help matters. He would not allow his footman
to tell intruders that he was out, as this would be encouraging him to lie,
and it was a waste of time to tell them he was busy.

These interruptions would have mattered less to a more methodical
man, but Wilberforce was all too easily diverted. A debtor, hopeless and
pathetic, might come in search of relief, a missionary might appear with
stories of outrages in West Africa, India or Botany Bay; a Yorkshire
constituent might call to complain of the state of the woollen industry;
one 'young female' burst in and announced, 'Mr. Wilberforce I have run

away' (he was relieved to discover that she had done so with a companion of her own sex). As his children grew up the games of marbles were succeeded by hide and seek, blind man's buff (the only game at which poor Wilberforce can have competed with them on equal terms), cricket and long reading sessions, but their summonses were as irresistible as ever. Soon he had the children of Thornton, Macaulay and Stephen to play with as well as his own.

Any one of these and a thousand other distractions were enough to divert Wilberforce's warm heart and butterfly mind from their chosen path. His concentration was fitful at the best of times. He once tried keeping a pebble in his shoe to remind himself of 'invisible things' and asked, 'Why should such secondary means be despised ?' He later admitted to his son Sam that want of application was his greatest fault. 'He said he thought the habit of such importance,' Sam remembered, 'that he would willingly consent to give up all his present knowledge. That he should not know one word even of Latin—that his whole memory of times past should be one universal blank; if at that price he could procure for himself the power of applying his mind to the employment in which he was engaged instead of sitting an hour over his work without giving ten minutes really to it.'[58] In the middle of a grave and critical meeting of the Abolitionists he would suddenly be captivated by the beauty of a flower or a tree and start telling his companions about it, only to be brought down to earth very sharply by his most remorseless walking stick, James Stephen. The same warm-heartedness which sometimes made Wilberforce set aside critically important work when he felt that his sympathies were needed, was, of course, one of the qualities which had made his leadership of his good causes so effective. It could, nevertheless, be exasperating at times.

He could, when provoked beyond endurance, be exceedingly offensive. He once used the botanical analogies, of which he was so fond, to describe a man who wished to represent himself as an associate of one of Wilberforce's societies. 'We must declare that his use of our name is utterly unwarrantable,' he wrote to Macaulay. 'He is like some vermin which will infest the most unwilling subject. It is the nature of things that the fairest trees and the finest fruits should be the prey of reptiles and grubs.'[59]

His friends delighted in telling stories showing his vagueness and the ease with which he could be diverted, for such stories emphasised the warmth of his character. But we should not allow these qualities to assume undue weight. If Wilberforce lacked the single-minded drive of a Macaulay or a Stephen he was by any other standards a most effective worker. He also had compensating virtues which they lacked, above all the ability to see how things must look to someone who was not committed, heart and soul, to the cause of Abolition. When dealing with officials he was shrewd and, at times, as obstinate as a mule. He resolved 'never to mention more than one subject to official men at one interview for if I do I find that all are forgotten'.[60] After his death a Colonial Office official who had had many dealings with him wrote to his sons: 'It is the fashion to speak of Wilberforce as a gentle, yielding character, but I can only say that he is the most obstinate, impractical fellow with whom I have ever had to do.'[61] His shrewdness at times led him near to cynicism. He once wrote to Samuel, 'One of the great secrets to be remembered, in order to enable us to press thro' life with comfort, is, not to expect too much from any new place, or plan, or from the Accomplishment of any new purpose.'[62] When he felt a moral obligation neither kindness nor prudence could divert him from his course. He once learnt that a man with a notoriously immoral character had been appointed to an important post abroad. He went to see the Minister responsible. 'I conceived that the honour of the country was involved, and therefore I plainly told him my mind, and that he would have to answer hereafter for his choice, but he was so angry that I thought he would have knocked me down.'[63]

His correspondence suffered from similar faults; quantity exterminated quality. He had every conceivable excuse: the volume of his mail was matched only by its variety. Often during the session he would receive over thirty letters for many days in succession. It would have been difficult for anyone to answer all these letters, but Wilberforce's eyes were soon strained by reading and writing and his days were already overflowing with work. He disliked using an amanuensis. A few selections from his correspondence will show its variety and how he had to wrench himself from one subject to another when dealing with it.

First there were his regular correspondents, Hannah More, Muncaster, Newton, Babington, Gisborne, Burgh, William Hey, Isaac Milner and James Stephen. He exchanged very long letters at regular intervals with all of these and many others. Then there was the correspondence concerning particular causes written to emperors, kings, presidents, ministers and bishops. He had another network of correspondents who kept him informed of conditions in their parts of the country. As his children grew up and went to school he began a long correspondence with them too. Finally there was a mass of unknown correspondents, constituents, admirers and suppliants which seemed to grow steadily in numbers.

He was constantly being asked for things. Clarkson asked him for a professorship for himself and a captaincy for his brother, Simeon for an honorary degree for his brother, Fletcher Christian's brother for forgiveness for the mutiny on the *Bounty*, Lord Dundonald and more humble correspondents for money. Lady Caroline Lamb asked him to visit a sick friend of her son's. Clergymen asked him for livings, constituents for places, Robert Raikes rather naïvely thought Wilberforce could get his son a position in the West Indies.

His opinion was as eagerly sought after as his assistance. A rich owner of coal mines wished to 'lay before you my sentiments respecting the necessity and propriety of erecting a Chapel or Church' for the benefit of his colliers. Lady Caroline Grahame consulted him about the propriety of her daughters singing songs, a practice to which he gave his qualified approval. Another correspondent tried to interest him in a new fire-extinguishing machine. A heart-broken Newton sent him verses about his wife soon after she had died, with a note of poignant pathos which warned him, 'There are sensibilities belonging to a happy marriage, which can no more be communicated by description than the taste of a pineapple.' Another poetical friend sent him a sonnet on his wig. Dr. Lempriere asked if he might dedicate the eleventh edition of his dictionary to Wilber-force in return for 'his great kindness'.[64] Mysterious packages arrived and, under the postal system of the time, had to be paid for. The first com-munication from Haiti cost him over £35. Once he rebelled at the expense. When an enormous package arrived from the West Indies he complained, 'But I have no correspondent in Demerara.' One admirer even sent him an antelope.

He answered all these letters and took great trouble to follow up the careers of people in whom he had taken an interest. He wrote a six-page letter to Macaulay about a youth he had placed on board a ship trading with China, who he heard had fallen into evil ways.[65] He persuaded the Duke of Gloucester to use his influence in favour of a reprieve for two criminals under sentence of death.[66] A letter from Rowland Hill, an Evangelical clergyman in Ireland, gives the authentic flavour of this side of his correspondence:

'Having already troubled you with two former applications I am ashamed to venture upon a third.

'By my first application you redeemed a thoughtless youth from the gallows whose crime had more the complexion of the trick of a knavish boy than the design of a desperate villain. He had therefore a petition for his life, but the petition was never presented. You discovered the mistake and procured him a pardon a few hours before he was to have suffered. His mother was a good but most afflicted woman. She found him an affectionate and obedient child till misled by others. I am happy to inform you the mercy he received was well bestowed.

'My next application was for a poor distressed widow once in affluence and though what was procured was very small yet your goodwill was equally the same.

'The last case speaks for itself. Mr. Bull's letter needs no explanation, while for the sake of his parents, the life of the wretched youth is earnestly requested. It is equally desired that his banishment may be procured for a considerable period of time.'[67]

Such letters as Hill's could clearly not be allowed to go unanswered; but Wilberforce, although incessantly complaining about the weight of his correspondence, never set about answering it in a purposeful manner. When months in arrears he would take a full page to apologise for the lateness of his letter and explain the poor state of his eyes. By the time he had reached the point of his letter his sight had often been squandered on such preliminaries and his writing degenerated into an illegible scrawl for the only part of it that mattered. They are unsatisfactory documents in other ways. He was in too great a hurry to take any trouble with his language, and at the same time he was too undisciplined to make them succinct. He splashes his thoughts down on the page as they occur to him. He rambles off the point and indulges himself in a series of diversions, parentheses and minute qualifications. They compare very unfavourably with the written works over which he took trouble, *Practical View*, his Letters to the Freeholders of York and to Talleyrand and his sketch of Pitt. It is hard to believe that they are written by a man with a gift for words and a reputation for wit.

The haphazard nature of Wilberforce's letters and his reputation for vagueness are shown in an amusing answer from Canning, to whom he had written from Bath in 1820.

'My dear Wilberforce,

Never was any thing so tantalising as your note of the 22nd which I have received this evening. It refers to a former letter, for which it makes a thousand apologies and explanations, all conspiring to satisfy me that *it* was such a letter as I should have been delighted to receive from you. And lo! *it* is not come to hand. Your packet of 22nd arrives safe—with your note of the same day—but the letter of an earlier date is missing. This is the very spite of fortune. Where can the letter be? Have you not dropped it in the Pump Room? or left it in your bathing jacket, or in the seat of your wheel-chair? or was it singed, in your breeches pocket, by the fire at the Old Rooms? Do feel among your memoranda for it: and pray send it to me as soon as you can find it.'[68]

He often made matters worse by embarking on quite unnecessary correspondence. A Mr. Roberts called on him by appointment and found that Wilberforce had forgotten the engagement and gone out. He sent him a letter accusing him of being too hurried and unmethodical. Wilberforce, instead of apologising abjectly but briefly, returned an interminable letter excusing his forgetfulness and explaining that he never had a moment to spare.[69] Roberts then became a regular correspondent, on whom Wilberforce lavished hours of the time which he complained he could never find.

Stephen was stern on this fault. 'Millions will sigh in hopeless wretched-ness,' he wrote, 'that Wilberforce's correspondents may not think him uncivil or unkind. Why if you were my Lord Wellington and I Masséna, I would undertake to draw off your whole attention to my grand move-ments, and ruin your army unperceived, by teasing your piquets and burning a few cottages on your flanks.'[70]

When he returned from Nice with Milner Wilberforce had an experi-ence which might have made a less scrupulous man take a different attitude towards his correspondence. He stayed with Pitt in Downing Street where 'one of the maid servants seeing a collection of forty or fifty letters on a chair, some opened, others unopened, believing them to be waste paper, threw them all unread into the fire. I dreaded the effect on my reputation in Yorkshire but happily no bad consequences ensued.'[71]

*

Charm is one of the most elusive of human qualities. Everyone who met him agreed that Wilberforce had it in abundance, but none of their accounts of him fully succeeded in recapturing it. This may be partly because the written sketches of him were made by his later friends, a grave and sober group. His sons were equally unsuccessful. Marianne Thornton, Henry's eldest daughter, was horrified to hear that they were writing their father's life. She was not frightened of 'dull Robert' and 'soapy Sam' producing 'anything worse than dull or heavy', but she could not bear the thought of Robert in particular trying to 'appreciate or describe that winged being and all his airy flight'. 'Why you might as well put a mole to talk about an eagle.'[72] The brothers recognised their limitations; when dealing with a feature of their father's character which Lord Milton had described as 'the close union between the most rigid principles and the most gay and playful disposition',[73] they admitted, 'the writers feel more deeply than any who may read these pages that to this great and leading feature of Mr. Wilberforce's character, they have been unable to do any justice in the necessary coldness of description.'[74]

Maria Edgeworth gives us some idea of the difficulties they faced after she met him in 1821. 'I cannot tell you how glad I am to have met him again,' she wrote, 'and to have had an opportunity of hearing his delightful conversation, and of seeing the extent and variety of his abilities. He is not at all anxious to merely talk. His thoughts flow in such abundance, and from so many sources, that they often cross one another; and sometimes a reporter would be quite at a loss. As he literally seems to speak all his thoughts as they occur, he produces what strikes him on both sides of any question. This often puzzles his hearers, but to me it is a proof of candour and sincerity; and it is both amusing and instructive to see him thus balancing accounts out loud. He is very lively and full of odd contortions:

no matter. His indulgent, benevolent temper strikes one particularly: he makes no pretension to superior sanctity or strictness.'[75]

Marianne herself once wrote down a whole morning's talk between Wilberforce and Sir James Mackintosh 'and two better talkers or more disposed to talk their best never were', but she burnt her paper the next day 'out of pure humanity to their memories'. In a way she was right; the most amusing conversations can be flat and banal when written down and of all forms of humour 'playfulness' transfers worst into print. But though she may have failed to recapture the full power of his charm, she came closer to doing so than anyone else. Beside her sketch Sir James Stephen seems stylised and Harford, Colquhoun, Gurney, Bowdler and the Wilberforce brothers all moles tunnelling away in vain pursuit of their eagle.

He was at his most captivating with children and it was as a child that Marianne first knew and loved him. 'Mr. Wilberforce seemed so entirely one of our family that I cannot describe my first impression of him any more than of my own father, indeed I can remember having a game of play with him earlier than with any one. He was as restless and as volatile as a child himself, and during the long and grave discussions that went on between him and my father and others, he was most thankful to refresh himself by throwing a ball or a bunch of flowers at me, or opening the glass door and going off with me for a race on the lawn "to warm his feet". I know one of my first lessons was I must never disturb Papa when he was talking or reading, but no such prohibition existed with Mr. Wilberforce. His love for, and enjoyment in, all children was remarkable.'[76]

He saw as much as possible of his own children. In London the time he could spend with them was restricted by business, but in the country he lived with them the whole time. He ate his meals with them, took them on 'little pleasurable excursions' and joined in their games. His wretched eyesight did not prevent him from playing cricket with them, but he was struck on the foot by a ball and put on his back for several weeks.

He was conscious of the importance of his responsibilities as a father, and always made allowances for those who might have been warped by their upbringings. 'Fox,' he would say, 'was truly amiable in private life, and great allowance ought to be made for him: his father was a profligate politician, and allowed him as much money to gamble as ever he wished';[77] Castlereagh's failings could be attributed to his Irish origins. He worried incessantly about the moral condition of his children and was always on the watch for the first flowering of 'true religion' in them, but he was wise enough not to attempt to force their religious feelings. He spent much time reading aloud to them and having them read to him. One of his sons remembered being read to from Robertson's *History of America*. 'I shall never forget the happy expedient, by which he impressed on me the

characters of the several Spanish chieftains. When the prayer bell cut
short our reading he would bid me mark how its heavy tones chimed in
with the epithets by which he had distinguished them. To this hour the
sound of a bell irresistibly reminds me of his exclamation, "there it goes
again, cruel Cortes, perfidious Pizarro".'[78]

Wilberforce was happiest when with his family, whether at home or on
frequent family holidays to the Lake District, to Bath, to various seaside
resorts or to country houses he had rented. He wrote in 1812, 'As to my
plan of life, I conceive that my chief objects should be—First; my
children. Secondly; Parliament. Thirdly; when I can spare time, my pen
to be employed in religious writing.' In London he took his children to
the British Museum, 'to see the great fish and the toy shops', to jugglers,
picnics and, after Waterloo, to stare at the Cossacks. John Bowdler's
description of an outing to Stowe shows the delight Wilberforce took in
these excursions, even if it shares the whimsical flavour of most reminiscences of his family life. 'We were still in the land of poetry, and music
too, for Mr. Wilberforce made the shades resound to his voice, singing
like a blackbird wherever he went. He always had the spirits of a boy, but
here not little Sam himself can beat him, though he does his best!' He
loved his children even when they were tiresome. He was once closeted
with a visitor when their conversation was interrupted by an appalling
uproar from the children's games on the floor above them. 'How can I be
worried with such trifles,' he asked with transparent sincerity, 'when I
have such constant remembrances of God's goodness to me?'[79]

At times he took a less saintly attitude. 'I sometimes fear,' he confessed
to his sister in 1818, 'that I continued too long a Bachelor. To you I may
open my secret infirmities, for tho' I love the dear children I am amused as
well as interested by them, yet now especially when we are in a small
house, where they keep up an incessant din almost; they really are a little
wearing, and it is at times a relief to get away from them for a quiet walk,
or after they are put to bed to sit in quiet to read or converse.'[80]

Wilberforce's influence on the Victorians was never greater than in his
family life. The regular family prayers which he instituted were a model
for the next generation. We are left with two different accounts of these
occasions, one very solemn in the Faringdon Diary:

'About a quarter before ten o'clock, the family assembled to prayers,
which were read by Wilberforce in the dining-room. As we passed from
the drawing-room I saw all the servants standing in regular order, the
women ranged in a line against the wall and the men the same. There were
7 women and 6 men. When the whole were collected in the dining-room,
all knelt down each against a chair or sopha, and Wilberforce knelt at a
table in the middle of the room, and after a little pause began to read a
prayer, which he did very slowly in a low, solemnly awful voice. This was

followed by two other prayers and the grace. It occupied about 10 minutes, and had the best effect as to the manner of it.

'After prayers were over, a long table covered with cold meat, tarts, etc., was drawn to a sopha on which sat Mrs. Wilberforce and Miss Hewitt. Wilberforce had boiled milk and bread, and tasted a little brandy and water which at night, he said, agrees better with him than wine.'[81]

This was in 1806; twenty-two years later Marianne Thornton gave her description of family prayers. 'The scene at prayers is a most curious one,' she writes, 'there is a bell which rings when Mr. Wilberforce begins to dress; another when he finishes dressing; upon which Mr. Barningham begins to play a hymn upon the organ and to sing a solo, and by degrees the family comes down to the entrance hall where the psalmody goes on; first one joins in and then another; Lizzy calling out, "Don't go near dear Mama, she sings so dreadfully out of tune, dear", and William, "Don't look at Papa, he does make such dreadful faces." So he does, waving his arms about, and occasionally pulling the leaves off the geraniums and smelling them, singing out louder and louder in a tone of hilarity. "Trust Him, praise Him, trust Him, praise Him, praise Him ever more." Sometimes he exclaims "Astonishing! How very affecting! Only think of Abraham, a fine old man, just a kind of man one should naturally pull off one's hat to, with long grey hairs, and looking like an old aloe—but you don't know what an aloe is perhaps: it's a tree—no a plant which flowers . . ." and he wanders off into a dissertation about plants and flowers.'[82]

One can see that all this was endearing and appreciate the warmth, enthusiasm, affection and simplicity that shine out of Marianne's memories. Wilberforce liked people and this was one of the central features of his charm. He liked talking to them, he was interested in their views, tolerant of their faults and sympathetic to their problems. He treated both adults and children as equals, not through any desire to flatter, but simply because it was natural for him to do so. Few of us are so free from vanity that we would resist being treated with such deference by a man of his distinction. He had a lack of vanity or self-importance which could be highly attractive. In 1817 he went with 'Lady D' to hear the sermon of Dr. Chalmers 'most awful on carnal and spiritual man'. The church was full, but instead of using his name to get in Wilberforce climbed over some iron palisades and in by a window. 'I was surveying the breach with a cautious and inquiring eye, when Lady D, no shrimp you must observe, entered boldly before me and proved that it was practicable.' He was told afterwards that 'all London has heard of your climbing in at that window'.[8] He also had the personality to turn men who had always disliked or distrusted him into friends after a very short meeting. Reginald Heber spoke for them all when he said after the final debate on the Slave Trade, 'How an hour's conversation can dissolve the prejudice of years!' He left an impression of goodness and tranquillity combined with gaiety, wit and an enormous zest for life.

We can understand the other qualities, but few traces of his humour survive. Mme de Staël, whose standards were as exacting as anyone's, called him 'the best converser I have met in this country. I have always heard that he was the most religious, but now I find that he is the wittiest man in England'. But, if the distinction can be made he could better be described as 'the most humorous man in England'. He seldom used sarcasm and his repartee was too well curbed to be memorable. We can still appreciate the crushing retorts of Dr. Johnson, the wit of Sheridan, Gibbon, Wilkes or Canning, but Wilberforce's humour depended, not so much on words, but on the way in which it was delivered. His vitality, his love of digressions and asides, and his talent for mimicry, all contributed to his gifts as a raconteur. His own delight in the story would carry along his audience. When written down on paper these stories are slight enough. Two of his favourites were the stories of Sheridan and the horse coper and Pitt and the French émigré.

'The story told of Sheridan is that meeting one day a horse-dealer to whom he owed a good deal of money he was somewhat embarrassed. The man came and pressed him to pay his bill. Mr. Sheridan could not escape because the dealer was on horseback and himself on foot. So he said to him "well it is very true I should have paid you before but come home now and I will give you a draft on my banker for the amount." On his way home he looked at the horse the dealer was on and said "a very pretty little thing that; I think it would just suit me. I have been looking out for one for Mrs. Sheridan: pray let me see him trot; one cannot altogether judge by a walk." The man trotted on to show his paces and Sheridan turning down the first alley made the best of his way out of the dealer's reach.'[84]

The second story was an illustration of the levity of the French. M. de Périgord, a distinguished émigré, called on Pitt soon after Marie Antoinette's execution. Naturally the conversation turned to the Queen. 'The Frenchman's feelings were quite overcome, and he exclaimed amidst violent sobbing, "Ah Monsieur Pitt, la pauvre Reine! La pauvre Reine!" These words had scarcely been uttered when he jumped up as if a new idea suddenly possessed him, and looking towards a little dog which came with him, he exclaimed, "Cependant, Monsieur Pitt, il faut vous faire voir mon petit chien danser." Then pulling a small kit out of his pocket, he began dancing about the room to the sound of the little instrument, and calling to the dog, "Fanchon, Fanchon, dansez, dansez," and the little animal instantly obeyed, and they cut such capers together that the minister's gravity was quite overcome and he burst into a loud laugh, hardly knowing whether he was most amused or astonished.'[85]

He could also enjoy stories against himself. 'I remember going to my old friend Lord —— in his last illness. I had spoken to him fully on religious matters many years before, and he had seemed to pay no attention to me. I heard that he was taken ill, and called upon him. When I had sat some time chatting with him, but without alluding to religious matters, another friend came in and asked, "How are you today ?" "Why," was his reply, "as well as I can be with Wilberforce sitting there and telling me that I am going to hell." '[86]

He was inclined to fall asleep, in church, in Parliament, or when listening to the admirable but dull plans of Robert Owen. This was mainly due to physical weakness, but it still pricked his tender conscience. He thought that sleeping on in the morning, 'late rising' as he called it, was a serious fault—'There was scarcely anything else equally injurious'—but when carried away by the pleasure of others' company he would sit up until all hours. Southey describes him as being 'such a *straggling* visitor,—he was longer a *going, going, going*, than a bad bale of goods at an auction',[87] and after his first evening at Wilberforce's home he made it a condition of any future visits that he should be allowed to leave by eleven o'clock.

Sir James Stephen gives us something of the flavour of his conversation.

'. . . Mr. Wilberforce was, by the gift of nature, among the most consummate actors of his time. Imagine David Garrick—talking not as a mime, but from the resources of his own mind, and the impulses of his own nature—to have personated in some other society the friends whom he had been dining at the Literary Club,—now uttering maxims of wisdom with Johnsonian dignity—then haranguing with a rapture like that of Burke—telling a good story with the unction of James Boswell—chuckling over a ludicrous jest with the childlike glee of Oliver Goldsmith—singing a ballad with all the taste of Percy—reciting poetry with the classical enthusiasm of Cumberland—and, at each successive change in this interlude, exhibiting the amenities of Sir Joshua—then brood awhile over this supposed monopolylogue, and there would emerge an image of the social William Wilberforce, always the same, and ever multiform, constraining his companions to laugh, to weep, to admire, to exult, and to meditate at his bidding.

'. . . a certain air of originality embellished the most trite and familiar of his observations. There was still an impress of novelty when he repeated for the twentieth time some favourite maxim, or told over again some well-known story. . . . The words however simple, which Wilberforce selected as the vehicle of any passion became in his use of them as replete with significance as those homely phrases with which Mrs. Siddons was accustomed to awaken the loudest echoes of the theatre.

'Scarcely any memorial of his table talk has survived him, nor is it difficult to explain the reasons. . . . Mr. Wilberforce turned on every topic which he touched a sort of galvanic stream of vivacity, humour, and warm-heartedness, which tended rather to volatise and to disperse, than to consolidate the substances on which it fell. He did not dispose of a laughable incident by one terse and pregnant jest; he rather used it as a toy to be tossed about and to be played with for a while, and then thrown aside. Even his wisdom demanded a certain breadth of space for its development; for it incorporated every illustration pleasant or pathetic which fell in his way and left behind it an impression more delightful than definite. Being himself amused and interested by everything, whatever he said became amusing or interesting.'[88]

Time may have taken Wilberforce's wit from us, but his sayings retain some force:

'Let the apparent temptation of profit be what it may, it can never be in the real interest of any nation to be unjust and inhuman.'[89]

'Economy is not inconsistent with generosity; on the contrary, unless people are as affluent as I was before my marriage, there can be no generosity without it.'[90]

'There is a vile and base sentiment current among men of the world, that if you wish to preserve a friend, you must guard against having any pecuniary transactions with him; but it is a caution altogether unworthy of a Christian bosom.'[91]

'The best course when any one is low spirited and distressed with anxieties, is to set them to action in doing good to others.'[92]

'Even if it were not a sin, as it certainly is, to marry for money, I should deem it one of the basest actions a gentleman could commit.'[93]

To a friend; 'I used to think you the most violent politician that I knew, but now I find you take in The Morning Chronicle and nothing else, I am only astonished at your moderation.'[94]

'London is the gangrene of our body politic.'[95]

He had his moments of gloom and they were more frequent than anyone suspected for he hid them well. He wrote to Babington in 1824, 'I sometimes think that I have the art (though I am sure undesignedly) of concealing from my most intimate associates my real character. One particular I doubt if you have ever observed. I ought however to say it is not constant: but I am at times much more disposed to melancholy than you would imagine.'[96]

The world saw only the vivacity, humour and conversational flair, which, combined with a deep interest in other people, however humble and dull, were the main pillars of Wilberforce's charm. They were supported by sympathy, kindness and a reputation for holiness without dullness. 'Do you remember Madame de Maintenon's exclamation?' asked Sir James Stephen. ' "Oh the misery of having to amuse an old King, qui n'est pas amusable!" Now if I were called upon to describe Wilberforce in one word, I should say he was the most "amusable" man I ever met with in my life. Instead of having to think what subjects will interest him, it is perfectly impossible to hit on one that does not. I never saw any one who touched on life at so many points; and this is the more remarkable in a man who is supposed to live absorbed in the contemplation of a future state.'[97] The absence of any vanity impressed the future Cardinal Newman: 'It is seldom indeed we may hope to see such simplicity and un-affected humility in one who has been so long moving in the intrigues of public life and the circles of private flattery.'[98]

It was his reputation for saintliness and rectitude that gave the point to one of Byron's favourite stories. Sheridan, incapably drunk, was found lying in the gutter by the watch. Asked for his name the great wit raised his head and hiccupped out the words, 'William Wilberforce!' It was, in its way, a tribute.

CHAPTER XXII

PARLIAMENT AND PERCEVAL, 1807–12

WILBERFORCE'S political life was spent in a period of Tory supremacy. He had entered Parliament in 1780, and from the fall of the Fox–North Coalition in 1784 until he retired from it in 1825, the succession of Tory Governments was interrupted only by the brief rule of the Talents in 1806–7. After Pitt's death Wilberforce had no personal ties with either party, but there is little doubt that he found the Tories more congenial. The Whigs might be more willing to lend the weight of their authority to particular reforms, but the Tories' political philosophy corresponded far more closely to his own. Wilberforce once made the startling statement that his political course had been shaped by Whig principles, and Whig historians, notably Sir James Stephen, were anxious to claim him as their own. But he was a Tory through and through; he never shed the political ideas he had inherited from Pitt and his religion intensified his conservatism, for every reform had to be weighed against the encouragement it might offer to revolution, chaos and, worst of all, atheism. He carried his Tory principles into county politics, where, although he would never sacrifice his independence by uniting with him, he lamented the West Indian magnate Lascelles's defeats at the hands of the Whig advocates of Abolition, Fawkes and Milton.

In 1807 he may have regretted the passing of the Talents. He was deeply grateful for their support of Abolition, he detected the burgeoning of true religion in Grenville and the issue on which they were dismissed was not dissimilar to the Bill he had himself put through the Commons. But the return to a Tory Government was made easier by the presence in it of Spencer Perceval, a man whom Wilberforce admired more than any other politician after Pitt's death. Perceval was Chancellor of the Exchequer and Leader of the House of Commons in the Portland Administration from 1807 to 1809 and Prime Minister from 1809 until his assassination in 1812.

Perceval had inherited all the purity of Pitt's private life, and though he had thirteen children to support he never attempted to benefit financially from his political offices. When Prime Minister and Chancellor of the

Exchequer he even held the latter office without remuneration. While many of those who had been raised to great and lucrative offices through Pitt's favour refused to subscribe to Wilberforce's fund to pay off his debts, Perceval, who owed him nothing, gave £1,000 at a time when he had only his earnings at the Bar to support his family. He was calm and courageous and a first-class debater, though not a great orator. He was also a deeply religious man, a fervent Protestant who opposed any relaxation of the laws against Roman Catholics and who would tolerate no compromise with the revolutionary atheists on the continent.

Had it been given more time, Wilberforce's friendship with Perceval might have grown as close as that with Pitt; Wilberforce regarded Perceval as being 'one of the most conscientious men I ever knew; the most instinctively obedient to the dictates of conscience, the least disposed to give pain to others, the most charitable and truly kind and generous creature I ever knew'. He had 'the sweetest of all possible tempers'. Wilberforce's religion would have been no barrier to such a friendship, but it is unlikely that Perceval or anyone else could ever have achieved the same influence over his mind as had been held by Pitt. It had been such an agonising experience to oppose Pitt in Parliament that he had allowed himself to be cajoled and argued out of many acts of opposition. He never had the same feeling of attachment to any other Prime Minister and his acts of opposition after 1806 were uninhibited by any personal feelings.

He had, on the other hand, no general grounds for opposition. He recognised that the nature of the war had changed and that to sue for peace was futile so long as Napoleon remained in power. The arrogance with which Napoleon forced the Spanish to accept his brother Joseph as their king confirmed him in this belief. 'Surely this is so heaping insult on injury,' he complained to Muncaster, 'that he might have foreseen that human nature would scarcely bear it. I have often thought that it might perhaps please God to pull down this giant when raised to his highest elevation, and apparently glorying the most reasonably, as well as the most proudly, in his strength.'[1] The brutality used against the Spanish partisans repelled him. 'To what a temper of hardness must that man have brought his mind,' he wrote again to Muncaster, 'who can coolly issue orders, that no quarter shall be given to the peasants taken in arms fighting for their natural monarch against a sovereign set over them by a foreign usurper. Well, we are taught by such instances to look forward to the day of retribution, and it will come.'[2]

He saw all politics through the eyes of an Abolitionist. When the Portuguese Royal Family were driven out of their own country he wrote in his diary, 'Portuguese court migrated to Brazil—pregnant with important consequences—especially in Abolition connection.'

The revolt in Spain raised all sorts of new hopes. The 'Spanish patriots' joined his long list of good causes; he realised that they must be preoccupied at present with the struggle for their own freedom but in this very struggle could not 'that generous temper of mind be produced, which will abhor oppression and cruelty, [and] consequently will abolish the Slave Trade'? He busied himself lobbying Ministers so that the Spanish representatives in England should hear the full Abolitionist case. He discovered that there were many priests with the rebels in Spain and presumably in Portugal. Could not they be influenced by 'the double motives of the spirit of liberty and of religion, to exert themselves for so glorious an object as ours'? Another hope, wilder and inconsistent with his idea of inflaming the priests against the Slave Trade, was 'that God, through the destruction of the Spanish political despotism, will also destroy the popish bondage and darkness, and (probably after much suffering) shine on them with the light of truth'.

For the moment he was content to give his support to the Spanish and to see that they were properly instructed on the merits of Abolition. Even those who had always opposed the war were disgusted by Napoleon's treatment of Spain. Sheridan went down to the House to deliver a speech that would 'electrify the country on the Spanish business . . . but the opportunity being delayed he going up-stairs got so drunk, as to make him manifestly and disgracefully besotted. Yet he seemed to remember a fair speech, for the topics were good; only he was like a man catching through a thick medium at the objects before him. Alas a most humiliating spectacle; yet the papers state him to have made a brilliant speech etc. So true is what Cobbett said of his friendship to the editors and reporters.'[3]

Wilberforce reluctantly accepted the war as a vile necessity, but he wished it to be waged with some sort of restraint. In 1808 he was in favour of allowing supplies of quinine to pass through the British blockade of France. Economic like military warfare should not be total.

Soon after the change of government his conscience was presented with a difficult problem. The French and the Russians had made peace at Tilsit on July 9, 1807 and the terms of the treaty included secret clauses to force Denmark and Sweden to join their alliance. The British Government heard of this agreement through their intelligence system; there was nothing they could do to thwart it, but Napoleon might be prevented from seizing the Danish fleet together with Denmark and his capacity for invading England thus reduced. A fleet under Gambier was therefore sent to Copenhagen. At the same time a British envoy demanded that Denmark should hand over her fleet and promised that it would be returned at the end of the war. When the Danes refused the city was bombarded by bomb-ships and rockets, while an army contingent attacked it from the land. A great part of Copenhagen was destroyed by the flames and the

Danes surrendered their fleet on September 5. Gambier wrote to Wilberforce:

> Prince of Wales, off Copenhagen
> Sept. 8, 1807.
>
> My dear Friend,
>
> I am sure you will be happy to hear that it has pleased God to bless our endeavours here for the service of the nation, and that we are in possession of the whole Danish navy at Copenhagen, consisting of eighteen sail of the line, eleven frigates, and eleven sloops, with a number of gun-boats, &c.
>
> Providence has favoured us in a most remarkable manner from the moment of our departure from England, every circumstance concurring to our help. Most thankful ought we to be for so favourable an issue in the attainment of an object of such importance, with a comparatively trifling loss. The poor Danes have suffered very much, and great distress must be felt by the inhabitants of Copenhagen. Having much upon my hands, I can only desire you will offer my affectionate remembrances to Mrs. Wilber-force.
>
> Yours ever most truly,
> J. Gambier.[4]

This violent and unprovoked attack upon a neutral power aroused criticism from other countries and from the Opposition at home. At first Wilberforce's thoughts seemed to be running along the same lines. 'How shocking,' he wrote in his diary on September 13, 'are the accounts from Copenhagen! Alas, alas! I cannot but greatly doubt the policy of changing so great a number of men from cold into most willing and energetic allies of France. They must think us the most unjust and cruel of bullying despots.'

He confessed afterwards that it had been extraordinarily difficult to keep his 'abstract reasonings on the case from being trampled underfoot by the host of feelings which the general view of the whole scene called into action'. Perceval had written to him before the action was finished announcing 'the *full conviction*, I believe of this Government, I can safely say, of *my own*, that unless either by treaty or by force we secured the possession of the Danish Fleet, that fleet would, to a certainty, have been completely French as the Fleet at Brest'.[5] After speaking with Gambier, a deeply religious man who approved of the expedition and ascribed its success to Providence, and to those who opposed it, he came to his own judgement. The expedition was justified—'our right clear, if self-defence clear'—for the Danes would be forced to become enemies, and if England did not seize their fleet Napoleon would. The management of the expedition had also been correct, so strong a force having been sent to Copenhagen that the Danes could have surrendered without disgrace. But the Government had been wrong in appropriating the fleet to its own use. 'We should have kept it as a sacred deposit, to be restored at the termination of the war.'[6] By failing to do so England had brought her motives into doubt and added to the inevitable injury to her national character.

The sailors should not have been deprived of their prize money, but it ought to have been paid from the Exchequer, not from the proceeds of the Danish seizures. He could not help wishing that the Government had acted on Christian principles. 'Oh that nations trusted more to God!' he wrote in his diary on October 20, 'and then if we had on Christian principles forborne, declaring we would not expose our good to be evil spoken of, I doubt not we should have been protected.'

He did what he could to help the homeless in Copenhagen. Fortunately most of the damage had been done by rockets rather than bombs and the loss of life was correspondingly low, but many houses had been destroyed by fire. Wilberforce therefore started 'a subscription for assisting the poorer of the individual sufferers to rebuild their houses'.

Another military adventure offended him more than the attack on Copenhagen. Driven by a desperate need to open up new areas for trade the Government had launched attacks on Buenos Aires in 1806 and 1807. Both attacks failed, although the city was in British hands for a short time, but since the first had taken place under the Talents and the second under Portland's administration, there was a general reluctance to hold an inquiry. Wilberforce had to vent his feelings in a letter to Bankes. 'Anything almost is better than a coalition,' he wrote in October 1809, 'and nothing is so likely to multiply expeditions, or to produce impunity for the most absurd. What, but its happening that both ins and outs were concerned in the Buenos Aires expedition, prevented some public censure of that most monstrous of all absurdities?—deliberately attempting to conquer South America, or when hoping to induce the natives to declare their independence, to set about conciliating their favour, by sacking one of their most populous towns.'[7]

Of all expeditions he thought the attack on Buenos Aires 'the most absurd in conception, and the worst planned as to execution', but by now 'expedition' had become almost as dirty a word as 'coalition'. In July 1809 a British force was sent to the Scheldt with the task of opening a second front against the French. But in the same month the defeat of Austria at Wagram, and the humiliating peace which followed, robbed the expedition of its original purpose. Instead of withdrawing it remained on the island of Walcheren, a fever-ridden swamp in the mouth of the Scheldt, where it first erected and then demolished fortifications. When the expedition finally evacuated Walcheren on December 22 nearly half of its members had died or fallen sick.

Wilberforce watched this fiasco with impatience. 'One point is clear,' he wrote on October 2, 'that there ought to be some great advantage in view from keeping Walcheren, considering the expense at which it seems likely to be held, and an expense in the article in which we can least of all afford to be extravagant.'

The House voted to hold an inquiry into the Walcheren affair and Wilberforce was a member of the secret committee, though Perceval objected to him 'as not enough of a party man to overbalance oppositionists'. These forebodings were justified, for he opposed the Government on point after point; but he followed his own conscience and refused to vote for the Opposition's more extravagant motions of censure.

*

In home affairs he also found it beyond him to give consistent support to the Government. In January 1809 a scandal broke which diverted the nation from all serious matters for the first months of the year. It was precisely the sort of issue on which Wilberforce's judgement could carry most weight.

The Duke of York, George III's second son, was Commander-in-Chief of the army; although he is now remembered mainly for leading his 10,000 men up and down the hill, the Duke did in fact fill this office with distinction and achieve many useful reforms. But he had a mistress, Mrs. Clarke, with whom he had parted and to whom he had given an annuity on condition that she behaved herself. When she failed to do so the Duke cancelled the annuity; Mrs. Clarke responded by threatening to print his letters to her and expose him, but he ignored her threats. On January 26 Colonel Wardle, a radical Member of Parliament, alleged that Mrs. Clarke, with the Duke's connivance, had been taking bribes from officers in return for promotions.

The nation greeted the scandal with relish. The survivors of Corunna returned home to find their friends gossiping about their Commander-in-Chief and no one interested in their victory. In the streets anyone tossing a coin would call Duke or Darling instead of heads or tails. Wilberforce's first reaction was to remove the hearing from the House, where anybody could listen to it from the public gallery, to 'a committee upstairs, and some parliamentary commission on oath'. He gave as his reason that 'all party bias and personal altercation, would be avoided'. But his diary shows him to have been more concerned that 'this melancholy business will do irreparable mischief to public morals, by accustoming the public to hear without emotion of shameless violations of decency'. His views on the corrupting effects of scandal and vice were consistent. He was realistic enough to realise that they would always exist, but he saw no reason why they should be paraded in public. He later quoted the case of Charles II. When that profligate monarch 'conducted himself improperly in Scotland with respect to a loose female, a deputation from the Kirk was sent to remonstrate with him. Their spokesman, Douglas, having left the rest of the deputation at a considerable distance, went up to His Majesty who expected a severe lecture, and merely said to him,

"When next your Majesty pleases to indulge yourself in practices like these, you should shut the window shutters, and avoid scandal".[8]

In this case his gloomiest forebodings were to be realised. Examination of witnesses soon established that Mrs. Clarke had received money from officers in return for helping them to be promoted. What was less clear was whether her help had been effective, for those of her clients who were promoted had all been recommended by other patrons. There was also some suspicion of Wardle's role, the other members showing anxiety that he should not have the opportunity of briefing his witnesses. Wilberforce found it depressing. 'Wardle's motion on the Duke of York,' he wrote in his diary on January 26, 'sad work. No apparent sense in the House of the guilt of adultery, only of the political offence. Spoke for any other proceeding than bar of House, and to be examining strumpets in present state of country.'

When the moment came for the examination of the strumpet, his gloom deepened. Mrs. Clarke is said to have boasted before her appearance that she would make half the House fall in love with her, and she seems, if anything, to have underestimated her own charms. She was pert, witty, coquettish and shameless. She freely admitted her dealings in commissions and did her best to involve the Duke in them. She claimed he knew she would receive a 'compliment' if the commission went through; she said she had shown him the draft she had been given and that he had had it changed for her.[9] She scored off her questioners, and her answers finally became so flippant that she was rebuked from the Chair. Even Wilberforce seems to have warmed to her; he wrote in his diary, 'House examining Mrs. Clarke for two hours—cross-examining her in the Old Bailey way—she elegantly dressed, consummately impudent, and very clever; clearly got the better in the tussle. . . . The House on watch for every double-entendre and in roars of laughter.'

At a later examination of Mrs. Clarke the theatrical atmosphere in the House must have been doubly offensive to Wilberforce. Her appearance was preceded by excited cries of 'Chair! Chair!' and a chair was brought into the chamber. But when Mrs. Clarke came in she explained that what she wanted was not to sit down but to go home, as she had been kept waiting eight hours and was very tired.[10] Although a charming witness, Mrs. Clarke was not a convincing one. She was evasive, her vindictiveness against the Duke was evident and she contradicted herself and the other witnesses, few of whose testimony inspired confidence. The House was also conscious that, although the Duke was effectively on trial, he was not present or represented, nor were the witnesses being examined on oath.

These considerations and the strong suspicion that there was a conspiracy against the Duke led the Saints to move an amendment to Wardle's motion, which Bankes put forward on March 10. They found the Duke innocent of personal corruption or of profiting from any such corruption, but concluded that he must have had suspicions of what was happening and recommended that he should not remain Commander-in-Chief.[11]

Wilberforce supported Bankes's amendment when he spoke on the subject on March 15.[12] After dealing severely with the moral aspects of the affair—he pointed out how the mistresses of princes were the sources and means of corruption—Wilberforce declared himself prepared to acquit the Duke of any real knowledge of Mrs. Clarke's transactions, but not of any suspicion of them. 'If he had not been blinded by his attachment to that woman, it was impossible that he should not have suspected, if not known, the corrupt practice that was carried on.'[13] The House should make some reparation to public morals and decency and recommend to the King that the Duke should no longer remain in command of the army.

'It was customary in that house to call things by very soft and gentle names. That which used to be called "adultery" was now only "living under the protection".'[14] Such delicate expressions struck at the root of the country's morals, and religion and morals were the best preservers of states. He quoted Machiavelli on this point. 'The rulers of all states . . . should take care that religion should be honoured, and all its ceremonies preserved inviolate, for there was not a more certain symptom of the destruction of states, than a contempt for religion and morals.'[15]

Even if the Duke had no suspicions of Mrs. Clarke, 'it was not at a time that all the continental nations were broken down by the armies of France, that this country should have a Commander-in-Chief who was liable to be blinded and duped by a woman (Hear! Hear!). It was well known that Buonaparte succeeded as much by his intrigues as by open force, and if he found that we had a Commander-in-Chief who was duped by his mistress, it would be easy for him to gain an ascendancy over such a woman, in order to command the most important secrets of the state.'[16]

Bankes's amendment was defeated by 95 votes, Wardle's motion by 224, but Wilberforce wrote to Muncaster on March 18: '. . . unless the Duke of York should resign before Monday, I am sanguine in my expectation, that we shall carry the question for his removal.'[17] Before the House met again he received a message from the Duke of Cumberland through Robert Thornton that the Duke of York had resigned;* he added that 'the King and all of them, extremely angry at me. Yet what could I do as an honest man short of what I have done?'[18]

On September 21, 1809 Wilberforce was shocked and surprised by what seemed to be an echo of the Pitt-Tierney affair. Canning's restless arrogance grew impatient with the failings of his colleagues before the

---

* He was reinstated in 1811 and gave a fine gesture of magnanimity by becoming patron of one of Wilberforce's dispensaries.

expedition was sent to Walcheren. He wrote a letter of complaint to Portland in which Castlereagh, who held the War Office, was criticised with especial bitterness. Portland dreaded a head-on clash between the two men and persuaded Canning to remain silent until the end of the session, when a reshuffle of offices might be arranged without offending either of them. It was hard for Canning to refuse, but by accepting he made himself seem to be secretly plotting the ruin of Castlereagh, while remaining on ostensibly friendly terms with him in cabinet. Castlereagh finally discovered the truth, called out Canning and gave him a slight wound. Both men resigned before the duel. Portland had a fit and died before the end of the year, leaving the wretched Perceval to patch together some sort of War Ministry.

Wilberforce's first reaction was predictable. 'What a humiliating thing it is!' he wrote in his diary, 'In what a spirit must our national counsellors have been deliberating!'[19] He wrote to Bankes on October 2: 'Could you have conceived any men's being so absurd, to say nothing of higher motives, as to make the public exhibition afforded by Castlereagh and Canning. I can only account for it in the former, to whom as the challenger it is nine parts in ten most probably to be ascribed, by his Irish education and habits. *Manent adhuc vestigia ruris.* I wish the King would declare that neither of them should ever serve him again in a public station. That would effectually prevent the spreading of the example.'[20] He had not suggested and would not have approved of making the same example of Pitt.

The next day he wrote again to Bankes, having heard a slanted version of the cause of the quarrel which shifted the nine-tenths of the blame from Castlereagh to Canning. He was now able to see the funny side of the affair. 'Indeed it is actually true,' he wrote, 'that when I read the paragraph I thought of cutting it out and transmitting it to you, lest your paper should be less just to the party concerned. The particular to which I allude, and which made me laugh heartily, was that of Lord ——'s having picked up and carried off one of the pistols, which one of the parties threw away after having fired it, and his gardener the other (like master like man). . . . But you perhaps have not heard as much as I have done of the noble Earl's provident parsimony, which indeed went beyond parsimony, for it not only made him take care of what was his own, but keep a sharp look-out for that which was another's.'[21]

It was a difficult matter in which to apportion the blame. Portland could scarcely be blamed for trying to preserve his ministry at a critical moment of the war; Canning was fully entitled to issue his criticism of Castlereagh, but could not demand a change of War Ministers in the middle of the Walcheren expedition; while Castlereagh's challenge was issued under the utmost provocation. Wilberforce in the end found against Castlereagh; his challenge, he discovered, had been issued 'after having chewed the cud of his resentment for twelve days'. It was thus sent not 'from the impulse of the first angry feelings', but as 'a cold-blooded measure of deliberate revenge'.

*

In 1808 Wilberforce's long residence at Clapham had ended. He had found his old way of life increasingly inconvenient and the cause of much wasted time. When Parliament was sitting he had to live in Palace Yard where he was defenceless against a host of uninvited guests. 'A residence near London,' he thought, 'would withdraw me from company, and give me more time. Yet I dread the separation which my leaving Broomfield would make from my chief friends, the Thorntons, Teignmouths, Stephens, Venn, Macaulay, with whom I now live like a brother.'[22] There were other reasons. If he moved to a large house, closer to Parliament than Clapham, but removed a discreet distance from the centre of the city, he could save money by having one home instead of two. Clapham also inspired a sort of spiritual pride, a self-righteous complacency among its sect, which was shown when a visiting clergyman preached there instead of Venn. Preaching to the Clapham Sect must have been the equivalent of singing at La Scala or playing on the centre court at Wimbledon. But the miserable substitute failed to realise the quality of his audience. 'He chose to extemporise,' was the chilling verdict, 'and that at Clapham.' Milner warned Wilberforce against the contagious danger of spiritual pride, though he thought him less susceptible to it than some of his friends.

All these reasons played their part in persuading him to move to Kensington Gore. He acquired a twenty-five-year lease on a large house standing on the site of the Albert Hall. Apart from the 'Nuisance' where he could escape from callers, Kensington Gore had a garden of three acres where he could sit out in the summer and read under the shade of the walnut and mulberry trees that grew there. James Stephen now lived next door in Hyde Park Gate. Although less than a mile from Hyde Park Corner, Kensington still enjoyed a rural atmosphere. Sir Leslie Stephen remembered: 'The Kensington of those days was still distinctly separate from London. A high wall divided Kensington Gardens from the Hounslow Road. There were still deer in the gardens, cavalry barracks close to Queen's Gate, and a turnpike at the top of Gloucester Road. The land upon which South Kensington has since arisen was a region of market gardens, where in our childhood we strolled with our nurse along genuine country lanes.'[23]

As anyone could have told him Wilberforce's new home was soon inundated with visitors. Among his more welcome guests were Pinckney, the American Ambassador, Perceval, who had taken Teignmouth's house at Clapham, and Southey. His old friends from Clapham were not deterred from visiting him by the distance, though John Venn must have been very irritated to have ridden over to Kensington for dinner only to find that his host had forgotten the engagement and gone out. General Miranda, the Latin-American revolutionary leader, was a frequent guest, as was John Bowdler, a young man whom Wilberforce perhaps saw as his successor in the management of his good causes.

Bowdler was born the year before Wilberforce became Member for Yorkshire, but in spite of the great difference in their ages, Wilberforce was influenced by his judgement. As early as 1807 he was asking Bowdler's advice: 'Oct 26 Evening. John Bowdler came, a truly amiable and most able young man, and above all truly pious and charmingly pleasant. Sat chatting with him too long. Much talk about education. He agreed that public school inadmissable, from its probable effects on eternal state.'[24] Bowdler was a brilliant man with a phenomenal memory. He knew enormous tracts of the classics and once learnt by heart a 30,000-line law book, an experience which he described as being 'most dry and like learning so many proper names'. His application was as remarkable. 'It is the testimony of one who for nearly twelve months divided with him the same narrow study,' Sir James Stephen wrote of Bowdler, 'that during the whole of this period he was never heard to utter an idle word, nor seen to pass an idle minute.'[25] Although a High Churchman he was a frequent contributor to the *Christian Observer*. He was an aloof, reserved and courteous man, but he unbent in Wilberforce's company. His health was always delicate and Wilberforce watched over it with a father's anxiety; when Bowdler suffered from a pulmonary disease in 1810 and had to travel abroad, Wilberforce wrote to Muncaster, 'But for my being married, I have thought that I would go as his companion.' Bowdler remained a High Churchman until his death in 1815 and it is a tribute to the tolerance of both men that his friendship with Wilberforce remained so close. But Wilberforce was soon to be deprived, both of Bowdler and of Perceval, to whom he looked for the moral leadership of the country.

Perceval had succeeded Portland at a time when the international outlook seemed worse than ever. After the alliance between Russia and France all of Europe had been forced to join the Continental System under which British cargoes, however they were carried, were liable to confiscation. Only through the Levant and the tenuous British hold on Portugal, could her goods filter through the embargo. After Austria had been crushed at Wagram in July 1809 any hope of forming another coalition disappeared. Perceval was also plagued by opposition at home, where his Government was narrowly based and low on ability. Canning and Castlereagh had disqualified themselves from holding office, while Grey and Grenville refused to consider joining him. Perceval gallantly struggled on and kept the Spanish campaign alive amidst a storm of abuse from the Opposition. He deserved Grattan's tribute: 'He is not a great man, sir;

and he is not a little man, sir, I will tell you what he is, he is a man who will go out in all weather.'[26] His position and his courage were similar to those of Pitt at bleak moments of the war, but he lacked Pitt's personal ascendancy over the Commons and all the orators in the House were against him. He was so short of talent that he had to take the portfolio of Chancellor of the Exchequer himself.

It is extraordinary what pains Perceval took to cultivate Wilberforce. They had already developed the greatest respect for each other when Perceval was leading the Commons during Portland's administration. One action showed him to be closer to Wilberforce's religious views than any other political leader of his time. In the winter of 1807–8 Wilberforce planned to go to Bath to restore his health, and he wrote to Perceval to find out when Parliament would meet again. Perceval sent him back a friendly letter saying that he had until Monday, January 16 to recuperate. Wilberforce at once wrote back pointing out that if Parliament met on a Monday many members would have to travel on Sunday. Perceval took the point, apologised in the most delightful manner, and put off the meeting until the next Thursday. At the time of the Duke of York scandal he and Wilberforce even seem to have been planning to introduce legislation against adultery.[27]

His generosity has already been seen in the contribution he made towards the payment of Pitt's debts. When Wilberforce found his seat for Yorkshire contested, Perceval displayed the same generosity together with great sensitivity; he wrote to a member of Wilberforce's Committee:

'The above is intended for Wilberforce's election subscription. I have hesitated about sending it before, on account of the peculiar situation in which I stand at the present moment. But I think it rather hard that, because I am Chancellor of the Exchequer, I should be deprived of the means which every body else has of showing either that he is a friend of W., or a friend to the Abolition of the slave trade. At the same time I can feel that W. himself may not like that my name should appear among the list of his subscribers, and I must therefore beg before you put it down, that you will consult W. on that point. The only difference will be, that you will apply it anonymously, if he disapproves of the appearance of my name (which I think he may do very rationally, and therefore certainly without any offence to me).'[28]

In his years in office he showed how close his views were to those of Wilberforce. 'I am fully impressed with the necessity of setting the face of government against the offensive and abominable project of interdicting the circulation of religious knowledge in India,'[29] he wrote in December 1807. In July 1808: 'The slave question, as far as Spain is concerned, is very interesting and if an opportunity occurs, you may depend upon my doing anything in my power that I think likely to be practicable and availing to forward the views you have upon it.'[30] When there were allegations of corrupt practices in Irish elections in 1809 he was anxious to secure Wilberforce's good opinion. He was never offended when Wilberforce voted against him. 'Good-natured in Perceval to ask me,' Wilberforce wrote after dining with him, 'considering my differing so much from him. A sweet-tempered man.' And again, 'Perceval is really a most generous creature, with many most excellent qualities'.

Perceval's administration was strengthened by the success of the war in the Peninsula, but at the end of 1810 its existence was threatened from another quarter. The King, deeply upset by the death of his favourite daughter, relapsed into madness. Another Regency Bill was introduced into Parliament, the Prince of Wales being made Regent but without the power to create peers and with his other powers curtailed for a year in case of the King's recovery. During these debates Wilberforce tacked an uneasy course between the two party lines, defending Pitt's memory from Romilly's attacks, making a tribute to Perceval, but voting with the Whigs on several amendments.

It would be hard to find two men more different and less sympathetic than the Prince Regent and his Prime Minister. The gross self-indulgence and irresponsibility of the one was in startling contrast to the puritan rectitude of the other. The country expected the Prince to change his ministers and bring back the Whigs under Grey and Grenville. But the Prince's views on the great political questions of the day were now much closer to Perceval's than to those of his old friends. He was in favour of waging the war with vigour and opposed to untimely experiments with emancipation and reform. It was also thought likely that the King would soon recover, in which case there was little point in changing governments. The Whigs did nothing to improve their chances by quarrelling over the division of the spoils of office. When the Prince's probationary year came to an end in February 1812, he decided to retain Perceval, much though he disliked him, his policy having proved too successful for him to be dismissed. The Whigs, who had counted on coming into power, refused the offer of sharing it.

Throughout this time the management of the war did not prevent Perceval from taking a deep interest in Wilberforce's causes. Even in Pitt's early days Wilberforce had never found so sympathetic a Prime Minister. Perceval was co-operative over the registration of slaves in Trinidad, helpful over the treatment of Dissenters and the dangers of war with America and 'very pleasing' when Wilberforce called to discuss 'the business of Africa and the East, also the East Indies'. He was the only Prime Minister of Wilberforce's time who might have sponsored missionary activity in India.

On May 11, 1812 Wilberforce stopped off at Babington's house in Downing Street for dinner. A group of friends including the Thorntons were also there, but Babington himself was delayed on Parliamentary business. Wilberforce was holding forth on Perceval's virtues when Babington came in 'greatly agitated, stating that Perceval had been shot in the lobby'. Perceval had been crossing the lobby of the House when a man called Bellingham approached him and shot him with a pistol; the bullet reached his heart and he died at once. Bellingham was a commercial agent whose business had been ruined by Orders in Council. He had sought compensation from the Government and, failing to find it, had been driven to this lunatic action of revenge. 'I went,' Wilberforce wrote, 'after calling at Perceval's and Arbuthnot's, who quite over-whelmed, to the House, to the Prison rooms, where the poor wretch Bellingham was. They were examining him. I carefully perused his face for some time, close to him—a striking face: at times he shed tears, or had shed them; but strikingly composed and mild, though haggard. Called William Smith, who close to Perceval when he dropped, and who thought it was myself till he looked in the face. Smith, with another, carried him into the Secretary's room. Poor Lord Arden quite wild with grief—"No, I know he is not here, he is gone to a better world." '31

Religion proved a powerful solace for the Saints and for Perceval's family. A week after the assassination Wilberforce wrote in his journal: 'Oh wonderful power of Christianity! Never can it have been seen, since our Saviour prayed for His murderers, in a more lovely form than on the occasion of poor dear Perceval's death. Stephen, who had at first been so much overcome by the stroke, had been this morning and found, praying for the wretched murderer, and thinking that his being known to be a friend of Perceval's might affect him, he went and devoted himself to trying to bring him to repentance. He found honest Butterworth trying to get admittance, and obtained it for him and Mr. Daniel Wilson, whom at my recommendation he had brought with him. The poor creature was much affected, and very humble and thankful, but spoke of himself as unfortunate rather than guilty, and said it was a necessary thing—strange perversion—no malice against Perceval. Poor Mrs. Perceval after the first grew very moderate and resigned, and with all her children knelt down by the body, and prayed for them and for the murderer's forgiveness. Oh wonderful power of Christianity! Is this the same person who could not bear to have him opposed by any one?'32

The House granted Perceval's family £50,000 and gave his widow an annuity of £2,000. Wilberforce was eager for the House to pass these motions unanimously, which it did, and he was therefore annoyed when a larger grant was then proposed. He voted in favour of the increase, but in his eyes the extra money was not worth the loss of the tribute of an undivided vote. 'Lady C for getting all the money that they could,' he wrote in his diary, 'how very low and mercenary people are!'33

CHAPTER XXIII

THE MEMBER FOR BRAMBER

SOON after Perceval's assassination Lord Sidmouth told Wilberforce that a dissolution of Parliament was imminent. He had now to make a decision which had been looming up for some time. Ever since his children had grown out of infancy it had been clear that he could not fulfil his duties both to them and to his Yorkshire constituents. He took his responsibilities as the County's representative most seriously. He wrote to Roberts, who had complained of his frittering his time, 'bearing in mind that I am member for Yorkshire I own I think it right that I should be present at the agitation of all public questions of moment, and for the same reason, that I should not shrink from the attendance on committees. The number of these to which I belonged in the last session was very great'.[1] 'I make all other business bend and give way to that of Parliament. I refuse all invitations for days on which the House sits. I commonly attend all the debate, instead of going away after the private business is over for two or three hours, and coming down again after a comfortable dinner; on the contrary I snatch a hasty meal, as I may, before the public business begins, in the short interval sometimes between the end of the private and the beginning of the public. I see little or nothing of my family during the session of parliament (though, blessed be God, of a more tender, excellent wife no man ever received "The gift from the Lord", you know the quotation), and I have staid till the very end of the session I believe, every year of the last twenty-three or twenty-four.'[2]

It made a deep impression on him when one of his sons began to cry as he picked him up and the nurse said, 'He always is afraid of strangers.' He could not bear to remain a stranger to them and if the choice ever had to be made between them and Yorkshire he knew that he must sacrifice his seat. It was in any case no longer crucial to him. During the Abolitionist campaign his position as representative of the greatest county in England had lent him authority, but his prestige was now enough for him to speak with equal weight from any pocket borough.

When confronted by a difficult decision it was Wilberforce's habit to put the various arguments down on paper. He did this on the question of Yorkshire on August 24, 1811.

'I wished to devote today specially to the important purpose of seeking God's direction on the question, whether or not I should resign Yorkshire; and if so, whether to come in for a small borough. I have not time now to record the arguments in full particularity. Babington and Stephen are clearly for my giving up the county, on the ground that neither my body nor my mind are equal to the pressure which it must bring upon me. The reasons for retiring from Yorkshire are chiefly,

'1. The state of my family—my eldest son just turned thirteen, and three other boys, and two girls. Now though I should commit the learning of my boys to others, yet the moral part of education should be greatly carried on by myself. They claim a father's heart, eye, and voice, and friendly intercourse. Now so long as I am M.P. for Yorkshire, it will, I fear, be impossible for me to give my heart and time to the work as I ought, unless I become a negligent M.P. such as does not become our great county. I even doubt whether I ought not to quit public life altogether, on the ground that if I remain in the House even for Bramber, which Lord Calthorpe kindly offers, I should still be so much of a political man, that the work of education will not be set to heartily. This consideration of education is, in great measure, the turning point with me; but,

'2. The state of my body and mind, especially the latter, intimate to me the solve senescentem,—particularly my memory, of the failure of which I find decisive proofs continually. . . .

'But there are some other considerations. I do not believe there would be any serious contest, and am not prompted to retire by the fear of being turned out, so that I may leave out altogether this class of considerations.'[3]

A few days later he visited the Speaker, who advised him strongly not to leave the House altogether. His friends' advice was conflicting: 'Babington strong for absolute retiring—Stephen and others for giving up Yorkshire —but Grant and Henry Thornton against my quitting the county.'[4] Stephen had put his views in a letter of startling honesty. Wilberforce's mind, he thought, was not decaying apart from his memory, while his speaking was as good as ever apart from the pitch of his voice. But 'of late I have at times seen or conceived I saw symptoms of deterioration in your bodily appearance, as if you were getting older faster than I could wish. Your spirits, too, I have thought not uniformly so high and so long on the wing as they used to be.'[5] He pressed Wilberforce to attend Parliament less often and to give up Yorkshire. The arguments for a change were overwhelming, but he shrank from the decision. 'When I consider what it is to relinquish voluntarily such a situation as that of member of Yorkshire in times like these,' he wrote to Babington, 'and I must add, without there appearing any person coming forward to occupy my place so far as espousing the cause of religion goes, I own I shudder at the thought. When I number up the considerations for retiring, I own they are very powerful.

But then it is like closing my account, and I seem to have done so little, and there seem some things which it would be so desirable to try to do before I quit parliament, that I shrink from retiring as from extinction.'[6] But by September 6 he had 'pretty well resolved against Yorkshire'.

When Sidmouth told him of the dissolution he had to make the decision. 'I shrink from absolutely deciding to resign my situation as from annihilation,' he wrote in his diary, 'yet my judgement commends it more and more; and it is not annihilation if I stay in the House, though not for Yorkshire.'[7] He announced his decision to Charles Duncombe, the Chairman of his Committee, two days later, making it clear that he was not influenced by the fear of opposition. The clothiers now supported him again and after winning in 1807 with everything against him he had nothing to fear in any future election. 'Several friends however,' he continued, 'on whose judgements I place great reliance, are so earnest with me not to quit parliament altogether, that I have agreed to accept the very kind offer of a dear friend, and through marriage a near relation,* which will probably place me in a seat in which my occasional attendance in the House of Commons will not be inconsistent with other claims.'[8]

His motives were widely misinterpreted. He was thought to be avoiding a contest and was offered seats at Westminster, Lewes and Dover. 'Would you believe it,' he asked, 'R really and gravely asked me to stand for Warwickshire, on the Birmingham interest, and be the business member. I am not yet quite insane.'[9] Others, realising that 'he could have walked over the course without the least show of opposition', could not understand his decision. It was thought that he might be angling for a vote of thanks as well as an invitation to remain as member for the County. When it became clear that he was in earnest a meeting of the County on nomination day did pass a unanimous vote of thanks for his services, which was followed by another from the freeholders of Hull. He watched the election with nostalgia. 'I feel somewhat like an old retired hunter,' he wrote, 'who grazing in a park, and hearing the cry of the hounds pricks up his ears and can scarce keep quiet or refrain from breaking out to join them.'

*

Wilberforce had been concerned for some time by the threat of war between England and America. In June 1811 he had written to Barbara about the King's madness and added, 'But the pain produced by this relapse is lost in the extreme concern I feel for the apparent probability of a war with America; may God avert it.' In the last debate of that session he made his anxiety clear. 'Deeply, sir, do I deplore the gloom which I see spreading over the western horizon; and I most earnestly trust that we are not to be involved in the misfortune of a new war, aggravated by

* Lord Calthorpe, Barbara's cousin.

possessing almost the character of civil strife—a war between two nations, who are children of the same family, and brothers in the same inheritance of human liberty.'[10]

Until the middle of the French wars the relationship between Britain and America had been cordial. The Americans were at first sympathetic towards the French Revolution and remembered how France had helped them achieve their own independence, but they soon recoiled from the excesses of the Terror. Pitt continued Shelburne's policy of conciliation and trade. In 1795 the Jay Treaty settled many of the differences outstanding between the two countries. American ships were allowed to trade in the Indian Ocean and, under certain circumstances, in the West Indies.

The questions of the frontier between America and Canada and the debts left over from the War of Independence were referred to arbitration. Shortage of British shipping in the early years of the French wars enabled American carriers to take over a large part of the trade in tropical produce. By 1798 the two countries were in an undeclared alliance; American and British men-of-war would join to protect convoys against French privateers. This state of co-operation continued until 1805, but there remained unsettled issues which, in less favourable circumstances, could become explosive.

The British navy kept up its numbers by the use of the press gang. Americans in port were often forcibly pressed and on the high seas American ships would be stopped and searched for British deserters. This issue was made more difficult by the fact that the two countries would frequently regard the same man as being their own citizen. The other difference concerned the rights of a belligerent in searching neutral ships for contraband. There was no agreement on these rights; it was a recognised rule of war that no neutral power could carry on a trade which had been closed to it in time of peace, but whether a re-export or 'broken voyage' constituted such a trade was undecided. It was equally clear that a belligerent could stop 'contraband' from entering an enemy port, but there was no satisfactory definition of contraband.

These issues remained dormant until 1805, in spite of the election of the Republican Jefferson in 1800; and during the Peace of Amiens the outstanding debts were settled. But the sale of Louisiana by the French made Jefferson deeply grateful to them and complicated the settlement of land frontiers with Canada. In 1805 the English began to interpret broken voyages more strictly, while the renewal of war with France reopened the question of pressing Americans.

It was against this 'gloom spreading over the western horizon' that the economic warfare between Britain and France was intensified. By the time that Napoleon had issued his Berlin Decree in November 1806, Perceval his Orders in Council in March 1807 and Napoleon his Milan

Decrees in November 1807, the position of neutrals had been made impossible. According to the British all vessels coming from enemy ports must go to Britain, pay customs there and buy licences to trade, but the French would confiscate any ship which had entered a British port. The United States responded by placing an embargo on trade with both belligerents. Economic warfare was waged throughout 1808 with unprecedented rigour, both England and France suffering as a result. In 1809 the continental embargoes were relaxed and smugglers and black market operators thrived once more. In 1810 Napoleon tightened his controls, causing an economic crisis in Britain and driving his bankrupt allies into rebellion. In November 1811 both sides relaxed their controls again and should relax trade revived in 1812.

The Americans had demanded in February 1811 that Britain should relax her Orders in Council. After lengthy prevarication and after the French controls had been eased, Britain followed suit in July 1812. But in June America, unaware that the *casus belli* was being removed, declared war. France's trade restrictions led her first into a debilitating war with Spain and finally into a disastrous invasion of Russia, England's brought upon her a pointless and tragic war with America.

But disputes over trade were not the only reasons for the war. The Americans suspected the British, unjustly, of having helped the Indians against them. The Louisiana purchase made the Americans covet Florida, which belonged to Spain, Britain's ally. Canada was an even greater prize. There was an expansionist mood in American politics that wished to sweep European powers out of the continent. On June 18 when Congress voted that war existed between the two countries it is significant that the New England states, which stood to lose most by trade restrictions, opposed the motion. The trade grievances were formidable in theory, but in practice these states were thriving by avoiding the rules laid down by both sides and they benefited from the temporary shortage of British shipping. When war was declared its pretext may have been restrictions on trade but its purpose was conquest.

Wilberforce was horrified; almost his first political action had been to oppose the war against the American colonists. He recognised and appreciated the contributions made by Americans from the early Quakers onwards to the Abolition of the Slave Trade. He wanted the two countries to join in enforcing Abolition and had written suggesting this idea to Jefferson in 1807 and to Jay in 1810. He had said in his letter to Jay, 'Really, the idea of a war between our two countries is perfectly horrible,'[11] and nothing had happened to change his mind. He liked their simplicity and good sense, though he admitted, 'I fear there is little spirit of religion in America.' Jay and Pinckney, both ambassadors from America to Britain, were among his friends.

Wilberforce's feelings towards the American War were even stronger than those he had held when he first broke with Pitt. In both cases he considered his country to have been in the right, but not to have taken every possible step to avoid the conflict. In February 1812 he was five months ahead of the Government when he wished to abandon the Orders in Council to appease America. 'I never was a warm friend to those measures,' he wrote to Roberts, 'or rather no friend at all, but an enemy to parts of them. I am sick at heart from the sad prospect of a war with America.'[12]

But after it had started he wrote to Hannah More, 'Alas! alas! this sad war with America! I never felt any public incident so deeply. Yet on the whole I thank God I can lay my head on my pillow in peace, for our government is not chargeable with the blood-guiltiness; but Madison, Jefferson, etc.'[13]

*

Another issue which came to a head at this time was the question of Roman Catholic Emancipation. Wilberforce had reluctantly supported Pitt's attempt to combine Emancipation with the Irish Union. He traced the troubles of Ireland to her religion, and accordingly opposed the increased grant in 1808 to the Roman Catholic Seminary at Maynooth. In his eyes to train more priests was to multiply Ireland's troubles. 'It is irreligion and immorality of which Ireland is sick,' he wrote in his diary. 'These popery has increased and fomented.' His great fear was that Emancipation would lead to the Disestablishment of the Church of England in Ireland. His own dislike of Catholicism was extreme. When Napoleon returned to power in 1815, Wilberforce, who as a lover of peace might have been appalled, wrote, 'It is a compensation to me that the Roman Catholic religion is stunted and injured by the change.'[14] But if his prejudices were against Emancipation, his common sense and desire for justice favoured it. In 1808 fears of the hierarchy stopped him speaking out firmly in favour of it. 'I strongly incline to their coming into parliament,' he wrote of the Catholics, 'though not to their seeing with other men's (priests') eyes.'[15]

In 1813 when the question of Emancipation was raised once more, it found him still undecided. Most of his friends were opposed to any concessions, Milner, William Hey and Dr. Burgh being particularly strong in their views. Alexander Knox wrote him a forty-page letter on the subject, to which he saw fit to add a four-page note apologising for its length.[16] Wilberforce considered them all 'sadly prejudiced'. Once the principle had already been conceded by giving Catholics the vote, whether they should also be allowed to sit in Parliament became a matter of expediency, and on balance expediency demanded that they should be admitted. He pursued this argument in a letter to William Hey:

'Whatever the Roman Catholics, if admitted into the House of Commons, could effect through the medium of law for establishing their hierarchy and injuring that of the Protestants in Ireland, they can do just as well (in one important respect better) through the medium of members of parliament, *called* Protestants, but who being elected by Roman Catholic voters, and having little or no real religion themselves, are implicitly subservient to their constituents' purposes. I say, they can serve the Roman Catholics even better in one respect, inasmuch as they do not call into action the opposite Protestant spirit in the same degree.

. . . And where can be the wisdom of retaining the prison dress, when you have set the men at liberty ?'[17]

He pursued the point further in conversation with Samuel in 1823. The representatives of the Catholics obeyed their wishes as much as if they were themselves Catholics. At the same time the Catholic electorate felt persecuted because they could not choose representatives of their own faith. They were thrown under the influence of the priests, 'which is often the grand fundamental evil of the Roman Catholic system. Hence it arises that the Roman Catholic religion is spreading so rapidly. On these grounds and not from regard of the Roman Catholics I vote for their nominal emancipation for nothing can in my opinion be more false than to call their admission into Parliament such. I think that it will in reality be the surest way to ruin their power and prevent their increase'.[18]

He spoke in favour of Emancipation on the same grounds,[19] although he knew that his speech would pain many of his closest friends. On his next visit to the Mores he saw the sisters preparing for an assault on him and boldly took the offensive. 'When the subject was first broached,' he remembered, 'I looked very grave, and immediately assailed them with the declaration: "How shocking it is that you who know so much of the misery which Popery has brought on Ireland, should advocate a system which perpetuates its galling yoke!" Patty, who was especially warm upon the subject, and was ready to attack me, was confounded by this sudden thrust; we had no dispute, and my visit passed off as happily as ever.'

His friends' reactions had been premature. The country was not yet prepared for Emancipation, and the Prince Regent was almost as opposed to it as the King. The Catholics had to wait until 1829 to be admitted to Parliament.

His letters and memoranda in 1813 on the Roman Catholic faith show that although he was prepared to tolerate it—'persecution for religious opinions is not only the wickedest, but one of the foolishest things in the world'[20]—he loathed it and saw its influence as entirely evil. But soon after his decision to speak for their Emancipation, his attitude towards the Catholics became less severe.

Perhaps the sympathetic reception given to his Abolitionist pleas by the Pope and Cardinal Consalvi helped to soften his attitude. In any case he wrote a letter to Hannah More in 1818, the tone of which is entirely different from anything he had written about Catholics since his conversion. Zachary Macaulay's brother had just returned from Rome. Wilberforce recounted one of his stories.

'He tells me that an Irish gentleman belonging to the Propaganda had lately a discussion with an Italian Catholic as to the salvability of heretics. The Irishman, having many Protestant relations, was unwilling to consign them over to wholesale destruction. He accordingly determined to refer the matter to His Holiness. "My son," says the old man, "whoever is seeking the truth with all his heart is a member of the Catholic Church whatever be his name." I wish our English popes were half as liberal.'[21]

As Wilberforce grew older his political ideas became more rigid but his tolerance for the Catholics increased. In 1831 he found himself in Bath with only one other lodger in the same building and Wilberforce felt sorry for this man, who was laid up on a sofa with rheumatic fever, visited him and sent him game, which his servant was too lazy or inefficient to buy.

'I soon afterwards was told he was a Roman Catholic. He is by profession a lawyer from Pontypool. I have since had several conversations with him, and find him a decided Roman Catholic, but a man apparently of great candour and moderation. I was a good deal surprised to receive from him an assurance that he had been reading with great pleasure in a book of my writing; and I found to my surprise, that quite unknown to me, Kendal had lent him the book. I durst not have done it, but the event has taught me that we may sometimes be too timid or delicate. Can you suggest any mode of dealing with my fellow lodger? Hitherto I have gone on to the plan of cultivating his favourable opinion by general kindness, sending him game, etc., and endeavouring to press on him the most important doctrines of true Christianity and of showing where the case is really so that *he may embrace those doctrines and still continue a good Roman Catholic.*'[22]*

The admission that the doctrines of true Christianity were not inconsistent with Roman Catholicism constitutes a reversal of the opinions that Wilberforce had held for most of his life, and it was one that he kept until his death. A year before he died he engaged a Roman Catholic tutor for his grandson William. When Samuel protested, Wilberforce replied, 'Dear little William's mother will always be on the spot, always on her guard,'[23] but if Wilberforce had taken the threat of Catholic propaganda seriously, he would not have relied on a fallible agency for the protection of his grandson's soul. There can, after all, have been no great difficulty in finding a suitable Protestant tutor.

* Author's italics.

Roman Catholic Emancipation could be renewed at any favourable time, and it was a question on which Wilberforce felt it necessary to pronounce, rather than a cause he cherished and actively promoted. The question of admitting missionaries to India was much closer to his heart. It may be remembered that in 1793 Wilberforce had scarcely finished tracing the workings of Providence in permitting his first promotion of missionaries to pass through the Commons, when all his work was undone by a 'little tumult in the Court of Proprietors'. The Charter of the East India Company was reviewed every twenty years, so that 1813 would be the last opportunity in Wilberforce's political life for him to expunge 'what I have long thought next to the Slave Trade, the foulest blot on the moral character of our country—the suffering our fellow-subjects (nay, they even stand towards us in the closer relation of our tenants) in the East Indies to remain without any effort on our part to enlighten and reform them, under the grossest, the darkest, and most depraving system of idolatrous superstition that almost ever existed upon earth'.[24]

He regarded the exclusion of missionaries from India as 'now the Slave Trade is abolished . . . by far the greatest of our national sins'; at times he gave the saving of these millions of doomed souls precedence even over Abolition, and he was not prepared to leave their future state to the unaided efforts of Providence. A stiff opposition could be expected from the Company and an unsympathetic reception from many members of the House. The mutiny of the sepoys at Vellore seven years before had been attributed to their fear of forcible conversion to Christianity. At the time Wilberforce vehemently denied that 'the late melancholy tragedy at Vellore' had any connection with the missionaries, but he realised that it must have hardened the Company's prejudices against them. There was a wide range of forces which he must bring into play against the entrenched interests of the Company and the indifference of most members, but they had to be mustered in the right order. The Established Church must be committed before the Dissenters came out in support of his plan.

His letter to Butterworth continues: 'I am but too well aware, that if the unbiassed judgment of the House of Commons were to decide the question, fatal indeed would be the issue. I am not without hopes of Mr. Perceval's lending himself to any moderate plan; but it will be necessary, I am persuaded, to call into action the whole force of the religious world. But on this subject, knowing with whom I have to do, I shall express myself without reserve, trusting to your candour for a fair construction of my sentiments. I am not without hopes of prevailing on a considerable party in the Church of England to interest themselves on the occasion: but I own I fear that if the Dissenters and Methodists come into action before our force from the Establishment has stirred, a great part of the latter will either desert our ranks, or be cold and reluctant followers. Now, if I mistake not, the organisation of the Dissenters, and still more of the Methodist body, is so complete, that any impulse may be speedily conveyed throughout the whole frame. It appears therefore, that it would be expedient for the Dissenters and Methodist bodies not to show themselves till the members of the Church have actually committed themselves (according to our parliamentary phrase), or till it be seen that they cannot be prevailed on to come forward.'[25]

He started his campaign early in 1812. He found Perceval in favour of missions but conscious of the great obstacles to establishing them. Before committing himself, the Prime Minister wished to see precisely what Wilberforce proposed. Wilberforce himself was still in some doubt about this. He had found the response from religious people disappointing, 'partly produced I think by the sectaries having had a notion that the Church of England to be established. Alas! alas! let us have some substance before we differ about form'.[26] He continued his lobbying throughout the session; he was even prepared to play politics to achieve his object. 'I have long conceived,' he wrote in his diary, 'that probably those who are interested for religion will be compelled to join the great body of commercial and political-economy men, who will I doubt not, contend for destroying the monopoly of the Company, and leaving the road to the East Indies free and open.'[27] He was prepared 'even to abolish the East India Company altogether, rather than not insure a passage for the entrance of light, and truth and moral improvement and happiness into that benighted and degraded region'.[28]

If the coldness of the religious was damaging to this cause, the assassination of Perceval came as a body blow. There was no member of the administration that succeeded him who could be expected to approach the problem with the same religious commitment. And some leverage had to be brought to bear on the House. On March 22, 1813 the debate on the East India Company's Charter opened and its indifference to the admission of missionaries became evident. 'The truth is,' Wilberforce wrote to William Hey, 'and a dreadful truth it is, that the opinions of nine-tenths, or at least of a vast majority of the House of Commons would be against any motion which the friends of religion might make.'

Eloquence alone could not hope to sway this majority; Wilberforce realised that the moment had come for an unprecedented demonstration of public support and he flung himself into the campaign to organise petitions with the same energy that he had shown over twenty years before in the first struggle for Abolition. He wrote to every one of his correspondents who had raised a petition against the Slave Trade, urging them to do the same in favour of the missionaries. 'You petitioned in the case of the Slave Trade,' he told one correspondent, 'and those petitions were eminently useful; so they would be now; and what is more, after having been talked of, their not coming would be highly injurious; so lose no time. The petitions should be from each place separately.'[29] He bullied and persuaded the reluctant. 'And can you venture thus to add your sanction to the opinion . . .' he asked, 'that our East India empire is safer under the protection of Brahma with all his obscenities and blood, than under that of God Almighty?'[30]

Raising petitions was now occupying him fully, but he considered it 'the greatest object which men ever pursued'. At first the response was sluggish, but his conviction and persistence seemed to breathe life into the movement. The whole Evangelical organisation came into motion behind him; the local associations of Abolitionists were mainly predisposed in favour of the missionaries; the Church Missionary Society, founded in 1799, by now had a formidable organisation of its own; a great public meeting held in London under its auspices aroused such enthusiasm that it was followed by others in the country; the *Christian Observer*, not content with lending its own weight to the campaign, gave birth to a more specialised offspring, the *Missionary Register*.

Wilberforce was expertly briefed during this campaign. Dr. Buchanan, one of Grant's proselytising chaplains, had returned to England in 1808. He was evidently a powerful speaker as well as a mine of information, for shortly after his return he delivered a sermon on 'The Star in the East' which 'kept the minds of a large auditory in a state of most lively sensation for an hour and twenty-five minutes'.[31] It was Buchanan who had drawn up the plan for the Church in India and provided the background for the circulars which the Clapham Sect distributed throughout the country.

On March 30, the House examined two men who had governed India in the past, Warren Hastings, now an old man, broken by his trial, and Lord Teignmouth. The House, according to Wilberforce's diary, was 'exceedingly civil to Mr. Hastings (not a premature gesture on its part); sufficiently so to Lord Teignmouth'. Warren Hastings was reluctant to voice any strong opinion, but he must have left many members uneasy after this exchange.

'What would be the political effects of the measure proposed respecting a church establishment for India?'

Hastings. . . . 'A surmise has gone forth of the intention of this government to force our religion on the consciences of the people in India . . . it has unhappily impressed itself with peculiar force on the minds of our native infantry—the men on whom we must depend in the last resort for our protection against any disturbances. . . . Much would depend on the conduct and demeanour of the person elevated to that sacred office. I dare not say all that is on my mind upon this subject, but it is one of great hazard.'[32]

Teignmouth was anxious to give every encouragement to missionaries, but the questions put to him were so skilfully slanted that he was never able to express his views. He had even to admit that the dangers attached to 'indiscreet zeal' were great. He was able to deliver some salvoes against the iniquities of the Hindu religion and express a low opinion of the moral character of its followers, but nothing he said would move the House as much as the fears of mutiny aroused by Hastings's evidence. Wilberforce wrote despondently to William Hey after the hearing: 'While we are going so far in favouring the Roman Catholics, shall Christianity be the only religion which is not to be tolerated in India?'[33]

The Lords were to examine witnesses on April 5, and it was crucial to the success of the cause that the bad impression made by the hearings in the Commons should not be repeated. The urgency was such that Wilberforce, Stephen, Grant, Henry Thornton and Babington met on Sunday afternoon to discuss the position. Afterwards Wilberforce stayed on to dinner at Thornton's house in Palace Yard, the only time he had done so on a Sunday since they had shared the house together.

As a result of this meeting Wilberforce called on Lord Grenville and wrote to Lord Wellesley. 'You know enough of life,' he told Hannah More, 'to be aware that in parliamentary measures of importance, more is to be done out of the House than in it.' His negotiations were successful and he was able to record in his diary: 'The House agreed that religion should be left out of the examination.' By these manoeuvres Wilberforce ensured that Parliament would not be influenced by the first-hand evidence, which inevitably would be dominated by the Anglo-Indians, while it would still receive the mass of petitions organised by his own side.

Easter week now interrupted the proceedings of the House. Wilberforce had intended to visit Lord Gambier during the recess, but abandoned his holiday to promote the Indian missions. He used these last days to lobby Baptists and bishops, noblemen and commoners. Most vital of all he continuously sought the support of the Government. At first their reaction was cool, but as the petitions and deputations accumulated they became more amenable. Finally, on May 27, Wilberforce recorded with triumph: 'Lord Castlereagh agreed to Lord Buckinghamshire's and our arrangement for East India Christianizing Resolutions—far surpassing my expectations.'[34] There remained, in Wilberforce's eyes, only Parliament between India and salvation.

On June 22 the debate was opened by Lord Castlereagh, with a restrained and short speech in favour of admitting missionaries. He was followed by Sir Henry Montgomery, an Anglo-Indian who forecast that if missionaries were allowed to circulate in India, there would be widespread riots and mutinies. Sir Henry added that he thought the moral character of Hindus greatly superior to that of Englishmen. He was more anxious 'to save the lives of the 30,000 of his fellow countrymen in India, than to save the souls of all the Hindoos by making them Christians at so dreadful a price'.[35] A short maiden speech from Lord Frederick Douglas followed and then Wilberforce rose. His speech almost monopolises Hansard's account of the debate and it is, for once, accurately reported, since it was reprinted verbatim from the version issued by Hatchard.

He started very calmly, denying that missionaries should be linked in any way with authority, and claiming that one of the tasks of the English in India was to enlighten the minds of its natives. He produced the examples of the Mahommedans, Sikhs and Buddhists to disprove assertions that Hindus could never be converted. He cited the existence of hundreds of thousands of Christians in the East Indies and contrasted this with the Anglo-Indians' statement that they knew of only one Indian convert. He then turned to the moral character of the Hindus which the Anglo-Indians had declared to be so exalted; and he quoted uncomplimentary opinions of it from foreign observers and officials and historians, ending with especially caustic views from judges. Having described the disease he produced the cure.

'That remedy, Sir, is Christianity, which I justly call the appropriate remedy; for Christianity then assumes her true character, no less than she performs her natural and proper office, when she takes under her protection those poor degraded beings, on whom philosophy looks down with disdain, or perhaps with contemptuous condescension. On the very first promulgation of Christianity, it was declared by its great Author, as "glad tidings to the poor"; and, ever faithful to her character, Christianity still delights to instruct the ignorant, to succour the needy, to comfort the sorrowful, to visit the forsaken. God forbid that we should have only to sit down in hopeless dejection, under the conviction, that though these evils exist they are not to be removed. Sir, such a supposition would be absolute blasphemy; to believe that the Almighty Being, to whom both we and our East Indian fellow-subjects owe our existence, has doomed them to continue for ever, incurably, in that wretched state of moral depravity and degradation, in which they have hitherto remained!

'The most able of our opponents has told us, that some classes of the natives are as much below others as the inferior animals are below the human species. Yes, Sir, I well know it; and it is because I wish to do away this unjust inequality, to raise these poor brutes out of their present degraded state to the just level of their nature, that I am now bringing before you their real character, and explaining to you their true condition.'

It was his supreme hope to see the Indians brought to the path of eternal happiness, but regard for their temporal well-being would itself justify the introduction of Christianity.

'The evils of Hindostan are family, fireside evils: they pervade the whole mass of the population, and embitter the domestic cup, in almost every family. Why need I, in this country, insist on the evils which arise merely out of the institution of Caste itself; a detestable expedient for keeping the lower orders of the community bowed down in an abject state of hopeless and irremediable vassalage? It is justly, Sir, the glory of this country, that no member of our free community is naturally precluded from rising into the highest classes in society. . . . Even where slavery has existed, it has commonly been possible (though in the West Indies, alas! artificial difficulties have been interposed), for individuals to burst their bonds, and assert the privileges of their nature. But the more cruel shackles of Caste are never to be shaken; as well might a dog, or any other of the brute creation, it is the honourable gentleman's own illustration, aspire to the dignity and rights of man. Christianity, independently of its effects on a future state of existence, has been acknowledged even by avowed sceptics, to be, beyond all other institutions that ever existed, favourable to the temporal interests and happiness of man: and never was there a country where there is greater need than in India for the diffusion of its genial influence.'

He proceeded with a more detailed examination of some effects of the Hindu religion. He dealt with the evils of polygamy and the prevalence of infanticide before embarking on a blood-curdling description of the practice of suttee (the burning of widows on their husbands' funeral pyres). He then turned to 'the various obscene and bloody rites of their idolatrous ceremonies, with all their unutterable abominations'.

'It has often been truly remarked, particularly I think by the historian of America, that the moral character of a people may commonly be known from the nature and attributes of the objects of its worship. On this principle, we might have anticipated the moral condition of the Hindoos, by ascertaining the character of their deities. If it was truly affirmed of the old pagan mythology, that scarcely a crime could be committed, the perpetrator of which might not plead in his justification, the precedent of one of the national gods; far more truly may it be said, that in the adventures of the countless rabble of Hindoo deities, you may find every possible variety of every practicable crime. Here also, more truly than of old, every vice has its patron as well as its example. Their divinities are absolute monsters of lust, injustice, wickedness and cruelty. In short, their religious system is one grand abomination. Not but that I know you may sometimes find, in the sacred books of the Hindoos, acknowledgements of the unity of the great Creator of all things; but just as, from a passage of the same sort in Cicero, it would be contrary alike to reason and experience to argue, that the common pagan mythology was not the religion of the bulk of mankind in the ancient world; so it is far more absurd and groundless, to contend that more or fewer of the 33,000,000 of Hindoo gods, with their several attributes and adventures, do not constitute the theology of the bulk of the natives of India. Both their civil and religious systems are radically and essentially the opposites of our own. Our religion is sublime, pure and beneficent. Theirs is mean, licentious, and cruel.'

Only imperative political necessity should deter us from the conversion of such people, and this necessity must be clearly proved. He considered that such proof had not been and never could be produced. 'For I should deem it almost morally impossible, that there could be any country in the state in which India is proved, but too clearly, now to be, which would not be likely to find Christianity the most powerful of all expedients for improving its morals, and promoting alike its temporal and eternal welfare.' He thought the opposite to be the case; so long as they proceeded with caution, to promote Christianity would be the surest way of strengthening England's government in India. He ended his speech with praise of the selfless dedication of Dr. Carey and the other missionaries who were already working in the East without provoking any disturbances. After various Anglo-Indians had repeated their objections to the motion, it was carried by 89 votes to 36.

This campaign and debate are of great interest; his speech on the Indian missions is acknowledged to be one of Wilberforce's best, and we are fortunate in having a complete record of it. Perhaps of all his speeches it is the one which we would have chosen to have preserved, for it contains not only some of his finest oratory, but also one of the most explicit statements of his religion. Normally when he introduced religion into his speeches, and particularly when he held forth on the retribution to be expected from any act of wickedness, it weakened his hold on the Commons. He was aware of this danger and was always on his guard against it. He had an exquisite sensitivity about how much religion the House would tolerate and would sometimes abandon a useful measure rather than make religion seem boring or ridiculous. He was once urged to promote a Bill to ensure that criminals should no longer be executed immediately after sentence, so that they should have every chance to be converted. While agreeing with the theory he thought that its discussion would lead to 'such profaneness and impiety that one person would ask, "how long do you think it necessary to give a man to become a Christian?" '[36] It is a rare gift for someone with the possession of revealed truth to realise that it cannot always be profitably inflicted on others, but Wilberforce saw the missions to India as of such critical importance as to justify the risk. He never put his religious beliefs to the House more fully or with such passionate sincerity, and they were never received with more respect. He later described his speech as having lasted 'two hours', 'near two hours' and 'above two hours', but an opponent said he spoke for three without tiring any of his audience.

In the later stages of the Bill he defended Dr. Carey, whose work in India he would compare favourably with the blind Milton embarking on *Paradise Lost*. Carey had been attacked on grounds of fanaticism. Wilberforce told the House his story, how as a poor cobbler working in his stall he had received the idea of converting the Indians to Christianity and of how his whole life had been shaped to this end. He had mastered classical and oriental languages and become the greatest European expert in Sanskrit. While running his mission and converting the Indians, he still found time to write grammars and dictionaries in several different languages. Lord Wellesley was so struck by his ability that he appointed Carey Professor of Sanskrit at the college in Calcutta. Carey made over the whole of his salary (between £1,000 and £1,500 a year) to his mission. 'By the way,' Wilberforce wrote afterwards, 'nothing ever gave me a more lively sense of the low and mercenary standard of your men of honour, than the manifest effect produced upon the House of Commons by my stating this last circumstance. It seemed to be the only thing which moved them.'[37]

The attacks on Carey had a sequel which must have given Wilberforce some satisfaction. 'A few days later the member who had made this charge came to me, and asked me in a manner which in a noted duellist could not be mistaken, "Pray, Mr. Wilberforce, do you know a Mr. Andrew Fuller, who has written to desire me to retract the statement which I made with reference to Dr. Carey?" "Yes", I answered with a smile, "I know him perfectly, but depend upon it you will make nothing of him in your way; he is a respectable Baptist minister at Kettering." In due time there came from India an authoritative contradiction of the slander. It was sent to me, and for two whole years did I take it in my pocket to the House of Commons to read it to the House whenever the author of the accusation should be present; but during that whole time he never once dared show himself in the House.'[38]

Other criticisms of the Indian missions lasted longer. Sydney Smith stormed away at the 'consecrated cobblers', while as late as 1831, the radical *Figaro in London* extended the attack to the whole Church in India. When four bishops had died soon after their arrival in Calcutta *Figaro* commented, 'We cannot but admire the justice of Providence in not giving to any one country more than its share of those evils to which humanity is deservedly subject. It has dealt out to each its curses and its blessings with an equal hand, and while we are free from the crocodiles, jackals and other ravenous animals by which India is infested, that country, as if to counterbalance the misery it is subject to from the disgusting brutes above mentioned, possesses in its climate an effectual preservative against *Bishops*.'[39]

The East India debate and its consequences are interesting in many ways. It showed, at its most spectacular, the Evangelical power to influence events by bringing public opinion to bear. For this campaign was peculiarly their own since its object could not have the same appeal to liberals and humanitarians as Abolition or Emancipation. It was a true test of their strength. The 837 petitions they raised with over half a million signatures were without precedent on this kind of issue. It was this indication of popular support which made the Government take the measure under its wing. Wilberforce acknowledged this in his diary: 'The petitions, of which a greater number than were ever known, have carried our question instrumentally, the good providence of God really.'[40] Almost as impressive as the volume of petitions was the fact that they had been raised from a nation whose initial response to them had been tepid. It was a new form of political manoeuvre, which was regarded by some as a horrifying innovation. The right to petition Parliament had long been a part of the Constitution, but its use on such a scale was first seen in the Abolitionist Campaign and brought to perfection over the India missions. This form of pressure was to be taken a step further in the final stages of the Emancipation Movement, when in the General Election of 1832 a list of all candidates was published with notes as to whether they were friendly, hostile or undecided on the question of slavery.

The violence of Wilberforce's denunciation of Hinduism was extreme. He acknowledged the beauty and the monotheistic philosophy of some sacred Hindu books only to contrast them with the religion actually practised by the great majority of Indians. Just as he thought that a less degraded Ireland would abandon popery, so he was supremely confident that, given the means of conversion, India, too, would see the light. Her present religion, after all, was 'one grand abomination'. Although he has been proved wrong it is hard to blame him, or to attribute his mistake solely to the strength of his own faith. The Hindu religion of Wilberforce's time, undiluted by Western influence, would have stuck in less sensitive gullets. It tolerated, encouraged or demanded a series of horrifying abuses. It did nothing to prevent infanticide, geronticide, polygamy or child marriages; the burning of widows, although not demanded in the oldest Hindu scriptures, had become a part of the religion and widows were burned alive by their families on their husbands' funeral pyres whether they wished to take this road to paradise or not. Wilberforce's speech contained an account of such a burning, in which the levity of the executioners formed a sickening contrast to the agonies of the victim. The practice of human sacrifice, although much less common than that of suttee, still prevailed in many parts of India. The caste system, an integral part of the religion, he rightly characterised as being worse than slavery. His sense of outrage might have overflowed had the activities of the thugs been known in 1813.

In the event many Indians were converted and there are some nine million Christians in that country today; but Wilberforce's visions of wholesale conversion have never been fulfilled. The effect of Christianity has been to soften Hinduism and to wear away some of the rough edges which excited Wilberforce's disgust; these abuses have been shed without weakening the religion in any way. He would have been bitterly disappointed by the result, but he would surely have thought the experiment justified by it.

If Wilberforce was wrong his critics were equally mistaken. The establishment of a Christian Church and missions in India did not provoke a bloody series of riots, nor were they wholly ineffective. One of the causes of the Indian Mutiny was a distrust of the changes that had been brought to the country, and a fear of forcible conversion to Christianity, however misconceived, must have played its part. How much the missions contributed to this fear it is impossible to say. As against this, one can set all the good works which Christianity has achieved and continues to achieve in India. It is one of its great strengths when contrasted with oriental religions that it encourages its followers to help others rather than to strive for an introspective perfection. This noble role has been filled by clergymen, missionaries and nuns from Dr. Carey to Mother Theresa.

Another aspect of the debate was that it gave official recognition to the theory that Britain had responsibilities as well as opportunities in India. A small beginning was made in providing funds for education. As a part of Wilberforce's plans for improving the Indians until they recognised the merits of Christianity they must be allowed to enjoy the blessings of English laws and institutions. The Government of India must rest on the affections of the governed. If any particular moment marked the change from looting to paternalism, from Trade to Empire, it was the renewal of the East India Company Charter in 1813. The religious opportunities opened up by this success caused Wilberforce to comment, 'We have laid the foundation stone of the grandest edifice that ever was raised in Asia.'[41]

CHAPTER XXIV

ENFORCING ABOLITION

ANY slaver who persisted in the Trade after 1807 could be punished only by fines and the confiscation of his ship; for some of them the risk was still justified by the reward. But in May 1811, Brougham steered a Bill through Parliament which made indulgence in the Trade a felony. The navy had already begun to enforce Abolition; a small squadron, all that could be spared from the blockade of the Continent, was sent to the Slave Coast in 1807 and ships in the West Indies were alerted. These measures, particularly the Slave Trade Felony Act, brought the British share of the Trade to an end. France and her allies were cut off from Africa for the duration of the war. America had abolished the Trade at the same time as Britain, and although her efforts to suppress it were less vigorous, her share of it was greatly reduced after 1807. From the time of the British Abolition until the end of the war the volume of the Atlantic Slave Trade dropped dramatically. Many native traders were ruined and the price of slaves on the coast fell in the absence of buyers.

Wilberforce had always advanced the rather unconvincing argument that the end of the Slave Trade would be followed by a Renaissance in Africa and the African Institution had been founded in 1807 to foster this development. In the event the Trade was not immediately replaced by any more wholesome form of commerce and the Slave Coast sank into a depression as a result. British exports fell to a third of their previous level. For this reason and because the Trade still survived, the African Institution became in practice an organisation for enforcing Abolition. Its membership was a measure of the new respectability of the cause. The leaders of both parties, Howick, Grenville and Perceval, joined it; the Duke of Gloucester was its president and the old Abolitionists were among its members; its first anniversary meeting was attended by fifty or sixty Members of Parliament.

Wilberforce's efforts to finish off the Trade were unrelenting. In 1811 we find him urging 'Yorke, first Lord of Admiralty, to send out ships of war to Africa, and clear the coast by a thorough sweep'. His friend, the flamboyant revolutionary General Miranda, triumphantly stormed into

Kensington Gore with the news that Venezuela had abolished the Trade. She was followed by Chile in 1811 and Buenos Aires in 1812. In 1813 Sweden became Britain's ally; Wilberforce urged Castlereagh to bring pressure to bear, and, under his persuasion, the Swedes, too, disowned the Trade. Although Abolition by these countries was welcome, none of them were owners of great tropical plantations or important carriers of slaves. On the other hand if Spain, Portugal and France could be persuaded to abolish, there would be nowhere for the slave ships to deliver their cargoes. But this proved to be a more difficult task.

We have already seen Wilberforce use the alliances with Spain and Portugal to educate them on Abolition. He could only obtain a treaty in which Portugal undertook to confine her share of the Trade to the parts of Africa in her possession. This concession was impossible to enforce and, for practical purposes, useless. In 1813 Wilberforce's irritation with his ungrateful allies was increased by 'Monsieur Funchal's project'. Under this scheme the Portuguese would be allowed absolute freedom to conduct the Trade south of Cape Palmas in return for abstention north of it, which would be enforced by a British right of seizure in those waters. To Wilberforce this seemed a shameful playing of games with a holy cause. He described the plan as 'full of hypocrisy, wickedness and cruelty', and gave vent to his feelings in a letter to Castlereagh:

'When I consider how closely we have been intertwining the interest of the Portuguese with our own, and how freely our blood and treasure have been lavished to preserve them in existence, I grow warmer, if not more indignant, than I ought to be at such treatment, and indeed at such conduct considered in itself—that with declarations in their mouths that they consider the Slave Trade unjust and inhuman . . . they should be striving for the right of availing themselves of the protection of our flag, for the purposes of bringing down on the natives of Africa miseries five times greater than any from which we have delivered them.'[1]

As the war drew towards its close Wilberforce saw a chance of an international agreement to outlaw the Trade. But he had lived with the war for so long that he dared hardly believe that it was ending. He had seen the French snatch victory out of defeat before and he watched anxiously for any reverse which Napoleon's genius might exploit. In September 1813, when on holiday at Sandgate he caught a distant glimpse of the struggle. One night he was worried by flashes of cannon on the French coast, which he thought might mean a defeat for the allies. Soon afterwards he was horrified to see a merchantman cut out by a French privateer and outraged to learn that there was no resistance because the signals officer was away shooting partridges.

His fears of a French recovery receded as the allied armies swept across France. On March 23 he heard from Marshal Beresford that 'all Gascony wild against Buonaparte—calling themselves English—showing the church and castle built by Edward The Black Prince, and saying, "It was yours, why do you not retake it?" '² On April 9 he wrote, 'How wonderful are the events of the last few days! After hearing that Buonaparte had dashed into the rear of the Allies it seemed doubtful what would happen: when suddenly we heard on Tuesday that they were marching on to Paris. Then we hoped the best; but how little expected that today, Saturday, we should hear of Buonaparte's accepting the Emperor of Russia's offer, renouncing the Throne, and agreeing to retire to Elba.'³ Napoleon's choice of exile held an especial irony for Wilberforce, who wrote to Stephen: 'Have you good authority for believing that Toussaint perished in Elba? If so, and if Buonaparte himself selected it, he is harder-hearted than Shakespeare would have rendered his greatest villains.'⁴*

Even now the war was to give him one more agonising decision. Czar Alexander of Russia had been anxious to secure the alliance of Sweden, in order to threaten Napoleon's northern flank. Sweden was ruled by an old marshal of Napoleon's, Prince Bernadotte, who exacted a hard bargain. He demanded as his price for joining the Allies that Norway, then part of Denmark, should be ceded to him. The Allies agreed and Denmark, being an ally, though an unwilling one, of Napoleon, had no say in the matter. None of the parties considered the wishes of the Norwegians.

After the war Bernadotte claimed his reward. The Danes surrendered Norway and evacuated their garrisons, but the Norwegians rose and refused to submit to the Swedes whom they loathed. Bernadotte called on Britain to honour her treaty obligations and blockade the Norwegian coast. The blockade and an invasion from Sweden forced the Norwegians to capitulate within a fortnight. If Norway had to be coerced this use of overwhelming force was probably the most merciful way of doing so. But Members of Parliament on both sides of the House felt deep displeasure about the operation, and the Whigs argued that it should never have been authorised. Wilberforce was torn between sympathy for the Norwegians— 'I consider the partitioning of states against their will a most despotic sacrifice of public rights'—and a desire not to betray the nation's honour by renouncing a treaty when it could no longer benefit her. The short answer was that dishonourable treaties lead to impossible dilemmas. Although he decided to support the Government as the lesser evil, Wilberforce seems to have reached this conclusion. 'The truth is, Norway would not starve. She would submit if she knew she must. We saved her from being conquered by prevailing on the Crown Prince to postpone the acquisition of Norway till after the European War, which was then doubtful, by promising that if by our common arms an enemy's country

---

* Wilberforce was misinformed. Toussaint, the Haitian hero, had died in a dungeon on the Swiss frontier.

was conquered, she should possess it. Yet the idea of starving these poor people is shocking. Oh how hideous are war's features when closely viewed!'[5]

After their triumph the Emperor of Russia and the King of Prussia visited London, the former bringing with him a troop of Cossacks and the latter Marshal Blücher. In spite of having no language in common Wilberforce and Blücher seem to have warmed to each other. The King of Prussia acknowledged his work on behalf of his suffering subjects with the gift of a set of Dresden china, 'the only thing I ever got by spouting'. He took his children to see the Cossacks at Portman Barracks. During Napoleon's retreat from Moscow the hardihood and ferocity of the Cossacks had become legendary, and all London flocked to gape at these dangerous allies. The Cossacks, unused to such treatment, became so neurotic that 'they could not bear to be looked at', but Wilberforce's charm rose to the occasion. He went round and shook hands with them all, and his friendliness and goodwill were so transparent that 'even the roughest of them, who looked as if he had never smiled in his life, unbent his ebon brows and relaxed the muscles of his iron face, and even kissed his hand when he came away'.[6]

When Wilberforce was summoned to meetings with both monarchs, his main concern was, of course, to convince them of the need for a General Abolition of the Slave Trade. He wrote a letter on this subject to Alexander, a task he approached with some trepidation. 'I am about to write to a real live emperor,' he told Gisborne, 'not merely such a sort of Birmingham emperor as Buonaparte;' the comparison might not have pleased the Spooners. He seems to have thought that such a letter should end with a flowery flourish.

'May you live, sire, to witness the blessed result of your beneficence, in a prevalence throughout those benighted regions of Christian light, and moral improvement, and social comfort; and to hear her sable children, when, in the language of Scripture, "They spread forth their hands unto God, call down not temporal only but everlasting blessings on the head of Alexander Emperor of the Russias, as the greatest of their earthly benefactors." '[7]

The fact that Russia had neither slaves nor interests in the Trade made it easier for Alexander to sympathise with Wilberforce, but it soon became clear that the French took a very different attitude. 'Their merchants,' he heard, 'are intent on gain anyhow. Gregoire and all the old amis-de-noirs men are in exceedingly bad odour.'[8] 'A fine return truly,' Brougham complained, 'and a pure sense of the benefits they have received, those base Bourbons are evincing! As for Alexander and the other allies, they may cheaply enough be Abolitionists, having not one negro—as I doubt not the Bourbons are all for abolishing villenage.'[9] Wilberforce worked through French allies, his old friend de Lageard, La Fayette, Sismondi, Madame de Staël and the German Baron Humboldt, whose South American expeditions had given him a vast reputation and left him with a loathing of all forms of slavery.

Wilberforce wrote a 'letter' to Talleyrand, which, like his letter to the Freeholders of York, grew into a full-length book. In it he gave a résumé of the arguments used in the campaign for Abolition and showed how they applied to the French colonies with even more force than to the English. The blacks already outnumbered the whites by ten to one in French colonies and excessive imports of negroes had been directly responsible for the revolt in St. Domingue. The merchants of Nantes had announced their intention of resettling that island with slaves and seemed to regard it as a matter presenting no great difficulty. He pleaded against such insanity. St. Domingue, he warned Talleyrand, could only be reconquered through an ocean of blood, in which army after army would perish. English traders had complained that Abolition would ruin them, but 'France had not even the poor excuse to plead, that the abolition would demand sacrifices, which she cannot afford to make. Not one solitary vessel, not a single seaman, not a livre of capital is now employed in the Slave Trade; not a single manufacturer or artisan is occupied in fabricating goods. She could only establish *by law* that discontinuance of the traffic, which, for twenty years, has subsisted *in fact*.'[10] If Liverpool, in spite of her doom-laden prophecies, had not suffered from the Abolition of the Trade, why should Nantes seek to revive it? He turned to regulation and described how the slaves might regard 'this wretched palliative'. 'Your enmity they can understand, your cruelty they can endure, sometimes even despise; but insult them not by your humanity, and allow not yourself, in the practice of these detestable and wicked barbarities, to indulge in complacencies of humanity and virtue.'[11] The letter is a fine example of Wilberforce's work, its close reasoning being interspersed with emotional and moral pleas of unusual force. It probably gives a truer impression of his speeches on Abolition than the versions published in Hansard.

Talleyrand replied with a disarming letter, full of flattery and committing himself to nothing. But Wilberforce, in Stephen's words, was 'praise-proof'. When pressed, Talleyrand admitted: 'La chose m'est démonstrée (à moi); il s'agit de la démonstrer à la France.' France was unreceptive; in her eyes the English, having been the greatest slave carriers in the world for almost a century, were now trying to cripple her colonies by denying them the new slaves which they needed and had not been able to ship during the war. The French colonies must be allowed five years in which to continue the Trade and restock their colonies before Abolition could be considered.

Castlereagh was representing Britain at the peace conference in Paris, but the Abolitionists remembered his old hostility to the cause and judged him to be 'a fish of the cold-blooded sort'. They decided to send their own representative to Paris, where he could both brief Castlereagh and see that he did not weaken. Wilberforce thought of filling this role himself but decided instead to send Macaulay, who was a less notorious figure and who spoke much better French. Macaulay took his responsibilities with the utmost seriousness. He pursued Castlereagh everywhere and deluged him with correspondence. He had been instructed, if he had a spare moment, to form a Bible Society in Paris,[12] and for all the good he was able to do for Abolition, he might as well have spent all his time on this task. Malouet, the French Minister for the Colonies, asked Macaulay if England intended to bind all the world. He also showed how seriously his Government had been considering the question by confusing Abolition with Emancipation.

Macaulay thought that Castlereagh had been indifferent, but in the hostile atmosphere of Paris, he could surely have achieved nothing more. He returned to England with a treaty in which France promised to abolish the Trade after five years and meanwhile to support England in pressing Abolition on other powers. For these concessions, he had surrendered England's only lever against France, the possession of her colonies.

The presentation of the Peace Treaty to the Commons put Wilberforce in a dilemma. To support it or to remain silent would be a betrayal of Africa, to oppose it would make him seem unpatriotic and reflect on his cause. Honesty prevailed. When Castlereagh brought in the Treaty, which was satisfactory in every other respect, Wilberforce struck a note of dissent. 'I cannot but conceive,' he said, 'that I behold in his hand the death-warrant of a multitude of innocent victims, men, women and children, whom I had fondly indulged the hope of having myself rescued from destruction.'[13] Nothing, he declared, would have induced him to sign the Treaty.

Shortly after the debate Wilberforce had an interview with the Emperor Alexander which must have given him some encouragement. 'He took me by the hand, very cordially, and assured me that he was much interested for my object, and very glad to see me. On my stating that the French would not in fact abolish at the time settled, he replied heartily, "We must make them"; and then correcting himself "we must keep them to it".[14] When Wilberforce expressed his disappointment over the Treaty, Alexander replied, 'What could be done when your own ambassador gave way?' The Czar's friendliness was clear enough, but it was also evident that he would not risk agreement on issues more important to Russia by pressing Abolition on the other powers. That was a task which could only be undertaken by England.

Wilberforce again found himself in a quandary; to press Abolition on the Government and to condemn its ministers for laxity could be interpreted as factious opposition. But the Government had to be persuaded to make a greater effort for Abolition at Vienna than it had at Paris or the question would be lost by default. As in the crisis over the Indian missions he appealed to the country, and its response was again overpowering. 800 petitions with over a million signatures were laid on the table of the House, figures that were unprecedented in parliamentary history. Such a demonstration of enthusiasm could not be ignored by the Government. 'The whole nation is bent upon the subject,' wrote Castlereagh, '. . . and Ministers must make it the basis of their policy.'[15] With this support Wilberforce had no difficulty in carrying an address on the subject to the Prince Regent on June 27 and on June 29 an amendment to an address on the peace.

Once the Government had adopted the cause Castlereagh conducted it with his usual efficiency, but both he and Wellington, who had been appointed ambassador in Paris, needed briefing. Stephen and Macaulay set out to provide a mass of evidence covering both the West Indies and Africa, while Wilberforce arranged the distribution in Paris of his letters to Talleyrand and the Freeholders of York. Wellington, when confronted by the result of Macaulay's researches, said that he could not see how on earth the French could fail to be convinced, but he had not yet gauged the mood of France. There was a total lack of sympathy with Abolition; in desperation Wilberforce asked Humboldt if the French would abandon the Trade in return for, say, Mauritius, or St. Lucia. He received a chilling answer. 'Elle n'est point ici, comme en Angleterre, une affaire d'argent, elle est liée uniquement à des passions nationales.'[16] He even advised against forming an Abolitionist Society on the grounds that it would infallibly attract radical members and thus bring the cause into further disrepute. The royalists on their return to power shunned any policy which had the slightest revolutionary associations. They were in no mood for fine distinctions and the memory of the old amis des noirs was enough to condemn Abolition. The atmosphere of reaction was so strong that the English were sometimes infected by it. When the Allies entered Paris for the second time, *The Times* urged: 'We would grind to powder the statue of the vain, obscene, heartless, atheistical Voltaire.'[17]

The French never considered the merits of Abolition seriously. It was prejudged both as a revolutionary and as an English measure. England was now loathed by most of France, and as Abolition was associated with England there was nothing that could be done to prevent the Trade being resumed. The Duke of Wellington wrote to Wilberforce that Louis XVIII was sympathetic, but isolated in his views. All that could be extracted from France was a promise in November 1814 not to allow their ships to trade north of the Niger. The reconquest of St. Domingue was abandoned for military rather than humanitarian reasons.

In October an account of the fitting out of nine slave ships at Le Havre with the help of Englishmen 'completely sickened my heart', wrote Wilberforce. 'How I would like to catch the Englishmen some day when on shore and send them to slave in New South Wales. I know not that in all my long experience of Abolitionism, I ever felt a keener paroxysm of grief and indignation. Oh that it might please God to dash to the ground that bloody cup which they are preparing to quaff with so much avidity. They really appear to my mind's eye to be so many demons exulting over their savage orgies with grim, ferocious joy.'[18]

At the Congress of Vienna the British Government was faithful to the cause. Russia, Prussia and Austria, none of whom were interested parties, made no objection to an international prohibition of the Trade, but Spain and Portugal demanded a period of grace to restock their colonies. On February 8, 1815 the powers agreed on a declaration condemning the Trade and resolving to end it as soon as possible. Wilberforce recognised this gesture for the palliative that it was, but he also felt that no more could have been achieved at the Congress.

Help came from an unlikely ally. On March 1 Napoleon landed in France and again seized power. He was anxious to placate his enemies and one of his first acts was to proclaim the immediate Abolition of the Slave Trade throughout France's possessions. After the Bourbons had been restored this proclamation was confirmed at the second Treaty of Paris and the French promised to replace it with a legitimate law. Lord Holland wrote to Wilberforce: 'There was no difficulty in abolishing the French slave trade last year but in the breasts of the Bourbons and their adherents either in France or in the colonies and the repugnance felt in 1814 to the measure *at Court* originated from their persuasion that, the principles of all Abolitionists as well as of all toleration in religion, are more or less connected with motions of political liberty which they know to be incompatible with their system of government. True French Royalists and many English Royalists too make no difference between you and me or between me and Tom Paine. We are all equally heretics in religion and Jacobins in politics.'[19]

In 1817 it was discovered that the prohibiting ordinance had not even been published. This was corrected the next year, but the Trade, although illegal, was not made a criminal offence and slavers continued to sail out brazenly from French ports until 1831 when the penalties were strengthened. But after Napoleon's return from exile the Slave Trade could only be continued legally by two countries, Portugal and Spain.

As these countries were both devout members of the Roman Catholic Church, Wilberforce thought that the Vatican might be persuaded to use its influence with them, in spite of Lord Holland's warning that 'you will not find his Holiness as much disposed to anathematize rapine and murder committed under the sanction of the powerful crown of Spain as to disdain the extravagances of the Catholics in Ireland'.[20] Wilberforce's friend John Harford was in Rome at the time and found himself appointed the Abolitionists' ambassador to the Holy See. Harford had become a friend of Cardinal Consalvi, the Papal Secretary of State. When Harford, who was not in Rome at the time, seemed to be neglecting his duties, Wilberforce wrote him a passionate letter:

'I cannot help regretting you not having endeavoured to interest the leading members of the Roman Church on behalf of the African Continent. The only obstinate continuers of the slave trade are now the Spaniards and the Portuguese, the nations most under the influence of the Romish Church; and instances of Spanish slave ships, and of Portuguese, also, have come to my knowledge attended with circumstances almost too dreadful to be described. In one case, a vessel of 160 to 180 tons contained, when she sailed from Africa, above 500 slaves, besides the sailors, &c; and how they were heaped together you may judge when I tell you that probably there would not be room for even 300 of them to lie on their backs. When they were taken, several were dying daily from suffocation, and the inexpressible (by any known word) combination of miseries resulting from cramming together into the hold of a ship at sea a vast number of human beings unused to that element, in a tropical climate, the men necessarily in chains, and shut down under hatches during the night. In this dreadful situation the flux is often generated, and then, from the impossibility of the people's getting to their tubs, from the comrade who is fettered not consenting to make a simultaneous effort to secure that convenience—from the quarrels and often the bitings of the legs of those who do try to crawl over and through the jammed bodies of their fellow-victims—such a mass of filth and horror is witnessed as is insufferable, even to the coarse but honest senses and feelings of our rough sailors. In another vessel, owing to the slaves being concealed under a false deck, the whole mass of them were on their hams, and the whole floor one large tub: this, in the stormy sea off the Cape of Good Hope, was the horrid condition of a slave-ship going from Mozambique to Rio. There, also, the daily deaths attested the fatal as well as cruel nature of the sufferings of the poor wretches. And nothing has been said of wives and children probably left behind—of being forced from their own country to be taken they know not where. Surely, surely, if the Pope, or if Consalvi were made aware of the real nature of these abominations, and of their unparalleled extent, they would exert themselves to put a stop to them.'[21]

On his return to Rome Harford had this letter translated and took it to Consalvi, but he found that, although sympathetic, none of the leading members of the Conclave were well informed about the Trade. Wilber-force therefore sent out a series of pamphlets including a superbly bound copy of his letter to Talleyrand for Consalvi or the Pope. Harford distri-buted these papers and obtained an interview with the Pope who 'expressed astonishment and pity' when shown Clarkson's print of the *Brookes*. When Harford started to ask for the Papal influence to be used with Spain and Portugal Pius VII interrupted: 'They cannot fail to adopt a similar policy.' He sent a letter to the court of Madrid urging its co-operation. Wilber-force was delighted by this news; 'why you are the very prince of negoci-ators,' he wrote to Harford, 'Lord Castlereagh himself could not have opened his business with more adroitness.'[22]

Portuguese Abolition was bought in 1815. In return for £750,000 Portugal signed a treaty confining her share of the traffic to the transport of slaves from south of the Equator to her own colonies. After Brazil had won her independence (1822–5) the Slave Trade became illegal for Portuguese. Spain at first resisted all inducements, but in 1817, in return for £400,000, she abandoned the Trade in the Northern Hemisphere. This was a greater sacrifice for her than for Portugal, since she lost access to Cuba, her main market for slaves. In 1820 Spain abolished the Trade entirely and in 1835 she imposed severe penalties against it.

If the laws passed by the different powers had been respected, the Slave Trade should have been utterly extinguished by the early 1820s. In the event it lasted for another forty years and the illegal Trade was even more horrible than its predecessor. Ships were built for speed now; slaves were crammed in mercilessly; prices on the Coast were low and in the Indies high, and few owners worried about their mortality rates. The *Brookes* as shown in Clarkson's drawing was a paradise compared to the holds of the nineteenth-century slavers. The incalculable suffering caused by the continuation of the Trade came about because only Britain, of all the nations that had abolished it, made a serious attempt to enforce her laws. At one time a sixth of the British Navy was employed in hunting down slave ships. The Abolitionists were ready to harass the Government at any sign of slackness, but nothing could be done against foreign slavers, unless other powers agreed to reciprocal rights of search. So long as there re-mained a market on the Coast, a colony which would accept the slavers' cargo and a flag under which they could sail without interference, the Trade would continue, its volume reduced but its horrors increased by Abolition.

Little could be done to help the slaves being carried by foreign ships, but smuggling into British colonies could be prevented. The direct trade from Africa had been ended by Brougham's Slave Trade Felony Act, but the failure to ban shipments of slaves between British colonies left a loop-hole for the smugglers. It was easy to take slaves from a foreign to a

British colony and pretend that they were a shipment from another British island. The supply of slaves in the foreign colony was renewed from Africa and the evil continued unabated. But Stephen, remorseless and inventive as ever, found a solution. If a record of all slaves was kept in a central register with details of their age, sex, name, height, colour, distinguishing marks and country of origin, it would become impossible to use the inter-colonial trade as a cloak for imports from abroad. Wilberforce persuaded Perceval to introduce Registration into Trinidad in 1812. Trinidad, acquired as a result of the war, had no Colonial Assembly and an Order in Council was sufficient.

The Registration system worked well, but it was adopted only by St. Lucia and Mauritius. Wilberforce had intended to follow the Order in Council with a Bill to make it compulsory in all British colonies, but he allowed himself to be dissuaded by Perceval and another opportunity did not occur until 1815. Lord Liverpool and his ministers then refused to support the Bill on the pretext that there was no evidence of smuggling. Stephen was disgusted by their decision and resolved to leave Parliament.

*

Another issue which coincided with Registration gives a rare example of Wilberforce trying to exact a political bargain. The price of wheat, and therefore of bread, fluctuated wildly according to the state of the previous harvest. To keep it from rising too much, foreign corn was allowed into the country at a nominal duty at a price of 66/– a quarter. During the war the supply of foreign corn had been insufficient to make up for bad harvests at home. In 1800 the price of wheat had soared to 142/10 a quarter and between 1804 and 1812 it averaged 88/11.[23] The end of the blockade was followed by a good harvest in 1813 and the price promptly collapsed. The agricultural interests, who had been busily cultivating marginal land, now faced ruin. A committee of the House examined the problem and recommended that the price at which foreign corn was admitted should be raised to 80/–.

This proposal aroused bitter hostility on the grounds that it threatened to raise the price of bread beyond the reach of the poor. There were riots in the streets and Members were pulled out of their carriages by the mob. Charles Grant and Arthur Young slept at Kensington Gore for safety. The Government needed Wilberforce's support for this unpopular measure and he needed their support for his Registration Bill. 'Much pressed to speak on Corn Bill,' he wrote on May 8, 1815, 'and told Huskisson I would, if government would support the Register Bill. It would not be right to change my opinion; but one may fairly take a more or less forward part from considerations of expediency.'[24] This was precisely as far as he was prepared to be pushed by expediency, and then only in theory. In practice the Government did not agree to his terms but his sense of duty still led him to support their Bill. It was not one of his happier efforts. Economics was never his subject and he would have done well to have remained silent on a question which divided Malthus and Ricardo. He showed much concern that Britain should not become dependent for her food supplies on countries which might be enemies in the future. To raise the price at which foreign corn could be admitted would be to encourage British agriculture and self-sufficiency.[25] Impeccable though such sentiments might be, he made no attempt to follow through his reasoning, to analyse what the change in price would mean to consumer and producer, or examine why the old price level had failed in its task. His speeches can be divided into two categories, those he wished to make and those he felt obliged to make. The latter are marked by hesitation and indecision. He was a judge rather than an advocate. They lack the power and conviction of his great speeches on subjects where he knew he was right.

His advocacy of the Corn Laws may not have been a great speech, but it was certainly a brave one. He wrote afterwards: 'I am sure that in coming forward, I performed a very painful act of duty, from a desire to please God, and to serve the interests of religion, and I humbly trust God will protect me and my family. If not, His will be done.'[26] The threat was real enough. Sir Joseph Bankes had his papers destroyed and was lucky to escape without his house being burnt. Wilberforce describes the precautions he took in a letter to his eldest son.

'Were you to enter the dining-room at family prayer time without having received some explanation of our appearance, you would probably begin to think that we were expecting a visit from the ex-emperor and his followers at Kensington Gore, and had prepared a military force to repel his assault. For you would see four soldiers and a sergeant, together with another stranger,* who as far as bodily strength would go, would play his part as well as any of them. The fact is, that we had some reason to apprehend mischief for our house, in consequence of the part which I judged it my duty to take on the Corn Bill; and as your mother, &c. was advised to evacuate the place, I preferred the expedient which had been adopted by Mr. Bankes, and several others of my friends, that of having four or five soldiers in my house—the very knowledge of their being there, rendering an attack improbable. But it was a curious instance of the rapid circulation of intelligence, that at Covent Garden market early on Saturday morning, John Sharman, who sells garden-stuff, being there to purchase for the supply of his shop was hooted after, with "So your old master has spoken for the Corn Bill," (I had spoken only the night before), "but his house shall pay for it." All however is hitherto quiet, and I trust will continue so. But I was aware of the danger when (to you I may say it, it was at my

* Bushel the Peace-officer.

prayers) I resolved to speak for the Bill; but I judged it my duty to show that I was in favour of the measure (though thinking 76s. a preferable importation price to 80s.). I thought that if I remained silent, many might say Mr. Wilberforce professes to trust in the protection of God, but you see when there is danger to be apprehended from speaking out, he takes care to protect himself by being silent. Again, I sometimes need parliamentary support for measures of a class not so popular as some others, as missionary questions, or any others of a religious kind. Now by coming forward and speaking my mind on the present occasion, I knew I should render people better disposed to support me in any of these cases, while on the other hand my remaining silent and snug as it might have been termed, would have produced a contrary disposition. I acted in short on the principle of "providing things honest in the sight of all men, and of adorning the doctrine of God our Saviour". But observe, I was clear in my judgement in favour of the Bill.'[27]

The presence of the soldiers was enough. Wilberforce was undisturbed by the mob and even found grounds for pleasure in the invasion of his home. 'The soldiers (Scotch) behave extremely well,' he wrote in his Journal. 'They come in to prayers, and pleased to do so.'[28] Before leaving the Corn Laws it is worth examining the way in which they worked, since his support for them has been cited as evidence of Wilberforce's 'reactionary' record in English politics. The Corn Laws, it is true, were intended to allow the price to rise up to 80/– and to this extent they favoured the agricultural interest at the expense of the poor. Wilberforce himself would have preferred a price of 76/–, but even at 80/– corn would have been cheaper than it had been throughout the last years of the blockade. In the event any influence they exerted on prices was marginal. In a year of rich harvests the price would fall below the old figure of 66/– at which foreign corn had been admitted. In 1820 it fell to 64/– and in November 1822 to 38/10.[29] As measures of protection the Corn Laws were inefficient; they did nothing to keep prices up in good harvests, and in bad they merely raised the price from 66/– to 80/–, a level well below the average price for the last eight years.

*

The Registration Bill was introduced to the Commons on July 5. Wilberforce had decided not to press it that session. The West Indians had united against it, and while their attitude was inconsistent—if, as they claimed there was no smuggling, it was hard to see why they found the Bill so objectionable—evidence was needed before it could be passed. In 1816 the campaign was opened by a salvo of propaganda from the West Indians, including a pamphlet by Marryat with vituperative passages on Wilberforce. He responded with what must have been maddening equanimity. 'Poor fellow!' he wrote, 'I hope I can bear him no ill will, but allow for and pity him.'[30] If all the accusations against him were true, he told the House, 'nothing but a special Providence could have prevented my being hanged full thirty years ago'.[31] But he was delayed again by a combination of factors. There had been a revolt in Barbados which had been suppressed with the usual savagery. The West Indians were certain to claim that it had been caused by the Abolitionists. In itself this would have been unimportant, but the negotiations with Spain over the Abolition of her Slave Trade had reached a very delicate point and could be upset by the slander that the Abolitionists were fomenting slave rebellions. The next year Registration was delayed yet again, this time for very different reasons. Wilberforce wrote to Macaulay:

'I have for some time been unwillingly yielding to a secret suggestion that it would be better perhaps to lie upon our oars in the Registry Bill, and West Indian cause. When parliament meets, the whole nation, depend upon it, will be looking for relief from its own burthens, and it would betray an ignorance of all tact to talk to them in such circumstances of the sufferings of the slaves in the West Indies. We should specially guard against appearing to have a world of our own, and to have little sympathy with the sufferings of our countrymen.'[32]

The Bill was never revived, but its purposes came to be achieved in an indirect way. The Government, influenced by the Abolitionists, urged the Colonies to adopt Registration, and since the registers would be safely in their own hands, the Colonial Assemblies were happy to make this meaningless gesture. In 1819 the trick was turned on them. The Secretary for the Colonies introduced a duplicate register to be kept in England. The Assemblies had only accepted the registers to show their goodwill, while intending to make sure that they were never used. But, having accepted them, they could find no reason to deny London duplicate copies.

CHAPTER XXV

PRIVATE LIFE, 1815-19

MANY of Wilberforce's closest friends and allies were lost during these years. Granville Sharp died in July 1813 and he was followed in September by Lord Muncaster. At the beginning of 1815 Wilberforce came to London to find Henry Thornton critically ill, 'I had no idea of his danger till to-day'. He wrote on January 11: 'He is so weak he could not talk for above a minute or two. His voice broken and feeble. Poor dear Henry!'[1] Four days later he wrote to Macaulay: 'Our dear friend is continually before my mind's eye, and his emaciated figure and face are very affecting. Above all, seeing poor Mrs. Thornton with her nine children makes my heart bleed. May it please God to raise him up again, in answer to the prayers of his many friends.'[2] Thornton then seemed to be recovering, but he had a relapse and died before Wilberforce could reach his side. Wilberforce himself became so ill that he could not attend the funeral.

Thornton's death was swiftly followed by that of John Bowdler. Bowdler was deeply devoted to the Thornton family and he had passed through agonies during Henry's illness. Two days after Thornton died Bowdler burst a blood vessel in his chambers. He died on February 1. Four years later Wilberforce wrote of him, 'Bowdler had a dignity—he would have become capable I assure you of thundering and lightening. And then he was the tenderest, and the humblest, and the most self-forgetting creature.'[3] Bowdler's funeral was scarcely over when the news arrived of the death of Dr. Buchanan, his ally in the battle for Indian missions. In September he was greatly shocked by the appearance of Mrs. Thornton. 'Till I saw her,' he tells Macaulay, 'I was sanguine in my hopes; I own I am now greatly alarmed.'[4] By the 27th he was preparing for the worst. 'I fear I have been misled into too favourable an opinion of Mrs. Thornton's case, and I have touched in conversing with her as strongly as I could on the guardianship of her children in the event of her death.'[5] On the 3rd, 'Macaulay and I were with her reading her a paper for his will—an affecting interview—I could scarcely understand her speaking; she is in a sweet state.'[6] She died on October 12 and Sir Robert Inglis became the guardian of the Thornton children.

The next year a heavy-handed Providence struck again. Wilberforce's sister who was married to James Stephen died unexpectedly. Wilberforce hurried down to console his friend, whom he found 'much affected, liable to strong paroxysms, at other times calm and pretty cheerful'. 'How affecting it is,' Wilberforce reflected, 'to leave the person we have known all our lives, on whom we should have been afraid to let the wind blow too roughly, to leave her in the cold ground alone! This quite strikes my imagination always on such occasions.'[7]

It is hard not to detect a note of satisfaction in Wilberforce's descriptions of these death-bed scenes. Death to him was a dispensation of Providence and therefore something which should be accepted although 'some tears of mortality will fall, when we see a friend descending into the dark valley of the shadow of death, and the mortal frame suffering its last agonies'.[8] The Heaven he believed in was a very personal place in which he could hope to meet all his old friends again. He was always anxious to extract a moral from a death or to divine the workings of Providence. He would analyse his own feelings with disconcerting honesty. 'How strangely are we constituted!' he wrote after Mrs. Thornton's death. 'I have often been more affected by a very trifle.' And on the anniversary of the death of his daughter Barbara he wrote: 'My dear wife's wounds bleed afresh on this anniversary. It is not really so with me.'[9] But compared to other Evangelicals he was very restrained in his treatment of the subject. Hannah More was perhaps the worst offender. She positively wallowed in the delicious agonies of the death-bed. 'I know of nothing so interesting,' she wrote, 'as the closing scenes of a champion of righteousness.'[10] In 1792 she visited the death-bed of Bishop Horne, 'a more delightful or edifying death-bed cannot well be imagined';[11] passing on to ease the last moments of a cousin of Wilberforce's she concluded, 'Two such dying beds, though near each other were not easy to be found.'[12] Death became a formalised moment. The champions of righteousness bowed out with sweetness, piety, patience and dignity. Suffering borne with courage could be allowed in the Evangelical accounts of death, but any other unpleasantness was firmly censored until they read like accounts of particularly moving funerals.

The death-beds of the wicked present a very different picture. Haunted by terror they suddenly realise, too late, the errors of their ways and are plucked out of life begging for a chance of repentance which they have not earned and are not allowed. The favourite actors in these unwholesome dramas include Paine, Gibbon and Voltaire. It was Wilberforce's nature to pity rather than to hate those whom he thought sinners, and this kind of self-righteous gloating over an enemy going to Hell would have been out of keeping with his character. But he did indulge, though never to the same degree as his friends, in sentimental piety over the deaths of the religious. On January 17, 1815 Bowdler had written him a long and moving letter about Henry Thornton's death. Wilberforce wrote on the back, 'Dear Bowdler day after dear Henry's death'; then when Bowdler had followed his friend into the grave he added 'delightful picture of a man just before his own seizure'.[13] Even his children were affected. In 1819 Samuel wrote to him with an account of the death of a school friend's father. He finished, 'Would you be so kind as to give me some account of the death of Mrs. Patty More?'[14]

Wilberforce's children were now growing up. He had decided against sending the boys to a public school because of 'its probable effects on eternal state'. They were sent instead to private schools, which were more a collection of pupils taken on by a clergyman than any school we would recognise today.

William, his eldest son, was worrying even as a child. He was moody and sulky, lazy in work and unenthusiastic over religion. Wilberforce thought he had suffered harm through fear of solitude.[15] Marianne Thornton declared that he 'never was endurable'.[16] But young Macaulay, who was at school with William, seemed to like him. . . . 'I am classed with Wilberforce,' he wrote to Zachary in February 1813, 'whom all the boys allow to be very clever, very droll, and very impudent. . . . We have had the first meeting of our debating society the other day, when a vote was moved for upon Wilberforce, but he getting up said, "Mr. President, I beg to second the motion". By this means he escaped.'[17] During the school play William was cast as the Pope and young Macaulay as Napoleon. The former ruined the performance by forgetting his lines.

Robert Isaac, the second son, was more a Spooner than a Wilberforce; he was conscientious, not as humorous as his brothers, methodical and thorough, a formidable worker and scholar. He was shy and lacked the charm of his two younger brothers but he was always considerate and kind. He was more patient than Samuel. They were both sent to a school at Nuneham Courtenay, run by the Rev. E. G. Marsh, and Robert remained there until he went to university. According to a story told by a friend and quoted with caution by Mr. Newsome, Samuel was so unhappy that he decided expulsion was the only answer. After failing to achieve this end by quarrelling with his tutor, he 'ran into the road before the cottage, then traversed by a score or two of London coaches a day, threw himself flat on the ground, in the very track of the coaches, and announced his intention of remaining there until he was sent home'.[18] This early example of passive resistance was entirely successful; it was typical of Samuel's impulsive, headstrong nature, but Robert, however miserable, could never have acted in such a way. He would instead have tried to reason his way out of his difficulties.

Samuel did not have as scholarly a mind as Robert, but he had a far stronger personality. He was impetuous and masterful. An early school report tells us, 'I must however in faithfulness observe that his *temper* needs much subjugation and softening. I have too often had to remark an overbearing and wayward disposition among his companions—and occasionally, a considerable want of meekness and modesty towards his elders.'[19] Samuel could get away with these faults; he had inherited much of Wilberforce's vivacity and charm; he too scribbled his letters, his thoughts outrunning his pen. Wilberforce loved all his children, but he probably loved Sam and Lizzy, his second daughter, the most. Samuel developed religious feelings early in his life. He wrote to his father in March 1819 at the age of fourteen: 'I think that given to choose, I should like by all means to become a clergyman that I might do my best to extend God's Kingdom upon this earth remembering the blessed promise that they who turn many to righteousness shall shine as the stars in the firmament.'[20] He also absorbed his share of the morbid side of Evangelism. Soon after the letter asking his father for an account of Patty More's death, he informed him that 'a gracious God has spared me until my fourteenth year when many other young persons stronger than myself have dropped into the tomb'.[21]

Henry, Wilberforce's fourth son, resembled him most closely in appearance and character. When Robert Isaac looked over the family correspondence after his father's death, he found his own letters had 'a formal rigidity which now looks to me inexpressibly ludicrous. . . . Yours,' he wrote to Samuel, 'are more lively and less constrained. . . . Henry's are untidy but affectionate and thoughtful.'[22] It was a fair thumbnail sketch of their characters. Like his father, Henry found it difficult to concentrate; he was such an irregular and illegible correspondent that Wilberforce's letters to him are full of gentle rebukes: 'It is not quite right for my dear Henry not to let me hear from him now and then.'[23] On July 26, 1818 he wrote to Henry, who was then eleven, 'You have long my dear Henry, had a sad habit of looking about you at Church. It has been in some degree the effect of that mental infirmity which I have often I believed noticed in you. But it is a practice of extreme importance and highly criminal in the sight of God.'[24] Wilberforce may have recognised his own faults in Henry. He too had let his attention wander in church and he even fell asleep there on a number of occasions. He too was an unreliable correspondent. Like Henry he had doubted whether he was strong enough to lead a truly religious life. Perhaps this is why his letters to Henry are even fuller of religious exhortations than those he wrote to his other children.

'Somebody told me two or three days ago,' Wilberforce wrote in 1818, 'that Henry was more like me, not only in Body, but in everything, than any of my children. I hope he will be better than ever I have been, and more active and useful to his fellow Creatures.'[25]

His correspondence with all his children, and indeed with his closest friends, was strongly religious in tone. He was relentless, though always kind, in pointing out their faults. It was an Evangelical convention that every letter from one 'serious' person to another should include some religious sentiment, and it was almost a compliment to criticise or point out the faults of your correspondent. 'You will guess what I mean to ask,' Bowdler once wrote to him, 'it is no common thing and what no common friend ever does—to be told of my faults.'[26] Stephen's letters to Wilberforce fairly bristle with reproof, and Wilberforce's to his children spared none of their faults. Robert could be intolerant and sulky, Sam too headstrong and Henry too scatterbrained, but never without having these shortcomings pointed out to them. Zachary Macaulay was even freer with his paternal criticism, but his son soon learnt how to deal with such rebukes, and by the time he was in his teens he was silencing if not convincing Zachary by the ingenuity of his answers. But Wilberforce's children took his comments to heart and reflections of his tone can be seen in their correspondence with each other.

He was eagerly on the watch for symptoms of 'the great change' in his children, the sign that they were becoming truly religious. He expected religion to come to them by growth from within, not in a flash of revelation. He compared the way he watched for the great change to a gardener walking up 'again and again to examine his fruit trees and see if his peaches are set; if they are swelling and becoming larger, finally if they are becoming ripe and rosy'.[27]

His letters to them, if serious, were overflowing with affection. Such love and such high expectations must sometimes have been daunting. 'Oh when I think of our name—what is expected from us and what religious advantages we have had—I tremble,' Lizzy wrote to Robert Isaac.

Barbara's letters to the children were as full of religious promptings as her husband's and even longer. Her concern over her children's souls expresses itself more shrilly than his; there is a note of incipient hysteria in many of her letters. She writes with the sort of gloom that might be expected of one of the 'professors' denounced by Marianne Thornton. Comparing her letters with Wilberforce's one feels that though they are similar in many ways, he was trying to ensure their entry into Heaven, she to rescue them from Hell. She certainly made a practice of expecting the worst. She was haunted by visions not only of Hell but also of death, particularly after Barbara, their eldest daughter, had died in 1821. Wilberforce shared her nightmares of their children dying before they had experienced 'the great change', but he was wise enough never to let these thoughts obtrude. He dashed them down instead in a 'book of private thoughts'[28] which he kept as a safety valve and marked 'For dearest B's perusal only'. 'I have been terrified by witnessing the death of good men's children while yet young I fear in a most alarming state, and the children God knoweth of better men than I am. . . . Alas! Alas! how deeply do I feel my own wretched incompetence as a parent in all particulars.'[29]

Barbara, unable to divert her worries in this way, wrote her children letters which contained not only doom-ridden religious passages but also warnings against the perils that beset their lives, skating on thin ice, eating raisins which 'are particularly clogging to the bowels', crossing the Channel during the Equinox, foreign cooking and other hazards. She continued to fret about such matters throughout her life and pestered her adult sons about going without overcoats, coughs, colds and rheumatism. She nagged poor Wilberforce about his appetite and forced him to eat until he had the dreaded feeling of being 'overloaded' which meant misery the next day. At times the children found her exasperating. Robert, more mature than his brothers and less able to see the funny side of her letters, was most often annoyed, but his self-control was strong. Barbara to him was always 'my dear mother' even when 'she used often to try me exceedingly'. Sam was more philosophical. He wrote to Wilberforce from Oxford: 'Tell dear Mama that my rooms are really very warm and comfortable, although I fear I shall hardly persuade her that they really are so.'[30] It is often more difficult for daughters to get on with their mothers and the Wilberforce family was no exception to this rule. Wilberforce once had to take Lizzy to task.

'It has often given me no little pain my dearest Lizzy,' he wrote, 'to witness little altercations between you and your mother, little rather in the occasions on which they arise, than in the real intrinsic importance of them. For I should not deal honestly with you if I did not state to you my real opinion, that they ought to be regarded as very serious blemishes in a religious character. Granting that there may be faults on both sides, I cannot forget a saying common among them, that it is the second blow that makes the battle. This applies full as accurately to the contest of the tongue as to any others. And you will not I am sure deny that the Obligation to abstain from any language that may tend to augment, or rather to keep up the irritation must press more strongly on you than on your Mother. I have often been strongly impressed by the Consideration that if any fellow creature happens to be present before whom you would be sorry to exhibit anything of the kind I allude to, you can abstain from it without any apparent difficulty; and therefore—but I need not draw an inference which I am sure will readily suggest itself to your own mind. Neither need I enlarge on the various motives which should prompt you to strive against an infirmity which you cannot but know to be wrong.'[31]

Such squabbles were rare. It was a happy family. Wilberforce never allowed piety to lapse into gloom, although one feels that Barbara might have, had she been left alone. Parents, he declared in his diary, 'Should labour to make religion as congenial as possible'. This was not only the sensible but also the right attitude. The Bible abounded with exhortations to joy and rejoicing in the knowledge of God. When a father sets his heart on his sons attaining some particular achievement in life, he is almost always disappointed. Wilberforce was not. His dearest dream, he often said, was that his sons should become clergymen and serve God, and three out of four of them did; as a bonus his favourite daughter married a clergyman.

William was his only failure and it soon became apparent that he was not cut out for the cloth. 'Oh my heart is quite sick about William', Wilberforce wrote in 1816, 'and that while there are some good traits, there should be such sad qualities. Oh how much I see the effects of our own indulgence, selfishness in one form or another his grand vice.'[32] William went up to Trinity College, Cambridge at the end of 1817, where he soon acquired expensive habits. Mr. Newsome has disinterred what followed from the pages of Wilberforce's diary.[33] In January 1819 Wilberforce complains: 'Wm buying another horse for 60 guineas and not behaving well about it tho' I most honourably to him. . . . Alas poor Wm sad work—I must draw in my expenditure some way or another.'[34] Extravagance was not his only vice. On March 15 Wilberforce wrote: 'A letter from H. Venn to-day strongly of opinion poor William should be taken from College, I fear rightly, on the ground that he won't read and therefore will be licentious and corrupted in mind as well as practice.'[35] Wilberforce was for once provoked into acting the part of the stern father. 'He took it all with good-humoured submission,' he wrote to Lady Olivia Sparrow. 'I stopped his allowance and yet he owned he could not say I had used him harshly, or that he could have expected anything different. He is now reading and going on well in all respects.'[36] But not for long; on March 28 Wilberforce wrote this intriguing entry in his diary:

'But the *grand* grief and shame is this sad business of poor Wm. His crime this last time has every aggravation. At the very moment of Blundell's body lying in his Rooms and his funeral to be the next day. To have been led into conviviality on a Sunday eve, to have been so drunk as to be beastly in a piously disposed friend's room and to have refused the hint of 2 friends . . . and Venn to spend the Sunday evening with him, alleging he wished to be alone; God grant this may have been at the time answered sincerely. Alas, alas! Yet I cannot abandon my trust in the promises of God.'

After this mysterious orgy William was removed from Cambridge and sent to study law under the supervision of John Owen, the secretary of the Bible Society. In January 1820 he married Owen's daughter, Mary, and a respectable future seemed assured.

CHAPTER XXVI

A SPLENDID ERROR

THE retreat of the French armies brought many foreigners to London, among whom was a woman Wilberforce may have met on his first trip abroad. She was anxious to renew the acquaintance. When Wilberforce and Pitt had made their tour of France, Necker, the French Prime Minister, had hinted at a match between the latter and his daughter. This daughter was now a famous figure in her own right.

At the beginning of 1814 Mme de Staël was in London, where she attended a great meeting in the Freemasons' Hall in aid of the German sufferers. She wrote of the occasion in her *Considérations sur la Révolution Française*: 'Mr. Wilberforce, the most loved and most highly regarded man in all England, could scarcely make himself heard, such was the applause that drowned his voice.'[1] She was a supporter of Abolition and determined now to meet its leader. She knew him to be an elusive quarry for any hostess and laid her traps with care. Wilberforce was first told by Sir Samuel Romilly that Mme de Staël wished to meet him more than any other man. The Duke of Gloucester then 'made me by her express desire fix a day for meeting her at dinner, chez lui'. There was no avoiding an open invitation to dinner from the one member of the Royal Family who supported Abolition, and Wilberforce, with his schizophrenic views on society, seems rather pleased to have been trapped. 'This is mere vanity, and perhaps curiosity,' he wrote after accepting the invitation, 'and I felt my vanity a little rising too on the occasion.'[2] Mme de Staël sent him a message that she was more religious than he realised, and he resolved to read her book *L'Allemagne* before meeting her 'in order not to excite her prejudices'.

On February 19 they met at the Duke of Gloucester's. Mme de Staël was effusive in her praise of Abolition; all Europe, she declared, shared her admiration for him, and she 'almost asked' him for copies of his books; she also invited him to two dinner parties, the first with the ubiquitous 'poet Rogers', the second with his old Abolitionist friends Harrowby and Mackintosh. Wilberforce was overwhelmed by all this attention and could think of no convincing excuse, but he soon had second thoughts.

353

'This would lead to an endless round of dinners,' he lamented, 'but it suits neither my mind or body. . . . I greatly doubt about the doing any good by dinings-out. . . . Oh how sad, that after trying to lead a Christian life for twenty-eight years, I should be at all staggered by worldly company —Mme de Staël, etc.'[3] He cancelled the first engagement and said that he would come in after dinner for the second, but when the time came he did not go at all. He was not to escape so easily. More invitations followed, he was asked to name the party and the day, and he finally found himself hoist, most astutely, with his own petard. His diary for March 4 reads '. . . Much unpleasant doubting what I ought to do about Mme de Staël. Lady S tells me that there has been much discussion whether I should go, and wagers laid; but Mme de Staël said she was sure I should come, because I had said I would.'

There was no resisting this appeal. Wilberforce went and enjoyed himself enormously, as perhaps he had dreaded. 'A cheerful, pleasant dinner,' he wrote in his diary. 'She talking of the final cause of creation— not utility but beauty—did not like Paley—wrote about Rousseau at fifteen, and thought differently at fifty. Evening, assembly, but I came away at half past eleven. A brilliant assembly of rank and talent.'[4]

The next day remorse set in. 'The whole scene', he wrote, 'was intoxicating even to me. The fever arising from it is not yet gone off. How dangerous then must such scenes be to young people in the hey-day of youth, and life, and spirits! . . . I am sure I durst not often venture into these scenes.' It would be hard to find a more perfect illustration of Lord Melbourne's comment on Wilberforce's diary: 'Perpetually vexing himself because he amused himself too well.'[5]

Nothing of this mood can have been in evidence the night before. 'Mr. Wilberforce', his hostess told Sir James Mackintosh, 'is the best converser I have met with in this country. I have always heard that he was the most religious, but I now find that he is the wittiest man in England.'[6] This little episode has the charm so often shared by encounters between prominent people from very different worlds. It also proved more useful than Wilberforce could have expected, for Mme de Staël later became one of his closest allies in the battle to end the French Slave Trade, and translated his works into French.

Four years after their meeting Wilberforce settled down to read her books. He wrote to Henry Bankes: 'I must say I am extremely struck with it; I had no idea she possessed so much sound political judgement, combined with considerable shrewdness in discernment of the characteristic traits of human nature in different classes and individuals. How clever are her remarks on the courtier minister, and how skilfully she slides over the weaker parts of her father's character. How much better and more true are her principles than those of our modern factious reformers.'[7]

Mme de Staël may never have understood Wilberforce's reluctance to meet her. She would certainly have considered herself to be a religious woman and would have been astonished to find that the Evangelicals disagreed on this point. While admitting her literary genius and good feelings, they argued that her religion was of a very questionable sort 'or rather a non-entity', in that it did not pervade her whole life. Hannah More, who admired her greatly, summed up these feelings in a letter to Wilberforce: 'In short she appears to me to be a splendid error.'[8]

*

Napoleon's return to power threw Wilberforce into confusion. On April 27, 1815 Whitbread introduced a motion in the Commons that a particular family was no bar to peace. Wilberforce was torn between a desire for peace and a sense of obligation to the Allies. 'I spoke ill,' he wrote in his diary, 'because indecisively as indeed I felt in one sense; for my own judgement would be for treating with Buonaparte if we were free: but we are so connected with the Allies, that we could not honestly separate from them, as agreeing to Whitbread's motion would substantially have been. Tierney very coarse and caustic. Whitbread ill-natured about my ingratitude for Abolition services. I could not reply, and better I should not; for alas, I was angry.'[9] His dislike of war was united to a distrust of the Government's optimism. Might they not be deceived, he asked, even as Pitt had so often been? He recognised the blessings for Europe 'if Buonaparte could be unhorsed', but he would have been more enthusiastic had the Bourbons been less strong Catholics. The nature of Louis XVIII's departure from England did nothing to reassure him. 'How sad it is,' he wrote in his journal, 'that Louis the Eighteenth should set out for France on this day, and thereby both himself spend Sunday in travelling, and keep numbers of others from public worship! . . . What folly! Is this the Roman Catholic religion? Is it philosophical enlargement of mind, alas!'[10]

Marshal Blücher did not forget Wilberforce's efforts on behalf of the suffering Prussians. After the battle of Waterloo he sent his aide-de-camp with dispatches for the Prince Regent. 'Did Marshal Blücher,' the Prince asked, 'give you any other charge?' 'Yes, sir, he charged me to acquaint Mr. Wilberforce with all that had passed.' 'Go to him yourself then by all means, you will be delighted with him.' Blücher wrote to the committee for the relief of his countrymen: 'I have fought two pitched battles, five engagements, masked three fortresses, taken two; but I have lost 22,000 men. Will the people of England be satisfied with me now? Desire Mr. Wilberforce to bestir himself.'[11] He duly did so, both for the Prussians and for a more local charity, a fund for the dependants of the dead and wounded of the 1st Life Guards, who were quartered at Knightsbridge.

Blücher later attributed the outstanding generosity of the English people towards his soldiers to three causes: the Duke of Wellington's description of their valour at Waterloo; the Prince Regent's command that collections should be made for them in all churches, and the exertions of Wilberforce on their behalf.[12]

Once the summer session was over he left on his usual holiday in the country, visiting the West before settling at Brighton, where he found a mountainous correspondence awaiting him. 'I cannot even read during the day all the letters which the morning's post has heaped upon me.'[13] He told Bankes that he would give him precedence 'over many business correspondents, who are clamouring around me, happily in dumb show, for otherwise no dog-kennel would ever give a more dissonant chorus of discordant sounds than my pro tempore study at Brighton'.[14] He found himself, to his distress, with little time to read and none to write.

His problems became worse when the Prince Regent and his Court descended on Brighton. He was inevitably summoned to the Pavilion, where he renewed his acquaintance with the Prince and the Duke of Clarence. One would have thought that Wilberforce could have found no common ground with one of the foremost rakes of his age, but when they met they seem to have got on well enough. Wilberforce could be staggeringly naïve at times and was always ready to give anyone the benefit of any moral doubt. After his first appearance in the Pavilion he wrote in his diary: 'Prince showed he had read Cobbett. Spoke strongly of the blasphemy of his late papers, and most justly.'

The next day Wilberforce returned to the Pavilion. 'The Prince came up to me and reminded me of my singing at the Duchess of Devonshire's ball in 1782, of the particular song, and of our then first knowing each other.' 'We are both much altered since, sir,' he replied. 'Yes,' said the Prince, 'the time which has gone by must have made a great alteration in us.' 'Something better than that too, I trust, sir.'[15] Some of the Court had been gossiping to the effect that Wilberforce would not dine at the Pavilion because of the looseness of the talk there. The Prince invited him to dine the following day and added 'that I should hear nothing in his house to give me pain'. Nor did he. He returned to the Pavilion often and found the Prince 'quite the English gentleman at the head of his own table'.

But the routine at the Pavilion ate into Wilberforce's precious time. He wrote to Hannah More: 'It is sad work. Dinner comes on table at six, at nine the dinner party goes into the other rooms, in one of which is music, in another cards, in others, and a long gallery 160 feet long, walking about, till about quarter or half-past twelve, and then, on the Prince's retiring, all of us depart. But really it is a large part of existence, from six to half-past twelve daily, or rather nightly.'[16]

When the Prince discovered that it was inconvenient for Wilberforce to attend the Pavilion so often he begged him 'in the handsomest way possible' to come when he wished and to suit his own convenience. He could, as Professor Coupland has pointed out, behave at times like the first gentleman of Europe. But Wilberforce left Brighton without regrets. 'Oh how thankful I am,' he reflected, 'that my wife is not one of the Pavilion-monger ladies, about to bring out her daughters!' And 'the Pavilion-going I find injurious even to myself; how much more so must it be to young people, especially young handsome women'.[17]

CHAPTER XXVII

THE BLEAK YEARS

THE French wars brought great hardships to England. Their cost swallowed up all the funds that should have been used for other purposes and it remains one of the very few periods when the standard of living in the country actually fell. In addition to all the normal sufferings and expenses of war, England had to endure a series of bad harvests. The Continental System cut her off from all her normal trade routes and food became ruinously expensive. These sacrifices were accepted so long as she lived under the menace of French invasion, but once this cloud was lifted she expected better things, and when they failed to come the pent-up grievances of the country overflowed. Liverpool's Government had only one answer to popular discontent, repression. The period from Waterloo until the economic recovery of 1820 was one of the most bitter in British history. No government has ever been more vilified than Liverpool's, nor any ministers so savaged as the two architects of its policy, Lords Sidmouth and Castlereagh.

The harvest of 1816 was disastrous. In August the price of corn rose past the 80/– at which the new Corn Laws allowed imports. In December it was 103/–. The bad harvest was accompanied by an industrial recession, for the continental countries were reviving their own industries and the markets for British manufacturers were greatly contracted. As a result wages and employment fell while the price of food remained at an inflated level. A spasm of rage and despair seized the workers. There were outbreaks of Luddism and disturbances throughout the country.

So far the pattern was sickeningly familiar; bad harvests and depression led to misery among the poor, which could only express itself in a series of futile protests against authority. Wilberforce and his friends set out to relieve the suffering in their usual way. During the economic crisis of 1812 they had founded the Association for the Relief of the Manufacturing and Labouring Poor. They now attempted to revive this society and they did so under the most august patronage. A great public meeting was called at the London Tavern on July 29, 1816. The Duke of York was in the chair and six resolutions were put to the meeting by the Duke of Kent, the Duke of Cambridge, the Archbishop of Canterbury, the Duke of Rutland, Lord Manvers, and the Bishop of London. But charity was no longer to be accepted with unquestioning gratitude. Lord Cochrane was in the audience, and this radical, embittered naval genius took charge of opposition to the platform, disrupted the proceedings and caused the Royal Dukes to leave amidst a storm of hisses.

The agitators denounced the Evangelicals' good works but they also copied their tactics. Hampden Clubs took the place of local branches of the Evangelical societies and played the same rôle in flooding Parliament with petitions. As their cause gained mass support their demands and leaders became more extreme. At first they had been led by Sir Francis Burdett and that veteran of protest, Major Cartwright. Burdett and Cartwright demanded equal constituencies, annual elections and household suffrage; by parliamentary standards they were extremists but they were not revolutionaries. The same could not be said for some of their successors. William Cobbett became the publicist of the movement; he conceived the idea of avoiding stamp duty on his *Political Register* by following the regular edition with a popular issue which cost only 2d and which came to be known as 'Twopenny Trash'. Cobbett was a journalist of genius; his language was inflammatory, and he loathed Wilberforce above all his many enemies, but he never incited the people to violence. Before he issued his cheap editions Cobbett had followed the line laid down by Burdett; now he took on more extreme views, those of the new leader of the radicals, Henry 'Orator' Hunt.

On November 15, 1816 Hunt spoke at a great open-air meeting in Spa Fields. He was accompanied by attendants with a cap of liberty on the end of a pike and a tricolour flag, green, white and red, the colours of the future British Republic. Hunt's speech was fiery but the meeting went off quietly enough; most of the enormous crowd signed a petition to the Prince Regent and deputed Burdett and Hunt to convey it. Burdett wisely declined the honour, but Hunt went and was twice turned away. When the meeting reassembled on December 2 the crowd was even larger and more excited than before. Hunt had replaced Burdett as the radicals' leader because his views were more extreme; he was now himself replaced for the same reason. Before Hunt arrived a group of out-and-out revolutionaries held a meeting on their own in a corner of the field. They then marched into the City, murdering a gunsmith on their way, and were finally dispersed by a force raised by the Lord Mayor.

As a riot the meeting at Spa Fields was not very serious, nor did it ever seem likely to topple the existing social order. There had been a certain amount of looting, disorder had prevailed for a day and one wretched gunsmith had been murdered. But in the sensitive atmosphere of 1816, observers recognised the trappings of revolution. The cap of liberty and the tricolour flag revived memories of the Terror in those who had hoped that such things had passed away for ever. At the opening of Parliament in January 1817, these gloomy forebodings seemed to be confirmed when the Prince Regent was hissed on his return to the Palace. Two panes of glass on his coach were pierced by a pellet or a stone, no one knew which. As in 1795, when George III had suffered a similar indignity, the Cabinet responded by tightening up the law.

A secret committee was appointed to look into the matter with Wilberforce as one of its members. Its report gave details of a plot to seize the Bank and the Tower, incite the Army to mutiny and carry out a revolution by force of arms. Lord Castlereagh then introduced four Bills into the Commons. Two of these were unexceptionable.* Another temporarily suspended Habeas Corpus, while the last restored severe restrictions upon the rights of public meetings. The Habeas Corpus measure aroused some opposition, but all four Bills passed easily into law. They were completely successful. The Opposition were already in a state of disarray. The Whigs felt that the violence of the radicals had robbed them of political victory, the radicals felt the same of the revolutionaries, and the revolutionaries were at loggerheads with one another. Cobbett, hounded by the Government for Stamp Duty on back numbers of the *Register*, quarrelled with Hunt and left for America, where in the absence of his enemies he found paradise: '. . . A hundred brace of wood-cocks a day—think of that! . . . And never to see the hang-dog face of a tax-gatherer. Think of that! No Alien Acts here. No long-sworded and whiskered Captains. No Judges escorted from town to town and sitting under the guard of dragoons. No packed juries of tenants. No Crosses. . . . No Bolton Fletchers. No hangings and rippings up. . . . No Castleses and Olivers. No Stewarts and Perries. No Cannings, Liverpools, Castlereaghs, Eldons, Ellenboroughs or Sidmouths. . . . No squeaking Wynnes. No Wilberforces. Think of *that*! No Wilberforces!'[1]

The radicals who remained found conditions less idyllic. Hunt called more meetings in Spa Fields, but few answered his summons. A march of protest by the 'Blanketeers' from Lancashire to London broke up in Staffordshire. After the passing of the Seditious Meetings Bill the radicals were driven underground and left few means other than revolution to express their views. A second and more violent march was organised, the conspirators thought secretly, but the authorities knew of their plans and arrested the ringleaders. On the strength of this plot to overthrow the Government Habeas Corpus was again suspended.

The conspirators were not alone in suffering from the new measures. Any sort of society became suspect. The Cambridge Union found itself

* They revived old laws for the protection of the monarch and against inciting mutiny.

obliged to suspend its meetings because its debates sometimes dealt with political questions. The Literary Society of Manchester, the Academical Society of Oxford, the City Philosophical Society of London—all met the same fate. A magistrate prevented a mineralogical society from meeting on the grounds that the study of mineralogy could lead to atheism.[2]

Sanity and a sense of shame were soon restored; the second suspension of Habeas Corpus had provoked more opposition than the first and London juries had displayed magnificent independence in refusing to convict rioters. On June 14, 1817 they were vindicated, for on that day the *Leeds Mercury* revealed that the conspiracy to march on London had been fomented by a man called Oliver, who posed as a member of the London political clubs, but was, in fact, an agent provocateur of Lord Sidmouth's. Oliver had not merely acted the part of the spy, to which no reasonable objection could be sustained, he had actively encouraged the conspirators to revolt in order to increase his reward when he betrayed them. Wilberforce's old opponent Lord Fitzwilliam endorsed the *Mercury*'s report, and a motion was made urging the House to investigate Oliver's activities. This revelation was followed by a series of acquittals of rioters and the Habeas Corpus Suspension Act was repealed when Parliament reassembled. If the Oliver scandal calmed the fears of the upper classes, the good harvest and economic recovery of 1817 removed the grievances of the workers. The speed with which normal life was resumed showed very clearly that it was poverty not political frustration which had caused the troubles and prosperity rather than coercion which had ended them.

But the prosperity of 1818 was a false start, and the frenzied business activity of that year was followed by another recession, although less serious and more localised than the last, only the textile industry being badly affected. Reductions of wages in the north were followed by strikes and riots, which, when they failed to achieve economic redress, became political in their ends. Parliamentary reform and the repeal of the Corn Laws* were their objectives and petitions to this effect flooded into Parliament. In July a mass meeting at Birmingham elected its own 'representative' and the orderly way in which this election was conducted did nothing to reassure the Government. Parliament had adjourned for the summer recess so the Coercion Laws could not be re-enacted, but Lord Sidmouth instructed the Lords-Lieutenant to take every step necessary to preserve order and to keep the yeomanry prepared for disturbances.

A great demonstration in favour of Reform was arranged in Manchester for August 16, and was to be attended by Hunt. The day of the meeting was awaited with eager anxiety, for it was the first since Sidmouth's

* In 1816–17 the price of wheat had fluctuated from 103/- to 152/6 but in 1819 it remained around 80/-, a level which seemed to indicate that the laws were beginning to work as intended.

proclamation. An enormous crowd gathered from neighbouring towns and when Henry Hunt arrived in his carriage he found an audience of 60,000 congregated on St. Peter's Fields. The crowd was unarmed and under perfect control; it had marched in with flags flying and drums beating. But when Hunt rose to speak a troop of cavalry pushed their way through to arrest him. They were hemmed in by the crowd and drew their sabres. A troop of hussars charged to their assistance, the crowd panicked and eleven people were killed, including two women, and several hundred wounded. In a few minutes St. Peter's Field was empty. Where a moment before the great meeting in favour of reform had gathered, the field was now occupied only by discarded revolutionary banners, the cavalry and the corpses of the dead.

The massacre at St. Peter's Field scandalised the country, reunited the radicals and restored respectability to their cause. Lord Fitzwilliam forfeited his Lord-Lieutenancy by taking the chair at a meeting of protest. Hunt, Burdett and Cartwright were reconciled, while Cobbett returned from America with melodramatic fanfare, bringing with him, to Byron's derision, the ashes of Thomas Paine.

> In digging up your bones, Tom Paine;
> Will Cobbett has done well:
> You visit him on earth again,
> He'll visit you in hell.

The radicals invented a name for the massacre which gave it the greatest possible emotional appeal. In bitter mockery they compared Wellington's victory over the French with Sidmouth's over his own countrymen and called it Peterloo. When Hunt entered London he was greeted by a crowd of 200,000 supporters. Mass meetings of protest were held throughout the north, and their very peacefulness and discipline were seen as signs of another conspiracy. The agitators could do no right; if they were violent they were clearly trying to overthrow the Government by force, if not they must be acting under some secret leadership.

The Government did nothing to improve matters. Without waiting for any details Lord Sidmouth sent a message of congratulation to the Manchester magistrates. The Six Acts were then passed through Parliament. Three of these Acts were reasonable enough: private military exercises were forbidden, delays in bringing cases to court removed and warrants made available for the search of arms. Other Acts made blasphemous and seditious literature liable to seizure and extended the Stamp Act to papers which had previously escaped it. The most controversial Act was that controlling public meetings. With certain exceptions it became an offence for anyone to attend a meeting who was not a resident of the parish in which it was held. While some control of the unlimited right of meetings may have been in the interest of public safety, such restrictions were certainly excessive. Soon after the Six Acts, much amended by the Whigs, were passed, a conspiracy to assassinate the entire Cabinet was discovered. This lunatic plot had been fostered by Lord Sidmouth's agents provocateurs, but it seemed to a horrified nation to have justified the severity of the Six Acts. After 1820 agitation died away; as in 1818 it did not survive a return of prosperity.

The rôle played by Wilberforce during these years, together with his support of Pitt's repressive policy, had led to bitter contrasts between his support for liberty abroad and his use of the moral authority he gained by doing so to grind it down in England. To a radical of his own time the spectacle of Wilberforce behaving in this way was more offensive than that of Castlereagh, Sidmouth, Eldon or Liverpool, from whom nothing better could be expected.

When he was appointed to the Secret Committee in February 1817, Wilberforce wrote: 'We are not to divulge; but this much I may say, though do not let it be repeated out of doors, that the seizing of the ringleaders on Sunday last prevented bloodshed from the Spa Fields mob on Monday. Hunt seems a foolish, mischief-making fellow but no conspirator, though the tool of worse and deeper villains. Cobbett is the most pernicious of all; but God will bless and keep us, I fear not, and it is highly gratifying that all the truly religious classes have nothing to do with the seditious proceedings. The blasphemous songs and papers of the seditious will disgust all who have any religion or any decency.'[3] This, of course, was a strong element in his loathing of the agitators. Seditious publications were bad enough but blasphemy was utterly beyond the pale. The radicals were still influenced by France and their agitation contained much atheism which gained them many enemies and no allies. The factory workers were desperate for employment under decent conditions, perhaps mildly in favour of parliamentary reform and wholly uninterested in atheist propaganda. The religious part of the country, which could be sympathetic to the first two objectives, was repelled by the last. By combining sedition and atheism the agitators played into the Government's hands, for bills to ban seditious and blasphemous publications would be supported by the religious community.

Wilberforce was prevented from attending the debate on the suspension of Habeas Corpus by a sudden illness. He wrote to Simeon, the Cambridge Evangelist, 'It has been a very great mortification to me, or rather it would be, were it not for the reflection that all is in higher hands, that I cannot attend the House to support the measures which have been taken, and are still in progress, for preserving the public peace. I assure you that in my judgement they are absolutely needed if we would not incur the danger of bloodshed and conflagration.'[4] But he hazarded in his diary:

'Perhaps, however, my not being able to attend the House, was kindly intended by Providence to prevent my needlessly differing from some who are friendly to my object of West India Reform.'[5] These quotations show how his mind had hardened since his attendance on the Secret Committee less than a month before when he had written to Macaulay, 'You and I agree in esteeming it to be the duty of every good subject to support government when he can. But then I own I feel that to draw on ourselves the ill-will, and worse than neutrality, of opposition on all West Indian questions, when we cannot have government as our friends, is to act in a way, which though it might become our duty if the ship were in danger of going down, is not to be expected from us unless in such critical circumstances. I have again and again been silent when I should have spoken against the democrats and even oppositionists, more especially against party, but for the consciousness that I had to look to the opposition rather than to government, as our supporters in the Registry Bill and West Indian matters.'[6] His new eagerness to speak out in support of the Government is evidence that during the last half of February he had decided the ship was in danger of going down. As soon as he recovered he spoke strongly in favour of the Seditious Meetings Bill. He followed this by a speech supporting the second suspension of Habeas Corpus, a speech which resulted in his famous clash with Burdett.

Speakers on both sides of the House acknowledged that the suspension of Habeas Corpus was an important infringement of the Constitution and one which could be justified only by a grave threat to the rule of law. The second suspension was more serious than the first, for it would continue during the summer recess when Parliament could no longer prevent Ministers from abusing their power. The questions at issue were firstly, did the disturbances in the country justify such a step? Secondly, was it the right step to take? and finally, could the Ministers be trusted to apply their powers without parliamentary control?

Wilberforce took the threat of revolution very seriously. He 'could readily conceive how the lower orders, that valuable portion of the community whose labour was so essential to the social system under which we live, might be tempted by the delusive and wicked principles instilled into their minds to direct their strength to the destruction of the government, and to the overthrow of every civil and religious establishment'.[7] He believed that there was a general spirit of disaffection caused by 'the dangerous political doctrines so actively propagated of late'. As for the danger of abuse 'he could not easily bring himself to apprehend that the noble Lord [Sidmouth] would so far forget the character he had always sustained, as to employ the authority intrusted to him to wicked or oppressive purposes'.[8] It was a choice of evils, but if the Ministers judged the measure to be necessary he must yield to their judgement.

Speakers before Wilberforce had harped on the activities of the spies and agents provocateurs, Castles, Reynolds and Oliver, but he blithely ignored the subject except for quoting Oliver as a reliable source on the organisation of the disaffected in London. His belief in the one-sided evidence heard by the Secret Committee and his faith in the humanity of Lord Sidmouth were equally naïve. One would have thought that Sidmouth's betrayal of Abolition would have left its mark.

But it was Wilberforce's support rather than his arguments which mattered. Nothing could show his importance more clearly than the way in which the Opposition singled out his speech for reply. Romilly addressed him rather like a dear child who had caused pain through no fault of its own,[9] reproaching him both for being credulous about the extent of disaffection and naïve about the harm that could be caused by the Bill. Brougham subjected the findings of the Secret Committee to his caustic wit. The report talked of the agitators having the means to finance a revolution, 'demands which the fortunes of the Dukes of Devonshire and Bedford would be incapable of answering'. He continued:

'This man of inexhaustible wealth was in fact so poor as to be unable to appear on his trial in court in the ordinary dress of the country, but was content to put up with the jacket and trousers of an old sailor. When the managers were arrested, they were found in a miserable garret, two or three in one bed, and in the depth of winter covered only with a single blanket. At least, therefore, if it were true that they had immense funds at their disposal, they had behaved most disinterestedly in appropriating no part of them to their own purposes. The subscriptions of which the first report said so much, amounted in the whole to £1. 2s.; and the whole scheme of summoning the Tower, taking the Bank, and seizing the bridges, was as contemptible in its reality, as the report had endeavoured to make it important in the representation. The cavalry was to consist of horses taken from hackney-coaches at a time of night when there were none in the streets; and the general who was to lead them had been appointed to his command, not so much because he could ride as because from his lameness he could not walk. All the craft in the Thames, like the Tower, was to be captured by a single rebel; and when a few barges had been furnished with one gun each, they were to proceed to the Nore, to capture all the first-rate men of war there stationed for the protection of the river.'[10]

Brougham described Wilberforce's asking the House if it could suppose that such a man as Lord Sidmouth would abuse his powers as being made with 'the simplicity of innocence'. Sir Francis Burdett was less charitable. On the third reading of the Bill he repeatedly referred to Wilberforce as 'the honourable and religious member', a gross breach of parliamentary etiquette.

'He confessed he was astonished at the concurrence in this measure of an honourable and religious gentleman who laid claim to superior piety as it unquestionably was of all others, the most hostile to vital christianity. . . . The honourable and religious gentleman no doubt recollected the denunciation of Jesus against the wicked: "I was hungry and ye gave me no meat; I was thirsty, and ye gave me no drink; I was naked and ye clothed me not; I was sick and in prison, and ye visited me not." How affecting was the last clause of this passage! "I was sick and in prison"; two of the greatest calamities that could befall human nature. But when to that was added, that the sick prisoner was deprived of every other consolation what could be said of those men who not only did not visit him themselves, but would not allow others to do so? . . . . The honourable and religious member was shocked the other day at the description of the Africans chained and carried into slavery. How happened it that the honourable and religious member (Order! order!) was not shocked at Englishmen being taken up under this act and treated like African slaves?'[11]

Wilberforce spoke impromptu in his own defence. After justifying the measures taken by the Government he turned on Burdett and asked, 'How can the honourable member talk thus of those religious principles on which the welfare of the community depends? I would fain believe that he desires as sincerely as I do myself to perpetuate to his country the blessings she enjoys. But if I could be base enough to seek the destruction of those institutions which we both profess to revere, I would tell him what instrument I would choose. I would take a man of great wealth, of patrician family, of personal popularity, aye and of respectable talents, and I am satisfied that such a one, while he scattered abroad the fire brands of sedition under pretence that he went all lengths for the people, would in reality be the best agent in the malevolent purpose of destroying their liberties and happiness.'[12] 'Religion had taught him a lesson on the subject —it had taught him to value the blessings which the country enjoyed, and to hand these down unimpaired to posterity.'[13]

It was the most severe rebuke he had allowed himself to utter since his rout of Courtenay over the prison at Cold Bath Fields, and it is ironic that both should have been in defence of such dubious causes. His diary for June 27 reads: 'B. forced me up in self-defence, and the House sided with me though I forgot what I meant to say.' Other members were more flattering. 'You know Burdett's manner when attacked,' one remembered, 'his head high, his body drawn up. His tall figure as he sat on the upper bench immediately behind was the higher of the two, even when Wilberforce stood up to speak. But when after speaking for a few minutes Wilberforce turned round to address him amidst the cheers of the House, he seemed like a pigmy in the grasp of a giant. I never saw such a display of moral superiority in my life.'[14]

Those who complained of Wilberforce's equivocation must have felt their case proved by his speech during the debate on spies and informers.[15] His diary's account of this debate reads: 'Fazakerley's motion—spoke, and better than usual—avowed openly my abominating the employing of spies and informers altogether, on the grounds of religion and morality. . . . But though I spoke better than usual, what I said not being palatable to either party, I was less than usual encouraged.'[16] The content of his speech would have needed hypnotic eloquence to earn applause from either side. His general denunciation of the use of spies went far beyond the attitude of the Opposition, but he then inexplicably refused to vote for the very moderate Opposition motion, which merely asked for an inquiry into the use of spies and informers to see if they were encouraging as well as reporting conspiracy. No one could be more outraged than Wilberforce when some technicality blocked one of the causes on which he had set his heart. He now voted against an inquiry on the technical grounds that the Secret Committee was not a proper body to hear such evidence.

On March 5 a similar motion was proposed. By this time enough allegations had been made by highly respected members—Bennet, Lord Milton, Lord Stanley, Brougham, Tierney and William Smith—to convince any impartial member that there might be some substance in them, enough at any rate to justify an inquiry for one who, like Wilberforce, considered the use of spies distasteful and unnecessary. But it was clear that he would vote against an inquiry and he did not even intend to speak until stung by taunts of Tierney.

'Surely the other side [the Government] must have been hard pressed indeed for an argument, when they snatched so greedily at a casual and hasty phrase, that the motion was framed to catch the vote of the hon. member for Bramber. It should never be forgotten, too, that the ridicule of this expression came from those who had not scrupled to practise trick after trick to catch the vote of that hon. member—from those who had spared no expense to catch it; not, indeed, to the profit of the hon. member himself (that was out of the question), but to the great loss of the public, whose money had been spent, time after time, in inquiries intended to satisfy the scrupulousness of his conscience. He did not wish to speak disrespectfully of the hon. member for Bramber, and, certainly, there was no individual more capable of giving effective support to ministers and their measures, when he chose to turn out [cheers and laughter]. What his vote would be upon the present occasion it was not, perhaps, easy to prophesy. If he had given a distinct and unequivocal pledge upon any question, he would doubtless redeem it; but here it was impossible to speak from experience, the case was of such rare occurrence: generally, his phraseology was happily adapted to suit either party; and if now and then he lost the balance of his argument, and tended a little to one side he quickly recovered himself, and deviated as much in an opposite direction as would make a fair division of his speech on both sides of the question' [continued cheers].[17]

Wilberforce 'wished not to speak; but at last forced up, and went off, through God's goodness, better than expected. Never did I give a clearer vote; for never would there have been a more long, intricate, complicated, unprofitable inquiry. Tierney gave the last prick, which forced me to rise; although not at all ill-naturedly I am glad to say. Nor was I ill-natured I hope: thank God I did not feel so.'[18]

He was not persuaded to support the motion by Tierney's optimistic manner: 'I have known the right honourable gentleman too long and too well not to know that he always appears most confident when his cause is desperate.'[19] The present motion was loose and indefinite and there was no reliable witness to Oliver's misdeeds. 'He felt convinced, that if the strictest investigation were to take place, all parties would come out of it with disgrace [a laugh]. His right hon. friend who spoke last, and himself were old soldiers in parliamentary warfare, and he certainly felt no anger at any observations which had dropped from him that night, because he felt that his right hon. friend had done no more than might be expected from him as leader of the opposition. But he would do what he conceived to be his duty, whatever might be the opinions, or whatever the sneers of his right hon. friend. As to the question more immediately before the House, if his hon. friend behind him [Mr. Bennet] or any hon. gentleman would pledge himself to bring forward any credible witness, who would prove that Oliver, or any other person, had instigated others to commit treason, he, for one, would give his vote for an instruction to the attorney-general to prosecute such a wretch. That he could be prosecuted he had no doubt; for on the common principle of our law, that there was no evil without a remedy, there must be a remedy for so monstrous an evil. Let such a motion be made, and he hereby pledged himself to support it.'[20]

He then launched into a denunciation of the system of using spies. 'The hired spy,' he declared, 'from anxiety to please his employer and to do himself credit would irritate instead of appeasing discontent, and would make a plot if he did not find one.'[21] This was precisely the contention of the opposition, but he then went on to say 'There was no man whose nature was more abhorrent from the employment of such agents than the noble Secretary of State for the home department.' He could hardly have provided a better example of the balancing act of which Tierney had complained. But he finished his speech with a dignified and effective defence.

'One word more, though on a subject on which it would not be pleasant for him to speak: he would ask, to what length must party feeling have reached in that House, when it was asserted, that because a person was not systematically opposed to every motion of government he could not form an honest opinion on any subject presented to him in Parliament [Cries of No! no! from the Opposition]. Well, if gentlemen were anxious to disclaim such an injustice, he hoped that himself and an hon. friend of his would in future be treated with somewhat more respect. . . . Let a definite motion be made and he would support it; that the present motion was of a different character was evident from the extraneous matter into which an acute and dear friend of his [William Smith] [a laugh] had wandered. He did not exactly know what that laugh meant, but if it was meant for his hon. friend, never was a laugh more misapplied, for he was convinced that his hon. friend had never acted in that House except from the most sincere motives of good to his country. The right hon. gentleman who had spoken last had amused the House a good deal by allusions to the chase, and by descanting on starting game. He could compare the present motion, and some others, like it, to nothing else than a pack of hounds in full cry, scouring the fields, and starting a hare in every corner [a laugh]. They might, so far as he was concerned, have the sport all to themselves, for he would not pretend to keep up with them.'[22]

At first sight Wilberforce's attitude was plausible. No hard evidence had been offered to prove that Oliver had incited others to treasonable acts, and it seemed that Oliver had proposed himself to the Government with the claim that he had discovered a conspiracy. Wilberforce, while condemning the Government for accepting his services, did not agree either that he was necessarily an agent provocateur or that, if he was, the Government knew of this side of his activities. But the arguments were superficial. If there had been convincing evidence that the Government had used Oliver as an agent provocateur, it would have stood condemned without an inquiry. In any case Oliver had done his work among the disaffected and witnesses against him would have had to come from their numbers. Whether such witnesses would have been 'credible' in Wilberforce's eyes is uncertain, but some radicals had been mentioned in speeches from the Opposition who had withstood Oliver's incitements and who should have made more satisfactory witnesses than, for example, those in the case of the Duke of York.

The fact that Wilberforce was unmoved by the horror felt by men like Romilly and Bennet, whose integrity he did respect, is as inexplicable as his continued faith in Lord Sidmouth. He did not feel, as in the Habeas Corpus debate, that the threat to the Constitution justified a temporary infringement of liberty. On the contrary he found it 'as unnecessary and impolitic as it was contrary to all the best principles of moral and religious justice, to employ the arts of depraved and mercenary falsehood for the discovery of truth'. His dislike of spies was as strong as anyone's and his inconsistency in opposing the motion was pointed out by the next two speakers. One can only agree with Mr. Philips, the framer of the motion, when he 'thought it extraordinary that the difficulty or extent of any inquiry should thus be urged as a reason for not entering into it'.[23] If Oliver had been a black quisling employed by the planters to stir up revolts in the West Indies and thus thwart the cause of freedom, Wilberforce would have hounded him down whatever the difficulties, for when his heart was set on an object like Abolition, Emancipation or the Indian Missions, complications existed only to be conquered. He disliked the use of spies, but not enough to break with the Government over the issue when the evidence was uncertain. If he had believed that Oliver was an agent provocateur as well as a spy he would have been forced to vote with the Opposition.

His performance in the debate on Peterloo was even less satisfactory. He had been increasingly concerned about unrest in the country, a condition which tragically he connected with blasphemy. His correspondents in the manufacturing districts shared his gloom and painted conditions in their areas in lurid colours. Morritt sent him a dismal account of affairs in Yorkshire: 'The West Riding of our country is in an alarming fermentation—the lower orders too generally corrupted, and the merchants and higher manufacturers scarcely daring to resist the tide of blasphemy and sedition.'[24] He was most concerned about this subject and wrote asking a friend in Sheffield 'to give me all the information you can concerning the state of mind of your lower orders'.[25] He was pressing the Attorney-General to bring forward the trial of the radical Carlile for blasphemy. 'Time ought to have been found for trying such a delinquent,' he wrote to Bankes. 'I grieve to hear that his poison, and that of such other venomous beings, is propagated extensively, and greedily sucked in by the lower orders in our manufacturing districts.'[26] He heard of pike drills at dead of night in Leicester. Another informant came back from Manchester with an account of Peterloo which convinced him that the magistrates 'have been unjust to themselves in not publishing what may be called their *case*'.[27]

His attitude in this crisis was very different to that of 1817. 'It is really true,' he wrote to Ralph Creyke, 'that seldom has a boy returned on a black Monday with more reluctance than I to St. Stephen's. . . . I dare not be too confident that we may not witness scenes of something nearer to civil war, than this land has exhibited since 1646, and if it should come to such extremities, the bitterness and cruelty with which the contest would be carried on, would be far greater than in that sad struggle.'[28] He took a less compromising line than in the earlier debates; to launch a parliamentary inquiry into the Peterloo massacre would be to sanction 'the proceedings of those bad men, who wished to produce anarchy and confusion, it would be the means of producing more discord and bloodshed than any other measure that could be devised'.[29] 'He insisted that the great body of the nation, at least the great body of the thinking part of it, approved of the steps the magistrates of Manchester had taken and would be dissatisfied if inquiry at the bar were instituted.'[30] He later complained[31] that this speech had been incorrectly reported and that he had sought neither to defend nor attack the magistrates, but simply to deny the need for a parliamentary inquiry. It seems at first sight that his attitude was indefensible, that if there was doubt about the correctness of the magistrates' action, this very doubt made an inquiry necessary. But Wilberforce was not alone in wanting the matter forgotten. Buxton took a far more severe view of the magistrates' conduct—'nothing has shaken my convictions,' he wrote to Gurney, 'that the Magistrates, Ministers, and all, have done exceedingly wrong';[32] but Buxton, too, voted against an inquiry. There was a feeling expressed in its bluntest form by Wellington that unless magistrates were supported now they would never stand firm again.[33]

Wilberforce followed his speech on Peterloo with unflinching support of the Six Acts.[34] He gave this support through a sense of duty rather than a general desire to support the Government. In fact, he was more anxious at this time to please the Opposition as he counted on their support for his slavery campaign. That he did not forfeit this support can be attributed partly to the fact that the Opposition, while delighted to attack and amend the Six Acts, realised that, had they been in office, they would have had to pass some sort of coercive measures themselves.[35]

There was one more incident which, although it took place later, can most conveniently be considered together with the repressive measures of 1816–20.

Wilberforce had founded the Proclamation Society long before in 1787; in 1802 it had been succeeded by the Society for the Suppression of Vice. Although meddlesome, sometimes obnoxious and often resented, this Society continued quietly with its work, prosecuting the purveyors of obscene, blasphemous and republican literature, until the post-war depression, when it found an enemy worth the name. During the years 1816 and 1819 there was a spate of blasphemous and seditious publications, with which the Society could barely keep pace. *Carlile's Political Register*, owned and edited by Richard Carlile, was one of the most influential of the republican newspapers, and as a sideline to these journalistic activities Carlile became a bookseller, reprinting, among other provocative works, Paine's *Age of Reason*. He soon found himself in trouble with the law, but he was a man of great courage and sincerity; in spite of frequent prison sentences he persisted in publishing his literature.

The outbreak of revolutionary propaganda was met by an unprecedented wave of prosecutions. Between 1816 and 1834 there were 183 prosecutions for seditious or blasphemous libel, or defamation of the King or his ministers. No less than 131 of these 186 cases took place in 1817 and in 1819–21.[36] Carlile was among those sent to prison in this period. His business was taken over by his wife until she suffered the same fate, and it was then managed by his sister, Mary Ann Carlile. In 1821 she too was arrested and prosecuted for selling a pamphlet entitled *An Appendix to Thomas Paine's Age of Reason*. She appeared at the Guildhall, and conducted her own defence which she started to read from notes some hundred pages long. She had got no further than page twelve when she was interrupted by the judge who refused to hear the remainder and sentenced her to one year's imprisonment and a fine of £500. The case had been initiated by the Society for the Suppression of Vice.

On March 26, 1823, Mary Ann Carlile petitioned the Commons for her release. She had already served her year's sentence. She was now confined in prison until she could find £500 to pay the fine. She had no capital and, therefore, no prospects of ever raising such a sum. This was not the sort of case in which one would expect Wilberforce to appear at his most magnanimous.

Joseph Hume presented the petition with a speech in which he challenged the Society 'to turn to the New Testament and show him one passage in which they were warranted in prosecuting men for the expression of opinions respecting religion'.[37] But quite apart from the injustice of the prosecution the punishment was excessive. Hume produced judgements and precedents which showed that the infliction of excessive fines was against all the principles of English justice. This was a key point and one which none of the other speakers attempted to answer. Fines were designed as punishment, not as means of raising revenue, and should therefore be tailored to the means of the convicted person. A fine of £500 to someone in Mary Ann Carlile's circumstances was the equivalent of a life sentence. It was useless to argue, as the Attorney General, Sir Robert Gifford, did, that she would be released when she had been deemed to have served the equivalent term to a fine of £500. To argue on these lines avoided Hume's point, which was to cast doubts whether such fines were in accordance with English law, and introduced a new and equally questionable one, the contention that, in some circumstances, the term of imprisonment should be decided, not by the courts, but by the King and hence by his ministers.

The Attorney General did not make a happy speech. Among other things, he said that if she had made a recantation he would have looked on her appeal with more leniency. He also made a statement which must have raised the hackles of every humanitarian in the House, 'The hon. gentleman [Hume] advanced another proposition more dangerous than any to which he had yet adverted. It was in effect, that the jury, before they pronounced on the guilt or innocence of a prisoner, were to consider what would be the punishment which would be inflicted. [No no.] No proposition could be more dangerous to the pure administration of justice. It was no matter what the punishment was to be.'[38] Ricardo, the great economist, spoke next and was quick to pounce on both points. He showed that juries were increasingly reluctant to convict for minor crimes to which the death penalty was still attached. When the Attorney General mentioned contrition, Ricardo continued, 'The demand of the attorney general was, that she must acknowledge that to be right, which she conscientiously believed to be wrong, before she entitled herself to any lenity; or in other words, she must commit an act of the most shameless duplicity, in order to become a proper object for the mercy of the crown.'[39] Ricardo argued that all prosecutions on religious grounds should be stopped. 'It savoured too much of the Inquisition to be received as genuine in a free country like England.'

Burdett repeated the point about excessive fines in his usual forceful style. Wilberforce then devoted most of his speech to a defence of the Society. Offences against public morals, he claimed, were the greatest of all offences and the least likely to be prosecuted, for although the damage done was enormous in the aggregate, no individual suffered greatly. 'For this reason it was that a small elect body of men employed in suppressing an act of this nature, by carrying the laws into action, was a great benefit to the nation.'[40] The Society had instituted thirty-two prosecutions, 'all for most detestable offences', and not one of them had failed. Its works had been praised by leading judges. Not, he hastened to say, that Christianity needed the suppression of its enemies. 'Christianity always has and always will triumph.' 'With regard to the unhappy woman,' he went on, 'I trust she may experience the mercy and long-suffering of that Being, against whose revealed word she has set herself in presumptuous array. The punishment, however, which she has justly incurred in this world cannot be remitted without holding out a prospect of impunity to similar offenders.'[41] He discharged a salvo against those who wished 'blasphemy to be closely defined'. He had once told one of them, 'I cannot help you, for I must honestly declare that if you desire to go as near as you safely can to blasphemy, I only hope that you will find that you have overstepped the mark, and incurred the punishment which you have tempted.'[42] 'Everything which is most valuable,' he finished, 'depends upon the preservation of the sacred institutions of the country. For your own sakes, as well as for the sake of your constituents, I implore you to preserve the religion and law of the land safe and inviolate.'[43]

It was not a convincing answer. Hume, Ricardo and Burdett had raised two main points, that Mary Ann Carlile's trial had been unfair, and that the fine on her had been monstrous. Wilberforce skirted the first point and made no reference at all to the second. The matter for him was simply not open to argument. He would not even swap texts with Hume. Atheism was absolutely beyond the pale; mercy to one atheist would encourage others; the stakes were too high for any compromise or weakness. Ricardo was right when he brought the Inquisition into the debate. Wilberforce's line of reasoning could as well have justified an auto da fé as a £500 fine. He was also inconsistent. He proudly maintained that Christianity needed no protection, that it would triumph whether it was attacked or not and then proceeded to implore the House, as a matter of the utmost urgency, to continue to persecute its enemies.

His sons felt no qualms about his speech. 'It was not without indignation,' they write, 'that he listened to the shallow and "very mischievous speeches" of these pretended friends of liberty. "I had hoped," he said in private, "that Ricardo* had become a Christian; I see now that he has only ceased to be a Jew." '[44] Ricardo, it is fair to say, had particularly offended Wilberforce by remarks which had nothing to do with the subject of the debate. After dealing with the Attorney General's statement that he would have looked on the matter differently had there been signs of contrition, Ricardo went on to castigate hypocrisy in general. Witnesses in court were asked before they gave evidence if they believed in a future state. If they answered 'no', they were permitted neither to take the oath nor to testify. But when they gave this answer, witnesses showed themselves to be honest men by the very action that led to their being judged incapable of giving truthful evidence, while an atheist who lied about religion was accepted as a reliable witness. Wilberforce was undoubtedly shocked by this attack on the system of giving an oath to tell the truth. 'I have heard with astonishment,' he said in his own speech, 'an honourable member behind me blame the practice of asking a witness, before his testimony was admitted, whether he believed in the Holy Scriptures. Has that hon. gentleman so little regard for the awful declaration "So help me God!" or can it be maintained that we have anything else to depend upon for the credibility of human testimony, than the attestation of the holy volume?'[45] It was not a matter which could be discussed with profit between the religious and the irreligious.

Wilberforce later talked about Ricardo to his family, and it is probably from this conversation that the sons took their quotation, although Samuel's notebook does not mention it. 'He spoke,' Samuel wrote, 'of what Mr. Ricardo had said in the House of Commons on the debate on the Society for the Suppression of Vice with the greatest regret. He said he had never expected to hear such a declaration made in the walls of a

* As always when making a disparaging remark Robert Isaac and Samuel left a blank in the place of Ricardo's name, though in this case few of their readers could have been left in any doubt of his identity. Clarkson alone is denied such anonymity.

British Parliament. He had regretted it the more on account of Mr. Ricardo's private character. He said he was a man of almost the clearest head of any man he knew. Very liberal towards the poor and taking great pains in schools etc.'[46]

*

Compared to the wretched Thomas Williams, Mary Ann Carlile was a willing and unrepentant victim. The sentence passed upon her, although exceedingly harsh, does not have the same callousness as condemning to ruin a man who had already repented. In other respects the second period of repressive legislation was more severe than the first. The Acts passed by the Liverpool Government in 1817–20 were more short-lived than those of Pitt, but they caused much deeper resentment at the time because measures excusable during the war were intolerable in time of peace. When Pitt enacted restrictions on the rights of assembly he was aiming at men who were forming Jacobin clubs while the country was fighting for its life against a Jacobin enemy. In Wilberforce's view the Parliamentary Opposition itself was verging on treason. The Bills against unlawful assembly were bitterly contested by the Opposition, but supported by the country, as could be seen in Wilberforce's dramatic meeting at York. But the Act of Pitt's which did the greatest damage to the working class, the Combinations Act, slipped through Parliament without serious opposition.

Wilberforce's support of Castlereagh is less easy to excuse. Castlereagh's case was weaker than Pitt's and the Opposition was much more moderate and constructive. Looking back on the two crises we can recognise that the country was not on the brink of revolution, but that it must have seemed so on both occasions. To Wilberforce revolution was a more dreadful prospect than to most men because of its attendant evils of atheism. His loathing of their irreligion poisoned his mind against the agitators and led to such outbursts as he made to the Attorney General over Carlile's prosecution. At this time he wrote in an otherwise light-hearted letter to Samuel, who had asked him for fireworks, 'If the parcel be not in time, you may have a special bonfire for Mr. Hunt, who deserves the distinction about as well as Guy Fawkes. For if he be not quite so desperate a conspirator, he has less than Guy to plead in his excuse.'[47]

When Wilberforce had taken the view that the threat to the constitution was so great that unpleasant measures must be accepted, one would expect him, as the leading philanthropist of his day, to be concerned that the suffering caused by these measures was as little as possible, and that they should be applied with justice. Having entrusted the Government with exceptional powers it was the responsibility of all Members of Parliament to see that those powers were not abused. But in the two most outrageous incidents of the crisis, the employment of Oliver and Peterloo, he opposed inquiries being instigated by the House. One can understand his voting against any motion of censure, but to vote against inquiries in such cases could be to vote for the suppression of the truth. Yet Wilberforce's faith in Sidmouth was such that he did not fear any revelations of abuse of power. Perhaps he dreaded the examination of witnesses who would proclaim their blasphemous and seditious views, which when reported might infect others.

The extraordinary part of Wilberforce's conduct was not that he supported the Government but that he did so with so few misgivings. He had a blind spot towards suffering caused by coercive legislation and was able to shrug it aside or ignore it in a way quite remarkable for so kind a man. Thus, soon after the Oliver Debate, he wrote in his diary, 'This is clear, that in Scripture no national crime is condemned so frequently, and few so strongly, as oppression and cruelty, and the not using our best endeavours to deliver our fellow creatures from them.'[48] But he was thinking of slavery and did not apply the same lessons to conditions at home.

Some ingenious explanations have been advanced to reconcile Wilberforce's humanity to the slaves with his severity to his own countrymen. Hazlitt maintained that he was genuinely anxious to do good, but that he would not risk courting unpopularity. Other radicals of his day regarded him as a sanctimonious hypocrite. The question did not trouble his sons who were more conservative than he and who reported his speeches with approval. The most damaging criticism in modern times has come from the Hammonds.[49] 'Wilberforce's point of view was quite different from that of Romilly, or Bennet or Sheridan. When it was proposed to suspend the Habeas Corpus or to give arbitrary powers over the lives of the working classes to Magistrates, they asked themselves whether such measures would not lead to the gross oppression of poor and defenceless people. Each of them had known such cases and brought them to light. Wilberforce asked himself a totally different question. He asked himself whether the Christian Religion and Social Order would not suffer if men whose principles and outlook he held in horror were allowed to unite and speak as they liked. His answer to this question led him to support authority in all circumstances.'[50] The way in which Wilberforce interpreted his religion reinforced his conservatism. If this life was no more than a brief interlude between two eternities the only important thing in it was the care of the human soul. Anything that menaced Christianity must be opposed and, to his mind, all agitation came under this heading, for he regarded the constitution and its religious and civil establishment as a whole. 'In questions where this disturbing element did not enter, where the demand was not that working men should be treated as persons with rights and liberties, but that suffering unnecessary from the point of view of discipline should cease, Wilberforce was a humane man.'[51]

Dr. Howse has compared these attacks with reproaching Columbus for not having also discovered Australia.[52] It is a neat analogy but the Hammonds' criticisms retain much of their force. One cannot expect anyone to be ahead of his time in every way. Wilberforce played a leading part in bringing to an end two of the most monstrous evils of his day, the Slave Trade and Slavery. He was a pioneer in the more humane treatment of weaker races and in raising the deplorably low moral tone of his own country. Many of those who opposed the Liverpool Government's oppressive measures also opposed some of Wilberforce's good causes. Cobbett, for example, saw the realities in England more clearly than Wilberforce; he often seems an entirely sympathetic character, as rough and prickly as his pseudonym, Peter Porcupine, but with a warmth of heart that extended to all his countrymen. Unfortunately, that was the limit of its extent. Cobbett's admirers cannot include many descendants of the African slaves whom he so totally despised and to whose oppressors he sold his literary genius. James Stephen, when confronted by such people, could equal the passion of the fieriest radical. 'This instance,' he wrote to Wilberforce in 1816, 'added to others confirms my antipathy to liberty boys and democrats. In all human character I know of nothing so detestable and contemptible as a democrat slave-master or defender of private slavery.'[53]

The democrat slave-masters, almost by definition, did nothing for the slaves, but Wilberforce did a great deal for the workers. He may have built churches and distributed Bibles when the most urgent need of the poor was food, but he also gave them much more food than any of his critics. The over-riding importance of religion to Wilberforce sometimes led him to sacrifice their temporal to spiritual interests, but it also preserved him from much of the arrogance and condescension of the acutely class-conscious age in which he lived. If all human souls were soon to be equal in the eyes of their Maker, the social rank of the bodies in which they were temporarily housed became of little importance to him. He assumed that it should also be unimportant to the poor. It was right for all classes to accept the station allotted to them by God, with the knowledge that it was only for a little time and that soon all would be equal.

He once talked to Samuel about this. 'He spoke of persons looking down with a species of contempt on those of lower birth than themselves. He said it was quite contrary to the precepts of Scriptures to "condescend to men of low estate".'[54] When discussing Dr. Carey, Sydney Smith's despised 'consecrated cobbler', he told Robert Isaac: 'It is a striking instance of the way in which Providence, to show the inutility of human rank, power and even talents, when it has a great design to execute selects

some mean and apparently, inefficient instrument.'[55] He also detested
servility. When a man wrote in fulsome terms hoping for him to use his
influence with Pitt, Wilberforce threw his letter on the ground and said,
'How much rather would I have the man spit in my face.'[56]

Wilberforce accepted the social structure both as a man of his age and
as a servant of God. He was himself entirely without social ambitions; he
refused offers of a peerage and honours and, after his conversion, chose
his friends from lower social classes than his old intimates at Goosetree's.
He reserved his deepest admiration for those who, like Dr. Carey, had
triumphed over social handicaps. A visitor to his own house was as likely
to meet a butcher, like Johnny Melon, or a penniless dissenting clergyman as a Duke or a cabinet minister. When Wilberforce cultivated the
great, he did so with the deliberate aim of using their influence to further
the cause of religion or Abolition.

He was not the sort of hypocrite who preaches philanthropy all day,
then goes home and bullies his dependants at night. He treated his
servants as an extension of the family he loved so much and his tolerance
of their oddities struck many of his friends as ludicrous.* When he bought
a property he would lower its rents by thirty or forty per cent, and allow
his distressed tenants to be years behind in their payments.

On a wider scale his personal generosity remained equal to every crisis.
In the same years that he was supporting Liverpool's legislation he was
also active in relieving the distress which had led to the new laws. In some
respects he was well ahead of his time. In December 1819, he suggested
the 'employment in public works for great numbers of the working
classes. The disproportion between the demand for labour and the
number of labourers would thus be lessened, by which wages would
materially rise.'[57] When a petition was presented to Parliament on behalf
of the Scottish poor the Government argued that it could not be expected
to help until the taxes on Scottish landowners had been raised to English
levels. Wilberforce opposed this proposal while admitting its justice. But
in a case of such desperate need he considered that justice must be sacrificed to mercy.

In education, too, he was ahead of his time. He supported the educational pioneers Bell and Lancaster and tried to apply the latter's revolutionary methods of teaching in Haiti. For Wilberforce education was
inevitably bound up with religion and we cannot be surprised that, with
so many religious schools to support, he never sponsored a secular one.
Zachary Macaulay showed a more impartial zeal for education when he
sat on the first Council of London University. These movements seem
modest enough nowadays and at times the condescension of their patrons
repels us, but in their day they seemed dangerous innovations. Even

* See pages 422-3.

Cobbett thought the movement for popular education 'despicable cant and nonsense',[58] while David Giddy, later President of the Royal Society, declared: 'However specious in theory the project might be, of giving education to the labouring classes . . . it would teach them to despise their lot in life . . . it would render them factious and refactory . . . it would enable them to read seditious pamphlets, vicious books, and publications against Christianity; it would render them insolent to their superiors, and in a few years the result would be that the legislature would find it necessary to direct the strong arm of power towards them.'[59]

These arguments might have had some appeal to the side of Wilberforce's nature which had voted for the Suspension of Habeas Corpus, but in the educational field his belief that 'if people were destined to be free, they must be made fit to enjoy their freedom' proved stronger than his fear that they should be seduced by the blasphemous pamphlets of his opponents. His genuine desire for education allowed him to give his sympathies, if not his patronage, to such secular schemes as that of Robert Owen of Lanark, the industrialist and philanthropist.

In December 1812 Owen of Lanark breakfasted with Wilberforce and stayed on 'long talking with me of his plan of education, and of rendering manufactures and morals compatible'. He returned soon afterwards to meet Wilberforce, Grant and Henry Thornton by appointment. 'When Mr. Owen was proceeding to detail his schemes, he gently hinted that the ladies present might be suffered to retire from a discussion which must prove beyond their comprehension. Mr. Wilberforce eagerly dissented from the proposition; and it was well for Mr. Owen that he yielded, for he had not read long before Grant, Henry Thornton and I were all fast asleep and the despised ladies were his only real audience.'[60] But when Owen's plan was put forward in Parliament, 'I forced to vote against it on the Christian ground'.[61] The next day he found 'Owen of Lanark truly placable and good-humoured; he said Vansittart and I right in voting against him'.

His humanity was shown in his loathing for 'our bloody laws', 'our murderous laws' and 'the barbarous custom of hanging'. He accompanied Elizabeth Fry on her saintly missions to Newgate and did much prison visiting on his own. He comforted condemned criminals and helped their families. He took their sufferings to heart. In February 1818 we find him 'up late from having been awake thinking of the slaves' wretched sufferings, and partly the two poor women about to be hanged for forgery this day. Alas, how bloody are our laws.' He intervened successfully in a number of cases and saved the lives of some young offenders. His vote and his voice in Parliament were at the disposal of those who sought to lessen the rigours of the Penal Laws.

Reform of these abuses was never one of his central causes, and he played rather the same supporting rôle to Romilly and Mackintosh as they had to his leadership of the Abolition Campaign. He also supported Bentham's and Howard's schemes for prison reform. In this field he was again ahead of his age, and in one respect he was ahead of the next generation of prison reformers. He regarded the main function of prison as being reform rather than correction. In his time this was a revolutionary opinion shared by few Members of Parliament. The next generation of progressive prison governors, men like Chesterton of Cold Bath Fields, agreed with this view of their functions, but applied it with a clumsy, if unintentional, brutality. Prisoners on the verge of reform, they argued, stood to be corrupted by their comrades. They therefore imposed long periods of solitary confinement and started 'the silent system', under which prisoners in no circumstances were allowed to exchange a word. Wilberforce's kindness and understanding of human needs kept him from such mistakes.

In the very years in which he was helping to cement the oppressive policies of Liverpool's Government Wilberforce was equally active in alleviating distress and supporting progressive causes in Parliament. In 1817 and 1819 he spoke in support of bills to reform the horrifying conditions under which chimney sweeps had to work. This was a simple issue of humanity, and not one which could cause a conflict between the philanthropist and the conservative in his nature. The same could be said of the successors of Sir Robert Peel's Factory Act of 1802, which sought to extend its benefits to children who were not apprentices. In 1815 and in 1818 Wilberforce supported Peel's attempts to limit the working day of all children in the textile industry to ten-and-a-half hours, and when that failed to twelve-and-a-half hours. Even this was too much for Parliament to accept and in 1819 the reformers were forced to agree to a thirteen-and-a-half-hour day. Both the Factory Acts and the Chimney Sweep Bills were interventions in the relationship between worker and employer. Hence they flouted the accepted economic doctrine of *laissez-faire*. They were also the first to recognize that conditions in factories could be controlled in a way impossible in the old cottage industries.

In 1817 and 1819 he also fought against the savagery of the Game Laws. The severity of these had been increased until any act of poaching was punishable by seven years' transportation. If the Corn Laws were passed by a parliament of landowners to protect their interests, the Game Laws gave the same sanctity to their pleasures. They were additionally offensive in that they were enforced by magistrates who were, for the most part, themselves landowners and preservers of game. The high regard in which Wilberforce held the country gentlemen, 'the very cement of our Society', did not blind him on this issue. He described the existing laws as 'so contrary to all our notions of private right, so injurious, so arbitrary in their operation that the sense of the greater part of mankind is in determined hostility to them'.[62] They 'subjected individuals to a severe penalty for an act which it was contrary to the natural feelings of mankind to say was in itself a crime. . . . He strongly objected to game being put on the same footing as other property'.[63]

*

This rapid survey of the humanitarian and progressive causes supported by Wilberforce is incomplete. It takes little account of the results of his personal generosity in the relief of suffering and hunger and none of the effect that his example of generosity had on others. He was responsible for the foundation of a mass of societies which, if sometimes self-righteous, patronising and priggish, were invariably warm-hearted and energetic. Wilberforce's efforts in Parliament were only a small part of his philanthropic work. Nevertheless the list of causes supported by him should be enough to give the lie to the criticism, originally made by Courtenay in 1792, and repeated by a long succession of literary parrots ever since, that he never did anything for a white man in his life, that he systematically opposed all progressive measures at home, that he was a 'reactionary' in his own country. All too often one reads in books, whose authors should know better, such statements as 'Wilberforce actually opposed legislation intended to improve factory conditions in contemporary England. Yet at the time no one criticized Wilberforce for this paradox.'[64] The absence of such criticism is not surprising, since Wilberforce supported every Bill presented to Parliament to improve conditions in factories. If the paradox is supposed to be the contrast betwen Wilberforce's humanity to the slaves and his acceptance of the evils of the social order at home, the author has compounded his error. Wilberforce, as we have seen, was constantly and violently abused on precisely these grounds by every spokesman of the radical party.

Wilberforce's social outlook, like almost everything else in his life, was dominated by his religion. When the country was quiet, the influence of his religion was entirely beneficial, it spurred him on to a series of charitable works. But in times of crisis, as the Hammonds have pointed out, it led to his fear of revolution subduing his natural kindness, and, occasionally, his powers of reason. Wilberforce's religion meant that he could never have the instinctive sympathy for the oppressed felt by the leading humanitarians in Parliament, though the latter's humanity would have been tested more severely had it been a Whig Government acting the part of the oppressor.

In one respect Wilberforce's religion gave him a great advantage over the humanitarians. Their instincts may sometimes have been surer, but his approach was much more effective. With the exception of Romilly none of the humanitarians were as purposeful as the Saints. When Wilberforce thought a matter crucially important he was not content with merely speaking in favour of it, he would lobby for it, arrange petitions, renew his motion inside Parliament and whip up support in the country until finally he was successful. He was also systematically generous. One cannot see men like Sheridan or Lord Holland sacrificing every luxury in life in order to give more money to charities, and yet this is what Wilberforce did from his conversion to his death. Wilberforce may have been less sure than them in his choice of causes, but when he adopted one he did so without reservations.

He responded instinctively to suffering, giving his money, his time and his voice with equal generosity. He would set himself against accepted economic dogmas by supporting government interference between labourer and employer (the Factories Act), tinkering with laws affecting other men's property (the Game Laws) and suggesting that the Government should create jobs for the unemployed by great programmes of public works. Even the Society for the Suppression of Vice played its part in this programme. While it suppressed many pleasures of the poor, its remorseless Sabbatarianism ensured that they would be allowed one day of rest in the week. The Sunday schools gave those who wished the chance to use this day in educating themselves.

For someone with so many sources of information, Wilberforce had strange misconceptions about the nature of his times. His faith in the integrity of Lords Castlereagh and Sidmouth must have driven men like Romilly to despair. His intelligence system, so useful in dealing with cases of want, broke down when it came to the discovery of sedition. His correspondents were mainly conservative men, many of them clergymen, who reacted violently to the slightest sign of unrest or irreligion. It was naïve of Wilberforce to share their alarm without making allowances for their views. But his credulity so far as clergymen were concerned was boundless, as can be seen in the 'Boers and Hottentots' fiasco, when without hesitation, he believed grossly exaggerated stories from missionaries, in the embarrassing statistics on 'the great Juggernaut of Orissa' which he quoted in the debate on Indian missions, and in the scandal of Cold Bath Fields. His faith in the integrity of the ministers and the reliability of his correspondents convinced him that the country was menaced by a band of sinister conspirators, who sought to corrupt its people, subvert its constitution and overthrow its religion, and that it was defended by a Government which was resolute but humane. When he saw the immortal souls of his countrymen threatened, he felt that a suspension of liberty was demanded. His nature did not lend itself to hatred, but in so far as it was possible for him to hate, he hated his enemies of 1816–19.

When he fought the Slave Trade, he analysed every defence that could be made of it, and was ready with answers for each point. His speeches on coercion are, in contrast, a mass of generalisations. He not only was without answers to the points made by Romilly, Bennet, Brougham and Tierney, but he does not even seem to have considered some of them seriously. Perhaps the critical nature of the threat, the same threat that in the prosecution of Williams had provoked him to a rare act of callousness, was such that he thought coercion advisable however slight the chance that it might be needed. But, judging by the unshaken conviction shown in his diary, it seems more likely that he allowed himself to be blinded by fear of atheism. Perhaps he missed his white negroes, he certainly needed another Clarkson to provide the kind of accurate brief that had served him so well in the Abolition Campaign.

The spectacle of a great philanthropist supporting repressive measures has jarred on radical nerves from Wilberforce's times to our own. But if one turns the question upside down and looks at him from a religious, rather than a sociological, point of view, one can almost create a new Wilberforce enigma. The question then becomes, why should a man who was a religious leader and a politician occupy so much of his time with causes which had nothing to do with religion and little connection with politics. Elie Halévy, writing with the objectivity of a foreigner and a knowledge equalled by few Englishmen, found the humanitarianism of Wilberforce and his friends more remarkable than their conservatism. He did not ask how the friends of the slaves could support the repression of Castlereagh and Sidmouth, but, 'How came the Evangelicals to temper their austere code with so much mercy?'[65]

CHAPTER XXVIII

THE ROYAL DIVORCE

IN 1795, nearly ten years after his illegal marriage to Mrs. Fitzherbert, the Prince of Wales had married Princess Caroline of Brunswick-Wolfenbüttel. He was drunk at the wedding and tried to leave before it was over. The course of their marriage ran true to its inauspicious beginning. In 1806 the Prince forced the Government to accept an inquiry into her behaviour from which she emerged with her reputation shaken, though the most serious charge against her, that of bearing an illegitimate child, was proved to be false. After 1815, when George III's health collapsed and that of the Prince Regent seemed very delicate, there was a chance that the latter's daughter, Princess Charlotte, might succeed in the near future.

While her husband consoled himself with his mistress, Lady Conyngham, known as the Vice-Queen, Caroline was travelling around Italy in equally deplorable company, but her daughter's prospects of succession made her cause attractive, and Brougham, impulsive opportunist as always, became her political adviser. His rôle in the scandal that followed can be interpreted in different ways. At times he seems interested only in personal and political gain, at others he is so dedicated to his client that he is prepared to sacrifice the country's interests to hers. Princess Charlotte died in 1817, but Brougham, though he had lost his best card, still saw chances of using Caroline to embarrass the Government and advance himself. In 1819, without consulting Caroline, he suggested that in return for an increase in her allowance of £15,000, she would renounce her title and promise never to return to England.

A few months later George III died. One of his successor's first acts was to instruct his ministers to bring divorce proceedings. Lord Liverpool replied that the evidence might not be convincing and hinted that the Queen had scope for accusations of her own. The King, after a display of petulance, agreed to grant his wife a large settlement provided that she never returned to England. Brougham's ambitions were inflated by this offer. He kept the bribe secret from the Queen for some time and then advised her to refuse it. Meanwhile he offered to keep the Queen out of

England in return for being made a K.C. Soon this seemed an inadequate reward and he began to think in terms of bringing down the Government. But the Queen had turned to other counsellors, notably Alderman Wood, a radical politician whom George IV once described as 'that beast Wood' and whom Victoria later made a Baronet.[1] Following Wood's advice she came to London and entered the city in triumph on June 6, 1820. She benefited enormously from the unpopularity of the Government. In the eyes of the mob she was a woman persecuted by the same men who had so recently trampled on their liberties. She assumed the reputation of a martyr.

Wilberforce watched her progress with alarm, mixed with the reluctant admiration which he seems to have felt for bold and shameless strumpets like the Queen and Mrs. Clarke. 'She approaches wisely, because boldly,' he wrote in his diary. 'Lodges at Alderman Wood's, Brougham in the house. How deeply interested all are, indeed, I feel it myself, about her! One can't help admiring her spirit, though I fear she has been very profligate. Bergami [her lover] left her at St. Omers.'[2]

The Government's reaction was to move for an inquiry by a Secret Committee, an action equivalent to putting the Queen on trial, but Wilberforce persuaded them to pause and give some time for a private settlement to be reached. The popularity of the Queen frightened him. He wrote in his diary, 'I fear lest it should please God to scourge us through the medium of this rupture between the King and Queen. If the soldiers should take up her cause, who knows what may happen—and is it very improbable?'[3] In the next few days the King made many important concessions to his wife. Her name and rights would be granted without reserve and notified at the foreign court where she chose to live. An address of thanks would be presented to her as well as the King by the Commons.

One bone of contention remained to which both parties attached surprising importance. The King had arranged that the Queen's name should not be read out in the liturgy during church services. She demanded that it should be, but her husband refused. Wilberforce favoured granting this concession since it was harmless and would prevent great dangers to the monarchy. He tried to persuade both sides to change their minds, but found them equally obdurate. Somewhat disingenuous attempts were made in the House of Commons to persuade the Queen that she was automatically included in the prayer for all the Royal Family. Denman, her solicitor general, a Whig and an enemy of slavery, replied morosely: 'If Her Majesty is included in any general prayer, it is in the prayer for all who are desolate and oppressed.'[4] Wilberforce decided to attempt a compromise. During the negotiations the Queen's representatives had suggested that some equivalent of the restoration of her name to the liturgy might be devised. 'I could not be persuaded,' he wrote in a memorandum, 'that if an Address should be carried by a great majority, assuring Her Majesty that her giving up the point should be regarded not as arising from any disposition to shrink from inquiry (an imputation to which her whole conduct had given the lie), but from a wish to give up her own opinion to the authority of the House of Commons, this very Address would constitute the equivalent desired.'[5]

But the Queen's popularity had intoxicated her. On June 20 as Wilberforce was about to go to bed he was disturbed by a knocking on the door, followed by 'a warm, expostulatory letter' from the Queen, in which he was told that 'Her Majesty assures Mr. Wilberforce that She *never will abandon this point* [the Liturgy]—as her honour is dearer to her than her life'.[6] In the morning she sent him a more moderate letter and he decided to go ahead with his Address. The House passed it by 391 to 124, 'an immense majority'. Wilberforce was chosen with three other members to present it to the Queen.

The next day, June 24, the four members dressed in full Court dress brought the Resolution to the Queen in Portland Street. Wilberforce had been warned that the mob was so violent that they should leave by a side door, but he thought that their lives were in no danger and, even if they had been, representatives of the House of Commons should not behave furtively. The Queen rejected their offer. They were jeered at by the mob and, according to some accounts, pelted. But Wilberforce wrote reassuring Barbara, 'Her [the Queen's] manner was extremely dignified, but very stern and haughty. There was a mob about the door, which if it had been night would have been very dangerous, but no stones were thrown.'[7]

He must have given a somewhat different account of the affair to the Thorntons, for Marianne remembered the day and later wrote to her niece Alice Forster:

'He used to go into ecstacies especially about flowers. When staying with us at the time of wicked Queen Caroline's trial (i.e. in 1820) he was one of a deputation of three from the House of Commons to persuade her to give up being crowned, for a large annual allowance. She was half drunk* I believe when they got there and she all but kicked them downstairs. Mr. Wilberforce came back very low and dis-spirited, thinking indeed that she would upset the monarchy; when stepping out of the library window before dinner he caught sight of a gorgeous moss-rose that grew up the wall, and seeing how it transfixed him I gathered it. Oh the beauty of it, Oh the goodness of God in giving us such alleviations in this hard world. The bell rang for dinner but there was no getting him to go in while he stood worshipping his flower and when he had lavished all other endearments and admirations he ended with "And Oh how unlike the Queen's countenance".'[8]

* There were many rumours that the Queen was an alcoholic. Brougham absolutely denies them in his memoirs (ii. 420). One must prefer his version.

Wilberforce was accused of trifling with the House of Commons by assuming that if they passed the Address, he would be able to arrange a compromise. He had a complete answer to this charge in a letter from Brougham written two days before which promised 'she will accede to your Address. I pledge myself.' As no contribution to the problem could now be served by this document and as its contents would put Brougham to shame, Wilberforce suppressed it, although by quoting it he could have cleared himself. He minded his own unpopularity only in so far as it affected his chances of bringing in legislation against Slavery. 'What a lesson it is to a man not to set his heart on low popularity, when after forty years' disinterested public service I am believed to be a perfect rascal! Oh what a comfort it is to have to fly for refuge to a God of unchangeable truth and love.'[9]

At this time he was diverted for a moment by a visit to the Duchess of Kent, where, for the only time in his life, he met the child whose reign was to be so influenced by him. 'She received me,' he wrote to Hannah More, 'with her fine animated child on the floor by her with its playthings, of which I soon became one.'[10] It would have been a consolation to Wilberforce had he known then how differently the Royal Family would conduct itself under Victoria.

Wilberforce's failure ended any hopes of compromise, and the Government decided to launch an inquiry into the Queen's conduct in the House of Lords. 'It will be long, painful, and disgusting,' he complained, 'and, what in my mind aggravates the evil, parliament is not clear in the matter. We marry our Kings and Queens contrary to the laws of God and of nature, and from this source proceed the evils which I am now anxious to avoid.'[11] The inquiry in the Lords was a necessary part of the Bill of Pains and Penalties which the Cabinet now introduced to dissolve the marriage and thus deprive the Queen of her title. It was to start on August 17. On the 5th, *The Times* printed a letter by Lord John Russell, appealing to Wilberforce to intervene again in the dispute. He had been thinking of an approach to the King, but he now felt hamstrung by this call from the Opposition. He then received a similar appeal, though this time conveyed to him in decent privacy, from William Lamb, the future Lord Melbourne. He came up to London for the first days of the proceedings, but finding no opening, retired again to his family in the country.

He would have found the scene in London most unedifying. He disapproved of public scandal on many grounds and in the summer of 1820 scandal ran riot. As August 12 passed many peers must have been pining for their grouse moors, but they were forced to remain in London in a heatwave, sweating, embarrassed and ashamed, to listen to the concocted perjury of a great number of Italian servants. Two hundred and fifty peers assembled every day to hear stories of connecting rooms, creaking springs and revealing bed linen.

The Queen herself hardly lent dignity to the proceedings by appearing in a black wig (she had fair hair) and a veil through which her face glowed brick red. Creevey was in the audience. 'To describe to you her appearance and manner is far beyond my powers,' he wrote to Miss Ord. 'I had been taught to believe she was as much improved in looks as in dignity of manners. It is therefore with much pain I am obliged to observe that the nearest resemblance I can recollect to this much-injured Princess is a toy which you used to call Fanny Royds.* There is another toy of a rabbit or cat, whose tail you squeeze under its body, and then out it jumps in half a minute off the ground into the air. The first of these toys you might suppose to represent the person of the Queen; the latter the manner by which she popped all at once into the House, made a *duck* at the throne, another to the Peers, and a concluding jump into the chair which was placed for her. . . . Such a back for variety and inequality of ground as you never beheld; with a few straggling ringlets on her neck, which I flatter myself from their appearance were not her Majesty's own property.'[12] Once in her chair, her posture there caused Lord Holland to remark, 'Instead of sleeping with Bergami, she sleeps with the Lords.'

The House of Lords had assumed its full judicial aspect. The Lord Chancellor presided, the prosecution was conducted by the legal officers of the Crown, while the Queen was represented by Brougham, Denman and other lawyers. It was not a setting in which she could expect a fair trial. However judicial the proceedings, they did not constitute a formal trial, but an inquiry which was part of a Bill brought in by the Government and supported by all its influence and by that of the Crown. No packed jury of tenants condemning a poacher to Botany Bay could have been more dependent on the favour of the prosecutor. Another unsatisfactory side to the proceedings was that while the Queen was, in effect, on trial for adultery, they did not allow her judges to take her husband's gross infidelity into consideration. Looking back on the scandal it seems certain that she did commit adultery, but only when abandoned, persecuted and disowned by a husband whose infidelities were far more frequent and more flagrant than her own. To have condemned the Queen without reference to the King's conduct would have been a travesty of justice. The Lords were thus placed in a dilemma: they could by passing the Bill return a verdict of guilty which they knew to be unfair and partial, or by rejecting it declare a woman innocent whom they believed to be guilty.

The London mob did not suffer from such mixed feelings. Ardent

* 'A Dutch toy with a round bottom, weighted with lead, so that it always jumps erect in whatever position it is laid.'

partisans of the Queen, they crowded round Parliament, cheered her defenders and hissed and jostled her enemies. There were moments which could have become ugly. The Duke of Wellington was surrounded by a hostile crowd which tried in vain to unhorse him. Lord Anglesey was cornered by the mob and told to show his loyalty to their idol. 'God save the Queen,' he replied, 'and may all your wives be like her.'[13]* On the whole the mob was astonishingly good-humoured.

The same could not be said for proceedings inside the House. Brougham struck an ominous note in his opening address with a passage which is still argued about by members of his profession. 'I put out of view at present the question of recrimination. . . . I dismiss for the present all other questions respecting the conduct or connexions of any parties previous to marriage. These I say not one word about; they are dangerous and tremendous questions, the consequences of discussing which, at the present moment, I will not even trust myself to describe. At present I hold them to be needless to the safety of my client; but when the necessity arises, an advocate knows but one duty, and, cost what it may, he must discharge it. Be the consequences what they may, to any other persons, powers, principalities, dominions or nations, an advocate is bound to do his duty; and I shall not fail to exert every means to put a stop to this Bill.'[14]

Brougham's audacity was staggering. He was serving notice that, if the Lords rejected the Queen's case when it was considered in isolation, he would be forced to turn to the attack. 'The ground, then,' Brougham wrote in his memoirs, 'was neither more nor less than impeaching the King's own title, by proving he had forfeited the crown. He had married a Roman Catholic [Mrs. Fitzherbert] while heir-apparent, and this is declared by the Act of Settlement to be a forfeiture of the crown, "as if he were naturally dead".'[15]

The Queen had been followed round Italy by agents of her husband who suborned her servants and collected damaging evidence about her friendship with Bergami. The evidence so gathered was assembled in a green bag. The first of the Crown witnesses was Teodoro Majocchi, a postilion whom the Queen had promoted to be her livery servant. As Majocchi appeared in the box the Queen 'having fixed her eyes on him, exclaimed, in a piercing tone, "Teodore! Teodore!"—or "Traditore! Traditore!" Her Majesty was immediately conducted to her retiring-room.'[16] Lady Charlotte Lindsay, who had once been a lady of her bed-chamber, made the waspish comment: 'I fear that on the wrong side of fifty a woman does not create much interest by being in a passion.'[17] Majocchi provided every evidence the Crown needed apart from actually

* Denman, although he defended the Queen with apparently passionate conviction, would never allow his own wife to meet her.

catching the Queen and Bergami *in flagrante delicto*. But the next day Brougham gave a superb display of destructive cross-examination which left Majocchi pathetically whimpering 'Non mi ricordo' (I do not remember) in answer to every question.

Brougham destroyed the credibility of the Italian witnesses, who had to be kept together and guarded against the vengeful mob. But some of his own witnesses made damaging admissions when cross-examined and one naval officer fainted under the strain. In the meantime feeling in the country caused acute concern. The army was openly sympathetic towards the Queen and the London mob committed to her. Creevey describes the scene of wild enthusiasm as the Queen went down the Thames. 'You know the Queen went down the river yesterday. I saw her pass the H of Commons on the deck of her state barge; the river and shores of it were then beginning to fill. Erskine, who was afterwards at Blackfriars Bridge, said he was sure there were 200,000 people collected to see her. . . . There was not a single vessel in the river that did not hoist their colours and man their yards for her, and it is with the greatest difficulty that the watermen on the Thames, who are all her partisans, are kept from destroying the hulk that lies off the H. of Commons to protect the witnesses in Cotton Garden.'[18] The King's unpopularity was not confined to London. Hannah More wrote to Wilberforce from the West Country that at a local dinner only five men out of fifty would drink his health.[19]

Denman summed up the Queen's case in an extraordinary speech which lasted for ten hours of sustained eloquence and passion. At the end, exhausted and perhaps mesmerised by his own eloquence, he quoted the parable of the woman taken in adultery, whom Christ had told to go and sin no more. It was an appalling blunder since the defence had maintained for two months that the Queen had not sinned at all. A rhyme appeared in the prints:

> Most gracious queen, we thee implore
> To go away and sin no more;
> Or if that effort be too great
> To go away at any rate.

There was another drama when the Lords debated the evidence. Lord Erskine, the great advocate and ex-Chancellor, fainted in the middle of a speech supporting the Queen. In the end the peers voted in favour of the second reading of the Bill by a majority of only twenty-eight. The third reading was passed by nine. Brougham had a new witness who was prepared to testify that he had tried to bribe the Queen's servants. He had not started on his attack on the King, and in the Lower House he could count on support to keep the debate alive for month after month. If the Bill had been presented to the Commons Wilberforce's opinion would have become of critical importance. Liverpool wrote him a lengthy letter, in which he tried to make out that the Lords' vote was a clear condemnation of the Queen,[20] but Wilberforce was already drifting towards her side. He wrote to Butterworth on November 2: 'I have studiously abstained from allowing myself to form any decided opinion on the Queen's case. But to you, confidentially, I will frankly confess, that the present inclination of my judgement is strongly against receiving the Bill. . . . Our Saviour's decision 5 Matthew 32. "He that putteth away his wife except for fornication, causeth her to commit adultery," appeared to me to bear very strongly on this question.'[21] The prospect of endless and humiliating hearings in the Commons with Brougham, supported by much of the country, moving for the King's impeachment, forced the Government to withdraw the Bill. Wilberforce received the news in the dramatic form of the early stage coaches from London arriving with their horses and drivers covered in white favours. 'Emblematic,' he commented sarcastically, 'I suppose of her innocence.'

The Queen had triumphed and the advisers who had urged her to reject Wilberforce's offer were vindicated. The threat of divorce proceedings, the only card the Government had to play against her, was now removed. In January 1821 her supporters pressed for the restoration of her name to the Liturgy. Wilberforce, after some doubt, decided to support the motion. 'That night I meant to vote for restoring her name, but was forced to go home by illness,' he wrote, 'though had the division come in a few days before I should have voted against it, on the grounds of the Queen's outrageously contumacious conduct.'[22] On February 13 he spoke on these lines. It was not a partisan speech, more a plea for keeping politics out of religion. After the motion was lost he wrote a letter which he thought would reach the King, urging that the Queen's name should be restored as a gesture.

Later in January the Queen was bought off. She accepted an offer of a house and £50,000 a year, neither of which could be worn with a martyr's crown.

George IV was to be crowned in July. The Queen claimed the right to be crowned with him, a right to which she was not legally entitled. The crowd cheered her as enthusiastically as ever on her way to the Abbey with Lord Hood. But Hood had only one ticket. The doorkeeper would not admit the Queen with him and, brave as she was, she did not dare enter alone. After a futile argument and an undignified dash from door to door she entered her coach and drove away to the accompaniment of hisses from the fickle crowd. She died the next month.

The King's hatred of her made him greet her death with indecent relish, and though not normally a vindictive man, he found it hard to forgive her advocates. He was, surprisingly, less annoyed by Brougham's threat to topple him from his throne than by the quotations he chose from Milton to show that the King was the true author of the proceedings:

Shape had none
Distinguishable in member joint or limb.

The King, Brougham learnt later, 'said I might have at least spared him the attack upon his shape. He was more vain of his person and of his slim figure than of almost anything else; and he said to Lord Donough-more . . . that he thought everybody allowed, whatever faults he might have, that his legs were not as I had described them.'[23] Denman's prospects at the bar were blighted by the King's refusal, for many years, to make him a K.C. His crime had been to compare his client's situation with that of Nero's wife.

CHAPTER XXIX

HAITI

WILBERFORCE'S fight against the Slave Trade gained him many peculiar correspondents. At the same time as he was lobbying Heads of State, writing to the foremost political and literary figures of the world and sending a copy of his works for the Pope's perusal, he would also be corresponding with obscure missionaries, seamen and slave owners. But none of his correspondence was more colourful than his exchanges with Henri Christophe, the Emperor of Haiti, a nation which has never been distinguished for the probity or administrative qualities of its rulers. From Dessalines to Papa Doc they have imposed a reign of terror on their wretched country. But during the last years of the French wars it seemed that Haiti had found in Henri Christophe a leader of true genius, under whom she might advance to the Black Renaissance of which the Abolitionists had dreamed for so long.

Henri Christophe was born a slave in the British island of St. Kitts, in spite of which he always retained an affection for his 'native country'. He served with distinction in the revolutionary and civil wars and once the turbulent forces of Haitian politics had thrown him into power he promptly arranged to be crowned King.* Christophe was a man of outstanding ability and imagination, with the objectivity to see his country's shortcomings and the confidence to tackle them. He realised that Haiti could never be safe while the threat of reconquest by France hung over her. She remained potentially the richest country in the New World and in the eyes of the French she was a colony which had revolted and which, but for the British blockade, would have been reconquered long ago. Napoleon had sent an expeditionary force under General Leclerc to subdue the Haitians during the Peace of Amiens. After initial successes Leclerc's army, decimated by yellow fever, harassed by the Blacks and cut off from France by the renewal of the war, wisely surrendered to the British. The conventions at Paris and Vienna took no account of Haiti and left the French at liberty to attack her again when

* Christophe was King of part of the old French colony of St. Domingue. The other part, also ruled by ex-slaves, was called the Haitian Republic.

they wished. Christophe's relationship with the Republic of Haiti was also stormy and sometimes the two countries were at war. So long as these threats remained Christophe needed to keep up a large standing army, though this was economically damaging and politically dangerous. Recognition by the British would give Haiti a new security against such dangers.

Christophe saw Haiti's second need as education, without which she could never raise herself from the miserable state in which the French had left her. Here again he must turn to England, both because the most advanced educational pioneers were English and because he could find in the Abolitionists a group of men able and willing to help him. Christophe's reasoning ran on the same lines as his feelings, his affection for England having been reinforced by her Abolition of the Slave Trade. He modelled his own dress and manner on that of George III whom he admired immensely. He never felt the same liking for Americans, partly because of their flirtations with Napoleon and partly because of their tolerance of slavery. Christophe would pace about the streets carrying a stout stick with which he would belabour any idler he saw. He was once taking an American merchant to task for a breach of Haitian regulations, when the man muttered, 'I wish I had you at Charleston now.' The King heard him, and abandoning his rule never to let anyone know he spoke English, replied, 'And how much do you think I should fetch?'[1]

The first letter Christophe sent Wilberforce must have reminded the latter of his mysterious correspondent from Demerara. It weighed eighty-five ounces and bore a carrying charge of £37. 10. Their early correspondence was about education. Wilberforce referred Christophe to the British and Foreign School Society, which followed Joseph Lancaster's system. Wilberforce had refused to become vice-president of the Lancaster schools on the grounds that 'emulation and vanity are the vital breath of the system', but Lancaster's methods were well suited to mass education where there could be few teachers. He claimed that 'one master may conduct a school of 1,000 children with perfect ease' and achieved this by an ingenious system under which monitors played the part of assistant masters and lesson boards were used. Lancaster taught Reading, Writing, Arithmetic and Needlework, and in an age when other schools enforced discipline with savage brutality he substituted humiliations for corporal punishments. Christophe, so far as flogging was concerned, inclined more to the views of Dr. Keate, but he adopted the rest of Lancaster's system. The first master, Thomas Gulliver, arrived in Haiti in September 1816.

The first school excited everyone by its success. In April 1817 Gulliver reported, 'My scholars possess great abilities, they make rapid progress in the English Language. It is now six months since I commenced to qualify some monitors and at present they are capable of teaching a class of thirty or forty boys. . . . They have advanced in six months to the sixth and seventh classes, and go through the four first rules of arithmetic in English with facility.'[2] The King inspected the school and expressed his satisfaction to Gulliver with the gift of a sheep and some coffee and sugar. By the end of 1817 there were five schools open in Haiti. In 1818 a Royal Academy was set up to provide secondary education. The progress made by the Haitian pupils convinced visitors that their race was not intellectually inferior to the white.

Christophe also founded hospitals under the superintendence of his Scottish doctor, Duncan Stewart, which were thought to be as good as any in England. He tried agricultural experiments, giving his soldiers small grants of land, and asking for English workmen to demonstrate the use of the plough. Schools for girls followed those for boys.

These developments were followed with eager excitement. English Abolitionists experienced the same feelings as liberals in France at the time of the American Revolution. Here in front of their eyes, all their arguments were being justified, all their dreams fulfilled. An independent Negro state, peopled by those who had been slaves, but enlightened and set upon improving itself, must soon bring the whole hideous edifice of slavery down in ruins. Sir Joseph Banks expressed his enthusiasm in a letter to Wilberforce: 'Were I five and twenty as I was when I embarked with Captain Cook, I am very sure I should not lose a day in embarking for Haiti. To see a set of human beings emerging from slavery, and making most rapid strides towards the perfection of civilization, must I think be the most delightful of all food for contemplation.'[3] Wilberforce lamented to Macaulay, 'Oh how I wish I was not old and you not too busy to go.' As it was he could do much to help. He wrote to Stephen, 'He has requested me to get for him seven schoolmasters, a tutor for his son, and seven professors for a Royal College he desires to found. Amongst these are a classical professor, a medical, a surgical, a mathematical, and a pharmaceutical chemist.' The King asked him to sit for a portrait and sent him one of himself and his son.

On November 18, 1816, Christophe wrote a long and friendly letter to Wilberforce. 'Je suis pénétré mon cher Wilberforce, des sentiments généreux et philanthropiques que vous m'exprimez, et je serais indigne de l'amitié pure que vous m'avez vouée, si je ne faisais tous mes efforts pour la mériter, en suivant les sages conseils que vous me donnez.'[4] The King said that he understood English perfectly and wished Wilberforce to write in that language. He expressed great satisfaction with the progress of the schools. The spreading of religion and morality would be more difficult in a country fresh from slavery and twenty years of revolutionary and civil wars, but he intended to see that it took place. But what must have excited Wilberforce most was Christophe's desire to dissociate his country from everything French, to eradicate the French language and replace it with English and to establish the Anglican Church in place of the Catholic. He launched into a lengthy passage in which he praised the English national character as brave, loyal, philanthropic, religious and honest and denounced the French as degenerate, degraded, vile and false. He contrasted Louis XVIII's vaunted religion with his authorisation of plots to enslave Haiti; he finished by begging Wilberforce to consider the portrait he had sent as that of two of his most sincere friends.

Wilberforce needed no such encouragement to spur on his efforts for Haiti. It was already too appealing a cause, but every letter he wrote to the King now contained some religious message. On October 8, 1818, he sent off an immense letter, which must have nearly brought their bills for carrying charges level. Wilberforce had tried and failed to obtain some recognition of Haitian independence from the meeting of the powers at Aix-la-Chapelle. He sent Clarkson as an emissary. 'Clarkson seems formed by Providence for the purpose,' he wrote in his diary. Clarkson was also acting directly for Henri Christophe, but although he impressed Czar Alexander by showing him letters of Christophe, he returned with no more than expressions of friendship. Nevertheless neither he nor Wilberforce thought the chances of a French invasion were very high. Together with this message of encouragement he was able to tell Christophe that the Spanish had joined with the Portuguese in abolishing the Slave Trade.

He had great difficulty in finding suitable candidates for employment in Haiti. Apart from the services and missionaries he found that the 'disinclination of men of good character to go abroad is very great unless they can find no way of maintaining themselves at home'.[5] Religion alone, he thought, could strengthen men to do their duty in the midst of temptations. He slipped easily into a discussion of the value of religion to the State and of the superiority of the Protestant system. He pointed out the support given by the religious to Abolition. He recommended the Protestant Sunday.

'A great variety of little works,' he continued, 'have been published in this country of late years for the purpose of inculcating useful knowledge and good works. Many of these though professing to be intended for the use of young people, may be read with advantage by persons of any age.'[6] He sent out a great number of these tracts for use in Christophe's new schools. 'A few copies of the different kinds that are very handsomely bound are intended for the use of your Majesty's own family who may be inclined to read them, and I cannot but flatter myself that they will derive both pleasure and profit from the perusal.'[7] He also sent Christophe a copy of the British Encyclopaedia, 'an excellent publication, in truth a library of itself', Dialogues on Political Economy and, to reinforce the King's Protestant leanings, Histories of the Jesuits and the Inquisition. Christophe cannot in fact have done more than toy with the idea of changing Churches.

He was a regular attendant at Mass and his country was firmly Catholic. He playfully gave the two Histories to his Roman Catholic Archbishop.

Wilberforce had discussed with Stephen the dangers posed by Christophe's armies. Now that he was convinced that France did not intend to invade Haiti, he felt bound to pass on his views. 'I am aware, indeed,' he wrote, 'that hitherto your Majesty has been under the necessity of considering yourself to be ready to repel the sudden assault of an invading enemy, rather than as administering the concerns of a Kingdom at peace with all the world. This we know has rendered it necessary for you to be a nation of soldiers. But surely it cannot be but that you would have notice from your friends in this country if the French court should be infatuated enough to renew their attempt. . . . I trust, therefore, that your Majesty may be able to allow your people to slide gradually into the various lines of civil industry, and get to keep them in a state in which they may be at any time able to come forward effectually for their own preservation, even more than for your Majesty's defence.'[8]

British recognition of Haiti depended on the attitude of the House of Commons, where feelings against 'the African cause' still ran high. There was also much goodwill and generosity to be tapped and he asked Christophe for a résumé of events in Haiti since 1790.

Of all the King's requirements the ploughmen proved the most difficult to fill. 'The honest rustics and their apparatus', as he called them in a letter to Christophe, did not embark until the end of 1819, and then they left Wilberforce full of misgivings. He wrote to Macaulay on November 9.

'My heart quite fails me at the idea of sending these . . . raw creatures into so distant, and to them, so strange a clime, without preparing them more for what they have to expect. I began my note meaning to entreat you to talk with them, especially on what I did not mention, the moral, or rather immoral state of society in Haiti . . . I desired them to confer with you about health, how to proceed on the first symptoms which you would state to them they ought to regard as indications of approaching sickness and how best to take precautions against its attacks.'[9]

The ploughmen came to no harm but neither were their implements successful. One was sent to a place so rocky that it could be tilled as well by the Haitians' primitive implements as by the iron ploughs bought by Wilberforce. The other could not persuade the local farmers to abandon their old ways. Both soon returned to England.[10]

Wilberforce's instincts about the danger of keeping so great an army proved to be right, though he had only seen one side of the King's character. He had exchanged letters with Christophe the visionary, the idealist and the philosopher, the King who was determined to prove his people the equals of any. He had had misgivings at times, as when he wrote to Thomas Harrison in September 1818. 'I am truly concerned at reading in the papers passages which afford but too much reason to fear that Christophe is again about to renew hostilities against the Haytian Republic as it is called, it is some palliation that he probably is afraid of being attacked by the French on that quarter. Still where power has once been tasted, one cannot help fearing the disposition to extend the means of gratification—nothing can be so ill judged with a view to interesting the Public in his behalf against any attack that might be made on him by the French Government.'[11] But he never knew Christophe the tyrant, or saw the means he used to drag his people into modern life. As time passed Christophe grew more violent, his demands increased and his rages became more frequent. In August 1820 he suffered a stroke followed by partial paralysis. His enemies rebelled, his own guard deserted him and he committed suicide.

Wilberforce heard the news on December 9. Shortly afterwards he wrote to the Reverend F. Wrangham:

'I cannot mention Hayti without interposing a word or two concerning this same *tyrant*, as now that he is fallen it seems the fashion to call Christophe. If he did deserve that name, it is then compatible with the warmest desire in a sovereign for the improvement and happiness of his people; and I must add that all the authentic accounts I ever heard of him have led me to believe that he was really a great man, with but few infirmities.'[12] A year later he wrote to Stephen, 'Poor Christophe! I cannot help grieving at the idea of his character's being left to the dogs and vultures to be devoured.'[13]

Wilberforce made a final effort to save some of Christophe's works. He had heard that de Vastey, one of Christophe's supporters, had been sentenced to death. He wrote to 'the Head of Haytian Government' asking for mercy for de Vastey, and imploring him not to destroy the schools that Christophe had started.[14] Both pleas were in vain. By the time Wilberforce wrote his letter, de Vastey had been dead nearly two months and the schools too were doomed. The country sank back into ignorance and disorder and once again provided the West Indian lobby with a debating point.

Henri Christophe's widow and daughters were allowed to leave Haiti. They arrived in England in the summer of 1821, and stayed until 1824, when they moved to the more congenial climate of Italy. They stayed in Clarkson's home for nearly a year. Long afterwards Clarkson confided to Benjamin Haydon that 'when Christophe's wife and daughters, all accomplished women, were brought or introduced by him to Wilberforce and others in high life, there was a sort of shrink at admitting them into high society'.[15] Wilberforce wrote to Mrs. Clarkson in March 1822, 'I am sure I should be cordially glad to render them any benefit, as would Mrs. Wilberforce also. But I have no time to spare and she has not at present spirit to undertake an office which would require a considerable share of them.'[16] Wilberforce's reluctance to receive the Haitians was attributed rather ungenerously by Clarkson to a refusal to recognise even royal negroes as social equals and by Henri Christophe's biographer to a dislike for the widow's bumptious escort Captain Sutherland. The reason he gave was more likely to be right. Their elder daughter had died on December 30 and Barbara might well have needed longer than two months to recover enough to face an invasion of royal Haitian ladies.

CHAPTER XXX

SLAVERY

WHEN the Abolitionists first united and formed their committee they had been in some doubt as to which to abolish, Slavery or the Slave Trade. They chose the latter, over Granville Sharp's protests, and rationalised their decision with the claim that once the Trade had been abolished planters would be forced by self-interest to take care of their slaves. As the slaves improved and acquired education and 'manners', it would become odious and impossible to keep them in a state of servitude. The end of the Slave Trade would lead almost by an organic process to the death of slavery, much as a tree can be killed by the removal of a strip of bark at its base. It might be possible to remove the bark but harder to fell the tree.

Having decided to abolish the Trade the Abolitionists let Slavery pass from their minds, except in as far as it affected the campaign for Abolition. But since the planters argued that they were transporting the slaves to far better circumstances than they had ever known before, the Abolitionists were forced to investigate conditions in the West Indies as well as in Africa. They discovered enough to justify a second crusade but one could understand their not wishing to deal with both at once. After producing horrifying examples of atrocities on the plantations they would often go on to deny an intention of freeing the slaves, but one would imagine that their discoveries had marked down slavery for destruction as soon as they had finished with the Trade.

It has been maintained that this was what Wilberforce did, that he always aimed at the abolition of Slavery as well as of the Slave Trade. The Abolitionists were indeed determined at the beginning of their campaign to end both evils. Wilberforce himself was first drawn to Abolition as much by the plight of the negroes in the West Indies as by that of the slaves on the Middle Passage. But at some stage in the campaign they seem to have lost sight of part of their original aim. Abolition proved to be far more difficult than they had expected and they knew that Emancipation, which violated sacred rights of property and raised untried constitutional issues, would be more difficult still.

But the main reason for the change was probably the development during the Abolition debates of the 'amelioration' argument, which arose from the planters' claim that Abolition would depopulate the West Indies. The Abolitionists discovered that the fall in the numbers of the slaves was very small, in spite of the barbarous way in which they were treated. Reasonable treatment, they argued, would ensure the return of a 'natural increase' in their numbers. The planters would be forced to improve the lot of their existing slaves if deprived of new ones by Abolition. The methods to be used would include not only improvements in the slaves' material well-being, but also the cultivation of their morals, the introduction of religion and the encouragement of marriage and family life. Abolition would therefore speedily end the worst of slavery; the improvement in the slaves' lot would be a continuous and painless process, which would end in their transformation into black equivalents of the sturdy yeomen and free peasantry whom Wilberforce imagined to populate his own country.

It would finally become so palpably wrong to keep such people slaves that the institution of slavery would wither away, or failing that be abolished without any difficulty. So confident was Wilberforce that the seed of freedom had been sown in the West Indies that, when on the eve of Abolition Lord Percy proposed that a date should be fixed for freeing the slaves' children, he said that he was glad the motion had been made, since it allowed him to show that far from favouring Emancipation, he was prepared to oppose it when put forward by others.[1]

This argument had two dangerous and obvious fallacies. In the first place it assumed that the planters would react to Abolition in a rational manner, an assumption which was unjustified by any action of theirs in the past. Their behaviour over the Foreign Slave Trade Bills had shown an inflexible obstinacy which bordered on a death wish. If the planters did not co-operate the whole amelioration argument fell to the ground.

The second fallacy was the assumption that improvements in the slaves' conditions would lead to their freedom. The Abolitionists had only to look at foreign colonies to see that this was not necessarily true. The Spanish treated their slaves very much better than the English, but Spanish slavery lasted longer than that of any other European power. In Spanish colonies the planters had to prepare their slaves for baptism and send them to mass on Sundays and festivals. If a slave wished to marry a woman from another plantation his master must buy her or sell him at a fair valuation. No married couple could be separated by sale. Slaves were encouraged to buy their own freedom and the conditions under which they could do so were controlled by an official known as the Protector of the Slaves. All slaves had allotments on which they could grow food and rear pigs; they were allowed 134 days a year for their cultivation. If a

Spanish slave was ill-treated he could apply for a licence to be sold com-
pulsorily to another owner. Infants could be emancipated before birth for
twenty-five dollars. The result of these lenient laws was that the free
black and coloured population of Spanish colonies became roughly
equal to that of the slaves.[2] But the institution of slavery was never
threatened, nor was this tolerance strong enough to survive a change in
economic circumstances. Cuba, for example, was the largest and, potentially, one of the richest of the sugar islands, and yet when a British expedition captured Havana in 1762 they found only 500 tons of sugar. This,
Cuba's output for the year, was a hundredth of that of Jamaica, a smaller
island.[3] The Spanish colonial regulations forbade any trade with foreigners and the Spanish market was not sufficient to absorb the output of
intensively cultivated colonies. The revolt in St. Domingue and the relaxation of controls changed the situation and Cuba began her rise to the
position of the greatest sugar producer in the world. As she did so the
conditions of the slaves in Cuba became as bad as elsewhere. It was too
early for the Abolitionists to learn the lesson that the treatment of slaves
depended as much on financial temptations as on legal safeguards, but
they should have known from the Spanish experience that amelioration
did not necessarily lead to emancipation.

They were in any case justified in making amelioration their first objective. Sir George Stephen, who elsewhere takes Wilberforce to task for
procrastination, admits that the first introduction in 1823 of a motion for
Emancipation was premature and that there was then no general basis of
support for it.[4] But long before 1823 it had become clear that the West
Indians, left to themselves, would do nothing to improve the conditions
of the slaves. James Stephen compared entrusting reform to the planters
to turning over the law of the country to 'the swell mob'. Amelioration,
apart from being desirable in itself, was, for a time, the only practicable
objective. It was also a necessary stepping stone between slavery and
freedom. For Emancipation to succeed Parliament must first be convinced
either that the slaves were ready for it or that the West Indians were so
reluctant to make any concessions that Emancipation was the only answer.

The campaign for the Abolition of Slavery was set into motion by the
West Indians' resistance to Registration, which in its turn was delayed by
a wish to secure Abolition of the Trade by other powers before proceeding
to new ground. But in 1817 Wilberforce seemed to be feeling his way
toward Emancipation. He wrote to Stephen on January 15: 'Reflection
renders me more and more confident that we shall, or at least that they
who live a few years will see the beginnings of great reforms in the West
Indies.'[5] The next year the opposition to Registration led the Abolitionists
to investigate the conditions of the slaves and they were so horrified by
their findings that they realised Registration alone was no cure for such

evils. The word 'Emancipation' now begins to occur in Wilberforce's correspondence. He heard at the beginning of 1818 of a planter who had murdered one of his slaves and had been punished only by a sentence of three months. 'My mind becomes so affected by the sad state of these poor injured wretches that it keeps me awake at night. Oh may God enable us to possess the nation with a due sense of their wrongs and that we may be the instruments of redressing them.'[6] On January 31 he was warned by Castlereagh not to press for Emancipation until the Abolition treaties with the other powers had been concluded. He took this warning to heart and allowed the next two years to pass without disturbing the attempts to achieve an international suppression of the Trade and the Registration of slaves in the West Indies. He also realised that it might seem insensitive to press for Emancipation when everyone else's attention was focused on the depression at home.

By 1821 Wilberforce was too old and too ill to take the lead in another protracted Parliamentary crusade. Emancipation promised to be as distant a goal as Abolition, for if the Abolitionists were stronger, their opponents' position was easier to defend. It was essential for him to choose a successor, and in his choice he faced the same problem which had confronted the Abolition Committee nearly forty years before. The stalwarts of the movement were all too old or too much associated with a particular party. His choice when it came must have seemed daring, for he selected a little known and inexperienced Member of Parliament, but his judgement was sound.

Thomas Fowell Buxton had much in common with Wilberforce. He too came from an old merchant family; he too was an Evangelical; he had a Quaker wife and mother and was the brother-in-law of Elizabeth Fry. The resemblance between their backgrounds was in contrast to the striking difference in their appearances. They must have seemed as ill-assorted a couple as Wilberforce and Milner in earlier days. Buxton was a huge man, tall, broad, athletic and devoted to the country sports he had loved since he was a boy. His old family gamekeeper, Abraham Plaistow, who taught him his field sports, remained his friend for life. He was a man of great physical and moral courage; he once swam out to a wreck in a gale without a rope and rescued a drowning sailor. He commented that the waves played with him as he might have with an orange. On another occasion Buxton was told that there was something badly wrong with his dog Prince; when he got home he found Prince covered with mud and running around biting everything he could see. Buxton saw him bite at least a dozen dogs, two boys and a man. Prince then set off towards London and Buxton followed on his horse, but the dog took no notice of his master's voice. Buxton, worried by the damage he might do if he reached London, decided that he was justified in risking his life to stop him. He leaped off his horse, seized Prince by the neck and secured him safely. The dog died, raving mad, the next day. Buxton could easily have killed him without any risk to himself, but, he explained, 'I was determined not to kill him, as I thought that if he should prove not to be mad, it would be such a satisfaction to the three persons whom he had bitten.'[7]

Unlike Wilberforce Buxton was not rich and he worked for seven years in a brewery before entering Parliament in 1818. But he made his mark two years earlier in a speech at the Mansion House on behalf of the distressed Spitalfields weavers. Wilberforce wrote him a letter of congratulation in which he looked forward to working on other causes with him in the future. He spoke in Parliament in favour of every motion for softening the Penal Code; he wished to abolish the death penalty for all crimes except murder.

On January 30, 1821, Buxton attended a meeting of the African Institution, having abandoned a day's shooting to do so. This sacrifice may have made him irritable. In any case he spoke his mind about the Society's inactivity and ineffectiveness. A few days later he met Wilberforce: 'I was quite astonished at Wilberforce yesterday. I had not seen him since my vehement reprobation of the African Institution. Yesterday he was warm to excess; over and over again he thanked me for the boldness and openness of my remarks, and said they had penetrated deeply into his heart.'[8] It seems likely that the sight of this vigorous young Abolitionist taking his leaders to task may first have persuaded Wilberforce that he had found his successor. He came to a decision on May 23 after listening to Buxton speak, with great eloquence, on Capital Punishment, and the next day offered him the leadership of the Anti-Slavery campaign.

Buxton, although favourably disposed to Emancipation, had not mastered the subject in the depth that he had his own causes, the reform of the Penal Code and of conditions in prisons. He delayed a full year and a half before accepting Wilberforce's offer. He was frightened that his work might make him responsible for a revolt of the slaves in the West Indies. 'If a servile war should break out,' he asked, 'and fifty thousand perish, how should I like that?' But he resolved this difficulty by deciding that if he had two sons he would rather choose to have one free and one dead than both living in slavery.[9]

There were several reasons for delaying the introduction of a Bill to abolish slavery. It must be demonstrated that the planters would do nothing on their own. The negotiations with other powers must not be disturbed and these negotiations stretched on interminably. Abolition Acts were brought about without too much difficulty, but it was a different matter persuading the other powers to enforce these Acts and impossible to get them to agree to mutual rights of search. France was the worst offender. She had in theory abolished the Trade in 1815, but in

1821 Macaulay wrote to Wilberforce: 'Think of a company formed at Nantes having twenty-four slave ships all ready to take up the Trade when the Spaniards and Portuguese should relinquish it.' Castlereagh and Wellington worked indefatigably to stop these abuses and it would have been foolish to introduce emancipation while they had any chance of success.

Information on the Slave Trade had come easily from the seamen who had been so mistreated in slave ships. The West Indies had no equivalent source. There was a general loyalty and cohesiveness in the islands which was lacking in the Trade and it was much more difficult to gather damning facts about slavery. The task of discovering about slavery fell on Macaulay and Stephen, the only two Abolitionists with first-hand experience of the West Indies. Stephen began his monumental indictment of the system while both he and Macaulay helped with the groundwork for Wilberforce's Manifesto against Slavery, which was published in 1823. By 1822 none of these reasons for delay applied with the same force. It was all too clear that the West Indians would do nothing constructive on their own, and every diplomatic overture seemed to have been exhausted.

On August 19, 1822, Wilberforce heard that Castlereagh, now Lord Londonderry, had committed suicide. 'I never was so shocked by any incident,' he wrote to Stephen. 'He really was the last man in the world who appeared likely to be carried away into the commission of such an act! So cool, so self-possessed. It is very curious to hear the newspapers speaking of incessant application to business, forgetting that by the weekly admission of a day of rest, which our Maker has graciously enjoined, our faculties would be preserved from the effects of this constant strain. . . . If he had suffered his mind to enjoy such occasional remission, it is highly probable the springs would never have snapped as they did, from over-tension. Alas! Alas! poor fellow! I did not think I should feel for him so very deeply.'[10] Wilberforce was more upset than he would have been had Castlereagh's suicide not followed soon after those of Whitbread and Romilly. He was also conscious that the Abolitionists had lost their most able diplomat and this must have been another factor in his decision to being forward a bill for Emancipation. Wilberforce tried to gather up the lost diplomatic reins. He wrote to Czar Alexander, sternly intimating 'that we should have no favourable opinion of his religious or moral character if he did not honestly exert his powers on our behalf'.[11] But Alexander's attitude remained the same as ever, one of distant sympathy. Wellington's exertions for the cause made Wilberforce declare, 'I shall love all generals the better for it as long as I live.'[12]

Canning took on Castlereagh's role and showed the same energy in fighting the Slave Trade. Brazil was in the process of achieving her independence and wanted British recognition. Canning wrote to Wilberforce on October 24, 1822, 'I expect every day an application by Brazil for the acknowledgment of that independence. Shall we be justified in making the Abolition of the Slave Trade by Brazil a *sine qua non* condition of any such acknowledgment? I incline to think so.'[13] But as time passed the damage that could be done to such negotiations by Emancipation became negligible.

Reluctance to offend ministers and a tendency to postpone difficult decisions were undoubted weaknesses of Wilberforce's. There was always some reason why any year should be unsuitable for raising a particular issue. He was criticised for this fault by men who otherwise had the deepest admiration and affection for him, by Romilly, Buxton and George Stephen. He would sometimes defend his procrastination on extraordinary grounds. In 1816 when he was agonised by the question of Registration he wrote the following note:

'Against precipitancy—Moses 80, Aaron 83 years old when God sent them to lead out the Israelites from Egypt. Abraham 100 years old when Isaac born. Our Saviour himself 30 years old before he came forth, having till then probably worked with his father at his trade.'[14]

In 1822 he had resolved his doubts and now felt conscious-stricken by his failure to raise the slaves' case earlier. 'We must now call on all good men,' he wrote in his diary, 'throughout the Kingdom to join us in abolishing this wicked system, and striving to render the degraded race by degrees a free peasantry.'[15] He was depressed by the decay in his faculties which he may have exaggerated and by the miserable state of his eyes. He did not feel up to the struggle. As he began work on his Manifesto[16] he missed his white negroes more than ever.

Once the decision was taken arrangements went ahead with breakneck speed. A society was founded in January for the mitigation and gradual abolition of slavery. He did not finish his Manifesto in time for the opening of Parliament. 'I am become heavy and lumbering,' he complained, 'and not able at once to start into a canter, as I could twenty years ago.'[17] He had to send part of it ahead to the printers, and it was not published until early in March. On March 19 he presented a petition against slavery from the Quakers. He was tired and confused when he rose and forgot some of his most important points. He was prepared for a bitter assault on the petition from the West Indies, but he was completely out-manoeuvred by Canning. 'Canning's generalship admirable, and his troops submissive. He let me exhaust my motions—that it be received, printed, etc. Then merely asked whether I meant to make a distinct motion? None of the friends of the Cause said a word. I, who had been thinking over the topic to be ready for reply, was quite confounded. All of us abattus. Never almost in my life was I so vexed by a parliamentary proceeding. I felt as if God had forsaken me, whom just before I had invoked; as if I had been wanting to the Cause etc. I could scarcely get to sleep, and was ashamed to see my friends, though they tell me the effect was better than I had conceived.'[18]

After this fiasco the campaign had to be planned more carefully. Wilberforce's Manifesto had prepared the ground and so impressed one West Indian proprietor that he declared, 'Its perusal has so affected me that should it cost me my whole property, I surrender it willingly.'[19] But he was resigned to the battle being a long one. To abolish slavery involved not only the need to violate others' property, something that went against all the ingrained prejudices of the times, but also to legislate on the internal affairs of colonies which, in their own legislative assemblies, enjoyed some form of self-government. This was a much more daring step than the regulation of a branch of commerce, yet the Slave Trade had taken nearly twenty years to abolish. The country and Parliament had to be convinced that Slavery was intolerable and that it would never be remedied by any action of the West Indians. Only when the colonists had failed to put their house in order could Parliament be expected to act for them. Before beginning an account of the Abolitionists' second crusade, it is worth examining the institution of slavery in British colonies and the forces ready to defend and attack it.

*

It was a commonplace claim of the defenders of slavery that West Indian slaves were far better off than English workmen. Their life of sun-kissed idleness, their well-fed and secure conditions, were contrasted with the dreary grind of a victim of the industrial revolution. From here it was an easy step to ridicule those who, like Wilberforce, sought to free the slaves while leaving the labourer in his misery. This distorted picture of slavery can be set against the violent attacks on it by the Abolitionists, notably by James Stephen.[20] The truth lay in between these two extreme views. But those who have sought to defend slavery on material grounds do not begin to understand the objections to it. Slavery consists of the total subjugation of one person to another, who may or may not abuse his power. The master may be a benevolent despot like 'Monk' Lewis, or a merciless sadist like Hodge, Huggins or the Mosses, whose brutality towards their slaves was to be a spur to the Emancipation Movement. Human nature being frail and easily corrupted by power, it is natural to expect a high degree of suffering on the part of the slaves. But cruelty is incidental to slavery; degradation is its very essence. To say that slavery is harmless if administered without cruelty is to reduce human beings to the level of animals. Sir George Stephen put it well in a letter to Harriet Beecher Stowe. He wrote of the Abolitionists: 'They even threatened to defeat their own heroic efforts in ameliorating a condition that amelioration only degrades; for of all the miserable spectacles on earth, the most miserable, and the most degraded, and the most hopeless, is that of the well conditioned and contented slave!'[21]

Any form of slavery was, therefore, obnoxious to the Abolitionists, but Parliament had to be convinced that the condition of British slaves was intolerable. It is difficult to assess if they were justified in this claim. In all the colonies except for those of Spain, the well-being of the slaves depended entirely on their masters' whim. But British colonies had perhaps the least legislative restrictions on the planters.

Manumission, the freeing of individual slaves either by their masters or by the purchase of their own liberty, was not encouraged in British colonies in the way that it was in Spanish. In many colonies there were taxes on manumission, while in others owners had to guarantee that the cost of maintaining freed slaves would not fall on the parish. Although the free coloured class was a great source of political stability, the island of Barbados in 1801 taxed the manumission of females more heavily than males,[22] to restrict their numbers. In Spanish colonies the price at which a slave could buy his freedom was set by the Protector of the Slaves and the highest price allowed by law was well below the value of a prime slave. In British colonies the master could and did hold his slave up for ransom and extract every penny he owned for the one thing in life he wanted. The result of this was that the free coloured population in British colonies never reached Spanish proportions; there were more manumitted slaves in Cuba than in all the British West Indies combined.

The slave, then, could not buy his freedom unless his master agreed; he was also tied to a particular plantation. If he married his family could be separated by sale at the whim of his owner. If the plantation went bankrupt the stock of slaves were sold by auction for debt. There were regulations concerning the treatment of slaves which varied from colony to colony. In Barbados, where the harshest code was to be found, it was no offence for a master to kill his slave in the course of punishment, while an outsider who murdered a slave laid himself open only to a small fine. In some colonies the murder of a slave was theoretically punishable by death. But in no British colonies did the courts allow the testimony of a slave against his master. Since the only witnesses of punishment were likely to be the ou er slaves this law allowed the master to do anything he wished. The excuse for the exclusion of their evidence was that the slaves, because of their ignorance of Christianity, could not understand the significance of oaths. But this was part of a vicious circle which held out no hope of an improvement in the slaves' conditions. Whatever laws were passed they must be enforced by the courts; the courts could not act without evidence; evidence could only be provided by other slaves; slaves could not testify until they were Christians; their masters would not allow them to become Christians.

The Church of England, in the West Indies, did not regard its obligations as extending to slaves. The Methodists, by far the most numerous
missionaries, were often persecuted and vilified, though some planters had
the sense to realise that the missionaries' work would foster order, sobriety
and morality as well as religion. Throughout the struggle for Emancipation the roles played by the Established and Dissenting Churches could
not have been in greater contrast. The latter tried both to convert and free
the slaves. The former not only denied them religious instruction and,
through the Bishops in the House of Lords, opposed all measures to free
them, but was also a large slave-owner. The Society for the Propagation
of the Gospel, a High Church Missionary society with which Wilberforce
had no connection, owned many slaves, to whom it made certain that the
Gospel was never propagated.[23]

In a sense the sort of amelioration which might be produced by religion
in the West Indies was as dangerous to the planters as to the Abolitionists.
Seeing a population of docile, tractable, religious slaves Parliament might
conclude either that they were clearly fit for freedom or that their conditions were so good that no changes were needed. Neither side knew which
argument would prevail but both had gains as well as losses to make from
amelioration; the planters would acquire more industrious and less
rebellious slaves, the Abolitionists some mitigation of an evil system.

*

Most of the slaves in the West Indies worked in the sugar fields. The
slave's ultimate sovereign would be the owner of his plantation, but he was
in all probability an absentee landlord. An agent would run the estate for
him; this agent was likely to be a professional man, with many estates to
run, and in his turn hired an overseer. Under the overseer there would be
a series of assistants and head negroes. These assistants to the overseers
were the immediate masters of the slaves.

So much of the evidence about the slaves' work is coloured by a desire
to justify or condemn the system, that it is difficult to discover how arduous it was. They had to work for long hours, some eleven hours a day on
average, but the planters said that this was because they could not be made
to work hard. They certainly came away from the fields with enough
energy to indulge in wild dancing and singing at night. They were allowed
Sundays and every other Saturday for the cultivation of their own allotments. Sugar was not only the most common crop but also the hardest on
the slaves, especially during the third of the year devoted to the harvest
and production of sugar. The process of producing sugar was kept going
continuously, day and night, and allowed to stop only from Saturday
evening to Sunday morning. Many of the slaves were exposed to intense
heat and others to the danger of having their limbs crushed in the rollers.

A hatchet was kept ready to sever their arms if this happened.[24] The slaves had to work harder and at more unpleasant tasks during the harvest than at any other time of year, and yet this was their favourite season; the activity and the atmosphere of feverish haste may have been a welcome relief from the monotony of the cane fields. They were also allowed to consume as much cane and cane-juice as they wished and there were fine opportunities for pilfering.

When the slave gangs went out to work at five in the morning they were accompanied by a head driver who carried a cart whip, which the West Indians claimed was a symbol of his authority,[25] and on some plantations this may have been so. But in the great majority of cases, it was all too functional. The driver was authorised to use his whip to spur on the slaves to work harder, like a coachman with tiring horses, or to punish them for unpunctuality, idleness or other minor offences. More severe floggings could be administered on the authority of the overseer. The whip was an essential part of slavery, its 'grand badge', Macaulay claimed: it was used to drive and punish the slave and the sound of its being cracked summoned them to work. Floggings as a rule were frequent rather than severe and not to be compared to those inflicted on the soldiers and sailors of the day. But there was no appeal from the sentence of the overseer and no control over his punishments.

The legal system protected the planters when they broke the law since the evidence of slaves was not admitted against them; but even if the physical evidence spoke for itself, as for example when the body of a slave was found mutilated, the jury of white planters would seldom convict the murderer and when they did the punishment usually fell well short of the crime. One planter, the infamous Arthur Hodge, was indeed hanged having first tortured at least sixty slaves to death. The uproar caused by his execution was such that the Governor proclaimed martial law.

'Monk' Lewis provides a pleasant contrast to Hodge. This famous Gothic romancer inherited two large estates in Jamaica. He was concerned about the future of his slaves, corresponded with Wilberforce and called on him to discuss the matter.[26] Unfortunately we do not know what advice he was given or how much of Lewis's regulations were inspired by Wilberforce. Although he had no reasons for misgivings about conditions on his properties, Lewis thought it his duty to make the perilous voyage to the West Indies to find out for himself. He arrived at his first plantation on a holiday and received a stronger impression of happiness and gaiety than he had ever had before. His arrival was treated as a cause for an indefinite extension of the holiday, and while his welcome was immense, less and less sugar was made and more and more stolen. Lewis was more amused than annoyed. Before he left Jamaica, he drafted a code on which his plantations were to be run. Labour in the fields was no longer to be driven by the lash. All punishments were to be entered in a register and a copy given to the culprit. Striking a slave was to be punished by dismissal. Every Saturday was to be kept free for the cultivation of the slaves' allotments and Sundays were to be days of rest. Allowances of food and clothing were laid down. He introduced ploughs to lighten field labour, particularly the back-breaking task of hoeing the sugar fields; he founded a hospital for sick slaves.

Lewis returned to Jamaica two years afterwards to see that his regulations were being observed. The slaves' joy at his return was so rapturous that those who should have been watching the cattle joined in and the animals escaped into a cane field and ruined it. He found that some of his improvements had foundered; the prize bulls he had sent out had all died and the ploughs had been misused and broken. But his regulations had been obeyed and the slaves had no complaints. Lewis then went on to his other property, which was too remote for him to have visited before. Here he 'expected to find a perfect paradise, and . . . found a perfect hell'. The slaves were being tyrannised by the trustee's underlings both black and white. 'All the blacks accused all the whites; all the whites accused all the blacks; and as far as I could make out, both parties were extremely in the right.'[27] Lewis dismissed the worst tyrants, pronounced his regulations, distributed presents and left the island. He contracted yellow fever on the ship home and died, a martyr to his own kindness.

One disturbing aspect of Lewis's experiment was that, although his slaves were well treated and although he had more women than men in his stock, their numbers declined. The 'unnatural' decrease in the numbers of the slaves was to feature both in the Abolition and Emancipation debates. In the first case the Abolitionists minimised it and forecast that it would be reversed by the better treatment and more equal balance between the sexes which would follow Abolition. In the second series of debates they made out the decrease to be as large as could be credible in order to prove that the slaves were still being mistreated. It is a difficult phenomenon to explain. Slaves in America, where they seem on the whole to have been treated at least as badly as in British colonies, nevertheless increased in numbers, while Lewis's slaves declined in spite of their excellent conditions. The infant mortality rate may not have been improved by Lewis's order that all babies should be plunged 'immediately upon their being born' into a tub of cold water. This, he was confident, 'infallibly preserved them from the danger of tetanus'. There does, however, seem to have been a corollary between the type of crop grown and the birth rate of the slaves. On sugar plantations slaves would decrease in numbers, on other plantations they would increase, and the more intense the cultivation of sugar the sharper the fall in population. After Emancipation the numbers of the Blacks again increased.

Most of the West Indian plantations fell somewhere in between Lewis's benign rule and Hodge's tyranny. As far as one can make such generalisations, the plantations administered by managers for rich absentee landlords seem to have been more humane, though when the manager was rewarded by a percentage of the profits the slaves were often driven too hard. Small plantations with resident owners had the worst reputation. Conditions were always degrading and often brutal, callous and unjust. But they were relieved by a certain rough bonhomie on the part of the planters which one meets over and over again in accounts of plantation life. Many planters regarded the slaves as their children and were genuinely outraged by the Abolitionist attacks. Lewis noticed on his first visit that his slaves addressed him with more familiarity than an English farmer would have used to his landlord.

The Spanish slaves responded to good treatment by seldom rebelling. Even during the height of the great revolt in St. Domingue the Spanish slaves in the other half of the island remained loyal. Judged by this yardstick British slavery does not emerge with credit, for there were frequent uprisings in the British West Indies. Some qualifications must be made. The greater number of whites and free negroes in Spanish colonies made rebellion less attractive, while the smaller volume of the Spanish Slave Trade meant that there were fewer dangerous Africans to lead the revolts. The English also imported very fierce tribesmen whom the other colonists would not buy. But the frequency of slave revolts still argues of great discontent, although the small casualties suffered by the whites on these occasions shows that the grievances of the slaves were general rather than directed against their masters. In America where the slaves certainly feared their owners more there were very few revolts. The suppression of slave rebellions was invariably merciless. Mass executions and hideous tortures showed what fears underlay the apparent good nature of the whites.

*

This then was the institution of slavery. Throughout the eighteenth century it had made an outstanding contribution to the wealth of the nation and the sugar islands had come to be the most treasured of all its possessions. By the time that Wilberforce launched the campaign for Emancipation their importance had greatly declined. Britain was fast becoming an industrial country, the first in the world, and her needs were now better suited by Free Trade and cheap raw materials than by protected colonies. But the West Indian interest still retained much of its strength in Parliament. A measure of this strength was provided when on May 22, 1823, the House debated a Bill to adjust the differences of duty on East and West Indian sugar. Wilberforce wrote in his diary, 'None interested for the question but the East Indians and a few of us anti-slavers, and the West Indians and government against us; so that 61 a less majority over 34 than might have been expected.'[28] According to Dr. Lushington, an eminent ecclesiastical lawyer who played a prominent role in the Emancipation campaign, the West Indian lobby could muster 56 votes in the Commons,[29] a figure consistent with the division on the sugar duties. The West Indian lobby had conducted the fight against Abolition, the Slave Traders having had little influence in Parliament. Abolition had not posed any real threat to the Planters' interests, indeed the abolition of the Foreign Slave Trade might have been drafted by one of them. But Emancipation, unless accompanied by very high compensation, would ruin them. They could therefore be trusted to exert their full strength against it. If the debate was to be waged on the condition of the slaves they had a better case than when defending the Slave Trade, which was so demonstrably wrong on every ground. If they had had the sense to implement the Commons resolutions on amelioration they could surely have prolonged slavery in the West Indies for another generation.

The enemy was stronger, but the Abolitionists were stronger too. When the Committee for Abolition had been founded in 1787 it had consisted of twelve people, none of whom were public figures and nine of whom were Quakers. The Anti-Slavery Society had the Duke of Gloucester as its president and five peers and fourteen Members of Parliament among its vice-presidents. Feeling in the country was still apathetic about slavery, but the Abolitionists knew that they had the organisation, the techniques and the cause to arouse it. Nor were they without allies; enough of the leading Whigs favoured Emancipation for the Abolitionists to hope that, when they returned to power, they would make it a government measure. There were also less disinterested allies. The East Indians resented a system which admitted West Indian sugar at a lower tariff than theirs. Whitmore, the East Indian leader in Parliament, was a vice-president of the Anti-Slavery Society, and had even been considered by Wilberforce as a possible successor.[30] His followers and the Abolitionists voted together on questions of the sugar duty and of slavery. The campaign to replace West with East Indian sugar might have been more successful if the latter had been of higher quality. The 'griping horrors of East India sugar' upset many a scrupulous stomach.

CHAPTER XXXI

THE CAMPAIGN AGAINST SLAVERY

ON May 15, 1823, a motion was introduced into the Commons: 'That the state of slavery is repugnant to the principles of the British constitution and of the Christian religion', and that it should gradually be abolished 'with as much expedition as may be found consistent with a due regard to the well-being of the parties concerned'. The motion, consisting as it did of a moral clarion call followed by a miserable qualification, reflects the hesitancy of its sponsors, and the scheme they produced was in keeping. Buxton emerged as the new leader of the campaign. He introduced the motion while Wilberforce merely spoke in its favour. Buxton argued, with some plausibility, that it was as wrong to enslave negroes at birth in the West Indies as to capture them and make them slaves in Africa. All slaves born after a certain date should therefore be free, and under this law slavery need not be abolished—'it will expire, it will, as it were, burn itself down into its socket and go out'. Meanwhile the last years of slavery should be made more bearable by the enactment of new regulations for the slaves' welfare. He had given a draft of these rules to Lord Bathurst, the Colonial Secretary; in future slaves should be attached to their estate rather than their owner, they should be admitted as witnesses, have a weekday free and be allowed to purchase their freedom in the Spanish manner. Religious instruction should be introduced and restraints on the master's right of punishment imposed.

Canning, the Leader of the House, rose immediately after Buxton. He agreed with many of the Abolitionists' points but argued against freeing the children of slaves as 'the least efficient and most hazardous' means of achieving Emancipation. He recommended instead that measures should be taken to improve the lot of the slaves so that they might eventually become fit for freedom. The Government would enforce these measures in the Crown colonies and recommend them to the colonial assemblies. If the latter refused to take action, the Government 'would not hesitate to come down to Parliament for counsel'.

Canning's arguments were so reasonable that the Abolitionists had to withdraw their motion. Wilberforce warned him that the Assemblies had always resisted reform, even when it was clearly in their own interests. But he believed that something might be achieved by determined government pressure. It was in any case obvious that Parliament would not consider legislation until the Assemblies had been given a chance to put their house in order.

Canning's position has never been clear. The first reaction of the Abolitionists was that he had betrayed their cause by undercutting it, rather as Dundas had when he proposed gradual Abolition. Canning himself had been a staunch Abolitionist, but he was speaking as the representative of a Government whose other members had had little sympathy with the cause. He was also suspected of having personal connections with the West Indies through his friendship with George Ellis. The West Indians allowed Canning's motion to pass without opposition because they could see that it had no teeth. So long as Emancipation must be preceded by amelioration and so long as the latter was in their hands, they were safe enough to continue their favourite tactic, prevarication.

Sir George Stephen understood this when he described Canning's resolutions as 'soothing, plausible and utterly impracticable'.[1] But he disagreed with those who thought they amounted to a betrayal of the cause, concocted in collusion with the planters. He saw Canning's speech rather as a response to the premature nature of Buxton's motion. In any case he regarded it as disastrous because it gave official recognition to Slavery. Stephen's objections are hard to follow. If Canning had not made his motion it is impossible to see in what way this could have hastened the day of Emancipation, and if any value were to be put on amelioration it must have been constructive. Wilberforce certainly thought so.

'We now stand in a perfectly new situation,' he said in his speech. 'We have now an acknowledgment on the part of government that the grievances of which we complain do exist, and that a remedy ought to be applied.'[2] Considering the difficulty experienced in reaching the same stage on Abolition, this was a satisfactory end to the first debate.

*

The Government's motion was greeted in the West Indies with incredulous horror. The Assembly of Jamaica passed a resolution containing this passage: 'A decree has gone forth whereby the inhabitants of this once valuable colony, hitherto esteemed the brightest jewel in the British Crown, are destined to be offered a propitiatory sacrifice at the altar of fanaticism.'[2] Every parish carried its own resolution of protest. There were dark prophecies of slave revolts and even talk of secession.

The most serious reaction to the proposals came not from the masters but from the slaves. The revolt in Demerara brought the whole issue alive and made it something about which people on either side could feel passionately. The campaign so far had been a phoney war, an exercise in shadow boxing. There had been a general agreement in Parliament, expressed through Canning's resolutions, that conditions on the plantations should be improved until the slaves were fit for freedom. There was an equally strong determination in the West Indies to resist any reforms; but the planters' tactics, agreement followed by obstruction, did not create the kind of atmosphere in which the public might take up the cause with their old Abolitionist fervour. The Abolitionists needed some dramatic event, a tangible enemy, or best of all a martyr. The planters duly provided them with one.

On May 23, 1823, Lord Bathurst informed the Governor of Demerara of the Commons' resolutions. He took literally Ellis's claim that the cart whip was now no more than a symbol of the driver's authority and demanded an immediate end to all flogging of women and to its use in the fields. Both Wilberforce and Macaulay thought he was moving too quickly. 'What!' Wilberforce exclaimed. 'Have they given such an order without preparation, and without explaining their purpose to the slaves— why it is positive madness!'[3] Macaulay wrote to him, 'The whip is the grand badge of slavery in the apprehension of the slaves, who feel it is the prominent mark of their servile state; its removal would naturally be but another name for emancipation. Our plan was certainly of a very different kind. They should have begun with all those reforms which would have had a wonderful influence, without seeming directly and suddenly to weaken the master's authority.'[4]

The Court of Proprietors temporised while wild rumours spread throughout the colony. Many of the slaves became convinced that the King had given them their freedom and that their masters were now cheating them of it. On August 18 a revolt broke out in two plantations, one of which was owned by the father of the future Liberal Prime Minister, W. E. Gladstone. The Governor's attempts to negotiate with the rebels met with a demand for the unconditional emancipation which, they claimed, was theirs by right. The Governor returned to Georgetown with some loss of dignity and that night 13,000 slaves from thirty-seven plantations joined the rebels. They were badly armed and easily subdued, but while they were in control of their plantations, their restraint was unusual. Whites were imprisoned but allowed to live and there was none of the usual looting or burning. This clemency was not returned. Nearly fifty slaves were hanged and three were given the dreadful sentence of 1,000 lashes and condemned to be worked in chains, two for the remainder of their lives.

The first reaction in England was to blame the Abolitionists for the revolt and cast the whole Emancipation movement under a cloud. Buxton wrote cheerfully, 'I much question whether there is a more unpopular individual than myself in the House just at this moment. For this I do not care.'[5] But as more news accumulated the Abolitionists' defensive attitude changed to one of outraged fury.

John Smith had been a Nonconformist missionary with a chapel on one of the plantations where the revolt started. He had not been happy in Demerara, for he loathed slavery and found some aspects of his work distressing. His efforts to bring religion to the slaves were obstructed at every turn by the authorities. He was also a consumptive and he suffered from the climate. On August 21 Smith was about to return to England for reasons of health when he was arrested and accused of complicity in the revolt. He was tried by court martial, convicted and sentenced to death, though with a recommendation for mercy. The Governor referred the case to England, but before a reply could be received Smith died in prison. The English Government had intended to reprieve him.[6]

The decision to try Smith by court martial was justified by the claim that he would never receive a fair trial from a jury of planters. But when the records of the trial were examined it was hard to see how he had benefited. Hearsay evidence was admitted for the prosecution 'to the third, the fourth, aye, even to the fifth degree', as Brougham later put it, while a defence witness was not allowed to relate a conversation in which he had himself taken part.[7] Smith's private journal and his religious views, although clearly irrelevant, were produced as evidence. The testimony of condemned slaves was admitted against him, slave evidence being allowed under a Dutch law which had continued in force after the British occupation of Demerara. Smith found a champion in Austin, the Church of England chaplain to the Georgetown garrison. Austin approached the case if anything prejudiced against Smith as a Dissenter and troublemaker, but he soon became convinced that Smith's religious instruction had prevented much bloodshed. He quoted one of the captured rebels as saying of killing: 'It is contrary to the religion we profess. We cannot give life and therefore we will not take it.'[8] Austin showed great courage in his support of Smith which earned him the vilification of the planters, the abuse of the colony's newspaper being mitigated only by the feebleness of its editor's pen.

'This wolf in sheep's clothing,' the *Guiana Chronicle* raged on February 7, 'this worthless animal, we have now fixed in a "tangible and credible shape", and. . . . Mr. Austin is the man! To find language sufficiently expressive to denote our abhorrence of this individual, is impossible. There is no language in the known world sufficiently strong for the purpose. . . . Mr. Austin's character is for ever gone. As a clergyman, as a preacher of the Doctrines of our Saviour, the fundamental principle of which is truth, he is sunk beyond redemption, his honour is forfeited; his name is blighted; and the pulpit cannot shield him from shame and disgrace. . . . Wherever he goes the finger of hatred shall point him out.'[9]

In the spring of 1824 Wilberforce suffered from a dangerous inflammation of the lungs. His family were deeply worried that he might make the sickness worse by overworking and expressed themselves with what he described as 'excessive solicitude'. He took this, like all his illnesses, philosophically. 'No man has been more favoured than I,' he would tell his sympathetic visitors, 'for even when I am ill my complaints occasion little suffering.'[10]

His sons were more concerned; Robert Isaac wrote: 'My father was first unwell Tuesday March 23rd 1824. Sunday 28th he was confined to his bed. Thursday night and Friday he was in great danger; he afterwards mended slowly, but was only out of bed once from March 28th to April 14th.

'Friday April 2nd; his cough was so bad that he was hardly allowed to speak at all. I was with him all the morning and about the only words I heard him say were, "How does dear Henry do?"' '[11] (Henry had had a slight feverish attack the day before.) Wilberforce had heard of Smith's death when on the brink of illness and the last entry in his diary before he was confined to his bed reads, 'Poor Smith the missionary died in prison at Demerara! The day of reckoning will come.'

He got up at the beginning of June and at once prepared for the debate on Smith. 'I very much wish, if my voice should be strong enough, to bear my testimony against the scandalous injustice exercised against poor Smith.'[12] When, on June 11, the debate took place, Wilberforce was disgusted with his own performance: 'I quite forgot my topics for a speech and made sad work of it.' But the Abolitionists had much the better of the debate; Lushington made a long and closely reasoned speech in which the methods used to obtain Smith's conviction were mercilessly exposed, while Brougham ripped to pieces the court martial's pretensions to legality. Smith had suffered from the worst features of Dutch and English law. The offence for which he was condemned to death was his failure to inform the authorities of the impending slave revolt. This crime carried the death penalty only under Dutch law, but the court martial which condemned him could be constituted only under British law. Smith's opponents had cited various legal authorities to support their case, Dutch, English and even one Frenchman who had, according to Brougham, 'as much to do with the question, in any conceivable view, as if he had been a Mogul doctor; yet his name, too, is brandished before us, as if to show the exuberance and variety of the stores at the command of my learned friends.'[13] He summed up this argument: 'One law takes from you the jurisdiction—the authority to try at all; and the other takes away the right to punish as you have punished. Between the horns of this dilemma I leave my learned friends.'[14]

The Abolitionists lost the vote by 146 to 193, but it was an encouraging result for them. Brougham's speech, according to one of the best historians of the Abolitionist movement, had 'dealt British slavery a blow from which it never recovered'.[15] The West Indian interest was of course solid against them and Canning, in an ingenious speech, had given Members grounds for opposing the motion without being convinced of the justice of the trial. The debate was conducted in a highly emotional atmosphere and interrupted by applause from both sides. The Abolitionists kept this emotion alive for the meeting of the Anti-Slavery Society on July 25. This meeting, a month before the publication of his essay on Milton, marks the first display to the public of the power of Macaulay's language. All the leading Abolitionists were there to hear him and the Duke of Gloucester occupied the chair. All except Zachary Macaulay listened with mounting excitement to the words of his son:

'When this country has been endangered either by arbitrary power or popular delusion, truth has still possessed one irresistible organ, and justice one inviolable tribunal. That organ has been an English press, and that tribunal an English jury. But in these wretched islands we see a press more hostile to truth than any censor, and juries more insensible to justice than any Star Chamber. In these islands alone is exemplified the full meaning of the most tremendous of the curses denounced against the apostate Hebrews, "I will curse your blessings".'

It had been said in defence of the court martial that a jury of planters would have behaved worse than it had. Macaulay made the most of this unguarded admission:

'Sir, I have always lived under the protection of the British laws, and therefore I am unable to imagine what could be worse; but, though I have small knowledge, I have a large faith. I by no means presume to set any limits to the possible injustice of a West Indian judicature. And since the colonists maintain that a jury composed of their own body not only possibly might but necessarily must, have acted with more iniquity than this Court Martial, I certainly shall not dispute the assertion, though I am utterly unable to conceive the mode.'[16]

Wilberforce punctuated this speech with exclamations of 'Capital!' and 'Wonderful!' After the speech he and Stephen each pumped one of Macaulay's hands and kept him there on the platform while the room shook with applause. Marianne Thornton was in the audience:

'I was so delighted with it that I should hardly have trusted my own feelings about it, but when I saw the grave old steady senators so carried away by the eloquence of the youthful orator, that even the decorum of the platform were forgotten, and the dignity of the Royal Duke compromised, by Mr. Wilberforce and Mr. Stephen catching hold of him as he was going back to his place, and keeping him there, each shaking a hand, while the very walls seemed to be coming down with the thunders of applause.'[17]

When Wilberforce replied he turned to Zachary Macaulay and said: 'My friend would doubtless willingly bear with all the base falsehoods, all the vile calumnies, all the detestable artifices which have been aimed against him, to render him the martyr and victim of our cause,* for the gratification he had this day enjoyed in hearing one so dear to him plead such a cause in such a manner.'[18]

Only Zachary Macaulay remained apparently unmoved by the occasion. 'Keen as his pleasure was,' wrote his grandson, 'he took it in his own sad way. From the first moment to the last, he never moved a muscle of his countenance, but sat with his eyes fixed on a piece of paper. While talking with his son that evening, he referred to what had passed only to remark that it was ungraceful in so young a man to speak with folded arms in the presence of royalty.'[19]

This was the last official notice taken of the death of Smith. But the temper of the Abolitionists had risen until they would never agree to any solution but Emancipation. Better still, they could now count the full strength of all the Nonconformist sects on their side. From 1824, Sir George Stephen judged, they played a part in the campaign second only to that of the Quakers, while the Bishops, second to the West India Committee, were their most relentless enemies.

In a sense it did not matter whether Smith was guilty or innocent. If he knew of an impending uprising the system of slavery put him in an impossible position. To tell the authorities would be to condemn many of his congregation to torture and death and to destroy all his own work. To withhold his information was to commit a capital offence and to risk having hundreds of deaths, black and white, on his conscience. Canning in his speech had admitted that Smith might be guilty but morally justified.[20] It was accordingly moral outrage, not resentment of a legal injustice, which inflamed the Abolitionists.

Before leaving the Smith case we must look at its poignant aftermath. Many years later the Secretary of the London Missionary Society was sorting out some old papers. He noticed a Bill which Smith had been forced to draw on the Society's funds to defray the cost of his trial. He looked at it casually and saw written in a minute hand the reference '2 Corinthians iv. 8, 9', and, turning to the text in his Bible, he read Smith's

---

* Zachary Macaulay was abused from all sides during the Emancipation campaign. He was singled out for vilification by the planters, attacked, most unfairly, by an old colleague from Sierra Leone, and finally assaulted by the younger Abolitionists as being unimaginative, old-fashioned and, final injustice, tepid in the cause. Once a correspondent addressed an envelope to him
'To that Prince of Cruelty, if he can be found,
     Z. Macaulay.
        London.'

last clandestine message to his friends. 'We are troubled on every side, yet not distressed; we are perplexed, but not in despair. Persecuted but not forsaken: cast down, but not destroyed.'[21]

*

Wilberforce's speech on Smith was the last important one he made in Parliament. When he compared it with those of the other Abolitionists he wondered if the time had come for him to resign. There was no pressing reason for him to remain. He had handed over Emancipation and there was now little he could do for the Cause which could not be achieved as well outside Parliament. He took the inflammation in his lungs as a warning against overwork and he would have considered it a betrayal of his principles to become an occasional attendant upon the House. But he had no immediate intention of retiring when he delivered his final speech on June 15, 1824 on a petition from Carlow against Slavery. In this speech he criticised the Government's failure to follow up the Resolutions of the previous year and pointed out how hopeless it was to rely on the planters to bring about any improvements.[22]

He left ten days later to stay with Lord Gambier, but on the road he suffered a new attack of illness. He was completely immobilised for a month and his health was left in such a shattered condition that he had to rest for the remainder of the year. His family and friends united to implore him to give up public life. After two severe illnesses in the last year it was all too clear to them that he was no longer strong enough. He recognised the truth of this but was tortured by the feeling that he had achieved so little in so many years in Parliament. He wrote to Harford:

'When I consider that my public life is nearly expired, and when I review the many years I have been in it, I am filled with the deepest compunction, from the consciousness of my having made so poor a use of the talents committed to my stewardship. The heart knows its own bitterness. We alone know ourselves, the opportunities we have enjoyed, and the comparative use we have made of them. But it is only to your friendly ear that I breathe out my secret sorrow. I might be supposed by others to be fishing for a compliment. Well, it is an unspeakable consolation that we serve a gracious Master who giveth liberally and upbraideth not.'[23]

A friend of his, Sir John Sinclair, suggested a compromise by which he would be made a peer and thus enabled to continue in public life without being subjected to the same strain as in the Commons. Wilberforce declined the honour on the grounds that 'as I had done nothing to make it naturally come to me, I must have endeavoured to go to it; and this would have been carving for myself, if I may use the expression, much more than a Christian ought to do'.[24] He was also worried that, if his children were thrown into association with the nobility, their religion would suffer. He saw the unhappiness and lack of piety in Lord Carrington's family as having been caused by his elevation to the peerage.[25]

The time had come for another memorandum:

REASONS FOR RETIRING NOW FROM PARLIAMENT[26]
(Feb. 1st, 1825)

I have long meant to retire when this parliament should terminate; consequently, the only doubt is, whether to retire now, or at the end of the approaching session.

The question then is, whether my qualified attendance during this session affords such a prospect of doing good as to warrant my continuance in parliament for its term?

Dr. Chambers does not deem it necessary to forbid my attendance altogether, but intimates fears that if an illness should occur, I might not have strength to stand it.

Had I no other promising course of usefulness, it might or rather would be right to run the risk of a seizure, in my present line. But,

1. I hope I may employ my pen to advantage if I retire into private life; and,

2. My life is just now peculiarly valuable to my family—all at periods of life and in circumstances which render it extremely desirable, according to appearances, that I should be continued to them.

I am not now much wanted in parliament; our cause has powerful advocates, who have taken their stations.

The example of a man's retiring when he feels his bodily and mental powers beginning to fail him, might probably be useful. The public have been so used to see persons turning a long-continued seat in parliament to account for obtaining rank &c., that the contrary example the more needed, and it ought to be exhibited by one who professes to act on Christian principles.

One reason for retirement which Wilberforce does not mention was Barbara's attitude. A woman so given to worrying over imaginary ailments was likely to have been driven almost to hysteria by two serious illnesses in so short a space of time. Certainly when Wilberforce made his decision to retire her relief was obvious. Mr. Newsome has written a graphic, if not entirely fair, description of the scene. ' "Thank God, the Die is cast," wrote the importunate Barbara, triumphant at last.'[27]

On February 17, 1825 Wilberforce wrote to Buxton asking him to apply on his behalf for the Chiltern Hundreds. 'It is the first place that I ever asked for myself, and for near thirty years for any one else.'[28] Buxton felt it 'just about the highest honour I could have; and yet it gives me unaffected pain, from a consciousness of my inability to be his successor'.[29] He reminded Wilberforce in his reply of the inscription which the Carthaginians placed on the tomb of Hannibal, 'We vehemently desired him in the day of battle.'[30]

He had been a Member of Parliament since 1780. Now nearly forty-five years later, the 'little fellow with his calico guts', who could not last a fortnight, had survived most of his contemporaries. He attended one final debate as a Member and thought, 'Never were there so many able speakers, though none so powerful as Pitt and Fox.'[31] He loved reminiscing about old times and his mind now must have been filled with nostalgia. So much had happened, so many fights had been lost and won, so many great men had come and gone since his triumphant return for Hull in 1780.

He must have cast his mind back to the first days in Parliament, watching Pitt's genius burst on the House and developing his own Parliamentary talents, getting to know the great figures of another age, North, Rockingham, Shelburne and Selwyn; enjoying the carefree years, which were to cause him such shame, at Goosetree's and Wimbledon, at Rayrigg and in France, gambling and going to balls, singing and mimicking Lord North. And then Pitt had become Prime Minister and Wilberforce, after his triumph in the Castle Yard, a serious political figure. He must have remembered the great debates between Pitt and Fox, and Sheridan's unbelievable denunciation of Warren Hastings. Then he had become 'serious' and taken up Abolition, and all the elation, disappointment and final triumph that he had experienced in that cause must have come back to him now. The course of Abolition had been intertwined with that of the French wars, which had occupied so much of his political life and done so much to constrict his views on domestic politics. The wars had been followed by depression at home and the beginnings of the fight to pull down the institution of slavery, a fight which he could not leave in other hands.

A series of names must also have flashed through his mind; those of his great contemporaries, Pitt, Fox, Windham, Sheridan, all now dead, Tierney, Mackintosh and Burdett, still alive, and active in Parliament; Castlereagh, Romilly and Whitbread, dead by their own hands. He must also have remembered his Abolitionist allies, both within Parliament and outside it, alive and dead, Granville Sharp, Ramsay, William Smith, Clarkson, old John Newton, Dickson, Dolben, the Thorntons, the Grants, Stephen and Macaulay, the Middletons, Babington, Milner, the More sisters, and many others, and its enemies, Thurlow, Addington, Jenkinson, Dundas, Ellis, Fuller and Edwards. And finally there were the younger men whom he was leaving in possession of the field, Buxton, Brougham, Canning and Lushington. He must have seen with pleasure the growing talents of his own and his friends' children, particularly the young Stephens and Macaulay.

CHAPTER XXXII

RETIREMENT

SHORTLY before he resigned from Parliament Wilberforce decided to move out of London altogether. There was a pleasant scene when he sold Kensington Gore, which Maria Edgworth recalls in an unpublished memoir. 'I must tell you an anecdote of Mr. Wilberforce. Mr. Wilberforce, you know, sold his house at Kensington Gore: the purchaser was a Chinaman, or I should say, the Keeper of a China shop in Oxford St, Mr. Mortlock. When the purchase money was paid, £10,000, and the deeds executed, Mr. Mortlock waited upon Mr. Wilberforce, and said "This house suits you, Mr. Wilberforce, so well in every respect, that I am sure your only motive in parting with it, is to raise the money, therefore permit me to return these title deeds. Accept this testimony of esteem due to your public character and talents".'[1] Wilberforce, of course, would not accept this wonderfully generous offer and bought a house with some land at Highwood Hill near Millhill 'beyond the dirt of the metropolis'. He looked forward to rural life. 'I shall be a little zemindar there,' he told Gisborne, '140 acres of land, cottages of my own, etc.'[2] He was in need of a rest; Marianne Thornton describes him at this time. 'He looks very thin and reduced and walks feebly,' she wrote, 'but really he is almost a proof already of the immortality of the soul for I never saw him in such spirits— or appear so keenly *alive* upon all subjects. He explained it by saying they had begun to feed him with roast beef again and that he was so highly animalized and exhilarated he hardly knew how to keep within due bounds. . . . "Here am I," he said, "a wreck left over for the next tide— but yet a-bounding in blessings and enjoyments." '[3]

His new house was not ready for him and he lived most of 1825 in a cottage at Uxbridge. An extract from his diary shows that retirement did not mean inactivity.

'March 24th. Inglis and two Thorntons came in the evening—staid all next day. Inglis extremely entertaining, and most kind. Not out of my dressing-room when they went, but Inglis chatted with me, and the girls shook hands. 27th. Macaulay and Tom came to dinner, and night. Tom infinitely overflowing with matter on all subjects, and most good-humoured. 28th. Macaulays off. Tom fertile and fluent to the last, and with unruffled good nature. Sir Stamford and Lady Raffles, and Dr. Morrison the Chinese scholar, came between one and two—Lord Gambier called, and we had an entertaining confabulation. Ward dined, and we had a very interesting evening. Good Morrison strongly censuring the luke-warmness of Christians, which prevents their devoting themselves to God's service, as missionaries for China. His plan that persons should become ministers of Chinese, and then settle on the borders. The Chinese a reading people; and he thinks by degrees you would introduce your knowledge and religion. Dear —— seems touched; may God direct him. Singular criminal law of the Battas, by which persons committing great crimes sentenced to be eat up alive; the injured party having the first choice—the ear claimed and eat, &c., until the mass fall on. The coup de grace, except in strong cases, given early. When Sir Stamford contended against the practice, the people urged, "what defence can we have for our morals?" '4

In the summer he set out on a series of visits to his friends and he found them so eager to have him to stay as to be embarrassing. He took the waters at Bath and stayed in December with his friend J. S. Harford at Blaise Castle near Bristol, where, in the inept language of his host, 'he slid insensibly into continuous descriptions of parliamentary scenes with which he had been connected'.5

He read or was read to for much of the day. His eyesight was now so bad that he often could not read or write for days on end. 'Half an hour's reading,' he lamented, 'injures my eyes more than an hour's penman-ship.'6 His illness continued to restrict him until well into the next year. In February 1825 he wrote to Buxton:

'It may appear like affectation for me to talk of being unable to write to absent friends—yet really—so it is very much however owing to my eyes not only being very indifferent but to the peculiarity of the complaint which is much worse when I first get up—and for the first 3 or 4 hours after rising. . . . The complaint appears to be of a nervous kind and it is rather curious that my bodily organs in general sympathise with it, for neither can I bear any exercise till some time after breakfast—I should bear a walk of 3 miles better after 2 o'clock than of half a mile before breakfast.'7

But his passion for literature triumphed over all physical handicaps. It was during these months that he settled down to a serious study of Sir Walter Scott. His old favourites, religious works, including the perennial Baxter also formed part of his diet. He was 'much interested by Pepys's Journal', and had read aloud to him 'Macdonnell's Demerara book—artful and false—Quarterly Review, and Edinburgh—Swiss Persecution—an able article by Tom Macaulay on Milton—rather too crowded, but several beautiful and forcible illustrations on colonial policy, etc.—about Claverhouse in Old Mortality—Sheridan's life by Tom Moore.'[8] This last work aroused him to a fury by its manifest party spirit and 'Moore's gross injustice to Pitt'.

He found time slipping away pleasantly but without anything useful having been achieved. He was inspired by a letter from Harford to go on a tour of Scotland, but he shrank from wasting the time. 'Week has been passing away after week,' he wrote, 'nay even month after month, in what too much resembles Shakespeare's expressive phrase of "Shapeless Indolence".'[9] But when his conscience was less obtrusive he would enjoy the idleness of retirement. He wrote in another letter to Harford: '[I] have begun to verify from experience the truth of Paley's remark, that as the pleasure of youth is found in action, that of age consists in ease.'[10]

Although when he accepted the Chiltern Hundreds he had lost the privilege held by Members of Parliament to 'frank' letters and have them sent for nothing, his correspondence did not diminish. But now he had more time to savour it, and it did not mount up unanswered as it had in other years.

He was able, too, to enter into family life more than before. He had lost his first child, Barbara, at the end of 1821, but the certainty that she was ready to meet her maker proved a great consolation to him.

'Blessed be God,' he wrote to Harford, 'the pain of the stroke was alleviated by many gracious mitigations—above all by the assured persuasion Mrs. W. and I have been able to indulge that our dear child is gone to a better world. The patience and resignation with which she bore what Baillie stated, a common friend, to be her great sufferings, her spirituality of mind and her humble confidence in the mercies of God ... were delightful evidence of her being prepared for the great change.

'On the very morn of the last day of her life, having desired her favourite maid servant to ask the physician then in the next room whether there was any hope of her living, she added, "But if not, all is well." The conviction of this truth has proved such a support to her dear mother's spirits, that she has been able to bear up surprisingly.'[11]

His eldest son, William, seemed to be settling down after his erratic career at Cambridge. The three other sons all went to Oriel College, Oxford, Robert Isaac in 1820, Samuel in 1823 and Henry in 1826. Wilberforce's choices of university and college have led to many conjectures. Cambridge in those days was the bastion of Evangelism with Simeon and Farish both in their prime. There was nothing like the same Evangelical strength and earnestness at Oxford and if he felt bound to send his other sons there after William's disgrace at Cambridge, why High Church Oriel rather than Evangelical St. Edmunds Hall?

Mr. Ford K. Brown has speculated that Wilberforce himself may have been repelled by some aspects of Evangelism and have turned towards the High Church. There may be some substance in this argument. Evangelicals were distinguished from other members of the Church of England not so much by doctrinal differences but by their earnestness, their attitude of mind. As their influence on the Church grew and it became more serious, it was unclear what their next achievement should be. The new generation of Evangelicals who had grown up in front of Wilberforce's eyes were bleak, dour, humourless men, bigoted, unimaginative, stupid, colourless and vulgar compared to the Milners, Venns and Newtons he had loved. Hannah More ascribed to this school of 'phraseologists' 'the unjust association which persons of refinement made between religion and bad taste'.[12] They, rather than the Evangelicals of his generation, provided the material for the great Victorian satires on the movement. There was little common ground between Wilberforce and Mr. Brocklehurst of *Jane Eyre*. Wilberforce may well have recoiled from the thought that his sons should be educated by such sterile creatures, without himself going over to the High Church. For Evangelism was a nebulous body and if he disapproved of part of it that was no reason to disown the whole.

Nor was it a sufficient reason for his choice of university. At Cambridge he could have left his sons under Simeon's wing, and Simeon was a man for whom he had the greatest respect, if not affection. William's escapades no doubt played their part, but Wilberforce had reached a preference for Oriel before William had gone to Trinity, and had tried to find a vacancy there for William in preference to Trinity.[13] This was in March 1817 and it must surely have been a last-minute decision for a man of his eminence to have failed to secure a place for his son in an Oxford college. But at this time his preference for Oxford was lukewarm, for, after failing with Oriel, his second choice was Trinity College, Cambridge. William's adventures confirmed his choice; Oxford was supposed to have more discipline and to produce greater respect for authority. The religious differences between the two universities had also closed. Cambridge might still be more Evangelical, but its Evangelism was turning into suspect channels, while Oxford was becoming more religious. Wilberforce had no reason to fear that his sons would be converted to another form of Christianity; he was more anxious that they should not waste their years at university as he and William had. He knew and liked Hawkins, the Provost of Oriel, and recognised that the college had become one of the foremost in the University. Wilberforce's indifference to party, religious or political, is shown in a letter written to William Gray in December 1830:

'It is curious to observe the effects of the Oxford system in producing on the minds of young men a strong propensity to what may be termed

Tory principles. From myself and the general tenour of our family and social circle, it might have been supposed that my children, though averse to party, would be inclined to adopt Liberal or, so far as would be consistent with party, Whig principles, but all my three Oxonians are strong friends to High Church and King doctrines. The effects I myself have witnessed would certainly induce me, had I to decide on the University to which any young protégé of mine should go, were he by natural temper or any other causes too prone to excess on the Tory side, I should decidedly send him to Cambridge, Trinity; were the opposite the case he should be fixed at Oriel, Oxford.'[14]

Astonishing! as he himself might have said. It is hard to say whether his assumption of Whig principles or his indifference to his sons' High Church doctrines are the more surprising. The former is a more extreme version of the professions of independence which so infuriated the Whigs when he consistently voted against them. His acceptance of the High Church doctrines of his sons may reflect a general softening of his own religious prejudices. By the standards of his time he had always been tolerant, but his tolerance had been well defined. He saw much to admire in individual Quakers, Methodists and High Churchmen although he disagreed with some of their beliefs. It was because the Evangelicals had the right approach rather than any particular tenets that he had spent so much time, money and effort in promoting their cause. By 1830 when he wrote to William Gray he was much less committed to it. If two years later he would engage a Roman Catholic tutor for his grandson it is not surprising to find him content to have High Churchmen as sons, so long as they were 'truly religious' High Churchmen.

On this subject as on others, Wilberforce has left us with contradictory memoranda. In 1823, Robert Isaac's third and Samuel's first year at Oxford, he said: 'The great reason why I should prefer Cambridge is that I think there is more true religion there. At Oxford there is more respect to appearances, more decorum among the irreligious part but there is less true piety than at Cambridge. Besides I think there is less distinction made between those who are really religious and those who are not so.'[15] In spite of this consideration, which one would have expected to be paramount, Wilberforce had tried to send his eldest son to Oxford, succeeded in sending his second and third sons there and three years later was to consign his fourth to this religious desert. His sons' performance at Oxford wiped out the memory of William's premature removal from Cambridge. Robert Isaac took Firsts in both Classics and Mathematics, Samuel a First in Mathematics and a Second in Classics, Henry a First in Classics and a Second in Mathematics. 'I have had three sons at Oxford,' he would tell his friends with pride, 'and all of them First Class men. Show me the man who can make the same boast.'[16] Samuel and Henry were also presidents of the Union, which had been founded as the Attic Society in 1823. During Henry's year the other two presidents were Manning and Gladstone.

These distinctions were not achieved without some concern at home. Wilberforce worried in case his other sons might follow the path taken by William; Barbara became frantically worried about the perils to their health and the danger that they might be dragged down to Hell by greedy whores. Perhaps she had heard of what Wilberforce called 'a very objectionable practice' prevailing at Trinity College, Cambridge: 'I mean having young women for bedmakers.'[17] In any case she wrote to Robert Isaac on July 9, 1823:

'Of course we all feel very anxious about dear Samuel's line of conduct at Oxford and the formation of his future character which so much depends on the course he runs there. May a gracious presence shield him from the many dangers of his trying tuition, for the universities are sadly trying, and grant that he may not only preserve his moral character— preserve his mind from taints of evil and give himself to his studies as a duty and with needful fervour—but also keep up his hitherto intended line of life, the Church, and grow more and more spiritual and fitter therefore for the sacred office . . . bear these things in mind, for much much indeed does your father desire to see him an excellent clergyman. It will go very near his heart in the way of grief and sorrow and perhaps shorten his days if Samuel does not choose that profession and prove worthy of being admitted into it.' She then turns to Robert: 'I fear lest the spiritual the evangelical and biblical growth of your mind should be hurt either from too much attention being drawn to learning and not time enough taken daily for God and religion—or from your company being not quite of the kind I wish as most desirable for you and most wanted by your best interests at present, or by your Sunday advantages being low and not truly evangelical and spiritual.'[18]

Even Lizzy joined in. She wrote to Robert Isaac about Samuel on October 11: 'His passions are so much more energetic than yours that I am sure if he lives as much in general society as you have done he will not go on well. He will be more led in his opinions and habits than ever you would be from the acquaintance he keeps. He will insensibly perhaps to himself take the character of the society in which he lives. Oh then what importance it is that he should live with decidedly religious men. My dear Robert I know you will forgive me if I say that I think Oxford has had this bad effect upon you, that it has led you too much to bury religion in your own bosom, not enough to see the distinction between the Christian and the amiable and good man of the world, that their grand design in life should be different—with the man of the world it is applause, distinction to obtain as a man of letters, but with the Christian, whatever may be the situation in which God has placed his lot, it should be a desire to please his God and saviour and to do good to his fellow creatures. Now, I feel convinced that my dear Robert acts from this motive inside his heart but what I think is and in this perhaps I am mistaken that externally you act too much from motives independently of religion. It has struck me so that perhaps I am mistaken. My dear Robert I sometimes wish that you and dear Sam, where there is real piety, were more disposed to get over manner and not as I fear to prefer a man for his elegant and gentlemanlike manners to one who has more piety.'[19]

Their letters back were becoming difficult to answer. Samuel wrote to Wilberforce from Oxford on June 21, 1823:

'I wish you would enlarge more on having acquaintances that are dreadfully irreligious. For instance at Oriel there are not perhaps above two or three men whom you can really call religious. Again the men generally who are most religious belong (I believe) to Wadham or St. Edmund's Hall and are *very very* low by birth and equally vulgar in manners and conduct. Would you have me form acquaintances with them?'[20] Samuel was also worried by reports that his father disapproved of his keeping a dog.

'I have a notion,' Wilberforce wrote to Samuel, 'that there is a very foolish practice, to call it by the softest name, of spending considerable sums in the fruit and wine of these wine drinkings, where I understood that there was no excess, every man being allowed to please himself as to the wine he drinks. But for a young man, the son perhaps of a clergyman who is straining to the utmost to maintain him at college, stinting himself, his wife and daughters in comforts necessary to their health, for such a young man to be giving claret and buying expensive fruit for his young companions is absolutely criminal. . . . Your situation is different, though, by the way, your father has given off giving claret except in some very special cases, and has entirely left off several other expensive articles, which are still exhibited by others of his rank.'[21]

Henry was nagged more by his father than Robert Isaac or Samuel. He was by nature a light, easy-going, pleasant character, like his father in his unregenerate days. If he had been almost anyone else's son he might not have entered the Church. 'The Inconstancy and Irresolution,' Wilberforce wrote to him in 1825, 'which you discover in your religious feelings and proceedings excite in you apprehensions that you are not a child of God.'[22] Henry was inattentive in church and full of doubts; he was an irregular and illegible correspondent, yet another characteristic he shared with his father.

'Though I can truly assure you,' Wilberforce wrote in May 1825, 'that a letter from you is so welcome a Guest, that not all the pains that may be required for decyphering its Hieroglyphics (a considerable amount I assure you when writing across renders the characters themselves additionally obscure) can render it unacceptable, yet when the Hand is small you must prepare for some little delay in receiving a reply to it. Your dear Mother's eyes are sometimes very indifferent . . . and mine are still worse. . . . A large sheet costs no more than a little one.'[23]

*

He kept a fatherly eye on the Emancipation campaign and envied the energy and good health which allowed Zachary Macaulay to continue to serve it. But he recognised that his own days of active service were gone for ever. He was reluctant to appear in any other rôle and needed much persuasion to take the chair at a great meeting of the Anti-Slavery Society on December 21, 1825. It seemed 'like wishing to retain the reins, when I can no longer hold them'. He added, 'I am a bee which has lost its sting.' But he yielded and was 'very kindly treated throughout'.[24]

He now saw the campaign as a spectator and some of its developments were hard for an old man to understand. He differed with Macaulay over the advisability of Female Anti-Slavery Associations, grounding his objections on St. Paul. 'I own I cannot relish the plan,' he wrote. 'All private exertions for such an object become their character, but for ladies to meet, to publish, to go from house to house stirring up petitions—these appear to me proceedings unsuited to the female character as delineated in Scripture.'[25] But he could still be stirred to the same anger as before. 'Really,' he wrote to Macaulay, 'when I hear of the horrors of the French, Spanish and Portuguese Slave Trades, I involuntarily exclaim, Lord, how long! Surely, surely the abominations will not be much longer tolerated'.[26]

*

He was always very kind to his dependants. In times of need he would allow his tenants to escape paying even the reduced rents that he normally charged them. In 1821 he wrote to Harford asking for his help in such a case.

Wilberforce had bought an estate at a place with the improbable name of Wickwick, with a rent roll of £810 which he promptly reduced to £580. The land was let to two farmers, both of whom were two years in arrears with their rent. One of these farmers, he thought, might have private means and could be turned out without hardship, but the other presented a difficult case. This man, Eyles, 'has no money, 13 children and seems a hard-working honest man. But I am assured that the land will be growing worse and worse in his possession, while I shall be losing my rent and he merely lingering on and barely maintaining himself. I think about 6 or 8 children are at home with him—I rather fear 8. Now I am aware that it is often false humanity to delay taking a painful step which must be taken at last . . . yet what is the poor man's family to do? I cannot suffer them to want, and yet on the other hand, perhaps by continuing them in their present situation, I am maintaining them entirely at my own expense, and not perhaps in the cheapest way. If you should happen to know of any person within your circle, whose kindness would prompt them to attend to such a case as this, it really would be a great relief to my mind.'[27]

A month later we find Wilberforce giving one of Eyles's sons a place in a school and taking one of his daughters into his service.

James Burningham was Wilberforce's amanuensis for five years, when he became very ill; 'both his eyes and his lungs appeared to fail him'. Wilberforce had him treated and kept him at home for fifteen months. His lungs recovered but his eyesight would not let him go back to his old work. Wilberforce tried to find him jobs, thought of setting him up in a bookshop, but recoiled because of his own close ties with Hatchard. 'I never could turn him out unprovided for,' he told Butterworth in 1819.[28] Nor did he. Nine years later Marianne Thornton found Burningham still in residence, his duties apparently confined to playing the organ at family prayers.[29]

His indulgence towards his servants and their familiarity with him was a standing joke among his friends. When he was travelling up to the Lake District in 1818 he made enquiries about coaches for them and was anxious to have them booked on one which allowed overnight stops 'considering the distance'.[30] After they had arrived they stayed at Keswick with Southey, who describes their visit:

'Wilberforce, also, has been here with all his household and such a household. The principle of the family seems to be that, provided the servants have faith, good works are not to be expected from them, and the utter disorder which prevails in consequence is truly farcical. The old coachman would figure upon the stage. Upon making some complaint about the horses, he told his master and mistress that since they had been in this country they had been so lake—and—river—and—mountain—and —valley—mad, that they had thought nothing which they ought to think of.'[31]

When Wilberforce moved into Highwood Hill on June 15, he brought an entourage with him. Marianne Thornton had visited him in his temporary quarters and described the scene:

'He has withdrawn from the world with a vengeance, for he is in so little a bit of a House or rather Hutch that some of his servants and most of his guests are sent off to the Inn, a mile away from the house, to sleep. Mrs. Wilberforce seems to like this hugger mugger way of going on, but I am right glad they are to move to Hendon. . . . There is something melancholy to me in all these changes at his advanced age, "The rolling stone gathers no moss" . . .

'Things go on in the old way the house thronged with servants who are all lame or impotent or blind, or kept from charity, an ex-secretary kept because he is grateful, and his wife because she nursed poor Barbara, and an old butler who they wish would not stay but then he is so attached, and his wife who was a cook but now she is so infirm. All this is rather as it should be however for one rather likes to see him so completely in character and would willingly despair of getting one's place changed at dinner and hear a chorus of Bells all day which nobody answers for the sake of seeing Mr. Wilberforce in his element.'[32]

He brought these dependants and their infirmities to Highwood with him. The house soon became plunged in the usual chaos. 'Many dinner bells ringing,' E. M. Forster described the scene, 'but no dinner, dissenting ministers ringing the door bell because they heard the dinner bell, the house a collection of rabbit hutches containing two married sons and their families,* the blind secretary and his family, the deaf butler and his.'[33] In the grounds William could be found making disastrous agricultural experiments. 'I wish William would keep company with his father instead of his cows,' Marianne wrote, 'It would be quite as profitable and much more agreeable.'[34]

In 1827 Wilberforce left this scene of happy confusion for a tour of Yorkshire. He had a nostalgic longing to revisit the scenes of his childhood and youth, but like most journeys of its kind it had its disappointments. The tour started off well enough with a visit to Yoxall Lodge. He had never seen the forest so beautiful as it was this spring. 'I never was here before till late in the year,' he wrote to Stephen, 'or saw the first foliage of the magnificent oak contrast with the dark holly, the flowering gorse, and the horse-chestnut.'[35] He travelled up through Derbyshire and noted the improvements brought about by new forestry. In Huddersfield, 'Smart came in, an honest warm-hearted shopkeeper, originally from Hull—knew me when himself a boy—remembered the ox roasted whole'.[36] But such living links with his youth were few. All too often when he enquired after an old friend, he was told, 'He died years ago.' 'How many far stronger and healthier than I, died early, while I still survive in spite of Warren's statement thirty-nine years ago!'[37] he wrote mournfully to Hannah More, 'My friends are daily dropping around me.'[38]

His tour covered every part of the County and finished with a visit to the house of his old adversary in Yorkshire politics, Lord Fitzwilliam. 'It is quite a palace,' he wrote to Samuel, 'and the whole apparatus in proportion. The domestic chaplain, a truly good, and from age a venerable man, told me that they dined daily in the servants' hall about seventy-six

---

* William married Mary Owens in 1820, Samuel Emily Sargent in 1828, Robert Isaac Agnes Wrangham in 1832 and Henry Mary Sargent in 1834 after his father's death.

of Lord Fitzwilliam's own household.'[39] He was delighted by his reception at Wentworth House. His host, he found, was 'all benevolence' and had 'a seraphic benignity about him'. He described his feelings to Stephen:

'I can truly say that the magnitude, wealth, and industrious population of our vast county, have made me feel even more than when I represented it in parliament the importance of the trust then committed to my care. The cordiality and kindness with which I have been received at this place [Wentworth House] has deeply affected me. Lord Fitzwilliam might well have been forgiven if he had conceived an unconquerable antipathy to me. When I was first elected county member it was in defiance of his old hereditary interest—I, a mere boy (but twenty-four), without a single acquaintance in the county, and not allowing him the recommendation even of one member, though with Sir George Savile's family connexion and name superadded to the Rockingham interest. And then I must have appeared to him to be identified with Mr. Pitt, against whom, not altogether without cause, he had conceived a deadly hostility, even imputing to him (though this was not merely different from the truth, but opposite to it), that Pitt had from the first disliked him. Yet in spite of all repelling principles so strongly has worked the general kindliness of his nature, that he, the old gentleman (gentleman I may truly term him, for a finer gentleman cannot be conceived), has behaved to us with an unaffected, unassuming friendliness, that at times has brought tears into my eyes. It has really brought powerfully to my feelings that better state in which all misconstructions will be done away, and all truly good men will love one another.'[40]

He returned to Highwood Hill in October 1827 and settled down to retirement. His routine was soon well established. He would rise at seven, pray, dress, hear his reader and meet the rest of the household for family prayers at half-past nine. This would last about half an hour, after which he would go for a short walk followed by breakfast, which 'was prolonged and animated by his unwearied powers of conversation'. After breakfast he would work and answer his letters. He resented interruptions at this time of the day. He was once asked to an amateur concert in the morning. 'What!' he said. 'Music in a morning? Why it would be as bad as dram-drinking.' By three o'clock his letters would be finished or the post gone and he would walk in the garden with his reader or a friend, his specially cut pockets bulging with books from which he quoted, breaking off constantly to point out the beauties of a flower or a tree. 'I am ready to think,' wrote Gurney, 'there could be no greater luxury than roaming with him in solitude over green fields and gardens and drawing out of his treasury things new and old.'[41] He would stay out until it was time for dinner, which was always before five. He would then lie down for an hour and a half. The evening would be spent in conversation and reading interrupted by perhaps another half-hour's prayer. 'The midnight hour was his zenith,' writes Gurney, 'and like the beautiful Cereus with all her petals extended, he was then in full bloom.'[42]

Gurney finishes his memoir of Wilberforce in retirement: 'But if he was lighted up, and in a small circle, where he was entirely at his ease, his powers of conversation were prodigious; a natural eloquence was poured out, strokes of gentle playfulness and satire fell on all sides, and the company were soon absorbed in admiration. It commonly took only one visit to gain over the most prejudiced stranger.'[43] A woman who had suffered under such prejudices visited Highwood and wrote an account as ecstatic as that of Gurney.[44] 'I have been in a delirium all the time that I staid here, from the excitement of being happier than for a long time past. . . . I shall have much to tell you at some future time, of sentiments and ideas of his, all so beautiful, and so true, and so indulgent. . . . Oh he is a dear, good, admirable old man!'

Wilberforce's days were still full. The visitor just quoted found that at midnight she had not started the letter she had intended to write in the morning. Apart from his ordinary guests he would encourage the young men for whose education he was paying to make his home theirs during the holidays. There were the poor to be visited, relieved and invited to join his family prayers.

Only one thing clouded his happiness. When he had first looked at Highwood he had noted with concern that it was a good three miles from any church and it was only on hearing that a chapel was to be built that he bought it. Now, three years later, nothing had been done. He decided to build the chapel himself. The local vicar, a Mr. Williams,* seemed at first to favour the project, but then turned to sudden and violent opposition, attacking Wilberforce from his pulpit and accusing him of being a liar, a hypocrite and inspired by mercenary motives. Pamphlets to the same effect followed the sermon. Wilberforce took these attacks with the same good nature he had shown in his political days, which can seldom have failed to exasperate his opponents: 'Poor fellow!' he wrote in his diary. 'I think I can truly say that I regret it chiefly on his own account.'[45]

On May 29 Wilberforce published all his correspondence with Williams together with his comments on it. He was conciliatory and reasonable throughout. But a year later, when Williams was still abusing him, his patience broke and he wrote to Henry Bankes:

* Wilberforce's encounters with those who bore his family Christian name were usually unfortunate. His eldest son William was his only unsatisfactory child; there was the wretched Williams, prosecuted and ruined by the Society for the Suppression of Vice, 'wicked Williams' with his absurd antics at the time of the Nore Mutiny, William IV, who as the Duke of Clarence led the attack on Abolition in the Lords, Williams the Mill Hill clergyman who tried to stop him building his chapel, and, recently, Mr. Eric Williams who has attacked him in *Capitalism and Slavery*.

'I solemnly assure you that this same Theodore [Williams] is one of the most unprincipled varlets that ever disgraced his profession. He has published a pamphlet against me, charging me in the plainest words with the grossest falsehoods and the basest endeavour to promote my own pecuniary gain under the mask of wishing to benefit my poor neighbours. His character is so well known in his own parish that tho' universally dreaded from his extortion and his violence, he cannot obtain any credit for his accusations. And I was assured by all my friends that I had far better leave his scurrility quite unanswered. In truth I can only account for his conduct and language by supposing him to be somewhat deranged.'

He added that Williams was in debt for £30,000 'in books, horses, pictures etc.'. His father had twice paid his debts and then broken with him. It was an interesting example of Wilberforce's controversial technique, an appearance of philosophic calm and detachment being broken by occasional diatribes which reveal his real feeling far better than the entries in his diary.

The Church Commissioners took Wilberforce's side in the dispute and he received sympathetic letters from a number of bishops. There were, however, many complications in erecting a chapel against the wishes of the incumbent. The chapel was built in his lifetime but only opened a few days after his death and the dispute with Williams was continued by his sons. The violence of Williams's feelings is puzzling. Wilberforce consulted him from the first, so that his attitude cannot be explained away as jealousy at interference in his parish. It does not have the ring of a High Church–Evangelical dispute, or Wilberforce would have been accused of Methodism, a charge which would have had much more chance of sticking than those of lying and self-interest. Again Wilberforce's Evangelism was fairly muted by now and non-Evangelical bishops supported him. One is left with the impression that Williams was an irrational, jealous and neurotically suspicious man.*

Wilberforce had lost many friends, just how many he had realised on his Yorkshire tour, but in retirement he made new ones. Sir James Mackintosh, always a political ally, now became a close personal friend. Mackintosh had moved into Clapham and built a house on land which had once belonged to Henry Thornton. He would have made a worthy member of the Sect. Industrious, humane and a renowned wit, he would have been its only member who could equal both Wilberforce's desire to do good and his ability to entertain. When the two old men met the sparks of wit flew and poor Marianne burnt her notebook 'out of pure humanity to their memories'.[47] 'What a paragon of a companion he is,' Wilberforce

---

* According to D. C. Boulger's life of Raffles (386–7), Williams came from a slave-owning family and hated Abolitionists. I am grateful to Bamber Gascoigne for telling me this.

wrote in his diary, 'quite unequalled. . . . He has been sitting chattering to the girls and myself for above an hour; and this extraordinary man spends, they tell me, much of his time in the circulating library room, at the end of the Common, and chats with the utmost freedom to all the passengers in the Clapham stage as he goes and comes from London.'[48] Mackintosh found Wilberforce 'quite as remarkable in this bright evening of his days as when I saw him in his glory many years ago'.[49]

James Harford was another old acquaintance who now became a close friend. He was a younger man than Wilberforce, with a Quaker up-bringing, though he himself was a strong member of the Church of England. Harford lived near Bristol and, as an important and devout West Country figure, he soon became friends with Hannah More and through an introduction from her met Wilberforce in 1812. Wilberforce enter-tained him to 'a mutton-chop dinner before the House of Commons', 'almost the only way in which I can see my friends during the sitting of Parliament', and asked him to use his spare room whenever he visited London. After the war Harford, as we have seen, became the Aboli-tionists' ambassador in Rome. In spite of the difference in their ages Wilberforce came to ask his advice, particularly after his retirement. They corresponded regularly, and Blaise Castle joined Barley Wood and Bath as havens in Wilberforce's tours of the West.

The peace of Wilberforce's retirement was soon to be shattered. He had not inherited the financial acumen of his merchant ancestors, but on the other hand he had never needed it. Before his conversion he had always had enough money to satisfy his desires. After it his own needs had been modest; he had lavished large sums on charities and the needy. These gifts had made some inroads into his capital, but he was left with enough to live out his days in comfort and pass on a decent competence to each of his children. He was careful with money so far as personal expenditure was concerned, because the more he saved the more he could give away. He would frequently thank God for giving him the means to do so much good, and that was the extent of his interest in money. He was happy to leave its management to others.

His sons took after him in this respect. Henry was wildly and Samuel fairly extravagant; only Robert seems to have inherited a shrewdness about money, probably along with his other Spooner attributes. But William brought financial disaster.

We have seen how Wilberforce felt obliged to remove him from Cam-bridge after a series of extravagances and misdeeds. William was placed at the Bar; he married into a leading Evangelical family and seemed set for a respectable career. But William suffered from illness, and on April 26, 1826, Wilberforce wrote an ominous letter to Babington:

'Your son George gave me his decided opinion that William my son's health would not stand practicing the law. . . . I believe William is likely to engage with Major Close to help him in taking up a great milk farm—of which there has been a pretty fair trial—the connection with so good a man as Close is a grand matter—but don't talk of this at present. Entre nous, I have been too expensive though it has chiefly been in improving my place and buying some shares at William's suggestion—but is it not better think you to sell land to pay off £5,000 or £6,000 and to provide William a capital of £15,000 or more if wanted, than to borrow on mortgage.'[50]

He went into more detail in a letter to the younger Henry Thornton over two years later, on December 29, 1828:

'I cannot recollect that I ever explained to you the circumstances which led me to acquiesce in my son's wish to take a great dairy farm near London. It is due to him to say that his having given up the law was a case of absolute necessity. He would have been in his grave ere now had he continued in it. . . . While he was in law, both Mr. Kindersley and Mr. Colman declared he was one of their most diligent pupils. As it is . . . he has only of late recovered his health. When forced to abandon the law, he tried to get into several modes of occupation . . . but all in vain. I have not time I find to explain matters fully. Suffice it to say that his present occupation seems likely to be a source of augmenting emolument to him. But I could not spare him all the capital necessary—a considerable part of it has been borrowed on mortgage. He stated to me a few days ago that owing to the staying abroad of a gentleman who had agreed to lend him £6,000, he was like to be put to extreme difficulties or inconveniences. Of this £6,000, I found £2,000 was to repay what your house had lent him till January. I myself have hoped to be able to supply him, having intended to sell some land near Beverley and Hull. . . . Indeed the house, in which I first drew my breath, though I cannot part with it without emotion, must with the premises be sold, and I am assured that I may hope to get from £5,000 to £6,000 for the whole. As much more I may expect from the land I intend to dispose of. I therefore request you to do me the real kindness of lending me the £6,000 for him (in truth £4,000, new loan, as two thousand of it are for yourselves) with the more confidence because I shall ere long be able to repay it. I assure you I shall consider *myself* as your creditor and you know enough of my property to know that the money is perfectly safe. I can truly assure you that I don't believe I have lessened my inheritance through the good providence of God which supplied me for many years with an increase of income from the Hull business. And though not a rich man as times go now, yet I have enough thank God to enable me to live in comfort. . . . If you wish William to converse with you on the business he would answer the summons I am persuaded. His manager is a man of tried integrity—have know him above 20 years.'[51]

But as Wilberforce wrote so optimistically of 'a source of augmenting emolument', the source was already bone dry. By 1829 William's losses were so heavy that recovery was impossible, but by struggling on he increased them. In November 1830 he had to go abroad to escape his creditors. Richard Spooner, Barbara's brother, was called in to salvage what he could.

The loss came at a time when Wilberforce could least afford it. Apart from his normal donations he had recently been lavishing money on his chapel, while his lowering of his tenants' rents had reduced his income. He was still the largest contributor to York charities. His family were not yet self-supporting and he had lent Macaulay £10,000 when the latter's devotion to Emancipation had lost him his fortune.[52]

'I must allow William £600 per annum more when I am able,' he wrote to Babington on March 14, 1831, 'Elizabeth £300 per annum, Sam £200 and Henry from 3 to 5 or 600'.[53] Robert was hoping to obtain a living soon. 'After much Consideration of Accounts,' he wrote, 'Mrs. W. and I become convinced that it is absolutely necessary to leave Highwood Hill—We could not go on here in any way without a greater Establishment and more Company than we can now maintain.'[54] In a postscript he added 'William's loss is full fifty or fifty [an indecipherable figure] thousand pounds.' He wrote the figures in Greek characters for secrecy's sake.

It was a staggering blow. £50,000 in 1831 must have been the equivalent of at least half a million pounds today, perhaps nearly a million. It is not possible to calculate how much Wilberforce was worth, since the surviving cash books do not deal with his agricultural or commercial investments, but this loss meant that he had to change his way of life and leave the home in which he had expected to end his days. He could have let William take the loss and become an exile on the continent, but he preferred to meet the debt himself. When the news broke, the response from his friends must have been most moving. There were many offers of contribution and no less than six individuals, including, to his eternal credit, Lord Fitzwilliam, offered to pay the debt off in its entirety. Another of these offers came from a West Indian. But Wilberforce refused all of them and accepted only contributions towards the building of his chapel.

For an old, feeble man with a large family to be suddenly deprived of the wealth to which he had been accustomed all his life was a blow which would have overwhelmed most people. Wilberforce never flinched under it. He made arrangements to leave Highwood Hill and let all his servants go except 'a man and a maid and my reader'.[55] 'What I shall miss most,' he confessed, 'will be my books and my garden, though I own I do feel a little the not being able to ask my friends to take a dinner or a bed with me, under my own roof.'[56] But he still counted his blessings and found them

abundant. 'I am bound to recognise in this dispensation the gracious mitigation of the severity of the stroke. It was not suffered to take place until
all my children were educated, and nearly all of them placed out in one
way or another; and by the delay, Mrs. Wilberforce and I are supplied
with a delightful asylum under the roofs of two of our own children. And
what better could we desire?'[57]

He told Harford: 'When I consider my situation and circumstances in
their whole extent, I should really deserve to be deemed a monster of
ingratitude if I were not ready to adopt the language of the Psalmist.
Surely goodness and mercy have followed me all the days of my life. . . . I
remember many years ago my dear friend the late Dean of Carlisle one
day when I was answering some invitation, half jokingly asking me "Do
you think you would be asked to so many dinners if you actually wanted
one?" This has now been put to the test and answered in the affirmative.'[58]

The discomforts and inconveniences of being without a home never
changed his mind. When Gurney saw him at Bath in 1833, within three
weeks of his death, Wilberforce said of his financial loss: 'I am afraid to
tell you what I feel about it, lest it seem like affectation. But rest assured
that the event has given me no uneasiness, none whatsoever! It has only
increased my happiness, for I have in consequence been spending the
winter with my son—the grateful witness of his Gospel labours.'[59]

Although the size of William's loss must have horrified Wilberforce at
the time, it cannot have come as a complete surprise to him. Samuel
remembered his father often saying: 'William is risking his own fortune
and *considering everything* I think it is the safest thing to let him do it. It
is I think an *innocent* employment and that is a great thing and I trust that
the degredation of it may be useful to him.'[60]

Poor Barbara was left the worst off as a result of William's folly. In
1837 she wrote to Samuel complaining 'how little your Father conceived
that the whole his widow should receive annually from the Wilberforce
fortune should be six hundred pounds without house or home or legacy to
set her out'.[61] She must have regretted the failure to accept all those
generous offers of help. It cannot always have been easy to be married to
a saint; fortunately her sons cared for her and supported her in her old age.

*

Soon after his move from Highwood Wilberforce felt ill. Robert Isaac was
in Germany studying the language. Barbara wrote him a letter in which
fear of being left to cope with her husband by herself struggled with an
equally strong fear of inflicting on her son the perils of travel. 'He felt
very odd about his head and I ventured to help him take this same medicine which immediately relieved his stomach from much wind though he
had not before felt anything but his head. Samuel thinks with me that this
mixture then prevented some attack. . . . It would certainly be a relief to

me when you return, though never put yourself into any danger either of
cholera or of Belgic war to come back.' On the former subject she continues: 'Mr. G. Babington says no dependence is to be placed on Chlorate
of Lime to remove contagion or infection and in one case where it has been
tried the disease appeared to be much increased by it. The only thing he
says to be depended on is Dr. C. Smith's *purified* nitre and vitrolic acid
poured on it and heated by hand.'[62]

On September 30 she returned to the attack. Robert having decided to
come back she warned him of the dangers of crossing the Channel during
the equinox. 'I have another caution to give you,' she went on remorselessly, 'and that is about "stewages"—do be careful for the newspapers
tell us of several travellers lately have been very ill I am not sure whether
some did not die, when on the continent, by some stewage which had
stood in copper for some hours. Be careful in going to good places and not
eating what looks greenish or bad coloured or tastes "oddly" or "unfortunately".'[63] The sea was rough when Robert Isaac crossed the channel
and, not surprisingly, he was very sick.

Wilberforce recovered from his illness. 'I cannot understand,' he said,
'why my life is spared so long, except it be to show that a man can be as
happy without a fortune as with one.'

*

In the middle of the financial crisis Wilberforce made his last appearance
in the chair of the Anti-Slavery Society at a great meeting in the Freemasons' Hall on May 15, 1830.

The cause had made little headway since his retirement from Parliament. Buxton had presented annual motions, Brougham, Lushington and
Denman had consistently and eloquently supported him and the temper
of Parliament was slowly turning. But Parliament's resolutions were ignored in the West Indies. In 1826, in response to the failure of the Colonial
Assemblies to implement any of its recommendations on amelioration, the
measures which in 1823 had been applied to Trinidad were drawn up
under various headings and sent out to the Colonial Assemblies. The
Resolutions of 1823 were passed through the Lords to give them extra
authority and the writing on the wall was clear when even Lord Eldon
spoke against slavery. But the West Indians could not read it. With the
exceptions of Grenada and Tobago the islands refused to enact any of
Parliament's more important resolutions. 'The progress of the colonies,'
Brougham said in 1828, 'is so slow as to be imperceptible to all human
eyes save their own.'[64] By May 1830 its pace had not increased.

Public feeling, first aroused by Smith's martyrdom, was warmed by the
West Indians' delays and cruelty. No Member of Parliament could find
any excuses for the suppression of a slave revolt in Jamaica in which
justice and mercy were equally abandoned. Magistrates who announced

before the trial began that they wished to hang the accused before the holidays, who refused to allow slaves who barely spoke English to be represented by Counsel, who admitted conflicting and hearsay evidence from slaves against other slaves, but never against their masters, epitomised what the House called 'the evils inseparably attendant upon a state of slavery'. The threats of secession to America made by extremists in the Colonial Assemblies irritated without intimidating the English Parliament. The lack of patriotism among the planters contrasted with the attitude of the free mulattoes and blacks, who had become impatient while remaining loyal. They had founded their own paper, *The Watchman*, which warned those who talked of secession 'that, if they dared to unfurl the flag of rebellion, every man of them would be hanged in twenty-four hours'.[65]

Secession was never a realistic threat; it would have led to universal uprisings among the slaves, supported by the free coloureds and other loyalists. The same spectre of St. Domingue that prevented Cuba from joining the other Spanish colonies in their wars of independence, bound the British sugar islands into the colonial system. But if they did not intend to secede, the West Indians' contemptuous treatment of Parliament's resolutions was suicidal. The most indifferent members must have realised long before 1830, that amelioration had failed and that emancipation had been forced upon them. It would surely have come earlier but for the confused state of politics at home. Governments and Ministers had changed with bewildering speed, while discontent with the system of electing members had become alarming. Sooner or later the Whigs must come in and that party—with its enlightened aristocrats in the House and its solid Nonconformist roots in the country—could be expected to end slavery for ever.

The strength of public feeling showed itself at the Anti-Slavery Meeting. Before other meetings of the Society George Stephen had pleaded with his friends to come and 'to secure at least an apology for an audience'.[66] Now the great hall was crammed with two thousand people and hundreds more were turned away at the doors. All the survivors of the first Crusade were there. Clarkson moved that 'the great leader in our cause' should take the chair, and Wilberforce, frail, bent and with his voice weakened by time and illness, replied with a tribute to his 'old friend and fellow labourer'.*

If the old enemies of slavery were there, so were the new and they were

---

* This was the last meeting of these two great enemies of Slavery. Their friendship lasted nearly fifty years without any quarrel or jealousy. But after Wilberforce's death his sons, encouraged by Sir James Stephen, launched an unprovoked and unjustified attack on Clarkson in their *Life* of their father. Clarkson successfully defended himself; the great men of the Abolitionist Movement sided with him and the brothers eventually apologised, but not until seven years after their attack, and five after Clarkson's reply to it. If Clarkson had not lived to an exceptional age, he would never have received their apology.[67]

no longer prepared to leave matters in the hands of their elders. George
Stephen was one of them.

'It was a goodly, a magnificent spectacle!' he wrote. 'Well do I remember saying to those around me what I sincerely felt—"Today the
slave is free!" And all appeared to share the same feeling; but, alas, the
very demon of procrastination seemed to have possessed our leaders. A
string of resolutions was proposed by Buxton; admirably worded;
admirably indignant, but—admirably prudent! They wound up with "an
unalterable determination to leave no proper and practicable means un-
attempted for effecting, at the earliest period, the entire abolition of
slavery throughout the British dominions". They were carried, and others
to the like effect; but it was too much for the patience of young Anti-
slavery England. Mr. Pownall, a member of the Anti-slavery committee,
was in the side gallery; careless of the prudish decorum that had hitherto
marked all our anniversary meetings, and in defiance of frowns and re-
monstrance, and cries of "Order!" Mr. Pownall would be heard, and was
heard. He moved an amendment in a few pithy words, deprecating indecision and delay, "That from and after the 1st of January, 1830, every
slave born within the King's dominions shall be free." It was a spark to
the mine! the shouts, the tumult of applause were such as I never heard
before, and never shall hear again. Cheers innumerable thundered from
every bench, hats and handkerchiefs were waved in every hand. Buxton
deprecated, Brougham interposed, Wilberforce waved his hand for
silence, but all was pantomime and dumb show. I did my best in a little
knot of some half-dozen young men to resist all attempts at suppression.
We would allow no silence and no appeals. At the first subsidence of the
tempest we began again, reserving our lungs till others were tired. We
soon became the fuglemen of the mighty host, nor did we rest, or allow
others to rest, till Wilberforce rose to put the amendment, which was
carried with a burst of exulting triumph that would have made the Falls of
Niagara inaudible at equal distance.'[68]

A General Election took place in 1830. Yorkshire was now entitled to
four county members and it returned four Abolitionists including
Brougham, who had no local connections. 'The election,' he wrote to
Wilberforce 'turned very much on Slavery; your name was in every
mouth, and your health the most enthusiastically received.'

Thomas Babington Macaulay was among the new members. Lady
Trevelyan remembered Wilberforce's reaction when he heard the news.
' "Your father," he told her, "has had great trials—obloquy, bad health,
many anxieties. One must feel as if Tom were given him for a recom-
pense." He was silent for a moment and then his mobile face lighted up,
and he clapped his hand to his ear, and cried: "Ah! I hear that shout
again. Hear! Hear! What a life it was!" '[69]

After the revolt of the young Abolitionists at the Freemasons' Hall, the movement was never the same again; it split into two streams. Buxton, Brougham, Lushington and others continued their Parliamentary motions and lobbying while Macaulay turned out his pamphlets and edited the *Anti-Slavery Reporter*. The young Abolitionists regarded these methods as being hopelessly old-fashioned and ineffective. They formed their own committee, the Agency Committee, which was dominated by vigorous uncompromising Quakers like James Cropper, Joseph Sturge and the Cooper brothers. They had one fundamental belief to which every dilemma was referred, everything else subordinated: 'To uphold slavery is a crime before God, and the condition must therefore be immediately abolished.' The Agency Committee appointed representatives throughout the country and instructed them to bring the crusade to the people. They held lectures, dogged West Indian speakers and challenged them to debates, founded affiliated societies and canvassed people in their houses.

'The old Anti-slavery Committee,' Stephen argues, 'had greatly erred in two particulars; they had relied too much on the influence of political rank and party strength, and they had limited their hope of popular support to a religious few detached from the people, and not only detached, but distrusted. They made no efforts to gain over the "respectable" as distinguished from the "pious", never dreaming that there were yet six thousand men in Israel who had not bowed the knee to Baal.

'To correct these errors before the first reformed election, was the work to which the 1,200 affiliated societies were immediately called. The agency lecturers paved the way; they placed the question in its proper light, throwing aside all party and political and hyper-religious feeling alike, and reducing the controversy to the simple point, that the state of slavery was criminal before God.'[70]

The first reaction of the traditional Abolitionists to their pugnacious offspring was one of injured and suspicious alarm. That it soon mellowed into co-operation is a tribute to their own warmth in the cause. The very existence of the Agency Committee was a criticism of its predecessors' work, work to which many of them had devoted their lives. If there had been jealous, vain and selfish men on the Anti-slavery Committee, the movement could have been split wide open in 1830 and 1831. Wilberforce, Buxton and Stephen did much to heal the rift by giving money and, more important, their endorsement to the Agency Committee. At times the Agency's committee went too far for even Wilberforce's patience. No man was more devoted to the cause than Zachary Macaulay, who had risked his health, sacrificed his fortune and dedicated his life to it. When some of the young Abolitionists accused him of being lukewarm Wilberforce admitted, 'This really shocks me beyond measure.'[71] When Buxton came under the same criticism, Wilberforce wrote to William Smith: 'I cannot bear remaining silent when you touch a string which vibrates in my inmost soul. I feel more indignant than I can well express at the unworthy treatment dear honest Buxton has experienced. . . . But do go to Buxton and say from me all that is affectionate.'[72] Clarkson wrote on similar lines, 'I cannot but speak in disgusted terms of the *Audacity*, and *Ingratitude* of the *Agency* anti-Slavery Committee.'[73]

*

Wilberforce's devotion to the Anti-Slavery cause was strong enough to lead him to endorse the Agency Movement, though their impetuous rabble rousing must have grated on his conservative soul. He could not keep abreast of political innovations in the same way. When the agitation for reform was at its height 'he spoke with much warmth for the suppression of *The Times* newspaper'.[74] After the Whigs finally came into power his main reaction seems to have been to compare the moral stature of their cabinet with that of their predecessors. 'Assuredly this Government is greatly to be preferred before the last,' he wrote approvingly, 'Brougham better than Copley, and several highly respectable besides, the Grants (Charles is in the Cabinet), Lord Althorp, Sir James Graham, Lord Grey himself, highly respectable as family men; Denman an honest fellow. The worst appointment is Holland, Duchy of Lancaster; he has much church patronage, which, though I love the man, I cannot think decorous.'[75]

Something more than respectable family men and decorous patrons of the Church was needed in the first years of the 1830s. Wilberforce completely misunderstood the crisis over Reform, and still clung to his old Pittite ideas. He wrote to Samuel on March 4, 1831: 'I will frankly confess to you that I almost tremble for the consequences of Lord Russell's plan of reform if it should be carried. I wish the qualification had been higher. . . . Much in the judgements we form on such practical questions depends on our period of life. I find myself now at seventy one and half far more timid and more indisposed to great changes.'[76] But he was mollified by the thought that 'the change will be for the benefit, and greatly so, of our poor West India clients'.[77]

In the autumn of 1831 he was ill again. He described his symptoms to Harford. 'I have had of late several seizures, which though we hope there is nothing very serious in them, yet have so much of an alarming character (inducing sometimes a temporary delirium: so that for hours I am utterly insensible) that they enforce the importance of attending to them without delay. The source of the evil appears to be the stomach and for disorders of this class, the Bath water is commonly deemed a peculiarly appropriate remedy.'[78]

The waters worked their usual wonders with him and he was soon able to join Harford at Blaise Castle. Here his concern about the political state of the country grew serious. Blaise Castle was only a few miles from Bristol and when the riots there broke out, Wilberforce was almost involved in them. The experience alarmed him and reduced Barbara to a frenzy of anxiety.

Sir Charles Wetherell, the Recorder of Bristol, was a leading opponent of the Reform Bill. When he arrived in the city his carriage was attacked and he only escaped from the mob by hiding and then disguising himself. The disturbances that followed were the worst since the Gordon Riots of 1780. The authorities panicked, withdrew their forces from the city and by doing so removed all restraints from the mob. From Blaise Castle Wilberforce and Harford could see 'the horizon reddened with the lurid glare of these devastating fires'.[79] Wilberforce wrote two letters to Samuel describing the scene:

'You will hear what dreadful work has been going on at Bristol for the last eight and forty hours. . . . Not a single gaol, I am assured is left undestroyed. The Bishop's Palace (and Deanery too I am told), burnt to the ground. The Custom House ditto, Mansion House ditto . . . strange to say (just as in the London riots), people were allowed to walk the streets in peace, and last night half the people in the square were looking on at the depredations committing by the other half. Well-dressed ladies walked about great part of the night staring as at a raree show. The redness of the sky from the conflagration was quite a dreadful sight to us in the distance. It is said they are endeavouring to organise a force for the defence of the city. It is very strange that this has been so long delayed. I'm assured pillage has latterly been the grand object. The deputation, I am told, were followed by a cart, in which, as they went along, they stowed the plunder. I have not said it to your mother, for fear of her becoming still more nervous (which need not be), by her finding me entertaining such cogitations, but if I perceive any grumblings of the volcano at Bath, before the lava bursts forth I shall hurry your mother to a certain quiet parsonage—though, alas! I cannot but fear for the Church in these days.'[80]

Wilberforce scented Revolution, Barbara was certain of it. 'Shall I send you the deeds, etc.' she wrote to Samuel, 'to take care of for the family, and the plate to bury in your garden? I think you will be safe in the Isle of Wight. Do not let my fears be mentioned; they say we should all appear brave and bold.'[81] But two days later their sense of perspective had returned:

'The Bristol riots, though in some particulars the accounts were as usual exaggerated, were quite horrible, and the *great* events as reported. But a striking instance was afforded how easily perpetrations, if I may use the word, the most horrible may be at once arrested by determined opposition. On Monday morning early the mobs were parading about without resistance. But on that morning the troops, a small body of dragoons, charged them repeatedly at full speed, and not sparing either the momentum or the sharpness of their swords, no attempt at making a head afterwards appeared. Afterwards the day was properly employed in appointing a great number of special constables and other civil force, and every night, as well as day, since has passed in perfect quiet. A great part of the plunder has been recovered, and numbers of criminals have been seized—some of them sent to a gaol about seven miles off; and happily the condemned cells have escaped the fury of the mob, and have afforded a stronghold for keeping the prisoners. I need not tell you in what a ferment of mind our host was thrown, indeed with great reason. He had been threatened with a visit at this place, and the best pictures were stowed away in safe custody. I am persuaded it has become indispensably necessary to form in all our great cities and neighbourhoods a civil police, properly armed and drilled. And thus, as usual, out of evil good may arise.'[82]

A few days later he visited the scene with Harford, whose civic pride was outraged. 'Frightful was the spectacle it presented,' he wrote, 'the Mansion House and Custom House, two large buildings, were laid in ruins—here and there tall and singed walls menaced a sudden downfall—large timbers, half-reduced to charcoal, stuck out . . . It was appalling to stand still and to contemplate the surrounding scene—presenting, as it did, so fearful an illustration of the consequences attendant on the prostration of law and order, which had led to the surrender of an ancient and venerable city to the rage of an insane populace, many of whom perished in a drunken state among the ruins. Mr. Wilberforce was anxious to examine and localise every principal feature of the recent outrages. . . .

'These painful scenes,' Harford continues, 'interfered not a little with the tranquil enjoyment of social intercourse which I had promised myself with our venerable guest during this visit. He looked older and was more bending than when we last met. But his animation and cheerfulness was unabated.'[83]

CHAPTER XXXIII

LAST DAYS

WILBERFORCE returned home and prepared to leave Highwood Hill for good, resigned to the loss of his garden and library, only to face a blow which caused him infinitely more pain.

Lizzy, his surviving daughter, had married an Evangelical clergyman called James. Wilberforce loved her with devotion and watched her confinement anxiously, giving thanks to God when she was safely delivered of a daughter. Then, soon afterwards, in February 1832 Lizzy fell ill with a pulmonary complaint. She, her husband and their baby moved down to Highwood Hill for the milder climate. Wilberforce wrote to Harford:

'She was extremely fatigued by the Journey and further medical advice was plainly necessary. For the first fortnight she appeared decidedly to improve, her pulse being less frequent, her cough rather less and her skin cooler, though she had been pursuing a restorative diet (bread twice daily and a little wine) without stimulating. But there has latterly been a sad drawback though not of the pulmonary kind of disease. We have engaged St. Boniface, the House in the Isle of Wight formerly Bowdler's (peace to his ashes *dear* Bowdler). . . . This house . . . is the best climate in Britain for a pulmonary case.'[1]

But these precautions were in vain. Lizzy died before she could be moved to St. Boniface. Mr. Newsome considers that the loss aged Wilberforce noticeably.[2] His faith sustained him through the agony of her death and he drew some consolation from the presence of her daughter. 'I was much impressed,' he wrote 'with the similarity in some respects of my own situation, to that of her dear little innocent who was undergoing the operation of vaccination. The infant gave up its little arm to the operator without suspicion or fear. But when it felt the puncture, which must have been sharp, no words can express the astonishment and grief that followed.'[3] But he seems to have found increasing comfort in the thought that he would soon be re-united with all the dear friends who had gone before him. 'I have often heard that sailors on a voyage will drink "friends astern" till they are half way over, then "friends ahead". With me it has been "friends ahead" this long time.'[4]

448

Brougham had been deeply distressed to hear of Wilberforce's financial disaster, and had done everything he could as Lord Chancellor in the Whig Government to ensure that he did not become 'a wanderer without any certain dwelling places'.[5] He placed James in the living of Rawmarsh and also looked for a living for Robert Isaac (Samuel had been Rector of Brighstone in the Isle of Wight since 1830). This was a more difficult task since Robert Isaac would not accept any living which did not include a vicarage suitable for his father and indeed had had qualms about accepting anything at all from Lord Brougham.

Finally scruples and difficulties were both overcome and Robert Isaac became vicar of East Farleigh near Maidstone, much to the relief of Samuel, who was finding the thought of having his mother as a permanent guest increasingly daunting. He had tried to persuade his parents to buy a small house near Brighstone and had written to Robert Isaac, 'I think that many reasons will occur to your mind why it would not be comfortable to have them positively *live* with us. My dear mother is not of a disposition in temper to be very long happy where she is not mistress,'[6] and later, 'I fear *entre nous* that two angels would not make my dear mother comfortable where she was to be a living visitor.'[7]

Barbara may have been an awkward guest, but Wilberforce was happy passing the last years of his life 'in this vagarious mode'. He visited his sons at East Farleigh and Brighstone and went on trips to Bath to take the waters there. He noticed the decline in his powers. 'Though I do not like to mention it to your mother,' he wrote to Samuel on July 12, 1832, 'I feel myself becoming more and more stupid and inefficient. I think it is chiefly a bodily disease, at least there, I hope, is the root of the disease. I am so languid after breakfast that, if I am read to, I infallibly subside into a drowsiness which, if not resisted by my getting up and walking, or taking for a few minutes the book Joseph may be reading to me, gradually slides into a state of complete stupor. . . . My memory is continually giving me fresh proofs of its decaying at an accelerated rate of progress.'[8] He found visitors tired him, even those who would otherwise have been welcome, like a Quaker from the American Colonisation Society, who spent some time with him in Bath at the end of 1831. 'The time was,' he wrote to Samuel, 'when such a visitor would have been no encumberance to me. But now that he takes me in hand when I am already tired by others (though it is only justice to him to say no one can be less intrusive or more obliging than he is), I do sink under it.'[9] Two days later he again wrote to Samuel, 'Our American friend has left us this morning. But, alas! he has requested me to write in his album. What a vile system is the album system!'[10]

His cheerfulness and high spirits lasted until the end of his life. Like many old men he had difficulty in absorbing new thoughts, but he de-

lighted in recounting his favourite stories. He also enjoyed arguing with
the Dean of Winchester, whom he met at Bath, about the degeneracy of
the times, Wilberforce taking the view that things were better than they
had been. He liked teasing the Dean. 'I now and then stroke up his plum-
age the wrong way to make him set up his bristles.'[11]

He also retained his restlessness. In the autumn of 1832 he visited old
friends in Clapham and there sat for Richmond. But he fidgeted around
too much to give the painter a chance, until it was arranged that one of
those present should ask him: 'Is it true that the last accounts from the
West Indies prove that the slaves are on the whole so much better off than
they were thought to be, that you have much altered your views as to
slavery?'

'I am astonished at you,' Wilberforce replied, 'What! a sensible man
like you believe such reports? Why, sir, they flog them with a whip as
thick as my arm,'[12] and he grasped his arm to make the point; but the
Reverend C. Forster,* who had been brave enough to ask the question,
remained unconvinced until the portrait was finished.

When he stayed with Samuel at Brighstone he would climb the downs,
go for rides in a pony cart or walk along the sea shore. He watched his
grand-children grow up with indulgent affection. 'This house,' he wrote
from Brighstone, 'is enlivened by a delightful infant which twaddles
about most captivatingly and begins to lisp out papa and mamma, with
more than Cicero's eloquence. . . . What a manifest benevolence there is in
the Almighty's having rendered young children so eminently attractive.'[13]

But it was in Robert Isaac's vicarage at East Farleigh that he found his
last real home. In the summer of 1832 Robert Isaac had married Agnes
Wrangham, the daughter of Archdeacon Wrangham, an intimate of
Sydney Smith's, an old friend of Wilberforce's, a poet, a scholar, a great
collector of books and the author of *The Civilisation of the Hindoos*.
Wilberforce pined for fresh air and exercise, but his health made exposure
to the weather dangerous. Robert Isaac built a special gravel walk for him
protected from the north wind. Wilberforce expressed his gratitude in his
diary. 'Gravel walk made expressly for me by dear Robert is extremely
valuable. I was not out of the garden all week. It is so clean and smooth
and sheltered.'[14] Agnes was pregnant and Wilberforce felt sometimes that
he and Barbara were being too much trouble. At times they may have
been, but Robert Isaac would never admit it. 'Dear Robert's affectionate
assurances last night,' Wilberforce wrote, 'when telling me of the pleasure
he (and I think he said Agnes also) had in our being with them, quite
melted me to tears. He has a cold and sometimes dry manner which does
no justice to his really kind heart.'[15]

* Forster married Laura Thornton, Henry's youngest daughter. He was E. M.
Forster's grandfather.

The vicarage was only a mile from Barham Court, where Lady Middleton had pleaded with him to take up Abolition nearly fifty years before. Any residence of Wilberforce's was liable to receive some exotic visitors and East Farleigh was no exception. Ramohun Roy, the Hindu philosopher and reformer, came over from Barham Court and told Wilberforce that one of his chief wishes when he left the East had been to meet him. Wilberforce gave him a copy of *Practical View*, and Ramohun Roy, not to be outdone in courtesy, sent him a book on Suttee. Prince Czartoriski brought his four-year-old son over and 'a dwarf about the same size'.

He invited Harford to visit him there. 'I really hope,' he wrote on February 6, 1833, 'that when you and Mrs. H. come to London or perhaps to *Ton*bridge, as is now the coxcomb mode of spelling it, you will allow us to have the pleasure of a short visit. . . .'[16] On the same day he wrote through his amanuensis to Lady Olivia Sparrow that his health was in a state 'of tolerably comfortable mediocrity. . . . Tho' I feel that I am becoming yearly more and more stiff and crazy'.[17] A few days later he mentions in a letter to William Smith 'having parted with my amanuensis, in the hope of promoting his benefit'.[18] His own writing is still strong and clear.

On April 2 he wrote again to Harford:

'Mrs. Wilberforce and I are still occupying our delightful quarters: and if it be a proof that our time has not passed away unpleasantly, that it has not hung heavily on our hands, never was that proof afforded in larger abundance, for tho' we have been residents here for very near 5 months Mrs. W. and myself can scarcely believe the calendar. I could imagine our stay had been for 5 or 6 weeks only. . . . Tho' your account of poor H. More's* situation is very distressing, it is better to know the truth and not remain in uncertainty. You will kindly keep me informed from time to time how matters are going on under her roof. . . .

'Our time for emigrating from our present much loved quarters is approaching and would have been still nearer but for one of those obstacles that often obstruct such intended gratifications—accidents arising from family circumstances. Another year—If it be not presumptuous for me to use such language, another year, I hope you and Mrs. H. will form in time a plan which will include us in its execution. Here, also, the ground was covered with snow a very few weeks ago. Tho' as with you it yielded to the warmth of the advancing day.'[19]

He had from the first been resigned to his financial loss, he was now deeply grateful for it. His letters and diary repeatedly make the same point. If he had not suffered this loss he could never have imposed himself on his sons for such long periods. 'How can I but rejoice rather than lament at a pecuniary loss, which has produced such a result as that of

* Hannah More was seriously ill, but she survived Wilberforce by two months.

bringing us to dwell under the roofs of our dear children, and witness their enjoyment of a large share of domestic comforts, and their conscientious discharge of the duties of the most important of all professions.'[20] 'It is really true,' he told Lady Olivia Sparrow, 'that our heavy loss has led to the solid and great increase of our enjoyments.'[21] He thanked Providence for furnishing him with 'quite an embarras des richesses in the habitation line'.

*

He had not quite finished with Slavery. The Agency Committee had used new and effective tactics at the General Election which followed the Reform Bill. For a year they had been quietly canvassing the classes which would be enfranchised. By 1832 they were ready to strike. A great number of electors had promised not to vote for those who would not, in their turn, promise to vote against Slavery. When the candidates opened their campaigns they were met by a mass of demands for Anti-Slavery pledges, which were unwelcome to the Whigs and odious to the Tories. The Committee published schedules in the daily papers showing under three headings the position on Emancipation of every candidate as favourable, unfavourable and doubtful. The first reformed parliament would in any case have returned a greater number of Abolitionists; the Agency Committee's campaign increased the proportion.

After the election the petitioning began. Wilberforce, who was still staying with Robert Isaac at East Farleigh, was persuaded to propose a petition against Slavery at Maidstone on April 12, 1833. It was his last appearance in public. His body and voice were both infirm and he had less than four months of life left to him, but he completed his speech, which was calm and moderate in tone. 'I trust,' he finished, 'that we now approach the very end of our career.' As he said these words, by some extraordinary coincidence a shaft of sunlight broke into the room and illuminated his face, in exactly the same way as Pitt's had been lit by the morning sun after his great speech for Abolition forty-one years before. Wilberforce, too, took it for a sign. 'The object,' he exclaimed with all his early fire, 'is bright before us, the light of heaven beams upon it, and is an earnest of success.'[22]

Later, when it was casually mentioned at dinner that the debate on Slavery was just starting, Wilberforce sprang out of his chair and cried out in a voice of great clarity, 'Hear, hear, hear.'

On April 20, 1833 he left East Farleigh for the last time and set out to visit Samuel at Brighstone. It was a bitterly cold spring. Barbara's new maid had had 'flu and he had delayed their departure for her sake and for their own. He was in good health at the time and ten days later he was well enough to write to Harford an irresistibly skilful letter of recommendation for a young surgeon.[23] But a few days later he was attacked by a bout of influenza, caught, no doubt, from the maid on the journey from Kent. He was taken to Bath, in the hopes that the waters there would do him some good, but he was past such aids. His strength visibly declined, and each of his old friends who visited him there noticed how much he had aged. Henry was with him and saw on June 25 that his knees and thighs were severely swollen. A fortnight later Henry wrote, 'The swelling of his legs made his breeches so unpleasant to him that he has had a pair of large, very loose trousers made. This makes a great alteration in his appearance and he is so much more infirm. The infirmity too which you know he has long had—the protrusion a posteriori is aggravated of late and greatly prevents his taking exercise.'[24]

He bore these sufferings and indignities with courage. He constantly found cause for thankfulness—that his illness was not more painful, that he was able to sleep, that he had kind friends to visit him and devoted servants to look after him, that he never suffered from headaches, and above all that he was still united to his beloved family. 'Think of what I should have done had I been left, as one hears of people quarrelling and separating. "In sickness and in health was the burden, and well has it been kept." ' Then Barbara came in and he told her: 'I was just praising you.'[25] At times he felt ashamed of having so many comforts.

Gurney visited him on July 11, having heard that Wilberforce had just suffered a severe bilious attack. 'I was then introduced,' he writes with unconscious humour, 'to an apartment up-stairs, where I found the veteran Christian reclining on a sofa with his feet wrapped in flannel.'[26] They had a spirited religious conversation, which ended with Wilberforce saying: 'With regard to myself, I have nothing whatsoever to urge, but the poor Publican's plea, "God be merciful to me a sinner." These words were spoken with peculiar feeling and emphasis, and have since called to my remembrance his definition of the word mercy—"Kindness to those that deserve punishment." '[27]

In July his family decided that he should be taken to London to consult Dr. Chambers. He was offered quarters in the house of his cousin, Lucy Smith in Cadogan Place and accepted them with a delightful compliment. Speaking of favours he said: 'One likes to confer them on every one, but only to receive them from real friends.'[28] He arrived in London on July 19. Parliament was still sitting and he was visited by many friends; when one of them asked how he was, Wilberforce answered, 'like a clock which is almost run down'. He was unable to walk and had to be carried into the garden on a chair. He had suffered from fits for the last two years, which would make him faint and lose his memory.[29] These became increasingly frequent and severe.

Among Wilberforce's last visitors were two young men, both sons of

Evangelicals and both destined for greatness. Gladstone was brought in to breakfast with him by Henry on July 25. 'He is cheerful and serene,' Gladstone wrote in his diary, 'a beautiful picture of old age in sight of immortality. Heard him pray with his family. Blessing and honour are upon his head.'[30]

Wilberforce remembered visiting his parents' house twelve years before and asked after Gladstone's mother 'in his silvery tones'.

It was Gladstone's only meeting with Wilberforce; Macaulay, of course, had known him all his life. He saw him for the last time on July 27, two days before his death. Wilberforce had just heard of the victory in the Commons for Emancipation and 'he exulted in the success . . . as much as the youngest and most ardent partisan. He was a very kind friend to me and I loved him much'.[31] Macaulay wrote to his sister: 'Wilberforce kept his faculties, and (except when he was actually in fits), his spirits, to the very last. He was cheerful and full of anecdotes only last Saturday. He owned that he enjoyed life much and that he had a great desire to live longer. Strange in a man who had, I should have said, so little to attach him to this world, and so firm a belief in another: in a man with an impaired fortune, a weak spine, and a worn-out stomach! . . . I was truly fond of him.'[32]

But his life was spared long enough to be crowned with one final blessing. When he was at Bath he had heard from Zachary Macaulay.

15th May 1833.

My dear Friend,
    This day ten years ago the abolition of slavery was first made a question in Parliament. Last night its death-blow was struck. I send you a copy of the debate. Stanley's allusion to you was quite overpowering, and electrified the House. My dear friend, let me unite with you in thanks to God for this mercy. . . .

On Friday, July 26, 1833, the Bill for the Abolition of Slavery passed its second reading in the House of Commons. It was a Government measure now and its success was assured. 'Thank God,' said Wilberforce, when he heard the news, 'that I should have lived to witness a day in which England is willing to give twenty millions sterling* for the Abolition of Slavery.'[33]

He was much better that evening, and on Saturday morning his improvement seemed to continue. He was taken out into the garden in a wheel chair and talked and prayed with animation. But on Saturday night he became weaker; on Sunday he suffered from a succession of fainting fits. In a coherent interval on Sunday night he said to Henry, 'I am in a very distressed state.' 'Yes, but you have your feet on the Rock.' 'I do not

---

* The sum with which the planters were to be compensated. It represented about half the market value of their slaves.

venture,' Wilberforce replied, 'to speak so positively; but I hope I have.' These are his last recorded words. He lapsed into a coma and died at three o'clock on the morning of Monday, July 29, 1833. He was within one month of his seventy-fourth birthday.

Barbara wrote a remarkably calm letter to William Smith:

'Why should I wish to detain in a sinking, emaciated suffering body, such a spirit from eternal joys, from a state where pain and sorrow and above all sin, are to be known no more? My loss is indeed beyond measure and expression great but to him, I trust, it is unspeakable gain and I ought to be full of thankfulness that such a treasure was spared to me, to his family, to his country and to the world so long, and recalled at last with so little *comparative* suffering, especially of acute pain, which the exquisite sensibility of his delicate frame so little enabled him to cope with. Thankful especially when I recall Dr. Chambers' opinion that prolonged life would only have led to protracted suffering and that he was threatened with death by a disease which kills by slow and afflicting progress.'[34]

When there is a long interval between the retirement and death of a public figure, he is often remembered during this time only in the past tense, so that when he finally dies the chief reaction is surprise that he was still alive. It was not so with Wilberforce. No sooner had he died than Brougham, as Lord Chancellor, organised an address to his sons asking that he should be buried in Westminster Abbey. He added in a personal note, 'Nearly all the members of both Houses would have joined, had the time allowed.' As it was, thirty-seven members of the Lords and nearly a hundred of the Commons signed these applications.

The two Houses suspended business to attend his funeral. The Speaker, the Lord Chancellor and the Duke of Gloucester were among his pall-bearers. His body was laid to rest in the north transept close to the tombs of Pitt and Fox. It was an unprecedented honour for a private individual who had died long after his retirement from Parliament, and it was echoed by the public response. A friend wrote to his sons: 'You would like to know that as I came towards it down the Strand, every third person I met going about their ordinary business was in mourning.'[35] The ripples spread across the Atlantic: his sons received reports of slaves in the West Indies and the free blacks in New York both going into mourning for him.

A year or so later a statue of him was erected in the North Aisle of the Abbey, with an epitaph which must surely have come from Macaulay's pen.

TO THE MEMORY OF

WILLIAM WILBERFORCE

(BORN IN HULL AUGUST 24TH 1759,
DIED IN LONDON JULY 29TH 1833;)
FOR NEARLY HALF A CENTURY A MEMBER OF THE HOUSE OF COMMONS,
AND, FOR SIX PARLIAMENTS DURING THAT PERIOD,
ONE OF THE TWO REPRESENTATIVES FOR YORKSHIRE.

IN AN AGE AND COUNTRY FERTILE IN GREAT AND GOOD MEN,
HE WAS AMONG THE FOREMOST OF THOSE WHO FIXED THE CHARACTER OF THEIR TIMES
BECAUSE TO HIGH AND VARIOUS TALENTS
TO WARM BENEVOLENCE, AND TO UNIVERSAL CANDOUR,
HE ADDED THE ABIDING ELOQUENCE OF A CHRISTIAN LIFE.

EMINENT AS HE WAS IN EVERY DEPARTMENT OF PUBLIC LABOUR,
AND A LEADER IN EVERY WORK OF CHARITY,
WHETHER TO RELIEVE THE TEMPORAL OR THE SPIRITUAL WANTS OF HIS FELLOW MEN
HIS NAME WILL EVER BE SPECIALLY IDENTIFIED
WITH THOSE EXERTIONS
WHICH, BY THE BLESSING OF GOD, REMOVED FROM ENGLAND
THE GUILT OF THE AFRICAN SLAVE TRADE,
AND PREPARED THE WAY FOR THE ABOLITION OF SLAVERY
IN EVERY COLONY OF THE EMPIRE:

IN THE PROSECUTION OF THESE OBJECTS,
HE RELIED, NOT IN VAIN, ON GOD;
BUT IN THE PROGRESS, HE WAS CALLED TO ENDURE
GREAT OBLOQUY AND GREAT OPPOSITION:
HE OUTLIVED, HOWEVER, ALL ENMITY:
AND, IN THE EVENING OF HIS DAYS,
WITHDREW FROM PUBLIC LIFE AND PUBLIC OBSERVATION
TO THE BOSOM OF HIS FAMILY.
YET HE DIED NOT UNNOTICED OR FORGOTTEN BY HIS COUNTRY:
THE PEERS AND COMMONS OF ENGLAND,
WITH THE LORD CHANCELLOR, AND THE SPEAKER, AT THEIR HEAD,
CARRIED HIM TO HIS FITTING PLACE
AMONG THE MIGHTY DEAD AROUND,
HERE TO REPOSE:
TILL, THROUGH THE MERITS OF JESUS CHRIST,
HIS ONLY REDEEMER AND SAVIOUR,
(WHOM, IN HIS LIFE AND IN HIS WRITINGS HE HAD DESIRED TO GLORIFY,)
HE SHALL RISE IN THE RESURRECTION OF THE JUST.

456

Notes

1. *Hull in the Eighteenth Century*, Jackson, 51.
2. Jackson, 264.
3. L. G. Pine, *The Family of Wilberforce* (*Wilberfoss*), 2–4.
4. Robert Isaac Wilberforce's Commonplace Book, 62–4, Wrangham MSS.
5. I. 4.
6. Bodleian MSS. E. 11. 121.
7. Robert Isaac Wilberforce's Commonplace Book, 4–5, Wrangham MSS.
8. I. 8.
9. Bodleian MSS. C. 4. 1–14.
10. Bodleian MSS. C. 4. 1–2.
11. Wrangham MSS.
12. Wrangham MSS.
13. Wrangham MSS.
14. Wrangham MSS.
15. Wrangham MSS.
16. Wrangham MSS.
17. Bodleian MSS. E. 11. 122.
18. I. 6–7.
19. Bodleian MSS. C. 4. 3.
20. Bodleian MSS. C. 4. 10.
21. I. 11.
22. Wrangham MSS. Gisborne to William Smith, April 15, 1834.
23. Ehrman, *The Younger Pitt*, 22–3.
24. Bodleian MSS. E. 11. 115
25. Corr. I. 246.
26. Lord Muncaster quoted by Sir John Legard. Bodleian MSS. D. 13. 361
27. Bodleian MSS. E. 11. 31–2.
28. Robert Isaac Wilberforce's Commonplace Book, 10, Wrangham MSS.
29. I. 13–14.

CHAPTER II (pp. 16–31)

1. Robert Isaac Wilberforce's Commonplace Book, 6, Wrangham MSS.
2. III. 417.
3. Bodleian MSS. E. 11. 129.

4. I. 17.
5. Hansard 22, 800–1
6. Hansard 22, 801.
7. I. 22.
8. I. 26.
9. Watson, *The Reign of George III*, 257.
10. I. 30.
11. I. 31.
12. Lansdowne MSS. Quoted Ehrman, 108.
13. I. 36–7.
14. I. 36.
15. I. 38–9.
16. I. 40, 44.
17. I. 44.
18. Coupland, *Wilberforce*, 288.
19. Quoted Robert Worthington Smith, 'Yorkshire Elections before the Reform Bill', *American Historical Review*, Vol. 74, No. 5, 1969.
20. I. 57.
21. Harford 20, 3–4. Wilberforce's Account of his own life as outlined to his friend John S. Harford. Included in Harford, *Recollections of William Wilberforce*.
22. I. 54.
23. I. 63.

CHAPTER III (pp. 32–53)

1. Forster, *Marianne Thornton*, 43.
2. Mary Bird's memorandum to Robert Isaac Wilberforce August 27, 1833, Wrangham MSS.
3. I. 72.
4. Wrangham MSS. Autobiographical memorandum.
5. Wrangham MSS. Autobiographical memorandum.
6. Duke MSS. September 30, 1785.
7. Wrangham MSS. 17.8.1786 to Major Cartwright.
8. I. 84.
9. Diary, October 25, 1785.
10. I. 88.
11. I. 89.
12. Journal, November 24–30, 1785. I. 89–93.
13. I. 96.
14. John Newton, *The Journal of a Slave Trader*, IX–XI.
15. Journal, I 100–1.
16. Bodleian MSS. D. 14. 285.
17. Bodleian MSS. D. 14. 285.
18. I. 103.
19. *Edinburgh Review*, January 1808.
20. Wrangham MSS.

21. Quoted F. K. Brown, p. 34.
22. Quoted F. K. Brown, p. 34.
23. Lord David Cecil, *Lord Melbourne*, 168.
24. Quoted Hennell, p. 11.
25. Quoted F. K. Brown, 36.
26. Ford K. Brown, 30.
27. Sydney Smith, Peter Plymley's letters, Letter X, quoted Brown, 369.
28. W. E. Gladstone, *Gleanings of Past Years*, Vol. 7.
29. Essays II. 195.
30. IV. 208.
31. W. E. Gladstone, *Gleanings of Past Years*, Vol. 7, 219.
32. Elizabeth Longford, *Wellington, Pillar of State*, 65.
33. 11.2.1815. IV. 242.
34. IV. 338.
35. III. 359.
36. III. 357.
37. IV. 246.
38. IV. 227.
39. Memorandum on duelling. Wrangham MSS.
40. Bodleian MSS. D. 15.173.
41. Elie Halévy, *History of the English People in the Nineteenth Century*, Vol. I, 432.
42. Bodleian MSS. E. 11.12.
43. I. 98.
44. Private Papers, 12–15.
45. I. 95.
46. Private Papers, 72–3.
47. Hansard 25. 1408–9.
48. V. 341.
49. V. 340–1.

CHAPTER IV (pp. 54–59)

1. I. 131.
2. F. K. Brown, 24.
3. G. O. Trevelyan, *The Early History of Charles James Fox*, 95.
4. Wrangham MSS. May 1787.
5. I. 248.
6. Duke MSS. 1789.
7. Bodleian MSS. D. 17. 7.

CHAPTER V (pp. 60–79)

1. Smith, *The Wealth of Nations*, I. 82.
2. Sir J. Stephen, *Essays in Ecclesiastical Biography*, II. 314.
3. Prince Hoare, *Memoirs of Granville Sharp*, 169.
4. Sir J. Stephen, *Essays*, II. 316.

5. Sir J. Stephen, II. 314.
6. Wrangham, MSS. Autobiographical Memoir.
7. Clarkson, *Abolition*, I. 210.
8. Clarkson, I. 225.
9. Clarkson, I. 241.
10. I, 150-1.
11. Clarkson I, 292.
12. Bodleian MSS. D. 17 8.
13. Clarkson I, 365.
14. Harford, *Recollections of William Wilberforce*, 90.
15. Quoted. I. 292.
16. Private Papers. 20.
17. Alethea Hayter, 49–50.
18. Wrangham MSS. 21 December, 1792.

CHAPTER VI (pp. 80–99)

1. I am indebted to Mr. George Patterson, the son of the present owner of Rayrigg, for this information.
2. I. 179.
3. Duke MSS. Wilberforce Papers. September 2–9, 1809.
4. I. 180–2.
5. I. 183.
6. Bodleian MSS. C. 4.14.
7. Bodleian MSS. C. 4.16.
8. I. 186–7.
9. I. 187.
10. I. 196.
11. Charles Chenevix Trench, *The Royal Malady*, 16.
12. J. H. Plumb, *The First Four Georges*, 142.
13. James Stephen, *Slavery delineated*. II, XIX.
14. Hansard 28, 63–7.
15. Hansard 28, 67–8.
16 Hansard 28, 68.
17. Hansard 28, 72–3.
18. Hansard 28, 74–6.
19. I. 225.
20. I. 228.
21. I. 229–30.
22. Clarkson, II, 155–6.
23. Abridgement of Minutes of Evidence. 1790, II, 191.
24. Abridgement of Minutes of Evidence. 1790, II, 197.
25. I. 255.
26. I. 257.
27. Clarkson, *Abolition*, II, 192.
28. I. 308–9.
29. Correspondence I. 75–6.

30. W. H. Bagehot, *Biographical Studies*, 291.
31. Burghardt du Bois, *Suppression of the African Slave Trade*, 15.
32. I. 297.

CHAPTER VII (pp. 100–114)

1. Hansard 29, 250–78.
2. Hansard 29, 278.
3. Hansard 29, 353.
4. Hansard 29, 356.
5. Duke MSS. Stephen Fuller Papers. Fuller to Committee of Correspondence, May 16, 1788.
6. Duke MSS. Stephen Fuller Papers. Fuller to Lord Sydney, January 29, 1788.
7. Duke MSS. Stephen Fuller Papers. Fuller to Committee of Correspondence; Jamaica. July 5, 1791.
8. Duke MSS. Stephen Fuller Papers. April 30, 1791, May 4, 1791.
9. I. 338.
10. I. 338.
11. I. 340.
12. I. 341.
13. I. 343.
14. Hansard 29, 1055–73.
15. Hansard 29, 1073.
16. Hansard 29, 1104–16.
17. Hansard 29, 1133–58.
18. Hansard 29, 1152.
19. Conversational Memoranda, I. 345.
20. II. 49–50.
21. Duke MSS. Stephen Fuller Papers. May 2, 1792 (loose Manuscripts).
22. I. 358.
23. Bodleian MSS. D. 13. 40.

CHAPTER VIII (pp. 115–121)

1. *The Life and Letters of Zachary Macaulay, by his granddaughter, Viscountess Knutsford*, 202.
2. Knutsford, 202–3.
3. Wrangham MSS. Autobiographical Memoir.
4. E. M. Forster, *Marianne Thornton*. 17.
5. Hennell, *John Venn and the Clapham Sect*. 172.
6. Sir James Stephen, *Essays in Ecclesiastical Biography*, 'The Evangelical Succession', 440.
7. Hennell, 21.
8. Hennell, 108.
9. Hennell, 170–1.
10. Hennell, 111.
11. Colquhoun, 180.

12. Quoted Howse, 68.
13. II. 25.
14. II. 27.

CHAPTER IX (pp. 122–129)

1. Anon, *Liverpool and Slavery*, 137.
2. Prince Hoare, *Granville Sharp*, 213.
3. Prince Hoare, 348.
4. G. O. Trevelyan, *The Life and Letters of Lord Macaulay*, I. 118.
5. Knutsford, 195–6.
6. Knutsford, 7.
7. Knutsford, 87.
8. Knutsford, 89.
9. Knutsford, 103.

CHAPTER X (pp. 130–142)

1. February 14, 1801, II. 12–13.
2. MS. Mem. II. 48.
3. Undated, II. 66.
4. Journal, December 1794, II. 69.
5. Letter to W. Hey, II. 70.
6. II. 72.
7. II. 72.
8. Keith Feiling, *The Second Tory Party*, 203.
9. II. 72.
10. II. 75–6.
11. II. 78.
12. II. 92.
13. Parliamentary History, Vol. 31, 1492–5.
14. II. 80.
15. II. 109.
16. October 24, 1795, II. 110.
17. Diary, October 26–9, 1795, II. 111.
18. Diary. November 16, 1795.
19. Parliamentary History, Vol. 32, 292–5.
20. Journal, November 22, 1795, II. 114–15.
21. The Rev. Miles Atkinson to his son at Cambridge. Quoted II. 125.
22. II. 131.
23. II. 134.
24. Duke MSS. Wilberforce Papers. September 21, 1795.
25. III. 538.
26. December 19, 1795.
27. Hansard 32, 762–3.
28. Hansard 32, 762.
29. Among Wrangham MSS.
30. Wrangham MSS.

CHAPTER XI (143–148)

1. II. 30–1.
2. II. 32.
3. II. 399 (Appendix).
4. II. 34.
5. II. 35.
6. Diary, Wrangham MSS.
7. Diary, Wrangham MSS.
8. II. 96.
9. II. 86.
10. Unpublished book on Yorkshire Election of 1807. Among Wrangham MSS.
11. Robert Worthington Smith, *Yorkshire Elections before the Reform Bill.*

CHAPTER XII (pp. 149–160)

1. Conversational Memoranda quoted II. 171.
2. Bodleian MSS. D. 13. 41. Wilberforce's son prudishly altered the wording to 'apply it to him by way of memento', II. 172.
3. II. 181.
4. Private Journal, Wrangham MSS.
5. Private Journal, Wrangham MSS.
6. Journal, January 29, 1797.
7. II. 199.
8. II. 199.
9. Wrangham MSS. 18.4.1797.
10. Bodleian MSS. C. 3. 27.
11. Bodleian MSS. C. 3. 29.
12. Henry Thornton to Hannah More, quoted II. 208.
13. II. 208.
14. Correspondence I. 167.
15. Quoted G. M. Trevelyan, *British History in the Nineteenth Century*, 52.
16. *Practical View*, First edition, 36.
17. Ibid. 185.
18. Ibid. 147–8.
19. Ibid. 194–6.
20. Ibid. 197.
21. Ibid. 297–8.
22. Ibid. 306–7.
23. Ibid. 318.
24. Ibid. 398.
25. Ibid. 393–4.
26. Ibid. 397–8.
27. Ibid. 405–6.
28. II. 61.
29. Lovat-Fraser, *Erskine*, 148.
30. Lovat-Fraser, 59.

31. Quoted L. P. Stryker, *For the Defence*, 367.
32. Lovat-Fraser, 60.
33. Francis Place, *Autobiography*, 170.

CHAPTER XIII (pp. 161–171)

1. II. 214.
2. Wrangham MSS.
3. General Abercromby quoted by J. S. Watson, 372.
4. Diary, May 5.
5. Private Journal. Wrangham MSS.
6. Private Journal. Wrangham MSS.
7. Quoted, Dorothy Pym, *Battersea Rise*, 195–6.
8. II. 220.
9. Forster, 42–3.
10. III. 434.
11. Bodleian MSS. D. 20.
12. Bodleian MSS. D. 20. 19.
13. Bodleian MSS. D. 20. 48–9.
14. Quoted *Cornhill Magazine*, December 1933. John Wilberforce, 'William Wilberforce's honeymoon'.
15. Bodleian MSS. D. 20. 34.
16. Bodleian MSS. D. 20. 35 see also Duke MSS. Wilberforce Papers, July 10, 1794.
17. Ibid. D. 16. 35.
18. Ibid. D. 16. 35.
19. Bodleian MSS. D. 20. 36–41.

CHAPTER XIV (pp. 172–187)

1. In speech in favour of Plunkett's Bill for removal of R.C. disabilities 1821.
2. Journal, August 24, 1797. II. 232.
3. II. 232.
4. II. 232–3.
5. November 10, 1797. II. 242–3.
6. Quoted Arthur Bryant, *Years of Endurance*, 219.
7. January 1, 1798. II. 249.
8. Journal, II. 250–1.
9. Diary, April 17.
10. II. 304–5.
11. Private Papers 223.
12. II. 306.
13. Corr. I. 93.
14. V. 232.
15. Diary, April 1, 1797.
16. Hansard 33, 570.
17. Hansard 33, 574.

18. 22.8.97. ii. 257.
19. II. 265.
20. Eric Williams, *History of the People of Trinidad and Tobago*, 65, 68.
21. II. 265–6.
22. Duke MSS. Wilberforce Papers. May 5, 1798.
23. Diary, May 27–30, 1798.
24. II. 281–2.
25. II. 283–4.
26. II. 284.
27. Quoted J. Holland Rose, *Pitt and the Great War*, 336.
28. Quoted J. Holland Rose. Ibid. 336.
29. Corr. I. 127.
30. II. 295.
31. Undated. About July 18. II. 298.

CHAPTER XV (pp. 188–207)

1. Hansard 34. 114.
2. Ibid. 114.
3. Ibid. 115.
4. II. 321.
5. II. 322.
6. II. 323.
7. Hansard 34, 981/4.
8. Hansard 34, 1481
9. Quoted Burdett's speech, Hansard 37 (1818) 485.
10. *The Town Crier*, 240-2.
11. Aris v.s. Dickey, described in W. M. Medland and Charles Weobly, *Criminal Trials*, Vol. I.
12. G. L. Chesterton, *Revelations of Prison Life*, 19–20.
13. Ibid. 55.
14. Hansard 17 (1810), 339.
15. Hansard 37 (1818), 494.
16. Parliamentary Register, April 9, 1799.
17. Diary, July 5 and 6, 1799.
18. Quoted Knutsford.
19. Diary, July 29, 1799.
20. Journal, August 25, 1799. II. 342.
21. II. 350.
22. Windham Papers II. 143. Quoted by Sir Arthur Bryant, *The Years of Endurance*, 295.
23. Diary, January 12, 1800.
24. January 5, 1800.
25. Quoted Bryant, 296.
26. Journal, April 13, 1800. II. 360.
27. II. 364.

28. These horrifying facts have been drawn from E. S. Turner's admirable history of cruelty to animals, *All Heaven in a Rage*.
29. Wilberforce to Hannah More, 25.4.1800. II. 366.
30. Sydney Smith, *Works*, 140–2.
31. Turner, 119.
32. Quoted Colquhoun, 441.
33. II. 367.
34. II. 377.
35. Correspondence I. 215.
36. II. 379.
37. II. 381.
38. II. 382.
39. Forster, 51.
40. II. 368. June 6, 1800.
41. Corr. I. 209.

CHAPTER XVI (pp. 208–221)

1. II. Appendix.
2. March 18, 1801. III. 6.
3. II. 326.
4. Bodleian MSS. E. 11. 139/140.
5. III. 22.
6. To Muncaster, December 10, 1801. III. 21.
7. September 7, 1802. III. 67.
8. September 7, 1802. III. 67.
9. Knutsford, 265.
10. M. G. Jones, *Hannah More*, 221.
11. Jones, 221.
12. Bodleian MSS. D. 20. 37.
13. Duke MSS. Wilberforce Papers, 1817 undated.
14. Duke MSS. Wilberforce Papers, July 10, 1794.
15. Much of it in the Duke MSS.
16. Forster, 140.
17. V. 254.
18. I. 238.
19. Ford K. Brown, 250.
20. Ford K. Brown, 357.
21. Diary, 12.2.1803.
22. Diary, 12.2.1803.
23. Corr. I. 261.
24. To Babington, March 22, III. 89.
25. Corr. I. 288.
26. To Muncaster, August 8. III. 112.
27. To Gisborne, October 18. III. 136.
28. To Gisborne, III. 137.
29. Journal, April 17, 1804. III. 153.
30. Journal, April 17, 1804. III. 153.

CHAPTER XVII (pp. 222–231)

1. III. 26.
2. III. 31–3.
3. 4.2.1802. III. 37.
4. To Muncaster, September 7, 1802.
5. February 21. III. 164.
6. Diary, May 30, 1804.
7. Wilberforce to Muncaster, July 6, 1804. III. 178.
8. To Gisborne, June 28. III. 181.
9. July 6. III. 182.
10. Diary, July 3, 1804.
11. Quoted Lord David Cecil, *Lord M*, 82.
12. Duke MSS. Wilberforce Papers. September 22, 1804.
13. Duke MSS. Wilberforce Papers. September 24, 1804.
14. III. 203–4.
15. Con Mem III. 211.
16. Hansard 3. 668.
17. Diary, 28.2.1805.
18. Diary, 1.3.1805.
19. III. 214.
20. III. 213.
21. Diary, 29.3.1805.
22. III. 217.
23. Diary, III. 188.
24. Diary, III. 191.

CHAPTER XVIII (pp. 232–244)

1. Sir George Stephen to Harriet Beecher Stowe, *Anti-Slavery Reminiscences*, Letter 5, 79.
2. Con Mem III. 218.
3. III. 219.
4. III. 218–19, R. I. Wilberforce Commonplace Book 70. Wrangham MSS.
5. III. 220.
6. Con Mem III. 221.
7. Hansard 4. 318.
8. III. 224.
9. Hansard 4. 362.
10. III. 224.
11. Diary, April 18, 1805.
12. Bodleian MSS. D. 13. 361.
13. Bodleian MSS. D. 13. 361.
14. Lord Macaulay, *Miscellaneous Writings*, Vol. II. 367.
15. III. 230.
16. III. 245.
17. Clarkson, *Abolition*, II. 506.

18. Duke MSS. Stephen Fuller Papers. Letterpress Box No. 2. 31.3.1795.
19. Brougham, *Statesmen of George III*, II. pp. 103–5.
20. Rogers, *Recollections*, 10.
21. Rogers, *Table Talk*, 83.
22. Corr. I. 23.
23. To Muncaster, 25.1.1806. III. 245.
24. III. 246.
25. Perceval to Wilberforce 29.1.1806. III. 248.

CHAPTER XIX (pp. 245–259)

1. Wrangham MSS.
2. Correspondence II. 70.
3. III. 257.
4. Duke MSS. Wilberforce Papers. February 4, 1806.
5. Diary, April 5, 1806.
6. Duke MSS. Wilberforce Papers. May 20, 1806.
7. Journal, May 25, 1806. III. 261–2.
8. To Stephen 27.5.1806. III. 263.
9. III. 273.
10. Bodleian MSS. B. 1.15.
11. Diary, January 31, 1807.
12. February 11, 1807. III. 293.
13. Hansard 8, 664.
14. Hansard 8, 667.
15. Diary, February 11, 1807.
16. Diary, February 12, 1807.
17. Hansard 8, 956.
18. Hansard 8, 977.
19. Diary, February 23, 1807.
20. Hansard 8, 975.
21. Hansard 8, 978–9.
22. III. 297.
23. Hansard 8, 986.
24. Diary, February 25, 1807.
25. III. 298.
26. III. 304.
27. E. Williams, *Capitalism and Slavery*, 181.
28. Frank J. Klingberg, *The Anti-Slavery Movement in England*, 101.
29. Lecky, *History of European Morals*, 6th edition, II. 153.

CHAPTER XX (pp. 260–271)

1. Wrangham MSS.
2. Corr. II. 1–2.
3. October 30, 1806. III. 282.
4. Wilberforce Museum, Hull MSS.

5. Manuscript Account of the Election of 1807 by David Russel, iii, 317, (Russel was one of Wilberforce's agents).
6. Creevey *Papers*, 166/7.
7. Songs, Epigrams, etc. of Yorkshire Contested Election, Leeds, 1807.
8. Wrangham MSS.
9. IV. 56.
10. Grimston. Unpublished Notes on Yorkshire Election 1807. Wrangham MSS.
11. Grimston, Wrangham MSS.
12. Grimston, Wrangham MSS.
13. Grimston, Wrangham MSS.
14. III. 324.
15. III. 324.
16. III. 335–6.
17. III. 328–9.
18. III. 330.
19. III. 331.
20. May 26, 1807. III. 326.
21. Grimston, Wrangham MSS.
22. Wilberforce Museum, Hull. Wilberforce to Montagu, 3.6.1807.
23. III. 332.

CHAPTER XXI (pp. 272–299)

1. Osbaldeston, *Memoirs* 11.
2. Osbaldeston, *Memoirs* 12.
3. Osbaldeston, *Memoirs* 13.
4. Bodleian MSS. D. 17. 286.
5. Louis Simond, *Journal of a Tour and Residence in Great Britain* (Edinburgh, 1817).
6. Harford, 3.
7. Harford, 70.
8. Joseph John Gurney, *Familiar sketch of the late William Wilberforce*.
9. Robert Southey, *Life and Correspondence*, iv. 316.
10. Colquhoun, 172.
11. III. 350.
12. Essays, II. 222.
13. Corr. II. 159.
14. Hannah More to Mrs. Bouverie quoted M. G. Jones, 90.
15. M. G. Jones, 193.
16. III. 461.
17. Newsome, 34. Wilberforce MSS. Fragments 29–30.
18. V. 132.
19. Diary, October 20, 1825.
20. Duke MSS. Wilberforce papers.8.12. 29.
21. IV. 123.
22. Corr. 1. 244.
23. Diary, August 18, 1812.

24. Bodleian MSS. E. 11. 80.
25. Bodleian MSS. E. 11. 7.
26. Bodleian MSS. E. 11. 93/94.
27. IV. 260.
28. Diary, October 10, 1818.
29. Diary, September 17, 1830.
30. Corr. I. 250.
31. Corr. I. 252.
32. Wrangham MSS.
33. V. 285.
34. Bodleian MSS. E. 11. 28–30.
35. III. 464.
36. Duke MSS. 22.10.25, 28.4.30, 6.2.33.
37. Thomas Moore's Diary, May 13, 1826.
38. Hansard 26, 855.
39. Corr. I. 219.
40. II. 414–16.
41. Hansard 36. 1249.
42. Hazlitt, *Spirit of the Age* (Everyman edition) 314.
43. James Boswell. Quoted J. Wesley Bready, *England Before and After Wesley.*
44. Wallas, *Life of Francis Place*, 147. Quoted F. K. Brown, 113.
45. V. 241.
46. V. 241.
47. Buxton, *Memoirs*, 90.
48. Stephen, *Essays* II. 256, 170.
49. V. 217.
50. Corr. II. 209.
51. Harford, 44.
52. I. 159.
53. Private Papers 62–3.
54. V. 241.
55. Hazlitt, *Spirit of the Age*, 315.
56. III. 57/8.
57. *Practical View*, 167.
58. Bodleian MSS. E. 11 3/4.
59. V. 6.
60. III. 34.
61. V. 243.
62. Bodleian MSS. d.9.116.
63. V. 244.
64. Wrangham MSS. (Clarkson).
    Bodleian MSS. C. 3 188 (Simeon).
    Bodleian MSS. D. 15 22 (Christian).
    Bodleian MSS. C. 146 (Dundonald).
    Bodleian MSS. D. 17 181 (Lamb).
    Bodleian MSS. D. 17 87 (Raikes).
    Bodleian MSS. D. 17 37 (Coal Mines).

Bodleian MSS. E. 11 38 (Grahame).
Wrangham MSS. July 1816 (Fire Extinguisher).
Wrangham MSS. 1792 (Newton).
Bodleian MSS. D. 17 54 (Whig).
Bodleian MSS. D. 17 110 Lempriere.
65. Wrangham MSS. 1818.
66. Bodleian MSS. C. 3 159.
67. Wrangham MSS. undated.
68. Duke MSS. Wilberforce Papers, December 24, 1820.
69. III. 527.
70. III. 487.
71. Wrangham MSS. Autobiographical Memoir.
72. Forster, 139.
73. V. 294.
74. V. 294.
75. Bodleian MSS. C. 257.
76. Forster, 42.
77. V. 249.
78. V. 249.
79. IV. 208.
80. Bodleian MSS. D. 16.15.
81. Faringdon Diary. Quoted Newsome, 33.
82. Forster, 137–8.
83. IV. 324.
84. Bodleian MSS. E. 11. 112.
85. V. 262.
86. V. 348.
87. Robert Southey, *Letters*, III. 99.
88. *Essays in Ecclesiastical Biography*, II. 218–21.
89. Letter to Freeholders of York, 104.
90. Correspondence II, 446.
91. V. 208.
92. IV. 53.
93. V. 333.
94. V. 48.
95. Corr. I. 219.
96. V. 228.
97. V. 315.
98. Quoted Newsome 85.

CHAPTER XXII (pp. 300–313)

1. III. 369.
2. III. 396.
3. Diary, June 14, 1808.
4. III. 344.
5. Duke MSS. Wilberforce Papers, August 26, 1807.

6. Wilberforce to Babington, III, 347.
7. III. 428.
8. Hansard 13. 591.
9. Hansard 12. 278.
10. Hansard 12. 446.
11. Hansard 13. 279.
12. Hansard 13. 578 et seq.
13. Hansard 13. 586.
14. Hansard 13. 590.
15. Hansard 13. 591.
16. Hansard 13. 592.
17. III. 405.
18. III. 406.
19. September 23, 1809.
20. III. 428.
21. III. 429.
22. III. 235.
23. Caroline Stephen, *Letters of Sir James Stephen*, quoted Newsome, 21.
24. Diary, October 26, 1807.
25. Stephen, *Essays*, 577.
26. Wrangham MSS. R. I. Wilberforce's Commonplace Book, 74.
27. Bodleian MSS. C. 3. 109.
28. Corr. II. 124.
29. Corr. II. 128.
30. Corr. II. 135.
31. IV. 24.
32. Journal, May 17, 1812.
33. Diary, May 13, 1812.

CHAPTER XXIII (pp. 314–331)

1. III. 526.
2. Ibid. 529–30.
3. III. 534–6.
4. Diary, August 24, 1811.
5. Corr. II. 209.
6. III. 541.
7. Diary, September 6, 1812.
8. IV. 56.
9. IV. 63.
10. Hansard (July 19, 1811).
11. Corr. II. 177.
12 IV. 17.
13. IV. 18.
14. Diary, March 25, 1815.
15. III. 362.
16. Duke MSS. Wilberforce Papers.

17. IV. 95–6.
18. Bodleian MSS. E. 11. 24/5.
19. Hansard 24. 1238.
20. Hansard 1821 (Plunkett's Bill for removal of R.C. disabilities).
21. Knutsford, 340.
22. Private Papers, 275–6.
23. Private Papers, 280.
24. To Butterworth, February 15, 1812, IV, 11.
25. To Butterworth IV. 11–12.
26. Diary, February 21, 1812.
27. Diary, February 14, 1812.
28. To Butterworth IV. 14.
29. IV. 104.
30. IV. 106.
31. Hole, *Early History of the C.M.S.* Quoted Howse, *Saints in Politics*, 82.
32. Hansard 25, 425.
33. IV. 109.
34. Diary, May 27, 1813.
35. Hansard 26. 830.
36. Bodleian MSS. E 11. 15.
37. Con Mem. Quoted IV. 124.
38. Con Mem. Quoted IV. 124.
39. *Figaro in London*, December 1831, 15, quoted Ford K. Brown, 427–8.
40. Diary, July 12, 1813.
41. Corr. II. 271.

CHAPTER XXIV (pp. 332–345)

1. IV. 136/7.
2. IV. 169.
3. IV. 170.
4. IV. 170.
5. Diary, May 13, 1814. IV. 185.
6. IV. 198.
7. IV. 182.
8. Diary, May 26, 1814.
9. Corr. II. 287/8.
10. Letter to Talleyrand, 43.
11. Letter to Talleyrand, 19.
12. Wilberforce to Lady Olivia Sparrow, May 3, 1814. Wilberforce Museum MSS.
13. IV. 187.
14. Diary, June 12, 1814.
15. Castlereagh Correspondence, 3rd Series II. 73. Quoted Howse 145.
16. IV. 212.
17. *Times*, July 10, 1815. Quoted Halévy, 14.
18. To Macaulay, IV. 217.

19. Duke MSS. Wilberforce Papers, November 13, 1815.
20. Ibid.
21. Duke MSS. Wilberforce Papers, 1816. Undated.
22. Harford, 79–82.
23. Watson, 520.
24. Diary, May 8, 1815.
25. Hansard 30. 116–18.
26. IV. 245.
27. IV. 246–8.
28. IV. 249.
29. Woodward, *Age of Reform*, 61.
30. Diary, February 14, 1816.
31. Hansard, May 22, 1816.
32. IV. 306.

CHAPTER XXV (pp. 346–352)

1. Diary, January 11, 1815.
2. IV. 229.
3. IV. 233.
4. IV. 271.
5. Diary, September 27, 1815.
6. Diary, October 3, 1815.
7. IV. 299–300.
8. IV. 273.
9. IV. 346.
10. Quoted Ford K. Brown, 457.
11. Ibid. 459.
12. Ibid. 459.
13. Duke MSS. Wilberforce Papers, January 17, 1815.
14. Bodleian MSS. D. 9. 6.
15. Newsome, 44.
16. Forster, 138.
17. Trevelyan, *Life and Letters of Lord Macaulay*, I. 40–1.
18. Newsome, 39.
19. Bodleian, C. 196. 44. undated.
20. Bodleian D 9. 3.
21. Bodleian D 9. 5 September 1819. Samuel was in fact entering his fifteenth year.
22. Wrangham MSS.
23. Wilberforce Museum.
24. Ibid.
25. Ibid.
26. Duke MSS. Wilberforce Papers, 1808 (undated).
27. Newsome, 49.
28. Wrangham MSS.
29. Wrangham MSS. Book of Private Thoughts, December 7, 1815.

30. Bodleian D. 9. 13.
31. Bodleian D. 9. 82.
32. Wrangham MSS. Book of Private Thoughts, September 4, 1816.
33. Newsome, 58. Mr. Newsome acknowledges his debt to Professor R. W. Smith of the University of Oregon for this and other references dealing with William's unfortunate career at Cambridge.
34. Diary, January 8, quoted Newsome 58.
35. Diary, March 15, quoted Newsome 58.
36. British Museum, Egerton MSS. 1964. Undated.

CHAPTER XXVI (pp. 353–357)

1. Quoted IV. 158.
2. IV. 159.
3. IV. 161–2.
4. Diary, March 18, 1814. IV. 164/5.
5. Lord David Cecil, 133.
6. IV. 167.
7. Corr. II. 410.
8. Duke MSS. Wilberforce Papers. March 21, 1814.
9. Diary, April 27, 1815.
10. IV. 180.
11. IV. 262.
12. Private Papers, 150.
13. IV. 276.
14. IV. 276.
15. IV. 277.
16. Corr. II. 332.
17. IV. 280.

CHAPTER XXVII (pp. 358–383)

1. *Political Register*, October 3, 1818. (XXXIV, 216).
2. Halévy, *Liberal Awakening*, 25.
3. IV. 308.
4. IV. 316.
5. Diary, March 5, 1817.
6. IV. 314–15.
7. Hansard 36. 1120.
8. Hansard 36. 1121.
9. Hansard 36. 1125 and 1127.
10. Hansard 36. 1134.
11. Hansard 36. 1246/7.
12. Hansard 36. 1246/7.
13. IV. 328.
14. IV. 329.
15. February 11, 1818. Hansard 37. 363/6.

16. IV. 369.
17. Hansard 37. 851/2.
18. Diary, March 5, 1818.
19. Hansard 37. 858.
20. Hansard 37. 859.
21. Hansard 37. 860.
22. Hansard 37. 860/1.
23. Hansard 37. 862.
24. V. 35.
25. V. 36.
26. V. 39.
27. V. 40.
28. V. 34.
29. Hansard 41. 135.
30. Hansard 41. 135.
31. Hansard 41. 320.
32. Buxton, 81.
33. Longford, *Wellington, Pillar of State*, 61.
34. Hansard 41. 800, 912.
35. Brougham, *Political Philosophy*, *III*, 184. Quoted Halévy, II. 75.
36. Woodward, 31.
37. Hansard 8. 712.
38. Hansard 8. 721/2.
39. Hansard 8. 722.
40. Hansard 8. 730.
41. Hansard 8. 731.
42. V. 173.
43. Hansard 8. 732.
44. V. 173.
45. Hansard VIII. 731.
46. Bodleian. Wilberforce MSS. E.11. Samuels' Fragments of his Father's Conversations. 3.
47. V. 38.
48. Diary, March 8, 1818.
49. J. E. and B. Hammond, mainly in *The Town Labourer*, 223–46.
50. *The Town Labourer*, 242.
51. *The Town Labourer*, 244–5.
52. *Saints in Politics*, 134.
53. IV. 293.
54. Bodleian MSS. E. 11. 20.
55. R. I. Wilberforce's Commonplace Book. Wrangham MSS. p. 13.
56. V. 345.
57. Hansard 41. 1168.
58. Quoted Howse, 99.
59. Hansard 9. 798–9. Quoted Howse, 99.
60. IV. 90-1.
61. Diary, December 16, 1819.

62. Hansard, March 19, 1819.
63. Hansard, February 12, 1817.
64. Rainsford, *The Slave Trade*, 188.
65. Halévy, 15.

CHAPTER XXVIII (pp. 384–392)

1. Woodward, 67.
2. Diary, June 6, 1820.
3. Diary, June 10, 1820.
4. Creevey, *Papers*, 1905 edition, 304.
5. V. 58/9.
6. Bodleian MSS. D. 13. 57.
7. V. 62.
8. Forster, 19.
9. Diary, July 6, 1820.
10. V. 71–2.
11. V. 67.
12. Creevey, 307.
13. Longford, 68.
14. Quoted Joanna Richardson, *The Disastrous Marriage*, 158.
15. Brougham, *Life and Times*, ii, 407.
16. Quoted Richardson, 160.
17. Quoted Richardson, 160.
18. Creevey, 318.
19. Wrangham MSS.
20. Duke MSS. Wilberforce Papers.
21. Wrangham MSS. November 2, 1820.
22. Diary, January 26, 1821.
23. Brougham, ii, 412.

CHAPTER XXIX (pp. 393–399)

1. Hubert Cole, *Christophe*, 213.
2. Cole, 242.
3. Corr. I. 358.
4. Corr. II. 368–9.
5. Corr. II. 368–9.
6. Corr. II. 376.
7. Corr. II. 376.
8. Corr. II. 381.
9. V. 42.
10. Cole, 256.
11. Duke MSS. Wilberforce Papers. September 8, 1818.
12. V. 82.
13. V. 108.
14. Corr. II. 391–5.
15. *Henri Christophe and Thomas Clarkson*, 79.
16. *Henri Christophe and Thomas Clarkson*, 79.

CHAPTER XXX (pp. 400–413)

1. Hansard 9. 142.
2. Matthieson, *British Slavery and Its Abolition, 1823–1838*, 35–8.
3. Hugh Thomas, *Cuba, or the Pursuit of Freedom*, 27.
4. *Anti-Slavery Recollections*, 61.
5. IV. 306.
6. Diary, January 7, 1818.
7. Buxton, *Memoirs*, 58.
8. Buxton, *Memoirs*, 105.
9. Buxton, *Memoirs*, 122.
10. V. 135.
11. V. 137.
12. V. 153.
13. Corr. II. 466.
14. IV. 307.
15. Diary, December 27, 1822.
16. 'An Appeal on behalf of the Negro Slaves', 1823.
17. V. 165.
18. Diary, March 19, 1823.
19. V. 168.
20. James Stephen, *The Slavery of the British West Indian Colonies Delineated*.
21. *Anti-Slavery Reminiscences*, 247.
22. Mathieson, 39.
23. L. J. Ragatz, *The Fall of the Planter Class in the British Caribbean*, 12, 423.
24. Matthieson, 64.
25. Hansard, 1823 9. 304.
26. Duke MSS. Wilberforce Papers 1814 undated. Correspondence II. 381–5.
27. Lewis, *Journal of a West Indian Proprietor*. Quoted Matthieson, 102.
28. Diary, May 22, 1823.
29. Anti-Slavery reporter, i. 7. Quoted Matthieson, 118.
30. V. 129.

CHAPTER XXXI (pp. 414–423)

1. Sir G. Stephen, 62.
2. Quoted Matthieson, 134.
3. V. 201.
4. V. 202.
5. Buxton, 143.
6. Canning's speech. Hansard 11. 1279.
7. Matthieson, 145.
8. Matthieson, 147.
9. Quoted Hansard 11. 1234/5.
10. V. 218.
11. Wrangham MSS. R. I. Wilberforce. Commonplace Book, 33.
12. V. 222. To Stephen.
13. Hansard 11, 1298.

14. Hansard 11, 1299.
15. Frank J. Klingberg, *The Anti-Slavery Movement in England*, 220.
16. Trevelyan, Life and Letters of Lord Macaulay, I. 115.
17. Forster, 128–9.
18. Trevelyan, I. 116.
19. Trevelyan, I. 116.
20. Hansard 11. 1286.
21. Buxton, 140.
22. Hansard 11. 1406/1416.
23. V. 230.
24. V. 229.
25. Bodleian MSS. 108/9.
26. V. 233–4
27. Newsome, 37.
28. V. 238.
29. Buxton, 152.
30. V. 239.
31. Diary, February 7, 1825.

CHAPTER XXXII (pp. 424–447)

1. Bodleian MSS. C. 3. 258.
2. V. 248.
3. Forster, 130.
4. V. 249/50.
5. V. 259.
6. Wilberforce Museum, Hull. To Henry, 18.9.26.
7. Duke MSS. Buxton Papers, February 17, 1826.
8. V. 257.
9. Duke MSS. Wilberforce Papers, October 6, 1825.
10. Duke MSS. Wilberforce Papers, December 5, 1825.
11. Duke MSS. Wilberforce Papers. January 16, 1822.
12. M. G. Jones, 234.
13. Newsome, 59.
14. Duke MSS. Wilberforce Papers, December 21, 1830.
15. Bodleian MSS. E. 11. 119/20.
16. Sir J. Stephen, *Essays*, II. 272–3.
17. Duke MSS. Wilberforce Papers, May 2, 1821, to Harford.
18. Wrangham MSS. July 9, 1823.
19. Wrangham MSS. October 11, 1823.
20. Bodleian MSS. D. 9. 10.
21. Private Papers. 217–18.
22. Wilberforce Museum, Hull.
23. Ibid.
24. V. 263.
25. V. 264.
26. V. 267.

27. Duke MSS. Wilberforce Papers. September 29, 1821.
28. Wrangham MSS. October 20, 1819.
29. Forster, 137.
30. Duke MSS. Wilberforce Papers. July 3, 1818.
31. Southey's *Life and Correspondence*, IV, 316.
32. Forster, 136.
33. Forster, 137.
34. Forster, 137.
35. V. 275.
36. V. 278.
37. V. 279.
38. V. 276.
39. V. 279.
40. V. 280–1.
41. Gurney, 10.
42. Gurney, 15/16.
43. Gurney, quoted V. 296. Not in Familiar Sketch.
44. V. 296–8.
45. Diary, May 24, 1829.
46. Wrangham MSS. May 21, 1830.
47. Forster, 139.
48. Diary, November 25, 1829.
49. V. 316.
50. Wrangham MSS.
51. Wrangham MSS.
52. Duke MSS. Wilberforce Cash Book.
53. Bodleian MSS. C. 3. 222.
54. Ibid.
55. Duke MSS. Wilberforce Papers, September 6, 1831.
56. V. 326.
57. V. 325.
58. Duke MSS. Wilberforce Papers, September 6, 1831.
59. Gurney, 42.
60. Wrangham MSS. Quoted Newsome, 131.
61. Quoted Newsome, 136.
62. Wrangham MSS. August 4, 1831.
63. Wrangham MSS. September 30, 1831.
64. Mathieson, 193.
65. Mathieson, 195.
66. Sir G. Stephen, 120.
67. The controversy can be followed in the brothers' life of Wilberforce, notably I. 141, Clarkson's structures on a life of William Wilberforce, 1838, The preface to the Correspondence of William Wilberforce 1840, H. C. Robinson. Exposure of Misrepresentations, in 1840, H. C. Robinson, Diary 1872, E. L. Griggs' Thomas Clarkson. There is correspondence between Clarkson and the Wilberforces. and the Wilberforce brothers and Stephen in the Wrangham MSS. The Bodleian MSS. has the correspondence between

Clarkson and Samuel Wilberforce, showing the restoration of friendly relations between the two families. The Duke MSS., William Smith Papers, show Clarkson's unsuccessful attempts to prevent the attack.

68. Sir G. Stephen, 120–2.
69. Trevelyan, I, 143.
70. Sir G. Stephen, 161–2.
71. Duke MSS. William Smith Papers, August 23, 1832.
72. Duke MSS. William Smith Papers, January 25, 1833.
73. Duke MSS. William Smith Papers, June 28, 1833.
74. Bodelian MSS. E. 11. 138.
75. Private Papers, 259.
76. Private Papers, 265.
77. Private Papers, 266.
78. Duke MSS. Wilberforce Papers, October 9, 1831.
79. Harford, 231.
80. Private Papers, 271–2.
81. Private Papers, 272.
82. Private Papers, 272–4.
83. Harford, 233–4.

CHAPTER XXXIII (pp. 448–455)

1. Duke MSS. Wilberforce Papers, February 21, 1832.
2. Newsome, 145.
3. V. 327.
4. V. 328.
5. Private Papers, 267.
6. Wrangham MSS. Quoted Newsome, 143.
7. Wrangham MSS. Quoted Newsome, 143.
8. Private Papers, 279–80.
9. Private Papers, 269.
10. Private Papers, 269.
11. Private Papers, 279.
12. V. 350.
13. V. 333.
14. Diary, December 1832. I am indebted to Mr. C. E. Wrangham for permission to use this and other quotations from his privately published memoir of his family's connection with East Farleigh.
15. Diary, December 1832.
16. Duke MSS. Wilberforce Papers, February 6, 1833.
17. Duke MSS. Wilberforce Papers, February 6, 1833.
18. Duke MSS. William Smith Papers, February 9, 1933.
19. Duke MSS. Wilberforce Papers, April 2, 1833.
20. V. 331.
21. V. 332.
22. V. 354.
23. Duke MSS. Wilberforce Papers, April 30, 1833.

24. Sandwitch MSS. B. 1. 23/4. Quoted Newsome, 145.
25. V. 359.
26. Gurney, 38.
27. Gurney, 41.
28. V. 366.
29. V. 372.
30. Morley, I. 106–7.
31. Duke MSS. Sir Edward Baines Papers, July 30, 1833.
32. Trevelyan, I. 319.
33. V. 370.
34. Duke MSS. William Smith Papers, August 17, 1833.
35. V. 376.

BIBLIOGRAPHY

Abbreviations: References to the biography of Wilberforce by his sons have been made with the volume number in Roman figures followed by the page number. No name has been given for references to this book.

The three main manuscript sources have been abbreviated to Wrangham MSS, Bodleian MSS and Duke MSS. Since the Duke University papers are arranged by date and the Wrangham collection is not yet catalogued, only the Bodleian Papers have reference numbers.

All references to the Parliamentary Debates/Hansard series are to Hansard.

MANUSCRIPT SOURCES

Wrangham Manuscripts

This collection is the possession of Mr. C. E. Wrangham, a great-great-grandson of Wilberforce's. It includes the major part of Wilberforce's diary, his religious journals, his memoranda on various subjects, a large collection of correspondence, Robert Isaac's Commonplace Book, and an unpublished account of the Yorkshire Election of 1807.

Bodleian Manuscripts

The Wrangham Manuscripts represent the papers kept by Robert Isaac Wilberforce, the Bodleian and Duke Manuscripts those of Samuel Wilberforce. The Bodleian has a large collection of the correspondence of William, Barbara and Samuel Wilberforce and a number of family albums, the most interesting of which are the Commonplace Books kept by Samuel and Barbara. It also has some essays written by William Wilberforce as a boy at Pocklington school.

Duke University Manuscripts

Duke University in North Carolina has acquired a collection of Wilberforce's correspondence which is substantial although not as large as those in the possession of Mr. Wrangham or the Bodleian Library. They also have Wilberforce's Cash Books. Some of the other manuscripts in the Duke archives are important for any student of Wilberforce, notably the William Smith Papers and the extensive collection of the correspondence of Stephen Fuller, the agent for Jamaica during the first years of the Abolitionist campaign.

Wilberforce Museum Manuscripts

This much smaller collection is lodged in the Wilberforce Museum, Hull, in the house where Wilberforce was born. It seems to have once belonged to Henry, Wilberforce's fourth son. Much of the correspondence is between Wilberforce and him. The museum also owns the part of the Diary not in the Wrangham collection.

PRINTED SOURCES

Annan, N. G. The Intellectual Aristocracy: Studies in Social History, a tribute to G. M. Trevelyan. Edited by J. H. Plumb. (1955)

Annual Register.

Anon. Liverpool and Slavery. An Historical Account of the Liverpool–Africa Slave Trade. (Liverpool 1884)

— Songs, Epigrams, etc., of the Yorkshire Contested Election. (Leeds 1807)

Anstey, Robert T. Capitalism and Slavery, a critique. (Economic History Review. Second Series XXI No. 2)

Barnes's Political Portraits.

Barnes, D. G. George III and William Pitt 1783–1806. (Stamford University Press 1939)

Birley, Sir Robert. The Discovery of Africa, some lessons for today. (Anti-Slavery Society 1968)

Bready, J. Wesley. England before and after Wesley. (Hodder and Stoughton 1938)

Briggs, Asa. The Age of Improvement. (Longmans 1959)

— William Cobbett. (O.U.P. 1967)

Brougham, Lord. Historical sketches of Statesmen who flourished in the time of George III. 2 vols. (Charles Knight 1845)

— The Life and Times of Henry Lord Brougham. (W. Blackwood 1871)

— Political Philosophy.

Brown, F. K. Fathers of the Victorians, the age of Wilberforce. (Cambridge 1961)

Bryant, Sir Arthur. The Years of Endurance. (Collins 1942)

— The Age of Elegance. (Collins 1954)

Burne, Alfred H. The Noble Duke of York. (Staples Press 1949)

Buxton, Sir Thomas Fowell. Memoirs. (John Murray 1848)

Buxton, Travers. William Wilberforce: the Story of a Great Crusade. (Religious Tract Society 1904)

Catterell, H. T. Judicial Cases concerning Negro Slavery. (Washington D.C. 1926–7)

Cecil, Lord David. Lord M. (Constable 1954)

— The Stricken Deer. (Constable 1929)

Chenevix Trench, Charles. The Royal Malady. (Longmans 1964)

Chesterton, G. L. Revelations of Prison Life. (Hurst and Blackett 1856)

Clarkson, Thomas. An Essay on Slavery. (Dublin 1786)

— The History of the Rise, Progress, and Accomplishment of the Abolition of the African Slave Trade by the British Parliament. (London 1808)

— Strictures on a Life of William Wilberforce by the Rev. R. Wilberforce and the Rev. S. Wilberforce; with a Correspondence between Lord Brougham and Mr. Clarkson; also a Supplement containing Remarks on the Edinburgh Review of Mr. Wilberforce's Life. (London 1838)

Clive, John. Thomas Babington Macaulay, the shaping of the Historian. (Secker and Warburg 1973)

Cobbett, William. The History of the last hundred days of English Freedom. (Labour Publishing Co. 1921)

— Political Register.

Cole, Hubert. Christophe, King of Haiti. (Eyre and Spottiswoode 1967)

Colquhoun, J. C. William Wilberforce, his friends and his times. (Longmans Green 1866)

Coupland, R. Wilberforce: a narrative. (Oxford 1923)

— The British Anti-Slavery Movement. (Thornton Butterworth 1933)

— The Empire in Those Days. (Macmillan 1935)

Creevey Papers. Edited by Sir Herbert Maxwell, Bt. (John Murray 1905)

Davidson, Basil. The African Slave Trade. (Little Brown 1961)

Dicey, A. V. Law and Public Opinion in England in the Nineteenth Century. (1905)

du Bois, W. E. B. The Suppression of the African Slave Trade to the United States of America 1638–1870. (New York 1896)

Edwards, Bryan. The History of the British Colonies in the West Indies. (3 vols. 1793–1801)

Ehrman, John. The Younger Pitt. The Years of Acclaim. (Oxford, Clarendon Press 1962)

Embree, A. T. Charles Grant and British Rule in India. (Allen and Unwin 1962)

The Farington Diary.

Feiling, Keith. The Second Tory Party, 1714–1832. (Macmillan 1938)

Forster, E. M. Marianne Thornton, 1797–1887. A domestic biography. (Edward Arnold 1956)

Fraser Lovat. J. A. Erskine. (Cambridge 1932)

Fyfe, Christopher. A Short History of Sierra Leone. (Longmans 1962)

Gladstone, W. E. Gleanings of Past Years. Vol. VII. (London 1879)

Gratus, J. The Great White Lie. (Hutchinson 1973)

The Greville Memoirs, a Journal of the Reigns of King George IV and King William IV. 3 vols. edited H. Reeve. (London 1874)

Griggs, Earl Leslie. Thomas Clarkson, the Friend of Slaves. (Allen and Unwin 1936)

Griggs, Earl Leslie and Prator, Clifford H. Henri Christophe and Thomas Clarkson. (University of California Press 1952)

Grimston. Notes on the Yorkshire Election of 1807. (Unpublished. Wrangham MSS)

Gurney, J. J. Familiar sketch of the late William Wilberforce. (Josiah Fletcher, Norwich 1838)

Halévy, Elie. History of the English People in the Nineteenth Century. Vol. I. England in 1815. Vol. II. The Liberal Awakening 1815–1830. (Benn 1949)

Hall, Helena. William Allen. (Charles Clarke 1953)

Hammond, J. L. and B. The Town Labourer 1760–1832. (London 1917)
— The Village Labourer 1760–1832 (London 1919)
— The Skilled Labourer 1760–1832. (London 1919)

Harford, J. S. Recollections of William Wilberforce, Esq., M.P. for the County of York during nearly thirty years. With brief notices of his personal friends and contemporaries. (Longmans Green 1864)

Hayter, Alethea. Opium and the Romantic Imagination. (Faber and Faber 1968)

Hazlitt, William. The Spirit of the Age. (1825)

Hennell, M. John Venn and the Clapham Sect. (Lutterworth Press 1958)

Holland, Lord. Memoirs of the Whig Party. 2 vols. (1852)

Howse, E. M. Saints in Politics, the Clapham Sect and the Growth of Freedom. (Allen and Unwin 1952)

Jackson, Gordon. Hull in the Eighteenth Century. (O.U.P. 1972)

Jaeger, Muriel. Before Victoria. (Chatto and Windus 1956)

Jones, M. G. Hannah More. (Cambridge 1952)

Kay, F. G. The Shameful Trade. (Muller 1967)

Klingberg, F. J. The Anti-Slavery Movement in England: a Study in English Humanitarianism. (Archon Books 1968)

Knutsford, Baroness. Life and Times of Zachary Macaulay. (Edward Arnold 1900)

Lascelles, E. C. P. Granville Sharp and the Freedom of Slaves in England. (O.U.P. 1928)

Lecky, W. E. H. A History of England in the Eighteenth Century. (Longmans Green 1899)
— History of European Morals. (London 1869)

Leighton, J. A. S. L. Smiths the Bankers. (National Provincial Bank 1958)

Lewis, M. G. Journal of a West Indian Proprietor. (1834)

Lipscombe, Patrick. Pitt and the Abolition Question: A Review of an Historical Controversy. (Leeds Philosophical and Literary Society. Vol. XII. 87–128)

Long, Edward. History of Jamaica. (1774)

Longford, Elizabeth. Wellington, Pillar of State. (Weidenfeld and Nicolson 1972)

Macaulay, Kenneth. The Colony of Sierra Leone vindicated. (London 1827)

Macaulay, Lord. Miscellaneous writings. (Longmans Green 1860)

MacInnes, C. M. England and Slavery. (Arrowsmith 1934)

Mackintosh, Sir James. Biographical notes.

M'Queen, J. The West India Colonies. (1824)

Matthieson, W. C. British Slavery and its Abolition, 1823–38. (Longmans 1926)

Medland, W. M. and Weobly, Charles. A collection of remarkable and interesting criminal trials, actions at law, etc. (1803)

Milner, Mary. The life of Isaac Milner. (1842)

Moore, Thomas. Diary.

More, Martha. Mendip Annals. (London 1859)

Morley, J. The Life of William Ewart Gladstone. 3 vols. (Macmillan 1903)

Newsome, David. The Parting of Friends: a study of the Wilberforces and Henry Manning. (John Murray 1966)

— Fathers and Sons. (Historical Journal VI No. 2 1963, 295–310)

Newton, John. Thoughts upon the African Slave Trade. (1788)

— The Journal of a Slave Trader 1750–54. Edited by Bernard Martin and Mark Spurrell. (Epworth Press 1962)

— The Life of John Newton with Selections from his Correspondence. (London 1855)

Osbaldeston, George. Squire Osbaldeston, His Memoirs. (Bodley Head 1926)

Pares, Richard. George III and the politicians. (O.U.P. 1954)

Parliamentary Debates (Hansard).

Philips, R. Public characters of 1800–1801. (London 1801)

Phillips, N. C. Yorkshire and English National Politics, 1783–84. (University of Canterbury, Christchurch, New Zealand 1961)

Pine, L. G. The Family of Wilberfoss (or Wilberforce). (Unpublished)

Place, Francis. The Autobiography of Francis Place 1771–1854. Edited by Mary Thrale. (Cambridge 1972)

Plumb, J. H. The First Four Georges. (Batsford 1956)

Pope-Hennessy, James. Sins of the Fathers. (Weidenfeld and Nicolson 1967)

Pym, Dorothy. Battersea Rise. (Jonathan Cape 1934)

Ragatz, L. J. Fall of the Planter Class in the British Caribbean. 1763–1833. (Century Co. 1928)

— A Guide for the study of British Caribbean History, 1763–1834, including the Abolition and Emancipation Movements. (U.S. Government Printing Office, 1932)

Rainsford, O. The Slave Trade. (John Murray 1971)

Ramsay, J. An Essay on the Treatment and Conversion of African Slaves in the British Sugar Colonies. (London 1784)

Rees, Alan M. Pitt and the Achievement of Abolition. (The Journal of Negro History XXXIX No. 3)

Richardson, Joanna. The Disastrous Marriage. (Jonathan Cape 1960)

Roberts, J. Memoirs of the Life and Correspondence of Mrs. Hannah More. (4 vols. 1834)

Robinson, H. C. Exposure of Misrepresentations in the Preface to the Correspondence of William Wilberforce. (Edward Moxon 1840)

— Diary. 1872.

Rogers, Samuel. Recollections. (Longmans Green 1859)

— Table Talk. (H. A. Rogers 1887)

Romilly, Sir A. Samuel. Memoirs of the Life of Sir Samuel Romilly. (London 1840)

Rose, J. Holland. Pitt and the National Revival. (G. Bell 1911)

— Pitt and the Great War. (G. Bell 1911)

— Pitt and Napoleon. (G. Bell 1912)

Rosebery, Earl of. Pitt. (London 1891)

Sharp, Granville. Memoirs. Edited by Prince Hoare. (London 1820)
— The Injustice and dangerous tendency of tolerating Slavery, or of admitting
    the least claim of private property in the persons of men, in England. (London
    1769)
Simond, Louis. Journal of a Tour and Residence in Great Britain. (Edinburgh
    1817)
Smith, Adam. The Wealth of Nations. (London 1776)
Smith, Sydney. Letters. (O.U.P. 1953)
Southey, Robert. Life and Correspondence. 6 vols. (London 1849–50)
— Essays, Moral and Political. 2 vols. (London 1832)
— Letters. 4 vols. (London 1856)
Stephen, Sir George. Anti-slavery recollections in a series of letters to Mrs.
    Beecher Stowe. (Hatchard 1854)
Stephen, James. The Slavery of the British West India Colonies delineated. 2
    vols. (London 1824, 1830)
— England enslaved by her own slave colonies. (London 1826).
Stephen, Sir James. Essays in ecclesiastical biography. 2 vols. (London 1849)
Thomas, Hugh. Cuba, or the pursuit of freedom. (Eyre and Spottiswoode 1971)
Thorpe, Robert. A letter to William Wilberforce. (London 1815)
— A Reply 'Point by Point'. (London 1815)
Trevelyan, G. M. British History in the Nineteenth Century. (Longmans 1922)
— Clio, a muse. (Longmans 1913)
Trevelyan, G. O. The Early Life of Charles James Fox. (Longmans Green 1881)
— The life and letters of Lord Macaulay. (Longmans Green 1878)
Turner, E. S. All Heaven in a Rage. (Michael Joseph 1964)
Victoria History of the County of Yorkshire.
Wallas, Graham. Life of Francis Place. (Longmans 1898)
Walpole, Horace. Letters. 6 vols. (London 1840)
Ward, W. E. F. The Royal Navy and the Slavers. (Allen and Unwin 1969)
Warner, Oliver. William Wilberforce and his Times. (Batsford 1962)
Watson, Stephen. The Reign of George III. (Oxford, Clarendon Press 1960)
Wesley, John. Thoughts on Slavery. (London 1774)
West, Richard. Back to Africa. (Jonathan Cape 1970)
Wilberforce, A. M. The Private Papers of William Wilberforce. (T. Fisher
    Unwin 1897)
Wilberforce, John. William Wilberforce's honeymoon. (Cornhill Magazine,
    December 1933)
Wilberforce, Robert Isaac and Samuel. The Life of William Wilberforce. 5 vols.
    (John Murray 1838)
— The Correspondence of William Wilberforce. 2 vols. (John Murray 1840)
Wilberforce, William. Practical View of the Prevailing Religious System of
    Professed Christians in the Higher and Middle Classes in this Country con-
    trasted with real Christianity. (London 1797)
— A letter on the Abolition of the Slave Trade; addressed to the Freeholders
    and other inhabitants of Yorkshire. (London 1807)
— A letter to His Excellency the Prince of Talleyrand Perigord on the subject
    of the Slave Trade. (London 1814)

—Appeal to the Religion, Justice, and Humanity of the Inhabitants of the British Empire on Behalf of the Negro Slaves in the West Indies. (London 1823)

Wilberforce, Yvette. William Wilberforce, an Essay. Foreword by C. E. Wrangham. (Privately printed 1967)

Williams, Eric. Capitalism and Slavery. (André Deutsch 1944)

— History of the people of Trinidad and Tobago. (André Deutsch 1964)

Woodward, Sir Llewellyn. The Age of Reform, 1815–1870. (Oxford, Clarendon Press 1962)

Worthington-Smith, Robert. Political organisation and canvassing. Yorkshire Elections before the Reform Bill. (American Historical Review vol. 74. No. 5. 1969)

Wrangham, C. E. East Farleigh. (Privately printed 1973)

Yorkshire Freeholder, A. Letter to William Wilberforce Esq. (Leeds 1807)

Index

Abolition of the Slave Trade, Committee for the: formation of, 70, 313; Wilberforce as Parliamentary leader of, 71–2; decision to concentrate first on slave trade rather than slavery, 72–3, 400; gathering of evidence, 73–7, 88, 91–2, 93–4; preparation of case, 85, 97; effects of French Revolution on, 98–9, 103, 107–8; popular campaigns, 106–7; increasing support for, 108–9; effect of war with France, 122–3; establishment of free colony in Sierra Leone, 123–9; Brougham, Stephen and Macaulay elected to, 227; preparation of case for Lords in 1805, 227–8; investigation of conditions of slavery, 402, 405. *See also* Anti-Slavery Society; slave trade; slavery

Academical Society of Oxford, 361

Acland, Sir Thomas, 215

Addington, Henry (later Viscount Sidmouth, q.v.), 110, 183, 208, 243; forms government, 210–11; cool about Abolition, 211; Pitt's support of, 212; criticism of his war policy, 217, 218, 219, 220; rift with Pitt, 220; opposition to Abolition, 222, 223, 224, 225; reconciled with Pitt, 228

Africa, and slave trade, 60–1, 86–90, 100, 103, 109, 111, 194–5, 227–8, 332, 340, 342

African Institution, 332, 402

Age of Reason (Paine), 10, 146, 258–60, 189, 371

Agency Committee, 444–5, 452

Alexander I, Czar, 334, 396; distant sympathy with Abolition, 335, 337, 405

Almack's club, 34, 56

Althorp, Lord, 445

America: and slave trade, 252, 318, 332; relationship between Britain and, 317–318; war with (1812), 318–19

American War of Independence, 12; Wilberforce's opposition to, 13, 19; Peace Treaty, 19–21

Amiens, Peace of (1803), 108, 212, 218, 222

Amis des Noirs, 91, 223, 338

Anglesey, Henry Paget, first Marquis of, 389

animals, cruelty to, 199–203

Annual Register, 152, 253

Anti Jacobin, 175

Anti-Slavery Reporter, 444

Anti-Slavery Society, 406–7, 413, 419, 431, 441, 442–3

Arden, Richard Pepper, 17, 22, 132, 242, 313

Aris (Keeper of Cold Bath Fields), 191, 192

Ashanti, King of, 76

Atkinson, Rev. Miles, 137, 138, 198

Austen, Jane, 279

Austerlitz, battle of (1805), 236, 237

Austin, Rev. Mr., 417

Australia, missions in, 120, 216

Austria, 339; makes peace with France (1797), 163, 174, (1809) 304, 310

Avignon, 33

Axbridge, 59, 143

Babington, George, 437, 441

Babington, Thomas, 10, 37, 115, 127, 237, 280, 287, 313, 325; character and friendship with Wilberforce, 96–7, 119;